t.s. eliot

t.s. eliot

The Making of an American Poet, 1888–1922

JAMES E. MILLER JR.

The Pennsylvania State University Press

University Park, Pennsylvania

Title-page illustration of T. S. Eliot used by permission of the Houghton Library, Harvard University (Call no. *AC9.El464.Zzx Box 2, env. 13a).

LIBRARY OF CONGRESS CATALOGING-IN-PUBLICATION DATA

Miller, James Edwin, 1920–
T. S. Eliot : the making of an American poet, 1888–1922 / James E. Miller, Jr.
p.   cm.
Includes bibliographical references and index.
ISBN 0-271-02681-2 (alk. paper)
1. Eliot, T. S. (Thomas Stearns), 1888–1965—Childhood and youth.
2. Eliot, T. S. (Thomas Stearns), 1888–1965—Knowledge—United States.
3. National characteristics, American, in literature.
4. Poets, American—20th century—Biography.
I. Title.

PS3509 .L43Z7856 2005
821´.912—dc22
2005005092

The Pennsylvania State University Press is a member of the
Association of American University Presses.

It is the policy of The Pennsylvania State University Press to use acid-free paper. This book is printed on Natures Natural, containing 50% post-consumer waste and meets the minimum requirements of American National Standard for Information Sciences—Permanence of Paper for Printed Library Materials, ANSI Z39.48–1992.

[contents]

The incubation period of *T. S. Eliot: The Making of an American Poet* is some thirty years, beginning in the early 1970s, and propelled by the publication of, and response to, my first book on Eliot, *T. S. Eliot's Personal Waste Land: Exorcism of the Demons,* in 1977. Since that book is out of print, as a sort of prolegomena to a preface, I propose a brief summary of its genesis, reception, and continuing influence.

A Backward Glance at Eliot's *Personal Waste Land*

In 1971, when Eliot's widow Valerie Eliot edited and published the manuscript version under the title *T. S. Eliot, The Waste Land: A Facsimile and Transcript of the Original Drafts, Including the Annotations of Ezra Pound,* she placed as an epigraph Eliot's own statement: "Various critics have done me the honour to interpret the poem in terms of criticism of the contemporary world, have considered it indeed, as an important bit of social criticism. To me it was only the relief of a personal and wholly insignificant grouse against life; it is just a piece of rhythmical grumbling" (*WLF,* 1). Although the instinct of many readers was to discount this statement, and even to point to the vagueness of its origins (it was quoted by a professor in a lecture, and recorded by Eliot's older brother, Henry), it is, in fact, quite in keeping with an entire series of such statements made by Eliot in public and for the record.

In 1931, in "Thoughts after Lambeth," Eliot comments: "When I wrote a poem called *The Waste Land* some of the more approving critics said that I had expressed the 'disillusionment of a generation,' which is nonsense. I may have expressed for them their own illusion of being disillusioned, but that did not form part of my intention" (*SE,* 324). When, in his 1959 *Paris Review* interview, Eliot was pressed on this statement, he in effect reaffirmed it: "No, it wasn't part of my conscious intention. I think that in *Thoughts after*

Lambeth, I was speaking of intentions more in a negative than in a positive sense, to say what was not my intention. I wonder what an 'intention' means! One wants to get something off one's chest. One doesn't know quite what it is that one wants to get off the chest until one's got it off." It was later in this same interview that Eliot made this astonishing statement (when asked to compare his two long poems): "By the time of the *Four Quartets,* I couldn't have written in the style of *The Waste Land.* In *The Waste Land,* I wasn't even bothering whether I understood what I was saying. These things, however, become easier to people with time. You get used to having *The Waste Land,* or *Ulysses,* about" (*INT,* 97, 105).

In his 1951 lecture, "Virgil and the Christian World," Eliot made perhaps his most intriguing statement about *The Waste Land* without naming the poem: "A poet may believe that he is expressing only his private experience; his lines may be for him only a means of talking about himself without giving himself away; yet for his readers what he has written may come to be the expression both of their own secret feelings and of the exultation or despair of a generation. He need not know what his poetry will come to mean to others; and a prophet need not understand the meaning of his prophetic utterance" (*OPP,* 137). In all of these statements, direct and oblique, about *The Waste Land,* Eliot emphasized more and more the personal, private matter that went into the poem and his astonishment at the way the poem came to be read as a public statement about the modern world.

In the last of the comments quoted above, he has perhaps put his feelings in their most complex language. Could it possibly be that Eliot believed he was expressing only his "private experience" in *The Waste Land*? That the lines of this most famous poem of the twentieth century were for the author "only a means of talking about himself without giving himself away"? *Giving himself away?* Giving what away? What was there to conceal? Presumably what nobody had, by the 1951 lecture, discovered, or at least discovered and revealed. Could it be that the 1919 essay "Tradition and the Individual Talent," with its elaborate and tortured "impersonal theory" of poetry, had been a sophistic or sophisticated defense for someone wanting to write poetry "talking about himself without giving himself away"?

It is of considerable interest that Cleanth Brooks waited until 1989 to reveal that he had sent his 1937 essay in manuscript ("*The Waste Land:* An Analysis," later titled "*The Waste Land:* Critique of the Myth") to Eliot, hoping to get his approval. Brooks had followed F. O. Matthiessen (Matthiessen, 92–93) in assuming that a Rupert Brooke letter had been an important source for some lines of *The Waste Land.* Eliot replied that he didn't recollect ever reading the Brooke letter, and added: "but actually this particular passage approximates more closely to a recollection of a personal experience of my own than anything else, and indeed is as nearly as I could remember a verbatim report [of the personal experience]" (Brooks, Cleanth, TWLPD, 321).

What is the passage in *The Waste Land* that Eliot described as a "verbatim report" of his "personal experience"? It is the opening lines of *The Waste Land*. Rupert Brooke described in his letter a friend's reaction upon hearing that England was at war with Germany. The friend "climbed a hill of gorse, and sat alone, looking at the sea. His mind was full of confused images, and the sense of strain. In answer to the word 'Germany,' a train of vague thoughts dragged across his brain.... The wide and restful beauty of Munich; the taste of beer; innumerable quiet, glittering cafés; the *Ring;* the swish of evening air in the face, as one skis down past the pines; a certain angle of the eyes in the face; long nights of drinking and singing and laughter ... certain friends; some tunes; the quiet length of evening over the Starnbergersee" (Matthiessen, 92–93). Readers familiar with the opening lines of *The Waste Land* could, like Matthiessen and Brooks, easily believe that this letter was a source for Eliot. But none would be likely to doubt Eliot's firm statement that the opening lines of *The Waste Land* were a "verbatim report" of his "personal experience." And his biography reveals that in 1911, during his academic year in Paris, Eliot did indeed visit Munich and the Starnbergersee nearby.

If there was increasing agreement over time that Eliot had reason to call *The Waste Land* a personal poem, critics were left with the even more baffling question: what is the nature of this personal dimension? The British poet Stephen Spender published his Penguin Modern Masters volume *T. S. Eliot* in 1976 and noted: "Eliot once referred to *The Waste Land* as an elegy. Whose elegy? His father's? Jean Verdenal's—mort aux Dardanelles in the war?" Spender's book does not identify sources; are we to assume that the remark was made by Eliot to Spender personally? Shortly after this passage, Spender wrote: "'Death by Water' crystallizes the *hidden elegy* that is in *The Waste Land*—hinted at, as we have seen, in 'Those are pearls that were his eyes'" (Spender, TSE, 111, 114, emphasis added). Although much younger than Eliot, Spender had come to know Eliot in the 1930s, and had included him in his critical work, *The Destructive Element: A Study of Modern Writers and Beliefs* (1936). Spender's personal acquaintance with Eliot and knowledge of his poetry renders it quite plausible that Eliot would comment to him in casual conversation on the elegiac nature of his most famous poem.

We might assume that with the publication in 1971 of *The Waste Land* manuscripts, Eliot's statements about his poem might have challenged reviewers and critics to find out what he meant, to look for clues for the concealed private experience. By and large the commentators on the poem, many of them a part of the critical establishment with vested interests in the received "public" reading of *The Waste Land*, found renewed confirmation of the traditional reading, and expressed their admiration for Ezra Pound's skill in revising and radically cutting the poem. There were some who made limited gestures to define the personal content of the poem as revealed by the manuscripts, but no very persuasive new reading seemed to emerge from the publication.

It was about this time that I came across "A New Interpretation of *The Waste Land*," by Canadian professor John Peter, published in the July 1952 issue of the British journal *Essays in Criticism*. Peter analyzed the poem as a dramatic representation of the speaker's falling in love with a "young man who afterwards met his death" by drowning. The article did not suggest that Eliot was the speaker, nor that he had based his poem on his own experience. But lawyers for Eliot reported to Peter that their client had read his article with "amazement and disgust" and said it was "absurd" and "completely erroneous"; they threatened to bring a lawsuit against Peter and the editor of *Essays in Criticism* if they did not withdraw and destroy the issue containing it. Peter offered to publish a retraction, but the solicitors were firm in their decision that he should not, perhaps because a published retraction would likely result in more embarrassment to Eliot. Peter and the journal quickly agreed to the withdrawal, and the matter not only seemed to be settled, but disappeared from public view.

But, after Eliot's death in 1965, Peter republished the article together with a long "Postscript" in *Essays in Criticism* in April 1969, in which he added details of what he frankly asserted was a biographical interpretation: the major identification was that of Phlebas the Phoenician as Jean Verdenal, the friend Eliot met in Paris during his year of study abroad in 1910–11. Inspired by Peter's article, the additional evidence of the facsimile, and Peter's letter to me that he did not plan to write anew about the matter, I set aside a book I was writing on the American long poem and wrote a short book, mining the *Waste Land* manuscripts that supported the thesis that the poem was in effect an elegy. I published the book in 1977 under the title, *T. S. Eliot's Personal Waste Land: Exorcism of the Demons*, and with an epigraph that would reveal the source of the second half of the title: "he is haunted by a demon, a demon against which he feels powerless, because in its first manifestation it has no face, no name, nothing; and the words, the poem he makes, are a kind of form of exorcism of this demon" (OPP, 107). The source of these lines is Eliot's "The Three Voices of Poetry," which is given the date 1953 in Eliot's volume *On Poetry and Poets*.

T. S. Eliot's Personal Waste Land provoked harsh criticism. Writing in the

Times Literary Supplement of October 28, 1977, Christopher Butler denounced "the homosexual interpretation of Eliot's life and work." Several reviewers felt that the book was persuasive. For example, in *The New York Times Book Review*, April 17, 1977, Robert Langbaum wrote: "By reminding us of the young Eliot's anguish, Miller's book serves as a corrective to the monumental figure Eliot cut in his later years," but noted that "a responsible biography" would have to be based on further information, especially an edition of the letters.

More than a generation later, the academic context for discussing the homoerotic aspects of literary works had been transformed, almost beyond recognition. The growth of scholarly interest in gay themes has broadened and deepened our understanding of what Eve Kosofsky Sedgwick has suggestively called "the epistemology of the closet." Wayne Koestenbaum in *Double Talk: The Erotics of Male Literary Collaboration* (1989) is but one of the many studies that have built on my reading of Eliot in *T. S. Eliot's Personal Waste Land*.

[a note on sources]

The main thrust of my 1977 book was not Eliot's life but his poetry, exploring ways in which the fragmentary details shaped and illuminated the poems. My reinterpretation of *The Waste Land* was not dependent on biographical reconstruction and thus the firm establishment of the full facts of Eliot's early life was unnecessary. Since then, *The Letters of T. S. Eliot, Volume One, 1898–1922*, edited by Valerie Eliot, was published in 1988. Eliot's widow arranged the correspondence chronologically up through 1922, covering some 640 pages, promising another volume in 1989, which has not yet appeared. The letters in Volume 1 are incomplete because, as the editor of his letters writes in the volume's introduction, "On the deaths of his mother and brother, in 1929 and 1947, TSE recovered his correspondence with them and burnt a good part of it, together with their side, thus removing the family record of his final school year [at Milton Academy in Massachusetts], his student days at Harvard and the period in Paris" (*LTSE1*, xv). In short, letters written during the first twenty-six years of his life (up to 1914) as well as letters to him from family members were destroyed.

Two sketchy "biographies" had appeared in the early seventies: Robert Sencourt's *T. S. Eliot: A Memoir* (1971) and T. S. Matthews's *Great Tom: Notes Towards the Definition of T. S. Eliot* (1974). But they did not have permission from Valerie Eliot for use of letters and other manuscript materials. The first groundbreaking biographical volume to appear making full use of unpublished letters and private papers was *Eliot's Early Years* (1977) by Lyndall Gordon. In 1984, Peter Ackroyd, who also had access to unpublished materials, produced his engaging and important *T. S. Eliot*. Gordon's second volume, *Eliot's New Life*, appeared in 1988. And in 1998, Gordon revised and combined her two volumes, publishing the magisterial *T. S. Eliot: An Imperfect Life*. In 2001 Carole Seymour-Jones, also drawing on much unpublished material, published a life of Eliot's first wife, entitled *Painted Shadow: A Life of Vivienne Eliot*.

In the writing of my biography, I have drawn from the archival materials in Gordon, Ackroyd, and Seymour-Jones. Not a conventional biography, my book is rather a supplement and complement to these works. It might be called a biographical interpretation. Over the years, more and more Eliot critics became convinced that indeed Eliot's poetry was a personal poetry, but the view did not bring about specific agreement as to how to read—or analyze—his personal poems. As for the several biographies that have been published, nearly all of them have been by British writers who, though skillful biographers, have tended to write skimpily about Eliot's American years—his first twenty-six years, excepting his 1910–11 year in Paris. I decided that I would write a biography (perhaps the first volume of a full biography) that would emphasize these formative years, covering Eliot's early life in St. Louis on the Mississippi River, his summering in New England, his education at Harvard (with a year in Paris), and his final settling in London, through the period of his writing and publishing *The Waste Land* and establishing his little magazine, *The Criterion*—i.e., through 1922.

Three books by Douglass Shand-Tucci have provided fresh material and insight into the goings-on at Harvard, Cambridge, and Boston in the years shortly before Eliot arrived—goings-on that would have been much the same in the first decade of the twentieth century. The first of these is entitled *Boston Bohemia, 1881–1900* (1995), the second is *The Art of Scandal: The Life and Times of Isabella Stewart Gardner* (1997), and the third is *The Crimson Letter: Harvard, Homosexuality, and the Shaping of American Culture* (2003). In the last of these, T. S. Eliot becomes something of a leading character. In short, these books must be factored into any imaginative re-creation of Eliot's college years.

Especially rich resources from Eliot's London years are the works of Virginia Woolf, particularly *The Diary of Virginia Woolf,* edited by Anne Olivier Bell, and *The Letters of Virginia Woolf,* edited by Nigel Nicolson and Joanne Trautmann, both in several volumes. A number of biographies have proved important sources for Eliot's life and his acquaintances, but one is particularly valuable: Michael Holroyd's *Lytton Strachey: The New Biography* (1994). Holroyd published his first biography of Strachey in the 1960s, and various revisions appeared in subsequent years. The 1994 version, some 780 pages in length, has to be the definitive biography of this fascinating rebel and it reveals that many individuals who figured in Strachey's life also figured in Eliot's.

Michael Hastings's play *Tom and Viv* (1985) has become a primary source for Eliot scholars because of Hastings's meticulous research, particularly his many interviews with Vivien's brother Maurice Haigh-Wood before writing it. The interviews took place over five months in 1980, when Maurice was eighty-six. He was clearly a primary source of information about its two main characters. I have drawn on the play as well as Hastings's long introduction.

As for Eliot's poetry beginning as a boy through 1922, I have tracked down all the poems and read and used them when called for in my biography. A signal event occurred in 1996 with the publication of *Inventions of the March Hare: Poems 1909–1917*, edited by Christopher Ricks. That edition made easily available for the first time Eliot's early, unpublished manuscripts of the Notebook poems, including poems Eliot had withheld from publication. I have also found useful John T. Mayer's *T. S. Eliot's Silent Voices* (1989), from which I have frequently quoted readings or interpretations of individual poems. Chapters 3, 5, 8, 10, and 11 all conclude with sections on Eliot's poetry as well as lists and sources for all of Eliot's poems written and/or published during each period. Readers interested in finding and reading any of Eliot's poems of this period should consult the appropriate list.

More recent Eliot scholarship has turned to an examination of his American roots. I must mention another of Ronald Bush's important additions to the body of Eliot criticism: "Nathaniel Hawthorne and T. S. Eliot's American Connection" (*Southern Review*, 1985). Eric Sigg's *The American T. S. Eliot: A Study of the Early Writings* places Eliot in an American aesthetic tradition; I have profited from his 1994 essay "Eliot as a Product of America." Lee Oser explores the American dimension in *T. S. Eliot and American Poetry* (1998). Manju Jain's *T. S. Eliot and American Philosophy: The Harvard Years* (1992) is an impressively researched book about the shaping of Eliot by his Harvard professors and the courses he took under them.

I have relied on Ronald Schuchard's *Eliot's Dark Angel: Intersections of Life and Art* (1999), especially chapter 1, "In the Lecture Halls," focusing on the extension courses Eliot gave in London from 1916 into 1919, and including syllabi, reading lists, term paper topics, and so forth—all valuable in revealing Eliot's views and understanding of the authors he had read and taught.

In the 1990s there began to appear a number of books exploring the relation of literary works to gender studies and to what has been dubbed "queer theory." In 1998, for example, Colleen Lamos explored erotic themes in *Deviant Modernism: Sexual and Textual Errancy in T. S. Eliot, James Joyce, and Marcel Proust*. George Chauncey's *Gay New York: Gender, Urban Culture, and the Making of the Gay Male World, 1890–1940* (1994) does not feature T. S. Eliot, but it explores a subject matter that is highly relevant to my understanding of Eliot.

If I were to express my appreciation for all the authors that have helped me write this biography, I would have to devote all my pages to that task.

However, special notice must go to James F. Loucks, compiler of "The Exile's Return: Fragment of a T. S. Eliot Chronology," with whom I carried on a long e-mail conversation and who provided me with leads, information, and encouragement. In my text, I have cited all works I have quoted and summarized, and I now express my gratitude to the authors of all of them.

I want to thank Peter Potter, Cherene Holland, Patty Mitchell, Steve Kress, Jennifer Norton, and all those at Penn State Press who have guided the manuscript through the stages of production—and also Jennifer Smith and Diana Witt. Many helped to make the book better; its flaws are those of the author alone.

Randall Jarrell (1914–65), poet, novelist, critic, served in the Air Force in World War II and attracted attention with the publication in 1945 of his volume of vivid but bitter war poems. Now largely forgotten, during his life he published a great deal of both poetry and prose, but ultimately it was as a critic that he had the greatest influence. In his essay entitled "Fifty Years of American Poetry," first delivered as a lecture in 1962, he said of T. S. Eliot: "Won't the future say to us in helpless astonishment: 'But did you actually believe that all those things about objective correlatives, classicism, the tradition, applied to *his* poetry? Surely you must have seen that he was one of the most subjective and daemonic poets who ever lived, the victim and helpless beneficiary of his own inexorable compulsions, obsessions? From a psychoanalytical point of view he was far and away the most interesting poet of your Century. But for you, of course, after the first few years, his poetry existed undersea, thousands of feet below the deluge of exegesis, explication, source listing, scholarship, and criticism that overwhelmed it. And yet how bravely and personally it survived, its eyes neither coral nor mother-of-Pearl but plainly human, full of human anguish!" (Jarrell, 314–15). The essay remains an excellent brief account of the American poetic renaissance that began in 1910 and lasted some fifty years, producing such remarkable poets as Robert Frost, Wallace Stevens, T. S. Eliot, Ezra Pound, William Carlos Williams, Marianne Moore, and John Crowe Ransom. Jarrell devoted a few paragraphs in his essay to these and other poets, bestowing both praise and blame.

When he came to Eliot, he remarked: "And then there is Eliot. During the last thirty or forty years Eliot has been so much the most famous and influential of American poets that it seems almost absurd to write about him, especially when everybody else already has" (314). Jarrell then wrote the words recorded above. In that passage, he assumed the voice of some future critic who is looking back at how the critical establishment reacted to the complex poetry of T. S. Eliot, generally adopting some approach to poetry that Eliot himself had set forth in his multitude of essays. It is a bit of prophecy that was to be fulfilled only after the passage of another half-century, when the leading Eliot critics and biographers revealed that they regarded Eliot's poems as personal poems, written out of and about his personal experiences—physical, mental, and emotional.

I had originally wanted to entitle my book *T. S. Eliot's Uranian Muse: The Making of an American Poet, 1888–1922*, because I had in mind a particular definition of the unusual word "Uranian" that comes from a special poem written by Eliot's friend and mentor, Ezra Pound, on a very memorable occasion. Pound had just finished his resurrection of a long poem from its premature burial in a mass of *Waste Land* manuscripts that Eliot had in frustration brought to him. The poem was entitled "Sage Homme" and was contained in a letter to Eliot (January 24, 1921). In it, Pound characterizes Eliot's poems as begotten by "the Uranian Muse," with a "Man" for a "Mother" and a "Muse" for a "Sire." The "printed Infancies" resulted from "Nuptials . . . doubly difficult" because "Ezra performed the caesarean Operation" (*LTSE1,* 498). In effect, Pound is invoking the "Uranian muse" because Eliot's poem was born by the union of two males, Eliot and Pound. "Uranian" was, in the early part of the twentieth century, in competition with other words to refer to same-sex love. Pound's poem is ambiguous, and no doubt intentionally so. At some deep level it reflects his response to the images of sexuality abundant in the *Waste Land* manuscripts. Of course, Pound never placed this private and intimately personal poem among his published poems (although it did appear in part in his 1950 volume of *Letters*).

But more important, my book combines an American account of the life and times of T. S. Eliot together with a comprehensive survey of the poetry he wrote from his first poems in 1902 through 1922, with the appearance of *The Waste Land*. It is only natural that, since Eliot began living in England in his twenty-sixth year and became a British citizen in the late 1920s, most of the biographies of Eliot have been written by British scholars. But as it is universally agreed that the early years of a poet's life are the most important in shaping his or her imagination, I set about writing this biography by focusing on his life in the city where he was born and went to his first schools, St. Louis, Missouri, and following him in the summers when he vacationed with his family in their Gloucester, Massachusetts, home perched on the Atlantic Ocean's edge. And I remained in pursuit of him when he finally came out from under the immediate presence of his family and was, in 1905 at the age of seventeen, on his own for one year at Milton Academy near Boston, and then from 1906 until 1914 at Harvard, first in undergraduate work and then in graduate work in philosophy—with the extraordinarily important exception of the year 1910–11, which he spent studying in Paris. I have attempted to deal, fully and frankly, with all aspects of his personal and public life, examining in detail his physical, intellectual, spiritual, imaginative, creative, and sexual growth—with special attention to relationships and friendships as well as beliefs, views, and opinions. And I have scrutinized (and utilized) Eliot's poetry throughout my book, with some sections devoted fully to the most revealingly personal—and impressive—poems. These passages are aimed not only at explication and evaluation of individual poems, but also and primarily at mining them for whatever biographical information might be buried in them.

We are told by Eliot that he knew exactly when and why he decided to become a poet. At the age of fourteen, in 1902, Eliot came across a copy of Edward Fitzgerald's free translation of *The Rubáiyát of Omar Khayyám* and it in effect took over his imagination. This influence affected his personal life deeply (about which more later), but of most importance he was inspired to set about writing verses of his own, most of which he later destroyed. But we accept the date of his birth as a poet as 1902, although the number of poems that survived during these very early years is scant. And we follow his development as a poet through 1922, the climactic year of the appearance of *The Waste Land,* which (as the preface indicates) is analyzed in my first Eliot book, *T. S. Eliot's Personal Waste Land: Exorcism of the Demons* (1977).

To clarify the value of a fresh approach to the intertwining of Eliot's life and work in this formative period, consider several passages from Eliot's prose in which, I believe, he reveals in condensed form his approach to the writing of poetry. The first of these comes from a letter to his Harvard friend, Conrad Aiken (January 10, 1916). In this letter Eliot opens with an explanation of why he has been too busy to write first by listing all of the problems in his life: He is teaching, rewriting his thesis, has a sick wife and financial worries, his "friend Jean Verdenal has been killed," conscription for military service is near and his "putative publisher will probably be conscripted," and "we are very blue about the war" and "living is going up. . . ." He then bursts into poetry: "King Bolo's big black bassturd kween / That airy fairy hairy un / She led the dance on Golder's Green / With Cardinal Bessarian // . . . King Bolo's big black bassturd kween / Her taste was kalm and classic / And as for anything obscene / She said it made her ass sick // . . . . King Bolo's big black bassturd kween / Was awf'ly sweet and pure / She said 'I don't know what you mean!' / When the chaplain whistled to her" (*LTSE 1,* 125–26).

At the time he wrote these lines, we now know, Eliot had displeased his mother and angered his father by marrying his first wife, Vivien, and then choosing to pursue a literary career in England rather than an academic career teaching philosophy in America. His father had refused to finance his son beyond the small allowance he had given him to supplement his Harvard fellowship for his supposed "one-year" (1914–15) of study abroad. In order to get out of graduate classes at Oxford and into the literary scene in London, Eliot turned down Harvard's offer of a renewal of his fellowship. Thus he was left with his father's meager subsidy. He was forced, therefore, during his second year in England, to take whatever jobs he could get to cover living expenses for him and his new wife. When he broke into his bawdy verses (about "King Bolo's kween") to his college friend who had heard them before, it was like breaking into a nervous laugh after describing some near-tragic experience.

Clearly Eliot had suffered mightily given all that he had been through in 1915, but the revelatory lines in his letter came later: "I *hope* to write, when I have more detachment. But I am having a wonderful life nevertheless. I have *lived* through material for a score of long poems, in the last six months. An entirely different life from that I looked forward to two years ago" (126). It is astonishing to hear Eliot describing his dire situation as a "wonderful life." The critical words here, however, are "I have *lived* through material for a score of long poems"; and it is surely the acquiring of this vital "material" ("lived through," not imagined) for poems that turned the desperate years into fruitful ones for Eliot. Important elements of that material are his troubled marriage with Vivien, Vivien's various illnesses, the death and loss of his Paris friend, Jean Verdenal.

Now consider a second passage that comes from one of Eliot's letters to John Hayward when Eliot was trying to find a way of improving the last of the *Four Quartets,* "Little Gidding," first published in 1942. Eliot wrote to Hayward that he was "particularly unhappy about Part II [which contains the lines about the 'familiar compound ghost']," and believed that it required "some sharpening of personal poignancy." Eliot then added: "The defect of the whole poem, I feel, is the lack of some acute personal reminiscence (never to be explicated, of course, but to give power from well below the surface) and I can *perhaps* supply this in Part II" (quoted in Gardner, CFQ, 67).

These are only two of many such passages that convinced me that Eliot's poems were all meant to be personal poems, written out of a great *intensity of passion and feeling* that had been aroused by some "acute personal reminiscence." Lying deep beneath the surface, this "reminiscence" is, says Eliot, "never to be explicated." Many critics would question whether it is possible that such power or effect can have a source that is never revealed, either by the poet or the reader.

Not long after writing the letter to Conrad Aiken quoted above (January 10, 1916) exulting in personal experiences that would furnish him material for his poetry, Eliot published the essay famous for its introduction of a "theory of impersonal poetry," entitled "Tradition and the Individual Talent." It was published in two parts in the September and December 1919 issues of the *Egoist,* a little magazine Eliot was helping to edit. In some three years, after telling his friend Conrad Aiken that he had "lived through material for a score of long poems," we find Eliot inventing this theory of poetry, in which he formulates his method for using not the biographical data of these experiences but rather the emotions evoked by them for the writing of poems. The essay was to become the first in the initial volume of Eliot's essays, *The Sacred Wood,* published in 1920, and remained in this prime position in his *Selected Essays* throughout Eliot's career. It concludes with a highly significant comment: "Poetry is not a turning loose of emotion, but an escape from emotion; it is not the expression of personality, but an escape from personality. But, of course, only those who have personality and emotions know what it means to want to escape from these things" (*SE,* 10, 11).

Here Eliot seems to be admitting that the "lived through" experiences he wrote to Aiken about could not, by their very nature, be the direct subject of his poems—as they would reveal too much about him, and his strangely mixed-up sexual feelings, i.e., distaste for a wife he seems never to have loved and passion for a friend killed in the Great War. He was no doubt aware of the reaction, or ambivalent response, to the poetry of comradeship written by the soldiers of that war, especially those whose companions (or "mates") were killed in the terrible and seemingly endless trench warfare—as, for example, Siegfried Sassoon (1886–1967) and Rupert Brooke (1887–1915). But Eliot never denies that "personality" and "emotion" have played a formative role in his poetics. On the contrary: To admit that poetry might "represent an escape from personality" is to confess that "personality" plays a large, if hidden, role in its composition.

Kristian Smidt, whose book *Poetry and Belief in the Work of T. S. Eliot* was first published in English in 1961 and appeared originally in Norwegian in 1949, wrote to Eliot enquiring as to the identity of the companion accompanying the title character in "The Love Song of J. Alfred Prufrock." Eliot wrote in his letter of reply: "As for 'The Love Song of J. Alfred Prufrock' anything I say now must be somewhat conjectural, as it was written so long ago that my memory may deceive me; but I am prepared to assert that the 'you' in 'The Love Song' is merely some friend or companion, presumably of the male sex, whom the speaker is at that moment addressing, and that it has no emotional content whatever" (quoted in Smidt, 85). This somewhat ambiguous comment, with what appears to be a defensive conclusion, needs to be placed beside another comment that Eliot made about "Prufrock" later in a 1962 interview in *Granite Review.* There he said that "'Prufrock' was partly a dramatic creation of a man of about 40 . . . and partly an expression of feeling of my own. . . . I always feel that dramatic characters who seem living creations have something of the author in them" (quoted in Bush, *TSESCS*, 241–42).

Accepting all of these passages stressing Eliot's murky or hidden presence in his poems as embodying his basic approach to poetic composition, I have tried to discover all of the various layers of meaning in the poems I analyze, as well as the personal "lived through material" underneath. But since, some years back, I was educated in literature classes devoted to the "new criticism," which attempted to divorce the work from the author, I have inevitably also tended to read a given poem as a work that stands alone, with a meaning independent from its relationship to a particular author.

In this book, I have focused on the events of Eliot's life, and whether minor or major, I have tried to concentrate on those elements that shaped Eliot into what he became. An early example is the book written by his grandfather, William Greenleaf Eliot (who died shortly before Eliot was born), entitled *Lectures to Young Men*—a book heretofore overlooked. It was widely circulated by the Young Men's Christian Association, and in it are to be found severe warnings about drinking alcohol, which results in "lust" and the "lewd and lavish act of sin"—the violation of a woman's purity.

It was perhaps strictures like this that led Eliot to become an avid fan of Edward Fitzgerald's translation of the *Rubáiyát of Omar Khayyám*. It not only inspired Eliot to begin the writing of poetry, but clearly in its celebration of drinking and the other pleasures of life, particularly physical, caused Eliot to become (as he affirmed) "atheistical, despairing, gloomy" (see Chapter 2, Section 1). In effect he found himself to be an American Omar. Unfortunately, Eliot destroyed the first poems that he wrote under Fitzgerald's/ Omar's influence, but the influence continued for the next ten years—as he remarked repeatedly throughout his later years.

As an undergraduate at Harvard, Eliot deepened his rebellion against his family's religiosity by associating with the Boston Bohemians, and particularly those who revolved around Isabella Stewart Gardner (Mrs. Jack), whose Boston house and museum became a center for those who were devoted to unconventional lifestyles and behavior. Eliot had a wider acquaintance of Mrs. Jack's followers than has heretofore been realized. And it should be no surprise that, when Eliot settled in London, he chose to become associated with the Bloomsbury Group, including Virginia and Leonard Woolf, the

Strachey family (especially Lytton), John Maynard Keynes, E. M. Forster, and others who were in some sense the British counterparts of Mrs. Jack's intellectual and sexual rebels.

In this work I have attempted to present a narrative of Eliot's life, essentially chronological, with necessary digressions to examine influences on him during crucial phases in his intellectual development, such as Henri Bergson and Havelock Ellis. Bertrand Russell's role in the married life of the Eliots is given close examination. Among other things, I have also attempted to detail the interdepartmental politics of the Harvard Philosophy Department at the time Eliot was there. In sum, my table of contents reveals the subjects treated as well as the structure of the work, and it provides an accessible index or, as one reader has said, a "bookmark" into the book.

When I was beginning work on this biography of Eliot some years ago, I was invited to teach American literature at the Sorbonne in Paris. I found an apartment located on the Left Bank, close to the Parthenon and within easy walking distance of the Sorbonne and the Luxembourg Gardens. On going over to teach my classes, I walked down a street named St. Jacques. It was only later that I found out that I passed on that walk the Pension Casaubon at 151 bis rue St. Jacques where Eliot and Jean Verdenal lived in 1910–11. After becoming aware of this remarkable fact, I decided that fate had indeed chosen me to write the biography I have written. At one point, I went with a French friend to knock on the door of that address, now containing a book shop, and we talked with the occupant. He led us to the central courtyard in back, which was like that in most Paris houses of that sort. We asked him whether there was contemporary awareness that the house was once called the Pension Casaubon and that the American poet T. S. Eliot had lived there while studying at the Sorbonne. He appeared vaguely familiar with the names and he indicated that the place was no longer a pension but did still rent apartments.

On another occasion while in Paris, I made my way with my French friend to St. Cloud, traveling there by car through somewhat crowded streets that slowed progress. Unfortunately we were not able to duplicate the system of travel, some eighty years before, of Eliot and Jean Verdenal, who took a boat on the Seine that meandered through Paris and outskirts until it arrived at the gardens—which included many kinds of flowers, including (as I recall) lilacs and hyacinths. Verdenal gave an unforgettable account of his and Eliot's visit there in April 1911 in his letter to Eliot a year later. In this letter Verdenal revealed that he had repeated that journey, alone and melancholic, the very day he was writing the letter, April 22. As we have noted in the preface, Eliot informed Cleanth Brooks that the opening lines of *The Waste Land* were a verbatim account of his personal experience. Thus we arrive at the biographical truth of the opening of *The Waste Land:* "April is the cruellest month, / Breeding lilacs out of the dead land," and the actual existence of the lilac and hyacinth gardens—and of the joke contained in the lines (with their telltale quotation marks): "'You gave me hyacinths first a year ago; / 'They called me the hyacinth girl.'"

I have tried to shed as much light on Eliot's life and poems during the first third of his life as the material allows. And I have tried to refrain from leaping hastily to conclusions, leaving alert readers, ultimately, on their own to interpret what I have discovered.

In writing this book, I have come to the conclusion that what we have not known about Eliot is out there in the public domain, available, not hidden away in library collections of papers and letters that have been placed off limits to scholars. The critic must simply *read,* closely, the published work, in the context of the life.

This manner of approaching Eliot has radically altered my understanding of Eliot's poetry—but my respect for the work has only grown. He is a great American poet—and this is the story of his making.

1888–1906

ORIGINS

1. Eliot's St. Louis and "The Head of the Family"

"In my end is my beginning," the poet writes in "East Coker." The story of T. S. Eliot's life is to some extent an account of his retracing Andrew Eliot's steps, further and further back to East Coker, and finally his interment there, in 1695, in St. Michael's, the village church. His first American ancestor, Andrew Eliot, had migrated in 1669 from the village of East Coker, Somerset County, England, to colonial Massachusetts. The original American Eliot became prominent enough to be appointed one of the judges who tried and sentenced to death by hanging some nineteen witches in the infamous Salem witchcraft trials in Massachusetts in 1692. In those same trials, an ancestor of Nathaniel Hawthorne (1804–64) had also voted to execute the witches, an act for which the novelist apologized in his introductory essay ("The Custom House") to his novel set in Puritan Salem, *The Scarlet Letter* (1850). Eric Sigg, in his "Eliot as a Product of America," has provided a remarkable genealogical tree, listing Eliot's "far-flung" "Literary Relatives," including James Russell Lowell, John Greenleaf Whittier, Henry Adams, Herman Melville, and Hawthorne (Sigg, 15–17). One of the few American authors T. S. Eliot never read was Melville, and one of the few American authors he read and referred to repeatedly in his critical essays was Hawthorne. Eliot would later call Hawthorne the "greatest" of New England writers, saying that "there is something in Hawthorne that can best be appreciated by the reader with Calvinism in his bones and witch-hanging (*not* witch-hunting) on his conscience" (*ALAL*, 14–15). Eliot would share this Puritan heritage with Hawthorne and partake of a Midwestern version in the city of his birth, St. Louis.

St. Louis was settled in 1764 as a trading post on the banks of the Mississippi River. When Eliot's grandfather, the Reverend William Greenleaf Eliot, was inspired by the missionary spirit to leave Boston, Massachusetts, for St. Louis, Missouri, in 1834, he settled in what was essentially a frontier town, more Southern than Northern, with a population heavily Irish Catholic and constantly outgrowing its civilized needs. The "river trade" of the Mississippi attracted not only easterners but also foreign immigrants, especially from Germany. By 1854, the railroad would extend from Cincinnati to St. Louis, which would become for a time—until overtaken by Chicago—the hub of the country's rapidly developing railroads. It became known as America's "gateway" to the West.

It was the river, however, that brought Ralph Waldo Emerson to St. Louis on Christmas day in 1852, as part of his extensive lecture tour of the West. He had read his "Fate," to become a chapter in his *Conduct of Life,* on December 16 in Cincinnati, and Gay Wilson Allen speculates on its effect: "His emphasis on the power of will to overcome obstacles and get things done must have appealed to men who were conquering nature by determination and effort, men who believed that Fate was on their side" (Allen, 566). For the seven lectures Emerson gave in St. Louis, he was paid $500. There is no record of his visit in the biography of William Greenleaf Eliot later written by Eliot's mother, but in a letter to his wife Lidian, Emerson provides us with a characterization of the man and the town: "This town interests me & I see kind adventurous people; Mr. Eliot, the Unitarian minister, is the Saint of the West, & has a sumptuous church, & crowds to hear his really good sermons. But I believe no thinking or even reading man is here in the 95000 souls. An abstractionist cannot live near the Mississippi River & the Iron Mountain." The Pacific Rail Road, he noted, was under construction as well as was one to New Orleans. "Such projects cannot consist with much literature, so we must excuse them if they cannot spell as well as Edith" (Emerson, *L,* 4:338–39).

Ronald Bush, in his essay "Nathaniel Hawthorne and T. S. Eliot's American Connection," has suggested that from the beginning Eliot would be "haunted" by two Emersons. The first was "a man who by identifying his own imagination with the Holy Spirit had become a monster of egotism." The second, closer to what Eliot would become: "Having rebelled in the name of poetry against forces that would have drawn him noiselessly into the New England fold, yet constantly aware of the claims of the spirit as he wrote, Eliot trod in the footsteps of a man who himself vacillated between religious rebellion and atonement" (Bush, NHTSE, 66).

Another giant of American literature would come to St. Louis in late October 1879 and would record "night views of the Mississippi" in his *Specimen Days*. There Walt Whitman wrote:"I have haunted the river every night lately, where I could get a look at the bridge by moonlight. It is indeed a structure of perfection and beauty unsurpassable, and I never tire of it" (Whitman, SD, 229). Whitman was looking at the "engineering and aesthetic masterpiece" of James Buchanan Eads, whose bridge, then the largest ever built, opened on July 4, 1874. Sigg describes the challenge posed to the builder: "the river's fifteen-hundred-foot width; powerful scouring currents and winter ice jams; wide swings in volume between low water and flood stage: and a sixty-foot change in the depth of bedrock" (Sigg, 23–24). It was the same bridge Eliot would later recall visiting "in flood time" (quoted in Anon., EFSL, 29).

St. Louis, the city Whitman described as "the centre of our national demesne," would be the birthplace of Thomas Stearns Eliot, born on September 26, 1888. Although Eliot's grandfather died in 1887, the year before Eliot was born, he was a more shaping presence in the house than Eliot's own father. During Eliot's early years, his mother was writing the "definitive" biography of his grandfather. The book was published in 1904 (when Eliot was sixteen) as *William Greenleaf Eliot: Minister, Educator, Philanthropist*, with a frontispiece portrait of the subject at age twenty-four above an ornately embellished signature. In the sober, self-assured expression of the grandfather can be found the eyes and facial lineaments of the grandson. The book opens with this inscription:"Written for my Children / 'Lest They Forget'" (Eliot, Charlotte, WGE, v). Eliot would surely have read his mother's book—and would not forget. In 1953, he spoke of the grandfather he never knew: "I was brought up to be very much aware of him: so much so, that as a child I thought of him as still the head of the family—a ruler for whom *in absentia* my grandmother stood as vicegerent. The standard of conduct was that which my grandfather had set; our moral judgments, our decisions between duty and self-indulgence, were taken as if, like Moses, he had brought down the tables of the Law, any deviation from which would be sinful" (ALAL, 4). Eliot's paternal grandmother had been born Abby Adams Cranch in Washington, D.C., and was married at age twenty to Eliot's grandfather in 1837. She was very much alive at the time of Eliot's birth in 1888, living on until 1908 in a house nearby the Eliot household.

Grandfather Eliot's accomplishments were remarkable, perhaps even intimidating. Not only did he found the First Congregational (Unitarian) Church of St. Louis, serving as its pastor until 1871, he also founded in 1857 Washington University, serving as its chancellor/president from 1871 until his death. In addition, he founded two preparatory schools, Smith Academy for boys and the Mary Institute for girls. His interest in education was in the blood, inasmuch as his great-grandfather was brother to the great-grandfather of Charles William Eliot, who served as president of Harvard College from 1869–1909. His life is summed up on the memorial plaque dedicated to him in his church: "His best monument is to be found in the many educational and philanthropic institutions of St. Louis to which he gave the disinterested labor of his life. The whole city was his parish and every soul needing him a parishioner" (Eliot, Charlotte, *WGE*, between pages 358–59).

The last words on the plaque refer indirectly to his role as one of the leaders in a band of determined Missourians who succeeded in keeping Missouri, a Southern-sympathizing state, from entering the war on the side of the South during the Civil War, 1861–65. One of the most interesting of his numerous publications is his *Life of Archer Alexander: From Slavery to Freedom* (1885). Archer Alexander was a slave in Missouri owned by a master who lived not far from St. Louis. Upon learning that Southern sympathizers had sawed through the wooden supports for a bridge over which approaching Union troops must come, Alexander walked five miles to the house of a Union sympathizer and revealed this critical information. He came under suspicion and was arrested, but he escaped and fled to St. Louis, and ended up working at Reverend Eliot's home. Eliot knew his harboring a runaway slave made him guilty of breaking the Fugitive Slave Law, but he (like Henry David Thoreau) pledged his fealty to a higher law and persisted in protecting Alexander. Even after Alexander was kidnapped and held in jail by "hired ruffians" outside St. Louis, Eliot succeeded through Union troops in discovering where he was held and in obtaining his return. Eventually, Archer was granted freedom. Charlotte Eliot writes that "at the request of his children, Dr. Eliot embodied the incidents of Archer Alexander's life in the form of a narrative which reads like fiction" (347). The book was first published in 1885, only shortly before the author's death in 1887. And in 1920 it found its way to London as one of the books Eliot asked his mother to send when she was packing for the move from St. Louis to Boston after his father's death.

By the time of the nineteenth century, the Eliots, like many other descendents of the Puritans in New England, had moved away from the Calvinism of the Puritan period and had become Unitarians—that is, believers in God but no longer believers in a trinity, and thus rejecting the divinity of Christ and a "holy spirit." As often described (and criticized), Unitarians believed in the perfectibility—or essential goodness—of humankind. But there were varieties of Unitarians, as in the case of Emerson. William Greenleaf Eliot belonged to a brand that was in many ways quite Calvinistic, with a clear-eyed view of humankind's propensity for evil. Charlotte C. Eliot devoted an entire chapter in her biography of Eliot's grandfather to the part he played in opposing the "social evil" (the circumlocution for "prostitution") that plagued St. Louis.

The problem the elder Eliot set about to address is described in volume 4 of the massive four-volume *Encyclopedia of the History of St. Louis*, published in 1899, under the title "Social Evil Ordinance": "The city council of St. Louis, in 1870, passed an ordinance designed 'to regulate and suppress' the social evil, by subjecting the keepers and inmates of immoral resorts to a rigid system of medical inspection and requiring them to pay certain fees, hospital dues, etc., at stated intervals." In effect, this amounted to "the licensing of prostitution," and outraged "the moral sense of the community." The very term, "licensing of prostitution," suggesting approval of it, ensured its failure. The legislature of Missouri thus "placed it beyond the power of any municipality to attempt to regulate the evil by giving to it the sanction of the law." So ended "the only attempt made in this country to 'regulate' the social evil by an enactment of this character" (Hyde and Conard, 2093).

The principal figure inspiring the outrage of the community, and thus inspiring the defeat of this approval of prostitution, was William Greenleaf Eliot. At the age of sixteen or shortly thereafter, T. S. Eliot would have read in words written by his mother about his grandfather: "In the 'St. Louis Democrat' of February 25, 1871, [W. G. Eliot] protested against the further passage of laws which would commit St. Louis to a system that had failed everywhere else. . . . His own conclusion was that the 'social evil,' considered as a sin and crime, should be treated like all other sins and crimes, to be 'prohibited by law and prevented as far as possible by the conjoined action of legal and moral force.' Faithfulness in this course would 'reduce the evil to its narrowest limit'" (Eliot, Charlotte, *WGE*, 300–301). Eliot's introduction, through his mother's book, to the complexities of the "social evil" at such a young age most likely intensified his adolescent urge to write the humorous and sexually explicit poems, which he began at an early age and continued throughout his life in the epic King Bolo verses.

In the spirit of a crusader, the elder Eliot kept track of the "social evil" around the country. After his success in ending the "regulation" of prostitutes in Missouri in 1874, he saw the "obnoxious law" raise its serpent-like head in the legislature of New York. His biographer describes the letter he wrote in protest, dated March 7, 1876, to the *New York Evening Express:* "He appealed to the editors of the paper to oppose the law, for the reason that it would 'do no good practically and infinite harm morally.' From his knowledge of the working of the system [i.e., regulation of the social evil] in Paris, Berlin, and all the leading cities of Europe, he knew that it did not prevent the consequences of wrong-doing, while it increased the extent of the evil, lowered the standard of public morality, and brought into contempt the sacredness of the family relation" (301). At no point does Charlotte Eliot reveal William Greenleaf Eliot's view of the "pox"—the deadly syphilis—that the "obnoxious law" was presumably designed to, and to some extent did, reduce. Was it, perhaps, as many crusaders believed it to be, God's righteous punishment?

Although the "obnoxious" ordinance was repealed in 1874, there is no evidence that the repeal decreased the level of prostitution. *A Tour of St. Louis; or The Inside Life of a Great City* appeared in 1878, by two "Members of the St. Louis Press," J. A. Dacus, Ph.D., and James W. Buel, and, in a chapter entitled "The Social Evil: Some of the Bad Phases of Metropolitan Life," the two journalists were sweeping in their claim: "We may say that St. Louis is truly a great seething, sinful city, where shameless bawds are to be enumerated by the thousands. And this evil is diffused over a large portion of the city. . . . The lower classes of fallen women to be found in the houses which line a portion of Christy Avenue, Seventh Street, Almond and Poplar Streets, and some portions of Sixth Street, are among the most degraded specimens of humanity to be found anywhere on the great round globe." There was, however, another group even more threatening: "These women are generally younger and handsomer in their appearance than those we have described above. . . . They inhabit gorgeously furnished, and, in some instances, elegant mansions where a train of servants are maintained. They dress gaudily if not elegantly, and they adorn their persons with flashing jewelry" (Dacus and Buel, 442–46). The city described here is the city as it was revealed by two investigative journalists ten years before T. S. Eliot's birth.

Eric Sigg depicts the city closer to Eliot's own time in his 1994 article, where he discusses the syncopated rhythms of ragtime as an influence on Eliot's poetry. He points out that Eliot's "family home lay only a short walk from the Chestnut Valley 'sporting district,' where inside the saloons and whorehouses along Chestnut and Market Streets St. Louis became the world's ragtime capital during the ten years before 1906." In fact, the owner of "the Rosebud Bar (at 2220 Market Street, six or seven blocks from the Eliot home at 2635 Locust), mounted a National Ragtime Contest for the 1904 St. Louis World's Fair" (Sigg, 20–21). Sigg's speculation that the young

Eliot may have overheard this original American music is plausible, but Eliot's later memories underscore the certainty that the neighborhood his family continued to live in became "shabby to a degree approaching slumminess" (ILUP, 422).

Even after the death of William Greenleaf Eliot in 1887, his books of lectures and sermons continued to circulate in Missouri and beyond. One of these, *Lectures to Young Men,* published in Boston in 1854, was circulated by an "International Historical Library of Y.M.C.A. Publications, Springfield Massachusetts." Copies of this small book, bearing the endorsement of the Young Men's Christian Association, would have been bound for all of the many YMCA hotel rooms existing throughout the country (there was a companion volume for the YWCA, *Lectures to Young Women*). Its presence in the Eliot household must have contributed to the feeling on the grandson's part that the grandfather was indeed present—as the head of the family, the one who laid down the moral law. In a lecture entitled "Leisure Time," the teenage Eliot—destined to become the leading arbiter of literary taste for the English-speaking world in the post–World War I period—would have found: "One might as well expect to gain strength to his body from sweetmeats and confectionary, as for his mind from works of fiction. The very best of them should be used as an occasional refreshment; considered as the daily food, they are absolutely pernicious." Even so-called religious novels were to be avoided, as well as "historical romances—from Waverley down to the latest of the fruitful brain of James" (Eliot, W. G., 74–75). The young Eliot, as we shall see, was later to find Henry James one of his favorite American authors.

It is in "Transgression," the book's longest lecture, that the "young man" would have heard the voice of his grandfather list, in the order of their heinousness, the terrible temptations he must at his peril avoid. The roads to ruin are several: first—alcohol, "the intoxicating cup," an indulgence leading to all the sins (86–107); second—"violation of the lord's day" (107–13); third—the "sin of gambling" (113–21); fourth—a "subject the most difficult of all, requiring at the same time plainness and delicacy in its treatment," i.e., lust, the "lewd and lavish act of sin" (121–27). To escape this last transgression, Grandfather Eliot recommended: "Of all the influences in society, calculated to purify and elevate man's character, that of virtuous and well-educated women is perhaps the strongest. . . . An essential part of the education of a young man is in woman's society. He needs it as much as he needs the education of books, and its neglect is equally pernicious" (123–24). For those who violate a woman's purity there is certain doom: "He who betrays her from her innocence is not less hateful in the eyes of God, than the serpent who brought sin into Paradise. He who is upon terms of friendship with her after she is betrayed, unless for the purpose of restoring her to virtue, is helping her to sink lower in her degradation, and himself goes down with her to the gates of hell" (124–25). This Old Testament wrath, evoking the serpent Satan and the "gates of hell," would strike many listeners as more Calvinistic than Unitarian in spirit and vocabulary. Yet William Greenleaf Eliot had no problem reconciling the two in his own religious view. To his fierce eye, there was no way in which such evil as he envisioned disappeared, fading into some transcendent good—as it did in the benign Unitarianism of Ralph Waldo Emerson.

At the end of "Transgression," Grandfather Eliot cautions young men to respect woman and venerate her virtue. He who does not "is sinking very fast; he is traveling very rapidly towards ruin." After a catalog of appeals—by the love of mother, her sacred memory, the affection for sisters, the indignation felt "if any one were to approach them with an impure word or look"—he closes: "I appeal to you by the respect which you cannot help feeling for the innocence and purity of womanhood, to keep your own purity of character and to avoid this worst contamination of sin" (126). Throughout his life, Eliot felt the need (in his grandfather's sense)—and said so—for the companionship of women. And at the same time, he was throughout his life in some sense haunted by "the innocence and purity of womanhood." As for Eliot's complex feelings about his mother, he came to believe her shaping influence to be the cause of some of his deepest personal problems.

2. Sons and Lovers: Sex and Satan

Notably absent from Eliot's 1953 remembrance of his family, left out of the picture and unnamed, is his own father, Henry Ware Eliot. Eliot's father may not have become a Unitarian minister as his own father had wished, but he absorbed deeply his father's association of sex with sin. He once wrote to his older brother, Thomas Lamb Eliot, a minister of the Unitarian church in Portland, Oregon, setting forth his view of sex education: "I cannot get up sympathy with Sex Hygien. It is a questionable fad. I do not approve of public instruction in sexual relations. When I teach my children to avoid the Devil I do not begin by giving them a letter of introduction to him and his crowd. I hope that a cure for syphilis will never be discovered. It is God's punishment for nastiness. Take it away and there will be more nastiness, and it will be necessary to emasculate our children to keep them clean" (quoted in Soldo, thesis, 62). The Puritan spirit was indeed alive in those fundamentalist-like Unitarians who became moral crusaders dedicated to stamping out alcohol and sex as allies of Satan.

Although Henry Ware Eliot did not own his father's eloquence, he wrote about his life in an unpublished account entitled *A Brief Autobiography*. There he describes his feeling toward his father as "not one of fear, but of reverential awe," his word as "law and gospel": "I knew that he was always right. He was very approachable, and yet I invariably felt that I was trespassing upon his time, so valuable for other things. He was not a stern man. His eyes were magnificent, and one felt that he could read one's inmost thoughts. It was impossible to tell him a falsehood. Undue familiarity was never attempted with him." And he reported the words of his father's Divinity School classmate Jas. Freeman Clarke: "How can one be familiar with the Day of Judgment?" (Eliot, H. W., Sr., 25). Henry's relationship with his father warmed later, but these impressions of his earliest years were indelibly imprinted on his imagination, ready to be summoned in the years of writing his autobiography, some sixty or so years later. His boyhood seemed to have been in many ways typically American, especially as lived in a frontier town in the nineteenth century—he rode horses, played football (one accident knocked out his teeth), tended home gardens and fruit trees (his brother took care of the cow), ganged together with other kids to make mischief and sometimes mayhem. The gangs differentiated themselves by nationality and religion—the French Catholics (high class and slave-holders), the Irish Catholics (domestic help), the German Lutherans (somewhere in between).

Probably his only act of disobedience involved his going against his father's wishes that he become a Unitarian minister. When he said that he preferred to enter the business world, his father replied: "Then your education is wasted." After a pause, he added: "Except it has made a man of you." The son commented on this scene: "It was the only sharp criticism I ever received from him. . . . My prejudice [against becoming a minister] was largely due to the fact that I was obliged to perform so many Church and Sunday School duties. 'Too much pudding choked the dog'" (45–46). Business offered no easy career. During a period of failed attempts, he borrowed heavily from his father, who was more than generous. His fortunes changed in 1874 when he went to work for the St. Louis Hydraulic-Press Brick Company. By the time Eliot was born in 1888, Henry Ware Eliot had risen to the top in the company and recouped his fortunes sufficiently to become a philanthropist, in part as "payment" for his father's generosity. But his successes decreased his presence at home. The house in which Eliot grew up was dominated by the extreme moral views of his grandfather and father regarding "transgressions," especially sexual; and these views were imposed and reinforced by powerful women, probably through prohibitions and significant silences at every turn, in every crack and crevice of adolescent growing pains.

Because Eliot destroyed much of the early correspondence upon the deaths of his mother and brother, biographers are dependent on scattered comments Eliot made about his early life in his own writings and others recorded by friends and acquaintances. One of the most diligent of the recorders was William Turner Levy, who knew Eliot from 1952 until Eliot's death in 1965. In the 1950s, when his doctors ordered him to give up smoking, Eliot began to eat candy as a substitute. Levy wrote: "He told me once that his puritanical upbringing had left him permanently scarred with an inability to indulge this pleasure. Indeed, when he was a boy, he told me, although he had the money he could never bring himself to enter a candy store and actually purchase a box of candy for himself" (Levy and Scherle, 53). On another occasion, when leaving a church service they had attended together in New York City, Eliot reminisced about his youth to Levy, who wrote: "Tom told me that the Church had defined good and evil for him, whereas, as a child, 'All that concerned my family was "right and wrong," what was "done and not done."' We walked silently behind the ladies for a few minutes and then Tom concluded his thought: 'It is necessary to realize that every act of ours results in positive good or positive evil. There's no escape from that!'" (120–21). In such comments, Eliot makes clear that his ultimate rejection of the Unitarian faith of his family lay in its mistaken conception of the innate goodness of human beings.

Again, in 1963, when Eliot, who was clearly dependent on the physical assistance of his second wife Valerie, visited New York briefly, Levy casually asked him if he now frequently thought about his childhood. Eliot answered: "More often lately, William. I had a dream the other night of my family as it was at that time. Curious. And I was thinking the other day of how as a child I never got anything new, always hand-me-downs from my brother. I remember a toby-dog my mother made for my brother and when he had outgrown any interest in it, it was given to me! And my favorite childhood toy was a rocking horse—with real skin. It was a very expensive one, but somehow my mother got it cheaply—for my brother. By the time I got it, there were cracks in the skin" (135). Henry Ware Eliot Jr. was some nine years older than Eliot, and the poet bonded more closely with Henry, who was generally supportive, than he did with his much older sisters.

Eliot's grumblings in this comment may appear to be meaningless recollections. But it is curious that they all derive from mildly unpleasant feelings about the circumstances of his growing up, resentments against his parents and his one brother. And they are confided to a young friend who is unfailingly sympathetic and deferential. Do these and other such glimpses into Eliot's feelings about his childhood hint at some deeper unease about those circumstances and those relationships? The missing context for the negative cast of these old-age memories may be provided by two comments he made regarding D. H. Lawrence. The first is found on the typescript of his lecture notes for the course he gave on contemporary literature at Harvard in 1932–33. Perhaps he actually included it in the oral delivery: "What he [Lawrence] says about mother love in the *Fantasia* is better than all the psychoanalysts" (Soldo, *TTSE*, 43). In one of three lectures Eliot delivered at the University of Virginia in 1933, in a passage on Lawrence—whose work he at first had appreciated but later came to condemn—appears the sentence: "As a criticism of the modern world, *Fantasia of the Unconscious* is a book to keep at hand and re-read" (*ASG*, 60).

Eliot's endorsement of Lawrence's *Fantasia* is all the more persuasive when considered in the context of Eliot's violent attacks on Lawrence's novels and stories during the latter part of his career and specifically in these Virginia lectures, published as *After Strange Gods: A Primer of Modern Heresy* (1934). In chapter 10 of *Fantasia,* entitled "Parent Love," Lawrence writes about the intricate sexual relationships of children and parents: "One parent, usually the mother, is the object of blind devotion, whilst the other parent, usually the father, is an object of resistance. The child is taught, however, that both parents should be loved, and only loved: and that love, gentleness, pity, charity, and all 'higher' emotions, these alone are genuine feelings, all the rest are false, to be rejected." This may seem innocent enough, but Lawrence sees dire consequences: "This is how introversion begins. The lower sexual centers are aroused. They find no sympathy, no connection, no response from outside, no expression. They are dynamically polarized by the upper centers within the individual. That is, the whole of the sexual or deeper sensual flow goes on upwards in the individual, to his own upper, from his own lower centers. The upper centers hold the lower in positive polarity. The flow goes on upwards." The ultimate result? "There *must* be some reaction. And so you get, first and foremost, self-consciousness, and intense consciousness in the upper self of the lower self. This is the first disaster. Then you get the upper body exploiting the lower body. You get the hands exploiting the sensual body, in feeling, fingering, and in masturbation. You get a pornographic longing with regard to the self. . . . You get the absolute lust for dirty stories, which so many men have. And you get various mild sex perversions, such as masturbation, and so on" (Lawrence, 166, 172–73). Could Eliot have come to realize through Lawrence that the obscene lyrics of his earlier years were induced by his parents, and primarily by his relationship with his mother?

Lawrence's prose is thickly repetitive and densely suggestive, the meaning emerging as from an obscure, meandering, and highly allusive poem. The reader is implicated, for example, in the "and so on" closing the quotation above, with Lawrence's implicit assumption that the reader's imagination can easily supply many other "perversions." The passage continues: "What does all this mean? It means that the activity of the lower psyche and lower body is polarized by the upper body. Eyes and ears want to gather sexual activity and knowledge. The mind becomes full of sex: and, always, in an introvert, of his *own* sex. . . . And today what have we but this? Almost inevitably we find in a child now an intense, precocious, secret sexual preoccupation. . . . A child and its own roused, inflamed sex, its own shame and masturbation, its own cruel, secret sexual excitement and sex *curiosity,* this is the greatest tragedy of our day. The child does not so much want to *act* as to *know.* The thought of actual sex connection is usually repulsive. There is an aversion from the normal coition act" (173–74). Eliot's critics later would be in unanimous agreement that this last sentence appears applicable to his many poems that portray or refer to the heterosexual act, inspiring the word *misogynist.*

The only critical question posed by these and other passages from Lawrence's *Fantasia* here does not relate to their scientific veracity but to T. S. Eliot's strong endorsement of them: Why was Eliot so profoundly impressed by Lawrence's discussion of the effect on a son of an all-encompassing, or "idealistic," mother-love? A key term for Lawrence, and one somewhat old-fashioned, is "introversion": it must have caught Eliot's attention at first because of its closeness to the term Havelock Ellis uses in his volume entitled *Sexual Inversion,* the first volume he published in his master work, *Studies in the Psychology of Sex* (to be discussed more fully later). Friends and acquaintances throughout Eliot's life referred to his reserve, his quiet presence and cautious or measured speech, his secretiveness in the guise of "Old Possum"—a nickname bestowed on him by his fellow American Ezra Pound and picked up by others. Eliot's awareness of this widespread perception of himself is revealed by his taking over "Old Possum" and using it as his own identity (as in *Old Possum's Book of Practical Cats* [1939]). He also surely saw one side of himself delineated by Lawrence in describing the introvert's intense curiosity in "mild perversions," his "lust for dirty stories"—that private side of Eliot that comes to the fore (as we shall see) in the correspondence with his Harvard friend Conrad Aiken and with his London mentor and fellow American expatriate, Ezra Pound, revealed for the first time in 1988 with the publication of *The Letters of T. S. Eliot.* Moreover, Eliot saw an explanation for the sexual failure of his first marriage, a failure that must have become clear soon after the vows were taken in 1915 and that endured through their life together, until Eliot's abandonment of his wife in 1932 and 1933—when he was delivering the lectures at Harvard and Virginia in which he endorsed Lawrence's *Fantasia of the Unconscious.*

Lawrence's argument could only have brought back to him the painfully mixed memories of his experience with his own mother, Charlotte Champe Stearns Eliot. His parents were both forty-five when he was born, the seventh and last child. His paternal grandmother, identified by Eliot as his grandfather's "vicegerent," lived on until 1908, when Eliot was twenty. The nine years separating Eliot from his older brother Henry meant that they could not have been playmates; and his four sisters—including Ada (nineteen years older) and Marian (eleven years older)—he would remember primarily as adults. In addition, there was an Irish Catholic nursemaid, Annie Dunne, who occasionally took the young Eliot to her Catholic services, which must have awed the boy in their contrast with his customary and severely simple Unitarian services. As the baby of the family Eliot was showered with abundant love and predominantly female attention. The pictures of the three- and four-year old Eliot in volume 1 of *The Letters,* one in the company of his mother-like sister Margaret, show him in feminine attire fully self-possessed—much like the notorious picture of Ernest Hemingway at a similar age.

Presiding over this powerful feminine presence surrounding the young Eliot, Charlotte Eliot was in a position to shape him after her own desires, transferring to the young Tom not only her own love of literature but also her own thwarted desire to become a recognized poet. Eliot would later arrange for the 1926 publication of her long dramatic poem *Savonarola,* where we find lines that foreshadow themes in her son's life and art: "Can penitence alone forgiveness earn? / Or must I not in purgatorial fire / Atone the baser promptings of desire?" (Eliot, Charlotte, *S*, 18). She was a reader and writer of books, and wrote essays and poems for religious magazines in support of her Unitarian faith. Born in Baltimore, educated in private schools in Boston, she was sent for her "college" education to the State Normal School at Framingham, Massachusetts, an education preparing a young lady for a teaching career until marriage. She taught in a number of schools and states, ending up at the St. Louis State Normal School—where she met her husband-to-be. During the early years of their marriage, at the time of her husband's business failures, she taught at the Mary Institute to support the family. Throughout her life, however, she devoted herself to charitable or reform work. It was her crusade that brought about the reform in Missouri of the relationship between children and the law. She was largely responsible for the adoption of the Probation Law of 1901 and the Juvenile Court Law of 1903. And it was her work that brought about in 1906 the creation of a house of detention for juveniles charged with crime, thus separating the young from the hardened criminals. But all these activities did not deflect her from her passionate interest in literature (Anon., EFSL, 39).

In a letter of April 3, 1910, to her twenty-two-year-old son at Harvard (on the verge of taking his M.A. in English literature), Charlotte Eliot's salutation is "My dear Boy." She writes: "I hope in your literary work you will receive early the recognition I strove for and failed." She then reminds her son that she longed for a "college course," but found that she had to begin teaching before reaching the age of nineteen. And she quotes for her son the description of her that accompanied her diploma back in 1862: "a young lady of unusual brilliancy as a scholar." Although Eliot's mother made these cryptic remarks about herself as a youth, her letter was most concerned about the possibility that Eliot would specialize in French literature and about his proposal to spend a year abroad studying: "Your being alone in Paris, the very words give me a chill" (LTSE1, 13).

The reputation of Paris as a city of seductiveness was widespread in America—so much so that Henry James was able to take it for granted in his *The Ambassadors* (1903). James wrote in his famous preface: "There was the dreadful little old tradition, one of the platitudes of the human comedy, that people's moral scheme *does* break down in Paris . . . that hundreds of thousands of more or less hypocritical or more or less cynical persons annually visit the place for the sake of that probable catastrophe, and that I came late in the day to work myself up about it" (James, Henry, AN, 316). Charlotte Eliot's view of the moral ambivalence of Paris could have been influenced by the views of her son's paternal grandfather whose biography she had written. Reverend Eliot had witnessed a Paris in which the "social evil" was regulated—and rampant—and indeed, France had no law against homosexuality because of the Napoleonic Code. Henry James served Eliot as a model both in his life (his expatriation) and his work—in all its moral complexity. Eliot would discuss him, along with his other favorite American author, Nathaniel Hawthorne, in one of his earliest critical essays, published in the James issue of the *Little Review*, August 1918, "The Hawthorne Aspect [of Henry James]." And in a brief essay, "In Memory," he would write that no one "who is not an American can *properly* appreciate James" (IMHJ, 44).

3. A Frail Youth, a Bookish Boy

Eliot was plagued by a congenital double hernia, forcing him to wear at an early age a corset-like truss (the editor of the *Letters* adds in a footnote that

Eliot remembered as a child, on seeing a naked boy in a book, asking his Nurse Annie why he wasn't wearing his truss). Fearful of a rupture, his mother forbade the rough-and-tumble horseplay that was characteristic of boys growing up in America, especially in a frontier town like St. Louis, and after Eliot entered school, any kind of physically demanding games or contact sports like football (Powel, 28–29; *LTSE1*, 10–11). The anti-intellectual environment of a frontier town could have been extraordinarily tortuous for a young boy who was in some way "different," particularly one who avoided sports and took to books—especially poetry. Eliot must have found himself the target of taunting ridicule, both painful and isolating. Had the other boys found out about Eliot's truss, they most likely would not have restrained themselves from much cruel humor.

If Mrs. Eliot's concern for the health of her youngest child led her to deny him the usual play with other children in their high-spirited pastimes and games of exploding and imploding energy, it also led her to supervise his immersion in books. Shakespeare was high on her prescribed reading list. In 1932, Eliot recalled his early bouts with the bard: "The only pleasure that I got from Shakespeare was the pleasure of being commended for reading him; had I been a child of more independent mind I should have refused to read him at all" (*UPUC*, 33). Clearly the young Eliot was clever enough to conceal his dislike of Shakespeare from his mother. In a letter to the head of Milton Academy (April 4, 1905) Mrs. Eliot proudly noted that her son had read nearly all of Shakespeare, whose work he admired and could quote from memory. In this same letter, she commented revealingly on her son's isolation. Because the family had continued to live in an old neighborhood in St. Louis from which most of the other families had moved out, Tom "desires companionship of which he has been thus deprived." When she added that she has talked with him as "with a man, which perhaps is not so good for him as if he had young people about him," she implied her own sense of failure (*LTSE1*, 6–7).

The young Eliot did discover, on his own, the collected works of Poe in the dentist's office and read him during his weekly visits over a two-year period. But he could not have realized until later the pleasures of freshly discovering works that had actually been denied him. In his introduction to the 1950 edition of *The Adventures of Huckleberry Finn*, he writes: "*Huckleberry Finn* is, no doubt, a book which boys enjoy. I cannot speak from memory: I suspect that a fear on the part of my parents lest I should acquire a premature taste for tobacco, and perhaps other habits of the hero of the story, kept the book out of my way. But *Huckleberry Finn* does not fall into the category of juvenile fiction. The opinion of my parents that it was a book unsuitable for boys left me, for most of my life, under the impression that it was a book suitable only for boys. Therefore it was only a few years ago that I read for the first time, and in that order, *Tom Sawyer* and *Huckleberry Finn*" (IHF, vii). It seems ironic that a boy growing up in St. Louis, Missouri, on the Mississippi River, should have been denied the pleasure of reading the masterpiece of one of the greatest of American writers and a fellow Missourian who had also grown up on the Mississippi River only a few miles upstream from St. Louis. Twain's *Huckleberry Finn* was first published in 1884 and Twain lived until 1910.

Eliot never attended the public schools of St. Louis. For his beginning years he was taken to Mrs. Lockwood's School by his nursemaid Annie Dunne, probably beginning in1894, and continuing there for the next four years (ages six to ten). In 1898, he began attendance as a "day boy" at the preparatory school established by his grandfather, Smith Academy. While on a break from Smith, from January 28 to February 19, 1899, the ten-year-old Eliot took his pencil and wrote and illustrated "fourteen numbers of 'A Weekly Magazine,' *The Fireside,* containing 'Fiction, Gossip, Theatre, Jokes and all interesting.'" He was a student there for seven years (ages ten to seventeen), graduating in 1905. After one year at Milton Academy in Milton, Massachusetts, from 1905 to 1906, he enrolled at Harvard in 1906 (*LTSE1*, xix).

The Eliot house bordered on the Mary Institute, the girls' school founded by Eliot's grandfather. As a child Eliot, together with his playmate and classmate Thomas H. McKittrick, would use the family key to enter the school's playground. Eliot recalled this experience in an address delivered at the Mary Institute in December 1959: "There was at the front of our house a sort of picket fence which divided our front yard from the schoolyard. This picket fence merged a little later as it passed the wall of the house into a high brick wall which concealed our back garden from the schoolyard and also concealed the schoolyard from our back garden. There was a door in this wall and there was a key to this door. . . . In the schoolyard I remember a mound on which stood a huge ailanthus tree. Oh, it seemed to me very big and round on this little mound" (quoted in Soldo, *TTSE,* 5).

Eliot connected his shyness to the nearness of the girls' playground to his childhood home: "Well, you know, either in spite of or perhaps because of this proximity it's interesting that I remained extremely shy with girls. And of course, when they were in the schoolyard I was always on the other side of the wall; and on one occasion I remember, when I ventured into the schoolyard a little too early when there were still a few on the premises and I saw them staring at me through a window, I took flight at once" (quoted in Soldo, thesis, 153). John Soldo has suggested that this enduring memory might well be present in "Burnt Norton," the first of the *Four Quartets,* where Eliot writes: "Footfalls echo in the memory / Down the passage which we did not take / Towards the door we never opened / Into the rose garden" (153). And a few lines later appear the relevant images: "the leaves were full of children, / Hidden excitedly, containing laughter."

The curriculum of Mrs. Lockwood's School was designed to induce students to become intellectually literate and socially acculturated. Eliot proved remarkably adept in the one, and somewhat retarded in the other. His fellow student, Thomas McKittrick, recalls him as a strong competitor: "I can still remember my unsuccessful efforts to keep pace with him in mastering subjects that boys of seven or eight were called upon to learn in the 1890s." So excellent was Eliot that he skipped a level when he entered Smith in 1898. This same student also remembers that "neither as a child nor as an undergraduate [at Smith Academy] did [Eliot] take an active part in the activities of his fellows. He was diffident and retiring" (quoted in Soldo, *TTSE,* 23–24, 26). These observations provided by one of Eliot's schoolmates at his first two schools focus on traits of intellect and personality that are to be repeatedly observed by those who knew him, friends and foes alike, throughout his life.

When Eliot made his centennial appearance at Washington University in 1953, he summarized his experience at Smith Academy fulsomely: "My memories of Smith Academy are on the whole happy ones. . . . There, one was taught, as is now increasingly rare everywhere, what I consider the essentials: Latin and Greek, together with Greek and Roman history, English and American history, elementary mathematics, French and German. Also English! I am happy to remember that in those days English composition was still called *Rhetoric.* . . . Mr. Hatch, who taught English, commended warmly my first poem, written as a class exercise, at the same time asking me suspiciously if I had had any help in writing it." Eliot concluded his description of his years at Smith by focusing on his classmates: "I remember it as a good school also because of the boys who were there with me: it seems to me that, for a school of small numbers, we were a well-mixed variety of local types" (*ALAL,* 5–6). The curriculum Eliot describes is indeed formidable, and if it was "increasingly rare," as he noted when he spoke in 1953, it has totally disappeared some fifty years later. Although at the end of his comment Eliot mentions his fellow students at Smith, he singles none out as special friends.

Since Eliot destroyed the family correspondence, we have little knowledge about his first year away from home, entirely on his own, enrolled at a preparatory school in Massachusetts, Milton Academy. It is one of the most elite preparatory schools of New England, close to Boston, enrolling the children of the rich and prominent generally destined for one of the seven Ivy League colleges. Two of Eliot's classmates there were Howard Morris, who later became his roommate at Harvard, and Scofield Thayer, behind Eliot but a longtime friend who sought Eliot out later in England and who was for a time (1919–25) editor of the *Dial*.

We do have a handful of letters from Eliot's mother to the school, making and completing arrangements for Eliot's study at Milton. On March 27, 1905, she asked the Head Master if he would "take a boy who has passed his finals for Harvard." She was holding him back "for the sake of his physical well being." On April 4, in possession of the catalog, she discussed courses and her son's capabilities, noting that he was "friendly," "of sweet nature, and every inch a gentleman, withal very modest and unassuming, yet very self-reliant too." Her concern was that without an early decision on their part she would have to engage rooms for Harvard. And, she noted, "we are willing to have him wandering a little from beaten paths this year and take somewhat miscellaneous course." After her signature, Eliot wrote in his own hand a formidable list of subjects passed, subjects he proposes to take, and books read—a dazzling reading list in English, Latin, Greek, French, history, and physics. Notably missing are Dante and the French poets that would prove so influential later. The July letters indicate that both she and Mr. Eliot prefer that he go to Milton rather than Harvard this year, thinking "it will do him good." On August 28, 1905, she wrote that after conferring with her son-in-law, Mr. Sheffield, she had settled on the best course of study, courses other than those in which he had passed his examinations. Thus her son would be spared going over the readings a second time, which "would induce a mental ennui." By the end of September she was writing about why he had to avoid strenuous sports: "Tom has never fully realized until now, when he is almost the only fellow debarred from football, his physical limitations." The last letter of May 1906 denied her son's request to swim in a quarry pond until she was better acquainted with the conditions, "because Mr. Eliot's sister was drowned in one." A footnote informs us that permission was given and on May 23 the Head Master wrote that "TSE seemed happier than he had been at first, and was mingling much more with his fellows" (*LTSE1*, 5–12).

After his year at Milton Academy, Eliot entered Harvard in October 1906. The years at Harvard would radically change his literary tastes, his ideas about life, his religious beliefs, and his relationships with his family. But before moving on to Eliot's Harvard years, we need to explore here and in

Chapter 2 some of the powerful and shaping influences outside those of the immediate family and home—especially influences deriving from the young Eliot's reading.

4. Early Landscapes, Later Poems

In a letter Eliot wrote to Marquis Childs of the *St. Louis Post-Dispatch,* October 15, 1930, he reminisced about another important woman in his life, Annie Dunne, and his boyhood in St. Louis: "The earliest personal influence I remember, besides that of my parents, was . . . Annie Dunne, to whom I was greatly attached; she used to take me to my first school, a Mrs. Lockwood's. . . ." And she took him to see the Mississippi when it was overflowing: "The river . . . made a deep impression on me; and it was a great treat to be taken down to the Eads Bridge in flood time. . . . I find that as one gets on in middle life the strength of early associations and the intensity of early impressions become more evident, and many little things, long forgotten, recur." And it was through Annie Dunne that the young Eliot found that his parent's Unitarian faith was not the only one to exist, as she took him with her "to the little Catholic church which then stood on the corner of Locust street and Jefferson avenue, when she went to make her devotions." Some of the "little things, long forgotten" he recalls: "the spring violets and the rather mangy buffalo which I photographed in Forest Park; the steamboats blowing in New Year's day, and so on" (quoted in Anon., EFSL, 28–29).

Of major significance in his remembrance of his youth was the Mississippi River: "I feel that there is something in having passed one's childhood beside the big river, which is incommunicable to those who have not. Of course my people were Northerners and New Englanders, and of course I have spent many years out of America altogether; but the Missouri and the Mississippi have made a deeper impression on me than any other part of the world" (29).

When in 1930 Eliot set down these early memories of his boyhood, he was some forty-two years old. He had long since abandoned the Unitarian faith of his family and had rather recently (in 1927) converted to the Church of England—or, as he always referred to it, Anglo-Catholicism; and his major poetic achievement lay behind him. It is possible that some of the seeds for his conversion had been sown by Annie Dunne and the impressive Catholic services to which she took him. Indeed, on an earlier occasion, in the *Criterion* for August 1927, he recalled that Annie had talked with him about the ways of proving the existence of God (WRIC, 179). And it is possible also that these memories were moving him toward his climactic poetic work, *Four Quartets* (begun in 1935 and completed in 1943), in which the Mississippi River becomes a powerful image introducing the third quartet, "The Dry Salvages."

On giving a reading of "The Dry Salvages" to the American Academy of Arts and Sciences in 1960, Eliot introduced his poem with a brief essay entitled "The Influence of Landscape upon the Poet," published, along with the poem, in the spring issue of *Daedalus*. Since he was accepting the academy's Emerson-Thoreau Award, he asked himself whether he had "any title to be a New England poet." His poetry, he answered, "shows traces of every environment" in which he had lived. His "personal landscape" was a composite—a montage of "landscapes" that figured importantly later in his poetry: "In St. Louis," out of "filial piety" for "the house that [his] grandfather had built," his family "lived on in a neighborhood which had become shabby to a degree approaching slumminess, after all our friends and acquaintances had moved further west. . . . So it was, that for nine months of the year my scenery was almost exclusively urban, and a good deal of it seedily, drably urban at that." Eliot elaborated: "My urban imagery was that of St. Louis, upon which that of Paris and London have been superimposed." But there was also America's great dividing river, the Mississippi, "as it passes between St. Louis and East St. Louis in Illinois . . . the most powerful feature of Nature in that environment" (ILUP, 421–22).

His "country landscape," however, was that of "coastal New England from June to October." He wrote: "In St. Louis I never tasted an oyster or a lobster—we were too far from the sea. In Massachusetts, the small boy who was a devoted bird watcher never saw his birds of the season when they were making their nests." Later impressions, such as those of the English landscape, would "fuse" with these early impressions, but the poet stressed that the English landscape impressed him in a way different than it did poets for whom it was their childhood environment. And, Eliot went on, he hoped his words would illuminate the poem about to be read and "substantiate, to some degree," his "claim to being, among other things, a New England poet." However, Eliot concluded, "this poem begins where I began, with the Mississippi; and . . . it ends, where I and my wife expect to end, at the parish church of the tiny village in Somerset" (423). Eliot then read the poem, which opens:

> I do not know much about gods; but I think that the river
> Is a strong brown god—sullen, untamed and intractable,
> Patient to some degree, at first recognized as a frontier;

Useful, untrustworthy, as a conveyor of commerce;
Then only a problem confronting the builder of bridges.
The problem once solved, the brown god is almost forgotten
By the dwellers in cities—

. . .

His rhythm was present in the nursery bedroom,
In the rank ailanthus of the April dooryard, In the smell of grapes
    on the autumn table,
And the evening circle in the winter gaslight.

(423, CPP, 130)

The imagery of Eliot's St. Louis childhood is here; as Sigg points out, a picture appears in the *Letters* showing "the tree trunk, Eliot, and a playmate . . . with *Ailanthus* foliage visible in the background" (Sigg, 29). The river of Eliot's childhood is here, as well as the river "of recorded history," "with its cargo of dead Negroes, cows and chicken coops, / The bitter apple and the bite in the apple. We can hear echoes of Whitman in the call to "fare forward, voyagers." But most clearly, in this poem, we can hear Eliot giving voice to his beginning.

In this essay, Eliot suggested the sources of much of the imagery that dominates many of his poems, and especially, in his two long masterpieces, the cities of *The Waste Land* and the river and coastal scenes of *Four Quartets*. Near the end of his career Eliot came to think of himself as not the "European" or "International" poet he had once thought himself to be, but rather the American poet that he had finally discovered himself to be all along.

[2]

1902–1914

EARLY INFLUENCES

1. Eliot at Fourteen: Atheistical, Despairing, Gloomy

In 1902, in either the third or fourth academic year of his five-year stay at Smith Academy, something remarkable happened that changed the fourteen-year-old Eliot. This event has not been hidden from the view of biographers. Eliot himself has made a series of references to it in a number of pieces written and published, ranging in years from 1919 (a time of personal crisis in Eliot's life) to 1959 (shortly after Eliot's second marriage and some five or six years before his death). When linked together the references appear to be a kind of reluctant and continuing public confession for which there was no one capable of granting absolution. In his review entitled "The Education of Taste" for the June 27, 1919, *Athenaeum* of J. W. Cunliffe's *English Literature During the Last Half-Century*, Eliot rushed to a full-speed condemnation of the book for its faulty notion about how the young develop a commitment to literature—but he paused at one point to say: "The first step in education is not a love of literature, but a passionate admiration for some one writer; and probably most of us, recalling our intellectual pubescence, can confess that it was an unexpected contact with some one book or poem which first, by apparent accident, revealed to us our capacities for enjoyment of literature. The mind of a boy of fourteen may be deadened by Shakespeare, and may burst into life on collision with Omar or the Blessed Damozel. And none of our tutors could have guessed what piece of printed book would precipitate this crisis" (EOT, 521).

As we have seen, Eliot's mother forced Shakespeare on her "literary" son, inadvertently inspiring in him a distaste for the English Bard. Eliot had himself precisely in mind when he speculated on what literary texts might light the fire of passion in a "boy of fourteen." As he later was to reveal, it was Edward Fitzgerald's "translation" of the *Rubáiyát of Omar Khayyám* that initially lit Eliot's fire—and led him to those writers of the aesthetic or pre-Raphaelite movement influenced by Omar (like Dante Gabriel Rosetti in "The Blessed Damozel") and who were fashionable during his time at Harvard. Eliot's use, and perhaps invention, of the term "intellectual pubescence" should be noted, as it aptly suggests the very real connection, however subterranean, between the physical (i.e., sexual) and intellectual turmoil in the tumultuous years of puberty.

In the some half-dozen references to or discussions of Fitzgerald's *Omar* in Eliot's prose, the fullest comes in his lectures at Harvard in 1932–33, published in 1933 as *The Use of Poetry and the Use of Criticism*. (I refer to this edition; the page numbers in the 1964 edition do not correspond.) He had accepted an invitation to lecture at Harvard in part, as we shall see, to sever permanently his unhappy relation with his wife, Vivien, whom he left alone in England. No doubt his state of mind contributed to the several times in the lectures when he drew from the private experiences of his own past. He said in his introduction, in a note entitled "On the Development of Taste in Poetry," "Recognizing the frequent deceptions of memory, I seem to remember that my early liking for the sort of verse that small boys do like vanished at about the age of twelve, leaving me for a couple of years with no sort of interest in poetry at all. I can recall clearly enough the moment when, at the age of fourteen or so, I happened to pick up a copy of Fitzgerald's *Omar* which was lying about, and the almost overwhelming introduction to a new world of feeling which this poem was the occasion of giving me. It was like a sudden conversion; the world appeared anew, painted with bright, delicious and painful colours. Thereupon I took the usual adolescent course with Byron, Shelley, Keats, Rossetti, Swinburne" (UPUC, 33).

Both Fitzgerald and his biographer have commented favorably on the *Rubáiyát of Omar Khayyám*. In sending his translation to a friend in 1877, Edward Fitzgerald said: "I know you will thank me (for the book), and I think you will feel a sort of *triste Plaisir* in it, as others besides myself have felt. *It is a desperate sort of thing, unfortunately at the bottom of all thinking men's minds; but made Music of.*" And in his *Edward Fitzgerald* (1905), A. C. Benson called the poem "probably the most beautiful and stately presentation of

Agnosticism ever made, with its resultant Epicureanism" (Benson, 114–15). Here are two typical stanzas:

XIII

Some for the Glories of This World; and some
Sigh for the Prophet's Paradise to come;
Ah, take the Cash, and let the Credit go,
Nor heed the rumble of a distant Drum!

XVI

The Worldly Hope men set their Hearts upon
Turn Ashes—or it prospers; and anon,
Like Snow upon the Desert's dusty Face,
Lighting a little hour or two—is gone.

(Fitzgerald, 84, 85)

Why, one might ask, was Fitzgerald's *Omar* lying about in a household in which the parents clearly censored what the children read? Curiously, one of Eliot's remote relatives whom Eliot would find still teaching at Harvard in 1906 when he became a freshman there—Charles Eliot Norton (1827–1908)—had written in 1869 a wildly enthusiastic review of the then anonymously translated second edition of *Omar* for the *North American Review*, a magazine that had links to Unitarian Boston and for which Norton had served as one of a series of distinguished editors. He wrote of the author of the *Rubáiyát*, first pointing out what Omar rejects: "Strokes of a vigorous imagination, strongly grasping the reality, constantly occur in his verse. His boldness of expression often runs into audacity. Things held sacred he treats with a free hand, and what he ventures to think he ventures also to speak. The bitter contrast between the wretchedness of men in this life and their undefined expectations of a better lot in another life moves him at times to contemptuous irony of human hopes and efforts, at times to indignant scorn of the supposed divine order of the universe." Norton next turns from what Omar rejects to what he affirms: "From the illusions of earth,—the palace of misery,—he turns to the real, if transient, gladness of wine, and celebrates the joys of self-forgetfulness in the embrace of the twisted tendrils of the grape. . . . He has no disposition to make terms with the true believers. He is unsparing in his rebukes of pretenders to religion, and in his satire of ministers" (Norton, 571). As we have seen, Eliot's parents were successful in keeping Mark Twain's "vulgar" but truly innocent *Huckleberry Finn* out of their son's hands, but failed to keep out a blasphemous book celebrating the very forms of behavior that the "head of the household," William Green-leaf Eliot, thought most sinful—drinking and devoted pursuit of sensuous pleasures.

Eliot felt the need to give a full paragraph of explanation, in his Harvard lectures of 1932–33, as to the nature of the influence of *Omar* on him, first emphasizing what it in fact was: "I take this period [of the influence of *Omar*] to have persisted until about my twenty-second year [the year he took his M.A. from Harvard and departed for an academic year in Paris, 1910–11]. Being a period of rapid assimilation, the end may not know the beginning, so different may the taste become. Like the first period of childhood, it is one beyond which I dare say many people never advance; so that such taste for poetry as they retain in later life is only a sentimental memory of the pleasures of youth, and is probably entwined with all our other sentimental retrospective feelings" (*UPUC*, 33–34).

Pointing out that "we must not confuse the intensity of the poetic experience in adolescence with the intense experience of poetry," Eliot turned to what his experience of *Omar* was not. At this period in one's life, a single poem or the work of a "single poet" may invade "the youthful consciousness" and assume "complete possession for a time." Such an experience can be much like "our youthful experiences of love, we do not so much see the person as infer the existence of some outside object which sets in motion these new and delightful feelings in which we are absorbed. The frequent result is an outburst of scribbling which we may call imitation, so long as we are aware of the meaning of the word 'imitations' which we employ. It is not deliberate choice of a poet to mimic, but writing under a kind of daemonic possession by one poet" (34–35). Eliot, of course, was writing these remarks long after he had given up *Omar* and embraced the religion that *Omar* rejected. And he was using his year of lectures at Harvard to launch his permanent separation from a wife whose "company" he could no longer tolerate.

"Youthful experiences of love"? If there were such experiences in Eliot's youth, the curtain had been closed on them by the destruction of all of Eliot's early correspondence. Given the surveillance of his parents, and the nature of the all-male preparatory schools he attended, there seems little likelihood that he experienced such boy-girl love firsthand. Moreover, at Harvard, in all of the surviving accounts of friends and acquaintances (some as we shall see discussing his strong friendships), there is no mention whatever of dating or girl-chasing—or even a yearning for girls. But even so, in Eliot's linking of his experience on reading *Omar* to the adolescent experience of first (sexual?) love, he seems to define the term he introduced earlier ("intellectual pubescence") as indeed encompassing both physical and mental responses, the sexual mingled with the intellectual. Released by his loss of faith from his fear of Satan, he surely felt free to engage in sexual experimentation (autoeroticism or homoeroticism); since the Kinsey report (*Sexual Behavior of the Human Male*, 1948) it has been generally agreed that such experimentation is a part of growing up. Indeed, Havelock Ellis had many years earlier reached similar conclusions in a work that Eliot, as we shall see, did read: *Studies in the Psychology of Sex*, 1897–1910, including especially volume 2, part 2: *Sexual Inversion*. How far, or in what ways, Eliot ventured in sexual experimentation is a question about which we can only speculate. The writer Thomas Bailey Aldrich (the popular author of *The Story of a Bad Boy*, 1870) wrote in his 1878 essay on *Omar*, "A Persian Poet": "Though the poet [of the *Rubáiyát*] sings of roses and wine and friendship, he has little to say of love, unlike Hafiz, Firdousi, and the rest. In one place Khayyám apostrophizes a 'beloved,' but whether it is friend or mistress we are left in the dark. Here, however, seems to be a very plain case:—'A book of Verses underneath the Bough, / A Jug of Wine, a Loaf of Bread—and Thou / Beside me singing in the Wilderness— / Oh, Wilderness were Paradise enow!' [XII]" (Aldrich, 425). Aldrich chose the word "seems" rather than "is" for good reason; the gender ambiguity in "Thou" surely seems as great as in "beloved." And, as we shall see in Chapter 11, in the discussion of one of Eliot's major poems, "Gerontion," the "Thou" in the original Persian poem by Omar did indeed refer to a "young boy."

One of Eliot's most revealing comments on Fitzgerald, made in 1938, was inspired by an essay in *Purpose: A Quarterly Magazine* (January–March 1938) by G. W. Stonier, "The Mystery of Ezra Pound." Stonier belittles Pound for copying so much of T. S. Eliot, citing among other lines the opening of "Gerontion": "Here I am, an old man in a dry month" (Stonier, 23). In the following issue of *Purpose* (April–June 1938), Eliot comes to Pound's defense, and states in the process: "The line quoted from 'Gerontion' was lifted bodily from a Life of Edward Fitzgerald—I think the one in the 'English Men of Letters' Series" (ORPC, 93). The biography Eliot refers to is the one quoted above by A. C. Benson, published in 1905. This revelation sheds a good deal of light on Eliot in his period of crisis at the time he was writing "Gerontion" in 1919, clearly identifying himself at some level with the Edward Fitzgerald portrayed in the Benson biography.

This identification will be explored more fully in Chapter 11, but it is useful to understand for the moment how fully Benson stressed feminine traits in his summary account of Fitzgerald's life—a central event of which was his unconsummated marriage to a woman that Benson calls "the greatest mistake of [his] life" (Benson, 39): "He seems . . . to have been one of those whose best friendships are reserved for men. . . . The truth is that there was a strong admixture of the feminine in Fitzgerald's character. As a rule the friendships of men are equal, unromantic comradeships, which take no account of such physical things as face and gesture and voice. But Fitzgerald had again an almost feminine observation of personal characteristics. Browne's wholesome, manly beauty [Browne, like the intimate male friends mentioned in this list, has figured importantly in Fitzgerald's interior as well as exterior life], the comeliness of Alfred Smith, the strength and vigour of Posh, the splendid majesty of Tennyson, the sweet-tempered smile of Cowell—all these played their part in determining the devotion of Fitzgerald" (172–73).

The climactic comment Eliot made about the influence of the *Rubáiyát* on him was made in an interview with Donald Hall, published first as "The Art of Poetry" in *The Paris Review* (Spring/Summer 1959) and later included in *The Paris Review: Second Series* (1963). Hall asked: "Do you remember the circumstances under which you began to write poetry in St. Louis when you were a boy?" Eliot's reply: "I began I think about the age of fourteen, under the inspiration of Fitzgerald's *Omar Khayyám*, to write a number of very gloomy and atheistical and despairing quatrains in the same style, which fortunately I suppressed completely—so completely that they don't exist. I never showed them to anybody. The first poem that shows is one which appeared first in the *Smith Academy Record*, and later in *The Harvard Advocate*, which was written as an exercise for my English teacher and was an imitation of Ben Jonson. He thought it very good for a boy of fifteen or sixteen." But Eliot's imitation of Fitzgerald continued throughout his undergraduate years: "Then I wrote a few at Harvard, just enough to qualify for election to an editorship on *The Harvard Advocate*, which I enjoyed. Then I had an outburst during my junior and senior years. I became much more prolific, under the influence first of Baudelaire and then of Jules Laforgue, whom I discovered I think in my junior year at Harvard" (INT, 92–93). We might assume that, since Eliot had previously dated his enthusiasm as lasting until 1910, he found no difficulty remaining faithful to Fitzgerald's *Omar* while accommodating the dark outlook of Baudelaire and the ironic masks of Jules Laforgue.

How seriously are we to take Eliot's characterizations of the moods that inspired his poetry from ages fourteen to twenty-two, from 1902 to 1910? His recollections do vary: in 1932–33—a time of great tension and uncertainty for him—he remembers that after reading *Omar* the world was "painted with bright, delicious, and painful colours"; years later, in 1959—after the tranquility brought by his second marriage—he remembers that

Omar inspired him to write a dark, despondent poetry—"very gloomy and atheistical and despairing." No doubt in some complicated way, the two recollections are not at odds. What seems clear is that Eliot's silent rebellion against his family's religion and behavioral strictures, beginning with the onset of puberty, was indeed authentic, as is shown in the early poetry that did not get destroyed, as well as in Eliot's behavior at Harvard as described by his friends—his drinking and smoking—and by his lifelong interest in pornography as revealed in his letters to Conrad Aiken and others. What happened to Eliot, then, in 1902 was profound, as was what happened in 1910, encompassing the turning-point year of his life lived for the first time abroad—and in Paris. Over and over again Eliot saw 1910–11 in Paris as the year toward which his life was somehow impelled, and during which his identity was radically changed, and after which nostalgia would always carry him back.

2. Poetic Beginnings: Merry Friars and Pleading Lovers

Eliot's early development as a poet derived in part from the exercises he prepared for class assignments. His first published poem, "A Fable for Feasters" (*PWEY*, 3), appeared in the February 1905 *Smith Academy Record*. In his essay "Byron," first published in 1937, Eliot remembered the writing of "A Fable": "To be told anecdotes of one's own childhood by an elderly relative is usually tedious; and a return, after many years, to the poetry of Byron is accompanied by a similar gloom: images come before the mind, and the recollection of some verses in the manner of *Don Juan,* tinged with that disillusion and cynicism only possible at the age of sixteen, which appeared in a school periodical" (*OPP,* 223–24).

"A Fable for Feasters" is an astonishing poem for a young man brought up to believe alcohol the most dangerous of all sins, given that it leads to all the other sins even more heinous. But by age sixteen, Eliot was already two years into his secret addiction to *Omar.* Although written after the manner of Lord Byron's *Don Juan* (1819–24), Eliot's poem by no means paints a portrait of a libertine or rake, but rather of an abbot and his fellow monks given over to the pleasures of wine and lavish feasts. Gluttony seems to be their only joy; there is no suggestion that their wine leads to the search for sensuous pleasures Eliot's grandfather had warned about. By setting his poem in a monastery, Eliot shields from the view of his teachers and parents his poetic model, Byron's *Don Juan.* Moreover, he provides a moral frame by means of which he scolds the friars for misbehaving. Young Eliot follows with great skill the *ottava rima* of his model (eight ten- or eleven-syllable lines rhyming ab ab ab cc) for his twelve-stanza poem: "In England, long before that royal Norman / King Henry VIII found out that monks were quacks, / And took their lands and money from the poor men, / And brought their abbeys tumbling at their backs, / There was a village founded by some Norman / Who levied on all travelers his tax; / Nearby this hamlet was a monastery / Inhabited by a band of friars merry" (*PWEY*, 3). The snake in the garden of this medieval merrymaking is an uninvited ghost who haunts their fantastic banquets in which they overindulge in strong drink and rich foods.

The Abbot vows to give a Christmas feast that would be "from ghosts and phantoms free." After four stanzas of unstinted drinking and eating, he and the monks are almost comatose: "Over their Christmas wassail the monks dozed, / A fine old drink, though now gone out of use— / His feet upon the table superposed / Each wisht he had not eaten so much goose. / The Abbot with proposing every toast / Had drank more than he ought t' have of grape juice. / The lights began to burn distinctly blue, / As in ghost stories lights most always do." At this critical moment the ghost seizes the opportunity to enter and grab the Abbot "roughly by the hair," and, leaving the friars to "gape and stare," he vanishes with his hostage "swiftly up the chimney." We might have guessed that the sixteen-year-old Eliot would not have dared to let such heavy consumption of spirits go unpunished. His most vivid and appealing scenes are of the merrymaking and overindulgence in food and drink, but his ending portrays the monks as properly chastened: "But after this the monks grew most devout, / And lived on milk and breakfast food entirely; / Each morn from four to five one took a knout / And flogged his mates 'till they grew good and friarly." The flogging (does it have sexual overtones?) reestablishes virtue—as any good New England Puritan would be aware. The poet uses his final words to reveal his source: "'We / Got the veracious record of these doings / From an old manuscript found in the ruins'" (6–8). The awkwardness of the phrasing and rhymes tends to undermine the poet's claims to truth—surely a wink of the eye to the reader revealing that the tale was meant to convey, not a serious moral, but a bit of amusement. There is something of the bizarre, too, in Eliot choosing in a school exercise to write about celibate monks—ironically prophetical of what he himself in a sense would attempt to become in the late 1920s and throughout most of the rest of his life. But Eliot was never to find the merriment in life that his celibate monks of 1905 were portrayed as enjoying— "enjoying," indeed, in spite of the poetic punishment dealt out to them in the end.

Another early poem drew high praise from Eliot's English teacher, Mr. Hatch. It appeared under the title "A Lyric" in the April 1905 *Smith Academy Record:* "If Time and Space, as Sages say / Are things which cannot be, / The sun which does not feel decay / No greater is than we. / So, why, Love, should we ever pray / To live a century? / The butterfly that lives a day / Has lived eternity. // The flowers I gave thee when the dew / Was trembling on the vine, / Were withered ere the wild bee flew / To suck the eglantine. / So let us haste to pluck anew / Nor mourn to see them pine, / And though our days of love be few / Yet let them be divine" (*PWEY*, 9). In completing a class assignment to imitate Ben Jonson, Eliot might well have had in mind his famous "Song: To Celia," which has the same eight-line stanzaic pattern, with alternating four- and three-stress iambic lines: "Drink to me only with thine eyes, / And I will pledge with mine; / Or leave a kiss within the cup, / And I'll not look for wine" (Jonson, 891–92). Eliot's poem, accomplished as it is, bears at the bottom of the page (the earliest surviving of Eliot's manuscripts) the words: "(Doggerel license No. 3, 271, 574)" (*PWEY, 33*).

It is not a surprise, given the elegance of Eliot's imitation, that his teacher wondered whether someone might not have helped him. Eliot did not immediately show this poem to his mother. "Some time later," Eliot recalled, "the issue [of the *Smith Academy Record*] was shown to my Mother, and she remarked . . . that she thought it better than anything in verse she had ever written. I knew what her verse meant to her. We did not discuss the matter further" (v, vi). That Eliot's mother would think so highly of a *carpe diem* love poem that her sixteen-year-old son had written may seem surprising. After all, the "wild bee" flying to "suck the eglantine" is quite sexually suggestive. But the action the speaker proposes immediately after the bee image is not to make love but to "pluck anew" and thus replace the bouquet that he had gathered earlier to give her, and which had since withered. The poem's ending—"And though our days of love be few / Yet let them be divine"—does emphasize the brevity of life (as the poem must), but is rendered innocent by the concluding and ambiguous word "divine," hovering as it does between the physical and the spiritual. Eliot does not record as to whether his mother inquired why he had not shown her the poem when it was published. We might guess that the pubescent boy felt the subject—"seize the day"—might have offended her sensibility.

The seventeen-year-old Eliot was selected to deliver the class ode upon the graduation of his class from Smith Academy in 1905. Apparently he did not give his fourteen-stanza poem a title, but it appears in *Poems Written in Early Youth* as "[At Graduation 1905]" (11–17). If there is any doubt about Eliot's testimony that he had been swept off his feet by *Omar*, this graduation poem would dissolve it. It opens: "Standing upon the shore of all we know / We linger for a moment doubtfully, / Then with a song upon our lips, sail we / Across the harbor bar—no chart to show, / No light to warn of rocks which lie below, / But let us yet put forth courageously. // As colonists embarking from the strand / To seek their fortunes on some foreign shore / Well know they lose what time shall not restore, / And when they leave they fully understand / That though again they see their fatherland / They there shall be as citizens no more." In a letter of August 19, 1943, to his friend John Hayward, Eliot wrote of his poem: "I hope you will be impressed by the pathos of the hopes which I expressed for the twentieth century and for the future of a day school which was dissolved through lack of pupils a few years later" (*PWEY*, 34). Eliot's outlook is somewhat bleak not only for the twentieth century and Smith Academy but also for his classmates and for himself.

Graduation addresses and odes are generally supposed to be inspirational, saying, in effect: now go forth and live a life of great achievement and fulfillment. Eliot, therefore, must have startled his listeners by his stark, if elegantly worded, pessimism about the future. Stanza XI is almost blithe in focusing on the fleeting quality of all human life: "We go; like flitting faces in a dream; / Out of thy care and tutelage we pass / Into the unknown world—class after class, / O queen of schools—a momentary gleam, / A bubble on the surface of the stream, / A drop of dew upon the morning grass." In the last two of the fourteen stanzas, Eliot apparently tries to slip into a more optimistic or positive mode—but the lameness of the imagery and diction suggests that his heart really isn't in what he is saying: "As thou to thy departing sons hast been / To those that follow may'st thou be no less; / A guide to warn them, and a friend to bless / Before they leave thy care for lands unseen; / And let thy motto be, proud and serene, / Still as the years pass by, the word 'Progress!' // So we are done; we may no more delay; / Thus is the end of every tale: 'Farewell,' / A word that echoes like a funeral bell / And one that we are ever loth to say. / But 'tis a call we cannot disobey, / *Exeunt omnes,* with a last 'farewell.'" We can imagine that his classmates might have gotten a bit restless, if not depressed, before the end of the declamation of this 112-line poem—with many of the stanzas sounding much like a "funeral bell." This would be the last poem in which Eliot would raise a toast to "Progress!" What is impressive about the word is its position at the very end of the penultimate stanza, rhyming with lines two and three ("less," "bless"), and the intricate problem Eliot had to solve (by use of the fillers, "proud and serene, / Still as the years pass by") in placing it there—where, of course, it had to appear not only for the sake of the rhyme—but as an affirming climax.

3. Missourian, New Englander: Double Identity

Until Eliot was seventeen years old he lived at home, first under the care of his nurse, who brought him to and from Mrs. Lockwood's School, and then as a day student at Smith Academy. In 1905–6 he was enrolled at Milton Academy in Massachusetts, and left St. Louis, to return again on visits but never again to live. St. Louis and its Mississippi River left deep impressions on the young Eliot, which would surface in his memory and be embedded in his poetry years later. As we have seen in Chapter 1 Eliot called St. Louis the root source of his "urban imagery," and then specified the deep source of his nonurban—or nature—imagery: "My country landscape, on the other hand, is that of coastal New England from June to October" (ILUP, 422).

Gloucester and its Dry Salvages off Cape Ann on the Massachusetts coast north of Boston also made their mark on the youth. The fishing port of Gloucester, settled first in 1623, attracted summer residents and artists as well to its stark and picturesque beauty. Eliot came with his family to the house his father built in the 1890s from the age of five (1893) until he went off for his year of study in Paris, 1910–11. After this period he paid only a couple of short visits to Gloucester on two of his rare trips back home from abroad. Eliot's brother Henry stressed the significance of the area to Eliot in a letter written on February 27, 1942, to the Gloucester library: "My brother spent some 20 summers as a child and a youth at Eastern Point where my father had a house on the top of the hill back of the old Beachcraft Hotel. The poem ["Dry Salvages"] reflects a very deep affection for these scenes" (quoted in Boyd, 121).

Although Tom was forbidden to participate in any school sports, his mother saw to it that he was given lessons in sailing. His friend at Harvard, W. G. Tinckom-Fernandez, recalled in 1938 visiting Eliot during the summers: "I used to descend on him at his summer home in East Gloucester on my way to Maine. There I saw him in a quiet, charming family circle of parents and sisters, whose affectionate understanding of his arduous scholarship and his untried gifts must have been an inspiration to him in those lean years he faced [later] in a foreign land. He used to take me sailing in his catboat, and he could handle a sheet with the best in Gloucester" (Tinckom-Fernandez, 48).

Samuel Eliot Morison, whom T. S. Eliot addressed as "cousin" in correspondence, writes of the importance of Eliot's Gloucester experiences: "He and his brother Henry, taught to sail by an ancient mariner of Gloucester, became familiar with these waters, and Henry continued to live on Cape

Ann for many years after Tom went to England. The young men talked with James B. Connolly, author of *Out of Gloucester,* and with numerous fishermen and sailors." Not only did the two Eliot brothers enjoy vacationing at Gloucester, but they steeped themselves in its lore and history: "They read the story of Anthony Thacher's shipwreck in 1635, which further identified them with Cape Ann, because one of the passengers was 'Mr. William Eliot of New Sarum,' conjecturally a relative. T. S. Eliot eventually came to believe that his first American ancestor was in the shipwreck. 'Did you know,' he wrote to me on 28 July 1964, 'that the Reverend Andrew Eliot was in the company with the Reverend Mr. Thatcher when they went ashore on Thatcher's Island? What they were doing there I cannot imagine.'" Cousin Samuel Eliot Morison goes on to dispute Eliot's assumption, asserting that there is "no evidence . . . of a relationship. Andrew Eliot of East Coker came over in about the year 1669, according to William Graeme Eliot's *Sketch of the Eliot Family* (1887)" (Morison, DSTS, 234).

Morison described the challenges of sailing in the ocean waters Eliot faced as a youth: "These waters off Cape Ann are a real test of seamanship for sailors of small boats. There are numerous rocky passages that you can thread if you are 'acquainted,' and the *Coast Pilot* warns you to sheer off if you are not; big ships do well to keep outside the entire collection of reefs." But Eliot and his brother developed the skills to steer their boat safely along the dangerous sea coast: "The Dry Salvages, as Eliot writes, is 'always a seamark to lay a course by.' Leaving it well to starboard when approaching Cape Ann from the north, you shape a south-southwest course to pass between Thacher's and The Londoner. . . . The Eliot brothers learned that when sailing down East, after turning Thacher's, you must either steer northnortheast to clear the Dry Salvages, or due north to pass Avery Ledge and Flat Ground" (235).

Cousin Morison was a great admirer of Eliot's "The Dry Salvages," the third of *Four Quartets,* but he takes issue with Eliot's head-note to the poem. Eliot writes: "The Dry Salvages—presumably *les trois sauvages*—is a small group of rocks, with a beacon, off the N.E. coast of Cape Ann, Massachusetts. *Salvages* is pronounced to rhyme with *assuages*" (CPP, 130). Morison comments: "We may first dispose of T. S. Eliot's theory that the 'Dry' of 'Dry Salvages' is a translation of the French 'Trois.' This particular ledge has a dry part, out of the water at high tide. 'Dry' is a not unusual designation along the Atlantic coast for ledges bare at high water, to distinguish them from others which, like the Little Salvages, are covered twice daily. . . . Moreover, 'Dry' appears on no map in connection with The Salvages until 1867, when any derivation from *trois* would be farfetched." As for the strange word "Salvages," Morison points out (citing several examples) that the older spelling of the word "savages," used commonly by early explorers and settlers of America for the Indians, was "salvages." Thus the word, Morison concludes, should be pronounced the same way we presently pronounce the word "savages" (Morison, DSTS, 236, 242–43). In answer to Morison's letter raising questions about Eliot's sources on these matters, Eliot in effect capitulated, saying that he "imagined" that his brother Henry was his source, adding: "But I myself can give no further explanation and it may be that mine owes more to my own imagination than to any explanation that I heard" (246).

The first reference to the Dry Salvages by Eliot in a poem was in the original manuscript for *The Waste Land*, but it appeared in a long description of a shipwreck off the New England coast, which Ezra Pound marked for deletion. Here are some of the discarded lines: "Kingfisher weather, with a light fair breeze, / Full canvas, and the eight sails drawing well. / We beat around the cape and laid our course / From the Dry Salvages to the eastern banks. / A porpoise snored upon the phosphorescent swell, / A triton rang the final warning bell / Astern, and the sea rolled, asleep. / Three knots, four knots, at dawn; at eight o'clock / And through the forenoon watch, the wind declined; / Then everything went wrong" (*WLF*, 62–65). Two historians of the Cape Ann area, Melvin Copeland and Elliot Rogers, have written in *The Saga of Cape Ann* (1960) of the Dry Salvages: "The hazards of navigation in the neighborhood of Thachers and Straightsmouth are rendered substantially more serious by the Salvages—the 'savage rocks'—which lie outside Straightsmouth. The Little Salvages are about a mile offshore and Big Salvages [the Dry Salvages], a half-mile farther out. On a clear day the Big Salvages glisten in the sun, whitened by the droppings of myriads of gulls, but in stormy weather those ledges have brought disaster to many a ship" (Copeland and Rogers, 132–33). Thus, as Eliot himself wrote in a publisher's preface to a collection of true tales, *Fishermen of the Banks:* "Gloucester has many widows" (PPFB, vii).

One critic, John Boyd, S.J., found the Eliot summer home still standing when he visited Gloucester in preparation for writing an article, "The Dry Salvages: Topography as Symbol," published in 1968. He reported that the house still stood "on Edgemoor Road. . . . The road was named for the large moor it bordered, still partially there though partially built upon, but in those days [of the Eliots] it swept spaciously down to the sea." The house had been built at a height to assure a remarkable scene from every window: "The Eliot house commanded a 270° panoramic view: northwestward and westward to the Gloucester Harbor and beyond in the direction of Boston, then, moving counterclockwise, southwestward towards Eastern Point Lighthouse, then southward and eastward over the entire expanse of the Atlantic Ocean, past what is now the Jesuit Eastern Point Retreat House . . . then north-eastward and northward over Brace's Cove, Bass Rocks, Thacher Island, Straitsmouth Island, and ultimately to Rockport, off which lie the rocks that give their name to the poem" (Boyd, 121). It is small wonder that the Eliot family hurried every summer out of their St. Louis house and made their way to Cape Ann for an extended stay in their Gloucester house.

In his preface to Edgar Ansel Mowrer's *This American World* (1928), Eliot recalled his ambivalent feelings about his American identity; his "family were New Englanders, who had been settled . . . for two generations in the South West—which was," in his time, "rapidly becoming merely the Middle West. The family guarded jealously its connections with New England." It was, however, much later that Eliot discovered the ambiguity of place in estab-lishing his identity: "It was not until years of maturity that I perceived that I myself had always been a New Englander in the South West, and a South Westerner in New England; when I was sent to school in New England I lost my southern accent without ever acquiring the accent of the native Bostonian" (PTAW, xiii–xiv).

Eliot found his feelings deeply embedded in the two highly different places, both of which were his home: "In New England I missed the long dark river, the ailanthus trees, the flaming cardinal birds, the high limestone bluffs where we searched for fossil shell-fish; in Missouri I missed the fir trees, the bay and goldenrod, the song-sparrows, the red granite and the blue sea of Massachusetts" (xiv). It is no accident that in recalling his past, he emphasized what he was missing in whichever place he was living. But it is clear that, though Eliot had deep roots in St. Louis, the roots of his family tree were far deeper in New England. It is hard for Europeans, with their firm national identities, to imagine the kind of confusion of personal iden-tity that many Americans such as Eliot experienced. It seems possible that Eliot became a "European" living in England in part because of this very confusion for him (who am I?) in America.

In his memoir of Eliot, Herbert Read quoted from a 1928 letter Eliot had sent to him: "I want to write an essay about the point of view of an American who wasn't an American, because he was born in the South and went to school in New England as a small boy with a nigger drawl, but who wasn't a southerner in the South because his people were northerners in a border state and looked down on all southerners and Virginians, and who so was never anything anywhere and who therefore felt himself to be more a Frenchman than an American and more an Englishman than a Frenchman and yet felt that the U.S.A. up to a hundred years ago was a family extension. It is also almost too difficult even for H[enry] J[ames] who for that matter wasn't an American at all, in that sense" (Read, 15). Clearly Eliot never got around to writing such an essay as described here, but his description of his confusion over his identity, although superficially humorous, sounds a deep note of genuine concern and uneasiness. As we shall see, after his father died in 1919, Eliot (then living in London) urged his mother to settle alongside family members who lived in and around Boston. Of course, the Eliots' deepest roots in time were in England, in the village of East Coker where Eliot himself in the end would finally be laid to rest—his identity still uncertain in his own mind as well as in that of the world.

4. A Soul's Paralysis: "Denying the Importunity of the Blood"

One of Eliot's poems written in 1929, "Animula," appears to be a kind of biographical summary or survey of his life, with Eliot looking back on it in a state of psychological shock or misery. It is perhaps significant that the time of the composition of the poem, October 9, 1929, followed by barely a month his mother's death on September 10, 1929. His father had died ten years earlier, in 1919. The poem seems to reveal a despairing, sometimes suicidal man. His wife Vivien's severe illness had proved a never-ending burden. Even though he often blamed himself for the failure of the marriage, he was only a few years away (1933) from the day he would walk out on Vivien, avoid any contact with her from then on, and never see her again, eventually having her committed to an institution. Even his conversion to Anglo-Catholicism had not brought the solace he seems to have anticipated; it seems quite possible that although Eliot had affirmed his faith, he continued to have doubts about its validity as he had earlier in philosophy had doubts about the validity of an "absolute."

In "Animula" (CPP, 70–71), Eliot appears to give a kaleidoscopic view of his emerging into the world as a baby and his growing to consciousness and adulthood. The Latin title means "little soul," and the first line comes from a passage in Dante's *Purgatorio* (Canto XVI, lines 85–88), in which Dante contemplates the origins and nature of the human soul and the necessity for its acquisition of discipline. Eliot opens with lines celebrating the awakening of the child to a world of wonder, a world engaging all the senses, a world of light and darkness, of dry warmth and chill dampness. He depicts the child as he moves "between the legs of tables and chairs," "rising," "falling," "grasping," "advancing boldly," and, when alarmed, "retreating to the corner of arm and knee." Eliot conjures up the pleasures of the child's world as he encounters the "fragrant brilliance of the Christmas tree," "the wind, the sunlight and the sea" and "studies the sunlit pattern on the floor," the shapes on a "silver tray." The child's world is a blend of "the actual and the fanciful," "what the fairies do and what the servants say." After the first full stop of the poem, the open acceptance somehow turns cautious, as life is now fraught with ever-increasing burdens, with perplexity and pain, strictures and controls: "The pain of living and the drug of dreams / Curl up the small soul in the window seat / Behind the *Encyclopaedia Britannica.*"

Bliss is lost in the past and pain moves to the fore. The "small soul" seems to be holding the heavy volume(s) of the *Encyclopaedia* up as a shield against the world. Then, after another full stop, the result of this "education" of the soul "issues" out into the world, inevitably shaped (or misshaped) by the imposition of restraints, strictures, and prohibitions—all positive physical engagement suppressed in favor of the intellectual, as symbolized by that greatest of all assemblages, in alphabetical (and meaningless) order, of the whole of human knowledge: the "simple soul" is unable to move forward or backward, "Fearing the warm reality, the offered good, / Denying the importunity of the blood, / Shadow of its own shadows, spectre in its own gloom, / Leaving disordered papers in a dusty room; / Living first in the silence after the viaticum." "Viaticum" is the Eucharist or communion given to one in danger of death. The speaker of the poem appears to be in extreme despondency.

"Animula" is, of course, like all of Eliot's poems, open to many interpretative approaches, even, in this instance, allegorical—especially given its origins in a line from Dante. And there are many allegorical interpretations that remain on a somewhat abstract level, neglecting the few specifics in the poem that tend to support a biographical reading (such references as to "what the servants say" and to reading the "*Encyclopaedia Britannica*" in the "window seat"). Eliot grew up under prohibitions and restrictions such as to force him inward to become, as popular speech would have it, a "bookworm," isolating him from other human beings, substituting intellectual for emotional resources to wall out the world. The poem appears to suggest that such a severe upbringing of the soul has produced a life in death, inasmuch as all of those affirmative elements—such as the "warm reality" of human love—have been extinguished in him and his life has become a living death.

What does it mean to "deny" the "importunity of the blood"? An obsolete meaning of "importune" is "to force" or "to impel": the "importunity of the blood" must refer to those natural forces within that impel an individual to experience sex. We might ask, has Eliot indeed denied those deepest sexual impulses within him, impulses that somehow relate to his friendships? The strange line, "Leaving disordered papers in a dusty room," seems so specifically detailed as to conjure up a vivid image, but the surrounding lines offer no flushing out of the scene. The line seems related, in strange ways, to some that appear near the end of *The Waste Land*, coming shortly after reference to "The awful daring of a moment's surrender": "By this, and this only, we [the speaker and a friend] have existed, / Which is not to be found in our obituaries / Or in memories draped by the beneficent spider / Or under seals broken by the lean solicitor / In our empty rooms" (*CPP*, 49). These lines, as I have argued in *T. S. Eliot's Personal Waste Land* (1977), appear to refer to Eliot's French friend whom he met during his year of study in Paris, 1910–11.

After the lines from "Animula" quoted above, and ending with the mention of "the viaticum," there appears the only stanza break in the poem followed by six additional lines. The narrative voice (the story of the "simple soul") shifts to an exhortation to prayer—and the poem becomes seemingly quite specific, giving actual names ("Guiterriez," "Boudin, "Floret"), but also vague, referring to nonspecific individuals ("this one," "that one"). Eliot himself has indicated that Floret is "so entirely imaginary that there is really no identification to be made, though perhaps it may suggest not wholly irrelevantly to some minds certain folklore memories." Guiterriez and Boudin represent, according to Eliot, "different types of career, the successful person of the machine age and someone killed in the last war [World War I]" (quoted in Stephenson, 49). It is of some interest to note that Eugène-Louis Boudin (1825–98) was a French painter who often depicted Normandy coastal scenes—that part of France Eliot remembered so vividly when he recalled his arrival in France in 1910 for his year in Paris, where his pension-mate turned out to be Jean Verdenal, later killed in the Great War (see Chapter 5, Section 2). The "us" in the final line ("Pray for us") identifies the "I"—the agonized narrator of the "simple soul"—with miscellaneous others of his generation, suggesting the universality of his spiritual plight in a materialistic age of machines and destructive wars. The final prayer reverses the plea made in the Lord's Prayer: "Pray for us now and at the hour of our death." Here the prayer is "for us now and at the hour of our birth," life having become a living death.

As "Animula" seems explicitly applicable to Eliot's early experiences in life, so it should prove a useful guide in the pages ahead as we trace Eliot's life from his Harvard years to the early 1920s, through the year of publication of *The Waste Land*, glancing when necessary to the years beyond (as here) to clarify the present being dealt with. As we have throughout our tracking of

Eliot's early years, we shall continue to identify what we take to be those critical situations, events, or experiences that brought him to the desperate state of mind manifested in the latter part of the poem and to explore them in depth through whatever materials are available—including especially, and foremost, his poems.

1906–1911

HARVARD: OUT FROM UNDER

1. Prologue: A Problematic Student

Eliot's career as an undergraduate student at Harvard began inauspiciously. In December of his beginning year, 1906, he was put on probation for poor grades and "for working at a lower rate than most freshmen"—even though he had "an excellent record of attendance" (*LTSE1*, xix). In History, Government, and Greek he earned Ds; in German a C+; and in English, unsatisfactory. Years later he told his second wife, Valerie, that "he 'loafed' for the first two years" at Harvard (xix). In fact, his schoolwork had begun to suffer in St. Louis while he was still enrolled at Smith Academy, and it improved only moderately if at all during his year at Milton. These were, of course, Eliot's pubescent years, when he had to come to terms with his deepening voice, his growth of a beard, his sexuality. At Harvard he was confronted for the first time with choosing for himself what courses he wanted to take. In response to a letter from Dean Wells at Harvard, Eliot's father wrote: "I am inclined to think that he has been permitted . . . to take courses all of which are difficult and two of which require much outside reading" (quoted in Soldo, *TTSE,* 49). Probation was a serious matter that could result in expulsion. Eliot pulled himself together and was able to boost his grades sufficiently to be removed from probation early in 1907.

An account of Eliot's relationship with one of his professors, Charles Townsend Copeland, offers a glimpse into the life of a Harvard student during Eliot's time there. He took the famous composition course English 12, as did innumerable other students who went on to become distinguished writers and editors—Maxwell Perkins, Van Wyck Brooks, John Dos Passos, Malcolm Cowley. In his book *Copey of Harvard*, J. Donald Adams quotes a letter Eliot wrote to him about his experience in Copeland's course, which he took when he was a junior, 1908–9: "I did indeed take the famous course called English 12 under Copeland's direction, but alas I was not one of his real following and I never really hit it off with him. I don't really think, to be quite candid, that the course was very profitable to me. . . . I think the difficulty was that I could not learn to write English according to the methods by which Copeland taught it" (quoted in Adams, 153–54).

Adams was able to publish in *Copey of Harvard* one of Eliot's essays written for English 12, entitled "The Defects of Kipling." It was Copeland's habit to go over his students' papers in their presence, making oral comments that the students were obliged there and then to copy onto their papers. Eliot's first paragraph begins: "As the novelty of certain innovations dies away, as the school of literature of which Mr. Kipling is the most illustrious representative, the exotic school, passes with all its blemishes exaggerated more and more into the hands of less able practitioners, so Kipling's fame is fading, and his unique charm is diminished." The young Eliot was obliged to write in the margin Copeland's comment: "A mouth-filling sentence." Further Copeland comments dutifully written down by Eliot included: "A harsh statement with some elements of truth"; "Youthful rashness is not likely to be one of your attributes, at least until you are middle-aged." Copeland's overall comment on Eliot's essay concluded: "Although it is a great pleasure to see that you can at last swing a long sentence, swing several, each growing out of the one before, you must now be on your guard against becoming pompous, orotund, and voluminous" (158–61, 163).

Though most readers of this essay would probably agree with the justness of Professor Copeland's comments, they must have stung the young Thomas Stearns Eliot. In looking over his essay around the time he permitted Adams to print it in his 1960 Copeland biography, Eliot wrote to Adams: "I am not very much impressed by my own essay which is, as Copeland remarked, unduly harsh. But, of course, it must be said that a large part of the work for which I admire Kipling was still unwritten at the date of this essay." One has to wonder why Eliot had chosen to write on Kipling's defects for Copeland.

Apparently, according to Adams, Copeland frequently held his students "spell-bound . . . in his repeated readings of Kipling's stories and verse" (163). Was the student trying to straighten out the teacher?

Whatever the reason for his choice, Eliot was to go on and edit a volume of Kipling's poems, *A Choice of Kipling's Verse,* published in 1942, to which he contributed a laudatory introductory essay, "Rudyard Kipling." It has no doubt astonished many of Eliot's appreciative readers to find him not only editing but praising Kipling's poetry. How can it be that T. S. Eliot, considered by many as the inventor of modernism in twentieth-century poetry, should find something to praise in Rudyard Kipling's somewhat traditional verses? The answer may be found in his concluding remarks, where Eliot writes: "I make the claim, that in speaking of Kipling we are entitled to say '*great* verse.' What other famous poets should be put into the category of great verse writers is a question which I do not here attempt to answer. That question is complicated by the fact that we should be dealing with matters as imprecise as the shape and size of a cloud or the beginning and end of a wave. . . . I can think of a number of poets who have written great poetry, only of a very few whom I should call great verse writers. And unless I am mistaken, Kipling's position in this class is not only high, but unique" (RK, 35–36). Although Eliot's criticism has had great influence on the nature and direction of modern criticism, the distinction he draws here between "poetry" and "verse" has not been picked up by many, if any, of his followers.

Eliot's brother Henry had taken Copeland's famous course a few years earlier, and indeed Copey is one of the Harvard professors that Henry included in his verses for *Harvard Celebrities:* "If wit and madness be as like as Pope and others tell, / Then Copey by the merest squeak escapes the padded cell. / Those merry quips, those airy jests he springs in English 8 / Mean spinal meningitis at no very distant date. And is it all spontaneous, or is it (hush!) a bluff? / And does he make them up o' nights, and crib them on his cuff? / Oh, wicked, clever cynic! How dare you be so sly? / How dare you read 'Peg Woffington' and make the Freshmen cry? You bold, delicious joker! You know it, yes, you do! / There's but one clever, clever Copey—and that one is you!" (Eliot, H. W., Jr., 15). *Peg Woffington* (1853), a novel by British writer Charles Reade, is based on an episode in the life of the celebrated, flirtatious Irish actress, Margaret Woffington.

This glimpse of Eliot's experience in the famed Professor Copeland's classroom is one of a kind—the only one that has survived from the Harvard years in any detail. Clearly Eliot did not want to pass on to posterity the information that could have been gleaned from his letters home. What we must work with in the absence of the material Eliot destroyed are the few clues and revelations that come from a variety of sources, including Eliot's essays, poems, and commentaries, as well as a few reminiscences of friends and acquaintances. Before encountering this elusive material, it should prove helpful to get a general impression of the Boston, Cambridge, and Harvard of Eliot's day.

2. Bohemian Boston at the Turn of the Century

Although Eliot had been away from home the academic year of 1905–6 attending Milton Academy in Massachusetts, near Boston, his mother and father retained their control from a distance. But when he arrived in Boston to attend Harvard beginning in October 1906, he was out from under parental supervision for the first time in his life. It would be most illuminating to have Eliot's feelings and impressions as expressed in his letters home, but as we have already observed, Eliot destroyed all the letters of his early years, both his and those of his correspondents, after his brother died in 1947. In the absence of letters or diaries from this period, Eliot critics and scholars have turned to memoirs of friends and associates and to Eliot's own recollections, which he scattered sparingly throughout his voluminous essays and journalistic writings.

Here is a summary thumbnail description of Eliot during his Harvard days from Steven Watson's *Strange Bedfellows: The First American Avant-Garde* (1991): "Bloodless, intellectual, nattily dressed, [Eliot] outwardly conformed to Harvard's social caste, aspiring to the clubs on Mount Auburn Street and the traditional literary clubs. But mostly he buried himself in his studies, which provided a well-polished shield for his intense shyness. Eliot's significant undergraduate experiences included his discovery of Symbolist poetry and his introspective wanderings around Boston, which he described as 'quite civilized but refined beyond the point of civilization.' They inspired such early poems as 'The Love Song of J. Alfred Prufrock'" (Watson, Steven, 33).

This description of Eliot as a Harvard undergraduate can be authenticated (but not necessarily verified) by any number of sources available to Watson, but he footnotes only his quotation of Eliot's characterization of Boston, taken from Eliot's two-part essay on Henry James ("In Memory [of Henry James]" and "The Hawthorne Aspect [of Henry James]") in the August 1918 issue of the *Little Review*. It is an isolated—i.e., parenthetical—statement, reading in its entirety: "The society of Boston was and is quite uncivilized but refined beyond the point of civilization" (HAHJ, 49). The statement seems at first to be saying a great deal, but on second glance seems to belong in the dialogue of an Oscar Wilde play—teasingly ambiguous. Do we define "uncivilized" as "barbaric"? Just what do "refined" and "beyond the point of civilization" mean? Does the "refined" link with "nattily dressed"; "beyond the point of civilization" with "bloodless"?

Just what might the young Eliot have encountered on his "introspective wanderings around Boston" beginning in October 1906? Eliot himself revealed something of the deeply personal nature of his habit of "big-city-rambling" in a letter from London to his Harvard friend Conrad Aiken, written on December 31, 1914, shortly after he had moved from Oxford to London. "Oxford is all very well, but I come back to London with great relief. I like London, now. In Oxford I have the feeling that I am not quite alive—that my body is walking about with a bit of my brain inside it, and nothing else. . . . How much more self-conscious one is in a big city! . . . Just at present this is an inconvenience, for I have been going through one of those nervous sexual attacks which I suffer from when alone in a city. Why I had almost none last fall I don't know—this is the worst since Paris. I never have them in the country. . . . One walks about the street with one's desires, and one's refinement rises up like a wall wherever opportunity approaches. I should be better off, I sometimes think, if I had disposed of my virginity and shyness several years ago: and indeed I still think sometimes that it would be well to do so before marriage" (*LTSE1*, 74–75). Here Eliot reveals himself as the "night city-rambler" he became, roaming first the streets of St. Louis and Boston—and, later, Paris and London.

We have already noted what the city-rambler Eliot might have run into in St. Louis had he ever escaped the oversight of his mother long enough to wander off the respectable main streets. What might he have run into in Boston? Douglass Shand-Tucci, in *Boston Bohemia* (1995, volume 1 of *Ralph Adams Cram: Life and Architecture*), gives us some idea of the possibilities (because Cram's homosexuality was well known, the subject was important for Shand-Tucci's biography): "Of the widespread prevalence of homosexuality in Boston there seems little doubt." Citing reports that "an awful lot was going on," Shand-Tucci adds, "and not least in the Turkish baths." And there are reliable "reports quoted by [Jonathan] Katz [in *Gay American History* (1992)] that, whether one speaks of men or women, in union or living promiscuously, Boston in the 1900s had a significant homosexual population among all classes and in all sections, from the slums to Back Bay" (Shand-Tucci, *BB*, 205).

The Intersexes, one of Shand-Tucci's sources, was first published ("privately printed") in 1908 under the pseudonym Xavier Mayne (who is described as the "Author of 'Imre: A Memorandum'"). In its reprinting by Arno Press in

1975 the author is revealed as an American, Edward Irenaeus Prime Steven-son. The full title of the book is *The Intersexes: A History of Similisexualism as a Problem in Social Life,* and a summary description appears on the title page: "Before we loathe the homosexual as anarchist against Nature, as renegade toward religion, as pariah in society, as monster in immorality, as criminal in law, let us feel sure that we have considered well whatever the complex mystery of Life presents as his defense." The dedication page reads: "To the memory of that pioneer in dispassionate, humane, scientific study of simili-sexualism, Dr. Richard von Krafft-Ebing, I inscribe this book, with humil-ity; remembering that without his suggestion and aid it would never have been begun nor carried on to its close."

The works described in the foregoing paragraphs will be important ref-erences later in this account of Eliot's life and times; but for an account of Boston at the time Eliot attended Harvard it should prove illuminating to quote from *The Intersexes* a passage from appendix C entitled "Uranianism in the United States of North America": "Certain smart clubs are well-known for their homosexual atmospheres, in New York, Boston, Washington, Chi-cago, New Orleans, St. Louis, and other centers. Resorts in the way of steam-baths and restaurants are plentifully known—to the initiated. With many such resorts there is no police-interference, though their proceedings and patronage, night by night, day by day, are perfectly plain." Mayne makes clear that the public baths were the centers for such sexual activity in the metropolises: "A special factor in homosexual uses of the vapour-bath estab-lishments (in larger cities) is the fact that in America these are kept open, and much patronized, during all night hours, and first morning ones; indeed some are never closed at all; in many examples a double staff of attendants being employed. In most such baths, each client has always a separate dressing-room, usually with a couch. What 'goes on' is under the guest's own lock and key, and without surveillance. New York, Boston, Washington, Chicago, St. Louis, San Francisco, Milwaukee, New Orleans, Philadelphia, are 'homosex-ual capitals'" (Mayne, 640).

The Dr. Richard von Krafft-Ebing (1840–1902) to whom *The Intersexes* is dedicated was a German neuropsychiatrist best known for his studies in "psychopathology" published in his *Psychopathia Sexualis,* translated into English in 1886 and widely known (its 17th edition appeared in 1924). It was singled out by Peter Gay in *The Tender Passion* (1986) as one of the "most resounding salvos" in an "accelerating cannonade of confession, celebration, medical and legal inquiry" in the latter nineteenth century. His book was a "culmination" rather than a "beginning," and brought Krafft-Ebing "fame, controversy, and continuous demands for revised editions, but what was new in it was mainly its calm manner of presentation, its detailed, orderly, even stylish way with sexual abnormalities" (Gay, 221, 223). Gay notes that Krafft-Ebing wrote in the preface to the first edition that it was his "sad prerogative" as a physician to "view the shadow side of life, of human weakness and wretchedness," and he warned that his book was addressed only to "serious researchers in the domains of natural science and jurisprudence" (230). To make sure prurient readers would be put off, he switched to a hybrid (but fairly transparent) Latin for the vividly intimate portions of the many narratives he printed, "cases" that quoted his patients suffering from a wide range of "perversions" (including homosexuality, sodomy and bestiality, and "anaesthesia sexualis" [absence of sexual feeling]).

As a matter of fact, *The Intersexes* goes out of its way in constructing its defense of "homosexualism," describing the achievements of many writers and musicians whose works were inspired and informed by their psychological-sexual nature and citing such figures as Walt Whitman and Richard Wagner. A widely popular work that preceded *The Intersexes* by some dozen years, Max Nordau's *Degeneration* (1895), presented a vivid attack on Whitman, Wagner, and other artists (or "aesthetes") as, indeed, "degenerates," in support of the catastrophic view that the "whole of civilized humanity" had been "converted to the aesthetics of the Dusk of the Nations" (Nordau, 7). Larzer Ziff writes in his *The American 1890s* (1966): "[In *Degeneration*] Nordau announced that degenerates are not always criminals, prostitutes, anarchists, and pronounced lunatics, but often artists and authors, since the same psychological features can be signaled as easily with the pen as with the knife." Although society had attempted to eliminate "depravity," it had "lost [its] energy" in the "twilight of the century":"Its vitality had been drained off in pursuit of the immense potentials of the new technology and had been sapped by the greater concentration of men in cities. The result was an outbreak of the unhealthy in the arts, an insistence on personality above custom, mysticism above tradition, and impulse above law" (Ziff, 136).

On his night wanderings through Boston, Eliot must have encountered many of the kinds of characters and scenes portrayed in these books, but did he ever encounter (day or night) the books themselves? We know of Eliot's interest in the psychological cases of "inversion" because, as we have seen, he read D. H. Lawrence's *Fantasia of the Unconscious* (1922) and found it full of the truth that Sigmund Freud—Eliot thought—had missed. And we know from such attacks on Freud that he must have read the Austrian father of psychoanalysis relatively early, certainly after Freud's first appearance in America in 1909 at Clark University, Worcester, Massachusetts, to deliver a series of lectures and to receive an honorary degree (along with Carl Jung and Sándor Ferenczi). Many of Harvard's professors (including William James) were in the audience, and it is even possible that Eliot attended. Or he might have chosen instead to go elsewhere in Worcester (near Boston) to take in a sideshow. We find this account of Freud's appearance in Massachusetts: "The *Boston Evening Transcript* sent a special correspondent. There was one notorious uninvited guest, Emma Goldman, whom the *Transcript* referred to as 'Satan,' and who happened to be in Worcester on a speaking tour. Forbidden by the police to rent a hall, she had talked, perhaps about her favorite subjects, anarchy and free love, to some three hundred people on a sympathizer's front lawn" (Hale, 5). The land of Puritanism had by the early 1900s traveled a far distance from its origins—and lost its propensity to condemn and execute those citizens who did not conform to conventional heterosexual practices under the sanctity of the marriage vow.

3. Bohemian Harvard and Isabella Stewart Gardner ("Mrs. Jack")

In a section entitled "Oh Harvard—Harvard," Douglass Shand-Tucci writes in *Boston Bohemia*: "By the nineties things had reached such a point that one author [Xavier Mayne, i.e., Edward Stevenson, in *The Intersexes*] was bold enough to report in 1908 that among American colleges at the end of the nineteenth and the beginning of the twentieth centuries Harvard and Princeton stood out for their homosexual auras" (Shand-Tucci, BB, 169). As in other places, "bohemian behavior" became identified with particular locales or neighborhoods. In giving a thumbnail sketch of one of Harvard's notorious bohemians, Shand-Tucci tells the story of a Harvard professor, Archibald Cary Coolidge, establishing "an Oxbridge-type residential complex in and around Randolph Hall, which he built in 1897 on Mount Auburn Street, a block from Harvard Yard along Harvard's Gold Coast. . . . Coolidge himself resided there for over two decades, living with and mentoring carefully vetted undergraduates in his elegant lodgings in Randolph Hall." Among the attractions he added over time to his dormitories was an "indoor swimming pool—an attraction not unrelated to Turkish baths and one that virtually constitutes in this context the collegiate homoerotic equivalent of that religious homoerotic architectural setting already considered here, the divided choir of an Anglo-American school chapel. (Coolidge also commissioned the famous artist Edward Penfield to adorn one of Randolph Hall's rooms with arresting murals celebrating Harvard athletes.)" (232–33).

Isabella Stewart Gardner (1840–1924), or, as she was known to friends, "Mrs. Jack," after her deceased husband, was the wealthy Boston widow who, according to Shand-Tucci, became the center of Boston bohemian life in the latter 1800s and early 1900s. Establishing her art-filled Venetian villa, Fenway Court, as the well-known Isabella Stewart Gardner Art Museum in Boston in 1903, she was aided in her selection of art by one of her fellow Bohemians, himself a Harvard graduate, Bernard Berenson. Shand-Tucci writes of her: "Gardner's sensitivity to gay young men was not just a case of finding non-threatening escorts, but was rooted in her experience with the three orphaned nephews of her husband, whom the Gardners raised." Joseph Peabody Gardner (known as Joe Jr.), William Amory Gardner (known as W. A. G.), and Augustus Peabody Gardner—all were gay, Joe Jr. committing suicide in 1886 over an unrequited love. Shand-Tucci concludes: "Isabella Stewart Gardner's experience of homosexuality was neither social nor trivial" (231). Coolidge, mentioned above, was another nephew. Letters to her in Boston from T. S. Eliot in England during the Great War reveal that he shared with her many friends and interests, suggesting that, during his seven years at Harvard (1906–10 and 1911–14), he often mingled with her circle of bohemian, or "aesthete," friends. The editor of Eliot's letters reveals in a footnote that Gardner's "guest book records two visits by TSE in 1912" (*LTSE1*, 93). It seems likely, by the tone of Eliot's letters to her, that he was a much more frequent visitor than this note indicates.

The young Eliot began his Harvard career in October 1906 by moving into one of the addresses along the bohemian "Gold Coast," on the same street as Coolidge's princely "dormitory": 52 Mount Auburn Street. There remain few firsthand accounts of Eliot at this time, but one of his friends, Leon Magaw Little, writing in the *Harvard Advocate* the year after Eliot's death (1966), remembered: "As a freshman, T. S. Eliot was of the type that welcomes friendships but is too reserved to seek them. However, his scholastic brilliance and his charming personality quickly brought to him a circle of friends of two quite divergent types, the intellectuals on the one hand and, on the other, many of those who were not considered in that category. His requirements seemed to be a reasonable amount of brains but above all a happy, keen sense of humor. Within the circles of these friends he was a very gay companion" (quoted in Soldo, *TTSE*, 53). Eliot himself had, in "The Aims of Education" (a series of lectures delivered at the University of Chicago in 1951), noted that at the Harvard of his day, there were two kinds of students: the "serious minded" and the "triflers" or "idlers." The latter manipulated their schedules so as to maximize the time of their long weekends— to be spent in whatever noneducational pursuits beckoned them (*TCTC*, 80).

In his second year, Eliot lived at 22 Russell Hall, sharing rooms with two other students: one of these was a friend of his Milton Academy days,

Howard Morris of Milwaukee. An acquaintance wrote years after: "Viewed in the later light of Eliot's career, it was one of the strangest combinations I have ever known. Morris weighs about 250 pounds, loves to eat and drink, and had few if any literary interests" (quoted in Soldo, *TTSE*, 53). In his third year, his last as an undergraduate, Eliot lived at 25 Holyoke Street. And in his fourth year, working on his M.A., he lived at 42 Apley Court, sharing rooms with Alan Seeger, a poet who later enlisted in the French Foreign Legion during World War I and was killed in the Battle of the Somme in 1916. His most famous poem, "I Have a Rendezvous with Death," appeared in the *North American Review* in October 1916. A fellow student and admirer of Seeger, when asked much later about his memories of T. S. Eliot, wrote that he was "chiefly impressed by his [Eliot's] sharing rooms with Alan Seeger who as I remember was far more colorful in undergraduate eyes and was considered something of an aesthete and was said to wear a golden fillet around his longish hair after washing it. So in my very slight acquaintance with Eliot, I was inclined to think of him as an aesthete too" (53).

In his abbreviated undergraduate career, Eliot was elected to two clubs, the Stylus and the Signet, sometimes described as the clubs for the literati. But during Eliot's time, they were known for much more. "It was through such clubs," writes Shand-Tucci, "that [Professor George] Santayana presided over aesthete Harvard. One such, recalled by Van Wyck Brooks [Harvard 1904], was 'the Stylus Club, [in] the straw-yellow wooden house [at] 41 Winthrop Street [still standing]. . . . [Professor] Pierre [Chaignon] La Rose [neé Peter Ross], Santayana's friend . . . [was also] in the circle of the Stylus . . . [and] personified the Pre-Raphaelite aestheticism and dilettantish Catholicism that flourished at Harvard. . . .' After taking his degree in 1895, [Pierre La Rose] stayed at Harvard to teach in the English department. He was dubbed 'the aesthete of Apley Court'" (Shand-Tucci, *BB*, 170). Thus he was one of the professors who attracted the attention of T. S. Eliot's older brother, Henry Ware Eliot (who, after two years at Washington University transferred to Harvard in 1900, graduating in 1902). Indeed, Henry portrayed Pierre La Rose in a brief portrait-poem published in *Harvard Celebrities,* 1901: "Mon dieu! What is it that it is! / A-walking on the Square? / We'll brush away the smoke—Voila! / Il est le bon Pierre! / He has the figure—is it not? / Petit et débonnaire! // At morn he punctures daily themes / With aphorisms neat, / At noon he bubbles with the sports / Upon Mount Auburn Street; / At eve he does the knobby stunt / With Mrs. Jack's *elite.* // See how the Radcliffe maidens turn / To rubber at his clothes; / He has a truly high-life way / Of turning out his toes. / The nifty Prince of Apley Court, / Our dainty, home-grown rose!" (Eliot, H. W., Jr., [25]). "Mrs. Jack," as we have seen, was the familiar nickname of the wealthy widow Isabella Stewart Gardner who was the presiding hostess—Shand-Tucci calls her "godmother" (Shand-Tucci, BB, 230)—for the Boston Bohemians. La Rose emerges from Henry Eliot's verses as a dandy, delicately balancing masculine and feminine traits.

Shand-Tucci further observes that among Boston's suburbs, Cambridge "contained Bohemia's heaviest concentration" of "*dandies,*" including Bertram Goodhue, the "aesthete" artist/architect, who "actually lived there, on Buckingham street." Shand-Tucci points out that Van Wyck Brooks recalled, in his *Autobiography,* that at the Stylus "everyone read Walter Pater's *Marius the Epicurean* (a defense of life as chiefly aesthetic appreciation), and the bookcases overflowed with Joris-Karl Huysmans and Oscar Wilde. Even Swinburne; Martin Green [in *The Mount Vernon Street Warrens*] observes that everywhere it was Swinburne who provided 'the litanies of aesthetic/erotic rebellion' so vital to the fin-de-siècle" (331).

In concluding an account of Eliot's "social life" as an undergraduate of Harvard in his unpublished M.A. thesis, Harford Willing Hare Powel Jr., writes: "It is important to observe that T. S. Eliot lived on the Gold Coast . . . in his freshman year, that he was something of a dandy in dress. . . . It becomes apparent that Eliot's career at Harvard was a mixture of opposites: he cut the figure of one of his 'triflers' [Eliot's term, meaning 'idlers' and 'sports'] and he took no courses that they would not have taken, yet he was obviously not a trifler." In a footnote to the word "dandy," Powel adds: "A group photograph of the *Advocate* board taken in 1909 shows Eliot wearing a high stiff collar ('gates ajar' style), a dark four-in-hand, and a dark suit. His hair is parted in the middle and is plastered down over each side of his head" (Powel, 38, 42, 72).

"A very gay companion," "an aesthete," "a dandy": these descriptions may be totally innocent, or they may be code phrases—as they are taken to be repeatedly in the bohemian culture explored so fully and convincingly in Shand-Tucci's *Boston Bohemians.* They seem to be the latter also in the book Shand-Tucci mentions above in his description of Cambridge, Charles Macomb Flandrau's *Harvard Episodes,* published by the Boston bohemian publishing firm Copeland and Day (publisher of Oscar Wilde and *The Yellow Book*) in 1897. It was a very popular book whose appearance coincided with the arrival at Harvard in 1898 of T. S. Eliot's older brother, Henry. It is hard to believe that he, with his genius in capturing the personalities of Harvard's professors in a few telling lines of verse, would not have taken delight in it and recommended it later to his younger brother.

As Shand-Tucci points out, most of the action of *Harvard Episodes* takes place on Harvard's Gold Coast, and its style seems modeled on a cross between the styles of Henry James and Oscar Wilde. The episode entitled "The Serpent's Tooth" opens with the principal character, Dickey Dawson, slightly sick and being visited in his rooms by three friends: "They had all, thus far, in their college life, ingeniously escaped going in for anything in particular and were in the habit of regarding themselves as a nucleus for a future society, to be composed of unrepresentative Harvard men. Little Dickey Dawson even went so far as to be almost ashamed of his own undeniable popularity; but, as he remarked apologetically, 'It is not always possible to avert success'" (Flandrau, *HE*, 57–58).

In the story's climactic scene, Dickey Dawson's mother visits her "sick" son in his rooms and happens to be there when the same three friends turn up unexpectedly. The conversation languishes, leading Mrs. Dawson to fill the silence with, "You have so many books, Richard." One of Dickey's friends jumps into the breach, saying, "Aren't his shelves attractive. . . . I think you would approve of everything there too, with the possible exception of this, which you undoubtedly know enough about to disapprove of." He then hands her a copy of Max Nordau's *Degeneration,* which she takes, observing, "Isn't it—isn't it—thick?" After an interval of stop-and-go conversation, in which it becomes clear that Dickey's mother did not know what she was holding, she observes as she "mechanically" turned the leaves of *Degeneration:* "I like reading. . . . I think it cultivates the observation." After Dickey's friends take their leave, she says to her son: "They're queer young men. . . . Do you like them very much, Richard?" He replies: "Oh, yes . . . you get to like people you see a great deal, I imagine" (Flandrau, *HE*, 72–76). The story concludes with no moment of literal revelation, but there seems to hover about the ambiguities of language (especially in the mother's hitting upon the word "queer") some measure of awareness that is, for her, beyond language.

There can be no doubt that Nordau's *Degeneration* was on Dickey's library shelf, not because Dickey agreed with its point of view, but rather because he found the book both amusing in its indiscriminate and abundant use of colorful invective aimed at fashionable authors and, at the same time, an inadvertent source of pornography in its descriptions of the very behavior ("degenerate") it was condemning. For example, most of the authors (listed above) that students encountered at the Stylus Club were luridly described by Nordau. Joris-Karl Huysmans, for example, is paired by Nordau with another French novelist, Maurice Barrès, in a summary—and vivid—condemnation: "If M. Huysmans in his [Duke Jean] Des Esseintes [in *À Rebours,* 1884] has shown us the Decadent with all his instincts perverted, *i.e.,* the complete Baudelairian with his anti-naturalism, his aesthetic folly and his anti-social Diabolism, another representative of decadent literature, M. Maurice Barrès, is the incarnation of the pure ego-mania of the incapacity of adaptation in the degenerate" (Nordau, 310). Nordau observes of Oscar Wilde: "Wilde obtained, by his buffoon mummery, a notoriety in the whole Anglo-Saxon world that his poems and dramas would never have acquired for him. I have no reason to trouble myself about these, since they are feeble imitations of Rossetti and Swinburne, and of dreary inanity. His prose essays, on the contrary, deserve attention because they exhibit all the features which enable us to recognize in the 'Aesthete' the comrade in art of the Decadent" (319). Nordau deals with Algernon Charles Swinburne by pairing him with Dante Gabriel Rossetti: "Swinburne is . . . a 'higher degenerate,' while Rossetti should be counted among Sollier's [*Psychologie de l'Idiot et de l'Imbecile*, 1891] imbeciles. Swinburne is not so emotional as Rossetti, but he stands on a much higher mental plane. His thought is false and frequently delirious, but he has thoughts, and they are clear and connected. He is mystical, but his mysticism partakes more of the depraved and the criminal than of the paradisiacal and divine" (94).

Charles Macomb Flandrau has disappeared from the usual reference books in use today. But he can be found in a brief entry in William Rose Benét's 1948 edition of *The Reader's Encyclopedia*. We learn there his dates (1871–1939) and that he is "especially remembered for *The Diary of a Freshman* (1901)" (Benét, 387). Henry Ware Eliot Jr. was enrolled at Harvard when the book appeared, and we might well imagine that it was widely read by both the faculty and students; it is entirely likely that Henry mentioned the book to his younger brother when he was preparing for Harvard. It gives a convincing account of Harvard at the time as recorded in the diary of Thomas (Tommy) Wood, who arrives from Perugia, Wisconsin, to find that the young man with whom he is to share rooms comes from an old New England family. The roommate provides much conversation for the diarist; indeed, he seems to have studied the style of Oscar Wilde. On one occasion he analyzes a third young man who also shares the rooms: "Duggie is passing through a phase. Even Bostonians sometimes pass through phases when they're very young. It doesn't happen often, though. The truth is, Duggie can't decide whether to be a Greek God or a college settlement. He'd really rather be a Greek god, only it's so immoral. He'll probably end, you know, by coming out of his trance some June morning and finding himself married. Then it will be too late to be either the one or the other" (Flandrau, *DF*, 245–46). If T. S. Eliot did chance to read *The Diary of a Freshman*, he would have marveled at the end of his own freshman year how closely it seemed patterned after Tommy Wood's, even including flunking his first examinations and being put on probation, during which time he was prohibited from cutting lectures.

4. A Fellow Poet: Conrad Aiken

"Cambridge, Massachusetts, or that part of it adjacent to Harvard College, was not at all the ugly manufacturing city it has become: it was still in many senses a village. Lilacs and white picket fences under elms, horse-drawn watering-carts to lay the dust in the blindingly dusty streets of summer, board-walks put down on the pavements every winter and taken up again every spring, sleighs and pungs in the snow, and the dreadful college bell reverberant over all" (Aiken, KB, 20). This description of the town surrounding Harvard College comes not from Eliot, but from Eliot's closest friend at Harvard, Conrad Aiken, remembering some forty years later (in 1949). Aiken was a year behind Eliot, but they came together in 1908 in their work on the college publication, *The Harvard Advocate.*

Here is the portrait of Eliot that Aiken painted after his sketch of Cambridge: "Were we gayer as undergraduates than those of today? At all events we were gay, and my earliest recollection of our sixty-year-old hero is of a singularly attractive, tall, and rather dapper young man, with a somewhat Lamian smile, who reeled out of the door of the Lampoon on a spring evening, and, catching sight of me, threw his arms about me—from the open windows above came the unmistakable uproar of a punch in progress. 'And that,' observed my astonished companion, 'if Tom remembers it tomorrow, will cause him to suffer agonies of shyness.' And no doubt he did: for he *was* shy" (20). Aiken goes on to compare his own shyness with Eliot's, noting how the two of them recognized the necessity of "disciplining oneself, lest one miss certain varieties of experience [dances and parties] which one did not naturally 'take' to" (20). The most interesting aspect of this portrait is that Eliot has just emerged from a "punch" party, where he clearly has partaken of that evil drink against which his grandfather, in *Lectures for a Young Man,* had warned him so severely. The drink has submerged his shyness sufficiently for him, still smiling his "Lamian smile," to embrace warmly his best Harvard friend. Aiken's description of Eliot's smile cannot be passed over lightly, recollected as it is by one poet applying it to another. In John Keats's "Lamia," the title character is a witch transformed from a serpent into a beautiful woman with a seductive and irresistible smile.

Aiken's portrait of Eliot is based upon an incident in the middle of Eliot's first four years at Harvard, from 1906 to 1910. (Because of his year at Smith Academy, Eliot was able to take a B.A. at Harvard after three years, in 1909, and an M.A. a year later, in 1910.) It is at about this same time that another fellow student, W. G. Tinckom-Fernandez, remembers Eliot in strikingly similar terms. Writing in a special Eliot issue of the *Harvard Advocate* for

December, 1938, he says: "To look back over more than a quarter of a century and try to recapture a personality from a remote and limited period, especially of one who was then as shy and reticent as he is probably still, is a difficult task. . . . Only now and then did he come to initiations and punch nights to expand, in the midst of our hilarity, into his quiet, subtle humor; and we saw as little of him at the Stylus and Signet. As president, during the first half of our final year, I made a desperate effort to get editorials from him; but by then he was working harder than ever in the graduate school" (Tinckom-Fernandez, 5–6).

If Eliot's tight-lipped, inner-directed personality represented little change from his former St. Louis self, there was an element distinctively new as represented by his keen interest in the writing of versified pornography, described by Aiken as a "series of hilariously naughty *parerga* [embellishments] which was devoted spasmodically to that singular and sterling character known as King Bolo, not to mention King Bolo's Queen, 'that airy fairy hairy 'un, who led the dance on Golder's Green with Cardinal Bessarion.' These admirable stanzas, notable at times for their penetrating social criticisms were to continue for years as a sort of cynical counterpoint to the study of Sanskrit and the treatise on epistemology" (Aiken, KB, 22). Eliot's letters to Aiken over the years offer innumerable written examples of the kind of humor that must have begun as verbal exchanges. Aiken refers to one of the most salacious or lascivious in his recollection: Eliot's "War Poem, for the $100 prize, entitled UP BOYS AND AT 'EM! Adapted to the tune of 'C. Columbo lived in Spain'" (23). Aiken doesn't dare quote this poem, but it appears in Eliot's letter to him dated September 30, 1914: "They pass'd a German warship. / The captain pac'd the quarterdeck / Parading in his corset. / What ho! they cry'd, we'll sink your ship! / And so they up and sink'd her. / But the cabin boy was sav'd alive / And bugger'd, in the sphincter." Eliot adds: "The poem was declined by several musical publishers on the ground that it paid too great a tribute to the charms of German youth to be acceptable to the English public. I acknowledg'd the force of the objection, but replied that it was only to be regarded as a punitive measure, and to show the readiness and devotion to duty of the British seaman" (LTSE1, 59). This little-noted side of Eliot no doubt blossomed during his Harvard days, especially in collusion with such friends as Aiken; and it endured not only beyond his religious conversion in 1927 but virtually to the end of his life.

However, the real basis for the lifelong friendship of Aiken and Eliot was their mutual—and obsessive—interest in the writing of poetry. Some years after Eliot's death, Aiken wrote (speaking in the third person): "From the moment they met, in the offices of the *Harvard Advocate* in 1908, for the next five years, this [the writing of poetry] was their constant concern. They exchanged poems and discussed them. How to find a new poetic language? We were feeling our way towards it, something less *poetic,* more inclusive, more quotidian, admitting even the vernacular, and lower in pitch: a new poetic voice, one in which one could *think.* How to do this and still manage to make it come out as poetry, this was the problem" (Aiken, *CJ,* 5). This recollection appeared in the 1971 publication of a poem Aiken had written in 1910, *The Clerk's Journal: Being the Diary of a Queer Man.* Aiken's poem is about an ordinary office clerk barely making a living in a mundane, boring job in an anonymous office in an anonymous building in an anonymous city: "Today, in bed, I wondered why / Year after year, so patiently, / I rose at dawn, breakfasted, / And toiled the day through, wearily, / And wearily came home, to bed" (11). The poem winds its way through fifteen pages of rhymed couplets introducing drab scenes of "invoices, ledgers, pens and ink, / . . . the nervous clink / Typewriters make" (14), "table-cloths embossed with egg" (17), "the moon snared in telephone wires" (26). The clerk, like Prufrock, finds himself unable to connect with women, represented in the poem by an anonymous waitress at a coffee-shop. The conclusion: "And I go on with tired feet.— / And life is paved with cobblestones" (26).

Aiken is right to observe that his poem, along with some of Edward Arlington Robinson's poems written even earlier ("maybe the earliest of the modernizers" [4–5]), are interesting forerunners of the modernist movement. Aiken's relationship with Eliot had its ups and downs, but it endured through the decades, even during the period when Aiken remained unknown while Eliot's fame skyrocketed. We'll return to that relationship in later chapters, particularly as Aiken described it in *Ushant: An Essay,* published in 1952, a curious work that is an autobiography in fictional form providing portraits (and assessments) of a lifetime's worth of friends and acquaintances all given appropriate names: T. S. Eliot is called Tsetse (a bloodsucking African fly whose bite causes sleeping sickness and other serious illnesses).

Eliot, of course, was aware of Aiken's comic portrayal of him in *Ushant,* but he never became aware of the poem Aiken wrote when in the late 1920s Eliot became an Anglo-Catholic. After Eliot died, Aiken discovered it among his papers and published it in his introduction ("A Memoir") to *The Clerk's Journal* in 1971: "Eliot's left us in the lurch / been and gone and joined the Church / he's been drinking holy water / when he knows he hadn't oughter / and it's made him awful sick / turning into Catholic / better be a Unitarian / or a plain humanitarian / truer mind and heart had he / before he took the Trinitee / for now he's put himself a-Cross / his great pain is our great loss / and Pure Thought's no longer pure / since he took the Sinai Cure" (7).

5. "A Very Gay Companion": Harold Peters

There have been many collections of reminiscences about T. S. Eliot published over the years, particularly in the *Harvard Advocate*. But it is only from his classmate L. M. Little that we learn of Eliot's "closest friend" during his time at Harvard. In his "Eliot: A Reminiscence" (Fall 1966), Little wrote that in his small circle of friends, Eliot was a "very gay companion. . . . [His] really closest friend was Harold Peters, and they were an odd but a very interesting pair. It was Peters who chided him about his frail physique, which led to his regular attendance at August's Gymnasium, in the basement of Apley Hall. He took this work seriously and developed into quite a muscular specimen. It also led to some boxing lessons somewhere in Boston's South End. He took up rowing in a wherry, and finally worked up to a singleshell. Peters also introduced him to small-boat cruising and they made many cruises between Marblehead and the Canadian border" (Little, 33). As we have seen in Section 3 above, Professor Pierre La Rose, the "aesthete of Apley Court," was ready to welcome such muscular young men as Peters already was and Eliot was trying to become.

Of course, Eliot had had training early in his life, provided by his mother, in the handling of boats off Cape Ann. But it is clear from Little's account that Peters was an athlete guiding a shy intellectual into physical feats he might not otherwise have attempted. In one of his letters to his cousin Samuel Eliot Morison about his life at Gloucester, Eliot wrote (July 28, 1964) the year before he died: "A friend with whom I used to cruise, Harold Peters, who is now dead, once had to tie up to a spar in the lee of that rock whose name I have forgotten near the lighthouse of Mount Desert where you now are. Mt. Desert Rock, I believe. We went ashore and talked to the lighthouse keeper" (Morison, DSTS, 246).

Little provides in his reminiscence a fuller account of the episode Eliot recalls: "The most spectacular episode of any in these cruises was when, in a 19-foot knockabout, before the days of power, they [Peters and Eliot] rounded Mt. Desert Rock in a dungeon of fog, a rough sea and a two-reef breeze. The log book, the next day, shows a sketch of Tom in the tender in a heavy wind unmooring from an enormous pile mooring at Duck Island. The title of the sketch is 'Heroic work by the swab.' They had spent an uncomfortable night at that mooring and had decided in spite of the continuing fog, wind and heavy sea, to leave there for Mt. Desert and a protected harbor." Though the two friends survived great danger, they recovered almost immediately. "So, now with three reefs, they headed inshore and finally anchored in the little land-locked harbor of Somesville. The last entry in the log for that day was 'Ashore for supper at Somes House, $1, excellent'" (Little, 33). Was Peters something of an artist as well as athlete, able to sketch in the log book his closest friend in action in the midst of this exciting event, verging on a disaster?

Both Little and Peters turn up in Eliot's letters to his mother, who must have had some measure of acquaintance with them given the nature of the references. We read in a letter of April 11, 1917: "Peters and Little (Leon) are no doubt patrolling the seas—they were in the naval reserve"; and May 13, 1917: "If the war goes on I shall be losing American friends too. I should like to know where Leon and Harold Peters are stationed now" (*LTSE1*, 174,180). Later on, in 1919, Peters turned up in London to visit Tom, forcing him to pass by an invitation from Ottoline Morrell (an important Bloomsbury hostess, as we shall see later) for a weekend gathering. In his letter of June 23, 1919, Eliot explained to her that the individual who had turned up was an officer in the American navy and "the oldest and loyalist [*sic*] American friend I have." He writes that "He was here about two months ago for two nights, and I begged him to come again before he went back to the States. He has been mine sweeping in the Orkneys; now he is suddenly demobilized, and came down from Liverpool entirely to see me before leaving Europe finally tomorrow. I got a wire from him, and when he arrived I realized that I should have to give up my weekend. . . . And I saw that it would be a bitter blow to him if he could not have me for the whole of the short time. He would never have got over it." Eliot felt the need to explain to Ottoline the one-time closeness of their relationship: "He had come from Liverpool only to see me, and he will probably never be in this country again, and he would not have understood, so I gave up. I could not let him think that anything was different from what it was five years ago. He had been almost the only man in my class at Harvard whom I could endure; and we had been through various adventures and physical risks together; . . . I could not let him go back to America thinking that our relations were altered" (306–7). The intensity of Eliot's prose here suggests the intensity of his feelings in tending to his "closest friend" after the friendship had long been over—at least for Eliot. It is remarkable that Eliot did not want Peters to think that their "relations had altered."

The letter confirms Little's statement that Peters was Eliot's "closest friend" at Harvard, and that their experiences together on the sea, especially the dangers they shared, were memorable and intimate. But Eliot reveals much about himself in his letter when he adds: "So I had to go to the theatre, which I detest, and walked for miles and miles yesterday showing him the East End and the docks; and I feel completely exhausted and especially depressed by my awareness of having lost contact with Americans and their ways, and by the hopelessness of ever making them understand so many things" (307). Eliot concludes by telling Ottoline Morrell (as he must socially) how much he would have preferred to have been with her for the weekend.

It is of some interest to note Vivien's view of Harold Peters, as expressed in a letter to Ottoline Morrell (June 25?, 1919): "What a fiasco about poor Tom's weekend. . . . The man who turned up is a friend of Tom's youth, an American with the development of an average boy of ten. *Boring!* He always makes me perfectly ill,—prostrate. He is so devoted to Tom that he has no other thought but to spend every minute of his leaves in just sitting, waiting for the few odd minutes Tom could spare him out of his days. He has been known to sit at the Bank, for *hours,* quite passive and contented, waiting for Tom to come out. This, you see, was his last leave, and he went back to America on Monday, and it would have simply broken his heart if Tom had left him" (307). The time of Peters's visits to Eliot, 1919 and again in 1920 (see below), was a time of increasing tensions between Eliot and his wife. With Eliot coming to realize that his marriage was the greatest mistake of his life, and his wife coming to realize that the marriage was empty of any meaning for her, the two found the sudden appearance out of his past of Tom's "closest friend" almost intolerable. Vivien's feelings were fraught with jealousy, and Tom's no doubt with embarrassment. For Harold Peters, how-ever, the past had not become really past and his devotion to Eliot appears to have been unabated.

Peters turns up along with several friends in 1920 on a yacht bound for a cruise in the Mediterranean. Eliot comments to his mother in a letter dated October 31, 1920: "I am very fond of Harold, but this visit has been much more of a strain and a responsibility than a pleasure. I want them to enjoy their stay, but they know no one in London, and could not be combined with the sort of intellectual society that I know, and it would mean giving up a great deal of time" (420). Who was Harold Peters? In a footnote to a letter mentioning him, the editor of *The Letters of T. S. Eliot* has informed us that Peters's birth year was 1888, identical with Eliot's, and his death occurred in 1941: "On leaving Harvard, Peters went into the real estate business, but took time to visit South America on one of the last of the square-riggers. In 1932 he sailed round the world for two years as skipper of an 85-foot auxil-iary schooner, having previously participated in the transatlantic race from Newport to Plymouth, and the Fastnet Race. He fell from a hoisted motor boat into dry dock at Marblehead [in 1941] and died from his injuries" (306).

The most interesting fact about Peters, which we do not learn from this footnote, is that Peters never married. We learn this from an account of his life in a publication published by Harvard University on the class of 1910; indeed, it is the first word we encounter in a kind of obituary, and stands alone under his name: "Unmarried." As we read on, we find out that he served in the Massachusetts Naval Militia during the Great War, and on his discharge spent most of the rest of his life at sea. The obituary concludes: "Peters' friends were numberless and from all walks of life and because his strongest characteristic was loyalty this was reflected back to him from all those who happily called themselves his friends" (Anon., OHP, 183–84).

The special elements of Peters's outer life are relatively easy to assemble and comprehend. What of the inner? One of Eliot's Ariel poems, "Marina" (CPP, 72–73), contains imagery that appears to have come out of his experiences at sea with Harold Peters. The poem opens: "What seas what shores what grey rocks and what islands / What water lapping the bow / And scent of pine and the woodthrush singing through the fog / What images return" (lines 1–4). According to one critic (B. C. Southam, *A Guide to the Selected Poems of T. S. Eliot* [1994]), "Eliot recorded on the manuscript of the poem ["Marina"] that the specific place he had in mind was Rogue Island, on the Maine coast, in whose vicinity he had sailed (sometimes in fog) during his years at Harvard" (Southam, 247). In explaining the poem to the artist who provided drawings for its first publication, Eliot said: "The scenery in which [the poem] is dressed up is Casco Bay, Maine. I am afraid no scenery except the Mississippi, the prairie and the North East Coast has ever made much impression on me" (247).

In fact, the scenery of the North East Coast dominates "Marina." Rogue Island is in Casco Bay and would have been passed both going to and coming from Mt. Desert Island, where Eliot and Peters had their adventure at sea, both dangerous and exciting—throwing them inescapably together, physically dependent on each other for a period of days. The following lines suggest the dangers they faced: "Bowsprit cracked with ice and paint cracked with heat. / I made this, I have forgotten / And remember. / The rigging weak and the canvas rotten / Between one June and another September. / Made this unknowing, half conscious, unknown, my own. / The garboard strake leaks, the seams need caulking" (lines 22–28). The title and the epigraph of "Marina" are elusive (and allusive) and need not detain us here. (Eliot himself has provided an explication of the poem's complex allusions, which may be found in Southam's *Guide* [246–48].)

The second grouping of lines of "Marina," following immediately the images Eliot clearly associated with his "closest friend" at Harvard, somberly incorporates four of the seven deadly sins (envy, pride, sloth, concupiscence): "Those who sharpen the tooth of the dog, meaning / Death / Those who glitter with the glory of the humming-bird, meaning / Death / Those who sit in the stye of contentment, meaning / Death / Those who suffer the ecstasy of the animals, meaning / Death" (lines 6–13). When Eliot wrote these lines, he had converted to Anglo-Catholicism, had sworn to chastity, and was devoting himself in large measure to writing "religious" poetry. If the poem is read as some kind of confessional (i.e., religious) poem, beneath all the layers of the learned allusions we may hear, however faintly, Eliot's own voice. Why otherwise does he associate the deadly sins with an episode in his life back during his Harvard days involving his sailing companion Harold Peters?

One of Eliot's biographers, Lyndall Gordon (in *Eliot's Early Years*), has provided a criticism of the attitude toward sexuality in "Marina"—but without taking into account Eliot's personal associations revealed in the poem: "[Eliot] felt the devil not so much in social wrongs, but within, and believed that the chief purpose of civilization was to cope with the notion of original sin. This defensible point of view found an unhappy focus in Eliot's routine identification of women with sin. He regarded lust as the most corrupting of all sins and, as a young man, he wished the flesh could be denied, burnt away by that refining fire he so often invoked. Soon after his conversion he wrote savagely that those who 'suffer the ecstasy of the animals' may look forward only to death" (Gordon, *EEY*, 137). It seems clear given the deep psychic origins of "Marina" that his savagery was not in this instance aimed at the sexuality of women (although there are many examples of this to be found in Eliot's poetry) but at the sexuality of human beings, including men. See in the next chapter, in the treatment of Dante's influence on Eliot, Eliot's identification of sex with religion, and his statement that "the love of man and woman (or for that matter of man and man) is only explained and made reasonable by the higher love, or else is simply the coupling of animals" (*SE*, 234, 235). The parenthetical statement in effect means that Eliot's concept of sexual love extended to the love of "man and man"— and embraced it as a love that could be "made reasonable by the higher love"—of God. Indeed "Marina" may be read, on the deepest personal level, as an attempt to transfigure, spiritually, such a love that lay in Eliot's past.

6. Practicing to Be a Poet: From Omar's Atheism to Laforgue's Masks

Of the surviving poems written during Eliot's early years, between 1904 and 1910 (ages sixteen through twenty-two), a few were published when written, ten in the *Harvard Advocate* and several in *Poems Written in Early Youth*. Only twelve copies of this privately printed volume were issued in 1950, but Valerie Eliot brought out a new edition in 1967. Many of the poems appeared for the first time in *Inventions of the March Hare* (1996), Christopher Ricks's edition of the Notebook poems, 1909–17. The three earliest poems were discussed in Chapter 2, "A Fable for Feasters," "A Lyric," and "[At Graduation 1905]," all from 1905. In October 1906, Eliot entered Harvard shortly after reaching the age of eighteen; he graduated with both a B.A. and an M.A. four years later, in June 1910, at age twenty-one. The poems reflect, therefore, Eliot's poetic development, beginning after his preparatory schooling and ending before his postgraduate year abroad in Paris (1910–11).

Eliot wrote most of these poems during the last two years of this period, and by and large they are unknown to his readers, as none of them ended up in his *Collected Poems*. A casual reading of the poems reveals two major thematic strands (or "plot situations") increasingly dominant: first, there is a recurring portrayal of conflicting male-female relationships so intense as to undermine the notion of the possibility of genuine romantic love between the sexes as portrayed by most lyric poets of the past; second, there is what might be called a portrayal of the distraught, despairing night-wanderer making his way through a nightmarish urban cityscape.

As to the question of Eliot's earliest sexual experiences, one biographer, T. S. Matthews in his *Great Tom: Notes Towards the Definition of T. S. Eliot,* has written: "Did he masturbate? Of course. And was he ashamed? Unspeakably. For an adolescent boy of his sort, as for a monk, 'purity' had one overriding sense: refraining from masturbation. The relief of a wet dream, although a sin, was by far the lesser sin. He had one other equivocal recourse, partly pornographic, partly purgative: he could write about it." Matthews assumes that Eliot's first sexual experiences were undoubtedly like those of most boys growing up in America: "It had been incumbent on his father to tell him . . . about these murky 'facts of life.' When? Ah, there was the rub: to hit on exactly the right moment. . . . Henry Eliot was a man who knew his duty and did it. He may have considered it no dereliction to prepare the way by first giving his thirteen-year-old son a book to read, as the general practice was in those days among such fathers and sons: *What Every Young Boy Should Know.* This book pretended to impart, in solemn and admonitory tones, all that an adolescent boy needed to know about sex. In fact, its only intelligible message was that masturbation results in impotence, madness, and often an early death" (Matthews, 21, 22). If the thirteen-year-old Eliot did come "accidentally" upon such a book lying in his room, it is interesting to remember that the year after he read this frightful book, at fourteen, Eliot came upon a copy of Fitzgerald's translation of Omar, and became an atheist.

The following commentaries on a select few of the early Eliot poems, focusing on the personal dimensions, might best be read in the company of the poems themselves. A complete list of these early poems appears at the end of this chapter with dates of composition (when known) and places of publication.

"Circe's Palace" (1908; PWEY, 20): Female Emasculation of the Male

In "Circe's Palace," which appeared in the *Harvard Advocate,* November 25, 1908, Eliot obliquely reveals his attitude toward women, depicting them all as mantraps, enticing men with promise of sexual excitement. The poem's point of view is that of one of Odysseus's shipmates entering Circe's palace. Surrounded by flowers of "fanged and red" petals with "hideous streak and stain," Circe lures her victims into her lair and there transforms them into beasts— panthers, pythons, peacocks. The latter walk about, "stately and slow," and look out "with the eyes / Of men whom we knew long ago." The range of the beasts, though at first glance seemingly narrow, encompasses four-footed, no-footed (ground-bound), and two-footed (winged) creatures, one overtly aggressive, another covertly aggressive, and the third passive and vulnerable.

As we have seen, Eliot repeatedly referred to sexual intercourse as the "coupling of beasts," and his imagery in "Circe's Palace" seems to portray such a reductive conception. There is reason to see Eliot's Circe as his archetypal representation of Woman, with her sexually centered control of men enabling her to reduce them to their animal natures. John T. Mayer writes of "Circe's Palace": "Beneath the poem's obvious décor of gothic terror, with panthers rising from lairs, hideously stained flowers, and a sluggish python, is Freudian revelation. It is the most personally revealing, if unconsciously so, of the *Poems Written in Early Youth.* It is also the first indication of one polarity of Eliot's view of woman in the earliest monologues, of woman as destructive, bent on emasculating men. Eliot's Circe embodies sexual threat, mastery and emasculation" (Mayer, 32).

"Nocturne" (1909; PWEY, 23): Eliot Kills Romeo to Rescue Him from Woman

With two poems written in 1909, "Nocturne" and "Opera," Eliot daringly took on classical works portraying passionate, romantic love: William Shakespeare's play, *Romeo and Juliet,* and Richard Wagner's opera, *Tristan and Isolde.* In the first of these (a sonnet), published in the *Harvard Advocate,* November 12, 1909, we find only in the last two lines of the octave that there is a speaker (presumably the poet) who is rewriting Shakespeare's play to conform to more realistic notions of the nature of love. Romeo is engaged with Juliet "in the usual debate / Of love, beneath a bored but courteous moon," when, the conversation "failing," Romeo strums his guitar and, "strikes some tune / Banal." At that point, out of "pity for their fate," the speaker becomes a revisionist author and has a servant stab Romeo to death. As the lady "sinks into a swoon," Romeo, his blood covering the "moonlit ground," smiles and "Rolls toward the moon a frenzied eye profound." There then appears an ambiguous parenthetical line: "(No need of 'Love forever?'—'Love next week?')." We may assume that this is the speaker's comment on his radical revision. The sonnet ends with a descriptive and an evaluative comment: "While female readers all in tears are drowned:— / 'The perfect climax all true lovers seek!'"

Lurking here is a play on the ambiguity of "perfect climax": dramatic or sexual, or both? No doubt both. Ronald Schuchard has called "Nocturne" Eliot's "first Laforguean poem": "the poet, in his 'best mode oblique,' an ironic mode designed to mask his underlying attitude toward the actions of his romantic personae, lets his mocking attitude emerge in the parodic description of his moonstruck hero, who, in the manner of Laforgue's Pierrot, 'Rolls toward the moon a frenzied eye profound.' With the depiction of that lunar impulse the nocturnal scene is closed" (Schuchard, 78). Although the female readers shed tears at Romeo's death and Juliet's loss, beneath the tears (the speaker suggests) is the realization that this "climax" is superior to Shakespeare's—in which both lovers die. Romeo has experienced his love—and, dead, will not need to adhere to the conventions that would tie him to his "beloved" forever in a union bound to disillusion: the sexual climax is outdistanced by this "perfect climax"—the entanglement of an enduring but hardly endurable relationship. The speaker's—and Eliot's—cynicism about romantic love is inescapable.

"Opera" (1909; IOMH, 17): "We have the tragic? oh no!"

In turning from *Romeo and Juliet* to Wagner's *Tristan and Isolde,* Eliot abandons his role as play director and/or revisionist to become a highly critical listener, characterizing first the instruments—the "fatalistic horns," the "passionate violins," the "ominous clarinet." The music produced (described as "love torturing itself") is, according to this listener, bizarrely, almost obscenely, extreme (perhaps sexually explicit, as many listeners feel): "Contorted in paroxysms / Flinging itself at the last / Limits of self-expression." Although both *Romeo and Juliet* and *Tristan and Isolde* are stories of romantic/sexual love tragically thwarted through death, which have moved audiences deeply over centuries, the twenty-one-year-old Eliot will have none of it: "We have the tragic? oh no!" This judgment is followed by a metaphor hard to unfold: "Life departs with a feeble smile / Into the indifferent." Life has departed on the stage, but in Eliot's metaphor he suggests that he has left the theater with a "feeble smile" and quite "indifferent" (or unmoved). The following statement is an exclamatory judgment: "These emotional experiences / Do not hold good at all." And the final statement of the poem is put in the first-person singular: "And I feel like the ghost of youth / At the undertakers' ball." Wagner's powerful music leaves this listener cold, a "ghost of youth," and the action of the opera no more meaningful than something as extravagantly meaningless (and repugnant) as a ball for, of all people, undertakers.

Whereas in the poem on *Romeo and Juliet* the reader may discover elements of irony à la Laforgue, in "Opera" (written, like "Nocturne," in November 1909) there seems to be a direct statement that Wagner's opera is a failure, even outright condemnation in such banal lines as "These emotional experiences / Do not hold good at all." An admirer of Eliot's *The Waste Land*, with its several and significant allusions to *Tristan and Isolde*, may feel some surprise on coming across this poem dismissing the Wagner opera out of hand. But we may well assume that Eliot was to exchange his contempt for Wagner for profound admiration upon receipt of the letters extravagantly praising Wagner, and particularly *Tristan and Isolde*, from his French friend Jean Verdenal (with whom he shared a pension in Paris during his academic year in 1910–11). Verdenal's letters to Eliot, and particularly his reaction to experiencing Wagner's operas in Paris, will be explored in depth in Chapter 5, Section 2. But it is worth noting here what John T. Mayer has written in *T. S. Eliot's Silent Voices*, after a brief analysis of "Opera," about Eliot's radically changed views: "Eliot, of course, eventually would use passages from this opera [*Tristan and Isolde*] to frame the Hyacinth garden episode in Part I of *The Waste Land*, and evoke in Part III's Song of the Thames-Daughters the role of the Rhine maidens in the *Ring*, as well as Brunnhilde's immolation. The Wagnerian references may be read as Eliot's private homage to Verdenal, to whom he owed his introduction to the riches of Wagner's world" (Mayer, 318).

"Humouresque (After J. Laforgue)" (1909; PWEY, 24; 10MH, 325): Concealing the Self behind Masks

Another poem written in November 1909 and published in the *Harvard Advocate,* January 1910, calls attention directly in the title to its source of inspiration: "Humouresque (After J. Laforgue)." This poem will be briefly discussed in Chapter 4, Section 7, but it requires a short comment in this sequence of the young Eliot's poetic efforts. The title, "Humouresque," refers to a short musical composition or exercise, whimsical or fanciful in tone. There is an authorial presence (an "I") in the poem whom we come to know only through his description of, and attitude toward, his dead marionette. It should be remembered that a marionette is a wooden puppet whose every feature is controlled by its human owner. Thus this dead marionette is a creation of the speaker—in some sense an extension of his personality. Psychologically, the dead marionette may represent a role or personality that the speaker has in the past assumed and now views, capriciously, as "dead." In the second and third stanzas, the speaker reveals his affection for this marionette: "But his deceaséd marionette / I rather liked: a common face, / (The kind of face that we forget) / Pinched in a comic, dull grimace; // Half bullying, half imploring air, / Mouth twisted to the latest tune; / His who-the-devil-are-you stare; / Translated, maybe, to the moon."

Could this in some sense be a self-portrait of T. S. Eliot in 1909, finishing his fourth year as an undergraduate/graduate student at Harvard? The critic John J. Soldo thinks so. He has written about the opening stanzas of "Humouresque": "This is the nervous humor of an intellectually astute, but emotionally insecure person, intent upon using humor as a protective shield to ward off invasions of his inner sanctum. . . . Here we see Eliot making himself a subject of his own poetry, in imitation of Laforgue's example" (Soldo, *TTSE*, 115). And, I would add, "without revealing what must remain suppressed or hidden." Having "translated" his dead marionette to the moon, Eliot quotes his pretentiously "superior" (i.e., superficial) comments there to the other moon inhabitants: "'The snappiest fashion since last spring's, / 'The newest style, on Earth, I swear. // 'Why don't you people get some class? / (Feebly contemptuous of nose) / 'Your damned thin moonlight, worse than gas— / 'Now in New York'—and so it goes." Soldo comments: "Through the colloquial speech, and the developing conversational tone, comes Eliot bantering himself about his Harvard dandy habits in dress. . . . And so Eliot, to use his own terms, was able to *objectify* his own feelings, his own self" (Soldo, *TTSE*, 115–16). If Soldo is right in his observations about what Eliot learned from Laforgue, as I think he is, they have the greatest significance for one of Eliot's masterpieces, which was completed in 1911, only some two years after "Humouresque": "The Love Song of J. Alfred Prufrock," discussed in Chapter 7.

"The Triumph of Bullshit" (1910; IOMH, 307): "For Christ's sake stick it up your ass"

Although this poem was written early during Eliot's academic year in Paris (1910–11), its negative attitude toward women had been shaped in Eliot several years before his arrival in Paris, probably, indeed, from a very young age. It ought to be read in the context of a letter that Eliot wrote to Conrad Aiken from London, on December 31, 1914, in which he refered to "those nervous sexual attacks" that he always suffered when he found himself alone in large cities—London, Paris, Boston, perhaps even St. Louis. As we have already observed, Eliot was a night-wanderer in the cities, and his motives were clear: "One walks about the street with one's desires, and one's refinement rises up like a wall whenever the opportunity approaches" (*LTSE1*, 75).

The feelings of "The Triumph of Bullshit" could easily have been formed from Eliot's frustrations described in his letter to Aiken. Christopher Ricks notes that the page in the original *Inventions of the March Hare* onto which Eliot had copied the poem had been torn out and sent with other such pages to Ezra Pound, and ended up finally in Yale's Beinecke Library. The poem was dated, according to Ricks, November 1910 or November 1916. He observes that it looks more like 1916, but since it is known that Eliot submitted the poem to Wyndham Lewis for publication in *Blast* before July 1915, he reluctantly accepts the first date, observing: "the later date might better fit the thought that TSE had 'patiently waited' and had been at the mercy of 'Ladies,' editorial and other." (We read in Wyndham Lewis's letter before July 1915 to Ezra Pound: "Eliot has sent me Bullshit" [*IOMH*, 308].) It seems odd for Ricks to think the later date more appropriate, given the number of misogynist remarks scattered through the whole of Eliot's poetry from the very beginning. The virulence of "The Triumph of Bullshit" seems far beyond anything called for in Eliot's sometime differences with editors in his career in London.

There is surely no Laforgue-like mask used by Eliot in "Triumph," and it cannot be set aside as an obvious piece of the kind of pornography that men sometimes share. It is a direct attack on the "ladies" addressed in each of the stanzas, and the self-portrait of Eliot that emerges is astonishing, consonant with the Eliot revealed in various descriptions of friends and acquaintances we have already seen. The poem represents a fantastic display of linguistic cunning, but beneath the glitter of the sounds of the multisyllabic words emerges an image of Eliot as, not comic, but soberly serious in his intensely negative feelings about women. The first lines of each of the three stanzas making up the body of the poem set forth the reasons for Eliot's fierce blast against women: "Ladies, on whom my attentions have waited / If you consider my merits are small"; "Ladies, who find my intentions ridiculous"; "Ladies, who think me unduely vociferous." The lines that close these three stanzas and the short fourth are essentially the same throughout: "For Christ's sake stick it up your ass." Ambiguity hangs over the pronoun "it," its antecedent never specifically identified. Could it be the poem itself which is addressed to those "ladies" who are the poem's target?

The body of each of the three first stanzas is made up of a sequence of adjectives that the speaker/poet applies to himself. In the first stanza the adjectives apply to the speaker's "merits." In order these are: "Etiolated, alembicated, / Orotund, tasteless, fantastical, / Monotonous, crotchety, constipated, / Impotent galamatias / Affected, possibly imitated." Definitions: "etiolated": puny or blanched; "alembicated": over-refined; "orotund": showy or pompous; "crotchety": eccentric; "affected": artificial or pretentious. Perhaps the most curious of these lines is "impotent galamatias," with no comma after impotent. Was this intentional or an oversight? Without the comma, the two words seem to mean, as Ricks points out, sterile and meaningless talk (OED "galimatias," IOMH, 309); even in this reading the suggestiveness of "impotent" resonates sexually.

In the second stanza the descriptions apply to the speaker/poet's "intentions": "Awkward insipid and horridly gauche / Pompous, pretentious, ineptly meticulous / Dull as the heart of a unbaked *brioche* / Floundering versicles feebly versiculous / Often attenuate, frequently crass / Attempts at emotions that turn out *isiculous*." Most of these words are familiar enough, except perhaps for "versicles": a short verse, especially one of those sung in church service by minister and congregation. "Versiculous" is apparently Eliot's invention, perhaps for the clerical manner and tone which he himself displayed. "Isiculous" (OED "isicle," "obsolete from 'cicle,'" IOMH, 309) is Eliot's invention to indicate his lack of human warmth (icicle-like).

In the third stanza, the descriptive list supplies fortification for the ladies who believe the speaker/poet to be "unduely vociferous." "Amiable cabotin making a noise / That people may cry out 'this stuff is too stiff for us'— / Ingenuous child with a box of new toys / Toy lions carnivorous, cannons fumiferous / Engines vaporous—all this will pass; / Quite innocent—'he only wants to make shiver us.'" Most of this is self-explanatory except for "cabotin": a strolling actor, overly theatrical, a charlatan. There is clearly sexual innuendo in the two quoted lines: "This stuff is too stiff for us"; "he only wants to make shiver us."

The final brief stanza, as Christopher Ricks has pointed out (309), parallels closely lines from Edward Fitzgerald's *Omar* (see discussion of the fourteen-year-old Eliot's infatuation with Fitzgerald's "translation" in Chapter 2, Section 1). From "The Triumph of Bullshit": "And when thyself with silver foot shalt pass / Among the Theories scattered on the grass / Take up my good intentions with the rest / And then for Christ's sake stick them up your ass."

From *Omar:* "And when Thyself with shining Foot shall pass / Among the Guests Star-scatter'd on the Grass, / And in thy joyous Errand reach the Spot / Where I made one—turn down an empty Glass!" (Fitzgerald, 106). It should be remembered, as detailed in Chapter 2, that Fitzgerald's *Omar* neglects love and treasures friendship (male-male bonding), and that Fitzgerald's own misogynistic attitudes were as fierce as Eliot's. These matters will be discussed in Chapter 11, Section 6, focusing on the Eliot poem that Fitzgerald essentially shaped, "Gerontion" (1919).

Lyndall Gordon, in her biography *T. S. Eliot: An Imperfect Life* (1998), writes a brief comment on "The Triumph of Bullshit," opening with the observation that the poem was written in Paris (November 1910): "The pressure of Eliot's own inhibition burst its barriers in a riot of obscene verse—exactly what his mother had feared in the immoral influence of Paris. Later, Eliot excised from his Notebook this start of an 'epic' about the sexual exploits of Christopher Columbus, King Bolo, and his Big Black Kween: 'The Triumph of Bullshit' (Eliot's is the first usage recorded in the *Oxford English Dictionary*) is the obverse of his polite refinement. It addresses 'Ladies' who find the attentions of the speaker . . . 'ineptly meticulous,' but he gets back at them with a rude retort at the close of each stanza: 'For Christ's sake stick it up your ass'" (Gordon, *EIL,* 54). Gordon does not mention that the poem was "excised from his Notebook" because Eliot wanted to get it published by sending it to Ezra Pound, his mentor, who offered it to Wyndham Lewis for his magazine *Blast.* But Gordon does mention the interesting fact that Eliot's title, "The Triumph of Bullshit," was, according to the OED, the first recorded usage of the word. This information must have come from the references to the poem by title that appeared in the published correspondence of Pound and Lewis.

7. Poems Written 1906–1910

Titles of poems are followed by dates of composition (when known) and dates of first publication in journals and books. POO: *Prufrock and Other Observations* (1917); PWEY: *Poems Written in Early Youth* (1967); IOMH: *Inventions of the March Hare* (1996).

"Song": "When we came home across the hill": *Harvard Advocate,* 24 May 1907; PWEY

"Song": "If space and time, as sages say": *Harvard Advocate,* 3 June 1907; variant version of "A Lyric," *Smith Academy Record,* April 1905; PWEY

"Before Morning": *Harvard Advocate,* 13 November 1908; *PWEY*

"Circe's Palace": *Harvard Advocate,* 25 November 1908; *PWEY*

"Song": "The moonflower opens to the moth": *Harvard Advocate,* 26 January 1909; *PWEY*

"On a Portrait": *Harvard Advocate,* 26 January 1909; *PWEY*

"Nocturne": *Harvard Advocate,* 12 November 1909; *PWEY*

"Opera" (November 1909); *IOMH*

"Humouresque (After J. Laforgue)" (November 1909); *Harvard Advocate,* 12 January 1910; *PWEY; IOMH*

"Conversation Galante" (November 1909); *Poetry,* September 1916; *POO; IOMH*

"Caprice" Series (1909–December 1910)

　　"First Caprice in North Cambridge" (November 1909); *IOMH*

　　"Second Caprice in North Cambridge" (November 1909); *IOMH*

　　"Fourth Caprice in Montparnasse" (December 1910); *IOMH*

"Convictions (Curtain Raiser)" (January 1910); *IOMH*

"Spleen": *Harvard Advocate,* 26 January 1910; *PWEY*

"First Debate between the Body and Soul" (January 1910); *IOMH*

"Easter: Sensations of April [I], ii" (April/May 1910); *IOMH*

"Silence" (June 1910); *IOMH*

"Ode": *Harvard Advocate,* 24 June 1910; reprinted the same day, *Boston Evening Transcript, Boston Evening Herald; PWEY*

"Mandarins" (August 1910); *IOMH*

"Goldfish (Essence of Summer Magazines) I–IV" (September 1910); *IOMH*

"Suite Clownesque I–IV" (October 1910); *IOMH*

"The Triumph of Bullshit" (November 1910); *IOMH*

$\begin{bmatrix} 4 \end{bmatrix}$

1906–1910

HARVARD INFLUENCES: TEACHERS, TEXTS, TEMPTATIONS

Teachers: (1) *Irving Babbitt: Human Imperfectibility,* 79; (2) *Barrett Wendell: The Inexperience of America,* 84; (3) *George Santayana: Philosopher of Reason,* 90; (4) *William Allan Neilson: Poetic Theorist,* 92; Texts: (5) *Dante and Eliot's "Persistent Concern with Sex,"* 93; (6) *Petronius's* Satyricon: *A "Serene Unmorality,"* 97; (7) *Symons/ Laforgue: The Ironic Mask,* 99; (8) *Havelock Ellis, "Sexual Inversion,"* 104; (9) *John Donne: Thought as Experience,* 107; Temptations: (10) *The Lure of Europe: Brooks's* The Wine of the Puritans, 110; (11) *"T. S. Eliot, the Quintessence of Harvard,"* 112

1. Irving Babbitt: Human Imperfectibility

The secret of how—and perhaps why—Eliot became such an allusive (and therefore elusive) poet is revealed in part in the authors and texts he studied at Harvard. From any point of view, the lists are overwhelming:

During his first year at Harvard, 1906–7, Eliot enrolled in the following courses: Mediaeval History, Greek Literature, Constitutional Government, German Grammar and Prose, and English Literature. For the latter course there were four lecturers: Professors LeBaron R. Briggs, Barrett Wendell, George Lyman Kittredge, and George Pierce Baker—all with national and some with international reputations. The Mediaeval History and Constitutional Government courses were large lecture courses, popular because they were relatively easy to pass.

In 1907–8: French Prose and Poetry and German Prose and Poetry, Greek Prose Composition, Greek Literature (Aristophanes, Thucydides, Aeschylus, Sophocles), History of Ancient Art, Philosophy, and Modern Philosophy—the latter course taught by George Santayana.

His third year, 1908–9: The Literary History of England and its Relations to that of the Continent from the Beginning to Chaucer, The Literary History of England and its Relations to that of the Continent from Chaucer to Elizabeth, Tendencies of European Literature in the Renaissance, English Composition, General View of Latin Poetry, The Roman Novel: Petronius and Apuleius. Eliot earned his undergraduate degree in 1909, the end of his third year, and his overall grade average was 2.70 (out of a possible 4, straight As). He decided, however, to wait a year and graduate with his class in 1910 (Powel, 46–48).

During 1909–10 Eliot took the following courses for an M.A. in English: Studies in the History of Allegory, taught by Professor William Allan Neilson; Chaucer, by Professors Neilson and Fred Norris Robinson; The Drama in England from the Miracle Plays to the Closing of the Theatres, by Professor George Pierce Baker; Studies in the Poets of the Romantic Period, by Professor Neilson; Literary Criticism in France, with Special Reference to the Nineteenth Century, by Professor Irving Babbitt; Philosophy of History: Ideals of Society, Religion, Art, and Science, in their Historical Development, by Professor Santayana. Eliot's grade average improved considerably for his graduate year: 3.75—verging on straight As (51–52).

Eliot's most extensive comment on the nature of his education at Harvard was made in a series of lectures delivered at the University of Chicago in November 1950, under the title "The Aims of Education": "On the wrong side of the balance sheet, I must put the unrestraint of the free elective system as practiced in my time. By passing examinations in a certain number of wholly unrelated subjects one could, in three or four years, obtain the certificate of education—the diploma of bachelor of arts. The only limitation was that you could not follow two courses in the same year if their lecture hours coincided. I knew one man whose principle of choice of courses was that the lectures should all fall on Tuesdays and Thursdays, with no lecture on Saturday: thus, he was free to spend four days a week in New York" (*TCTC*, 79–80). How did the elective system work? A description appeared in the Harvard *Lampoon*, October 4, 1909 (the advisee is given the name of his graduation year): "Typical Scene: Adviser—Have you chosen your courses? / 1913—Yes, sir. / Adviser—Do you like them? / 1913—Yes, sir. / Adviser—Do they conflict? / 1913—No, sir. Adviser—Then take them" (Powel, 37, 38).

The free elective system for courses was adopted by Harvard President Charles William Eliot (a distant relative of T. S. Eliot's) on his taking over the office in 1869, and had originated in Germany. It was fiercely opposed by many prominent faculty members, including Irving Babbitt and Barrett

Wendell, and it is clear that Eliot absorbed their feelings about the system and about the president who imposed it. Indeed, Babbitt had a personal reason for detesting the elective system. He had taken his master's degree from Harvard's Department of Classics in 1893 with honors. After teaching elsewhere for a year, he returned to Harvard with an appointment in Classics. But in the meantime, President Charles William Eliot had abolished the classical language requirements at Harvard, causing enrollments to decline rapidly. Babbitt's appointment, therefore, was made in French rather than classics, a move he took as a betrayal. One of his students, Van Wyck Brooks, has painted a portrait of him, giving "the reason for his exasperation that characterized his manner . . . [as partly because] he was miscast as a professor of French, a 'cheap and nasty substitute for Latin,' as he called it once, when he had wished to teach the classics. Convinced that French literature lacked, as he put it, 'inwardness,' he studied it 'chiefly to annihilate it,' said Paul Elmer More [like Eliot, a Babbitt student and disciple]" (Brooks, Van Wyck, *AA,* 124).

In his book *Literature and the American College* (1908), in a chapter entitled "Literature and the College," Babbitt wrote a stinging attack on the elective system: "Our educators, in their anxiety not to thwart native aptitudes, encourage the individual in an in-breeding of his own temperament, which, beginning in the kindergarten, is carried upward through the college by the elective system, and receives its final consecration in his specialty. . . . Have we escaped from the pedantry of authority and prescription, which was the bane of the old education, only to lapse into the pedantry of individualism? One is sometimes tempted to acquiesce in Luther's comparison of mankind to a drunken peasant on horseback, who, if propped up on one side, slips over on the other" (Babbitt, *LAC,* 121).

In another chapter, "The College and the Democratic Spirit," Babbitt reveals the philosophy behind his condemnation of the elective system: "In one sense the purpose of the college is not to encourage the democratic spirit, but on the contrary to check the drift toward a pure democracy. If our definition of humanism has any value, what is needed is not democracy alone, nor again an unmixed aristocracy, but a blending of the two—an aristocratic and selective democracy" (113). It would be hard to overestimate the impact on the young Eliot of Babbitt's "humanism." In essence, Babbitt's "humanism" is contained in the phrase, "an aristocratic and selective democracy." As we have seen, Eliot had lost his faith at the age of fourteen upon reading Edward Fitzgerald's translation of *The Rubáiyát of Omar Khayyám.* Anyone of Eliot's temperament would have been in search of something to believe in to replace the "atheistical" pain he felt inside. No doubt the Eliot lineage and the prominent social and economic position of his immediate family (even though "marooned" in vulgar St. Louis) helped to shape Eliot's conservative, somewhat aristocratic view of the world. It was Babbitt's philosophy that was to capture his allegiance at Harvard, particularly as it was a philosophy that had many other disciples at Harvard and elsewhere, including Paul Elmer More and Barrett Wendell.

In "A Commentary," appearing in the *Criterion* for October 1933, written on the occasion of Babbitt's death that same year, Eliot reminisced about his experience in his classes twenty-four years earlier. Babbitt was not a popular professor—but a special few became attached. Of his two books, *Literature and the American College* (1908) and *The New Laokoon: An Essay on the Confusion of the Arts* (1910), Eliot regarded the first as more important. Babbitt's "outspoken contempt for the methods of teaching in vogue had given him a reputation for unpopularity which attracted to him some discerning graduates and undergraduates at Harvard. . . . His classes in those days were small, and could be conducted informally round a small table. For Babbitt . . . was at his best with a small group of pupils" (ACIB, 115).

Eliot described him as entering the classroom "with a pile of books, papers and notes, which he shifted and shuffled throughout the hour; beginning to talk before he sat down, beginning anywhere and ending anywhere, he gave us the impression that a lifetime was too short for telling us all that he wanted to say." The lectures Eliot attended were supposed to be "concerned with French Literary Criticism; but they had a great deal to do with Aristotle, Longinus and Dionysius of Halicarnassus; they touched frequently upon Buddhism, Confucius, Rousseau, and contemporary political and religious movements. Somehow or other one read a number of books, Aristotle's *Politics* or La Fontaine's *Fables,* just because Babbitt assumed that any educated man had already read them." But Eliot discerned the real source of his appeal: "What held the lectures or talks together was his intellectual passion, one might say intellectual fury; what made them cohere was the constant recurrence of his dominant ideas; what gave them delight was their informality, the demand which they made upon one's mental agility, and the frankness with which he discussed the things that he disliked, and which his pupils came to dislike too" (115–16). The few students Babbitt did have, like Eliot, became lifelong disciples.

Eliot's comment is a classic tribute to a college mentor who in his influence made a difference in the way the young Eliot saw the world—and perhaps restored stability to a life that had been both delighted and destabilized by the poetry of *Omar,* dedicated as it was to wine, song, and the sensuous pleasures. From Babbitt's chapter in *Literature and the American College* entitled "Two Types of Humanitarians: Bacon and Rousseau," Eliot was to take much that would shape his view of the nature of literature, literary history, and literary theory as revealed in essays and books that he would write much later. Babbitt took Francis Bacon (1561–1626) as a symbol of the scientific fallacy, which looked upon man as simply a part of nature who could be defined in scientific or naturalistic terms and who could, by applying the intellect, bring about infinite human progress; and he took Jean-Jacques Rousseau (1712–78) as a symbol of the romantic fallacy, elevating feelings over intellect and culminating in the anarchy of the romantic movement, with its worship of individuality and belief in the perfectibility of humankind. Thus both are "humanitarians" but not humanists: "What is important in man in the eyes of the humanist is not his power to act on the world, but his power to act upon himself. This is at once the highest and most difficult task he can set himself if carried out with reference to a humane principle of selection, or what amounts to the same thing, to a true principle of restraint. . . . That man is most human who can check his faculty, even if it be his master-faculty, and his passion, even his ruling passion, in its mid-career and temper it by its opposite" (Babbitt, *LAC*, 100–101). Implicit in this description of Babbitt's "humanist" is that he is behaving as he does because his intellect and feelings are in balance, neither subordinated to the other.

Thus Babbitt's philosophy tends to undermine the notion of "democratic education" and the tradition in America of education for the entire citizenry; it also has implications for the entire democratic tradition in America as established by the founding democratic documents ("all men are created equal"), especially in the American tendency to declare to be "right" what the majority endorses. For example, Van Wyck Brooks wrote: "Irving Babbitt was all for authority and formalistic discipline as against the Jeffersonian vision he connected with Rousseau, the traditionally American belief that men, freed from unjust social conditions, were sufficiently good to be trusted to rule themselves" (Brooks, Van Wyck, *AA*, 110). Several times Babbitt refers to Alexis de Tocqueville's reservations about America in his *Democracy in America* (1835–39): "The final test of democracy, as Tocqueville has said, will be its power to produce and encourage the superior individual." Moreover, "Tocqueville remarks that the contempt for antiquity is one of the chief dangers of a democracy, and adds with true insight that the study of the classics, therefore, has special value for a democratic community" (Babbitt, *LAC*, 127, 129). "Classics" were for Babbitt primarily the major literary works of Greece and Rome. But some later works were admissible: "The average student of modern languages should have a general grounding in the Middle Ages, and should have above all the knowledge of mediaeval life that comes from a careful study of Dante and Chaucer." The enemies of the classics are the "moderns," admissible only in company with the classics: "The classics with the modern foreground will be safeguarded against dryness and stagnation; the moderns with the classical background will be saved from impressionism and superficiality" (179–80).

In his piece in the *Criterion* on Babbitt's death, Eliot reveals how he remained even after twenty-four years Babbitt's disciple: "The errors against which Babbitt fought are errors from which we are not immune. We insist upon 'educating' too many people; and Heaven knows what for. Thirty years ago Babbitt was a young tutor of insecure position, when he began almost single handed (though perhaps under the approving eye of Charles Norton) to attack the system which Charles Eliot of Harvard had built up and popularized throughout the country; to the end of his life he opposed the heresies of the school of John Dewey" (ACIB, 117). Dewey (1859–1952) became a principal proponent of democratic education in America in the early twentieth century, proposing "learning by doing"; he became the prime target for those who believed (like Eliot) in some form of an elitist educational system. Of the many professors Eliot encountered at Harvard, it was perhaps Babbitt who made the deepest imprint of all.

2. Barrett Wendell: The Inexperience of America

The conservative views of Babbitt that the young Eliot absorbed were reinforced or intensified by the reactionary views of Barrett Wendell. Tom Eliot would have heard about this professor from his brother Henry, who wrote a Gilbert-and-Sullivan-like ditty about him: "Please make a careful study of this truthful illustration, / And take especial notice of the subtle connotation. / The atmosphere of London is so well suggested there, / You'd think you were in (Rotton Row) instead of Harvard Square. / How palpably inadequate my feeble talents are / To tell what Harvard culture owes to this, its guiding star! / Coherence, mass, and unity in Barrett are combined, / To edify the vulgar, and abash the unrefined" (Eliot, H. W., Jr., 8).

Wendell was clearly an unforgettable professor and had a special appeal to the male students of Harvard. In *Copey of Harvard*, J. Donald Adams writes: "Wendell had his limitations: he was rabidly an Anglophile, and was to write and speak condescendingly of American literature. . . . He was an undergraduate favorite: the boys in his courses were in the first place fascinated by his obvious and unmistakable role as a man of the world; he exuded sophistication and elegance of dress and manner. They were fascinated, too, by his little mannerisms; his constant twirling, as he lectured, of his watch chain." But his principal attraction was his tendency to surprise his class with off-color comments: "Above all, they were captured by his bawdiness, and sat forward on their seats, expectantly waiting for one more departure from the accepted norm of academic behavior. Indeed, one former student of his recalls that Wendell was pleased whenever someone turned in a theme on a broad subject like the mores of the ladies of an ancient profession who adorned the houses on Bulfinch street. Compositions like these were likely to receive an A" (Adams, 97–98). Van Wyck Brooks's memory confirms the extreme conservatism of Wendell: "That the world had been steadily going to the dogs since the time of Dante was the complaint ... of Barrett Wendell, who deplored the American Revolution that had sundered us from England and the guidance of the British ruling class" (Brooks, Van Wyck, AA, 110).

The depth of Wendell's influence on Eliot may be judged by the authority he would later invest in what is perhaps Wendell's most important book, *A Literary History of America,* published in 1900 by Charles Scribner's Sons. The title is a tip-off that Wendell did not believe there was an *American Literature!* In 1919 Eliot published a review in the *Athenaeum* of *A History of American Literature* (volume 2 of the American Supplement to *The Cambridge History of English Literature*). Sounding a supercilious note in a commentary much like that of Wendell's, Eliot wrote: "Hawthorne, Poe and Whitman are all pathetic creatures; they are none of them so great as they might have been. But the lack of intelligent literary society is not responsible for their shortcomings; it is much more certainly responsible for some of their merits. The *originality,* if not the full mental capability, of these men was brought out, forced out, by the starved environment." Eliot wrote with the assurance of his knowledge as to the cause of the inferiority of American writers: "What the Americans, in point of fact, did suffer from was the defect of society in the larger sense, not from exiguity of *intelligentsia*—intelligentsia would have spoiled their distinction. Their world was thin; it was not corrupt enough. Worst of all it was second hand; it was not original and self-dependent— it was a shadow. Poe and Whitman, like bulbs in a glass bottle, could only exhaust what was in them. Hawthorne, more tentacular and inquisitive, sucked every actual germ of nourishment out of his granite soil; but the soil was mostly granite" (AL, 237). Eliot's metaphors might be so bright here as to blind his readers to the superficiality of his meaning.

In his condemnatory review of *A History of American Literature,* Eliot noted that the book that "remains the best reference" on the society from which the writers sprang is none other than Barrett Wendell's *A Literary History of America,* published some twenty years before. A close look at Wendell's book will reveal a great deal of the origin of Eliot's views of American history and American literature. Wendell saw the first fundamental mistake America made was in fighting for and winning independence from England: "If the American colonies had failed in their heroic attempt to assert independence of England, there can be little question that by this time the imperial dominance of our language, our law, and our ideals would be assured throughout the world. The American Revolution, then, disuniting the English-speaking race, has had on history an effect which those who cherish the moral and political heritage of our language may well grow to feel in some sense tragic" (Wendell, *LHA*, 106).

What about Wendell's view of the first of America's two founding documents, the Declaration of Independence? He seized upon a phrase referring to the Declaration appearing in a letter written in 1856 by one Rufus Choate: "the glittering and sounding generalities of natural right which make up the Declaration of Independence." Wendell commented: "This phrase, 'glittering generality,' is commonly used of empty rhetoric: Mr. Choate used it of a piece of rhetoric which American tradition is apt to believe the least empty in our history. . . . Now, to describe the Declaration of Independence as a tissue of glittering generalities is by no means to tell its whole story; but so to describe it is probably as near the truth as to accept it for a sober statement of historic fact. Not that Jefferson, who wrote it, or his compatriots who signed it, were insincere; the chances are that they believed what they said. But the fact that in a moment of high passion a man believes a thing does not make it true" (106).

In a chapter called "The Antislavery Movement," Wendell's sentiments appear to be against abolitionists, who derived their arguments, according to him, from "Unitarianism and Transcendentalism." Thus: "If human nature is essentially good, if evil is merely the consequence of what modern evolutionists might call artificial environment, it follows that relaxation of environment, releasing men from temporary bondage, must change things for the better" (339). Having presented the weakest of the arguments for abolition, Wendell then spent several pages giving sympathetic treatment to the arguments *for* slavery. He wrote: "In the first place, the institution of slavery was honestly regarded by many people as one more phase of the more comprehensive institution which really lies at the basis of modern civilization; namely, property. Property in any form involves deprivation. Property in land, for example, deprives many human beings of access to many portions of the earth." Thus Wendell argued that "slavery, whatever its evils, was really a form of property, and that an attack on slavery therefore involved a general attack on the whole basis of civilization" (343–45).

Wendell clearly had no idea of the unconscious ironies he had embedded in his incredibly obtuse prose, crying out to the reader to unmask the subtextual hypocrisy. Nor did he realize how pompously antidemocratic and arrogant he sounded in a concluding passage. He observed that an antislavery legend had arisen in which the abolitionists have so badly maligned the anti-abolitionists, whose "chief heroism lay in their unflinching devotion to an unpopular principle" (i.e., favoring slavery on the basis of "property rights"), that they have corrupted later generations: "In so far as this legend has led the growing generation of American youth to assume that because you happen to think a given form of property wrong, you have a natural right to confiscate it forthwith, the antislavery movement has perhaps tended to weaken the security of American institutions. At least in Massachusetts, too, the prevalence of this movement seems permanently to have lowered the personal dignity of public life, by substituting for the traditional rule of the conservative gentry the obvious dominance of the less educated classes" (356).

The more we peruse Wendell's book, the more we become convinced of the origins of many of the ideas T. S. Eliot will express in the decades after he leaves Harvard.

On Unitarianism: "According to the old creed, which held salvation from Adam's fall to be attainable only through God's grace, won by the mediation of Jesus Christ, the divine character of Christ was essential to redemption; without his superhuman aid all human beings were irrevocably doomed. But the moment you assumed human nature to contain adequate seeds of good, the necessity for a divine Redeemer disappeared, and redemption became only a matter of divine convenience. The second person of the Trinity having thus lost his mystic office, the third spread wing and vanished into the radiance of a new heaven. In this glorious region the New England Unitarians discerned singly and alone the one God, who had made man in his image" (278). No doubt Eliot would be responsive to this attack on his family's faith from which he turned at first to atheism, but later to Anglo-Catholicism.

The depravity of cities: "Now, whatever your philosophy, this dogma [the depravity of human nature] does account for such social phenomena as occur in densely populated lands where economic pressure is strong. In our own great cities you need a buoyant spirit and hopefully unobservant eye to perceive much besides evil; and if you compare Boston or New York with London or Paris, you can hardly avoid discerning, beneath the European civilization which is externally lovelier than ours, depths of foulness to which we have not yet sunk" (278–79). So much for the red-light districts of America's large cities.

On Emerson: "According as our individuality responds or not to the idealism which touched him, we may find him repellent or sympathetic; and although it may hardly be asserted, it may fairly be surmised, that even in Emerson's most memorable utterances the future may find no considerable truth not better phrased by others. For in his effort to express truth, just as in his whole knowledge of life, he was limited by the national inexperience which throughout his time still protected New England" (327). If Wendell were to walk into a college class on American literature, he would find nothing taught about Barrett Wendell, but several essays and poems by Ralph Waldo Emerson read and discussed aloud, including particularly the very American "Self-Reliance"—with its very American observation that "A foolish consistency is the hobgoblin of little minds."

On Thoreau: "Now, Thoreau's philosophic speculations so surely appeal to powerful minds who find them sympathetic that we may well admit them to involve more than they instantly reveal to minds not disposed to sympathize. Even their admirers, however, must admit them to be colored throughout by the unflagging self-consciousness involved in Thoreau's eccentric, harmless life. Perhaps, like Emerson, Thoreau had the true gift of vision; but surely he could never report his visions in terms which may suffer us to forget himself. The glass which he offers to our eyes is always tinctured with his own disturbing individuality" (336). No American author has had more influence worldwide than Thoreau, as in India, for example, through Mohandas K. Gandhi.

On Hawthorne: "Of course the man has limits. Comparing his work with the contemporary work of England. . . . One grows aware . . . of its unmistakable rusticity; in turns of thought as well as phrase one feels monotony, provincialism, a certain thinness. Throughout, one feels again that tendency to shrink from things of the flesh which to some foreign minds makes American writing seem either emasculate or hypocritical. . . . One and all of these limits, however, prove, like his merits, to be deeply characteristic of the New England which surrounded his life" (434). So much for *The Scarlet Letter.*

On Melville: "Herman Melville, with his books about the South Seas, which Robert Louis Stevenson is said to have declared the best ever written, and with his novels of maritime adventure, began a career of literary promise, which never came to fruition" (229). So much for *Moby Dick*—a book that Eliot never read!

On Whitman: "Now, eccentricity of manner, however unavoidable, is apt to indicate that art has strayed dangerously far from its vital origin. Oddity is no part of solid artistic development; however beautiful or impressive, it is rather an excrescent outgrowth, bound to prove abortive, and at the same time to sap life from a parent stock which without it might grow more loftily and strongly. Walt Whitman's style is of this excrescent, abortive kind. . . . It is a style which in the history of literature suggests a familiar phase of decline" (476–77). Whitman's "excrescent" style marked the innovation of free verse in poetry, an innovation that had its influence on, among others, T. S. Eliot and Ezra Pound—and has not yet run its full course.

On the future of American literature: "The history of such future as we can now discern must be that of a growing world-democracy. The most threatening future danger, then, is often held to lurk in those dogged systems of authority which still strive to strangle humane aspirations. . . . If in the conflicts to come, democracy shall overpower excellence, or if excellence, seeking refuge in freshly imperious assertion of authority, shall prove democracy another futile dream, the ways before us are dark. The more one dreads such darkness, the more gleams of counsel and help one may find in the simple, helpful literature of inexperienced, renascent New England. There, for a while, the warring ideals of democracy and of excellence were once reconciled, dwelling confidently in some earthly semblance of peace" (434–35). Wendell did not foresee that the twentieth-century struggle would be between "democracy and totalitarianism"—not between "democracy and excellence."

Wendell, in his Harvard courses and in his widely read *Literary History of America,* was a pioneer in turning scholarly attention to the distinctiveness of American literature. But his prevailing view was one of condescension. As Van Wyck Brooks put it: "For Harvard ears these writers were 'of little lasting potence,' Barrett Wendell's phrase for all of them, and as [William Dean] Howells put it, Wendell gave his readers the impression that American literature was 'not worth the attention of people meaning to be critical'" (Brooks, Van Wyck, *AA,* 114).

We shall refer again to Wendell's views as we come across Eliot's expression of similar sentiments throughout the rest of his life. But there may be one other connection between Eliot and Wendell: the latter's book, entitled *Stelligeri, and Other Essays Concerning America* (1893), expresses a great fear for America's future: "The floodgates are opened. Europe is emptying itself into our Eastern seaports; Asia overflowing the barriers we have tried to erect on our Western coast; Africa sapping our life to the southward. And meantime the New England country is depopulated, and the lowlands drained by the Mississippi are breeding swarms of demagogues. And so on, and so on, and so on" (Wendell, *SOE,* 16). These remarks are fully consonant with many sentiments Eliot was later to express; they also raise the question of racism. A notable example of Eliot's adoption of these sentiments is to be found in his opening lecture of a series he delivered at the University of Virginia in 1933, entitled *After Strange Gods*. He began by saying that he had become much interested, after reading *I'll Take My Stand*, in the "agrarian movement in the south." The book cited was published in 1930, and included essays by twelve conservative Southerners (including John Crowe Ransom and Allen Tate), and presented views closely aligned with those of Barrett Wendell discussed above. Eliot told his Southern audience that the Civil War "was certainly the greatest disaster in the whole of American history," and that though neither side had actually recovered, the South had a better chance of establishing a "native culture . . . [having been] less industrialized and less invaded by foreign races" than the North (*ASG*, 15–16).

It seems clear from the documentation that Professors Babbitt and Wendell did wield an important influence on Eliot's views. Most college students are highly susceptible to the charismatic teacher. But it should also be pointed out that there were many other influences that helped to shape, one way or another, Eliot's beliefs. And it might be argued, indeed, that Eliot himself had reached a stage in his intellectual growth at which he was psychologically in need of, or ready for, some such conservative or reactionary views as those of Babbitt and Wendell. Had he been otherwise psychologically constituted at this vulnerable moment in his life, he might have turned to a liberal or radical mentor. But his inward-directed personality, with its weak sense of personal identity both spiritually and sexually, its need for, but lack of, a powerful structuring authority, reached out to the right rather than to the left, to elitism, authoritarianism, dogmatism.

3. George Santayana: Philosopher of Reason

There were clearly other professors who influenced Eliot, among them George Santayana and William Allan Neilson. But the influence of these others was not nearly so marked as that of Babbitt and Wendell. In a letter of August 4, 1920, to Sydney Schiff, Eliot writes: "I have never liked Santayana myself, because I have always felt that his attitude was essentially feminine, and that his philosophy was a dressing up of himself rather than an interest in things. But still I think one ought to read *Reason in Common Sense* [the first of the five volumes making up *The Life of Reason*] or one other volume. His *Athenaeum* things were exceptionally bad. He is not quite like anyone else" (*LTSE1*, 395). Eliot could not have been sympathetic with Santayana's philosophical materialism, which was underpinned by his basic belief in science. One critic summarizes: "According to *The Life of Reason*

(1906), matter is all that exists. What then of thought and feeling? The answer is that they are by-products of the body, 'a lyric cry in the midst of business,' 'a wanton music' babbled by the brain and wholly without efficacy in turning the wheels of the bodily machine" (Spiller et al., 1275).

It is possible that in the two years (1907–8 and 1909–10) of coursework with Santayana, something happened that cooled the relationship between Eliot and his professor. When Eliot returned from his year in Paris in the fall of 1911 to start work on a doctoral degree in philosophy, he did not turn to Santayana, and Santayana was to leave his professorship and America when, on the death of his mother, he became financially independent in 1912. Santayana once set down his view of Eliot in an undated note (quoted in John McCormick's 1987 biography of Santayana): "The thought of T. S. Eliot is subterranean without being profound. He does not describe the obvious— why should he? Nor does he trace the great lines of the hidden skeleton and vital organs of anything historical: he traces rather some part of the fine network of veins and nerves beneath the surface, necessarily picking his way in that labyrinth somewhat arbitrarily, according to his prejudices and caprice. (E.g., hanging his essay on Dante on the alleged fact that he is easy to read.) This peep-and-run intuition appears in his leading ideas, as well as in the detail of his appreciations" (McCormick, 416). Dante was the first of the figures addressed in Santayana's *Three Philosophical Poets* (1910), and would have figured in his course, Philosophy of History, which Eliot took in 1909–10. Moreover, in the preface to his book on Dante published in 1929, Eliot cited Santayana's essay as one of the works that contributed to his views of Dante.

Santayana had entered Harvard in 1882, nearly a quarter of a century before Eliot, and the milieu he found was quite similar to that which Eliot was to enter in 1906—the same clubs, the same Harvard publications, the same kinds of associations. For Santayana that was an ambiguously homosexual milieu, and included the notorious Pierre Chaignon de La Rose (see Chapter 3, Section 3). According to Santayana's biographer, there is persuasive evidence of Santayana's "frank preference for homosexual over heterosexual attachment," especially found in early love sonnets exchanged between him and Ward Thoron when both were undergraduates at Harvard (49). In the light of this background, Santayana's novel, *The Last Puritan* (1936), portraying strong male bonding by its protagonist (and no strong male-female relationships), becomes comprehensible. Immediately upon inheriting his mother's wealth, Santayana resigned from Harvard and left for Europe, never to return to live in America, but he was always identified as an "American writer."

Santayana's attitude toward America somewhat matched that of Barrett Wendell in intensity and much of it would have appealed to Eliot. Born a

Spanish Catholic, Santayana was brought to America to live with his mother at the age of eight. Although he attended all of the "right" schools, including Harvard, he never felt himself assimilated as an American. He rejected the literal truth of all religions, including his own Catholicism, but he maintained a lifelong interest in—and wrote about—the psychological power of religion, particularly its ritual. He disdained the American "genteel tradition" and found no competing genuine tradition, but only contemporaneousness, the *present* of business and machines, the *now*. American ingenuity he found dedicated to American materialism. See especially his "Marginal Notes on Civilization in the United States" and "Americanism" (in *Santayana on America* [1968], ed. Richard Colton Lyon). Eliot shared many of these attitudes, and his ultimate decision to settle in Europe rather than remain in America might well have been reinforced by the example of Santayana. Like Henry James, he provided an important model for Eliot.

4. William Allan Neilson: Poetic Theorist

William Allan Neilson was the professor in two of Eliot's M.A. courses—Studies in the History of Allegories and Studies in the Poets of the Romantic Period. In effect, at the same time Eliot was hearing Irving Babbitt attack the romantic writers from Rousseau onward, he was studying Keats, Shelley, and Byron with Neilson. Neilson's book, *Essentials of Poetry: Lowell Lectures, 1911,* was published in 1912 and probably contained much of the material that Eliot heard in Neilson's classes. In laying out the "essentials of poetry," Neilson found it necessary to deal with Wordsworth. Some twenty-eight pages into his discussion, he writes: "Nothing has been so far said as to *emotion* . . . Wordsworth, among many illuminating and profound utterances on this theme, has called poetry 'the spontaneous overflow of powerful feelings'; and again, speaking of poetry as having truth for its object, he says that such truth must be 'carried alive into the heart by passion.'" Neilson takes exception to Wordsworth's vocabulary: "The term 'emotion,' however, as used by Wordsworth . . . is not an entirely happy one. It points in the right general direction, but hardly hits the mark. . . . The quality aimed at may . . . I believe, more fitly be termed intensity" (Neilson, 28–29).

"Intensity" becomes in Neilson's scheme the crowning "essential" of poetry, to which a central chapter of his book is devoted. Again rejecting the terms "emotion," "feeling," and "passion," Neilson writes: "These terms are apt to be interpreted in too narrow or too wide a sense for our purpose. It may be regarded as a matter of degree: the degree of vividness with which the imaginative conception is visualized, the degree with which the intellect seizes its aesthetic problem and selects and arranges the essential elements, the degree of force and precision and fullness with which the fact is perceived and remembered" (170). By assigning a role to intellect (selecting and arranging the "aesthetic problem") in achieving the desired "intensity," Neilson depersonalizes what Wordsworth personalized with the word "emotion," as in "emotion recollected in tranquillity."

In "Tradition and the Individual Talent," Eliot also rejects Wordsworth's formulation: "We must believe that 'emotion recollected in tranquility' is an inexact formula. For it is neither emotion, nor recollection, nor, without distortion of meaning, tranquility. It is a concentration, and a new thing resulting from the concentration, of a very great number of experiences which to the practical and active person would not seem to be experiences at all; it is a concentration which does not happen consciously or of deliberation. . . . Of course this is not quite the whole story. There is a great deal, in the writing of poetry, which must be conscious and deliberate" (SE, 10). Eliot's term "concentration" is sufficiently close to Neilson's "intensity" to suggest they are headed in similar directions in revising Wordsworth.

But there is no doubt that Eliot's language is crisper, more lucid, more pointed. Whatever Eliot found useful in Neilson's "essentials of poetry," he would have necessarily made it his own by his own language. We might assume, however, that he learned something regarding the complications of theorizing about the nature of poetry from the care and inclusiveness with which Neilson worked out his "essentials." When in the early 1940s Eliot was struggling to revise part 2 of "Little Gidding" in Four Quartets, he wrote to John Hayward: "The defect of the whole poem, I feel, is the lack of some acute personal reminiscence (never to be explicated, of course, but to give power from well below the surface)" (Gardner, CFQ, 67). Intensity, concentration, acuteness—the words meld in meaning; and Eliot seems to be applying his "intellect," as suggested by Neilson, to solve the "aesthetic problem" with which he is confronted in his revision.

No doubt there were others who influenced Eliot's conception of the sources of poetry, but Professor Neilson must be given his share of credit for having helped shape the views of the future innovator of modernism.

5. Dante and Eliot's "Persistent Concern with Sex"

In 1926, in an essay entitled "The Poetry of T. S. Eliot" (Appendix B in *Principles of Literary Criticism,* 2nd edition), I. A. Richards writes: "The critical question in all cases is whether the poem is worth the trouble it entails. For *The Waste Land* this is considerable. . . . There is Canto XXVI of the *Purgatorio* to be studied—the relevance of the close of that canto to the whole of Mr. Eliot's work must be insisted upon. It illuminates his persistent concern with sex, the problem of our generation, as religion was the problem of the last. There is the central position of Tiresias in the poem to be puzzled out—the cryptic form of the note which Mr. Eliot writes on this point is just a little tiresome. It is a way of underlining the fact that the poem is concerned with many aspects of the one fact of sex, a hint that is perhaps neither indispensable nor entirely successful" (Richards, PTSE, 291–92). Richards's insights in this early examination of *The Waste Land*, touched off by Eliot's use of Dante, have never been explored in the depth they invite. My discussion of Eliot and Dante will concentrate on the ramifications of Richards's comments.

Eliot's views of Dante have appeared in a number of pieces scattered over the years, one of the most readable of which is "What Dante Means to Me," a talk given at the Italian Institute, London, July 4, 1950. Eliot recalled his first encounter with Dante forty years before (in 1910) when he "began to puzzle out the *Divine Comedy*" with "a prose translation beside the text": "and when I thought I had grasped the meaning of a passage which especially delighted me, I committed it to memory; so that, for some years, I was able to recite a large part of one canto or another to myself, lying in bed or on a railway journey. Heaven knows what it would have sounded like, had I recited it aloud; but it was by this means that I steeped myself in Dante's poetry." Eliot then turned to a review of his past attempts to express the debt he owed to Dante's somehow profound shaping of his poetry: "And now it is twenty years since I set down all that my meagre attainments qualified me to say about Dante [Eliot's book *Dante* had appeared in 1929]. But I thought it not uninteresting to myself, and possibly to others, to try to record in what my own debt to Dante consists. I do not think I can explain everything, even to myself; but as I still, after forty years, regard his poetry as the most persistent and deepest influence upon my own verse, I should like to establish at least some of the reasons for it" (WDMM, 125).

Earlier, in his Harvard lectures of 1932–33, published as *The Use of Poetry and the Use of Criticism*, Eliot took note of Richards's comments, calling them "acute" and then adding: "I readily admit the importance of Canto XXVI, and it was shrewd of Mr. Richards to notice it; but in his contrast of sex and religion he makes a distinction which is too subtle for me to grasp" (UPUC, 126–27). What was shrewd of Richards to notice was the relevance to *The Waste Land* of Canto XXVI of the *Purgatorio*—that is, the canto of

"The Lustful," portraying the straying bands of sodomites, hermaphrodites, and other such devotees of lust, with one of whom, the Provençal poet Arnaut Daniel, the speaker of *The Waste Land* identifies directly in the closing lines of the poem. What is to be made of Eliot's statement that Richards's "contrast of sex and religion" is a "distinction which is too subtle" for him to "grasp"?

In his book on Dante (published in 1929 and included in his *Selected Essays* [1932]), in a discussion of the *Vita Nuova*, Eliot made the direct link between sex and religion that he assumed Dante himself had made in his narrative. Falling in love at first sight, at the age of nine, with the unknown young girl Beatrice, Dante felt both his "vital" and his "animal" spirits tremble. It is this love that is never expressed, let alone consummated, that both tortures and inspires Dante over the years, until finally he meets Beatrice in the *Paradiso* and she leads him through the heavens to the supreme experience of viewing the divine essence and hearing the chorus of angels. Eliot says that Dante's attitude in his initial meeting with Beatrice "can only be understood" by finding "meaning in *final causes* rather than in origins." In other words, his full reaction is not to be found in "what he *consciously* felt on his meeting with Beatrice, but rather as a description of what that meant on mature reflection about it." Thus the "final cause is the attraction towards God." In this way, sex and religion are inevitably bound together. Eliot goes on to write: "A great deal of sentiment has been spilt, especially in the eighteenth and nineteenth centuries, upon idealizing the reciprocal feelings of man and woman towards each other, which various realists have been irritated to denounce: this sentiment ignoring the fact that the love of man and woman (or for that matter of man and man) is only explained and made reasonable by the higher love, or else is simply the coupling of animals" (SE, 234–35).

Perhaps the most astonishing part of Eliot's statement is his parenthetical insertion near the end. Eliot seems to be saying that sexual intercourse of "man and woman (or for that matter of man and man)" is elevated above the simple "coupling of animals" and "made reasonable by the higher love," defined earlier as "attraction towards God." A little later Eliot explains: "The system of Dante's organization of sensibility—the contrast between higher and lower carnal love, the transition from Beatrice live to Beatrice dead, rising to the Cult of the Virgin, seems to me to be his own" (235). Of course there was never a consummated "carnal love" between Dante and Beatrice— but it is clear that Dante's "carnal" ardor was aroused at age nine when he first saw her. Presumably, if we accept all of what Eliot has explicitly said, he has given endorsement to "carnal love"—man-woman, man-man—when it is of the higher rather than the lower kind.

Eliot gives his endorsement to Dante's use of psychology in his work: "The *Vita Nuova* . . . is, I believe, a very sound psychological treatise on something related to what is now called 'sublimation.' There is also a practical sense of realities behind it, which is antiromantic: not to expect more from *life* than it can give or more from *human* beings than they can give; to look to *death* for what life cannot give" (235). Eliot's intensity here conveys the impression that he is not only talking about Dante's views, but his own as they have evolved by 1929, when he was some forty-one years old, converted to Anglo-Catholicism, and trapped in a miserable marriage from which he would soon flee (in 1932).

In one of the essay's closing paragraphs, Eliot advises readers to pick up the *Divine Comedy* before the *Vita Nuova*: "The first reading of the *Vita Nuova* gives nothing but Pre-Raphaelite quaintness" (236). By invoking the pre-Raphaelites, Eliot reveals the "quaint" way to Dante at the Harvard of his day. There was at that time, writes Van Wyck Brooks in his *Autobiography*, "a semi-serious cult of royalism . . . led by Ralph Adams Cram . . . though this could not rival the cult of Dante, which Mrs. Jack Gardner also embraced and which had been established at Harvard for two generations. It had given birth, with the Dante Society, to Longfellow's and Norton's translations and to Lowell's and Santayana's important essays" (Brooks, Van Wyck, AA, 111). Douglass Shand-Tucci, in *Boston Bohemia*, tracks the nineteenth-century movements—"Pre-Raphaelitism to aestheticism to Decadence"—up to the literally Gay Nineties, a decade that spilled over into the early 1900s, including T. S. Eliot's time at Harvard. What Eliot says about carnal love (man-woman, or "for that matter" man-man) "made reasonable by the higher love" appears to be what Shand-Tucci is describing near the end of his book: "How fitting that the symbol of so much of this—the endpoint of Plato's and Dante's ladder of love begun in physical beauty and erotic impulse, as of the true knights' quest for right achievement, self-mastery, and salvation as understood in the Arthurian legend [architect and author Ralph Adams] Cram made his own in *Excalibur* (the best thing, he always insisted, that he ever wrote)—how fitting, indeed, that this symbol should be blazoned at the center as the finale of Ashmont's high altar . . . : the splendid gilt-bronze tabernacle relief by the goldsmith James Wooley that depicts the Holy Grail" (Shand-Tucci, BB, 452).

What was the central, intuitive belief of the Dante Cult around Harvard during Eliot's day? We may assume we have the answer in Eliot's reply to Richards's reference to the poet's "persistent concern with sex"—in Eliot's linking of sex and religion. It seems essentially the same as that which Shand-Tucci presents in *Boston Bohemia*, in his discussion of the "endpoint" of "Plato's and Dante's ladder of love": discovery of the holy grail. In a blank-verse play *Excaliber* (1895), Boston's great (and gay) architect Ralph Adams Cram portrayed a protagonist-knight foregoing "carnal love" to discover—ultimately—divine love. As Shand-Tucci observes, the passion of love from Plato onward has often been portrayed as divertible in other directions, especially religious or idealistic (265). And Shand-Tucci also calls attention to the fact that the sexologist Havelock Ellis, in his *Studies in the Psychology of Sex,* explores this kind of diversion or displacement under the title "The Auto-Erotic Factor in Religion" (Ellis, AE, 310–25). In his opening paragraph Ellis writes: "Love and religion are the two most volcanic emotions to which the human organism is liable, and it is not surprising that, when there is a disturbance in one of these spheres, the vibrations should readily extend to the other. Nor is it surprising that the two emotions should have a dynamic relation to each other, and that the auto-erotic impulse, being the more primitive and fundamental of the two impulses, should be able to pass its unexpended energy over to the religious emotion, there to find the expansion hitherto denied it, the love of the human becoming the love of the divine" (Ellis, AE, 310). Ellis's *Studies in the Psychology of Sex* was published between 1897 and 1910 and would have been available during Eliot's Harvard days. Indeed, Manju Jain, drawing on Eliot's class notes in her important study *T. S. Eliot and American Philosophy: The Harvard Years* (1992), notes that Eliot "copies Havelock Ellis's assertion in *The Psychology of Sex* that love and religion are the two most volcanic emotions to which the human organism is liable" (Jain, 172). And as we shall see, Eliot read Havelock Ellis, especially the volume entitled *Sexual Inversion.*

6. Petronius's *Satyricon:* A "Serene Unmorality"

During his third academic year at Harvard, Eliot took a course in the Roman novel taught by Professor Clifford H. Moore, where he read two bawdy tales with the greatest of intensity: Petronius's *Satyricon* and Apuleius's *The Golden Ass.* The first of these works was clearly Eliot's favorite, as it would provide epigraphs for his first collection of essays, *The Sacred Wood* (1920), and for his first long poem, *The Waste Land* (1922). Since both of the epigraphs were in Latin and, even when translated, would not reveal the nature of the novel from which they were taken, they caused little stir. But such use suggests that Eliot was influenced by Moore's course and that he had developed a lasting appreciation particularly for the *Satyricon.* In Eliot's *Selected Essays,* first published in 1932, the last essay is entitled "Charles Whibley." Few of Eliot's readers know who Whibley was. In fact, he was a conservative literary journalist who befriended Eliot at a critical moment, securing him a position at the publishing firm of Faber and Faber (then Faber & Gwyer) in the 1920s. In addition to his literary columns in the press, Whibley wrote introductions to translations of the two Roman tales Eliot had studied at Harvard, and Eliot praised them and Whibley highly. His essay in *Selected Essays* is part of *Charles Whibley: A Memoir*, written on the occasion of Whibley's death in 1931 and published as an *English Association Pamphlet* (No. 80, December 1931).

It is somewhat strange that Eliot would have chosen epigraphs for two of his early books from an author as controversial as Petronius. Those unappreciative of his complex, satiric masterpiece tend to see the *Satyricon,* in the words of one translator, William Arrowsmith, as "merely the story of a trio of picaresque perverts told by a pornographer of genius" (Arrowsmith, *S,* xiv). Part of the fragmentary first-person narration of the protagonist Encolpius involves the lustful rivalry with his fellow travelers Ascyltus and the poet Eumolpus over the comely Giton. Eliot, of course, could read the original Latin, but here is a scene from Arrowsmith's translation: Encolpius has just asked Giton if he had made supper, whereupon Giton breaks down, and with prodding and threats begins to speak. "'It's that man,' he sobbed, 'the one you call your brother, your friend Ascyltus. He ran up to my garret a little while ago and tried to take me by force. When I screamed for help, he pulled out his sword.' . . . Furious at such treachery, I rushed to Ascyltus and shook my fist in his face. 'What do you say to that?' I yelled. 'You male whore, you! You bugger! Even your breath stinks of buggery!'" (26). The narrative unfolds, depicting such behavior as commonplace, without moral (or immoral) significance, and has led many to condemn the work as not just obscene but corruptive of society's morals. Or, as Whibley put it: "With such characters, how should the romance satisfy the sensibility of the Prude? . . . A French critic in an admirable phrase once praised the 'serene unmorality' of Petronius, and the most scrupulous can do no more than confess that the author of the *Satyricon* did not twist his creatures to suit the standard of law" (Whibley, xiv–xv).

Xavier Mayne, author of the 1908 volume *The Intersexes: A History of Similisexualism* (discussed in Chapter 3, Section 2), assesses the book briefly: "Was Petronius, voluptuary, critic and literary dilettante—Petronius the brilliant 'Arbiter' of the Neronian court-circle—personally homosexual? There is good cause to argue it, by indirect conclusions, as well as from the first great pederastic novel that we know of, the *Satyricon.*" Mayne's point is that Petronius's work, in spite of its somewhat satiric or lurid events, is indeed a sympathetic treatment of the boy Giton: "The story's real action condenses in the furious jealousy of the hero Encolpius and his companion Ascylt[u]s, for the favours of Giton. The passing-over of the lad, now to one rival now to another, with a hint of his boyish constancy of heart for Encolpius, is the theme that holds the loose texture of the tale together. Giton rather wins us, [in] spite of his effeminateness, and his want of moral fibre" (Mayne, 290–91).

When Eliot praised Whibley's essay on the *Satyricon,* he chose to quote a long passage that stresses, not the satiric or comic elements of the book, but the realism of the social scene—including the sexual behavior—and its commonplace recurrence in the contemporary world:

> You may meet Encolpius today [he says] without surprise or misunderstanding. He haunts the bars of the Strand, or hides him in the dismal alleys of Gray's Inn Road. One there was (one of how many!) who after a brilliant career at the University, found the highway his natural home, and forthwith deserted the groves of learning for the common hedgerow of adventure. The race-course knew him, and the pavement of London; blacklegs and touts were his chosen companions; now and again he would appear among his old associates, and enjoy a taste of Trimalchio's banquet, complaining the while that the money spent on his appetite might have been better employed in the backing of horses. Though long since he forgot he was a gentleman, he always remembered that he was a scholar, and, despite his drunken blackguardism, he still took refuge in Horace from the grime and squalor of his favourite career. Not long since he was discovered in a cellar, hungry and disheveled; a tallow candle crammed into a beer-bottle was his only light; yet so reckless was his irresponsibility that he forgot his pinched belly and his ragged coat, and sat on the stone floor, reciting Virgil to another of his profession. Thus, if you doubt the essential truth of Petronius, you may see his grim comedy enacted every day. . . . (Whibley, quoted in SE, 448–49)

Twentieth-century Boston or Paris, St. Louis or New York, could substitute here for London. Eliot's recurrent image in his poems of the decadent city in the modern world comes in part from Petronius.

7. Symons/Laforgue: The Ironic Mask

In a letter dated August 8, 1917, to the British poet Robert Nichols, then teaching at the Imperial University in Tokyo, Eliot wrote about the difficulty he was having in forgetting what he had already written and in beginning "quite afresh, with only the technical experience preserved": "This struggle to preserve the advantages of practice and at the same time *to defecate the emotions* [emphasis added] one has expressed already is one of the hardest I know. I wonder if you will agree with me." This astonishing metaphor comes immediately before one of the most ardent comments about Jules Laforgue ever made by Eliot: "I remember getting hold of Laforgue years ago at Harvard, purely through reading [Arthur] Symons [*The Symbolist Movement in Literature* (1899)], and then sending to Paris for the texts. I puzzled it out as best I could, not finding half the words in my dictionary, and it was several years later before I came across anyone who had read him or could be persuaded to read him. I do feel more grateful to him than to anyone else, and I do not think that I have come across any other writer since who has meant so much to me as he did at that particular moment, or that particular year" (*LTSE1*, 191).

In a review of Peter Quennell's *Baudelaire and the Symbolists* (1929), in the *Criterion* for January, 1930, Eliot again remembers his first encounter with Laforgue: "Mr. Symons' book . . . was a very good book for its time; it did make the reader want to read the poets Mr. Symons wrote about. I myself owe Mr. Symons a great debt: but for having read his book, I should not, in the year 1908, have heard of Laforgue or Rimbaud; I should probably not have begun to read Verlaine; and but for reading Verlaine, I should not have heard of Corbière. So the Symons book is one of those which have affected the course of my life" (quoted in Howarth, 103–4). What, we might inquire, aroused the young Eliot's interest in the Symons book? The work seems to violate much of what Eliot was to call for later in criticism.

Indeed, Symons provided titillating gossip and biographical data that would naturally pique the interest of a twenty-year-old girl-shy male, a student at Harvard, and a wanderer of the streets of Boston. In his chapter on Arthur Rimbaud, Symons narrates the story of Rimbaud sending manuscripts of his poems to Paul Verlaine and being invited by the latter to come to Paris as "Verlaine's guest": "The boy of seventeen . . . astonished the whole Parnasse. . . . The meeting brought about one of those lamentable and admirable [*sic*] disasters which make and unmake careers." At first the two poets were filled only with "admiration and astonishment" for each other: But this "passed gradually into a more personal feeling, and it was under the influence of Rimbaud that the long vagabondage of Verlaine's life began. The two poets wandered together through Belgium, England, and again Belgium, from July 1872 to August 1873, when there occurred that tragic parting at Brussels which left Verlaine a prisoner for eighteen months, and sent Rimbaud back to his family" (Symons, 34–35). Symons narrates only these sparse details in the Rimbaud-Verlaine relationship, but they are enough to fire a young reader's imagination. (He does not reveal that Verlaine gave up his wife, home, and job to run away with Rimbaud; or that their relationship ended up in a drunken brawl in which Rimbaud fired a gun and wounded Verlaine.) Without passing or implying any moral judgment, Symons concludes in his final paragraph on Rimbaud: "[He] had his influence upon Verlaine, and his influence upon Verlaine was above all the influence of the man of action upon the man of sensation; the influence of what is simple, narrow, emphatic, upon what is subtle, complex, growing. Verlaine's rich, sensitive nature was just then trying to realize itself . . ." (41). So the scandalous homosexual experience, in fact, worked to Verlaine's development, Symons assures the young Eliot.

Symons opens his following chapter on Paul Verlaine with an account of receiving a telegram in early 1896 informing him of Verlaine's death. Symons now becomes a central character in his own book, explaining how through his reaction to Verlaine's death he came to comprehend the importance of Verlaine's life: "With all his pains, misfortunes, and the calamities which followed him step by step all his life, I think few men ever got so much out of their lives, or lived so fully, so intensely, with such a genius for living. That, indeed, is why he was a great poet. Verlaine was a man who gave its full value to every moment, who got out of every moment all that moment had to give him. It was not always, not often, perhaps, pleasure. But it was energy, the vital force of a nature which was always receiving and giving out, never at rest, never passive, or indifferent, or hesitating" (42). The rapture of Symons's prose elevates Verlaine above any kind of moral context. Symons does, however, after many pages, come around to the haunting fact that Verlaine had been imprisoned for eighteen months, and reveals that in prison, Verlaine's conversion to Roman Catholicism took place: "With that promptitude of abandonment which was his genius, he grasped feverishly at the succour of God and the Church, he abased himself before the immaculate purity of the Virgin" (52). The young Eliot must have been astonished at such goings-on: he could not have imagined such events taking place back in St. Louis; and still an atheist after reading *Omar* at fourteen, he must have marveled at Verlaine's conversion—an episode that perhaps sowed some of the seeds that would come to fruition later in Eliot's own conversion to Anglo-Catholicism.

It is not widely known that the sexologist Havelock Ellis accompanied Arthur Symons on a trip to Paris during 1889 and 1890, the one seeking medical and anthropological materials, the other looking for literary figures and new works of literature. But they obviously shared information. "During their stay, they met many of the leaders of the Decadent Movement, and others associated with it, Verlaine, Mallarmé . . . Huysmans, to whom they were introduced by Remy de Gourmont" (Thornton, 50). It is interesting to compare Ellis's account in *Sexual Inversion* (a work, as we shall see, that Eliot had read) of Verlaine and Rimbaud with Symons's account quoted above. Ellis is explicit: "A man who possessed in fullest measure the irresponsible impressionability of genius, Verlaine—as his work shows and as he himself admitted—all his life oscillated between normal and homosexual love, at one period attracted to women, at another to men. He was without doubt, it seems to me, bisexual." Ellis then focuses on the Verlaine/Rimbaud affair: "An early connection with another young poet, Arthur Rimbaud, terminated in a violent quarrel with his friend, and led to Verlaine's imprisonment at Mons. In after-years he gave expression to the exalted passion of this relationship—*mon grand péché radieux* [my great radiant transgression]—in *Laeti et Errabundi,* published in the volume entitled *Parallèlement;* and in later poems he has told of less passionate and less sensual relationships which yet were more than friendships, for instance, in the poem, '*Mon ami, ma plus belle amitié, ma Meilleure,*' in *Bonheur*" (Ellis, 51, 57).

Of Laforgue's art, Symons says: "It is an art of the nerves . . . and it is what all art would tend towards if we followed our nerves on all their journeys. There is in it all the restlessness of modern life, the haste to escape from whatever weighs too heavily on the liberty of the moment, that capricious liberty which demands only room enough to hurry itself weary. It is distressingly conscious of the unhappiness of mortality, but it plays somewhat uneasily, at a disdainful indifference. And it is out of these elements of caprice, fear, contempt, linked together by an embracing laughter, that it makes its existence." In short, Laforgue keeps an ironic distance from the realities, often painful, of everyday life: "sentiment is squeezed out of the world before [he] begins to play at ball with it. . . . He has invented . . . an inflexible politeness towards man, woman, and destiny. He composes love-poems hat in hand, and smiles with an exasperating tolerance before all the transformations of the eternal feminine. He is very conscious of death, but his *blague* [hoaxing] of death is, above all things, gentlemanly. He will not permit himself, at any moment, the luxury of dropping the mask: not at any moment" (Symons, 60–61).

The young Eliot was inspired by Symons's book of revelations, and he particularly liked the essay on Laforgue, taking from it and his further reading in Laforgue's poems Laforgue's ironic masks as his model for a new kind of poetry. He tried out his Laforgue stance in a few of his *Harvard Advocate* poems, including "Nocturne," "Spleen," and "Humouresque." "Humouresque," a six-stanza poem, appeared in the *Harvard Advocate* on January 12, 1910, boldly proclaiming its "source"—"Humouresque / (After J. Laforgue)": "One of my marionettes is dead, / Though not yet tired of the game— / But weak in body as in head, / (A jumping-jack has such a frame), // But this deceaséd marionette / I rather liked: a common face, / (The kind of face that we forget) / Pinched in a comic, dull grimace; // Half bullying, half imploring air, / Mouth twisted to the latest tune; / His who-the-devil-are-you stare; / Translated, maybe, to the moon" (*PWEY*, 24). Eliot's poem appears to derive directly from Laforgue's lines found in Symons: "Encore un de mes pierrots mort; / Mort d'un chronique orphelinisme; / C'etait un coeur plein de dandyisme / Lunaire, en un drôle de corps" (Symons, 57). (Again one of my pierrots is dead; / Dead of a chronic orphanhood; / His was a heart full of dandyism / Lunar (honest), in a body of a queer fellow.)

The last stanza of Eliot's poem reads: "Logic a marionette's, all wrong / Of premises, yet in some star / A hero!—Where would he belong? / But, even at that, what mask *bizarre!*" (*PWEY*, 25). Both Eliot and his model, Laforgue, succeed, through the death of their marionettes (the "masked" poets are manipulating the puppet strings), in making oblique comments, devoid of sentimentality, on the human realities of alienation, despair, death. Eliot, however, in his last stanza seems to step out of his role as the mask-wearer to comment on, rather than from, the mask. His skill in mask-wearing would improve enormously in just a few years, beginning with "The Love Song of J. Alfred Prufrock." Laforgue would remain a complex influence on Eliot into the 1920s, but there would come a time, as we shall see, when in the later poetry Laforgue's grasp on Eliot's imagination weakened.

The poetic "mask" has some similarities to the one used in what Xavier Mayne, author of *The Intersexes: A History of Similisexualism,* called Uranian (i.e., homosexual) love. It is of importance to set the nature of this other "mask" alongside Laforgue's notions. Mayne points out that the "normal" man can tell the lady he loves of his passion without fear of being ostracized. He can even discuss his love with his friends, and their response is likely to be sympathy. On the other hand, "the Uranian must often 'go through' the most overwhelming, soul-prostrating of loves, finding his nerves and mind and body beaten down under the passion, his days and nights vilified or poisoned by it, all without his doing anything so persistently as to hide his sentiment forever from the object of it! To hide it from his closest friends, from suspicion by the world! Hide it he must. . . . Ever the Mask, the shuddering concealment, the anguish of hidden passion that burns his life away!" Indeed, he must become a skillful pretender, he must "take pains to appear sexually interested in women, to be intimate with women, to seem to relish open, and frequently obscene, sexual talk about women. This last is much in his programme for hiding sexual indifference or downright physical aversion to women. The Mask, ever the Mask! It becomes like the natural face of the wearer" (Mayne, 85–87). If Havelock Ellis's view of genius as described in his discussion of Verlaine above is valid, it is surely likely that there are cases in which the poetic mask and the Uranian mask are one and the same.

8. Havelock Ellis, "Sexual Inversion"

As we have seen in Chapter 3, Sections 2 and 3, the undergraduates at Harvard during Eliot's day, as portrayed in the novels of Charles Macomb Flandrau, were familiar with Max Nordau's *Degeneration* and its blast at the degenerate writers, artists, and poets of all countries, including America. Harvard, along with other major universities, was among the targets at which Nordau aimed his vituperative charges. The major work that took the opposite, or semiscientific and objective point of view, was Havelock Ellis's multivolume *Studies in the Psychology of Sex*. As the main title suggests, Ellis's ambition was to cover all aspects of human sexuality without moral judgment but with scientific accuracy. The volume entitled *Sexual Inversion*, although appearing fourth in the final publication, was actually the first volume to appear in 1897. It was then published with two authors listed, Havelock Ellis and John Addington Symonds (1840–93). Symonds was a British historian who was homosexual and who campaigned discreetly for legal reform of laws that he believed punished individuals for a congenital condition. For an account of Symonds's collaboration with Ellis, see Wayne Koestenbaum's *Double Talk: The Erotics of Male Literary Collaboration* (1989). Ellis, who was heterosexual, revised subsequent publications of *Sexual Inversion* in order to deprive sexual bigots the ammunition for attacking the book: he removed Symonds's name as co-author and removed much of the material Symonds had supplied for original publication of the book.

We have seen that Eliot took notes from a reading of Ellis's *Studies in the Psychology of Sex* (Jain, 172). We can now affirm that Eliot read Ellis's *Sexual Inversion*, not because he ever wrote about it, but because of an episode related in Edward Butscher's biography, *Conrad Aiken: Poet of White Horse Vale* (1988). The incident took place at Harvard and involved three of Santayana's students, Conrad Aiken, T. S. Eliot, and George Boas. It seems to have occurred in either 1911 or 1912. Eliot was in Paris for the academic year 1910–11, and did not return for graduate work until the fall of 1911. Santayana, as we have already mentioned, left Harvard in June of 1912, having inherited enough money to give up teaching. Butscher introduces the relevant episode by indicating that the three graduate students, who shared each other's company frequently, had come together and continued a "recurrent topic of debate and humor," about the "absent Santayana, to whom Aiken remained loyal." Thus the conversation took place after June 1912, when Santayana had left Harvard permanently. The three students first discussed Santayana's philosophy: "Aiken remained loyal [to Santayana]," but "Eliot now claimed to discern the lineaments of a 'charlatan' in Santayana's systemless system, and Boas denigrated what he viewed as a lack of logical rigor in his theories. Eliot dismissed both Santayana and Bergson for having reduced philosophy to mere 'psychology,' which, ironically, was the same charge Santayana leveled against Bergson, but the three young men in lighter moments also enjoyed speculating as to whether the former Harvard don was actually a homosexual" (Butscher, 199). At this point, the reader must go to the notes in the back pages of the book to continue the story.

In the note, easily missed in the crowded note pages, a determined reader can find the following: "In later years, Aiken spoke to Ted R. Spivey with deep feeling about Santayana's influence 'on his thought and work and even spoke of an influence Santayana had at the time on T. S. Eliot but which Eliot was careful to cover up.'" There follows a companion note for page 199: "Boas letter to the author, July 20, 1979: 'Since I didn't know the meaning of either the term [homosexual] or the acts referred to . . . I wasn't much enlightened. (Eliot after some awkward questions on my part got me to read Havelock Ellis).' [Bruce] Kuklick [author of *The Rise of American Philosophy* (1977)] reports that Harvard students tended to regard Santayana as an 'unconscious homosexual'" (473–74). Obviously Eliot had to have read Ellis and thought his work good enough to recommend to others.

Succeeding generations have used different words for same-sex love—as suggested by the popularity today of the word "gay." At the beginning, in Ellis's opening chapter of *Sexual Inversion*, we find him discussing the several terms that have been in some kind of competition for general use at the time of his writing, including that in his title, "sexual inversion," and also "Uranianism," "sodomy," "buggery," "hermaphroditism," and "homosexuality." For an account of the various terms used for "homosexual," including "gay," see George Chauncey's introduction to his comprehensive 1994 study, *Gay New York: Gender, Urban Culture, and the Making of the Gay Male World* (Chauncey, 1–29). A related term that has come into general use since the middle of the twentieth century is "closet": to "live in the closet" is to live a secret gay life. The most useful book for discovering its use (and background) is Eve Kosofsky Sedgwick's 1990 volume, *Epistemology of the Closet;* see especially chapter 1 (Sedgwick, 65–90).

Ellis's introduction to *Sexual Inversion* is clearly meant to suggest that some of the most revered writers and artists of the past could have been, seemed to have been, or were sexual inverts or homosexuals. Among the artists Ellis discusses are Michelangelo and Shakespeare, but more important for Eliot, surely, is Ellis's treatment of the various writers about whom Eliot had strong opinions; for example, Edward Fitzgerald, Byron, Walt Whitman, Verlaine, Arthur Rimbaud, and Oscar Wilde.

Here is a part of Ellis's discussion of Edward Fitzgerald: "In a writer of the first order, Edward Fitzgerald, to whom we owe the immortal and highly individualized version of *Omar Khayyám,* it is easy to trace an element of homosexuality, though it appears never to have reached full and conscious development. Fitzgerald was an eccentric person who, though rich and on friendly terms with some of the most distinguished men of his time, was always out of harmony with his environment." One episode in his life paralleled in part a similar one in Eliot's: "He felt himself called on to marry, very unhappily, a woman whom he had never been in love with and with whom he had nothing in common. All his affections were for his male friends." Ellis mentions two deep friendships—first with "W. K. Browne, whom he glorified in *Euphranor* [a work of fiction]," and the other, Joseph Fletcher, a fisherman he called Posh, "6 feet tall, said to be the best of Suffolk type, both in body and character" (Ellis, SI, 50).

Ellis's comments on Fitzgerald seem designed to draw the reader into admiring him, neither making nor implying any negative moral judgments about his sexuality. As we have seen, Fitzgerald was, for ten years, Eliot's favorite poet and idol from the age of fourteen. One might think that Eliot, on reading Ellis's volume and finding there Edward Fitzgerald a leading "character," would have stopped pointing out his passion for him until near the end of his life. But in fact, in one poem, "Gerontion," written in 1919 and published in *Ara Vos Prec* in 1920, Eliot used many lines found in Fitzgerald's letters and often quoted in A. C. Benson's biography, *Edward Fitzgerald,* of the English Men of Letters Series (1905). The use of these descriptive lines in "Gerontion," in many ways an Eliot self-portrait, suggests that indeed Eliot identified with Fitzgerald in spite of his appearance in the Ellis book. At one point, when Ezra Pound was "revising" *The Waste Land* and getting it ready for publication, he proposed eliminating "Phlebas the Phoenician" (Part IV). When Eliot counterproposed that he should probably publish "Gerontion" as the opening section of *The Waste Land,* Pound discouraged him from doing so. See especially Chapter 11, Section 6, and the extended analysis of "Gerontion."

Ellis spends much space on Walt Whitman, but since Eliot's attitude toward Whitman's poetry was ambivalent there is no need to examine closely here what Ellis's point of view was. But his major focus was on the "Calamus" poems of comradeship: Whitman "would most certainly have refused to admit that he was the subject of inverted sexuality. It remains true, however, that 'manly love' occupies in his work a predominance which it would scarcely hold in the feelings of the 'average man,' whom Whitman wishes to honor. . . . Although a man of remarkable physical vigor, he never felt inclined to marry. It remains somewhat difficult to classify him from the sexual point of view, but we can scarcely fail to recognize the presence of a homosexual tendency" (52–53). We might well conclude that Eliot's tendency to dismiss Whitman was not because he was the poet of "manly love" but rather because he was the poet of democracy, which Eliot openly disdained. There is, for example, Eliot's use of the word "Calamus" in his never collected poem, "Ode on Independence Day, July 4th 1918" (discussed in my book *T. S. Eliot's Personal Waste Land*, 1977).

Two French poets discussed by Ellis are among those Eliot did admire: Paul Verlaine and Arthur Rimbaud. Recall that Ellis and Symons had traveled together to France, and they were both interested in the French poets, one focused on their sexuality, the other on their poetry. As we have already seen, it was reading Symons's book, *The Symbolist Movement in Literature* (1899), that inspired Eliot's interest in the work of Jules Laforgue and other French poets.

It is hard to estimate the influence of Ellis on Eliot. Probably the most important aspect of that influence was that its reasoned and unprejudiced discussion of "sexual inverts" or "homosexuals" reassured Eliot of the normality of his interest in the works of writers and artists, whatever their sexuality. And it may also have reassured him in whatever uneasiness he felt about his own sexuality and the obscure ways in which it might be reflected in his poetry.

9. John Donne: Thought as Experience

In his essay "Donne in Our Time" in *A Garland for John Donne: 1631–1931*, Eliot revises the tercentenary dates in describing his introduction to Donne: "For my own experience . . . our time is roughly 1906–1931. I mean that Professor Briggs used to read, with great persuasiveness and charm, verses of

Donne to the Freshmen at Harvard assembled in what was called, as I remember, 'English A.' I confess that I have now forgotten what Professor Briggs told us about the poet; but I know that whatever he said, his own words and his quotations were enough to attract to private reading at least one Freshman who had already absorbed some of the Elizabethan dramatists, but who had not yet approached the metaphysicals." Though sure of the timing of his own personal involvement with Donne, Eliot says that he "cannot account for his general emergence toward tercentenary fame. I know that when I came to London [in 1914] I heard more of Donne, in social conversation, than I had heard before" (DIOT, 3).

It is interesting to observe that in "Donne in Our Time," Eliot downplayed the sensual element in Donne's poems: "I suspect that we can easily exaggerate the erotic element as well [as the mystical element in Donne's poetry]. No one now is likely to follow Sir Edmund Gosse in reading Donne's *Elegies* as exact biography. My intention here is not to whitewash the evidence of a dissipated or immoral youth; but merely to affirm that we have no satisfactory evidence, and that it is a point of the very slightest interest anyhow." Thus Eliot suggests that Donne was a poet of the imagination, not relying on personal experience for the subject matter of his poetry: "The courtly cynicism was a poetic convention of the time; Donne's sometimes scoffing attitude towards the fickleness of women may be hardly more than immature bravado. . . . Nor can I take very seriously Donne's later remorse or repentance. It is pleasant in youth to think that one is a gay dog, and it is pleasant in age to think that one *was* a gay dog; because as we grow old we all like to think that we have changed, developed and improved; people shrink from acknowledging that they are exactly the same at fifty as they were at twenty-five" (10–11).

As so often in his critical essays, Eliot here starts down a path seemingly generalizing from his own experience, but injecting ambiguity by lapsing into the use of the impersonal "one." As in his reply to Richards's observation about Eliot's "persistent concern with sex," Eliot seems to want to dismiss that element in Donne that probably most appealed to him when he first heard his freshman professor read the poems aloud in class ("it is a point of the very slightest interest anyhow"). Curiously, Donne, like Dante (but each in his own way), brings together sex and religion in his poems, enabling Eliot to claim their inevitable interrelationship or identity. Eliot describes the nature of Donne's love poems, apparently assuming them to be representative, as presenting the essence of Donne's poetry: "In the poem—'I wonder by my troth, what thou, and I . . . [the first line of Donne's poem "The Good-Morrow"]'—the *idea* is thoroughly teased and touseled. The choice and arrangement of words is simple and direct and felicitous. There is a star-tling directness (as often at the beginning of Donne's poems) about the idea, which must have occurred to many lovers, of the abrupt break and alteration of *the new life* [emphasis added]." Eliot goes on to suggest that what seems at first glance the speaker's sexual desire is undercut by Donne's style: "These *trouvailles* [windfalls, discoveries] themselves are enough to set Donne apart from some of his imitators: Cowley never found anything so good. But the usual course for Donne is not to pursue the meaning of the idea, but to arrest it, to play catlike with it, to develop dialectically, to extract every minim of the emotion suspended in it. And as to the poetic justification of this method of dialectic I have no doubts" (12–13). Eliot has quoted the first line of Donne's poem "The Good-Morrow," in which Donne transfigures the pas-sion of sexual love into a deeply spiritual love—"And now good-morrow to our waking souls" (line 8 of "The Good-Morrow"). Indeed, carnal love is transfigured into divine love, infusing Dante's *Vita Nuova,* the new life.

Eliot's well-known essay "The Metaphysical Poets," which sets forth his theory of a "dissociation of sensibility" in English poetry beginning after Donne and his school, was first published in 1921 as a review of an anthol-ogy of seventeenth-century poetry. This early essay reveals some of Eliot's thinking about the way a poet's imagination works—or ought to work: "A thought to Donne was an experience; it modified his sensibility. When a poet's mind is perfectly equipped for its work, it is constantly amalgamating disparate experience; the ordinary man's experience is chaotic, irregular, frag-mentary. The latter falls in love, or reads Spinoza, and these two experiences have nothing to do with each other, or with the noise of the typewriter or the smell of cooking; in the mind of the poet these experiences are always forming new wholes" (*SE,* 247). Donne's sensibility, thus described, is pre-sumably not dissociated, i.e., his thought separated or disconnected from his feelings caused by his various, and chaotic, experiences.

But Donne and his fellow "metaphysical poets" were more or less the last to engage in the task "of trying to find the verbal equivalent for states of mind and feeling" (248) for over two centuries—until the advent of Eliot and his contemporaries. Eliot's observations born of contemplating Donne led in this essay to some of his most relevant notions about the nature of modern poetry: "It appears likely that poets in our civilization, as it exists at present, must be *difficult.* Our civilization comprehends great variety and complexity, and this variety and complexity, playing upon a refined sensi-bility, must produce various and complex results. The poet must become more and more comprehensive, more allusive, more indirect, in order to force, to dislocate if necessary, language into his meaning. . . . Hence we get something which looks very much like the conceit—we get, in fact, a method curiously similar to that of the 'metaphysical poets,' similar also in its use of obscure words and of simple phrasing." Eliot cites no poets writing in English who meet the demands of the modern age in the way he suggests as necessary, but he does cite two French poets: "Jules Laforgue, and Tristan Corbière in many of his poems, are nearer to the 'school of Donne' than any modern English poet" (248–49). Certain of the Harvard influences are here—in the linking of Donne with Laforgue—beginning to converge. Of course, when writing these words in 1921, Eliot was only a year away from publishing *The Waste Land,* which would seem to fulfill all those attributes he describes here, attributes that were inspired by his reading primarily of Donne.

10. The Lure of Europe: Brooks's *The Wine of the Puritans*

Van Wyck Brooks, Harvard Class of 1907, published his first book, *The Wine of the Puritans,* in England in 1908 and in America in 1909. Eliot claimed the book for review in the *Harvard Advocate,* and his review appeared May 7, 1909. Eliot's eagerness to review the book suggests that he was already uncertain if he would, after finishing his education, remain in America or, like Henry Adams and Henry James, become an international citizen spending much or most of his life abroad. Brooks's book explored this question for the young American with intellectual or artistic interests. Eliot in his review stated that the book exposed the "reasons for the failure of American life (at present)." He added: "The more sensitive of us may find ourselves shivering under the operation." The book, he wrote, would challenge those "double-dealers with themselves," Americans who are lured by the Old World but remain in America because of business or other reasons, such as a sense of obligation or duty—this last reason "implying a real sacrifice." For such Americans the book will prove a "definition of their discontent" (quoted in Howarth, 110).

Brooks's *Wine of the Puritans* is cast in the form of a dialogue, with both speakers confronting the question as to whether it is best for an American interested in "culture" and "tradition" to stay in the United States or settle abroad. It is not exactly the Socratic method, because neither conversationalist has authority over the other. By using such a format, Brooks avoids being pinned down to any particular view, but is able to explore even conflicting views judiciously. For example, at one point near the end, one of the participants exclaims: "It's all so vague, so difficult [helping America "get" a "tradition"]. You can't deliberately *establish* an American tradition. Walt Whitman was on the right track, possibly: but you can't build literally on *cosmos*. Universal comradeship means a great deal, but for practical purposes it means—nothing. It means just 'Yawp'" (Brooks, Van Wyck, TWOP, 56). There is in this rather exasperated comment a left-handed endorsement of Whitman (note the immediate qualification of "possibly"), which is abandoned in the end by using one of Whitman's neologisms against him: "I sound my barbaric yawp."

Many of the passages of the book would have attracted Eliot's attention, by and large reinforcing his already acquired criticism of his native land: "The native-born Puritan race is the dominant race everywhere [in America], socially at least, deeply tinged with those Puritan ideals, provincial and material still. The New England idea, adequate for a small province, naturally became inadequate for the expression of a great nation. Adapted as this idea was to the needs of a frugal, intellectual people whose development was strictly intensive rather than extensive, it was unable to meet the needs of great prosperity, imperialism and cosmopolitanism" (5). The American educational system seems unable to correct this national isolation: "In college one in every two is really enthusiastic about something larger than buying and selling. And the enthusiasm comes to an end with college. They seem, every one, to pass through their moments of undergraduate idealism as if it were all a dream, as if after all the world were shabbily real and there were no help for them" (29–30). A primary problem, of course, is that of identity—or the lack of a past: "For the Americans alone among all the races of the world, cannot seek for any interpretation of life in their own remote antiquity, simply because the childhood of America is the childhood of another country. We have no myths, there is nothing childlike in our past, and when we look to our ancestors to help us we find them almost as grown-up and self-conscious as we ourselves" (37).

At the close of the book, Brooks tries to counter the negative views that have multiplied throughout the brief sixty-page text: "We Americans do not feel the inspiration of American life because we shut ourselves off from understanding it. Everything in America is in a state of distraction, of divorce. Our humour is not our life, our politics and religion are outside ourselves, we are intelligent without instinct. And we further divorce ourselves by living abroad." Behind these problems lies a basic misunderstanding: "We consider it more honourable to trade than to create, whereas the farmer who produces wheat and barley is nearer the civilized ideal than the broker who negotiates them in Wall Street. By his labour he is actually bringing something into the world, not merely transferring something already produced.

And the artist also creates." In the end Brooks offers hope: "But I think a day will come when the names of Denver and Sioux City will have a traditional and antique dignity like Damascus and Perugia—and when it will not seem to us grotesque that they have" (59).

It is likely that Brooks's first book helped Eliot in making one of the most critical and determining decisions of his life—to settle ultimately in the land of his ancestors, England, for his life and career. Ironically, Brooks came to see Eliot's self-exile as a betrayal of himself and his country. In his autobiography, Brooks said he did not object to Eliot's "leaving his country and becoming a British subject," but he did object to Eliot's making "a popular intellectual cause of attacking what gave America its uniqueness and distinction" (Brooks, Van Wyck, *AA*, 510).

11. "T. S. Eliot, the Quintessence of Harvard"

As Eliot was a perceptive reader as well as a reviewer of Van Wyck Brooks's first book, *The Wine of the Puritans*, so he was a focal point in the chapter "Harvard: 1904–1907" in one of Brooks's last books, the first volume of his autobiography, *Scenes and Portraits: Memories of Childhood and Youth* (1954). Although Brooks and Eliot overlapped at Harvard for only one year, they were immersed in essentially the same environment—classes, clubs, publications, associations. Although they both confronted the choice of remaining in America or finding a career in Europe, Eliot chose England, and Brooks threw in his lot with America, helping to establish—or, rather, discover—the very tradition he and Eliot had originally felt did not exist, essentially in such of his works as *The Pilgrimage of Henry James* (1925), *The Flowering of New England* (1936), and *The Times of Melville and Whitman* (1947).

In his remembrance of his—and Eliot's—days at Harvard, Brooks levels a serious indictment: "That the world had been steadily going to the dogs since the time of Dante was the complaint . . . of Barrett Wendell, who deplored the American Revolution that had sundered us from England and the guidance of the British ruling class. Irving Babbitt was all for authority and formalistic discipline as against the Jeffersonian vision he connected with Rousseau, the traditionally American belief that men, freed from unjust social conditions, were sufficiently good to be trusted to rule themselves." As serious, and perhaps more so, was Santayana's criticism of America: "Then there was Santayana who described himself as an 'American writer,' or said he could not be described as anything else, but whom Lee Simonson remembered as always 'gazing over our heads as if looking for the sail that was to bear him home.' He was repelled by everything that characterized American life, preferring a world 'run by cardinals and engineers,' rejecting as 'all a harvest of leaves' the New England Renaissance and its best essayists, historians, romancers and poets. His smiling contempt for the efforts of men to better the world and humanity was reflected in a host of Harvard minds that were reversing the whole tendency of the great New England epoch, dismissing its faith in progress as 'the babble of dreamers.'" Brooks blamed his, and Eliot's, Harvard professors for their yearning for the old rather than welcoming the new: "One and all tended to revert, temperamentally, if not in fact, to the old European rigidities of the medieval order, to the cause of 'the altar and the throne,' hierarchy and clericalism, against the fluidities that were bred by American living" (Brooks, Van Wyck, *AA*, 110).

Brooks extended his criticism beyond Harvard to Cambridge and Boston, characterizing the whole culture encountered by Harvard students in the early decades of the twentieth century. First, there was a reactionary religious movement: "In reaction against the Puritanism of the New England forbears an Anglo-Catholic movement throve in Boston, and there was a semiserious cult of royalism also, with a branch of the Jacobite Order of the White Rose. The members offered expiation on the annual feast of St. Charles the Martyr [England's Charles I, whose beheading in 1649 led to establishment of the Commonwealth and rule by the Puritan Oliver Cromwell until the restoration of the monarchy in 1660], led by Ralph Adams Cram, the prior of the chapter, the architect-disciple of Henry Adams." In addition to this semireligious movement, there was a similarly reactionary literary movement: "The cult of Dante, which Mrs. Jack Gardner also embraced. . . . Dante was an omnipresent interest like the dramatists of Shakespeare's time, who were constantly studied and performed as well. Another Harvard note of the moment was the Sanskrit that Babbitt had studied with Lanman and that spread the renunciatory attitude." France, too, made its contribution to this reactionary movement: "The French Symbolist poets, steeped in mediaeval reverie, were a new mode of the young, some of whom discovered these poets in the library of the Union in *The Symbolist Movement in Literature* of Arthur Symons. . . . Dean Briggs was only one professor who talked of Donne familiarly as a poet about whom everyone went to extremes, whom people inordinately hated or loved and whom he personally cherished as one who preeminently 'made the far-fetched worth fetching'" (111–12).

Brooks cataloged all of the remarkable influences and more in stretching to reach a climax toward which his prose was driving: "When one added these tastes together, the royalism and the classicism, the Anglo-Catholicism, the cults of Donne and Dante, the Sanskrit, the Elizabethan dramatists and the French Symbolist poets, one arrived at T. S. Eliot, the quintessence of Harvard. Together they shaped his opposition to the 'cheerfulness, optimism and hopefulness' that stood for the point of view of the great days of the past, as they shaped also his inevitable vogue in an age prepared to feel with him that poetry can be found in suffering and through suffering only." Not surprisingly, Brooks asserts that these forces lay behind Eliot's leaving America and becoming a "European": "They shaped the course that led him, quite logically, to England, to which others were drawn temporarily, or only in part, to be drawn back later by powerful elements in their own minds of which at the time perhaps they were unaware. For the 'European virus,' as Henry James had called it, attacked its American victims in varying degrees, but in some degree or other it attacked most literary minds at Harvard because America there seemed nugatory" (112–13).

When T. S. Eliot went off to study in France in October 1910, he was embarking on a new phase of his life, one that would lead further and further from American soil, one that would lead, eventually, to his later decision to settle in England and, much later, in his startling declaration in the preface to *For Lancelot Andrewes* (1928), that he was a "classicist in literature, royalist in politics, and anglo-catholic in religion." All the seeds were sown at Harvard.

1910–1911

T. S. ELIOT IN PARIS

1. The Primacy of Paris, 1910–1911

To understand what happened to Eliot in Paris during his year of study there, 1910–11, it is best first to look ahead at Eliot's state of mind and imagination some decades after that magical year. In 1934, in the April issue of the *Criterion,* a journal that Eliot then edited in London, Eliot filled his regular column "A Commentary" with words written in praise of the French writer Henri Massis's *Evocations* (*Souvenirs* 1905–11): "The book should be, for anybody, an interesting and valuable document upon a period; but has a more personal interest for me, inasmuch as M. Massis is my contemporary, and the period of which he writes includes the time of my own brief residence in Paris" (ACHM, 451). At the time of that "brief residence," Eliot was twenty-two. In 1934, Eliot experienced the arrival of his forty-sixth year. His year in Paris lay nearly a quarter-century in his past, and much had happened in his life in the intervening time. But clearly the experiences of 1910–11 in Paris remained intact and vivid in his memory and imagination.

Eliot's little essay is not so much devoted to the book under review as to Eliot's nostalgic remembrance of things past. In his first paragraph he quotes Massis's comment lifted from Charles Péguy: "je vais fonder un parti, le parti des hommes de quarante ans; vous en serez aussi, mon garçon. Un jour, vous serez mûr" (I am going to found a party, the party of forty-year-old men. One day, you will be mature) (451, my translation). The mature Eliot—or, as he called himself later in the essay, the *quadrégenaire*—described the England and America of 1910 as "intellectual desert[s]" in contrast to the France of 1910, in which there was everywhere intellectual ferment. Many of the figures that Eliot mentions in his review will be found scattered throughout Jean Verdenal's letters (see below), the best concrete evidence of what Paris was like for young Eliot: Péguy himself, Barrès, Gide, Claudel, Verlaine, and so on. It may be the summoning up of all those names that brought back so vividly to Eliot his memory of Verdenal, a scene that seems so vibrant and compelling in its intensity that it bursts forth and takes over in the middle of the essay: "I am willing to admit that my own retrospect is touched by a sentimental sunset, the memory of a friend coming across the Luxembourg Gardens in the late afternoon, waving a branch of lilac, a friend who was later (so far as I could find out) to be mixed with the mud of Gallipolli" (452). The "outburst"—it seems irrepressible in the relaxed intellectual context surrounding it—is perhaps the most revealing comment by Eliot on Verdenal that has survived. It is consonant with the dedicatory quotation from Dante that appears in his *Poems, 1909–1925,* below the 1917 dedication to Verdenal in the first grouping of poems, *Prufrock and Other Observations* (1917): "For Jean Verdenal, 1889–1915 / mort aux Dardanelles / Or puoi la aquantitate / Comprender dell' amor ch'a te me scalda, / Quando dismento nostra vanitate / Trattando l'ombre come cosa salda" (*CPP,* 3). (Now canst thou comprehend / the measure of the love which warms me toward thee, / when I forget our nothingness, / and treat shades as a solid thing [Dante, *Purgatorio,* 267]).

If the image of Verdenal coming across the Luxembourg Gardens bearing a branch of lilac in his hands burned brightly in Eliot's memory, so did the image of "the *camelots* cheering the *cuirassiers* who were sent to disperse them, because they represented the Army, all the time that they were trying to stampede their horses." The incident described involved the Camelots du Roi of the Action Française of Charles Maurras, a writer turned political leader in the extreme right movement that was both antidemocratic and anti-Semitic. Maurras was described in an editorial note in *La Nouvelle Revue Française* in March 1913 (Eliot continued to subscribe to the *Revue* after he returned to Harvard) as embracing three conservative traditions—"classique, catholique, monarchique"—uncannily close to Eliot's self-description in 1928 as a "classicist in literature, royalist in politics, and anglo-catholic in religion" (*FLA,* 7). Eliot had been recruited by Verdenal as one of Maurras's admirers, but there can be no doubt that Eliot genuinely came to admire Maurras. In the street scene he depicted, Eliot clearly gave his approval to the disruptive mob of *camelots,* and he added enigmatically: "Perhaps France will be the last country to be conquered by the mob" (ACHM, 453). Eliot had been prepared by his Harvard professors to become a follower of Maurras, especially in the rightist views of Barrett Wendell (deploring America's breakaway from England, thus depriving the country of the wisdom of the British monarchy), and in part by the antidemocratic philosophy of Babbitt (see Chapter 4, Sections 1 and 2).

Thus, this 1934 "Commentary" touches on personal and intellectual attachments that began in Eliot's Paris year and were to remain, as we shall see, concerns for him for his entire life. Before beginning an examination in detail of that year, we should take note of another remark that Eliot made in a letter of January 10, 1916, written to his Harvard friend Conrad Aiken. Eliot said that he had not written because he had been "frightfully busy" teaching in secondary school in England, trying to rewrite his thesis in philosophy that he had drafted at Harvard, to which he had returned after Paris. In his catalog of the time-consuming and emotionally draining experiences he was facing he wrote: "my wife has been very ill. . . . I have been taken up with the worries of finance and Vivien's health . . . my friend Jean Verdenal has been killed." He reassured Aiken: "*I hope* to write, when I have more detachment. . . . I have *lived* through material for a score of long poems, in the last six months" (LTSE1, 125–26). That material clearly included not only his wife's sickness, which was unsettling their marriage, but also the devastating reality of Verdenal's death. It is noteworthy that in this casual statement Eliot identifies his personal—"*lived* through"—experience as the source for the "material" of his poems. (This statement must be taken into account in any analysis of what Eliot meant by his later formulation, in "Tradition and the Individual Talent," of an "impersonal theory of poetry.") Of course, Eliot's "long poem," *The Waste Land* (though brief parts of it were drafted much earlier), would not appear until 1922. But it should prove useful to keep that poem in mind as we sort through whatever biographical materials survive for a reconstruction of that critical Paris year.

2. Jean Verdenal: "*Mon Meilleur Ami*"

When T. S. Eliot sailed for France in October 1910, his social and literary views had been shaped by his education at Harvard—both in and out of the classroom. He went to France with great expectations about what he might encounter there, inspired in part by Irving Babbitt, who had encouraged his going. He went as well to attend classes at the Sorbonne, and particularly to hear the lectures of Henri Bergson at the Collège de France. Eliot's tutor in French was the novelist Alain-Fournier (1886–1914, killed in the war), who introduced Eliot to his brother-in-law, Jacques Rivière. The latter was secretary of *La Nouvelle Revue Française,* founded in 1909 by (among others) André Gide, with the purpose of publishing the important new post-Symbolist writers. Thus Eliot was thrust immediately into the avant-garde of French literature, and by reading *La Nouvelle Revue Française* was able to keep up with the latest in French poetry and prose. In addition to Gide himself, Eliot could find in the *Revue*'s pages such contemporary writers as Paul Claudel, Jean Giraudoux, Charles Péguy, and Paul Valéry.

Eliot found rooms at the Left-Bank Pension Casaubon at 151 bis rue St. Jacques, near the Sorbonne, and among the other tenants he met Jean Verdenal. Most of what is known about Verdenal comes from two critics who sought out his relatives long after his death: George Watson, in "Quest for a Frenchman" (1976), reports what he learned from Pierre Verdenal, a younger brother of Jean, and Claudio Perinot, in "Jean Verdenal: T. S. Eliot's French Friend" (1996), summarizes the information he obtained from one of Verdenal's nephews, named Jean after his uncle. Verdenal was both attractive and charming (his picture appears in volume 1 of *The Letters of T. S. Eliot*), and he became the focal point of all of the most profound memories Eliot carried away with him from Paris after his one-year stay. Studying to be a doctor, like his father before him, Verdenal was some two years younger than Eliot. He had come to Paris from his home in Pau in the French Pyrenees, and had settled into the Pension Casaubon—because the Verdenal family members were longtime friends of the Casaubons. He must have shared to a degree Eliot's sense of wonder at being alone—and free, personally and intellectually—in Paris.

Although Verdenal was a medical student, perhaps in accord with his father's wishes, his interests were mainly literary, and were astonishingly close to Eliot's: in his library were volumes of the works of Stéphane Mallarmé and Jules Laforgue. One of his (and his family's) political interests was in Charles Maurras and the Action Française. The right-wing political movement of early twentieth-century France viewed the overthrow of the monarchy during the French Revolution as the origin of all of the problems faced by contemporary France and called for the rule of an elite under a strong leader. Verdenal's influence on Eliot was incalculable, both personally and intellectually. Theirs was an encounter that changed Eliot's life and left its stamp on him and on both his prose and poetry, as we shall see, over his lifetime. There was correspondence between the two, first when Eliot left temporarily on a trip through Europe and then when Eliot returned to America in 1911, but only seven of Verdenal's letters have survived.

On his way through France to Pau to seek out the Verdenal family, George Watson planned to stop in Paris to look up Verdenal's military records. He knew from Eliot's dedicatory epigraph, which remained in volumes of his collected poems from 1917 (*Prufrock and Other Observations*) until 1952 (*The Complete Poems and Plays, 1909–1950*), that Verdenal had been killed in the Dardanelles during World War I. But since the French government forwarded Watson's request to examine the military records of Jean Verdenal to the Verdenal family, Verdenal's younger brother wrote to Watson enclosing the hand-written service record of Jean Verdenal. In it Watson found out the following bare facts: "Jean Jules Verdenal, born 11 May 1890 at Pau, medical student in Paris; granted deferment on his military service in 1911, again in 1912; renounced any further deferment in March 1913, when he entered the eighteenth infantry regiment; became a medical officer in November 1914, after the war had broken out, and entered a section of medical attendants in February 1915, when he joined the 175th infantry regiment. . . . Killed by the enemy on the 2nd May 1915 in the Dardanelles" (Watson, George, 466–67).

After conveying this information, Watson continues: "Then follows, in another hand, a citation dated 30 April 1915 awarded: 'Scarcely recovered from pleurisy, he did not hesitate to spend much of the night in the water up to his waist helping to evacuate the wounded by sea, thus giving a notable example of self-sacrifice.'" Watson speculates that Verdenal participated in the initial "Anglo-French attack on Gallipoli [April 25, 1915], designed to help Russia by knocking Turkey out of the war." And he further reports: "Some weeks after his death . . . his commanding officer wrote this citation on his conduct: 'Verdenal, assistant medical officer, performed his duties with courage and devotion. He was killed on the 2nd May 1915 while dressing a wounded man on the field of battle'" (467). In the various accounts that have been written about the attack on Gallipoli, the battlefield was as much in the water as it was on land, especially when it became clear that the troops would have to be withdrawn. Verdenal might well have been tending the wounded as they were heading off the beaches toward the vessels that would carry them away. As for personal interests, Watson learned that Verdenal had a keen interest in literature and excelled in school, particularly in languages. Watson was able to confirm that Jean Verdenal (along with his family) were, like Eliot, admirers of Charles Maurras and his Action Française (468–69).

Perinot's article, "Jean Verdenal: T. S. Eliot's French Friend," is written as a dialogue, in which Perinot poses a series of questions and records, presumably verbatim, the answers given by the nephew, Jean Verdenal. Asked to describe his Uncle Jean as a child, he replied: "Jean, as a boy, was a bit delicate, you might say. He was rather an introvert and rarely easy-going. He changed somewhat as he grew. Yet, we all remember him as being honest, serious and not malicious at heart, at all." Asked about Jean's schooling, M. Verdenal replied: "From the start, Jean was . . . always top of the class, in every subject. A remarkable student. Even in English. . . . And though there were tens of English Students, mother tongue I mean, one year Jean managed to beat them, too. He seemed to have a natural inclination for languages." On responding to a question about Jean's "cultural background," M. Verdenal said his grandfather and his uncles all loved the classics, "Knew them . . . by heart," including Balzac, Stendhal, Flaubert, even Dante in French, and that Jean "in particular loved poetry. He was well-known for his inspired readings. He found an enduring satisfaction in Mallarmé, among others" (Perinot, 267–69).

The nephew went on to list other attractions: Kant and Hegel, Goethe and Schiller in German, Shelley, Tennyson, Shakespeare, and the Bible. He notes that Verdenal "was a kind of mystic . . . he did have a strong inner life, a personal spiritual life. He was a profound believer and rather shunned the exterior rites of religion" (268–70). Permitted to browse through a "good deal of miscellanea" that had belonged to Jean Verdenal, Perinot found programs for operas, including much of Wagner. He also found many notes on philosophy recorded from Bergson's lectures, as well as from conversations, such as one with "[Matthew] Prichard and Milhaud," two fellow lodgers (we'll return to these lodgers later in another context). And Perinot found other notes set down from the reading of particular books by such authors as William James—because Verdenal was "particularly interested in psychology" (no doubt the work was James's massive study, *The Principles of Psychology*, 1890). Authors of the books personally owned by Jean Verdenal included Laforgue, Verlaine, Charles-Louis Philippe, Anatole France, Gide, Claudel, Baudelaire, Maeterlinck, and Schiller (271–72).

The only other information about Eliot's friend and the close and complex nature of their relationship, except for the scattered references to Verdenal that Eliot made in a few of his letters to his mother and friends, is contained in a handful of letters written by Verdenal to Eliot. Of the seven letters from Verdenal to Eliot, the first two were written some time in July 1911, after they had already spent ten or so months together and would soon be parted by Eliot's return to Harvard. They were addressed to Eliot when he was absent from Paris on a trip through northern Italy and southern Germany, settling in Munich long enough to receive mail. The first two letters are addressed to him there.

In the first letter (mid-July 1911) we encounter immediately the informality and joshing of friends: "Mon cher ami, Je suis impatient de vous voir trouver du papier à Bavière, et d'en recevoir un échantillon couvert de votre belle écriture avant que la bière allemande n'ait engourdi votre esprit" ("My dear friend, I am waiting impatiently to hear that you have found some notepaper in Bavaria, and to receive an example of it covered with your beautiful handwriting, before German beer has dulled your wits"). The character of the intellectual exchange that is already in place by the time these letters are written is suggested by the nature and range of allusions in this letter. Verdenal reports that he had the night before just finished reading Charles-Louis Philippe's *Mother and Child* ("a good and beautiful book; wholesome as bread and milk"), and almost immediately launches into an attack on "intellectual criticism"—the kind of academic criticism written by those who would be unable to understand or appreciate Philippe's work. Verdenal's description of this criticism is set forth by one confident of his reader's assent in what he is saying: "Reason, in criticism, should be reserved for demolishing, for hammering charlatans, for hammering phoneys and falsifiers of art until they are laid low. The good things stand out of their own accord; they have to be talked about to make them known, as you lend a book to a friend. Any attempt on the part of the intelligence to demonstrate the beauty of a work of art is, undoubtedly, a contradiction in terms" (*LTSE1*, 20–22).

That an enthusiasm for Philippe's novels of Paris lowlife (the "dregs," the poor) was one shared by the two friends was revealed when Eliot later, in 1932, wrote a preface to an English translation of another of Philippe's novels, *Bubu of Montparnasse*, which he confesses to have read when he "first came to Paris" in 1910, and which had become for him a "symbol of the Paris of that time"—a book that is an almost unrelieved portrayal of the "prostitutes and mackerels of the Boulevard Sébastopol." Eliot commented: "[Philippe] had a gift which is rare enough: the ability not to think, not to generalize. To be able to select, out of personal experience, what is really significant, to be able not to corrupt it by afterthoughts, is as rare as imaginative invention" (*PBOM*, vii, x–xi). It is likely that Eliot's respect for Philippe's talent was inspired by reading about—perhaps attending—André Gide's tribute to Philippe delivered in Paris in November 1910 (Hargrove, 39–41).

In his next letter to Eliot in Munich (mid-July 1911), Verdenal spends a long second paragraph describing Paris on "14th July, Bastille Day," concluding: "the evening is filled with an ever-mounting sensual excitement; sweat makes the girls' hair stick to their temples; lottery wheels spin; a merry-go-round, attractively lit and alluring, also revolves, and with every jerk of the wooden horses, the whores brace their supple busts and a shapely leg can be glimpsed through the slit of a 'fashionably split skirt'; a heavy, sensuous gust flows warmly by" (*LTSE1*, 24). The description could well have come out of Philippe's *Bubu of Montparnasse*, but without any mention of the danger lurking in the seductive scene—the "Pox" (syphilis) that becomes the center of Philippe's focus in the latter half of his book. But that Verdenal felt free to write to Eliot about such a sensual scene, with seductive whores displaying their wares, reveals the depth of intimacy that they had come to share. How many nights had the two of them spent wandering through the sex-haunted streets of Paris filled with "sensual excitement" and physical allure?

Using this description of Paris as a stepping stone, Verdenal characterizes the Parisian populace (or "working class") as having become "materialistic," an "evolution" like that of the "aristocracy in the eighteenth century," resulting in the suppression of "good inner impulses" in a devotion to thinking "rationally," or a dedication to "complete intellectualism." In contrast, Verdenal observes, there is aspiration among the contemporary elite "towards the Idea," revealing itself in the arts, especially "modern poetry," taking the form of a "return to Christianity, whether Catholic or Galilean and evangelical." Verdenal then introduces the names of a number of writers to suggest the variety of this latter—and obviously more desirable—essentially religious tendency, the list showing in itself "the sorting to be done" when he and Eliot get together again: "[Paul] Verlaine [1844–96: poet, early Symbolist], [Joris-Karl] Huysmans [1848–1907: novelist], [Maurice] Barrès [1862–1923: novelist], Francis Jammes [1868–1938: poet and novelist], [Charles] Péguy [1873–1914: essayist and poet], [Paul] Bourget [1852–1935: novelist and critic], [Paul-Louis-Charles-Marie] Claudel [1868–1955: poet and dramatist], [Louis] Le Cardonnel [1862–1936: poet], etc." (24).

Whatever the sorting Verdenal and Eliot might have undertaken in subsequent discussions of these writers, the dominant tendency bound to emerge would have been idealistic and religious. "The main thing is to say," Verdenal himself concluded, "in the case of each, *how far he can influence our inner life towards the knowledge of the supreme good.*" This "reading list" suggests something of the nature of the discussions that went on between them during the visits back and forth in their rooms in the Left-Bank pension, and it reveals as well something of the ultimate impact the interchange made on Eliot's subsequent intellectual (and religious) development. Verdenal's letter, excluding postscripts, concludes: "My dear fellow, I shall be here in September, and very pleased to see you again; all friendly greetings. Jean Verdenal." In one of three postscripts, however, Verdenal added a recommendation that Eliot go see some Wagner in Munich, mentioning that he had just seen the *Götter-dämmerung,* "the end of which must be one of the highest points ever reached by man" (27).

In the remaining five letters, all but the first written in 1912, this warm glow of anticipation of renewed encounter turns to apprehension or foreboding of permanent separation and loss. In the brief letter of October 17, 1911, written only a month or so after Eliot's departure from Paris for America, Verdenal opens with the admonition, "Don't think I have forgotten you." He then goes on to explain that he is preoccupied with preparing for and taking examinations: "I am too young. . . . I am . . . exhausted but appropriately exhilarated by the tension." He then hastily expresses his pleasure in receiving Eliot's letter and adds self-confidently: "we will talk together some other time" (27).

Some four months later, on February 5, 1912, Verdenal pens the longest of his letters to Eliot. He mentions that his exhaustion over the "drudgery" of the examinations has left him "feeling very lazy," and describes his attempt to reestablish "contact with life" in Paris after return from a "blissful provincial" holiday: "I am at a loss to know what to hang on to—few friends (my best friend is away), no acquaintances, since I deliberately dropped them all some months ago, no habits with which to fill time intelligently, and the rain is coming down." In his loneliness, he "fall[s] back upon his books" but finds they do not hold at bay those "vague surges of melancholy." He must, he adds, avoid "above all . . . chasing deliberately after some artificial ideal" (31). Thus in a blow he rejects for a time the reading list he had sent Eliot for future discussion in his mid-July 1911 letter.

Revealing that he has been going frequently to Wagner's operas, Verdenal says that he is "beginning to get the hang of *The Ring:* Each time the plot becomes clearer and the obscure passages take on a meaning. *Tristan and Isolde* is terribly moving at the first hearing, and leaves you prostrate with ecstasy and thirsting to get back to it again. . . . I am not making much sense, it is all so confused and difficult, and impossible to put into words. . . . However, I should be happy to know that you too are able to hear some Wagner in America" (31). Verdenal's mention of *Tristan and Isolde* is remarkable, given the allusions that Eliot will make to it in *The Waste Land.* That the opera left Verdenal "prostrate with ecstasy" suggests an orgasmic effect that was overpowering, and that left him "thirsting" for more. Verdenal's lapse into inarticulateness ("I am not making much sense") suggests that he feels he has revealed himself too fully, but the whole passage addressed to his absent friend points obliquely to his longing to share with his friend, in each other's presence, the overpowering effect of Wagner's music.

That this effect of Wagner's music is intensely sexual is suggested by ample testimony in various psychological studies of sex and music. In *The Tender Passion* (1986), Peter Gay writes: "[Wagner] acknowledged that some of his compositions were poems about love—*Tristan und Isolde,* indeed, was a 'monument' to it. . . . It is arguable (and has been argued) that *Tristan* is far more than a love story, but it made Wagner's munificent patron, King Ludwig II of Bavaria, literally swoon, and the impression it leaves on its audiences remains that of a long drawn out and reiterated representation of sexual congress." The music markedly emphasizes "the love scenes with its luxuriant themes and flowing rhythms rising, rising, and those final satiated moments with Tristan breathing his last in Isolde's arms; it evokes the thrilling journey to what the French call the little death, which seals sexual intercourse happily completed. In such representations, the regressive pull toward primitive feelings is almost irresistible, sublimation far from complete, with the erotic sources of the composition unmistakable, consciously exploited" (Gay, 264–65).

Verdenal's experience of listening to *Tristan and Isolde* seems to be exactly what Peter Gay so aptly describes—sexual feelings rising in intensity to the moment of climax. Apparently Eliot had seen a production of the opera in Boston in 1909, before ever going to Paris, and it led to his writing a 1909 poem ("Opera") that appears contemptuous of the music. After describing in the first stanza the music he has heard at a performance of *Tristan and Isolde* ("Writhing in and out / Contorted in paroxysms"), in the second stanza he writes: "We have the tragic? Oh no! / Life departs with a feeble smile / Into the indifferent. / These emotional experiences / Do not hold good at all, / And I feel like the ghost of youth / At the undertaker's ball" (*IOMH*, 17). But later in life a conversation Eliot had with Igor Stravinsky led the composer to believe that Wagner's *Tristan and Isolde* had been "one of the most passionate experiences of his [Eliot's] life" (119). Obviously Verdenal changed Eliot's view of the opera. Indeed, Eliot used two highly significant quotations from the opera at the start of *The Waste Land:* "Frisch weht der Wind / Der Heimat zu / Mein Irisch Kind, / Wo weilest du?" (lines 31–34 [*Tristan and Isolde,* act 1, verses 5–8: "Fresh blows the wind / To the homeland; / My Irish child, / Where do you tarry?"]). These hopeful lines from the opera express Tristan's exhilaration in his expected return to his beloved's arms. After seven intervening lines introducing the "hyacinth girl," which have inspired much interpretive controversy, appears a single line from *Tristan and Isolde:* "Oed' und leer das Meer" (line 42 [*Tristan,* act 3, verse 24: "Sea, desolate and empty"]). The stark line embodies intense feelings of loneliness and despair.

In paragraph four of this letter of February 5, 1912, Verdenal writes that he is occupying the same room at 151 bis rue St. Jacques that Eliot had occupied the year before, with "the bed in a little recess." But he finds "the pattern of the wallpaper" inexplicably upsetting and annoying: "Damn. It occurred to me a moment ago to send you a little piece of wallpaper—then I immediately realized that the idea was not mine but that I had got it from a letter by J. Laforgue, so I will abstain" (*LTSE1*, 32). Valerie Eliot provides a footnote in her edition of *The Letters of T. S. Eliot,* quoting from a Laforgue letter of September 1881 addressed to his sister: "What can I send you as a souvenir of this time? From the corner behind the chest of drawers in my room I have cut a piece of wallpaper. Treasure it" (29). From the former bed, to the familiar wallpaper pattern, to the shared poet Laforgue, Verdenal seems almost overcome by memories of his year with Eliot.

After bemoaning the loss of spontaneity and enthusiasm he once had, Verdenal asks: "Will my enthusiasms [*ardeurs*], now as operative as damp squibs, ever be able to flower fully? The hope still remains with me, my dear fellow, a sweet and serious hope, as yet veiled but tomorrow, perhaps, wreathed in smiles." Verdenal's paragraph trails off into silence; he frequently uses ellipses to indicate his own elisions. But the immediately following paragraph begins: "My dear friend, we are not very far, you and I, from the point beyond which people lose that indefinable influence and emotive power over each other, which is reborn when they come together again. It is not only time which causes forgetfulness—distance (space) is an important factor" (Eliot would remember and refer to this passage in a 1917 letter to his cousin, Eleanor Hinkley: "I remember Jean Verdenal saying to me when I left Paris that Space more than Time would separate us. I think one feels space less in a short letter" [192]). The melancholy expressed in this letter by Verdenal ("I was not made to be a melancholic") is inspired by feeling a confusing mixture of Eliot's felt presence and his absolute absence as he goes to bed in the room that had formerly been his friend's. In the remainder of the letter, Verdenal apologizes profusely for not having written more often ("that is the excuse for the length of this letter and its disjointedness"). The implication seems to be that Eliot has been a more frequent correspondent, but has now lapsed into waiting silence. In any event, Verdenal commands: "Send me news of yourself, with evocative details, as you know how; shake off your elegant indolence and grant me a little time filched from your studies, however unworthy of it I may be." After some description of the occupants and life at 151 bis rue St. Jacques, Verdenal signs off: "Dear friend, I shake your hand. Jean Verdenal" (32).

But still the letter does not end. Verdenal adds: "I am copying out here a sentence by André Gide, which has given me enormous pleasure during the last few days: 'Alternative—Ou d'aller encore une fois, ô forêt pleine de mystère, jusqu'à ce lieu que je connais où, dans une eau morte et brunie, trempent et s'amollissent encore les feuilles des ans passés, les feuilles des printemps adorables'" (30). The translation provided in the *Letters* is as follows: "The Alternative:—Or to go once more, O forest filled with mystery, to that place I know, where, in darkened, stagnant water, the leaves of bygone years are still steeping and softening—the leaves of adorable springtimes." The lines are the penultimate paragraph of Gide's 1896 work *Paludes* (from Latin *Palus,* a swamp), translated into English by George D. Painter as *Marshlands* (1953).

It might prove useful to glance next at this passage in Painter's translation: "Alternative: Or shall I go yet once more, oh forest full of mystery—to the place I know, where in a brown dead water the leaves still soak and soften, the leaves of fallen years, of lost delicious Aprils?" (Gide, 93). This appears to be an enigmatic passage from one of Gide's more enigmatic works. The quotation is the penultimate sentence of Gide's work, and as translated by Painter poses a question. Can it be in some indirect way connected to the opening lines of *The Waste Land:* "April is the cruellest month, breeding / Lilacs out of the dead land, mixing / Memory and desire, stirring / Dull roots with spring rain. Winter kept us warm, covering / Earth in forgetful snow, feeding / A little life with dried tubers. / Summer surprised us, coming over the Starnbergersee" (*CPP,* 37). The Starnbergersee is a lake resort near Munich, the city Eliot was visiting after his academic year in Paris, and the city to which Verdenal addressed the first two letters examined above. "Memory and desire" are evoked as much by Verdenal's Gide quotation as by Eliot's opening *Waste Land* lines.

We might assume that Eliot, had he not already read Gide's *Paludes,* sought it out to discover the context of the quotation Verdenal shared with him. Had he done so, he would have found in it something of the fragmentary method often said to characterize Gide's poetry, together with an incoherent plot evoking the bleak theme suggested by the title, *Marshlands* (bogs or swamps characterized by "stagnant" or "dead" water), much like a *waste land.* Gide's central "character," living in Paris, desultorily writing a novel entitled *Marshlands,* exclaims at one point, "What I want to express is the emotion my life has given me: the boredom, the emptiness, the monotony" (Gide, 20). At another point, he writes: "All through life I shall have struggled towards a little greater light. I have seen, ah! all round me, crowds of beings languishing in too narrow rooms; the sun never entered them; great panes of tinted glass brought them, about midday, discoloured refractions of its light.

It was the hour when, in the alleys below, one stifled in the breathless heat; rays, that could find no space to diffuse themselves, concentrated between the walls of the houses an unhealthy shimmering" (81). In short, the title *Marshlands* is used as an extended metaphor for contemporary life.

It is clear that the title, "Alternative," on this last page of the calculatedly incoherent narrative of the novel, is an alternative to the futile and meaningless activities of modern life in Paris described recurrently in the body of the book. In "Alternative," the tone is no longer light, comic, or frivolous, but earnest, revelatory, deeply felt. Verdenal copied out for Eliot only the first paragraph on that last page. The final paragraph reads: "It is there [by the "brown dead water"] that my broken resolutions take their deepest rest, there that my thoughts are reduced, at long last, to little or nothing" (93). The place so strongly desired is clearly the place of "memory and desire," a place beyond "thought" (or rationality) for recollecting the ecstasies of earlier springs (or Aprils) associated with "broken resolutions"—the self's forbidden pleasures. It is perhaps these "unconscious" and unrealized memories that have rendered life empty and without purpose, as so vividly portrayed throughout a land of waste in *Marshlands*.

In an introductory note to his book, Gide writes: "Before I explain my book to others, I am waiting for others to explain it to me. . . . What interests me most in my book, is what I have put in without being aware of it—the part that belongs to the unconscious, which I should like to call, the part that belongs to God." Gide wrote this after finishing his book, just as Eliot suddenly recollected "The awful daring of a moment's surrender" at the end of *The Waste Land*. Like Eliot, Gide seems to be sighting or signaling a way out of the waste land (or marshlands), confronting and accepting a "memory" embodying a "desire" that endures in one's whole life—and sustains one's sanity.

Verdenal's closing postscript in that same letter of February 5 reads: "Excuse the handwriting—the spelling, the style and the crossings out—but I was in the habit of sometimes coming down to your room in an old jacket, collarless and in slippers." The room, we should remember, is Eliot's old room, where Verdenal is composing his letter to his "dear friend." Rooms at 151 bis rue St. Jacques figure importantly in the relationship of Eliot and Verdenal and in their memories of each other after their separation, as this letter reveals. Although the word "room" appears twice in *The Waste Land* (in "A Game of Chess," line 106, and "The Fire Sermon," line 254), the word "rooms" appears only once: in "What the Thunder Said," line 409, in the context of one of the most enigmatic (and controversial) passages in the poem, lines 400–409: "DA / *Datta*: what have we given? / My friend, blood shaking my heart / The awful daring of a moment's surrender / Which an age of prudence can never retract / By this, and this only, we have existed / Which is not to be found in our obituaries / Or in memories draped by the beneficent spider / Or under seals broken by the lean solicitor / In our empty rooms" (lines 401–10).

The *Waste Land* manuscripts reveal that after "Datta," the words "we brother" originally appeared, rendering the two friends experiencing the "awful daring of a moment's surrender" unmistakably masculine (*WLF*, 77). They had often been interpreted, before the manuscripts were published in 1971, as male and female, as in Cleanth Brooks's "*The Waste Land:* Critique of the Myth," in which he takes the key line, "the awful daring of a moment's surrender," as having "sexual meaning" in reference to sex as "propagation of the race" (Brooks, Cleanth, TWLCM, 163). Similarly, Grover Smith, in *T. S. Eliot's Poetry and Plays,* sees the "surrender" as a "yielding to lust," like the lust enacted in "The Fire Sermon" by the typist and "young man carbuncular"—a lust to which Tiresias (the poem's most important personage, according to Eliot) "has already confessed": "This alone, the craven surrender to a tyranny of the blood, has secretly dominated the quester's whole existence, though it is 'not to be found in our obituaries'" (Smith, Grover, PP, 96). Though the *Waste Land* manuscripts appeared as long ago as 1971, Eliot critics and scholars have not come to terms with the obvious masculinity of the two individuals who experience that "awful daring of a moment's surrender" that is clearly sexual.

Verdenal's next letter to Eliot is dated April 22, 1912, a little over two months after his last, and is perhaps the emotional climax in the correspondence: it conjures up vividly the happy time the year before when the two friends were together. Does the month of April, the beginning of spring, have a special significance for Verdenal? His opening paragraph reads: "My dear friend, a persistent blaze of spring sunshine prompted me to go out into the woods today. The little boat carried me gently to Saint Cloud between translucent green rows of tender young leaves drenched in light. At Saint Cloud, the explosion of spring was less conspicuous, being crystallized into the artificial lines of the great avenues; it was a delicate, unreal scene, even fairy-like, I would say, if that word had not been too much bandied about and distorted." We do not find out until paragraph two what seems to have been the principal determinant of Verdenal's itinerary on this April day: "So, this evening, when I got back, I thought of writing to you, because *you* were especially called to mind by the contact with a landscape we appreciated together" (*LTSE1*, 34). A day in April, a visit to Saint Cloud to see alone what Verdenal and Eliot had seen together the year before, witnessing again that "explosion of spring" in the seemingly instantaneous appearance of a multitude of flowers of every species.

The Seine meanders through some of the most beautiful garden and park country in France to St. Cloud, a town on the left bank of the Seine with the Bois de Boulogne across on the right bank. "Picturesquely built on a hill-slope, St. Cloud overlooks the river, the Bois de Boulogne and Paris; and, lying amid the foliage of its magnificent park and numerous villa gardens, it is one of the favorite resorts of the Parisians. The palace of St. Cloud, which had been a summer residence for Napoleon I, Louis XVIII, Charles X, Louis Philippe and Napoleon III, was burned by the Prussians in 1870 along with part of the village. In spite of the damage inflicted on the park at the same period its magnificent avenues and ornamental water still make it one of the pleasantest spots in the neighborhood of Paris." This contemporaneous description comes from the 11th edition of the *Encyclopaedia Britannica,* published in 1911, and describes what Eliot and Verdenal actually saw on their trip to St. Cloud (*EB*, vol. 23, p. 1019). What the description does not say is that the "villa gardens" are a multitude of flower gardens, which could have conceivably contained the lilac and the hyacinth.

In the closing lines of *The Waste Land,* after the references to "the awful daring of a moment's surrender," after references to "our obituaries" and "empty rooms," Eliot writes in the original version:

Damyata. ~~the wind was fair, and~~ the boat responded
~~rudder~~.
Gaily, to the hand expert with sail and ~~wheel.~~
oar.
would have
The sea was calm, ~~and~~ your heart responded
obedient
Gaily, when invited, beating ~~responsive~~
~~You over on the shore~~
To controlling hands. ~~I left without you~~
~~There I leave you~~
~~Clasping empty hands,~~ I ~~sit~~/sat upon ~~the~~/a shore
the arid plain
Fishing, with ~~the/a desolate sunset~~ behind me /

~~Can~~/Shall I at least set my ~~own~~ land~~s~~
~~Which now at last my~~/the kingdom in order? (*WLF*, 79)

Lurking among the images of the passage appear to be glimpses of the experience that Verdenal refers to in his letter—the experience in which both Verdenal and Eliot—in a "little boat"—made the trip in April 1911 that Verdenal repeats alone in April 1912. (A year before Verdenal wrote his nostalgic April 1912 letter, Eliot returned to Paris from his visit to London on April 25, 1911, as described in an exuberant letter to his cousin Eleanor Hinkley, discussed below.)

The watery scenes quoted above from the early version of *The Waste Land* are likely the mingling of two such scenes, that on the Seine on the way to St. Cloud in April 1911, and that on the boat that carried Eliot alone back to America in October 1912. The prominence of April in the event— both the date of the Verdenal's nostalgic letter of 1912 and the probable date of the visit to St. Cloud in 1911—motivated Eliot to open his long poem *The Waste Land,* based on "material" he had "lived through," with the phrase "April is the cruellest month." The clue to the second phrase of the poem, "breeding / Lilacs out of the dead land," may be found in that nostalgic remembrance of Verdenal "coming across the Luxembourg Gardens in the late afternoon, waving a branch of lilacs." The next two phrases logically follow: "mixing / Memory and desire, stirring / Dull roots with spring rain." Of course the vocabulary of the passage—"breeding," "stirring / Dull roots"— is fraught with sexual (even phallic) suggestions. In his language here, Eliot may have unconsciously remembered words from Philippe's novel, *Bubu of Montparnasse,* which he and Verdenal had so enthusiastically read and shared: "A man walks carrying with him all the properties of his life, and they churn about in his head. Something he sees awakens them, something else excites them. For our flesh has retained all our *memories,* and we mingle them with our *desires"* (Phillippe, 25–26; emphasis added).

Moving back from the end of *The Waste Land* to its opening, we might concentrate on the hyacinth garden episode as written originally in the manuscript: "You gave me hyacinths first a year ago; / 'They called me the hyacinth girl.' / —Yet when we came back, late, from the hyacinth garden, / Your arms full, and your hair wet, I could not / Speak, and my eyes failed, I was neither / Living nor dead, and I knew nothing, / Looking into the heart of light, the silence" (*WLF,* 7). No doubt when Eliot and Verdenal went to St. Cloud in April 1911, they came back late in the day to Paris. Did Verdenal pick the hyacinths at St. Cloud to give to Eliot? And when we turn in the *Waste Land* manuscripts to Part II ("A Game of Chess"), lines 49–50, we find: "I remember / The hyacinth garden. Those are pearls that were his eyes, yes!" (19). Here we find the hyacinth garden linked to the "drowned Phoenician sailor" by a key line first heard from Madame Sosostris, the

"famous clairvoyante" in the poem's opening, referring to Phlebas the Phoe-
nician in Part IV. Have we reached the deepest levels of the poem's origins,
perhaps, and come face to face with "Jean Verdenal (1889–1915), *mort aux
Dardanelles?*"

In the letter of April 1912, Verdenal goes on to share with Eliot his inner
struggle to emerge from his "melancholic state": "I am beginning to be less
afraid of life and to see truths less artificially." He feels "both younger and
more mature," which, he thinks, "is no doubt the prelude to some new pur-
suit of the absolute." As in previous letters, he identifies the object of his
pursuit as the "ideal," which is "an *inner impulse* and not an attraction from
outside." The "ideal" is "inherent in the impulse of life itself," but it "cannot
be appeased by the achievement of any goal." It is the "Ideal" which "1) Leads
us to believe that life has a purpose" and "2) Makes that purpose unknow-
able." After this heavy philosophical breathing, Verdenal suddenly exclaims:
"Excuse this blather." And he turns to a brief discussion of the movements
in art (cubism, futurism), expressing dismay at the creation of "new schools
every six months." And he concludes: "Goodbye, my dear fellow, write to me
whenever the thoughts occur to you. I hope you are doing splendid things
in America, and that radiant blooms are germinating. Jean Verdenal" (*LTSE1*,
34–35). Is it too much to venture that the flower metaphor—"radiant blooms
are germinating"—has special meaning for both Verdenal and Eliot?

On August 26, 1912, Verdenal wrote his penultimate letter to Eliot, appar-
ently from his temporary address, which was added in a postscript (Hôtel-
Dieu, place du Parvis, Nôtre Dame). He notes at the opening that he has been
away from Paris on a month-long "health-giving holiday, 'well-showered
and with muscles in trim,'" and has plunged into preparation for medical
examinations, mobilizing "every scrap of [his] meagre medical knowledge."
The second—and last—paragraph: "And then this evening, on the stroke of
ten (all the bells in the area are ringing and, almost at the same time, comes
a tinkling of fairly distant chimes, soon blotted out by the measured pealing
of a deeper bell, do you remember?) suddenly I think of you as ten o'clock
is striking. And your image is there in front of me, and so I am writing you
this little note. But now, a hurried, very hurried good night . . . because
I must get back to work. Jean Verdenal" (35). *Do you remember?* Whatever
Eliot might have answered in a now-destroyed letter, he may also have given
his answer in *The Waste Land's* third line: "Memory and desire, stirring /
Dull roots with spring rain." What is the moment remembered so intensely,
at ten o'clock at night, called up by the "tinkling . . . of distant chimes, soon
blotted out by the measured pealing of a deeper bell"? The sensuality of
the images suggests a primary candidate: "The awful daring of a moment's

surrender." Eliot might well have been remembering this dream-like bell in Part v of *The Waste Land:* "And upside down in air were towers / *Tolling reminiscent bells,* that kept the hours" (lines 382–83, emphasis added).

Verdenal's last extant letter to Eliot is dated December 26, 1912. He reports the good news—that he has come to the end of his "boring examination," preparation for which made his head "rather like a department store stocked with anything and everything to hoodwink the public." To counter this overemphasis on the merely "practical," Verdenal pledges that his "thought will continue to develop freely and that [his] heart will respond to the calls of life. . . ." In short, he proposes to give himself "an organized scheme of literary and philosophical study." And he is pleased that Eliot is engaged in serious study (graduate work in philosophy at Harvard), remarking that Eliot's "delicate taste and perspicacity will be put to better use than in dealing with futile matters" (*LTSE1, 36*).

Verdenal then extends best wishes to Eliot in language fraught with ambiguity: "I wish you, for the coming year, an oft-renewed ardour—ardour, flame—but its source is in the heart, and here it is that our wishes must be prudent. 'Bring good upon me, O Lord, whether I ask for it or not, and remove evil from me, even though I ask for it'" (36). The movement of Verdenal's subject appears to be from the surface to the subtextual, with ambiguous personal reference in the latter. "Ardour," a favorite word for Verdenal, here defined with the synonym "flame," appeared as well in the long letter of February 5, 1911 (translated as "enthusiasm"), in a similarly ambiguous context. His wishes are for Eliot at the beginning, but he slips into the plural in mid-sentence—"and here it is *our wishes* must be prudent." Prudent? "The awful daring of a moment's surrender / Which an age of *prudence* can never retract" (emphasis added). From the second-person "you" to the first-person plural "our" to the first-person "I"—Verdenal's movement of thought is difficult to follow. What kind of "evil" is it that either Verdenal or Eliot is likely to "wish for"?

Although Eliot's letters to Verdenal were lost, there survives one of his letters to his cousin Eleanor Hinkley, of April 26, 1911—a date that places it *before* any of Verdenal's letters explored above. In it Eliot describes something of his relationship with Verdenal at the pension 151 bis rue St. Jacques as it has developed several months after initial acquaintance. It is made more understandable in the context of the whole of Verdenal's correspondence, and especially those letters written after Eliot's departure for America in October 1911, when it is gradually becoming clear to Verdenal that time is rushing past and would (as it turned out and as Verdenal feared) separate them forever. In his letter of April 22, 1912, Verdenal is moved by the arrival of spring, and especially April, to take time off from his busy schedule of study for an outing in a boat to St. Cloud, where the two had gone together the year before. Verdenal is writing a year (1912) after the event, while Eliot is writing to his cousin a year (1911) earlier, at a time close to the initial event. He has just returned from London to Paris and the *femme du chambre* welcomes him home like a member of the family, telling him he is "getting fat," and relaying all the news about his friends at the pension.

The most important news in Eliot's letter of April 26, 1911, to his cousin is that Verdenal has changed rooms at the pension, and is now occupying one larger and giving onto the garden. Eliot reports: "So then I had to go [at the insistence of the *femme du chambre*] into M. Verdenal's room to see how the garden did. Byplay at this point, because M. Verdenal was in the garden, and because I threw a lump of sugar at him." This "byplay" is perhaps the most important news of the letter, as Eliot seems to have little to say, apologizing: "I have no news equally amusing to repay with. I feel rather guilty about that, I do: for Paris has burst out, during my absence, into full spring; and it is such a revelation that I feel that I ought to make it known" (17–20). Eliot's tossing of the lump of sugar at his friend Verdenal in the garden outside his room may seem insignificant in itself, but it is the kind of gesture that reveals something of the depth of their emotional bonding—especially in the light of Eliot's well-known (and lifelong) reserve and formality in all his relationships. In a novel by Henry James, one of Eliot's favorite writers from youth onward, the gesture might well stand as a profound revelation. Indeed, it suggests the deep warmth of the relationship as we have recovered it from Verdenal's letters.

After Eliot's sudden and inexplicable marriage in 1915 and his settling down in London, his thoughts must have frequently returned to his carefree days in Paris. In a letter to his mother, dated January 22, 1921, Eliot mentions a trip he had made alone to Paris in the week before Christmas, in December 1920. And where did he stay? Like an emotional magnet, the rooms at his Left-Bank pension occupied in 1910–11 pulled him back: he stayed again at 151 bis rue St. Jacques: "I stayed at my old pension Casaubon, you know the old people are all dead, and the grandson is now proprietor. . . . If I had not met such a number of new people there Paris would be desolate for me with pre-war memories of Jean Verdenal and the others" (432–34). The feelings of "desolation" Eliot expresses here at Verdenal's loss were to endure, as we have seen in the outburst with which we began above—in the indelible image Eliot has fixed in his imagination some twenty-five years after the event (vividly recollected in 1934): "the memory of a friend coming across the Luxembourg Gardens in the late afternoon, waving a branch of lilacs."

That Eliot had returned in 1920 to the Pension Casaubon where he had come to know Jean Verdenal some years after his death, and the emotions he felt there, must have been on his mind when he wrote his introduction to a volume entitled *Poems of Tennyson* in 1936, reprinted in his *Selected Essays* as "In Memoriam." Eliot quotes a passage from Tennyson's *In Memoriam* describing his visit to the empty house of his dead friend, Arthur Henry Hallam: "Dark house, by which once more I stand / Here in the long un- lovely street, / Doors, where my heart was used to beat / So quickly, wait- ing for a hand, // A hand that can be clasp'd no more— / Behold me, for I cannot sleep, / And like a guilty thing I creep / At earliest morning to the door. // He is not there; but far away / The noise of life begins again / And ghastly thro' the drizzling rain / On the bald street breaks the blank day" (*SE,* 291). Eliot commented: "This is great poetry, economical of words, a universal emotion related to a particular place; and it gives me the shudder that I fail to get from anything in *Maud.* But such a passage, by itself, is not *In Memoriam: In Memoriam* is the whole poem. It is unique: it is a long poem made by putting together lyrics, which have only the unity and continuity of a diary, the concentrated diary of a man confessing himself. It is a diary of which we have to read every word" (291).

The question arises: why did this poem give T. S. Eliot the "shudder" of genuine response that he records in this essay, a shudder that causes him to say, simply, "This is great poetry, economical of words, a universal emotion"? Eliot's extravagant claims for the lines seem strangely remote from the pas- sionate intensity of his highly personal response. We might readily agree on the universality of the inconsolable sense of loss as it becomes mixed with guilt ("like a guilty thing I creep"), and the sense deepening to feelings of futility and meaninglessness, as the poet turns back to "the noise of life"— as in "on the bald street breaks the blank day." However *great, economical,* or *universal* Tennyson's lines, the particular circumstances of his grief appear unique: he and Arthur Hallam became close friends at Cambridge, where both were undergraduates; later Hallam became engaged to Tennyson's sister. Hallam's sudden death at the age of twenty-four (in 1833) affected Tennyson profoundly, and he at once began the long elegy that was published as *In Memoriam* in 1850. Eliot's emphasis on the universality of the emotion in Tennyson's lyric suggests his own deep identification with it—and inspires wonder as to whether there is not a similar structure of circumstances in Eliot's own life. We already know, of course, what Eliot does not reveal in his comment: that he too had lost a beloved friend, and that he too had returned to the place—Pension Casaubon—of their meeting and brief but intense friendship.

Robert Sencourt, in his *T. S. Eliot: A Memoir* (1971), writes of the impact of his Paris experience on Eliot:"The friend whose memory lingered longest with him was a medical student, Jean Verdenal, who in a life tragically cut short at Gallipoli also found time to be a poet. In letters at the Houghton Library, Harvard, I found the record of this affinity of hearts" (Sencourt, 32). Sencourt wrote out of personal acquaintance with Eliot over a period of years, and his characterization of the letters appears persuasive in the light of our exploration of them. In a footnote, Sencourt records a "biographical" interpretation of a part of *The Waste Land* that was becoming current as he was writing his memoir: "Jean Verdenal, as Phlebas the Phoenician, has left a profound imprint on *The Waste Land*." Sencourt cites John Peter's "New Interpretation of *The Waste Land*" in *Essays in Criticism* (April 1, 1969) discussed above, which appears to be consonant with what we have discovered in Verdenal's letters.

One of the young British poets Eliot published when he went to work for Faber and Faber in the mid-twenties was Stephen Spender, who later wrote *T. S. Eliot* (1976), part of the Penguin Modern Master Series. A young friend of the poet in the latter part of Eliot's life, Spender wrote in this volume: "Eliot once referred to *The Waste Land* as an elegy. Whose elegy? His father's? Jean Verdenal's—mort aux Dardanelles in the war?" (Spender, *TSE*, 111). A few pages later, Spender remarked: "'Death by Water' crystallizes the hidden elegy that is in *The Waste Land*—hinted at, as we have seen, in 'Those are pearls that were his eyes.' The passage has, however, an innocence of cleansing waters which seems outside both the sordidness and the apocalyptic fire of the rest of the poem. It seems an escape from a mood, and perhaps that is its virtue" (114). Unfortunately, Spender does not provide the context for Eliot's labeling his masterpiece an "elegy."

3. Matthew Prichard: A Blurred Portrait

We have dealt briefly in Chapter 3, Section 3 ("Bohemian Harvard and Isabella Stewart Gardner ["Mrs. Jack"])" with Eliot's involvement with the group of nonconformists surrounding Mrs. Jack, her three homosexual nephews, and her house/art-museum known as Fenway Court in Boston. We must return to that scene and the sources we used to create it to find out something about Matthew Stuart Prichard. Although the Prichard name can be found in *The Letters of T. S. Eliot,* especially in Jean Verdenal's letters to Eliot and in a few letters by Eliot, the quickest way to find out important facts about him is to begin with Douglass Shand-Tucci's *Boston Bohemia.* In chapter 6, "The Figure in the Carpet" (the title borrowed, of course, from Henry James), in the section entitled "The Aesthetic Movement in Boston," we learn first that Edward Perry Warren (or Ned), a rich man with an inherited fortune, began endowing in the 1880s the Boston Museum of Fine Arts, thus enabling it to possess and exhibit "one of the great classical sculpture collections of the world." He was widely known as a homosexual, even publishing "a three volume work entitled *A Defense of Uranian* [i.e., homosexual] *Love*." And it turned out that Ned's most intimate friend, Matthew Prichard of Sussex, England, was assistant director of the museum. As he was a part of Oscar Wilde's circle, Prichard's sexual preferences were known by some of the trustees of the museum as well as others. For example, a "collection of poems published in Paris *after* the Wilde trial [in 1895] by Alfred Douglas included one poem dedicated *to* Prichard" (Shand-Tucci, BB, 220–21).

And the reason that Prichard did not suffer due to his sexual orientation was, according to Shand-Tucci, that unlike Warren, who was strikingly effeminate and flaunted his sex preference in his writing, Prichard was "not only very masculine . . . but handsome as well; his sexual temperament was much less important than that his 'bearing and behavior, including his emotional attachment to others of his sex, did not affront current codes of conduct.'" The result was that Warren remained an outsider, a fact which he resented, while Prichard "became increasingly influential in Boston and a key figure in the aesthete network" (220–22; quotation from Gay, 212). In the Gardner Museum, as Fenway Court is now called, there was hidden away a guest suite, with bath and small kitchen, which Mrs. Jack made available to special friends and their guests for overnight stays, among whom were her nephew Amory Gardner, the artist John Singer Sargent, the museum curator Okakura Kakuzo, and Prichard (Shand-Tucci, BB, 229).

Although Isabella Gardner seldom turns up in Eliot's letters, it is clear that Eliot had, while attending Harvard, become close friends of several individuals associated with Mrs. Jack, some of them also connected with the other major art museum in the city, the Boston Museum of Fine Arts. Only three letters from Eliot to her appear in the 1988 volume of his correspondence, but they reveal that he formed a closer bond with her and her crowd of "followers" than has been previously realized. In the first of these, dated April 4, 1915, Eliot (then still at Oxford) inquires as to the whereabouts of their mutual acquaintances, Prichard among them. Having just met a friend of hers who had come to England from Boston at a meeting of the Buddhist Society—one Henry Furst—Eliot had learned from him that he knew "Matt Prichard" but did not know where he was at that time. Eliot did discover from Furst, however, that Prichard had been in Freiburg, Germany, when Eliot was studying in Marburg just as the Great War broke out. As we shall see, Eliot was able to get out of Germany and to England before being permanently detained in Germany. Eliot wrote that Furst "showed me a photograph and a letter of poor Matt Prichard, of whom I had heard nothing whatever. . . . As I seem to have lost contact with Furst, and am not in touch with other of Matt's friends, I should be more than indebted to you if you would let me have word about him: if he is eventually released, especially. Furst spoke of him as very happy, in being able to help other people in the camp. I can imagine its bringing out exclusively the best in his restless spirit; and now that I know that he is there, it seems to me the happiest and best and most appropriate thing for him at such a time as this: a certain curious symbolism about it" (*LTSE1*, 93).

From the intensity of Eliot's remarks about Prichard, we must conclude that his relationship with Matt Prichard had been quite close. We learn in a footnote: "Prichard, whom TSE had last seen in September 1911, was interned by the Germans for the duration of the war. He had known Mrs. Gardner in his Boston days and they kept in touch when he left America in 1907." It is certainly interesting to discover that Eliot had "last seen" Prichard in Munich in 1911, which suggests what Verdenal's letters confirm (see below)—that during his 1910–11 year in Paris Matt had turned up with various friends, and had come to know Verdenal and continued to see him after Eliot returned to America in October 1911. At this meeting of the Buddhist Society, Eliot had also heard Henry Furst mention the name of Okakura, whom Eliot had known in Boston. We are told in another footnote: "Okakura Kakuzo (1862–1913), Japanese scholar and writer. From 1906 until his death he was curator of the Department of Chinese and Japanese Art at the Boston Museum of Fine Arts. Author of *The Book of Tea* (New York, 1906). He took TSE to meet Matisse in 1910." We find out from these letters and footnotes that more friends—and quite interesting individuals in their own right—turned up in Paris during Eliot's year's stay there than we had previously realized (93).

The name Matthew Stuart Prichard turns up five times in Verdenal's letters. It is useful to view these references by Verdenal to Prichard before we settle on a finished, if somewhat blurred, portrait. In Verdenal's letter, dated [mid-July 1911], in the third and final postscript: "Another thing I forgot to tell you is that, the previous week, I had the pleasure of going several times with Prichard to drink mineral water and eat French beans, in various restaurants. A fine, strong nature, but a little stiff until one gets to know him." The editor provides a footnote with minimal information about Prichard:

"Matthew Stuart Prichard (1865–1936), English Aesthete to whom TSE had an introduction from Henry Eliot. After leaving Marlborough College, Prichard read law at New College Oxford. In 1902 he became secretary to the director of the Boston Museum of Fine Arts." Note the editor's quaint, and perhaps revealing, description of Prichard as an "English aesthete" (23–25). In his brief letter of October 17, [1911], Verdenal adds a postscript: "I have lunched occasionally with Prichard, who seems to me to be on the wrong course—an 'artificial' course, I should say, in relation to morality (?)" (27). The question mark is Verdenal's: Did Verdenal and Prichard discuss philosophy or ethics? Verdenal's remark seems based on conversations, and with him these tended to be philosophical or literary.

In his letter of February 5, 1912, Verdenal presents his fullest portrait of Prichard, deepening our understanding of Verdenal himself as well as clarifying the brief remark in his last letter about "morality": "I see Prichard occasionally for lunch in a vegetarian restaurant which looks like a shop (it is one). The dishes have strange names, like those of some unknown religion; initiates think nothing at ordering 'a *protose* of peppers' [?] or a nuttalene [?]. These names, smacking of organic chemistry, correspond to substances which pretend to be meat without being so, just as there are bottles of unfermented grape-juice pretending to be wine." Clearly Verdenal is less than enthusiastic about these dishes: "I hate this sort of thing. Vegetarians are praiseworthy people; there are habitués among them, elderly spinsters especially, foreign women-students, technicians from some university laboratory or other, and Hyperboreans—they are conscious of performing a rite as they consume their Bulgarian curds; they are convinced people, demonstrating to others that 'it is quite easy to do without meat.' It is wonderful to be able to enthuse about such things, and a sign of greatness of soul" (31).

It is not such people, however, to whom Verdenal objects, but to his fellow diner: "The worthy Prichard's conversation is still more or less the same; although he preaches in favour of life and action, he is one of the most hidebound individuals I know—some times he can be ever so slightly boring. Yet I like his sincerity, his instinct for vital truths, and his goodness, although it is sometimes directed towards useless matters (are there useless matters?)." After talking with Prichard an hour or so, he is "left with a headache." Verdenal objects to his "mixing up physics and metaphysics (in connection with colours)." Moreover, he is irritated by the "absolute nature of some of his assertions": "I cannot see what lies behind them, what is important. His bony face, with its small, deep-set eyes hides what, exactly? I don't think we understand each other very well and our friendship is not progressing. I will tell you about it some other time. (Don't attach any great value to my

present judgements; excuse my stupefied state with the thought that it is per-
haps only temporary)" (31). These remarks reveal as much about Verdenal as
they do about Prichard, especially his ability to make quick (and accurate)
judgments about people he encounters.

Verdenal took up the matter of Prichard in his last surviving letter to
Eliot, written December 26, 1912. Given his final view of Prichard, it is
not surprising that he confined it to a postscript, making his words about
him the last of Verdenal's words Eliot would read: "I have seen the worthy
Prichard again; he delivered himself of a mass of ridiculous opinions about
a host of works of art, and repeated theories from which he more or less
refuses to budge. He hasn't, I think, sufficient grounding in philosophy and
science to avoid being taken in by charlatans" (36).

To the question we began with—Who was Matthew Stuart Prichard?—
we must conclude that we have no "conclusive" answer. More detailed infor-
mation is to be found about Prichard in Douglass Shand-Tucci's biography
of Mrs. Jack, *The Art of Scandal: The Life and Times of Isabella Stewart Gardner*
(1997), but not about the Eliot-Verdenal connection. Shand-Tucci's descrip-
tion of Prichard explains how he and Gardner came to hit it off: He "was a
wonderfully gifted, forceful, and persuasive man possessed of many attributes
Gardner sought in a man (a Dantesque profile and an athletic body among
them) and a few she obviously worked around (he was distinctly a misogy-
nist)" (Shand-Tucci, AS, 238). Of course, much of the original source mate-
rial for finding out about the Prichard-Eliot relationship was destroyed by
Eliot himself when he saw to the burning of his early letters. But when the
fragments we have rescued from the "rubble" we have sifted through are
closely examined, we might find out how they fit in with the life of Eliot
that we have been in search of.

4. Henri Bergson: A Brief Conversion

In his column dubbed "A Commentary" for the April 1934 issue of the *Crite-
rion,* in which he made his seemingly involuntary remark about his memory
of Jean Verdenal, Eliot wrote of his impressions of Paris during his year there:
"Younger generations can hardly realize the intellectual desert of England
and America during the first decade and more of this century. In the English
desert, to be sure, flourished a few tall and handsome cactuses, as well as James
and Conrad (for whom the climate, in contrast to their own, was relatively
favorable); in America, the desert extended *à perte de vue* [as far as the eye
can see], without the least prospect of even desert vegetables." Eliot's personal

experiences had obviously skewed his negative view of his native and adopted countries—and enabled him to enthrone Paris, where he found "a most exciting variety of ideas" and thinkers who "provided types of skepticism for younger men to be attracted by and to repudiate." Even in education, Paris was more impressive, i.e., creatively productive: "At the Sorbonne, [Émile] Faguet [literary critic, defender of tradition (France, 297)] was an authority to be attacked violently; the sociologists, [Émile] Durkheim and [Lucien] Lévy-Bruhl, held new doctrines; [Pierre] Janet was the great psychologist; at the Collège de France, [Alfred] Loisy [modernist theologian of unorthodox views (Harvey, 420)] enjoyed his somewhat scandalous distinction; and over all swung the spider-like figure of Bergson. His metaphysic was said to throw some light upon the new ways of painting, and discussion of Bergson was apt to be involved with discussion of Matisse and Picasso" (ACHM, 451–52).

This outpouring of names of French scholars, thinkers, and writers captures some of the intellectual ferment that was Paris for Eliot, and it puts an impressive spotlight on the philosopher at the peak whom Eliot connects with the new in art: "over all swung the spider-like figure of Bergson." Did Bergson, to extend Eliot's metaphor, spin webs of words that stunned and bound his listeners in philosophical positions that later some of them (including Eliot) would feel the need to escape?

Henri Bergson (1859–1941), this looming intellectual presence, can be found in nutshell summaries in various reference works, such as: "At the time of his death in 1941, in the France dominated by the Nazis, Bergson was a relatively forgotten man, forgotten by the cultivated public and given little attention by the professional philosopher. Yet in the first two decades of this century he was lionized by the former and respected and often received enthusiastically by the latter" (Magill, 767–68). In the 1995 edition of the *New Oxford Companion to Literature in French,* Rhiannon Goldthorpe calls Bergson "one of the most influential French philosophers of his age. In 1900 he was appointed to a chair at the Collège de France, where his lectures became a fashionable Parisian cult. He was awarded the Nobel Prize for Literature in 1927. His thought encompassed metaphysics, science, psychology, aesthetics, ethics, and religion, and he developed a philosophical method which reacted markedly against the scientific and analytic approach of contemporary positivism" (quoted in France, 83).

Drawing on Eliot's own reminiscence in the 1944 essay "What France Means to You," Nancy D. Hargrove has briefly summarized Eliot's involvement in the Bergson lectures in her fascinating essay, "'Un Présent Parfait': Eliot and La Vie Parisienne, 1910–1911": "Chief among [Eliot's] intellectual experiences was attending Bergson's famous lectures, which he gave on

May 1911, the date given on the manuscript seems questionable. Habib writes: "Eliot's manuscript reveals that even at this early stage he had severe misgivings about Bergson's thought. . . . The Bergson manuscript [also] confirms not only that Eliot was familiar with Bradley's ideas as early as this but that he preferred them to Bergson's" (Habib, 40–41).

Habib's discussion of Eliot's intricate arguments concludes "with an appraisal of how Eliot's engagement with Bergson may have been integrated with the influences of Babbitt, Santayana, Symons, and Laforgue in shaping Eliot's aesthetics, poetry and their connections with philosophy."

But first, Habib summarizes the main points of objection that Eliot made in his draft essay to the philosophy of Bergson by pointing out that Eliot "focuses on issues central to certain debates with a resonance in poetry, theology and social thought as well as philosophy"; he believed that "the most fundamental of these was the heated dispute between realism and idealism." Habib then suggests dividing Eliot's paper "into three broad stages: firstly, he denies Bergson's claim that consciousness and matter are essentially different, a claim based on certain dualisms. . . . Eliot then questions Bergson's notions of space and time, basically denying the priority Bergson accords to time over space. Finally, Eliot rejects Bergson's attempt to do away with the distinction between realism and idealism" (40–42).

In Habib's complex analysis of the effect of Bergson's thought on Eliot, he poses questions as to why Eliot reacted so forcefully against Bergson and how to reconcile that reaction with "Bergson's evident influence on Eliot's poetry" (54). Of course, the philosophical texts with which poets might disagree can still have an indirect influence on their poetry. Critics will continue to find what appear to be Bergsonian elements in Eliot's poetry and even in his essays. The problem often is that a particular aspect or element in a poem or essay may seem to come—and may come—from any number of possible sources. And the writer may be unaware of any influence at all.

5. Charles Maurras: The Action Française

It is interesting that in his nostalgic "Commentary" about his Paris of 1910, published in the *Criterion* in April 1934, Eliot does not mention the name of Charles Maurras. But there is the vivid image, discussed above, of Maurras's Camelots du Roi skirmishing in the streets of Paris with the mounted soldiers whose horses the Camelots "stampede." Maurras's fingerprints are all over the little essay. Indeed, although Eliot does not say so, he is reviewing the book *Evocations* in the first place not only because it is by his friend Henri

Massis, but because that friend was a French supporter of Charles Maurras, and in his writing reflected Maurras's reactionary positions. Eliot does not reveal what the skirmish in the streets was about, which is a strange omission because one of the notorious and much publicized anti-Semitic successes of a harassment campaign by the Camelots du Roi took place while Eliot was in Paris.

In his book *The Action Française: Die-Hard Reactionaries in Twentieth-Century France* (1962), Edward R. Tannenbaum provides a vivid account of this event: "These young rowdies [Camelots du Roi] gained notoriety in February 1911 when they tried to stop the presentation of Henri Bernstein's *Après-Moi* at the Théâtre Français. In addition to being a Jew, Bernstein had deserted the army during his period of military service. The Camelots and Lycéens vowed not to allow their national theater to be desecrated by such an author, and they interrupted the opening performance of his play by hooting him until the police threw them out." These "young rowdies" did not give up, but continued working their way into the theater and harassing the actors "by interjecting facetious comments into their dialogue." Tannenbaum continues:"Each night the crowd in front of the theater grew larger and attracted 'patriots' who were not connected with the movement. Bernstein fought duels with [Leon] Daudet [one of the founders of the newspaper, *L'Action Française*, 1908], and other Action Française leaders, but the government finally persuaded him to withdraw *Après-Moi* from the boards" (Tannenbaum, 100). This confrontation clearly had serious consequences, and it reveals the kind of ugliness in racist behavior not to be found in the somewhat innocent skirmish in the street scene Eliot describes. Given his rapt attention while in Paris to the writings and actions of Charles Maurras and his Camelots, it is surprising that he didn't recall this particular incident in his glowing remembrance of 1910 Paris.

As a matter of fact, the movement that Maurras led had its racist beginnings in the agitation of those who would not accept the possible innocence of Captain Dreyfus, convicted of treason and sent into exile in 1894. Although a second trial in 1899 did not find Dreyfus innocent, the court reduced his sentence because of "extenuating circumstances"; shortly afterward, Dreyfus was granted a pardon by the government. Then some years later, in 1906, Dreyfus's 1894 sentence of guilt was reversed to innocent by a Cour de Cassation (appeals court). Maurras joined with other anti-Semitic rightists in 1899 to establish the Action Française Society and its new mouthpiece, *L'Action Française* (which became a daily in 1908). The movement proclaimed itself as monarchist (but was repudiated by the Comte de Paris) and Catholic (but Maurras's books were listed on the Catholic Church's Index).

Maurras was a steady contributor, sometimes signing his pieces with the name "Criton." The paper was sold in the streets by the Camelots du Roi, who also resorted to acts of hooliganism to draw attention to various reactionary causes. Foreigners, and particularly Jews, were especially targeted. Typical is a letter that appeared in *L'Action Française* of January 6, 1909: "A horde of Russians, men and women, has invaded the schools, especially the Faculties of Medicine and Letters. These individuals are ridiculously dressed, speak hardly any French, and affect a rudeness toward their French comrades that is typical of their native land. To be sure, everything is for their benefit. . . . The whole educational machine built by our fathers is now functioning for the benefit of the foreigner" (Tannenbaum, 261).

Maurras's biographers agree that one of the shaping events of his life was his becoming partially deaf at the age of fourteen. As did Eliot's double hernia, so did Maurras's deafness cut him off from the usual kinds of associations for an adolescent boy. His overprotective mother and his affliction both tended to isolate him from others, forcing him to develop an inner life of his own: "Maurras's deafness, his scrawny appearance, and his unsociable habits made him unattractive to most girls. . . . Both his close associates and his enemies agree that as a man Maurras viewed women with contempt and used them to satisfy his physical needs without expressing the slightest spark of affection for them. He never married and he seems never to have had a steady mistress. From the time of his childhood he had few playmates and no lovers. Whatever 'caused' him to be this way, this was the way he was" (46–47; based on personal interviews with Maurice Pujo, Henri Massis, Albert Bayet, and Émile Buré, a group containing both friends and foes of Maurras).

Maurras's attitudes and intellectual development are so similar to those of Eliot that there seems little wonder that Eliot gravitated to him after Verdenal's introduction. On his first trip out of France in 1896, Maurras "asked himself what made England and Germany stronger than France. His answer was that those nations had dynastic monarchies but that France was being corrupted by a democratic regime." Thus he became a monarchist. Well-read in the Greek and Roman classics and an admirer of an ideal Greece, "he dismissed contemporary civilization as contemptible." Indeed, he "was the archetype of the aesthete, the snob, the contemner of the masses and of things that are not beautiful." He "praised the statue of the 'Lamented Young Man' in the National Museum in Athens: 'Ripe, adolescent, brought to the supreme moment of his virile springtime—the soul, as firm as the flesh, gives off emotion without receiving any in return.'" And he "detested anything that he considered feminine or effeminate, whether it was Romantic literature or what he called 'sentimental' socialism" (49–51).

In spite of his condemnation of romanticism, Maurras's own literary works have been described as—indeed—romantic! Julien Benda, in *Belphegor* (1918), writes:"In *Anthinea* [1901], and *L'Avenir de L'Intelligence* [1905] [two of Maurras's most important works, the first travel sketches and the second critical essays], we have the classic spirit taken as the theme of romantic exaltation" (Benda, 157). One critic, George Bernanos, has written persuasively of the gulf between Maurras's work and his life:"Nothing can be understood about Maurras if one judges the man from his writings, for the writings are not the man. It was for himself, for his personal security, that the author of *Enquête* [*sur la Monarchie*] constructed that vast defensive system of which he was at the same time the master and the prisoner" (quoted in Tannenbaum, 51). The *Enquête* was an inquiry conducted in 1900 to determine whether or not important public personages would welcome a return of the monarchy.

Maurras's self-contradictions and bizarre views did not deter T. S. Eliot from remaining steadfast in his friendship and admiration for the leader of the Action Française—even through that leader's active support of the Petain regime in Nazi-occupied France during World War II and his imprisonment as a collaborator afterward. (Many others in the Action Française movement were active supporters of Henri Petain, including Henri Massis, author of *Evocations,* the book that Eliot so lavishly praised in his 1934 review in the *Criterion.*) Maurras was arrested in 1948 and his followers worldwide rallied to his support. Kenneth Asher in his 1998 essay, "T. S. Eliot and Charles Maurras," writes:"Eliot offers a testimonial on behalf of the man to whom he owed so much. In 1948 he acknowledges the tremendous influence of Maurras on him and other like-minded young people: 'Maurras, for certain of us, represented a sort of Virgil who led us to the gates of the temple' ('L'Hommage [de l'etranger,' *Aspects de la France et du Monde* 2 (April 25, 1948)], 6). And, Eliot argues, Maurras's essential ideas are not outdated: 'his conceptions of the monarchy and of hierarchy . . . [are] kin to my own, as they are to English conservatives, for whom these ideas remain intact despite the modern world'" (Asher, TSECM, 27).

Maurras died in 1952, shortly after his release from prison. Eliot's intellectual attachment to Maurras reveals many of the subrational (or primal) elements of his personal attachment to Verdenal during what can only be called the watershed year of Eliot's life—1910–11 in Paris. Just as Eliot dedicated his important first book, *Prufrock and Other Observations,* to Jean Verdenal with a declaration of love in an epigraph from Dante, so he dedicated his little—but important—book of essays on *Dante* (1929) to Charles Maurras, and on the dedication page quoted a phrase from Maurras's "Conseil de Dante": "La sensibilité, sauvée d' elle-même / et conduite dans l'ordre, est devenue / un principe de perfection" (Sensibility, preserved in itself / and exercised in order, has become / a principle of perfection). This dedication was not reprinted with "Dante" in Eliot's *Selected Essays.*

In almost every respect, Eliot's year in Paris marked the major turning point in his life. With Jean Verdenal Eliot enjoyed a companionship—personal, literary, intellectual—deeper and more profound than he would ever find later in any relationship, male or female. And in Charles Maurras, he reached the outer limits of his intellectual development, and would sort through, modify, and perhaps refine his social and religious beliefs, but would no longer be open to any radical or fundamental changes in his views. Kenneth Asher's summary statement in "T. S. Eliot and Charles Maurras" suggests the far-reaching effect of his Paris year: "At the most basic level, Eliot's creative work represents not a quest for faith but for Order understood in the Maurrasian sense. In *The Waste Land,* for example, the eroded tradition is conceived of as a series of interlocking rituals designed to contain the manifestations of Original Sin. Indeed the welter of mythologies in the poem presupposes their common sufficiency to answer a constant human need: the ritualistic regulation of impulse, especially sexuality" (Asher, TSECM, 28).

Later, in a French piece entitled "What France Means to You," which appeared in *La France Libre,* June 8, 1944, Eliot summed up in his own words the effect of his year in Paris: "I believe that it was exceptional good fortune for a young man to discover Paris in the year 1910. *The Nouvelle Revue Française* was still truly new. . . . One always had a chance of noticing Anatole France, along the quays: and one could buy the latest book of Gide or of Claudel the same day of its publication. Sometimes Paris was all the past; sometimes all the future: and the two aspects combined in a present perfect." That Eliot's prose, in speaking of Paris, would become poetry is explained in his next revelation: "It wasn't an accident that led me to Paris. For several years, France represented mainly, to my eyes, la *poésie*" (WFMY, 94; my translation).

6. Finding the Personal in the Poem: Drafts of "Portrait" and "Prufrock"

In a sense, Eliot found his poetic self during his Paris year, producing some of his best known and most highly praised poems, including "Portrait of a Lady" and "The Love Song of J. Alfred Prufrock." As we have noted before, Eliot himself referred to specific experiences that became embodied, one way or another, in particular poems. Eliot confirmed Conrad Aiken's identification of the Boston lady portrayed in "Portrait of a Lady," as we shall see; and Eliot identified the person to whom he as speaker addressed the opening of

"The Love Song of J. Alfred Prufrock" ("Let us go, then, *you* and I") as an unnamed, but real, *male* companion. In both cases he could have denied, but did not, that the speaker in the poem was Eliot himself. Given such examples of Eliot's acknowledgment of the personal origins of his poems, we might well expect to find Eliot somewhere, somehow lurking in all of his poems. My readings will constitute searches for him in each case.

The poems Eliot wrote between 1910 and 1914 are listed at the end of this chapter, with dates of composition (when known or estimated) and publication. It should be noted that in some cases the texts cited and examined here are of early—and different—versions, often differing from texts found in Eliot's *Complete Poems*. I find that the early versions of poems, not yet revised, are likely to contain more of the personal elements I am seeking. These early versions I have used generously in the two poems analyzed below, "Portrait of a Lady" and "The Love Song of J. Alfred Prufrock."

"Portrait of a Lady" (November 1910; IOMH, 327–33)

In his autobiographical fiction, *Ushant,* Conrad Aiken revealed in one of the many paragraphs devoted to an aggressive questioning of the relationship of "art and sex," that Eliot's "lady" in "Portrait of a Lady" did in fact have an original in life: "the oh so precious, the oh so exquisite, Madeleine, the Jamesian lady of ladies, the enchantress of the Beacon Hill drawing-room— who, like another Circe, had made strange shapes of Wild Michael [Thomas T. McCabe] and the Tsetse [Eliot]." Aiken adds that the lady "was afterwards to be essentialized and ridiculed (and his own pose with it) in Tsetse's *Portrait d'une Femme*" (Aiken, U, 186). Even before *Ushant,* Aiken had found occasion to comment on the source of "Portrait." In the piece he called "King Bolo and Others" contributed to the 1948/49 volume on the occasion of Eliot's sixtieth birthday, *T. S. Eliot: A Symposium,* Aiken refers to the period of their undergraduate days as distinguished by wild creativeness in the development of the comic strip and American slang—both of which gave Eliot "enormous pleasure": "This rich native creativeness was to be reflected, of course, in his poetry, notably in Prufrock, just as our dear deplorable friend, Miss X, the *precieuse ridicule* to end all preciosity, serving tea so exquisitely among her bric-a-brac, was to be pinned like a butterfly to a page in 'Portrait of a Lady.'" As for the "King Bolo" mentioned in Aiken's title, as we have already discussed, it refers to one of the bawdy poems he, Eliot, and others had fun quoting (Aiken, KB, 21–22).

Eliot confirmed Aiken's statement about "Portrait of a Lady" in a letter he wrote Ezra Pound, February 2 [1915], enclosing a copy of his poem and thanking him for efforts to publish the poem. He finds the poem "cruder and awkwarder and more juvenile every time I copy it. The only ~~enrichmant~~ enhancement which time has brought is the fact that by this time there are two or three other ladies who, if it is ever printed, may vie for the honour of having sat for it. It will please you, I hope, to hear that I had a Christmas card from the lady, bearing the 'ringing greetings of friend to friend at this season of high festival.'" In her footnote to this letter, Valerie Eliot provides valuable data on Eliot's "lady": "Miss Adeleine Moffatt, the subject of the poem, lived behind the State House in Boston and invited selected Harvard undergraduates to tea. During a visit to London in 1927 she asked the Eliots to dine, offering 'a modest choice of dates to sacrifice yourselves on the altar of New England,' but they were away" (*LTSE1*, 86). Pound was successful in getting Eliot's poem published in the September 1915 issue of *Others* and he included it (along with several other Eliot poems) in his *Catholic Anthology 1914–1915*, published in November 1915.

Like Aiken in "King Bolo and Others," Eliot moves in his letter to Pound from mention of "Portrait" to mention of his bawdy poems: "I fear that King Bolo and his Big Black Kween will never burst into print. I understand that Priapism, Narcissism etc., are not approved of." ("Priapism" is defined in the OED as "persistent erection of the penis"; Eliot linking it with "Narcissism" [same-sex love] is significant.) Both Aiken and Eliot seem to imply, in their associating "Portrait" with Eliot's bawdy poems, that "Portrait" has an implicit or subtextual dimension of the bawdy. Are we to assume, as does Valerie Eliot, that the poem is about Miss Adeleine Moffatt, or is the title misleading? Just as we very quickly learn that the title of "The Love Song of J. Alfred Prufrock" is "misleading"—the poem is no "song," and certainly not a "love song"—so we might assume that since the "lady" in "Portrait of a Lady" is not really in any serious sense a "lady," we might focus our attention elsewhere in search of the poem's "subject." What if Eliot had called his poem "The Silent Refusal of a Drawing-Room Narcissus"?

In the manuscript draft of "Portrait of a Lady," Eliot presents a series of challenging allusions, first in the poem's title (to Henry James's novel, 1881), and then in epigraphs for each of the poem's three parts: first, to John Webster's *The White Devil* ("I have caught an everlasting cold"); second, to Christopher Marlowe's *The Jew of Malta* ("'Thou has committed—' / 'Fornication—but that was in another country / And besides, the wench is dead'"); and the third, to Jules Laforgue's "Locutions des Pierrots" (Asides of Pierrots) part 16, 1–2, 9–10 ("Je ne suis qu'un viveur Lunaire / Qui fait des ronds dans les bassins / . . . Devenez un legendaire / Au seuil des siècles charlatans!" ["I'm only a man about the moon / Who makes circles in pool and pond / . . . make the legendary grade, / The phoney ages starting soon"] [Laforgue, 224–25]). Of these four, only two remained in the published version—James in the title, and Marlowe in what became an epigraph for the entire poem. Neither allusion seems to help elucidate Eliot's meaning; on the contrary, each seems to be in conflict with the other. James's *Portrait of a Lady* does portray a genuine lady: not the scheming, cold-blooded Madam Merle often cited, but the heroine and would-be victim Isabel Archer; Eliot's "lady" has some of the superficial aspects of a Jamesian lady, but none of the genuine sophistication and subtlety.

And the Marlowe quotation, with its admission of fornication with a "wench" who is irrelevant since now dead, seems to do violence to the restraints, diversions, and suppressions so evident in the "nonaction" of Eliot's poem. Grover Smith at first finds Eliot's epigraph anomalous, but then decides that it represents Eliot's moral condemnation of the young man who refuses to "fornicate": "It [the epigraph] becomes clearer if taken as Eliot's blunt but probably afterthoughted chiding of the young man's attitude. For, though exaggerative, its bravado corresponds in moral callousness to the surface tone of the poem itself. By penetrating to the depths of the lady's lonely and empty life, the young man has committed a psychological rape; this is far worse than fornication, for he has not respected her human condition" (Smith, Grover, *PP*, 14). This seems to be a violent misreading of the poem: the young man does no penetrating, sexual or psychological, but remains silent through the lady's monologue. She indeed is the obvious aggressor, he the fleeing Prufrockian character. In short, Smith seems to be saying that had the young man accepted the "lady's" veiled invitation to "fornicate," he would have acted the role of a gentleman—and cleared Eliot of being identified as the young man.

But Eliot is writing about his own experience in real social situations, and his psychic-sexual relationship to the young man must be explored in depth. Indeed, his confession to Pound that since his writing of the poem, three or so other women have also sat for the portrait already "painted"—lending it (somehow) enhancement—makes clear that it is his own portrait, not that of a fictional character, that appears alongside the lady. Moreover, the mention of "narcissism" in Eliot's letter to Pound seems somehow relevant to the self-portrait Eliot painted in his poem. Linking "narcissism" to "priapism," as Eliot links them in his comment, suggests the "bawdy" as primarily linked with man-man sex.

Part I of "Portrait" takes place in December, Part II in April (lilac-time), Part III in October, the lady having become aware that her "friend" is going abroad (to Paris, no doubt, like Eliot himself). We hear only the lady's voice in the poem, but we silently read the various extraordinary reactions of the friend. In the beginning, the lady makes clear that her passion for genuine "friendship" is intense, and that she believes that she will find it in her visitor: "To find a friend who has those qualities / So rare and strange and so unvalued too / Who has, and gives / Those qualities upon which friendship lives / How much it means that I say this to you! / Without these friendships—life, what *cauchemar* [nightmare]!" (*IOMH*, 327, lines 24–29). We learn from the friend that he believes that what the lady says is only a fraction of what she feels: "And so the conversation slips / Among the velleities and carefully caught regrets" (327, lines 14–15). In response to the concert music that accompanies, metaphorically, the lady's elaborate and graceful comments on friendship, the young man begins to hear a tom-tom, "Hammering a prelude of its own / Capricious monotone" (328, lines 34–35). Such a "primitive" instrument is highly suggestive sexually, and inspires the young man to "take the air, in a tobacco trance" (328, line 37)—i.e., a speedy departure, a retreat into a bar for a drink and then home, safe outside the seeming clutches of this overly friendly lady.

In Part II, the lady's vocal meditations suggest something of her complex, but unrevealed, past: "Yet with these April sunsets, that somehow recall / My buried life, and Paris in the Spring, / I feel immeasurably at peace, and find the world / To be wonderful and youthful, after all" (328, lines 12–15). This moment of affirmation is almost immediately followed by recognition of a bleak future: "But what have I, but what have I, my friend, / "To give you, what can you receive from me? / "—Only the friendship and the sympathy / "Of one about to reach her journey's end." / "I shall sit here, serving tea to friends" (329, lines 30–34). Such a remark immediately inspires wonder as to just how old indeed the lady is. But before the reader has time to ponder the question, the young man takes his hat and starts for the door. And he paints a rather bleak picture of his own life, as he spends his mornings in the park reading the paper (the comics, sporting pages, and various sensational items of crimes, etc.): "I keep my countenance—, / I remain self-possessed" (329, lines 43–44). Indeed? But there is an intrusion into this composure, brought about by the common or popular song played by a mechanical street piano and "the smell of hyacinths across the garden— / Recall things that other people have desired— / Are these ideas right or wrong?" (329, lines 47–49). The sound of music and smell of hyacinths (phallic in form) awaken the young man's senses—ultimately sexual, bringing in their wake moral uneasiness. What the lilacs and the lady could not do, street-music sounds and hyacinth scents achieve. A reader is bound to wonder why.

In the last part of "Portrait," the lady knows already that her young man is going abroad. He becomes unsettled at her suggestion that perhaps he might write to her. Then she assesses anew their nonrelationship: "I have been wondering frequently of late / —(And our beginnings never know our ends!)— / Why we have not developed into friends" (330, lines 13–15) All their friends had thought, she says, that they would "relate"—but they did not. And she adds, almost desperately: "You will write, at any rate. / Perhaps it is not too late" (330, lines 23–24). The young man, who had arrived this October evening feeling that he was climbing the steps on his hands and knees, now goes through a sequence of animal roles: dancing "like a dancing bear," whistling or crying "like a parrot," chattering "like an ape." After his clumsy departure, he begins to envision the consequences. What if she "should die some afternoon / . . . Should die, and leave me sitting pen in hand / . . . Not knowing what to feel, nor if I understand" (331, lines 30, 32, 35). He concludes, wondering whether she would "not have the advantage after all?" In short, he finds that despite all of the devices he has used to fend her off, she has penetrated his psychic wall. The final line: "And should I have the right to smile?" (331, lines 37, 40). Whatever he does or does not do, this young man will end up damning himself. He might ultimately find someone in the run-down streets he roams with whom he could lose his virginity (cf. his December 1914 letter to C. Aiken discussed in Chapter 3, Section 2, where he "walks about the street with one's desires" [*LTSE1*, 75])—but never in a drawing room with a "lady" of his own family's social class!

"The Love Song of J. Alfred Prufrock (Prufrock among the Women)"

"Prufrock's Pervigilium" (*July, August 1911, 1912; IOMH, 39–47*)

With the publication of the manuscript of "The Love Song of J. Alfred Prufrock" by Christopher Ricks in *Inventions of the March Hare*, we are able to see the poem in the process of becoming the poem we know. The text of the manuscript poem is dated (after the last lines) July–August 1911, when Eliot was in Munich at the end of his European tour near the finish of his academic year in Paris. As we have learned in Section 2 of this chapter, Eliot received letters from his Parisian friend Jean Verdenal while he was in Munich—finishing "Prufrock." Some parts of the poem (including the Prince Hamlet lines) had been written earlier in 1910, before Eliot left for Paris. A major cut Eliot made before publication was nearly the whole (but not all) of "Prufrock's Pervigilium," an "insert" not completed presumably until 1912, which Aiken (according to Eliot) advised cutting (Gordon, EEY,

45). We learn from the manuscript that "Prufrock" once had a parenthetical subtitle, "(Prufrock among the Women)."

And we also learn that its original epigraph was "'Sovegna vos al temps de mon dolor'— / Poi s'ascose nel foco che gli affina" ("'Be mindful in due time of my pain.' Then he hid him in the fire which refines them"). These lines come at the end of Dante's *Purgatorio*, Canto XXVI, and are spoken by Arnaut Daniel, one of those who "failed to restrain their carnal appetites within the limits prescribed by the social institutions of humanity," or who "had not even observed the laws laid down by nature" (Dante, *Purgatorio*, 331, 322–223). It is perhaps the most important revelation of the manuscript of the "Love Song," linking Prufrock to the band of those brought together in Purgatory for the sin of same-sex lust—a lust that transcended "normal" sexual desire and that came to be known early in the twentieth century as Uranian or homosexual, identified not as "lust" but as same-sex love. With this revelation, the original subtitle, "Prufrock among the Women," makes some sense: the poem portrays a man who cannot love—feel sexual desire for— women; the question of same-sex love is not confronted in the poem except by inference, obliquely. Some might well conclude that it is the main theme, even though not overtly sounded, in the poem. (Although Eliot deleted reference to the "Rein of Lust" Canto (*Purgatorio*, Canto XXVI) from "Prufrock," he would introduce it again and again in later poems, including a poem entitled "Ode on Independence Day, July 4th 1918," *The Waste Land*, "Ash Wednesday," and *Four Quartets* (in "Little Gidding").

The evidence is that Eliot felt "The Love Song of J. Alfred Prufrock" had a personal dimension. There is the assertion by the poet, often ignored or discounted, that there was indeed a companion for the poem's speaker. In response to a query from Kristian Smidt, when writing his *Poetry and Belief in the Work of T. S. Eliot* (1949, 1961), Eliot wrote: "As for 'The Love Song of J. Alfred Prufrock' anything I say now must be somewhat conjectural, as it was written so long ago that my memory may deceive me; but I am prepared to assert that the 'you' in 'The Love Song' is merely some friend or companion, presumably of the male sex, whom the speaker is at that moment addressing, and that it has *no emotional content whatever*" (Smidt, 85; emphasis added). Eliot may have been remembering the writing of the poem, but he may also have been remembering one of the experiences on which the poem is based. Eliot's statement—that the companion of Prufrock being of the "male sex" has "no emotional content whatever"—seems revealingly gratuitous. Such a statement from the author can only signal to the alert reader that it might be interesting to explore what "emotional content" it was Eliot wanted to dismiss so irrevocably. The discarded epigraph, with its suggestion of Uranianism, might well point to the general nature of Eliot's concern.

Later, near the end of his career, Eliot was asked about "Prufrock" in a 1962 interview published in the *Granite Review.* He said that Prufrock "was partly a dramatic creation of a man of about 40 . . . and partly an expression of feelings of my own." He then made a significant generalization: "I always feel that dramatic characters who seem living creations have something of the author in them" (quoted in Bush, *TSESCS,* 241–42). The nature of what Eliot meant here might well be suggested by Stephen Spender in his autobiography, *World within World,* when he describes one of his first meetings with Eliot in London. Spender announced that he was choosing the smoked eel from the menu: "I was surprised to hear him say: 'I don't think I dare eat smoked eel,' thus unconsciously paraphrasing Mr. Prufrock who asks himself: 'Do I dare to eat a peach?'" Spender quotes Eliot on another occasion saying: "I daren't take cake, and jam's too much trouble." Spender then comments that he suddenly realized that "the effectiveness of the line, 'Shall I part my hair behind? Do I dare to eat a peach?' is precisely that it is in the poet's own idiomatic voice" (Spender, *WW,* 146).

Related to all of these observations is the fact that Eliot wrote the discarded passage "Prufrock's Pervigilium," which once stood at the very center of the poem. This title echoes the irony of the poem title "The Love Song of J. Alfred Prufrock," which portrays a man who cannot love women—and thus the opposite of a love poem. *Pervigilium Veneris (The Vigil of Venus)* is a Latin poem that celebrates man-woman love. According to the contemporaneous *Encyclopaedia Britannica,* 11th edition, "Pervigilium was the term for a nocturnal festival in honour of some divinity, especially Bona Dea [goddess of fauna]." Little is known about the author or the date of composition of *Pervigilium Veneris,* but the *Encyclopaedia* says that it "was written professedly in early spring on the eve of a three-nights' festival of Venus (probably April 1–3). It describes in poetical language the annual awakening of the vegetable and animal world through the goddess" (*EB,* vol. 21, p. 281). "Prufrock's Pervigilium," on the other hand, is set not in the country but, ironically, in the city, and portrays a world not awakening but going to sleep (or indeed dying).

It is interesting to note that later, in *The Waste Land,* Eliot will include a line from *Pervigilum Veneris* in the list of "fragments" he quotes at the end: "Quando fiam uti chlidon—O swallow swallow." This line may be translated "When shall I be like the swallow—O swallow, swallow," and differs from the original line: "When shall I be like the swallow and my voice no longer dumb?" (*Pervigilium,* 115). The poet of *The Vigil of Venus* is wondering when he will be violated like Philomela and motivated to song (the story of Tereus and Philomela is briefly retold in the preceding stanza); as, perhaps, the poet of *The Waste Land* is wondering when he will regain his poetic gift, stilled with the death of his friend and the advent of his unhappy marriage. Each verse of *The Vigil of Venus*—and the last stanza containing the quotation Eliot used—ends with a refrain: "Are ye loveless or love-lorn? Yours be love tomorrow morn!" (106–15). This seems to be the prayer of the poet, a prayer for return of the ability to love. This passionate plea works in somewhat the same ironic way in "Prufrock's Pervigilium."

The second stanza of "Prufrock's Pervigilium" suggests the passage's persistent dreariness: "And when the evening fought itself awake / And the world was peeling oranges and reading evening papers / And boys were smoking cigarettes, drifted helplessly together / In the fan of light spread out by the drugstore on the corner / Then I have gone at night through narrow streets, / Where evil houses leaning all together / Pointed a ribald finger at me in the darkness / Whispering all together, chuckled at me in the darkness" (*IOMH*, 43, lines 10–17). As in Eliot's other night-wandering city poems, there is no Venus, but more likely a Circe lurking and luring in the darkness, and no love, but doubtless some kind of sex hidden there somewhere—for a fee. Near the end of the poem the poet, as dawn is approaching, describes himself observing the day approach: "I fumbled to the window to experience the world / And to hear my Madness singing, sitting on the kerbstone / [A blind old drunken man who sings and mutters, / With broken boot heels stained in many gutters] / And as he sang the world began to fall apart . . ." (43, lines 28–32). This is an individual who is searching the streets for something luring him on, but that he cannot bring himself to accept—any more than he can accept the seemingly proffered relationships in the drawing room he frequents during the daylight. In the "Pervigilium" passage, Eliot's authorial voice tends to dominate, while that of his Prufrock persona recedes.

Had Eliot kept his original subtitle and epigraph, and had he kept "Prufrock's Pervigilium" in the middle of his poem, the poem's sexual dimension would have been more clearly visible. The fact that he revised his poem as he did does not mean that he eliminated this sexual dimension, but rather that he buried it more deeply, resulting in the confusion of his explicators. It is interesting to observe that, in eliminating this long passage, Eliot did not lose the lines altogether. Some of them made it into the final version of "Prufrock," while others turned up in other poems. The final lines of "Prufrock's Pervigilium," however, certainly offer an aspect of Prufrock's experience hard to reconcile with the Prufrock we have come to know: "—I have seen the darkness creep along the wall / I have heard my Madness chatter before day / I have seen the world roll up into a ball / Then suddenly dissolve and fall away" (44, lines 35–38). Something quite different emerges in the use of some of this imagery in the final version of "Prufrock": "Would it have been worth while, / To have bitten off the matter with a smile, / To have squeezed the universe into a ball / To roll it toward some overwhelming question" (45, lines 90–93; CPP, 6). There is less baldness of statement, more sophisticated weariness in the revised passage.

I think it appropriate to read "The Love Song of J. Alfred Prufrock" as a portrayal of a man who not only cannot love women, but who is unable to reconcile himself to his own nature. His agonized frustration is essentially sexual, but it extends to all the frustrations universally felt when contemplating the elusive meaning of life—and death. Thus those who cannot identify with Prufrock's sexual frustrations have no difficulty in sharing all his other frustrations. Some critics have debated the question as to whether Prufrock goes out to make a visit or stays home and imagines the "events" of the poem. It is a question that does not matter. The poem is made up of a multitude of Eliot's experiences in big cities—St. Louis, Boston, Paris, and even London (which he visited in April 1911). These are all cities on important bodies of water—the Mississippi, Boston Bay, the Seine, and the Thames—and thus subject to fogs of the kind Prufrock describes. There were important museums in all these cities where Eliot could have witnessed the women who "come and go / Talking of Michelangelo." Even Boston's Gardner Museum had its Michelangelo. (An implicit meaning of this line is often missed: Michelangelo's male nudes have well-built, sexually potent bodies naturally attractive to female art-lovers; the women coming and going would not, of course, mention this dimension in their admiring comments.)

There is no reason not to believe, as Eliot has said, that Prufrock has a companion to accompany him—whether the excursion is "real" or imagined. Indeed, it is clear that in Boston Eliot often went around the city (and the Gloucester Bay waters) with his "really closest" friend, Harold Peters, from whom Eliot learned to box (and thus put in shape his "frail physique") (Crawford, 124). In Paris, of course, Eliot's closest friend was Jean Verdenal, and we have already noted from Verdenal's letters to Eliot that they became close companions in their explorations of Paris—including the seamy side of Montparnasse as described in the fiction of Charles-Louis Philippe.

Thus "The Love Song of J. Alfred Prufrock" is a montage bringing together as one several cities, friends, streets, drawing rooms, casual encounters. Near the opening of the poem the sexual suggestiveness is heavy, with the two city-wanderers going "through certain half-deserted streets / The muttering retreats / Of restless nights in one night cheap hotels / And sawdust restaurants with oyster shells." The reference to the red-light district is clear in the phrase, "one night cheap hotels," where the prostitutes, male and female, ply their trade in the big cities. But it is clear that Prufrock has not frequented these "houses of ill-repute." As the poem moves along, attention swerves from the external city streets to the internal examination of life as Prufrock lives—or does not live—it.

Much of Prufrock's commentary seems that of someone bored with life: "*For* I have known them all already, known them all / Have known the evenings, mornings, after-noons, / I have measured out my life with coffee spoons" (*IOMH,* 40, lines 49–51). Especially he has known the "eyes"—"The eyes that fix you in a formulated phrase, / And when I am formulated, sprawling on a pin / When I am pinned and wriggling on the wall, / Then how should I begin? / —To spit out all the butt-ends of my days and ways?" (40, lines 56–60). These appear to be thoughts of a social conformist ready to rebel, ready to let down his hair and go out on a spree. But, alas, he is constitutionally incapable of such a rebellion. He identifies with those "lonely men in shirt sleeves, leaning out of windows" watching life pass them by, and he thinks to himself: "I should have been a pair of ragged claws / Scuttling across the floors of silent seas" (40, lines 72–74; *CPP,* 5). These depressing thoughts come immediately after what seems to have been an opportunity passed by, evoked only by an image of sight ("arms that are braceleted and white and bare / [But in the lamplight, downed with light brown hair]") and an image of smell ("Is it . . . perfume from a dress / That makes me so digress?") (*IOMH,* 41, lines 63–66; *CPP,* 5). If this really was a neglected opportunity, Prufrock can contemplate it only as a digression from his thoughts about his own shortcomings.

Indeed, soon after this seemingly missed opportunity, Prufrock confronts the reality that he would never have had "the strength to force the moment to its crisis." He has lived his life in a state of terror, and, in spite of his weeping, fasting, and praying, he has seen his "head (grown slightly bald) brought in upon a platter" (as in Salome's presentation of the head of John the Baptist to Herod, included in Oscar Wilde's opera *Salomê*): "I have seen the moment of my greatness flicker / And I have seen the eternal Footman hold my coat, and snicker— / And in short, I was afraid" (*IOMH,* 45, lines 84–86; *CPP,* 6). Moreover, had Prufrock indeed forced "the moment to its crisis"— i.e., had "bitten off the matter with a smile" and had "squeezed the universe into a ball / To roll it toward some overwhelming question" (like Andrew Marvell in "To His Coy Mistress") the question remains, "would it have been worth while" if the lady in question, "settling a pillow by her head," should have said: "That is not what I meant, at all. / That is not it, at all" (*IOMH,*

45, lines 96–98; *CPP*, 6). Prufrock continues agonizing over whether it would have been worth it, balancing somehow "sunsets and the dooryards and the sprinkled streets" as well as novels, teacups, and "skirts that trail along the floor." At a moment when the speech seems spiraling out of control, Prufrock brings himself up short: "It is impossible to say just what I mean! / Perhaps it will make you wonder and smile: / But as if a magic lantern threw the nerves in patterns on the screen" (*IOMH*, 45, lines 104–6). At this point Prufrock reimagines and repeats the dreaded reply with only slight variation: "That is not it, at all; / That is not what I meant, at all" (46, lines 109–10).

At this critical moment the poem takes a surprising turn: "No! I am not Hamlet, nor am meant to be; / Am an attendant lord—, one that will do / To swell a progress, start a scene or two, / Advise the prince: withal, an easy tool, / Deferential, glad to be of use, / Politic, cautious, and meticulous, / Full of high sentence, but a bit obtuse; / At times, indeed, appear ridiculous; / Almost, at times, the Fool" (46, lines 111–19). This passage was the first written for "Prufrock," and one about which Ezra Pound, who thought the poem on the whole superb, had his doubts. However the lines might relate to the rest of the poem, they are cleverly composed, showing Prufrock studiously trying out for all the parts in a Shakespeare play and deciding finally upon, in the final word of the final line, the Fool. But the reader should recall that Shakespeare's Fools are often wise.

After this digression, Prufrock returns to the reality of his condition—growing old and having to decide how to live, what to do, where to go, how to be. First he wonders about fashion—should he wear "the bottoms" of his "trousers rolled"? Cuffs on pants were just coming into fashion—and one had to decide. Should he part his "hair behind"? Also a new fashion. Did he dare, indeed, to "eat a peach"? After all this indecisiveness, Prufrock pronounces: "I shall wear white flannel trousers, and walk upon the beach. / I have heard the mermaids singing, each to each" (46, lines 123–24; *CPP*, 7). In his "Song" (1633), John Donne wrote: "Teach me to hear mermaids singing." Prufrock has heard them singing to each other, but not to him. Yet simply hearing them singing puts him in some jeopardy, if these mermaids are indeed the sirens that only Odysseus, bound to the mast, has listened to and survived.

There comes next the only single line of the entire poem: "I do not think that they will sing to me." Is this the moment that Prufrock realizes his sexuality does not extend to women, mermaids symbolizing the eternal female somehow purified? Or is it that the mermaids, with their fish tails, pose no sexual threat in a relationship? "In relation to man the mermaid is usually of evil issue if not of evil intent. She has generally to be bribed or compelled to utter her prophecy or bestow her gifts, and whether as wife or paramour she brings disaster in her train" (*EB*, vol. 18, p. 171). Perhaps Prufrock has been lucky that they have not sung to him.

The poem closes ambiguously: "We have lingered in the chambers of the sea / By seamaids [sea-girls in *CPP*] wreathed with seaweed red and brown / Till human voices wake us, and we drown" (*IOMH*, 46, lines 129–31; *CPP*, 7). Have all the women of the poem become, metaphorically, the "seamaids wreathed with seaweed" in this passage? In what sense have Prufrock and his male companion "lingered in the chambers of the sea"; are these "chambers" somehow a metaphor for the streets, art museums, and drawing rooms where we have observed them? And how is it that "human voices" waking them result in their drowning? The action of the poem has been imagined, including, most obviously, the under-sea conclusion; and with the intrusion of actual "human voices" the imagined action fades away like a drowning vessel, taking with it the imaginers.

However special Prufrock's plight, there are many themes and passages in "The Love Song" that have universal appeal. It is not only Prufrock who has thought to himself, desperately, about the dailiness of life, "There will be time, there will be time / To prepare a face to meet the faces that you meet." Nor does one need to identify with Prufrock to marvel at the surprising profundity of these lines: "[I] have known the evenings, mornings, afternoons, / I have measured out my life with coffee spoons." And it takes no large leap of sympathy to share Prufrock's fear when he confesses, "I have seen the moment of my greatness flicker / And I have seen the eternal Footman hold my coat, and snicker." These and other such passages have made this poem probably the most popular of Eliot's poems.

7. Poems Written 1910–1914

The poems of 1910 through 1914 are divided into four roughly interrelated groups. Titles of poems are followed by dates of composition (when known) and dates of first publication in journals and books. "Mayer" refers to John T. Mayer's *T. S. Eliot's Silent Voices* (1989), in which Mayer estimates dates of composition. "Leyris" refers to Pierre Leyris, French translator of Eliot's work *T. S. Eliot Poèmes, 1910–1930* (1947), for which John Hayward (Eliot's British friend and longtime apartment mate) provided notes and dates of composition. *POO: Prufrock and Other Observations* (1917); *IOMH: Inventions of the March Hare* (1996).

Night-Wandering and Tea-Time Encounters

"Preludes" (October 1910–November 1911); *Blast,* July 1915; *POO; IOMH*
    I. "Prelude in Dorchester (Houses)" (October 1910)
    II. "Prelude in Roxbury" (October 1910)
    III. "(Morgendämmerung) Prelude in Roxbury" (July 1911, Leyris)
    IV. "Abenddämmerung" (November 1911, Leyris)
"Portrait of a Lady" (November 1910); *Others,* September 1915; *POO; IOMH*

City Streets, Bars, Garrets

"Entretien dans un parc" (February 1911); *IOMH*
"Bacchus and Ariadne: 2nd Debate between the Body and Soul" (February 1911); *IOMH*
"Interlude in a Bar" (February 1911); *IOMH*
"The smoke that gathers blue and sinks" (February 1911); *IOMH*
"Rhapsody on a Windy Night" (March 1911); *Blast,* July 1915; *POO; IOMH*
"He said: this universe is very clever" (March 1911); *IOMH*
"Inside the gloom" (March 1911, Mayer); *IOMH*
"Interlude in London" (April 1911); *IOMH*
"Ballade pour la grosse Lulu" (July 1911); *IOMH*
"The Little Passion: From 'An Agony in the Garret'" (1911–14, Mayer); *IOMH*
"La Figlia Che Piange" (November 1911, Leyris); *Poetry,* September 1916; *POO*

Prufrock Among the Women

"The Love Song of J. Alfred Prufrock (Prufrock among the Women)"; "Prufrock's Pervigilium" (July and August 1911; 1912); *Poetry,* June 1915; *POO; IOMH*

An Anguished Cry

"Do I know how I feel: Do I know what I think?" (1911 or 1912, Mayer); *IOMH*

[6]

1911–1914
ELIOT ABSORBED IN PHILOSOPHICAL STUDIES

1. Prologue: The Rise of Harvard's Philosophy Department and the
Santayana Controversy

The Harvard philosophy department that T. S. Eliot found upon entering its graduate program in 1911 had been shaped some three decades or so earlier. Eliot's distant cousin, Charles W. Eliot, had served as president of Harvard from 1869 to 1909 and was credited in *Three Centuries of Harvard, 1636–1936* (1936) by Samuel Eliot Morison (another distant cousin) with having maneu-vered the appointment of "three out of four of Harvard's matchless philo-sophical foursome." The first of these was George Herbert Palmer, who took his B.A. at Harvard in 1864, "translated from the Greek Department to a vacant instructorship in 1872." Next was William James, who, "after a haphazard Jamesian education (schools and private tutors in three or four countries, painting with La Farge under William Morris Hunt, chemistry and anatomy in the Lawrence Scientific School, medicine in the Harvard Medical School)" was appointed an instructor in physiology in 1872; he "established the first American psychological laboratory in 1876, and became Assistant Professor of Philosophy four years later." Third was Josiah Royce, of California, educated at "Göttingen, and Johns Hopkins," who "substituted

for James in 1882–83, and remained at Cambridge for the rest of his days."
And last was George Santayana, who took his degree from Harvard in 1886,
and "shortly after began the second stage of his captivity among the puri-
tans." Clearly the last of the "matchless foursome," in Morison's view, was
Santayana—not only numerically but also in intellectual stature (Morison,
TCH, 353–54).

Morison does not give credit to President Eliot for Santayana's appoint-
ment for good reason: the President actually opposed it. The story is espe-
cially interesting in that it bears some similarities to the story much later
of what happened when the philosophy department could not agree on the
hiring of T. S. Eliot (related in this chapter's epilogue). Santayana took his
B.A. (summa cum laude) at Harvard in 1886 and was awarded a two-year
fellowship for study in Germany. He returned to Harvard and completed his
doctoral dissertation in philosophy in 1889 and was appointed an instructor
in philosophy. His biographer John McCormick relates the story of what
happened when Santayana was proposed for appointment to an assistant pro-
fessorship in 1898. President Eliot wrote to a member of the department,
Hugo Münsterberg: "I agree with you that Dr. Santayana's qualities give a
useful variety to the Philosophical Department, and that he is an original
writer of proved capacity. I suppose the fact to be that I have doubts and
fears about a man so abnormal as Dr. Santayana." After quoting this passage,
McCormick comments: "Since Eliot was not alleging psychiatric disorder,
his use of 'abnormal' probably meant 'homosexual'" (McCormick, 97).
Material supporting McCormick's assertion has been presented in Chapters
3 and 4.

The remainder of President Eliot's letter to Münsterberg seems to con-
firm this characterization: "The withdrawn, contemplative man who takes
no part in the everyday work of the institution, or of the world, seems to me
to be a person of very uncertain future value. He does not dig ditches, or
lay bricks, or write school-books; his product is not of the ordinary useful,
though humble, kind. What will it be? It may be something of the highest
utility; but on the other hand, it may be something futile, or even harmful,
because unnatural and untimely" (97). The words are not only ambiguous but
highly suggestive—"withdrawn," "even harmful," "unnatural and untimely."
In spite of his objection, President Eliot capitulated to the consensus in the
department. Santayana had the support of Josiah Royce, William James, and
Hugo Münsterberg, with only George Herbert Palmer expressing reserva-
tions about his appointment. When President Eliot answered Münsterberg's
rejoinder to the letter quoted above, he replied that his "doubts" had been
answered: "I have read with much interest and admiration your third note

about Mr. Santayana. I am very glad that you can say of him that he is a 'strong and healthy man,' and 'a good, gay, fresh companion.' That testimony strikes me as important" (97).

2. The Decline and Fall of Harvard Philosophy in Eliot's Day and After

On his return to Harvard from Paris in October 1911, T. S. Eliot plunged immediately into philosophy courses preparing him for a doctoral degree in philosophy. Harvard's distinguished department, assembled in the late nineteenth century, remained intact. Even before going to Paris, Eliot had enrolled in some philosophy courses: George Herbert Palmer's survey of ancient philosophers; and George Santayana's survey of modern philosophy, plus his course in the historical development of the ideals of society, religion, art, and science (based on Santayana's *Life of Reason,* 1905–6).

At the time Eliot began his graduate studies, philosophy had reached a critical point in its development as a "body of knowledge" or academic field. It was still widely thought that "truths" could be validated or invalidated by the careful use of language. The more care taken in the refinement and use of language, the less meaningful the "truths" seemed to be, and the result was the proliferation of philosophical works that were not only colossally boring but virtually unreadable. In fact, the field of philosophy was in turmoil, in the subtle process of change so that philosophers who had been respected fell out of favor within a short time and some philosophers (like Eliot) who were writing works (like his dissertation) soon found themselves and their works a part of the rapidly fading "philosophical" past. A full account of Eliot's education in philosophy is to be found in Manju Jain's 1992 book, *T. S. Eliot and American Philosophy: The Harvard Years* (1992). She visited the Harvard Archives, discovering all the courses he had taken, both graduate and undergraduate, and the names of the professors who taught them, which she included in an appendix to her book (252–56). The courses I have listed below are limited to Eliot's graduate courses in philosophy at Harvard and suggest something of the formidable and seemingly chaotic field he had entered, as well as the challenges he faced.

1911–12: *First semester:* experimental psychology, with Professor Herbert Sidney Langfeld; ethics, with George Herbert Palmer; Plato and other Greek thinkers, with James Haughton Woods; elementary Sanskrit, with Charles Rockwell Lanman. *Second semester:* ethics with Palmer, Plato with Woods, and Sanskrit with Lanman continued; a course on Descartes, Spinoza, and Leibniz with George Plimpton Adams.

1912–13: *First semester:* seminar on the nature of reality, with Charles Montague Bakewell; seminar on the philosophy of religion, with a visiting professor from Germany, Rudolf Eucken; the Yoga philosophical system in Sanskrit, with Woods; a study of some Theravada Buddhist texts, with Lanman. *Second semester:* the nature of reality with Bakewell, Yoga philosophy with Woods, and Buddhism with Lanman continued; a course on Kant, with Bakewell; and a course in modern logic, with Karl Schmidt.

1913–14: *First semester:* a seminar on various types of scientific method, with Josiah Royce; a seminar on the nature of reality, with R. F. A. Hoernlé. *Second semester:* scientific method with Royce continued; a history of ethics, with Ralph Barton Perry. During the second semester, Bertrand Russell came to Harvard to deliver the Lowell Lectures, entitled "Our Knowledge of the External World." Russell also offered two courses, one in logic and another on theories of knowledge. Eliot's encounter with Russell at Harvard was important, and Russell would figure importantly in Eliot's future in London.

Those readers familiar with the kinds of courses taught in philosophy departments in the latter half of the twentieth century will recognize some strange aspects of Eliot's program of study. For example, Eliot took courses in psychology, in scientific method, in religion, in Yoga, and in Buddhism that would not generally be found in the curriculum of contemporary departments of philosophy. The quarrels and discussions inspired by the advent in the middle of the nineteenth century of Charles Darwin's "theory of evolution," in effect demonstrating that human beings had closer connections to animals than to angels, forced philosophy to redefine itself as an academic discipline. Philosophy found itself reassessing its traditional position as to the basic or fundamental body of knowledge of the university, forced to decide whether to encompass or ignore science and religion, which by many had come to seem—in the light of Darwinism—quite incompatible.

In a letter opposing Harvard President Lowell's proposal to appoint the anti-idealist philosopher Arthur Lovejoy to the Harvard Department of Philosophy in 1912, a senior member, Hugo Münsterberg, paints a useful picture of the department in Eliot's time: "Harvard ought to ask not only whether a man handles philosophy skillfully, but also what kind of philosophy he handles. Harvard's tradition has been a distinctive leaning toward idealism." Realizing that the term "idealism" hardly applied to James's "pragmatism" and Santayana's "scientism," Münsterberg went on: "In the case of James and Santayana, the pure theoretical metaphysics can hardly be called of idealistic brand, and yet the moral idealism of the one and the aesthetic idealism of the other blended with their general metaphysics so fully that the total impression of the philosophy teaching in Harvard has been an idealistic one, and just this distinctive character has been the source of the strength of the influence." Münsterberg concluded with a somewhat fuzzy claim of unity: "This general unity has always left room for a great variety and no doubt the students of philosophy profit from the manifoldness of the influence" (Jain, 71).

Of the four philosophical stars who had been appointed to positions during President Eliot's early years—George Herbert Palmer, William James, Josiah Royce, and George Santayana—Münsterberg mentions only two, James and Santayana. The other two, Palmer and Royce, were so well known for their commitment to the reigning idealism (holding that the vital element in comprehending reality is the mental or spiritual) that he did not need to mention them. Of all these stars, James would retire in 1907 (and die in 1910), Santayana would resign in 1912, and Palmer would retire in 1913 (but remain to have a say in appointments). In short, three of the four were gone before Eliot finished his work, and Royce died in 1916—but not before he had read and approved Eliot's dissertation.

In the very year that Münsterberg was extolling the idealism dominating Harvard's philosophy department, 1912, a book appeared entitled *The New Realism: Cooperative Studies in Philosophy*, presenting six essays proclaiming the advent of a "new philosophy": "The historical significance of the new realism appears most clearly in its relations with 'naive realism,' 'dualism,' and 'subjectivism.' The new realism is primarily a doctrine concerning the relation between the knowing process and the thing known; and as such it is the latest phase of a movement of thought which has already passed through the three phases just indicated. Neorealism, in other words, seeks to deal with the same problem that has given rise to 'naive realism,' 'dualism,' and 'subjectivism'; and to profit by the errors as well as the discoveries for which these doctrines have been responsible" (Holt, Perry, et al., 2). Two of the authors were from Harvard: Edwin Holt and Ralph Barton Perry; two were from Columbia: W. P. Montague and Walter B. Pitkin; one was from Rutgers: Walter T. Marvin; and another from Princeton: E. G. Spaulding.

In the introduction to *The New Realism*, under a subtitle "The Scrupulous Use of Words," appears a passage that is perhaps the most prophetic in the book. The passage describes first the emphasis of the centrality of "words" in philosophy, creating "need . . . of a great fastidiousness and nicety in the use of words." Indeed, a "regard for words is, in philosophy, the surest proof of a sensitive scientific conscience; for words are the instruments of philosophical procedure, and deserve the same care as the lancet of the surgeon or the balance of the chemist. A complacent and superior disregard of words is as fatuous as it is offensive." This was followed by an almost comic discussion of the misuse of words: "What is the good of words if they aren't important enough to quarrel over? . . . If you called a woman a chimpanzee instead of an angel, wouldn't there be a quarrel about a word? If you're not going to argue about words, what are you going to argue about? Are you going to convey your meaning to me by moving your ears? The church and the heresies always used to fight about words, because they are the only things worth fighting about" (21–22). This focus on the critical importance of language anticipates some of the most radical changes that lay ahead for philosophy.

Eliot was quite aware of this book and its importance, and referred to it a number of times long after he had separated himself from the "profession" of philosophy. Indeed, Eliot's view of his experience in the Harvard Department of Philosophy changed over the years, and we can trace the change—and also gain insight into his shifting philosophical beliefs as systems of philosophy came and went—in a series of four miscellaneous pieces published over the remaining decades of his life: 1918, 1935, 1952, 1964, the last dealing with the belated publication of Eliot's thesis in 1964.

In a 1918 essay entitled "New Philosophers," Eliot reviewed three philosophical works: J. S. Mackenzie's *Elements of Constructive Philosophy,* DeWitt H. Parker's *The Self and Nature,* and James Gibson's *Locke's Theory of Knowledge.* Eliot notes that the "philosophical market does not at the present time manifest much liveliness. It is, indeed, very dull, if we compare it with the active first decade or first twelve years of the century." It was then (while Eliot was still at Harvard), that there "appeared the most important writings of Mr. Russell and M. Bergson, the vogue of William James was at its height, and the New Realists in America were dusting the arena under the imperial and slightly amused gaze of Mr. Santayana." Eliot then comments on the apparent decline of philosophy: "With the exception of a book or two by Professor Dewey, Mr. Russell's late volume of reprinted essays [*Mysticism and Logic, and Other Essays,* 1917?], and possibly Professor Holt's *Freudian Wish,* there have been no notable productions during the last few years; especially in the States, Realists and Pragmatists are engrossed in social and political questions—League of Nations, International Ethics, etc." (NP, 296).

Eliot notes that one of the books he is reviewing, *The Self and Nature,* was written by DeWitt H. Parker, who as a student had "been a pupil of the New Realists at Harvard at the moment when their philosophy still wore the morning dew." And he adds: "The degree of purity in which he transmits their impulse may be taken as a measure of its potency. In America this New Realism has counted, and probably will have counted for a good deal in the history of general ideas; for in America, as in Germany, the mental agitations of philosophers in universities largely supply the place of the less official activity of intellectual London or Paris." What has happened in philosophy since Eliot's study of it and his reviewing of these books in 1918 is indeed extraordinary: "That a school of philosophy so much like materialism should prosper is important in America; that it should have cast out the older theological Idealism is miraculous. The Realists have won their victory simply by concentrating on scientific methods; leaving the implications as to theology still implicit. They have not wholly extirpated theology from philosophy; they have disturbed it and left it to take root again as best it can" (296). The revolutionary changes in American philosophy Eliot lists in 1918 are remarkable, given that the harbinger book had appeared only six years before, and Eliot himself had left Harvard only four years before and had sent his finished dissertation to Harvard only two years before.

Some seventeen years later, in 1935, Walter B. Pitkin, one of the six New Realists of 1912, published a book entitled *A Short Introduction to the History of Human Stupidity*, and Eliot reviewed it for *The New English Weekly*. In this review Eliot made one of his most extensive as well as important statements about *The New Realism*. First, he recalled his first encounter with it: "The Six Realists whose co-operative work, *The New Realism*, made a considerable stir in the philosophic departments of American universities in that year [1912]—and I was then in the philosophical department of an American university—were animated by a missionary zeal against the Hegelian Idealism which was the orthodox doctrine of the philosophical departments of American universities at the time, and which had begun to turn manifestly mouldy." Eliot then looked back at the idealism that had prevailed at Harvard when he was a student: "This Idealism was an inheritance from the times in which philosophy was generally taught by retired non-conformist ministers, the better qualified of whom had passed some years in German universities, and who accepted the Ethics of Kant and the Mysticism of Schleiermacher. It is handled with tender reverence and admirable restraint by George Santayana in his essay on 'The Genteel Tradition in American Philosophy.'" Although the six realists brought about radical changes in the predominant idealism, some of which were "to the good," their "New Realism, like most pre-War philosophies, seems now as demoded as ladies' hats of the same period" (V&R, 151).

Some twenty or more years after his Pitkin review—in 1952—Eliot wrote an introduction to Josef Pieper's *Leisure, the Basis of Culture,* finally finding a book of philosophy he could endorse. In his introductory essay, Eliot placed the book within the scope of his philosophical education. He opened by focusing on the question, "Where are the great philosophers?" and defining the felt need for "new authority to express *insight* and *wisdom*": "To those who pine for philosophy in this ampler sense, logical positivism is the most conspicuous object of censure. Certainly, logical positivism is not a very nourishing diet for more than the small minority which has been conditioned to it. When the time of its exhaustion arrives, it will probably appear, in retrospect, to have been for our age the counterpart of surrealism: for as surrealism seemed to provide a method of producing works of art without imagination so logical positivism seems to provide a method of philosophizing without insight and wisdom" (ILBC, 11–12).

Eliot added that he thought that "logical positivism will have proved of service by explorations of thought which we shall, in future, be unable to ignore." Moreover, he said, he believed "that the sickness of philosophy, an obscure recognition of which moves those who complain of its decline, has been present too long to be attributable to any particular contemporary school of thought." In search of the answer to a question about philosophy Eliot once again dives into his own past: "At the time when I myself was a student of philosophy—I speak of a period some thirty-five to forty years ago—the philosopher was beginning to suffer from a feeling of inferiority to the exact scientist." Indeed, the mathematician appeared to be "the man best qualified to philosophize. Those students of philosophy who had not come to philosophy from mathematics did their best (at least, in the university in which my studies were conducted) to try to become imitation mathematicians—at least to the extent of acquainting themselves with the paraphernalia of symbolic logic." Moreover, other sciences came to the fore: "Some familiarity with contemporary physics and with contemporary biology was also prized: a philosophical argument supported by illustrations from one of these sciences was more respectable than one which lacked them—even if the supporting evidence was sometimes irrelevant" (12–13). Eliot then concluded that he now believes—though he "was unconscious of it" at the time he was a student studying it—that his "dissatisfaction with philosophy as a *profession*" lay in "the divorce of philosophy from theology" (14–15).

Eliot's next major comment on his graduate experience at Harvard comes in his preface to the publication in 1964 (the year before his death) of his dissertation on F. H. Bradley under the title *Knowledge and Experience in the Philosophy of F. H. Bradley*. There, Eliot explains that Professor Anne Bolgan of the University of Alaska had persuaded him, after reading the work in manuscript, to permit its publication under her editorship. After Eliot presented, in the opening paragraph of his brief preface, an exact description of the requirements he faced on entering the philosophy department's graduate program, he then proceeded to relate briefly the events following his departure from America in 1914 on a Sheldon Traveling Fellowship to study philosophy abroad, concluding with an account of finishing his dissertation and dispatching it "across the Atlantic for the judgment of the Harvard Department of Philosophy" (*KEPB*, 9–10).

Perhaps the most amazing aspect about Eliot's preface to his dissertation is his disavowal of it as a work of philosophy: "Forty-six years after my academic philosophizing came to an end, I find myself unable to think in the terminology of this essay. Indeed, I do not pretend to understand it. As philosophizing, it may appear to most modern philosophers to be quaintly antiquated." Eliot then explained his motive for agreeing to its publication: "I can present this book only as a curiosity of biographical interest, which shows, as my wife observed at once, how closely my own prose style was formed on that of Bradley and how little it has changed in all these years. It was she who urged me to publish it; and to her I dedicate it" (10–11). (It was, of course, Eliot's second wife Valerie to whom he referred.)

3. Eliot and Oriental Philosophies and Religions

Over a third of the courses that Eliot took in his graduate work at Harvard were in Oriental languages, philosophies, and religions. Two of the most useful studies of the influence on Eliot of these courses are Cleo McNelly Kearns, *T. S. Eliot and Indic Traditions: A Study in Poetry and Belief* (1987); and Jeffrey M. Perl and Andrew P. Tuck, "The Hidden Advantage of Tradition: On the Significance of T. S. Eliot's Indic Studies," published in *Philosophy East and West: A Quarterly of Asian and Comparative Thought* (April 1985). Eliot was enrolled in courses on topics such as Sanskrit and Yoga in each of his three years in the graduate program. Such courses were radically different from his courses in Western philosophy. Indeed, a number of them involved the learning of new languages—Sanskrit, the religious and classical language of India from 1200 BCE; and Pali, the Prakrit language (the vernacular Indic language of the ancient and medieval period) of the Buddhist scriptures.

Learning Sanskrit would have enabled Eliot to read the Vedas, books of Hinduism's sacred writings, and the Upanishads, prose treatises containing the Hindu philosophy focusing on the unity of Atman, the individual self, and Brahman, the supreme impersonal being: enlightenment leads one (Atman) to discover one's self identical to/with Brahman, the transcendent being, or world soul. Sanskrit would also have enabled Eliot to read the *Bhagavad-Gita,* that portion of India's great epic (*Mahabharata*) that presents a dialogue between its hero Arjuna and his charioteer, Krishna—an incarnate descendant of a deity. It is a popular book of devotion in India, with emphasis on the way of faith and salvation. Those readers familiar with Eliot's infamous footnotes for *The Waste Land* will remember references to some of these texts (see Kearns; Perl and Tuck).

One of Eliot's courses with J. H. Woods was devoted to Yoga, a branch of Hindu philosophy prescribing the physical and mental disciplines used to free the practitioner from the material world in order to attain union with the transcendent being (or "ultimate principle"). The textbook that Woods developed from the course has what seems like an endless title, perhaps appropriate given his subject (note that a "sūtra" is a collection of aphorisms on how to live one's life): *The Yoga-System of Patañjali or The ancient Hindu Doctrine of concentration of Mind embracing the Mnemonic Rules, called Yoga-Sūtras, of Patañjali and the comment, called Yoga Bhāshya, attributed to Veda-Vyāsa and the explanation, called Tattva-Vaiçāradī, of Vāchaspati-Micra* . . . (Harvard Oriental Series, 1914).

Following are a few scattered samples from book 1, "Concentration": Sūtra 2 opens: "Yoga is the restriction of the fluctuations of mind-stuff" (Woods, 8). Sūtra 33: "By the cultivation of friendliness towards happiness and compassion towards pain and joy towards merit and indifference towards demerit [the yogin should attain] the undisturbed calm of the mind-stuff" (71). Sūtra 41: "[The mind-stuff] from which, as from a precious gem, fluctuations have dwindled away, is, with reference either to the knower or to the process-of-knowing or to the object-to-be-known, in the state of resting upon [one] of these [three] and in the state of being tinged by [one] of these [three], and [thus] is in the balanced-state" (77–78). These quotations convey something of the nature of the rules set forth in the Yoga-sūtras for transcending the self that Eliot would have encountered.

And to what end? In the fourth and final book of *The Yoga-System*, in Sūtra 31, we get some notion of the successful outcome of the Yoga exercises: "Then, because of the endlessness of knowledge from which all obscuring defilements have passed away, what is yet to be known amounts to little." This somewhat startling statement is followed by an explanation: "The knowledge which is freed from all obscurations by hindrances and by karma [reaching Brahman or transcendent being] becomes endless. The *sattva* [purity or goodness] of the obscured knowledge overwhelmed by the *tamas* [dullness or inertia] which obscures it, and kept in motion here and there only by the *rajas* [passions], is set free [from the *tamas*] and becomes fit for the process-knowing. In this case when it has become rid of defilement by any of the defilements of the covering, it becomes endless." The comforting conclusion comes next: "In consequence of the endlessness of knowledge what is yet to be known amounts to little, to no more than a firefly in the sky. On which point it has been said 'A blind man pierced a jewel; one without fingers strung it on a cord; one without a neck put it on; a dumb man paid honour to it'" (342). Many Western readers are likely to find the riddles posed in this passage beyond their grasp—which may in some obscure way be the point.

Eliot seems to have preferred, among his Oriental studies, the Buddhist or Pali texts he encountered in a course he took with Professor Lanman in his second graduate year and in a course with Professor Masaharu Anesaki in his third year, Schools of Religion and Philosophical Thought in Japan, which apparently included the varieties of Buddhism in both Japan and China. Eliot's mastery of the Pali language would have enabled him to read Buddhist texts in the original. But when he footnotes "The Fire Sermon" (Part III of *The Waste Land*), he cites Henry Clarke Warren's *Buddhism in Translations*. Warren's "Fire Sermon" is in effect a blast against all the senses (eye, ear, nose, tongue, the body) and an appeal to the divestment of all—*all*—passion in order to attain that freedom which is the "holy life" (Warren, 351–53). In Eliot's poem "Gerontion" (1919), written before *The Waste Land,* the speaker exclaims "I have lost my sight, smell, hearing, taste and touch"—the senses as introduced in the original "Fire Sermon." But as we shall note later, the protagonist's loss of his senses does not bring him to the "holy life." Eliot's use of his Oriental studies was by no means confined to "Gerontion" and *The Waste Land*. Many of his poems not yet written would reflect this influence, and particularly his last poem, so religious in nature, *Four Quartets,* published in final form in 1943.

Eliot's early dismissal of American writers, including Emerson, seems puzzling in the light of his quickened interest in Indic religions, a major influence on the transcendentalists—Emerson principal among them. Eliot's Professor Charles Rockwell Lanman, in an address published as *The Beginnings of Hindu Pantheism* (1890), concluded: "The doctrine of the absolute unity finds perhaps its most striking expression in Sanskrit in the Katha Upanishad; but nowhere, neither in Sanskrit nor in English, has it been presented with more vigor, truthfulness, and beauty of form than by Emerson in his famous lines [in his poem "Brahma"] paraphrasing the Sanskrit passage. They are conceived as if uttered by the All-pervading Spirit" (Lanman, 23). Lanman then proceeds to quote the entire Emerson poem:

> If the red slayer think he slays,
> Or if the slain think he is slain,
> They know not well the subtle ways
> I keep, and pass, and turn again.

Far or forgot to me is near,
Shadow and sunlight are the same,
The vanished gods to me appear,
And one to me are shame and fame.

They reckon ill who leave me out;
When me they fly, I am the wings;
I am the doubter and the doubt,
And I the hymn the Brahmin sings.

The strong gods pine for my abode,
And pine in vain the sacred Seven;
But thou, meek lover of the good!
Find me, and turn thy back on heaven.

(Lanman, 23–24)

Although Lanman introduces the lines by praising them, in his final re-marks he turns away from them to the religion Eliot himself was finally to embrace: "What a prospect, dark and void,—this Supreme Spirit, before whom all human endeavor, all noble ambition, all hope, all love, is blighted! What a contrast, a relief, when we turn from this to the teachings of the gentle Nazarene!" (24). This final remark may give us insight into the way Lanman presented his Oriental religious texts to his students—in a context that is not placed in contest with their assumed Christianity.

In his most extensive reminiscence of his encounter with the Oriental philosophies, in an aside in *After Strange Gods,* Eliot wrote: "Two years spent in the study of Sanskrit under Charles Lanman, and a year in the mazes of Patanjali's metaphysics under the guidance of James Woods, left me in a state of enlightened mystification. A good half of the effort of understanding what the Indian philosophers were after—and their subtleties make most of the great European philosophers look like schoolboys—lay in trying to erase from my mind all the categories and kinds of distinction common to Euro-pean philosophy from the time of the Greeks." Eliot then explained why he rejected these philosophies: "My previous and concomitant study of Euro-pean philosophy was hardly better than an obstacle. And I came to the con-clusion—seeing also that the 'influence' of Brahmin and Buddhist thought upon Europe, as in Schopenhauer, Hartmann, and Deussen, had largely been through romantic misunderstanding—that my only hope of really penetrat-ing to the heart of that mystery would lie in forgetting how to think and feel as an American or a European: which for practical as well as sentimen-tal reasons, I did not wish to do" (*ASG*, 40–41).

Eliot had formed a bias in favor of Buddhism before he ever became a student of philosophy. In his essay "What Is Minor Poetry?" (1944), Eliot describes a reading experience with which many readers can identify: "In a family library there may be a book which somebody bought at the time it was published, because it was highly spoken of, and which nobody read. It was in this way that I came across, as a boy, a poem for which I have preserved a warm affection: *The Light of Asia,* by Sir Edwin Arnold. It is a long epic poem on the life of Gautama Buddha: I must have had a latent sympathy for the subject-matter, for I read it through with gusto, and more than once." The impact of this poem on Eliot seems similar to—and preceded—the impact of Fitzgerald's Omar: "I have never had the curiosity to find out anything about the author but to this day it seems to me a good poem, and when I meet anyone else who has read and liked it, I feel drawn to that person" (*OPP,* 38). While at Oxford in 1915, he reported in a letter of April 4 to Mrs. Jack Gardner that he had attended meetings of the Buddhist Society, where he had met a friend of Mrs. Gardner (*LTSE1,* 93). And Stephen Spender evidently heard Eliot tell an acquaintance that as late as 1922, when he was writing *The Waste Land,* he was tempted to become a Buddhist (Spender, *TSE,* 20).

A reader familiar with Eliot's early dismay at the "thinness" of American culture, and particularly at its watered-down Puritanism in the form of an essentially secularized religion—Unitarianism—may wonder at his fear, expressed in *After Strange Gods,* of forgetting "how to think and feel as an American or European." It must be remembered that in *After Strange Gods* he is delivering an address in the American South (Virginia) in 1933, and he is extraordinarily sensitive (as we shall see later) to the Southernness of his audience. In an attempt to clarify his point about the vast differences separating Indian and Western philosophy and religion, Eliot continues: "And I should imagine that the same choice would hold good for Chinese thought: though I believe that the Chinese mind is very much nearer to the Anglo-Saxon than is the Indian. China is—or was until the missionaries initiated her into Western thought, and blazed a path for John Dewey—a country of tradition; Confucius was not born into a vacuum; and a network of rites and customs, even if regarded by philosophers in a spirit of benign skepticism, makes a world of difference." "But," Eliot concludes, "Confucius has become the philosopher of the rebellious Protestant. And I cannot but feel that in some respects Irving Babbitt, with the noblest intentions, has merely made matters worse instead of better" (*ASG,* 41).

John Dewey is, of course, Eliot's cultural target, representing everything intellectually that Eliot opposed—as, for example, Dewey's fervent belief in education for all in a democracy. But Eliot's Harvard mentor Babbitt, who had been influential in inspiring Eliot to study philosophy in France for a year, had by 1933 (the year of Eliot's lecture) become something of a target for Eliot because of Babbitt's religious—or rather his nonreligious—beliefs. Babbitt's dilution of whatever little traditional religious belief remained in him by belief in the wisdom of Confucius was an affront that drew Eliot's ire. In *After Strange Gods,* Eliot said of Babbitt: "His attitude towards Christianity seems to me that of a man who had had no *emotional* acquaintance with any but some debased and uncultured form: I judge entirely on his public pronouncements and not at all on any information about his upbringing. . . . His addiction to the philosophy of Confucius is evidence [of trying to compensate for the lack of a living tradition]: the popularity of Confucius among our contemporaries is significant" (39–40). Note, first, the importance given the word *emotional* by italicizing it. Eliot's somewhat contemptuous remark is surprising, given what we know about Eliot's own early disenchantment with his parents' Unitarianism—which Eliot early disdained and which he refused to consider as a genuine branch of Christianity.

Eliot's argument with Babbitt and his religious beliefs continued after Babbitt's death. Babbitt died in 1933, and Eliot devoted a good deal of his lead essay to him in a book entitled *Revelation,* edited by John Baillie. In this essay, Eliot attacked Babbitt's posthumous publication, *The Dhammapada: Translated from the Pali with an Essay on Buddha and the Occident* (1936). Eliot begins a long semi-digression: "The problem is why Babbitt, with such a mind and equipment as, it would seem, could only be supported by Christianity, should have turned to primitive Buddhism (Hinayana) instead. But first it will help us if we can form some conclusion about what he made of Buddhism" (RI, 16). The next six pages of Eliot's essay are devoted to the deficiencies of Babbitt's understanding of both Buddhism and Christianity. Whatever is certain or uncertain about Babbitt's beliefs and Eliot's disagreements with them, it is certain that by the mid-1930s Eliot's sympathetic feelings about Buddhism and his own earlier leanings toward it had somewhat soured.

This brief and sketchy account of what Eliot encountered in his extensive studies in Oriental religions in graduate study, and his recollections of that period in his life, may be sufficient to serve as a background for Eliot's attitudes, both conscious and unconscious, toward his studies at Harvard in traditional or conventional Western philosophy. Eastern philosophy assumes a mystic structure of the universe that can be known only through certain ritualistic or meditative forms of behavior, while Western philosophy assumes a knowable structure of reality that might be clarified through using language to set forth proofs. In Eastern philosophy, the truths are imbedded in sacred texts, scrutiny and understanding of which may lead, through proper responses, to a shared enlightenment generally beyond words. Intuition, insight, feelings are key. In Western philosophy, reality holds the secret truths that must be ferreted out by careful definition and argument. Reason, intellect, common sense are key. But in Eliot's day, psychology and Western religion were taught as "philosophy," and may have supplied a convenient bridge between the "philosophies" of the East and the West.

4. Psychology as Philosophical, Religion as Psychological, Mysticism as Magical

By the time that Eliot was a graduate student, psychology (as a study of the workings of the "mind") had developed as a research discipline, but it had not yet found its own department at universities: thus it was adopted by philosophy—still debating the precise location of "reality," in the "mind" or in the "world"—or in some obscure binding of the two. In 1911–12 Eliot enrolled in Professor Herbert Sidney Langfeld's yearlong Philosophy 21, which was in fact "experimental psychology," with a lecture and four hours of laboratory each week. And in 1912–13, he took Professor Hugo Münsterberg's Philosophy 20b, a seminar focusing on the "mind and body"; also during this year he took Philosophy 20h with a visiting professor from Germany, Rudolf Eucken, in the philosophy of religion. Eliot seldom commented, after he "left" philosophy, on his professors other than those he greatly admired. In the case of Eucken, he recalled: "No one who had not witnessed the event could imagine the conviction in the tone of Professor Eucken as he pounded the table and exclaimed *Was ist Geist? Geist ist . . .* [What is soul? Soul is . . .]" (quoted in Howarth, 207). But of course, all of Eliot's other philosophy courses—especially those in Indian philosophy—frequently touched on matters psychological and religious.

William James was a distinguished and leading proponent of the field of psychology, yet he was a member of Harvard's Department of Philosophy. His credentials in psychology were established when he published his two-volume work, *The Principles of Psychology,* in 1890, introducing the metaphor, "stream of consciousness," that was to shape modern literature in the early twentieth century. His series of lectures on *Pragmatism,* published in 1907, established his credentials in philosophy; he helped to divert philosophy from the dead-end imprisonment of Hegelian idealism and its attempt to discover or create an Absolute—leading it from the bogs of abstraction to the firm fields of concreteness, and thus helping to move it from the irrelevant to the relevant as to how human beings do or should live their lives. And finally, his *The Varieties of Religious Experience* (1902) established James's credentials in the field of religion, especially mysticism in all its varieties, where psychology, philosophy, and religious beliefs intersected and intermingled. Although Eliot never took a course with James, he was clearly influenced by him and his brother, master novelist Henry James. Eliot's debt to William James is summed up in the final sentence of Eliot's 1917 review of one of James's published lectures (delivered in 1898), "Human Immortality: Two Supposed Objections to the Doctrine": "It would be easy to pick the lecture to pieces; its binding fluid is its attack upon dogmatic disbelief, not any constructive theory. But James has an exceptional quality of always leaving his reader with the feeling that the world is full of possibilities—in a philosopher, a rare and valuable quality; and what seems skepticism or inconsistency or vagueness in others, James has the knack of communicating a sense of sincere adventurousness" (WJOI, 547). From a committed philosopher, "sincere adventurousness" as a label would have been severe criticism; from T. S. Eliot, it is a high compliment indeed.

Eliot critics and scholars have in the later 1980s and the 1990s brought to light previously ignored or undiscovered miscellaneous graduate-school notecards and essay manuscripts in libraries (chiefly the Houghton Library at Harvard and the King's College Library in Cambridge, England). Since much of the material is undated, and since all of it relates to the various courses Eliot was taking at Harvard, 1911–14, it has an uncertain authenticity: does any particular sentence Eliot wrote, or quoted from one of his sources, represent his own view, or a view he explored or experimented with for a particular audience and a particular class presentation? Among these materials, according to Manju Jain in *T. S. Eliot and American Philosophy,* are some fifty-nine index cards that "can be roughly classified into four groups: Greek philosophy; the anthropology and the psychology of religion; clinical psychology, concerned mostly with individual cases of pathological states of consciousness as they relate to mystical phenomena; and theological writing on mysticism" (Jain, 161–62).

These cards are remarkable for revealing the wide range of reading in various aspects of psychology and religion, including abnormal psychology, that Eliot was doing at this period of his life. From Josiah Morse's *Pathological Aspects of Religion,* according to Jain, Eliot "copies Havelock Ellis's assertion in *The Psychology of Sex* that love and religion are the two most volcanic emotions to which the human organism is liable" (172). What Jain does not say is that the love referred to here is "auto-erotic." Morse goes on to quote

Ellis's next sentence, which we've encountered in Chapter 4, Section 5: "Nor is it surprising that the two emotions should have a dynamic relation to each other, and that the auto-erotic impulse being the more primitive and fundamental of the two impulses should be able to pass its unexpended energy over to the religious emotion, there to find the expansion hitherto denied it, the love of the human becoming the love of the divine" (Morse, 18). Did Eliot not finish reading the paragraph, or could he not bear to write the key term "auto-erotic"?

Jain also relates that Eliot noted, from his reading of *Pathological Aspects of Religion,* Max Nordau's assertion (in *Degeneration*) that "mysticism is a characteristic of degeneration" (Jain, 172). In fact, Morse places Nordau's observation alongside several others, all of them taking varied positions on the meaning of mysticism: "Some consider [mysticism] the product of a diseased brain, or gross ignorance; others as divine inspiration, or intuition; some find its seat in subconsciousness or the Unconscious, others regard it as the highest flight of human reason; others in terms of feeling and emotion, and not a few make it a compound of all psychic activities." Morse presents all of these views as well as Max Nordau's view in *Degeneration* that "mysticism is a characteristic of degeneration" (Morse, 69).

From *Etudes de l'histoire et de psychologie du mysticisme* (1908), by Henri Delacroix, Eliot "takes down details of the lives of St. Theresa and Mme. Guyon. He is particularly interested in the fact that both of them had a low physical vitality. Eliot copies in considerable detail their experiences, as recorded by Delacroix, of visions, ecstasy, rapture, and unification with the divine which results in an abolition of the ego and is attained after various stages." Jain points out that Eliot copies "Delacroix's view that the subconscious has specialized in religious activity, but it also dominates everyday life into which it sometimes introduces its operations. The characteristics of the final state are abolition of individual consciousness; immense and insentient joy and continuous ecstasy; divine automatism; the apostolic life; the rejection by the subject of certain states incompatible with the divine; and then the divine command is withheld, there is the impossibility of acting, and complete '*aboulie*' [lack of will]." Eliot circled these last two lines. Jain emphasizes their "special significance for him in view of the fact that he renders this state of paralysis in poems such as 'Prufrock,' and later, in 1921 he admitted to suffering an '*aboulie*' and emotional derangement which had been a lifelong affliction" (Jain, 172–73). This last admission, made in a letter dated November 6, 1921, to Richard Aldington, occurred at a time when he was writing *The Waste Land.*

Another French psychologist Eliot was reading at this time, according to Jain, was Pierre Janet, author of two works: *The Mental State of Hystericals,* published in 1901, and *The Major Symptoms of Hysteria,* a series of lectures given at Harvard University in 1906 and published in 1907: "Janet's studies of hysterical patients . . . demonstrated to him that hysteria had played an important role in the history of all religion and superstition, and that the visionary experiences of the mystics, together with their concomitant phys- ical actions, were no different from the symptoms exhibited by the hysteri- cal patients in his care. He claimed, therefore, that hysterical patients helped in an understanding of religious and mystical experience. . . . Hysteria was a form of degeneration, and the most revered of the 'ecstatics' had never thought of anything higher than the monotonous interrogations of his patients." Eliot "appears to have deliberately gone out of his way to choose bizarre instances" to copy, "partly in a spirit of fun, for he was no doubt also struck by their absurdity. . . . [He copied] the banal details of the case of a man who interested himself passionately in spiritualism and then acquired delusions of a malignant spirit" that would "torment him" (168–70).

Whereas these French psychologists Eliot was reading and recording on his notecards tended to see mysticism as a symptom of mental illness, two other writers he was reading on the subject were clearly more sympa- thetic to the mystical tradition: the American William James in *The Varieties of Religious Experience* (1902) and England's Evelyn Underhill in *Mysticism* (1911).

According to Jain, Eliot copied out of James's book part of a passage on "states of consciousness" concerning the "truth" James drew from the results of his experiments with nitrous oxide: "that our normal waking conscious- ness, rational consciousness as we call it, is but one special type of con- sciousness, whilst all about it, parted from it by the filmiest of screens, there lie potential forms of consciousness entirely different" (174). After the pas- sage Eliot copied, James goes on in *Varieties* to write:

> We may go through life without suspecting their existence; but apply the requisite stimulus, and at a touch they are there in all their completeness, definite types of mentality which probably some- where have their field of application and adaptation. No account of the universe in its totality can be final which leaves these other forms of consciousness quite disregarded. How to regard them is the question—for they are so discontinuous with ordinary conscious- ness. Yet they may determine attitudes though they cannot furnish formulas, and open a region though they fail to give a map. At any rate, they forbid a premature closing of our accounts with reality.

> Looking back on my own experiences, they all converge towards a kind of insight to which I cannot help ascribing some metaphysical significance. The keynote of it is invariably a reconciliation. It is as if the opposites of the world, whose contradictoriness and conflict make all our difficulties and troubles, were melted into unity. . . . I feel as if it must mean something, something like what the Hegelian philosophy means, if one could only lay hold of it more clearly. (James, William, 349–50)

This passage, with all its intuitive speculation, is probably as close as James could ever come to affirming some kind of religious belief—and it comes as the report of an experiment in the use of nitrous oxide. According to Jain, Eliot took careful note of James's list of four characteristics of "mystical states of consciousness": *Ineffability,* "it defies expression"; *Noetic quality,* "insight into depths of truth unplumbed by the discursive intellect"; *Transiency,* "cannot be sustained for long"; and *Passivity,* "the mystic feels as if his own will were in abeyance, and indeed sometimes as if he were grasped and held by a superior power" (Jain, 74–75; James, William, 342–44).

Although Eliot read James's *Varieties* with great care and took many notes—especially of James's sources (Jain, 174–76)—he felt more at home with the religious tone of Evelyn Underhill's *Mysticism.* A clue as to Eliot's preference may well be found in the absence of Dante's name in the index to *Varieties* and the vivid presence of Dante in *Mysticism,* not only in the index, but also in passages crucial to Underhill's explorations and affirmations. Eliot took particular note of Underhill's account in part 2 of *Mysticism* of what she calls "The Mystic Way." According to Jain, Eliot listed the phases as follows: "Revelation of Divine Reality, Purgation, Illumination, Dark Night of the Soul, and Union" (195). In fact, Underhill's terms are for what she calls the "five great stages" of "the normal development of mystic consciousness" as it "oscillates between pain and pleasure states": "1. Awakening or Conversion; 2. Self-knowledge or Purgation; 3. Illumination; 4. Surrender, or the Dark Night; 5. Union." Throughout her book, Underhill compares and contrasts the mysticism of the West and East, and after citing the five stages she observes: "Unitive life the goal of the Mystic Way—Annihilation of Self the end of Oriental Mysticism—Christian Mysticism denies this interpretation of Union—Finds in it the enhancement not the suppression of life" (Underhill, 167).

Eliot also, as Jain observes, took note of Underhill's discussion of the principal symbols mystics use in describing their experiences (Jain, 194). Underhill writes: "The three great classes of symbols which I propose to consider, appeal to three deep cravings of the self, three great expressions of man's restlessness, which only mystic truth can fully satisfy. The first is the craving which makes him a pilgrim and wanderer. It is the longing to go out from his normal world in search of a lost home, a 'better country'; an Eldorado, a Sarras, a Heavenly Syon. The next is that craving of heart for heart, of the soul for its perfect mate, which makes him a lover. The third is the craving for inward purity and perfection, which makes him an ascetic, and in the last resort a saint" (Underhill, 126–27). One or another of these symbols becomes dominant in the traditional mystics in accord with their temperaments: "A. Those [mystics] who conceive the Perfect as a beatific vision exterior to them will find in the doctrine of Emanations something which answers to their inward experience, will feel the process of their entrance into reality to be a quest. . . . B. Those for whom mysticism is above all things an intimate and personal relation . . . will fall back upon imagery drawn largely from the language of earthly passion. . . . C. Those who are conscious rather of the Divine as a Transcendent Life . . . and of a strange spiritual seed within them by whose development man . . . attains his end, will see the mystic life as involving inward change rather than outgoing search" (128–29). Underhill summarizes: "We may fairly take as their [the three groups of mystics] characteristic forms of symbolic expression the Mystic Quest, the Marriage of the Soul, and the 'Great Work' of the Spiritual Alchemists" (129).

The chapter in Underhill's book that probably attracted Eliot's closest attention is the one entitled "Mysticism and Theology," where Eliot encountered the two doctrines of Emanations and Immanence (Jain, 194–95). According to Underhill, Divine Reality has been presented by the great mystics under two apparently contradictory modes: "The opinion which is represented in its most extreme form by the theory of *Emanations,* declares His utter *transcendence.* This view appears early in the history of Greek philosophy. It is developed by Dionysius, by the Kabalists, by Dante: and is implied in the language of Rulman Merswin, St. John of the Cross and many other Christian ecstatics. . . . Such a way of conceiving reality accords with the type of mind which William James called the 'sick soul.'" But the "theory of Immanence" is "at the opposite pole": "To the holders of this theory, who commonly belong to James's 'healthy minded' or optimistic class, the quest of the Absolute is no long journey, but a realization of something which is implicit in the self and in the universe: an opening of the eyes of the soul upon the Reality in which it is bathed." Indeed it appears, seemingly, anywhere and everywhere: "The Absolute Whom all seek does not hold Himself aloof from an imperfect material universe, but dwells within the flux of things: stands as it were at the very threshold of consciousness and knocks, awaiting the self's slow discovery of her treasures. . . . Unless safeguarded by limiting dogmas, the theory of Immanence taken alone, is notoriously apt to degenerate into pantheism" (Underhill, 97–99).

As this last sentence suggests, and as Eliot observed, the religious dogmas play a vital part in Underhill's conception of mysticism. Jain writes that Eliot "copies Underhill's assertion that 'the dogmas of Christianity,' whether or not accepted on the scientific plane, 'are necessary to an adequate description of mystical experience'" (Jain, 195). Underhill cites as one example the Christian dogma of the incarnation: "The Incarnation, which is for traditional Christianity synonymous with the historical birth and earthly life of Christ, is for mystics of a certain type, not only this but also a perpetual Cosmic and personal process. It is an everlasting bringing forth, in the universe and also in the individual ascending soul, of the divine and perfect life, the pure character of God, of which the one historical life dramatized the essential constituents. Hence the soul, like the physical embryo, resumes in its upward progress the spiritual life-history of the race" (Underhill, 118).

In reading Underhill, Eliot found rather explicitly set forth the reasons for his dissatisfactions with his family's Unitarian faith—which by this time he had already abandoned. And moreover, Eliot found in Underhill's repeated citations from Dante and *The Divine Comedy* support for his own admiration for Dante's work, and valid reasons to begin looking at the poem as something more than a great work of literature. Here is the entry for Dante that Underhill included in an appendix setting forth a "Historical Sketch of European Mysticism": "In Italy Dante (1265–1321) is forcing human language to express one of the most sublime visions of the Absolute which has ever been crystallized into speech. He inherits and fuses into one that loving and artistic reading of reality which was the heart of Franciscan mysticism, and that other ordered vision of the transcendental world which the Dominicans through Aquinas poured into the stream of European thought. For the one the spiritual world was all love: for the other all law. For Dante it was both." In the third book of Dante's work is found the climax of his religious "restitution": "In the 'Paradiso' his stupendous genius apprehends and shows to us a Beatific Vision in which the symbolic systems of all great mystics, and many whom the world does not call mystics—of Dionysius, Richard, St. Bernard, Mechthild, Aquinas, and countless others—are included and explained" (462). The influences on Eliot were many, but his reading of Underhill's *Mysticism,* and especially her use of Dante in her "argument," clearly must be counted as a major factor in his conversion to Anglo-Catholicism some years later.

5. Eliot and the Elusive Absolute

In June 1913, Eliot purchased a copy of *Appearance and Reality* by British philosopher F. H. Bradley (Gordon, *EEY*, 49). He would eventually complete a dissertation entitled *Experience and the Objects of Knowledge in the Philosophy of F. H. Bradley*. Eliot finished his coursework on his doctorate at the end of the 1913–14 academic year and traveled to Europe to attend lectures at the University of Marburg in Germany in June 1914; his plans were interrupted by the war and he consequently settled in England. His life abroad must be left to later chapters, but the story of his study of philosophy, including the writing of his dissertation, must be included here. Although Eliot had begun his dissertation at Harvard, he did not complete it (or his revision of it) until early 1916 when he was settled in London. Eliot sent the finished dissertation to his Harvard adviser, Josiah Royce, who approved it enthusiastically, calling it the "work of an expert." Prevented from traveling to the U.S. for the necessary final exams, Eliot was never formally awarded the doctoral degree. As we have noted, the dissertation was published in 1964 under the title *Knowledge and Experience in the Philosophy of F. H. Bradley.*

Eliot's thoughts about his dissertation and the field of philosophy in general are discussed in a letter Eliot wrote to Norbert Weiner dated January 6, 1915, at a time when he was trying to finish his dissertation. Weiner (who would become famous years later as a pioneer of information theory) was ten years younger than Eliot, had taken a Ph.D. at Harvard at age eighteen, and was on a Sheldon Traveling Fellowship to study with Bertrand Russell at Cambridge (*LTSE1*, 66 n. 3). Eliot was returning Weiner's essay "on relativism," which sparked Eliot's discussion. Eliot found himself in "cordial" agreement with the doctrine of Relativism, but it needed to be "worked out." He characterized "all philosophising" as a "perversion of reality" for the simple reason that "no philosophic theory makes any difference to practice." In effect, it can never be tested: "It is an attempt to organise the confused and contradictory world of common sense, and an attempt which invariably meets with partial failure—and with partial success. It invariably involves cramming both feet into one shoe: almost every philosophy seems to begin as a revolt of common sense against some other theory, and ends—as it becomes itself more developed and approaches completeness—by itself becoming equally preposterous—to everyone but its author." Although all theories "are certainly . . . implicit in the inexact experience of every day," Eliot concluded, when "extracted they make the world appear as strange as Bottom in his ass's head" (79–80). Since Eliot was not to finish and send off his completed dissertation on Bradley until a year later, it would appear likely that something of this negative attitude would find its way into his philosophical discussions in it—consciously, or unconsciously.

We have just noted Eliot's interest in passages of Evelyn Underhill's *Mysticism* evoking the Absolute. He brings the matter up in his letter to Weiner as central to his philosophical exploration of Bradley. Following the passage quoted above, he writes: "These are all obvious remarks which I need not weary you with: but the upshot is (or would be if I continued till I had really expressed my meaning) that relativism, strictly interpreted, is not an antidote for the other systems: one can have a relative absolute if one likes, for it is all one if one call the Absolute, Reality or Value. It does not exist for me, but I cannot say that it does not exist for Mr. Bradley." Eliot had by this time wound his way to the point of questioning the very existence of philosophy: "And Mr. Bradley may say that the Absolute is implied *for* me *in* my thought—and who is to be the referee? . . . The only reason why relativism does not do away with philosophy altogether, after all, is that there is no such thing to abolish! There is art, and there is science. And there are works of art, and perhaps of science, which would never have occurred had not many people been under the impression that there was philosophy" (80–81). This passage makes clear why, at the deepest level, Eliot was to choose art (or poetry) over philosophy for a career.

Eliot goes on to describe his purposes in the writing (or revision) of his dissertation, which might be useful for any reader attempting to read it today: "I took a piece of fairly technical philosophy for my thesis, and my relativism made me see so many sides to questions that I became hopelessly involved, and wrote a thesis perfectly unintelligible to anyone but myself; and so I wished to rewrite it. It's about Bradley's theory of judgment, and I think the second version will be entirely destructive. I shall attack first 'Reality,' second 'Idea' or ideal content, and then try to show sufficient reason for attempting to get along without any theory of judgment whatsoever" (81).

Bradley's principal beliefs have been described succinctly by the authority Richard Wollheim in a review of Eliot's published dissertation entitled "Eliot, Bradley, and Immediate Experience" in the *New Statesman,* March 13, 1964. Wollheim's brief explanation of the points of view of Eliot and Bradley is especially helpful for those unfamiliar with the history of philosophy: "As a philosopher Bradley at once belonged to and also rejected the tendencies of his day. For while he was unable to accept the old dualism between mind and nature, he found equally untenable any of the new distinctions that were being drawn within mental philosophy. All of them, according to him, committed the cardinal sin of analysis, which is to treat what can be distinguished as though it were different." Wollheim finds in effect what Eliot had come to see, i.e., that Bradley himself ultimately committed the error he had set out to expose and transcend: "Indeed it might be said that by a process of exaggeration that is typical of metaphysics, he grossly generalized the essential connection that he had rightly detected as holding between an idea and its meaning, and argued that everything was related to everything else in just this inner kind of way. And for anyone who believes this, it must follow that the ideas, categories, classifications that we impose upon the world falsify it, by suggesting real divisions where really there are none: although, as Bradley was quick to see, even to state the doctrine like this, is already error, for what are 'we' and 'it' but themselves unjustified abstractions?" In this last paragraph, Wollheim is essentially describing how the notion of the Absolute emerges from Bradley's theory—as in his argument "that everything was related to everything else in just this inner kind of way." And in a later passage he writes: "As a metaphysical counterpart to this doctrine about thought Bradley was led to postulate, as underlying all our knowledge, a primitive fused condition, known as Immediate Experience" (Wollheim, 401).

Eliot's language in his dissertation is shot through with this kind of ambiguity. Here are some passages from his concluding chapter, including its closing sentence: "To the builder of the system, the identity binding together the appearance and the reality is evident; to anyone outside of the system it is not evident. To the builder the process is the process of reality, for thought and reality are one; to a critic, the process is perhaps only the process of the builder's thought. From the critic's standpoint the metaphysician's world may be real only as the child's bogey is real. The one thinks of reality in terms of his system; the other thinks of the system in terms of the indefinite social reality. There occurs, in short, just what is sure to occur in a world in which subject and predicate are not one." Clearly we find no philosophical summary of a well-argued system, but rather an agnosticism about all philosophical systems embodied in words: "Metaphysical systems are condemned to go up like a rocket and come down like a stick. . . . The Absolute, we find, does not fall within any of the classes of objects; it is neither real nor unreal nor imaginary. . . . A metaphysic may be accepted or rejected without our assuming that from the practical point of view it is either true or false. . . . If I have insisted on the practical (pragmatic?) in the constitution and meaning of objects, it is because the practical is a practical metaphysic. And this emphasis upon practice—upon the relativity and the instrumentality of knowledge—is what impels us toward the Absolute" (KEPB, 167–69). Readers of these closing pages of Eliot's dissertation may well wonder whether, in Eliot's inner eye, Bradley's metaphysical system had "come down like a stick." His concluding sentence is underwhelming in its affirmation of the Bradleyan metaphysic: it is certainly not an acceptance of the Absolute but an assertion of being "impelled" toward it.

Eliot published two essays ("The Development of Leibniz' Monadism" and "Leibniz' Monads and Bradley's Finite Centres") in the *Monist* for October 1916, and these have been included at the end of his published dissertation. In these pieces Eliot seems more secure of his own doubts about the "reality" of Bradley's Absolute: "I suggest that from the 'pluralism' of Leibniz there is only a step to the 'absolute zero' of Bradley, and that Bradley's Absolute dissolves at a touch into its constituents. . . . Leibniz does not succeed in establishing the reality of several substances. On the other hand, just as Leibniz's pluralism is ultimately based upon faith, so Bradley's universe, actual only in finite centres, is only by an act of faith unified. Upon inspection, it falls away into the isolated finite experiences out of which it is put together." In sum, Eliot shows great skepticism as to the possibility of the Absolute being finally captured by language: "The Absolute responds only to an imaginary demand of thought, and satisfies only an imaginary demand of feeling. Pretending to be something which makes finite centers cohere, it turns out to be merely the assertion that they do. And this assertion is only true so far as we here and now find it to be so" (200–202). "Bradley's Absolute dissolves at a touch into its constituents"; "Pretending to be something which makes finite centres cohere, [the Absolute] turns out to be merely the assertion that they do": Such passages reinforce a reader's impression that in Eliot's view Bradley's Absolute is not only elusive but, finally, simply and only a creation of language, and thus highly insubstantial.

The several years that Eliot spent reading closely the works of Bradley and writing and revising his dissertation were bound to leave their mark. After Bradley's death in 1924, Eliot himself provided an assessment of Bradley's philosophy and writing, which first appeared in the *Times Literary Supplement*, December 29, 1927, and was then published in Eliot's 1928 volume, *For Lancelot Andrewes: Essays on Style and Order*. Eliot found the secret of Bradley's powerful effect in what he characterized as "the great gift of style." There is probably no better way to understand Eliot's own style than to follow his zestful exploration of Bradley's prose. Here are some of the generalizations and examples Eliot set forth in his essay; most of the generalizations could be applied to Eliot, and similar examples found in his essays. "Bradley always assumed, with what will remain for those who did not know him a curious blend of humility and irony, an attitude of extreme diffidence about his own work. . . . The first words of the Preface to his *Principles of Logic* are: 'The following work makes no claim to supply any systematic treatment of logic'" (*FLA*, 53). Eliot referred to "Bradley's polemical irony and his obvious zest in using it, his habit of discomfiting an opponent with a sudden profession of ignorance, of inability to understand, or of incapacity for abstruse thought" (54)—all of which are easily applicable to Eliot's style. Eliot further observed: "Of wisdom Bradley had a large share; wisdom consists largely of skepticism and uncynical disillusion; and of these Bradley had a large share" (60).

It might be claimed that Eliot was not only an innovator in poetry, heralding the modernist period in the early twentieth century, but also an innovator in prose, introducing an informality and a skeptical common sense in a highly readable prose style that provided the basis for a modernist criticism. Using himself a "curious blend of humility and irony," Eliot often apologized for what seemed to be contradictions in his critical principles by saying that he had moved on to new positions and could be bound only by what he at the moment of writing really believed, not by statements made in the past. Laforgue apparently helped Eliot to find a poetic character both humble and ironic, and Bradley helped him to discover a prose voice of similar nature.

6. Epilogue: The Eliot Controversy

We began this chapter with a prologue about George Santayana, citing his biographer's account (John McCormick, *George Santayana* [1987]) of Santayana's presumed homosexuality and the problems it caused him at Harvard. And we now end with an epilogue in which Santayana's sexuality becomes relevant and important in a move by the Harvard Department of Philosophy in 1919 to hire T. S. Eliot.

It is of some interest before turning to Eliot to observe that Bruce Kuklick, in his chapter on Santayana in *The Rise of American Philosophy: Cambridge, Massachusetts, 1860–1930* (1977), finds it useful in a section entitled "Career at Harvard" to set forth evidence as to Santayana's sexuality: "One of the factors influencing [Santayana's] decision to leave teaching was his relations with Cambridge and his department. A small coterie of students idolized him. His fastidious black dress—he wore an exotic European cape— and his aloof, removed demeanor epitomized for them the only sane style of life. For most others he was supercilious, vain, and offensive. Santayana also had a peculiar belief that he might have been an unconscious homosexual during his Harvard years, and, in fact, some students thought he was a homosexual." In contrast to his loyal student following, Santayana's fellow faculty members "only grudgingly accepted him, and as his view became more distinct they grew more suspicious. The other philosophers had all developed a robust religious orientation—an academic version of nineteenth-century muscular Christianity—in the face of mechanistic interpretations of science. . . . They never admired Santayana's aestheticism or his belief that religion was a form of poetry. He was, said James, 'unworldly,' 'a spectator rather than an actor by temperament,' and Harvard needed 'a specimen' of someone like him" (Kuklick, 365–66).

It turns out that T. S. Eliot was one of the few Harvard graduate students (other than those who later became professors at Harvard) to make it into Kuklick's *The Rise of American Philosophy*. He is buried in a footnote but it is a long one in an account of the philosophy department's move to hire replacements for the distinguished professors that were retiring or dying: "As an administrator [James Haughton] Woods was energetic and ingenious. At the same time he was tempting [Bertrand] Russell, he came within an inch of getting T. S. Eliot, who had just completed his dissertation under Royce, to come back to Harvard as an instructor. Eliot was apparently set to return from England when a wartime emergency caused the cancellation of his boat." Woods was "bitterly disappointed," so, at the end of the war he tried again to bring Eliot to Harvard. "But both [Ralph Barton] Perry and [George Herbert] Palmer—still a departmental force—appear to have over-ruled Woods, although they granted Eliot's genius. Perry believed Eliot was a 'sort of attenuated Santayana,' too 'rare and overrefined'; Palmer that 'a certain softness of moral fibre' had allowed a 'weak aestheticism' to turn Eliot's head. The memory of Santayana appears to have been operating in cases other than this" (410).

Recall that in 1919, at the time this debate over the hiring of Eliot was going on in Harvard's philosophy department, Eliot was living in London with his wife Vivien and was launched on a writing career with a number of successes to his credit—including his first book, *Prufrock and Other Observations* (1917); he was on the verge of publishing (in 1920) another book of poems and his first book of essays. No matter what Harvard offered, it was unlikely that he could be lured back permanently to an American academic career.

A fuller account of Harvard's consideration of Eliot's appointment in 1919 is to be found in the generous quotations from letters in Manju Jain's *T. S. Eliot and American Philosophy*, in a chapter entitled "Eliot and Harvard: 'An Attenuated Santayana'?" The key players, unaware of Eliot's commitment to the course he had taken in his life, were the then chair James Haughton Woods, Ralph Barton Perry (a former department chair), R. F. A. Hoernlé (the chairman in 1919), and the single carry-over, George Herbert Palmer. Eliot had twice been a student in Woods's yearlong classes, the first on Plato and other Greek philosophers, the second on Yoga and Buddhist philosophical texts. Pushing for Eliot's appointment, Woods was supported by Hoernlé, who had taught Eliot in a seminar on the nature of reality.

Eliot had taken a course in the history of ancient philosophy under Palmer in 1907 and a course in ethics in 1911–12. Palmer raised the most serious doubts, as reported to Perry in a letter from Hoernlé: "Palmer thinks that Eliot has failed to make good his early promise and that he has allowed himself to be turned into weak aestheticism by the influence of certain literary cliques in London." Palmer remembered Eliot as having "a mind of extraordinary power and sensitiveness," but that "love of beauty, which might have been his strength, had turned out to be his weakness, by reason of a certain softness of moral fibre" (quoted in Jain, 34–35). Palmer had seen Eliot on his recent trip to America in 1915 and had been "deeply disappointed by the change" in him, and had suggested to him "as plainly as he dared the dangers which he was running" (35). The language Palmer used was strangely and ambiguously forceful, hinting at things left unsaid.

Ralph Barton Perry, with whom Eliot had studied the history of ethics, wrote that the man to be selected for the open position should be "a man with a knowledge of history and politics and a man of solid character and live interests, rather than a man whose interest in philosophy is bookish and literary." While Mrs. Perry thought Eliot to be "an exceptionally thoughtful and sensitive person of whom great things may be expected," Perry thought that Eliot might "turn out to be the man to play a role similar to that played" by Santayana (34). When pressed again about Eliot's appointment, Perry wrote to Hoernlé: "I think we ought to know something more about his present state of mind as he was very young, and undergoing rapid change when we last had a good opportunity to know him." It would, concluded Perry, be a great blunder "to put into a position of such great influence a man who was so rare and over-refined as to be out of sympathy with the current social and political movements." And in another letter addressed to Woods, Perry wrote significantly: "If he is a sort of attenuated Santayana, in other words if his recent poetry is now the most typical thing about him, I do not believe that he would be the right man to be permanently in charge of students concentrating in philosophy. Our great hope beyond my convictions is in the economic and political, rather than in the literary applications of philosophy" (35).

The phrases used to describe Eliot's personality summoned by Palmer and Perry are remarkable for their thrust and power, their extraordinary suggestiveness: "weak aestheticism," "softness of moral fibre," "the dangers [Eliot] was running," "rare and over-refined," an "attenuated Santayana." These do not clash with—indeed they tend to complement—the kinds of comments that Eliot's friends and acquaintances made about him (cf. Conrad Aiken's "dapper young man," "a somewhat Lamian smile," "shy" but "disciplined," "Europeanized" and "carrying a cane").

In referring to Eliot's "recent poetry," surely Perry had in mind "The Love Song of J. Alfred Prufrock." It is likely that Eliot was never to find out how *personal* his reputedly impersonal poem had seemed to Harvard's philosophy department. Although it has been long assumed that Eliot could have had the position at Harvard if he had wanted it (certainly his family in America believed so), it seems unlikely that the Department of Philosophy could come to an agreement on hiring him, not because of his academic record but because of his Santayana-like personality.

1914–1915
AMERICAN CHAOS VERSUS ENGLISH TRADITION

(1) *Philosophy in Marburg, War in Europe*, 191; (2) *London Interlude: Pound and Russell*, 196; (3) *Oxford, 1914–1915: Reconsidering Philosophy*, 203; (4) *New Friends and Old: Culpin, Blanshard, Pound, Lewis*, 207; (5) *The Mystery of Emily Hale:* "The Aspern Papers *in Reverse,*" 211

1. Philosophy in Marburg, War in Europe

In March 1914, Eliot was awarded a Sheldon Traveling Fellowship for the coming academic year, 1914–15, to study philosophy at Merton College, Oxford, where the subject of his dissertation, F. H. Bradley, had taught and where Bradley's student, Harold Joachim, offered classes in which Eliot intended to enroll. We do not have Eliot's letter to his father informing him of the fellowship, but we have his father's four-line reply—the only letter from his father to appear in *The Letters of T. S. Eliot*, dated April 11, 1914: "I am much pleased that you have rec[eive]d the Scholarship, on ac[coun]t of the honor, as you couldn't get it unless you deserved it. You have never been a 'burden' to me, my dear fellow. A parent is always in debt to a son who has been as dutiful and affectionate as you have been. Yrs. P." (*LTSE1*, 37). We are left to imagine the nature of the self-deprecating letter Eliot must have written—primarily from the word "burden," which he must have used to describe himself in relation to his father. And the reserved words of praise from father to son—"dutiful and affectionate"—suggest something of the depth of reserve on both sides in what seemed to have been a mainly formal relationship. Eliot included minor messages to his father in letters to his mother for the next five years, until his father's early death on January 8,

1919, by which time it had become clear to the father that his son had not been as "dutiful" as he had expected.

In June of 1914 Eliot left America earlier than his fellowship dictated in order to travel in Europe, visiting cities he had come to know rather well during his 1910–11 year in France—Paris, Munich, and apparently London—and continuing to Marburg, Germany, where he planned to attend lectures given by the German philosopher Rudolf Eucken at the University of Marburg. No doubt Eliot would have visited his friend Jean Verdenal in France had he been able to track him down. But Verdenal, whose military service had been deferred in 1911 and 1912 to allow him to study medicine in Paris, had renounced further deferment in March 1913, and entered the eighteenth infantry regiment in the French army, where he was to be appointed a "medical officer" in November 1914 (Watson, George, 467). In early July 1914, Eliot passed through London, according to the chronology provided by Valerie Eliot in her edition for the first volume of Eliot's letters (oddly, she does not mention his visits to Paris and Munich) (*LTSE1*, xxi). It may be that the only evidence to indicate that Eliot "passed through" London is that a letter was posted there to his favorite cousin (on his mother's side), Eleanor Hinkley—a letter that he had written while on board the ship crossing the Atlantic and postmarked "London 7 July 1914" (37). Eliot assumes a familiar voice in describing his voyage to his cousin: "Free from the cares and irks of city life, indifferent to my whilom duties, I sit in my snug little cabin lazily watching the little clouds slip across the sky and the trunks slide across the floor. From my tiny round window I can see a flock of lovely birds dip and skim athwart the zenith (sparrows I believe—I am not much on ornithology)" (37–39). It is important to remember that, during Eliot's early days, ocean travel to Europe was not only prolonged but also rough and uncomfortable.

What little we know about Eliot's life in Europe in 1914 before his settling down in England is to be found in the few letters he wrote from Marburg to two faithful correspondents: two to his Harvard friend Conrad Aiken, and one to his cousin Eleanor. In a letter dated July 19 to Aiken (then in London), Eliot asked Aiken to pick up a valise Eliot had left with American Express in London and send it to him in Germany. The letter is filled with the details of a young, somewhat world-weary and hard-to-impress sightseer visiting cities and museums that he hasn't seen before: "Bruges is charming if you like that sort of thing . . . but has a sort of post-putridity about it, the sort which infects small old towns and old things generally—Italy stinks the same way, except up in the lakes." In some of his remarks, Eliot sounded somewhat like a forerunner of the "ugly American": "Flanders on the whole I don't care for; it is neither French nor German, and seems to combine the defects of both." But Eliot conceded that Flanders is "unique, and the paintings are *stunning!*" He then listed the cities and their "treasures": Bruges, Antwerp, Brussels, Ghent; Memling, van Eyck, Matsys, David, Breughel, Rubens—"really great stuff." Eliot concluded his comments on the art he has seen by listing "*three* great *St. Sebastians*": "1) Mantegna (ca d'Oro) [in Venice] 2) Antonello of Messina (Bergamo) [in Lombardy, Italy] 3) Memling (Brussels)." (His viewing these St. Sebastians, as we shall see later, figured in two of Eliot's extraordinary poems written during this period, "The Love Song of St. Sebastian" and "The Death of St. Narcissus.")

In this same letter to his confidante Aiken, Eliot included a sample of the "*stuff*" he had been writing—in reality a continuation of two bawdy poetic "epics" that he had shared with Aiken in their days together at Harvard about one Columbo and a King Bolo: "Now while Columbo and his men / Were drinking ice cream soda / In burst King Bolo's big black queen / That famous old breech l(oader). / Just then they rang the bell for lunch / And served up—Fried Hyenas; / And Columbo said 'Will you take tail? / Or just a bit of p(enis)?'" As we have already noted in Chapter 3, Section 4, Aiken had become acquainted with the bawdy side of Eliot's poetic production at Harvard, including ditties about characters called Columbo and King Bolo with his "big black queen." Not only was the young Eliot gifted as a bawdy poet, but he reveals in his early letters a gift for comic drawings. Alongside his poem in his letter to Aiken is a "portrait" of the head of King Bolo smoking a huge cigar above the inscription "Viva Bolo!!"

In this and other letters we have the valuable commentaries of Eliot on his own poems—the only poems of his on which he was anxious to make explicatory comments. After quoting the above lines, Eliot explains: "The bracketed portions we owe to the restorations of the editor, Prof. Dr. Hasenpfeffer (Halle), with the assistance of his two inseparable friends, Dr. Hans Frigger (the celebrated poet) and Herr Schnitzel (aus Wien). How much we owe to the hardwon intuition of this truly great scholar! The editor also justly observes: 'There seems to be a double entendre about the last two lines, but the fine flavour of the jest has not survived the centuries'.—Yet we hope that such genius as his may penetrate this enigma" (*LTSE1*, 40–43). No doubt such jesting (and outrageously salacious punning) with his fellow undergraduate helped release the tensions that were bound to build up with such dedicated devotion to the elusive ideas (including an elusive absolute) of academic philosophy.

Less than a week after this first letter from Marburg to Aiken, Eliot wrote again on July 25, 1914, describing the routine of his life in Marburg: "I find myself very well fixed here *chez* the Herr Pfarrer, his wife, and his daughter

Hannah. The people are extremely kind, the quarters comfortable, the view from my windows (south) excellent—over roofs and hills—the house is on the side of the hill, and the hill is steep—the food is excellent—I find that I like German food!" Indeed, Eliot seemed to be settling into life in Germany with surprising satisfaction: "I like the German people! and we have five meals a day. I stuff myself; the Frau Pfarrer thinks I don't eat enough. Then I swim (there are baths) or walk (there are beautiful walks among the woods) but not far, because I must always be back in time for the next meal" (43–44). Eliot's letter, however, seems to have as its main purpose to share with his friend his ambitious plan for writing a sequence of poems tentatively entitled "Descent from the Cross." Included was a "part" called *Love Song of St. Sebastian,* as well as two untitled passages with first lines:"Oh little voices of the throats of men" and "Appearances appearances he said." (A selection of these poems and others written during this period will be discussed later.)

Eliot's final letter sent from Marburg, dated July 26, 1914, is addressed to his cousin Eleanor Hinkley, then enrolled in Radcliffe College, sister college to Harvard in Cambridge, Massachusetts. It is filled with details of Eliot's contented daily life in Marburg, revealing little awareness of the approaching war that was within days to engulf the whole of Europe. It is surely the most fully (and amusingly) illustrated of all Eliot's letters: simple line-drawings, or caricatures, of himself and members of the family with whom he was living. Eliot opened: "Here I am, safely out of harm's way, settled in the bosom of the family of the Lutheran Pastor, and the church is right across the street. I have just been to church, and feel good as gold. This will not be an exciting summer, but I think a pleasant one, though I hope you will not circulate any gossip about me and the Pastor's daughter." There was indeed a "Pastor's daughter" named Hannah, who did needlework in the evening with her mother until asked by Frau Pfarrer to "play a bit of Beethoven" on the piano. Marburg is, Eliot wrote, "more a miniature compact city than a small town, as it has very good shops, and a cunning little street car that runs round the town on one track, and little narrow streets." The University had 2,500 students who appear "a little cub-like and uncouth, but . . . fearfully polite." Eliot's chatty letter touched on the view, walks, the "peaceful" life, mutual friends, and his looking forward to making "some amusing acquaintances" in his approaching attendance at summer-school. He closed by describing a scene on the boat crossing over with fellow Bostonians that is uncannily prophetic of the coming mood: "You should have seen us round the piano on the 4th July, singing 'Rally, rally round the Flag, Boys!'" (48–51).

Although it was not widely realized at the time, war had become inevitable by the time Eliot had passed through London in early July on his way to Germany. In late June 1914, the Archduke Franz Ferdinand, heir to Austria's throne, was assassinated by a Serbian revolutionary. Austria declared war on Serbia on July 28, 1914, followed by Austria's ally, Germany, declaring war on Russia on August 1 and on France on August 3. On August 4, Great Britain declared war on Germany. (The United States delayed entering the war until 1917.) Thus began the Great War, "the war to end all wars," fought mainly in the muddy French trenches, that continued for four years and devastated Europe, and whose peace settlement in November 1918 laid the groundwork for World War II. Soon after his July 26 letter to his cousin, Eliot found that the university lecture series had been canceled: his most important task was to find a way to get out of Germany and find his way to England.

When Germany declared war against Russia on August 1, it imposed a "blackout" (to mobilize and get armies in place) throughout the country that finally forced all the foreigners living in Germany to realize that they were in the wrong place at the wrong time. That realization was heightened shortly after, when first France and then Great Britain declared war on Germany. The blackout intensified, cutting Germany off from other countries that might become enemies. When Eliot did make it out, he wrote to his cousin from London that "The Germans treated us royally, but we had to stay in Marburg 2 weeks without any outside communications" (51). After the two-week blackout ended, around August 15 and 16, the foreigners were left to their own devices to get out of the country the best way they could—with nationals of enemy countries, of course, given the closest scrutiny.

Eliot did not find it easy to get from Germany to England. A letter he wrote to his mother from London (August 23, 1914) concentrates on the harrowing experience he had trying to get along in Germany after the war had begun and then trying to get out of Germany to England (51–54). It is worthy of note that Eliot addressed his letter to "Dear Mother," without a mention anywhere in it of his father. It was not, he writes, until the day after the declaration of war with Russia that Eliot and his fellow students came to realize the "seriousness" of their position, when they were informed that the summer course in which they had enrolled would not continue. Money was an immediate problem, as there was no way to get it from home in the emergency. The German families with whom students were living were astonishingly generous in offering them free room and board. Finally, after the blackout, Eliot began a several-day zigzag journey out of Germany, with minimal sleep and food: the goal was to get to London via Rotterdam in the Netherlands.

First he made his way to Frankfurt, a trip that usually took a bit over an hour now taking Eliot five hours. The train was crowded with soldiers on their way to the front, making frequent stops for more soldiers who were bidding farewell to their families. As though giving the kernel of a poem, Eliot described a haunting image: "I shall never forget one woman's face as she tried to wave goodbye. I could not see his face. . . . I am sure she had no hope of seeing him again." After spending the night in Frankfurt, Eliot had to make his way to Cologne, where he had a choice of taking a boat down the Rhine (a trip of some three days) or another train. He chose the train, arriving in Cologne at 10 PM that night. He decided to wait up for a 3:00 AM train to the Netherlands border, which he reached the next day at 3 PM. Although expecting to be challenged at the border, Eliot was waved along when recognized as an American (Eliot surmised that Germany was "making a strong bid for American sympathy"). He finally reached Rotterdam that same day at 10 PM and got, he says, "the last room in the hotel." After a day of waiting in Rotterdam, he took a train for Flushing—i.e., Vlissingen, a Netherlands seaport offering boat trips to England. From there he took a boat offering overnight passage to London, arriving the following night. Up to that point Eliot had been "persuaded of the rightness of the German cause . . . to a certain extent, til [he] found that the English papers were making exact contradictions of the German" (53–54).

In London Eliot joined his Harvard friend Conrad Aiken, renting a room in the same cheap Bloomsbury boarding house at 28 Bedford Place, Russell Square, that Aiken was occupying. Aiken was desperately trying to get passage on one of the crowded liners that were sailing for America, finally getting space not many days after Eliot's arrival. In the brief period (August 22 to October 6, 1914) while Eliot was in London before going on to Oxford, he was to establish some of the most important relationships of his life. But the period must have seemed to him filled with more uncertainties than he had ever faced before, primarily because of the chaos brought about by the outbreak of the war.

2. London Interlude: Pound and Russell

In a September 8 letter, some two weeks after arriving in London, Eliot wrote to his brother, addressed as "My dear Henry." Eliot characterized life in London as all "noise and rumour": "Hot weather, all windows open, many babies, pianos, street piano accordions, singers, hummers, whistlers." A major noise was created by men hawking newspapers: "GREAT GERMAN DISASTER!" or "LIST OF ENGLISH DEAD AND WOUNDED." In spite of the noisy distractions, Eliot reported, he found it "quite possible to work": "The noises of a city so large as London don't distract one much; they become attached to the city and depersonalize themselves." He added, however, that his liking for London had not supplanted his love of Paris: "I think I should love Paris now more than ever, if I could see her in these times. There seems to have come a wonderful calmness and fortitude over Paris, from what I hear." To those looking back from the twenty-first century, Eliot's opinions about the war at its beginning are indeed interesting: "I am anxious that Germany should be beaten; but I think it is silly to hold up one's hands at German 'atrocities' and 'violations of neutrality.' The Germans are perfectly justified in violating Belgium—they are fighting for their existence—but the English are more than justified in turning to defend a treaty." To this rather astonishing comment Eliot added a somewhat ambiguous statement about Germany: "But the Germans are bad diplomats. It is not against German 'crimes,' but against German 'civilisation'—all this system of officers and professors—that I protest. But very useful to the world if kept in place" (54–56).

On the same day that he wrote to his brother, Eliot again wrote to his cousin Eleanor Hinkley, confessing that he had come to like London very much, but he was puzzled by Englishmen, finding them "a bit conventional: I don't know just what conventionality is; it doesn't involve snobbishness, because I am a thorough snob myself; but I should have thought of it as perhaps the one quality which all my [English] friends lacked." Further exploring the English character, Eliot wrote: "It's very so much easier to know what a Frenchman or an American is thinking about, than an Englishman. Perhaps partly that a Frenchman is so analytical and selfconscious that he dislikes to have anything going on inside him that he can't put into words, while an Englishman is content simply to live." Eliot saw this as "a virtue," also manifested in the "way they have been fighting in France." As for the war, having come to see how people in both Germany and France "have taken the affair . . . has made it impossible for me to adopt a wholly partisan attitude, or even to rejoice or despair wholeheartedly, though I should certainly want to fight against the Germans if at all." He explained: "I have been to some of the towns about which they have been fighting; and I know that men I have known, including one of my best friends, must be fighting each other. So it's hard for me to write interestingly about the war" (56–58). This best friend is surely Jean Verdenal, and Eliot's use of the term echoes Verdenal's "meilleur ami," referring to Eliot in his letter of February 5, 1912. (Eliot himself tried to join the American armed forces when the United States entered the war in 1917, as we shall see.)

But his letter had opened with a vivid description of his immediate scene in London: "Here I am in Shady Bloomsbury, the noisiest place in the world, a neighborhood at present given over to artists, musicians, hackwriters, Americans, Russians, French, Belgians, Italians, Spaniards, and Japanese; formerly Germans also—these have now retired, including our waiter, a small inefficient person, but, as one lady observed, 'What's to prevent him putting arsenic in our tea?'" Bloomsbury, which Eliot dubbed "a delightfully seedy part of town," was roughly equivalent to New York's bohemian Greenwich Village, attracting poets, novelists, painters, as well as social and sexual nonconformists. It was home to the British Museum as well as Harold Monro's Poetry Bookshop, established in 1913. And of course, it was soon to become famous, or notorious, as the home of the Bloomsbury Group.

Aiken had entered this scene earlier in the summer of 1914, armed with letters of introduction to several poets, including Ezra Pound. He also brought his own poetry as well as Eliot's "Prufrock" and "La Figlia Che Piange." Aiken had mentioned Eliot's name when Pound had asked Aiken if he could recommend any young poet "genuinely modern." Aiken replied (as Pound remembered the conversation) that Eliot was a "guy at Harvard doing funny stuff." Aiken remembered the encounter with Pound differently: he had been trying to interest several editors in Eliot's "The Love Song of J. Alfred Prufrock," including Harold Monro, editor of *Poetry & Drama*. Monro read the poem, announced that the author was "absolutely insane" and "practically threw" the manuscript back at him. It was then that Aiken went to Pound (Carpenter, 257–59).

Eliot sought out Ezra Pound on September 22, 1914, at his Holland Place Chambers address and began one of the most important relationships of his life. Pound had been born in Idaho in 1885 (three years before Eliot's birth in St. Louis), brought up in Pennsylvania, and had attended Hamilton College and the University of Pennsylvania. After a brief period of teaching at Wabash College in Indiana, he was dismissed for offering his room to a stranded burlesque performer, and in 1908 he set off for Italy, where, in Venice, he published his first book of poems, *A Lume Spento*. He next took off for London, where he published additional volumes, most notably *Personae* and *Exultations* in 1909, and *Canzoni* in 1911. By the time Eliot came for his visit, Pound had served as "secretary" for the Irish poet William Butler Yeats and had established a professional relationship with (among many writers and critics) the English philosopher-poet T. E. Hulme. And more important for Eliot, he had become the "foreign correspondent" for a magazine entitled *Poetry,* established in 1912 in Chicago by Harriet Monroe; she had collected money from the city's rich meat packers and railroad builders to provide a cultural dimension to a city that Carl Sandburg called "Hog Butcher for the World." Most magazines of the time, both in England and America, published poems only as "fillers." *Poetry* was unusual in that it was devoted entirely to poetry, and it *paid* poets for the publication of their poems.

Although Eliot had not met Pound until his September 1914 visit, he had read some of Pound's early poetry and had not liked it. He remembered in his *Paris Review* interview that, as an undergraduate at Harvard an associate of his then editing the *Harvard Advocate,* W. G. Tinckom-Fernandez, had given him some of Pound's early volumes to read, saying, "This is up your street; you ought to like this." Eliot confessed in the interview: "Well, I didn't, really. It seemed to me rather fancy old-fashioned romantic stuff, cloak-and-dagger stuff. I wasn't much impressed by it. When I went to see Pound, I was not particularly an admirer of his work" (INT, 95). Indeed, after his visit to Pound, Eliot wrote an aside in a letter to Aiken (September 30, 1914): "By the way, Pound is rather intelligent as a talker: his verse is well-meaning but touchingly incompetent; but his remarks are sometimes good" (*LTSE1,* 59). Of course, Eliot's opinion of Pound and his work was to change radically over the next few years.

Pound was impressed by the young Eliot on his first visit and wrote to Harriet Monroe at *Poetry* about him, even though he had not yet seen any of Eliot's poems. It was not until a subsequent visit that Eliot handed Pound a draft of "Prufrock." Pound read it and immediately announced his opinion, writing to Monroe: "I was jolly well right about Eliot. He has sent in the best poem I have yet had or seen from an American. PRAY GOD IT BE NOT A SINGLE AND UNIQUE SUCCESS. He has taken it back to get it ready for the press and you shall have it in a few days." Although Pound's opinion was extraordinary and almost rapturous, it does not in retrospect seem extravagant: "[Eliot] is the only American I know of who has made what I can call adequate preparation for writing. He has actually trained himself *and* modernized himself *on his own.* . . . It is such a comfort to meet a man and not have to tell him to wash his face, wipe his feet, and remember the date (1914) on the calendar" (quoted in Carpenter, 258).

Although Monroe received "Prufrock" in October of 1914, it did not appear in *Poetry* until June 1915. It is not clear what caused the delay in publication, but it was evident that Harriet Monroe had doubts about Eliot's poem. In a reply to a long letter from the editor of *Poetry* on a variety of matters including "Prufrock," Pound first replied curtly on November 9, 1914: "Your letter—the long one—to hand is the most dreary and discouraging document that I have been called upon to read for a very long time. Your objection to Eliot is the climax." Later the same day, Pound opened a long reply: "No, most emphatically I will not ask Eliot to write down to any audience whatsoever. I dare say my instinct was sound enough when I volunteered to quit the magazine quietly a year ago. Neither will I send you Eliot's address in order that he may be insulted" (Pound, *L*, 44–47). The remainder of the letter was devoted to less controversial topics; but in a letter of January 31, 1915, to Monroe, Pound rejected her specific objections to "Prufrock": "Now as to Eliot: 'Mr. Prufrock' does not 'go off at the end.' It is a portrait of a failure, or of a character which fails, and it would be false art to make it end on a note of triumph. I dislike the paragraph about Hamlet, but it is an early and cherished bit and T. E. won't give it up, and as it is the only portion of the poem that most readers will like at first reading, I don't see that it will do much harm. For the rest: a portrait satire on futility can't end by turning that quintessence of futility, Mr. P. into a reformed character breathing out fire and ozone" (50).

This exchange provides a glimpse into Harriet Monroe's role as the editor of *Poetry* magazine, as well as some insight into Pound's arbitrary and what some would call "high-handed" ways of dealing with her—using his richly colloquial American speech. In Ellen Williams's comprehensive study of this relationship, *Harriet Monroe and the Poetry Renaissance* (1977), we learn that Monroe was not alone in finding fault with the poem. Pound cited only Ford Madox Hueffer and Harold Monro as expressing any interest in it in England, and in America only Vachel Lindsay praised it to Monroe (Williams, 127–28). The appearance of "Prufrock" in *Poetry* in June 1915 marked the first major step in Eliot's recognition as a poet; though little noted at the time, the poem would eventually establish itself as probably Eliot's most frequently published, as well as one of the most quoted poems of the twentieth century.

While Pound became a key player in Eliot's developing career as a poet, Eliot encountered another individual in London about the same time who would figure importantly in his personal life. While walking one day in New Oxford Street in October 1914, Eliot ran into one of his Harvard philosophy professors, Bertrand Russell (*LTSE1*, xxii). During Eliot's last semester of graduate work in the spring of 1914, Russell had delivered his Lowell Lectures, "Our Knowledge of the External World"; he had also taught two courses, one on logic, the other on theories of knowledge. Eliot had sat in on Russell's course on logic and probably his lectures as well. By that time, Eliot was known as one of the most promising of students in philosophy at Harvard. As we discover in his *Autobiography*, Russell had his twelve students in to tea once a week. Eliot, Russell notes, "subsequently wrote a poem about it, called 'Mr. Apollinax.'" He never revealed that he wrote poetry, even though he had already written the then unpublished "Portrait of a Lady" and "Prufrock."

Eliot was "extraordinarily silent," but attracted his attention when, in response to Russell's praise of Heraclitus, he remarked: "Yes, he always reminds me of Villon." Russell found Eliot's remark "so good" that he "always wished he would make another" (Russell, *A*, 220–21). According to Russell's biographer, Russell remembered Eliot's remark because for him François Villon was "the very personification of the value and danger of submitting to the 'central fire' of the human soul"; and moreover, in 1914, "Heraclitus too held a special place in his imagination; in 'Mysticism and Logic' Heraclitus is exalted as the paradigm of the 'highest eminence' that it is possible to achieve: 'the true union of the mystic and the man of science.'" For Eliot to link the two, however tenuously, inspired Russell to believe that "somewhere beneath Eliot's own civilised crust there was, after all, some fire" (Monk, 350).

When they met in October 1914 in New Oxford Street, Russell (a vociferous pacifist) recalled asking Eliot "what he thought of the War. 'I don't know,' he replied, 'I only know I am not a pacifist.' That is to say, he considered any excuse good enough for homicide" (Russell, *A*, 242). Russell's pacifism was so deeply ingrained that he became an active and vocal member of the No-Conscription Fellowship and publicly courted prosecution for "impeding recruiting and discipline." Indeed, he was tried, fined, and imprisoned for a brief time (Monk, 416, 456–68). In effect, he was able to exploit his fame as a philosopher and writer for a cause in which he deeply believed. His relationship with Eliot later in 1915, after Eliot found himself married, was to become quite close as well as extremely complicated.

Ezra Pound and Bertrand Russell provided Eliot astonishingly easy entry into English literary and intellectual society, both bohemian and sophisticated. His fellow American, Pound, seemed to have connections in every nook and cranny (including journals and magazines) of the London literary scene—having been there since 1908. And Eliot's British philosophy professor Russell, becoming a kind of father-figure for the young Eliot, linked him with a social scene—the Bloomsbury Group—that has been called the "most brilliant intellectual and social circle of our century." In fact, this characterization is found on the cover of Leon Edel's highly praised volume, *Bloomsbury: A House of Lions* (1979), a "group biography" of the crowd that would surround Eliot in his early London years.

Eliot's final letter from London during this period, September 30 [1914], at least as published in volume 1 of his *Letters* (1988), is addressed to Conrad Aiken, and though carrying the return address of Merton College, Oxford, was actually sent from the Bedford Place address as Eliot explains in his opening paragraph. Eliot wrote that he had stayed in London for a few extra days because of the possibility of dining in the next day or so with Yeats and the Pounds. But more important, he revealed that Pound was "going to print 'Prufrock' in *Poetry* and pay for it," and moreover wanted him to "bring out a Vol. after the War." Eliot added: "The devil of it is that I have done nothing good since J. A[lfred] P[rufrock] and writhe in impotence. The stuff I sent you is not good, is very forced in execution, though the idea was right, I think." Eliot's reference to Prufrock naturally carried his imagination back to Paris, and he said wistfully: "Sometimes I think—if I could only get back to Paris. But I know I never will, for long. I must learn to talk English" (*LTSE1*, 58). (Later, Eliot's American friends would be surprised indeed at how British he sounded in his speech.)

This series of thoughts led Eliot into a meandering series of ideas about the nature of poetry's genuine inspiration: "Anyway, I'm in the worry way now. Too many minor considerations. Does anything kill as petty worries do? And in America we worry all the time. That, in fact, is I think the great use of suffering, if it's *tragic* suffering—it takes you away from yourself—and petty suffering does exactly the reverse, and kills your inspiration." These thoughts led Eliot to what he believed was behind his present lack of inspiration: "I think now that all my good stuff was done before I had begun to worry—three years ago. I sometimes think it would be better to be just a clerk in a post office with nothing to worry about—but the consciousness of having made a failure of one's life. Or a millionaire, ditto." A reader might wonder whether there was indeed "tragic suffering" behind the work done "three years ago"—behind Prufrock and other poems. In his next comment Eliot seemed to be on the verge of some such conception as that of "impersonal poetry": "The thing is to be able to look at one's life as if it were somebody's else—(I much prefer to say somebody else's). That is difficult in England, almost impossible in America—But it may be all right in the long run, (if I can get over it), perhaps *tant mieux* [so much the better]. . . . Anyway, it's interesting to cut yourself to pieces once in a while, and wait to see what fragments will sprout" (58–59). This letter seems to suggest that indeed Eliot was not in England to study philosophy—but to settle in and become what he wanted to be—a poet.

Eliot suddenly changed the subject and playfully offered Aiken a bawdy war poem entitled "UP BOYS AND AT 'EM!" (see Chapter 3, Section 4). Eliot ended his letter with a strange comment revealing his own longing for sex: "I should find it very stimulating to have several women fall in love with me—several, because that makes the practical side less evident." An ordinary reader might puzzle over the use of the word "practical" in this last comment, but surely one meaning is that he would not have to entangle himself with any one of the "several" and thus tie himself down in any way. He asked Aiken: "Do you think it possible, if I brought out the 'Inventions of the March Hare,' and gave a few lectures, at 5 PM with wax candles, that I could become a sentimental Tommy?" This question is notable on two counts. It appears to be the first mention in the letters of the title of Eliot's then unpublished notebook, on which Eliot had inked the title, then drew a line through it, according to a note to "Inventions. . . ." Second, Eliot's reference to his becoming a "Sentimental Tommy" is not only witty but revealing. A note informs us: "A whimsical thrust at the Poetry Bookshop where such events occurred, combined with J. M. Barrie's title, *Sentimental Tommy* (1896), and a play on [Eliot's] name" (58–59). Eve Kosofsky Sedgwick, in *Epistemology of the Closet,* places Barrie's novel and its sequel *Tommy and Grizel* (1900) in a "post-Romantic tradition of fictional meditations on the subject . . . of male homosexual panic": "'Sentimental' Tommy . . . the hero . . . is treated throughout each of these astonishingly acute and self-hating novels both as a man with a specific, crippling moral and psychological defect and as the very type of the great creative artist" (Sedgwick, 183, 195).

3. Oxford, 1914–1915: Reconsidering Philosophy

In the letters Eliot wrote while studying philosophy at Oxford during 1914 and 1915, under the tutelage of F. H. Bradley's most distinguished student, Harold Joachim, Eliot revealed himself confronting crucial decisions: most especially whether he would go back to Harvard and become a professor of philosophy, as his parents wanted, or whether he would remain in England and find ways to fulfill his ambition to become a poet, a career on which he was already tentatively launched through the flattering support of Ezra Pound. The year at Oxford ended with the most puzzling action of Eliot's life: his marriage to Vivien Haigh-Wood on June 26, 1915, an event that has mystified both his biographers and critics (discussed in Chapter 8, Sections 1 and 2). This academic year was marked by the increasing involvement of Great Britain in the war—which not only affected the daily lives of all those living in Europe, but also made extremely difficult both transoceanic communication and travel.

One of Eliot's professors at Harvard, J. H. Woods, had asked Eliot to report to him what he was studying and to send him materials and even notes from lectures and discussions that would cast light on the philosophy of Oxford's Joachim. Eliot dutifully reported in a letter of November 9 [1914] that he was following three courses of lectures during the first term: Joachim's on the *Ethics* of Aristotle, R. G. Collingwood's on Aristotle's *de Anima*, and J. A. Smith's on logic (Eliot's comment: Smith's lectures represent "the purest strain of old fashioned Hegelianism to be found in England"). In addition,

Eliot and one other student were slated to read Aristotle's *Posterior Analytics* with Joachim. There were to be conferences and "informals" scheduled during the week. Eliot reported enthusiastically on many courses and readings, illustrating why he was such a good student. He observed little originality in Oxford philosophy but praised the scholarship and the teaching: "For anyone who is going to teach the Oxford discipline is admirable. It has impressed on my mind the value . . . of personal instruction in small classes and individually . . . and the value of careful study of original texts in the original tongue—in contrast to the synoptic course" (LTSE1, 67–68).

In a letter of October 14 from Merton College, Oxford, to his close cousin Eleanor Hinkley, he expressed his preference for the British educational milieu, which he had by then scarcely sampled. Assuming that everyone would want to know how he liked Oxford, he wrote: "I like it quite well enough to wish that I had come here earlier and spent two or three years; perhaps even before the end of my college course at home, for I am sure that I should have got more profit from both my work and my play. . . . I should have gotten along with the undergraduates better and made more friends than I made at Harvard, though I should be very sorry to have to give up those whom I did make" (61). Similarly, in a letter of the same date to a fellow Harvard student who had also studied at Oxford, William C. Greene, Eliot wrote: "I wish now that I had taken a year—several years—here first and done my Harvard work later, instead of beginning my house at the roof. I have begun to entertain the highest respect for English methods of teaching in addition to the disapproval for our own which I had acquired through experience" (65).

In writing to Conrad Aiken on November 16, however, Eliot revealed a greater disenchantment with his country and his field of study than he did to either his cousin or former classmate. As a place to live long-term: "I conclude that London is a pleasant place when the road to Paris is *gesperrt* [closed]." And he then observed that all "university towns" are the same "the world over" in that they do not provide the "intellectual stimulus" for the writing of poetry: "Only the most matter of fact people could write verse here, I assure you" (68). Believing Aiken had been too lenient in criticizing his verse, Eliot called it "strained and intellectual. I know the kind of verse I want, and I know that this isn't it, and I know why. I shan't do anything that will satisfy me (as some of my old stuff *does* satisfy me—whether it be good or not) for years. . . . Not in the life I have been leading for several years." He then said ambiguously, "And I don't know whether I want to" (69). What is it Eliot does not know?—whether he wants to write poetry? Or whether he wants to go on leading the life that somehow does not lead him to write the kind of poetry he wants to write?

In two later letters to Aiken, Eliot seems to have reached a decision. On December 31, 1914, during a six-week vacation from classes, Eliot wrote from London: "Oxford is all very well, but I come back to London with great relief. I like London now. In Oxford I have the feeling that I am not quite alive—that my body is walking about with a bit of my brain inside it, and nothing else. As you know, I hate university towns and university people, who are the same everywhere, with pregnant wives, sprawling children, many books, and hideous pictures on the walls" (74). Eliot illustrated his feeling by drawing two outside bell pulls, one for "visitors" and the other for "professors and their wives." This second would "have no bell" and thus admit none of the undesirables. Eliot added this implausible (but revealing) exhortation: "Come let us desert our wives and fly to a land where there are Medici prints, nothing but concubinage and conversation." Sobering suddenly, Eliot spoke in his own voice: "Oxford is very pretty, but I don't like to be dead. I don't think I should stay there another year, in any case; but I should not mind being in London, to work at the British Museum" (74). Eliot next brought Aiken up to date on their mutual friends: "Weiner, like a great wonderful fat toad bloated with wisdom, has returned to Cambridge; Scofield Thayer . . . promises to be a fine dilettante and talker if he loses all literary ambition, has also gone to Cambridge to see Santayana" (75). Then comes the passage on nervous nocturnal ramblings previously discussed in Chapter 3, Section 2.

Eliot's letter to Aiken of February 25, 1915, is filled with uncertainty: "I do not know my own plans for the future." He had just received a telegram from Harvard telling him that he would be renominated for the Oxford fellowship: "Oxford I do not enjoy," Eliot complains, with its "execrable" food and climate, his "indigestion, constipation, and colds," and "the university atmosphere." Although he did not think he could ever "come to like England—a people which is satisfied with such disgusting food *is not* civilised"—he dreaded the notion of returning to Harvard: "the nausea of factory whistles at seven and twelve o'clock (one doesn't mind it so much at night—one doesn't *see*, then) and the college bell, and the people in Cambridge whom one fights against and who absorb one all the same." The diatribe turns at this point into a confession: "The great need is to know one's own mind, and I don't know that: whether I want to get married, and have a family, and live in America all my life, and compromise and conceal my opinions and forfeit my independence for the sake of my children's future; or save my money and retire at fifty to a table on the boulevard, regarding the world placidly through the fumes of an aperitif at 5 PM." After such a confession, Eliot seemed surprised, perhaps even frightened, by his frankness:

"How thin either life seems! And perhaps it is merely dyspepsia speaking" (87–88).

The most revealing of Eliot's comments about the uncertainty of his plans for the future are found in the January 6, 1915, letter (discussed above) that he wrote to his fellow student at Harvard, Norbert Weiner, then in Cambridge on a Sheldon Traveling Fellowship. The entire letter reads like a confession by Eliot that he finds himself preparing for a profession in which he can no longer believe. As Eliot felt his way through his criticism of philosophy, he made his way over to the alternative for him—art (or poetry), and the word "Value" provided a bridge: "Some philosophies are only a play upon this ambiguity of the word Reality. In a way the most valuable is the most real, and the beauty of a work of art is in this way more real to me than its ultimate (or relatively ultimate) physical constituents." Eliot was in effect revealing that he has learned what he calls "the lesson of relativism": "to avoid philosophy and devote oneself to either *real* art or *real* science. (For philosophy is an unloved guest in either company). Still, this would be to draw a sharp line, and relativism preaches compromise" (80).

Surprisingly, Eliot at this point in his thinking invoked the name of the one philosophy professor at Harvard that he was generally thought to have rejected: "For *me,* as for Santayana, philosophy is chiefly literary criticism and conversation about life; and you have the logic, which seems to me of great value. The only reason why relativism does not do away with philosophy altogether, after all, is that there is no such thing to abolish!" So much for the very field to which he had devoted several years of preparation for a lifetime career. If philosophy did not exist, what did? "There is art, and there is science. And there are works of art, and perhaps of science, which would never have occurred had not many people been under the impression that there was philosophy" (81).

Eliot broke the news to his advisers at Harvard, in a letter to his former professor J. H. Woods of January 28, 1915, writing that he had embarked on a radical revision of his dissertation. Eliot had come to Oxford on his Sheldon Traveling Fellowship in order to study under one of Bradley's most distinguished students, Harold H. Joachim, and after one term of study with him, Eliot reported for the first time that he had not received what he had anticipated: "I did not often really 'get anywhere' with [Joachim], though this failure was due no doubt as much to my fatal disposition toward scepticism as to his Hegelianism." Recognizing that he prefers "criticism" to "construction," Eliot decided to "recast" his thesis according to the more satisfying "historical aspect of philosophy." In a kind of confession, Eliot put the best light he could on his reversing directions in his work on Bradley: "I had great difficulty, even agony, with the first draft, owing to my attempt to reach a positive conclusion; and so I should like to turn it into a criticism and valuation of the Bradleian metaphysic—for it seems to me that those best qualified for such tasks are those who have held a doctrine and no longer hold it" (84).

4. New Friends and Old: Culpin, Blanshard, Pound, Lewis

In his letter of November 27, 1914, Eliot mentioned to his cousin Eleanor Hinkley that he was planning to spend a "fortnight" at the seashore with two new friends, "one an Amurrican, the other an Englishman" (72). After the seashore holiday, he wrote another letter (January 3, 1915) containing vivid descriptions of these new "friends": One was "the most intelligent of the Englishmen at Merton"; the other was "an American, who, if not intelligent, was at least an excellent butt for discourse, as he defended with great zeal all the great American fallacies, and exhibited all the typical American middle class confusion of thought." With zest, Eliot explained his meaning: this "typical American"—Brand Blanshard—was "anxious to be broadminded (that is, to be vague), to have wide interests (that is to say, diffuse ones), to be tolerant (of the wrong things) etc. . . . though I think he has come to regard me as an unscrupulous sophist—as I always took either the ultra conservative or the ultra radical view" (78). Evidently Eliot's time abroad had not mellowed his notions about his countrymen.

Eliot's English friend was Karl Henry Culpin, who, born in 1893, was some five years younger than Eliot. He was studying history and economics, and was born of a German father and an English mother. He was (according to an editor's note in the *Letters*) Eliot's "closest friend at Merton." Drawing in part on a letter Eliot wrote June 24, 1963, to R. H. C. Davis, describing his Oxford friends, the first of Eliot's biographers, Robert Sencourt, calls Eliot's friendship with Culpin one of "the deepest . . . of his life" (Sencourt, 46–48). Culpin was "of darkish complexion and normal physique. . . . As soon as Tom and Karl started talking to each other, each knew that he had found an ideal companion. The Yorkshireman's brain was brilliant enough to keep pace with the American's, and this exercise was the more stimulating because it was not centred on philosophy or literature but history and economics." When presented with a copy of Eliot's *Prufrock* volume, Culpin immediately recognized that "here was the great new poet of the age." Unfortunately, Culpin was called into the British army after his graduation and died on May 15, 1917, from the wounds he received near Fresnois. Much of Sencourt's information comes from Culpin's family, his mother and his sister Mary, both of whom continued to visit Eliot after Culpin's death. Sencourt was able to interview the Culpin family members in the writing of his biography (54–55).

The other vacationer at Swanage was Brand Blanshard, the "Amurrican" whom Eliot, slipping into Pound-speak, noted in his letter to his cousin. Blanshard was a Midwesterner and had attended the University of Michigan, and was, like Culpin, younger than Eliot. We know more about him not only because of Eliot's unflattering description, but also because he left two personal accounts of the seaside fortnight much later in life, the first ("Eliot in Memory") published in *The Yale Review*, 1965, and the other ("Eliot at Oxford") twenty years later, in *The Southern Review*, Autumn 1985. In the second of these, Blanshard clearly wished to evoke some of the flavor of the Oxford that he and Eliot experienced back in 1914–15: "The cab that a student bid for on getting off the train at Oxford was horse drawn, and horses pulled the streetcars up and down the High." When installed in a college— Merton, in the case of these three—"one was automatically a gentleman, for the class system was still strong: a man old enough perhaps to be your grandfather waited on you like a footman, built a fire daily in your grate, served in your rooms (and I mean rooms) a hearty English breakfast and a lunch of bread and cheese." Each morning "you were supposed to pull out" from under the bed a tin tub, refilled daily, "leap into [it], throw water over your quivering torso, and then rub down . . . a Spartan regimen . . . we . . . thrived on." The evening meal was served in the dining halls, "crowded with portraits of past students—Hobbes and Locke and Johnson and Wesley and Newman and Swinburne and Ruskin and Arnold and Gladstone and Asquith." Blanshard's "first impression of Eliot, an impression never removed, was that he was friendly, and ready with his smile [later he calls it "that Mona Lisa smile"], he was shy, reticent, and reserved" (Blanshard, EAO, 27–28, 32).

When Blanshard recalled that holiday with Culpin and Eliot, he remembered that they had engaged separate rooms in a house in the village and took meals in a dining room with a fireplace. One memory of Eliot fixed itself in Blanshard's mind: "Eliot's figure as he sat at the dining room table each morning with a huge volume of Russell and Whitehead's *Principia Mathematica* propped open before him. He had a certain facility in dealing with its kind of symbols; he said that manipulating them gave him a curious sense of power" (32). Blanshard's memories of the young Eliot at Oxford underscore Eliot's impressive scholarship. The "tag ends of Latin, Greek, and other tongues . . . strewed about his poems" really did mean that he was at home in the languages (Blanshard, EIM, 217).

But Blanshard also spoke of Eliot's being "at home on the water." He recalled "a race between two Merton fours in which Eliot stroke one boat and I was in the other. His boat won handily. He pulled a good oar." Blanshard concludes with the observation: "I don't think he found much more fun than I did in this sort of rowing; one could easily become a galley slave; and on a cold and rainy day it could be miserable. Still, it helped to keep us fit, and it made an excellent preface to tea and talk before a fire" (Blanshard, EAO, 33).

In both of his essays, Blanshard remembered Eliot as distant: "By temperament he was a born Englishman. He abominated indiscriminate sociability; he never wore his heart on his sleeve; he was reserved, shy, economical of speech, rather frostily formal of manner as a hedge against invading familiarity." Indeed, Eliot was aloof, and his "aloofness was at once his strength and his weakness. I used to feel that he sat apart from the rest of us, looking at us with his thoughtful, interested, appraising brown eyes, but with feelings that were singularly disengaged. This made it possible for him, as it did for Hegel, to view the *genus homo* with a curiously scientific objectivity." Toward the end of Eliot's life, much later than the Oxford days, Blanshard found his preferences bizarre: "His tastes, like his intellect, were fastidious and individual (at the last luncheon I had with him he ordered seagull's eggs); and when one's preferences are sharply and reflectively defined, the enjoyments of the many are likely to seem bleak. And so they were for Eliot. To some critics his poetry has seemed warm and full of pity. That is not my impression of the poet or his poetry" (Blanshard, EIM, 220).

During his Oxford year, Eliot seems to have sealed his relationship with Ezra Pound and to have begun his entry into Pound's fascinating circle of artists and "isms." In his February 2, 1915, letter to Pound in London, Eliot addressed his fellow American poet as "My dear Pound," and enclosed another of his poems for Pound to place ("Portrait of a Lady"). He reported to Pound that he had read his "article on the Vortex," and commented: "I distrust and detest Aesthetics, when it cuts loose from the Object, and vapours in the void, but you have not done that. The closer one keeps to the Artist's discussion of his technique the better, I think, and the only kind of art worth talking about is the art one happens to like." Eliot concluded his comment on Pound's "Vortex" piece with approval: "I was fearful lest you should hitch it up to Bergson or James or some philosopher, and was relieved to find that Vorticism was not a philosophy." He signed off "Thomas S. Eliot," and enclosed "one small verse" (already sent to Aiken), "Suppressed Complex." He said "it is not good, but everything else . . . is worse. . . . Burn it" (LTSE1, 86–87). One critic sees the eight-line poem as "a fantasy of male bravado," the title suggesting "disturbed behavior," with "a premonition of violation," and the male "flight" at the end having "ominous overtones for Eliot's marriage" (Mayer, 178–82).

At one point in this February 1915 letter, Eliot, talking as freely about his bawdy poems as he had to Aiken, reported the results of his sending some of his work, no doubt at the suggestion of Pound, to *Blast,* the new magazine that Wyndham Lewis had begun to publish: "I have corresponded with Lewis, but his puritanical principles seem to bar my way to Publicity. I fear that King Bolo and His Big Black Kween will never burst into print. I understand that Priapism, Narcissism etc., are not approved of" (*LTSE1,* 86). As we've noted in Chapter 5, Section 6, Eliot's characterization of his bawdy verses with these two revealing nouns—priapism and narcissism—strongly suggests homoeroticism. Indeed, Eliot's bawdy poetry portrayed all conceivable kinds of sexual behavior. *Blast,* the painter-author Wyndham Lewis's magazine, was founded to promote the movement he had "invented" called Vorticism. The movement is often connected to a similar movement in Italy labeled "futurism," and for Lewis related to his own way of painting—a kind of half-way abstraction. Only two issues of *Blast* appeared, one in 1914 and the other in 1915 (including Eliot's "Preludes" and "Rhapsody on a Windy Night"), but the beginning of the war was not a nourishing environment for such experimental movements.

Contributors to *Blast* included Pound, Rebecca West, and T. E. Hulme. As we have seen, Lewis had rejected some of Eliot's bawdy poems, but all three—Eliot, Pound, and Lewis—took delight in them, as is revealed in Lewis's January 1915 letter to Pound: "Eliot has sent me 'Bullshit' & the Ballad for Big Louise. They are excellent bits of scholarly ribaldry. I am longing to print them in *Blast;* but stick to my naive determination to have no 'Words Ending in -Uck, -Unt, and -Ugger'" (quoted in Carpenter, 261). These poems by the bawdy Eliot have been rescued for posterity in *Inventions of the March Hare* (1996).

Eliot met Lewis, who was to figure importantly in his early poetic career, in 1915 at the Pounds' apartment at 6 Holland Place Chambers in Kensington. The three men now together in London were all American born. Lewis had moved as a child to England and had received all his education there, and thus had a particularly European view of Americans. In his later recollection of this momentous first meeting, "Early London Environment," Lewis characterized the self-satisfied Ezra as good as saying: 'Yor ole uncle Ezz is wise to wot youse thinking. Waaal Wynd damn I'se teeling *yew,* he's a lot better'n he looks!" (Lewis, ELE, 26).

In that 1949 memoir, Lewis recalled that the meeting took place in the famed "triangular sitting room, in which all of Ezra's social life was transacted."

Lewis, who would go on to paint Eliot's portrait in 1949, described him with a painter's sensitivity: "As I entered the room I discovered an agreeable stranger parked up one of the sides of the triangle. He softly growled at me, as we shook hands. American. A graceful neck I noted, with what elsewhere [in *Blasting and Bombardiering*] I have described as 'a Gioconda smile.'" Lewis hastened to add: "Though not feminine—besides being physically large his personality visibly moved within the male pale—there *were* dimples in the warm dark skin; undoubtedly he used his eyes a little like a Leonardo. He was a very attractive fellow then; a sort of looks unusual this side of the Atlantic." Lewis was surprised at his own response: "I liked him, though I may say not at all connecting him with texts Ezra had shown me about some fictional character dreadfully troubled with old age, in which the lines (for it had been verse) 'I am growing old, I am growing old, I shall wear the bottoms of my trousers rolled'—a feature, apparently, of the humiliations reserved for the superannuated—I was unable to make head or tail of" (25).

In *Blasting and Bombardiering* (1937), Lewis described Eliot as speaking in a "prepossessing, ponderous, exactly-articulated drawl." He was, he said, "a very attractive young Prufrock indeed, with an alert and dancing eye— *moqueur* [mocker] to the marrow, bashfully ironic, blushfully *tacquineur* [teaser]." Lewis's image of Eliot as "a Prufrock to whom the mermaids would decidedly have sung," have sung "at the tops of their voices," depicts the young Eliot as one who might easily have become entangled in Romantic attachments (Lewis, BB, 282–83).

5. The Mystery of Emily Hale: "*The Aspern Papers* in Reverse"

Of Eliot's strong bonding with other men there is abundant evidence. When we try to shed light on the significant women in Eliot's life, we encounter first—Emily Hale. There is little reference to her in Eliot's published letters, and those to be found confined, with one exception, to his letters to his cousin Eleanor Hinkley (the exception is a letter to Conrad Aiken). Before we encounter Emily Hale's name in any of Eliot's letters, however, we find her mentioned in a footnote to his letter of April 26, 1911, to his cousin. The note identifies the cousin to whom he is writing as the daughter of his mother's sister who studied drama under the famed Professor George Pierce Baker of Radcliffe College, and "through amateur theatricals at [Eleanor's] family house, 1 Berkeley Place, Cambridge, Mass., . . . TSE met and fell in love with Emily Hale (1891–1969)" (*LTSE1*, 17). During his year in Oxford, Eliot's letters reveal two brief references to Emily: one in an October 14,

1914, letter to Eleanor, in which Eliot expresses interest in Emily's health as she seems to be launching her acting career; and the other in a November 21 letter to Conrad Aiken, in which Eliot asks Aiken to send her "some red or pink roses" at her first performance in a "Cambridge Dramatic Play" together with a card he encloses in the letter (64–65, 69–70).

And now we must break with chronology in discussing Emily Hale. Near the end of his life (Eliot died in 1965), in "the sixties," we are told, Eliot wrote a "private paper" from which Valerie Eliot quoted in the introduction to her edition of *The Letters of T. S. Eliot*. It seems a little strange that Eliot's widow would publish what Eliot appears to have designated a "private paper." Since Eliot had forbidden any authorized biographies, this paper seems to be directed at future unauthorized biographers. Indeed, Valerie Eliot was aware that Eliot had at one point decided to destroy all his letters, and it was only at her intervention (according to her) that Eliot relented. In their evenings of reading to each other, she writes: "I took every opportunity to introduce a poet's letters, until, eventually, he burst out laughing, and said he would relent on condition that I did the selecting and editing" (xv). But those letters from Emily to him he had burned in 1957. He had already burned the letters to and from his mother and brother upon their deaths in 1929 and 1947.

In her introduction Valerie Eliot tells us that "before he left for Europe in 1914, he told her [Emily] that he was in love with her. He had no reason to believe, from the way in which his declaration was received, that his feelings were returned 'in any degree whatever.' They exchanged a few letters, 'on a purely friendly basis,' while he was up at Oxford" (xvii). Those letters from Emily have not survived. But there was much correspondence with Emily Hale "between 1932 and 1947—when Vivien died after seven years in a mental home." This is of course the year Eliot became free to marry again—but did not. Valerie Eliot goes on to recount that "TSE liked to think [during the course of this correspondence] that his letters to her would be preserved and made public fifty years after they were dead. He was, however, 'disagreeably surprised' when she informed him in 1956 that she was giving the letters to Princeton University Library during their lifetime." And then, Valerie Eliot goes on, continuing to quote from the private paper: "It seemed to him 'that her disposing of the letters in that way at that time threw some light upon the kind of interest which he took, or had come to take, in these letters. *The Aspern Papers* in reverse.'" When he heard in January 1957 from the librarian that the letters would be sealed until fifty years from the death of the survivor [2019], Eliot asked "a friend to incinerate Emily Hale's letters to him" (xvi).

What was Eliot upset about? He had already admitted thinking that both sides of the correspondence would eventually be open to the public fifty years after the survivor's death. So why did he resent her placing his letters to her in a library where their preservation would be assured? His phrase, "*The Aspern Papers* in reverse," is revealing. In Henry James's story the narrator, an admirer and critic in search of more material relating to the renowned, long-dead American poet Jeffrey Aspern, duplicitously tries to obtain the papers from the poet's aged mistress, Juliana, who guards them possessively. He goes to Venice where she and her middle-aged niece Tina are living in an ancient, run-down palace and rents rooms there, intending to flatter the niece into aiding him. One night Juliana catches him ransacking her desk and calls him "a publishing scoundrel!" He flees, ashamed, and Juliana dies from the strain. Tina, trying to be true to Juliana's wishes, offers the papers to him but only as a "relative," meaning only if he marries her. He leaves in alarm—and when he returns, conflicted but ready to accept, she tells him that she has burned the papers, "one by one." In the end, the papers are burned by the one whose affections had been trifled with. In Eliot's case, it is he the poet who burns the letters, while Emily, in giving them to the library, fulfills his own wishes to preserve them.

What motive does Eliot ascribe to Emily? "Her disposing of the letters in that way" showed "the kind of interest she took, or had come to take, in these letters. *The Aspern Papers* in reverse." Did he think she was spiteful at Eliot's not marrying her? Or did he feel guilt at how he had treated her? He may have unwittingly taken on the mantle of his beloved Henry James, who also enacted a sort of *Aspern Papers* in reverse.

James's biographer Leon Edel has written that the "evil" in the tale "lay in the invasion of privacy, the failure to enter into human feeling." He draws comparisons between the work and the life: James reacted to the suicide of his close friend Constance Fenimore Woolfson by racing to Venice to destroy their correspondence. "His task was the opposite of his narrator in *The Aspern Papers*. To make away with, rather than preserve" (Edel, *HJ*, 237, 365). Whatever Eliot meant by the analogy at the end of his life, we do know that at the time of Eliot's year at Oxford, he was, according to his private paper, in love with Emily Hale.

Various biographies have treated the relationship. The first to be published on Eliot (*T. S. Eliot: A Memoir*, 1971) was written by Robert Sencourt, a long-time friend of Eliot's, and does not discuss Emily Hale. The next biography, T. S. Matthews's *Great Tom* (1974), tries to come to terms with the nature of Eliot's relationship with her. In introducing his extensive speculation, Matthews suggests the difficulty of summoning the right words: "It was more than a friendship, definitely not a flirtation, something a little less than a love affair but very like a long engagement. A forty-eight-year-long smile and shake of the hand? Not to Emily's mind, and not on Emily's part. She was his oldest friend, and perhaps his closest" (Matthews, 139).

Lyndall Gordon, whose *Eliot's Early Years* appeared in 1977, writes: "It is not yet known how deeply Eliot fell in love with Emily Hale, but Helen Gardner suggests that it was she who inspired Eliot's nostalgia, twenty years later in the rose-garden of Burnt Norton [a house in Gloucestershire and title of the first of *Four Quartets*], for his youthful love and another life that might have been. Emily Hale never married. She became a teacher of drama . . . and over the course of her life exchanged about two thousand letters with Eliot. This is little to go on, but it is worth noting that the rose-garden is the last of several similar garden pieces in which Eliot recalled a moment of romantic intoxication with a woman" (Gordon, EEY, 55). In the second volume of her biography, *Eliot's New Life* (1988), Gordon included extensive discussion of the relationship, and a list of Eliot's works for which Hale presumably was in some sense "T. S. E.'s muse." Her chapter 4, "Lady of Silences," was devoted entirely to Emily Hale (Gordon, ENL, 146–90). By the time Gordon wrote her revised biography, combining her first two volumes in one, entitled *T. S. Eliot: An Imperfect Life* (1998), her chapter 7 dealing solely with Hale was significantly given the title "Enter Beatrice" (Gordon, EIL, 233–83).

Appearing between Gordon's first two volumes was Peter Ackroyd's *T. S. Eliot* (1984). He points out Eliot's refusal of friend Mary Trevelyan's 1949 marriage proposal. In a long letter to her, Eliot "explained that his past affection for someone else (no doubt Emily Hale) rendered any new relationship impossible for him" (Ackroyd, 306; a footnote on p. 362 credits Humphrey Carpenter for the information). Eliot's refusal of Trevelyan's marriage proposal occurred two years after Vivien's death. Why hadn't Eliot married Emily Hale? Ackroyd notes that they were so close that in 1936, the one year when she didn't come to England to visit him, he went to America (229).

There are any number of problems for a biographer who sets out to portray Emily Hale as the great love of Eliot's life. There is, to begin with, his first marriage in 1915 to Vivien Haigh-Wood, shortly after he had presumably "fallen in love with" Emily Hale, and perhaps even had proposed. And to complicate the problem further, there is Eliot's almost inexplicable second marriage in 1957 to his secretary at Faber and Faber, several decades his junior: he was sixty-eight, she was thirty. Emily Hale lived until 1969 (Gordon, EIL, 527).

In his study of the early poetry as "essentially a psychic poetry," John T. Mayer, in *T. S. Eliot's Silent Voices* (1989), provides a perceptive analysis. He points out that "Eliot's highly moralistic upbringing in a world dominated by women and his own innate naiveté inhibited his developing a mature view of sexuality. . . . For much of his life, Eliot seems to have thought of sex as the 'coupling of beasts.'" Further, Mayer asserts that Eliot's mother "lived the grandfather's code of self-denial and passed on its Manichaean tendencies to her son. Untouchable, she is the primal model of the Idealized Woman of the early poetry, and after Eliot met Emily Hale, she fuses with the Mother to form a composite figure who metamorphoses into the remote and pure Lady of religious inspiration in the later works, symbol of the negative way, the way of denial." Mayer concludes: "Against this backdrop, it is not entirely surprising that Eliot portrays Woman as devouring Body or bloodless Spirit, repulsive Flesh or Abstract Ideal, Threat or Wraith. In this poetry, a real woman is not to be found" (Mayer, 36–37). It appears that Mayer's theory explains why, on the death of his alienated wife in 1947, Eliot did not seize the opportunity to marry Emily Hale: a conventional marriage leading to sex would have toppled the idealized lady from her pedestal.

By the end of his Oxford year, Eliot had through Pound met a number of important figures in the world of the arts, poetry, and publishing. And he had seen some of his major early poems published, not the least of which was the appearance of "The Love Song of J. Alfred Prufrock" in *Poetry* magazine in June 1915. Although he found time for the academic study of philosophy at Oxford and for a start on the major revision of his doctoral thesis on the philosopher F. H. Bradley, he had lost his interest—and in some sense his belief—in philosophy. By the time he finished his work at Oxford, he was confronted with the critical decision of his life—to pursue an academic career in America or to stay in London and write poetry. There is no sign that he was drawn back to Boston because of the presence there of Emily Hale.

1915

AN INEXPLICABLE MARRIAGE AND THE CONSEQUENCES

1. A Sudden Marriage at the Registry Office

In Eliot's letter to his cousin Eleanor Hinkley, April 24, 1915, we find the first mention of the woman who would become his wife only two months later—on June 26. She was one of several English girls his age he had met at the dances he attended at the large hotels on Saturday nights—two especially were "very good dancers." Eliot was quite the dancer himself, "dip[ing] in [his] one-step" and the two English girls "caught the American style very quickly." Eliot dined and took tea with them, finding them "quite different" from any he had known in America or in London—"charmingly sophisticated (even 'disillusioned') without being hardened." Eliot went on to comment revealingly (given his father's strictures against smoking) that he took "great pleasure in seeing women smoke" and all of them apparently did. The two girls Eliot had come to know had names he found "amusing": "Phyllis" and "Vivien" (LTSE I, 97). Vivien was born Vivienne Haigh-Wood, the name that appeared on official records, including the marriage documents. She had changed the spelling, and was called both. For consistency, we will use "Vivien" throughout. Shortly after the posting of this letter, Vivien would become Mrs. Thomas Stearns Eliot. Eliot would almost instantly discover how little he knew about the "English girl" he found himself bound to until his separation from her some eighteen years later.

But besides meeting at dances, we also know that Eliot had met Vivien at a luncheon in the rooms of his friend and fellow student at the Milton Academy and Harvard, Scofield Thayer, then completing two years of postgraduate study at Oxford. Vivien, who was working as a governess in Cambridge the winter of 1914–15, was a close friend of Thayer's cousin Lucy (Seymour-Jones, 17). We know that all four spent time punting on the River Cherwell. One year after the marriage, Eliot wrote to Thayer on May 7, 1916: "Can it be that a year ago you and I were charming the eyes (and ears) of Char-flappers from one virginal punt, I by my voracity for bread and butter and you by Sidneian showers of discourse upon Art, Life, Sex and Philosophy?" (*LTSE1*, 137). A sadder memory of these days would occur in Vivien's diary for July 28, 1935, when, now abandoned by Eliot, she visited Oxford alone and recalled punting on the river with Lucy and him (Eliot, Vivien, UD). One of her surviving sketches is of a punt moored on the river under a willow (Seymour-Jones, 2; the sketch is reproduced there and in Hastings's *Tom and Viv*). "The River Girl" is what she was called by "Eliot's social friends (Lady Ottoline Morrell, St. John Hutchinson and his wife, Virginia and Leonard Woolf, the Sitwells, the Aldous Huxleys)" (Spender, *TSE*, 46). In her biography of Vivien, *Painted Shadow: A Life of Vivienne Eliot* (2001), Carole Seymour-Jones quotes Osbert Sitwell's unpublished memoir for a contemporary definition: "'River-Girl' was a term used by the contemporary press to describe 'that kind of young person—the rather pretty young girl who could be seen, accompanied by an undergraduate, floating down the river in a punt on a summer afternoon.'" And she notes that Stephen Spender found "a trace of mockery in this name. She had a history of illness and 'nerves'" (quoted in Seymour-Jones, 16–17). But Spender is writing in 1976 and the young Eliot could have had no such thoughts or knowledge.

The record shows that on June 26, 1915, at the Hampstead Registry Office, in a northwest suburb of London, Thomas Stearns Eliot, Bachelor, and Vivienne Haigh-Wood, Spinster, appeared and signed the register. They gave their ages as twenty-six, though Vivien had already turned twenty-seven. They were accompanied by two witnesses, her aunt Lillia C. Symes and her friend Lucy Thayer. Eliot signed himself as "of no occupation" and listed his father's occupation as "Brick Manufacturer." Vivien's father was described as an "Artist (Painter)" (*LTSE1*, 98–99). What is clear is that the marriage had been hasty, the ceremony was civil, not religious, and no members of the immediate family of either bride or groom had been present. Indeed, the families had not even been informed in advance of the event.

Although the facts are sparse, there has been no lack of speculation about the marriage. Perhaps the most bizarre such guesswork is that of Logan Pearsall Smith, who reportedly told Cyril Connolly: "Eliot had compromised Miss Haigh-Wood . . . and then felt obliged as an American gentleman, the New England code being stricter than ours, to propose to her. This would account for the furtive nature of the ceremony, and for his subsequent recoiling from his conjugal privileges" (Matthews, 43–44). Anyone familiar with Eliot would have known that he was incapable of "compromising" any woman. And there is no evidence elsewhere, in Vivien's extensive diaries for example, of such a "compromise." The diaries, it is true, only cover 1914, 1919, and the years from their separation, 1932–33, through 1936. Still there is no recollection of such a compromise; rather there is evidence that Vivien had already had sexual affairs.

Eliot's own comments about his marriage shift radically over the years, beginning with excited pleasure and moving quickly to expressions of some degree of mental, emotional, and even physical pain. In the "private paper" discussed at the end of Chapter 7, written near the end of his life, a kind of *apologia,* he wrote as if in answer to a question posed by his second wife: "To explain my sudden marriage to Vivienne Haigh-Wood would require a good many words, and yet the explanation would probably remain unintelligible. I was still, as I came to believe a year later, in love with Miss Hale. I cannot however make that assertion with any confidence: it may have been merely my reaction against my misery with Vivienne and desire to revert to an earlier situation" (*LTSE1,* xvii). It is astonishing how what appears at first glance to be in the nature of a confession or revelation is almost meticulously undercut by Eliot's repeated expression of uncertainty about his motives.

He continues, however, with statements of certainty: "I was very immature for my age, very timid, very inexperienced. And I had a gnawing doubt, which I could not altogether conceal from myself, about my choice of a profession—that of a university teacher of philosophy. I had had three years in the Harvard Graduate School, at my father's expense, preparing to take my Doctorate in Philosophy: after which I should have found a post somewhere in a college or university." The tone here is persuasive, and is confirmed by the various letters we have reviewed in Chapter 7. Then he touches on the emotions that were to inform his actions: "Yet my heart was not in the study, nor had I any confidence in my ability to distinguish myself in this profession. I must still have yearned to write poetry" (xvii). Is it not possible that his motivation for marriage, conscious or unconscious, was to make it impossible for his family to compel him to become an American academic, thus becoming what he did not want to be in a field in which he no longer believed in a country in which he no longer chose to live?

Looking back upon that turning point in his life, Eliot pays tribute to the indisputable catalyst in his poetic development: "Then in 1914 . . . my meeting with Ezra Pound changed my life. He was enthusiastic about my poems, and gave me such praise and encouragement as I had long since ceased to hope for. I was happier in England, even in wartime, than I had been in America: Pound urged me to stay . . . and encouraged me to write verse again" (xvii; ellipses in *Letters*). There follows finally a direct answer to the question that had started Eliot down the path of this broad review of the past: "I think that all I wanted of Vivienne was a flirtation or a mild affair: I was too shy and unpracticed to achieve either with anybody. I believe that I came to persuade myself that I was in love with her simply because I wanted to burn my boats and commit myself to staying in England. And she persuaded herself (also under the influence of Pound) that she would save the poet by keeping him in England" (xvii).

At the end of this private paper, in a single sentence, Eliot seems indeed to bare his soul: "To her the marriage brought no happiness . . . to me, it brought the state of mind out of which came *The Waste Land*" (xvii; ellipsis in *Letters*). Of course, *The Waste Land* was some seven years away, but here in 1915 is, in the profoundest emotional sense, its beginning. Compare Eliot's contemporaneous remark to Conrad Aiken already quoted: "I have *lived* through material for a score of long poems in the last six months" (126). Eliot cites Pound as the individual most responsible in persuading him to stay in England and write poetry; either overtly or covertly, Pound seems to have been behind Eliot's otherwise inexplicable act. The gist of Eliot's private paper is that at its deepest level, his motive for marrying was to ensure that, instead of returning to America for a career in the teaching of philosophy, he could stay in England for a career in literature. Indeed, Eliot expresses just that sentiment in a newly discovered letter (which was brought to my attention by James Loucks in an e-mail, December 9, 1998), reported in the November 2, 1991, edition of the *New York Times* by Craig R. Whitney: "In 1946, Eliot wrote to console [his friend] Mrs. [Geoffrey] Tandy on the collapse of her own marriage. He said he had made 'a complete mess of my personal life' and married 'the wrong woman.' . . . He did so, he said, to escape from 'a maddening feeling of failure and inferiority' caused by 'trying to make myself into a philosopher and future professor of philosophy'" (*NYT,* 13). The marriage ultimately helped Eliot defy his parents' determined plans for their son's future; but it no doubt had unforeseen consequences, as we shall see, for Eliot's psyche as well as his physical well-being.

2. Who Was Vivien?

Vivien Haigh-Wood was the eldest child of Rose and Charles Haigh-Wood, wealthy middle- to upper-class landowners. Her father was a portrait and landscape painter and her brother, eight years her junior, was the right age to be caught up quickly in the Great War as an infantry officer. Her father and his family had houses in Hampstead, in Anglesey, and other properties in Dublin; the family was clearly at a social level in which Eliot felt comfortable. Since Charles Haigh-Wood was in effect a free spirit, he and his family traveled frequently abroad. And indeed it was on a family trip to Switzerland that Vivien met Lucy Thayer, who later, through her cousin Scofield, then at Oxford, had been instrumental in Vivien's introduction to Eliot. Vivien herself was, at the beginning, lively and high spirited, a good bit shorter than Eliot (who was about six feet) but trim and graceful. She was a good swimmer and an accomplished ballroom dancer. One of the fullest descriptions of Vivien at this time is provided by Brigit Patmore, who knew them and even went dancing with them at the time: "[Vivien] was slim and rather small, but by no means insignificant. Light brown hair and shining gray eyes. The shape of her face was narrowed to a pointed oval chin and her mouth was good—it did not split up her face when she smiled, but was small and sweet enough to kiss. Added to this, she did not quiver, as so sensitive a person might, but shimmered with intelligence" (Patmore, 84–85). As we shall see, this portrait is not one that other of Eliot's friends and associates of the time would agree with—but it might have been what Eliot saw when he first encountered her.

Patmore gives an even fuller description of Eliot himself in these early years: "T. S. Eliot was unspectacular and one hunted for an explanation of his undoubted force. But no, it was not 'tender rancour' [Henry James's description of Hawthorne]; in a gentle way he was pleased with nobody—all well short of his desired perfection—but this unending judgment was unspoken." From this assessment of Eliot's general demeanor, Patmore goes on to paint the physical details: "His mouth had turned-up corners, not with merriment, but some kind of restriction—perhaps the bit between his teeth—for he was careful never to say anything indiscreet. Yet how winning and cordial he could be when the wide mouth smiled and the lines from both sides of the strong, well-shaped nose looked humorous and really genial." There was, however, one feature that did not join in this cordiality: "But the eyes, not yet inquisitorial as they became later, but cold dark grey, wide open and suiting finely the forehead so wide and high, but not too high." And finally the sum: "As he was tall, Tom's head did not look out of proportion, as it would have in a smaller man. He was distinguished in appearance, perhaps handsome but one longed for a grace, a carelessness which would have let him approach beauty" (84).

We know from her diary that Vivien, before she met Eliot, had had a passionate affair with a man called B. (one Charles Buckle). According to her diary entry for February 26, 1914, she became engaged to him. The private encounters of the two were frequent and about evenly divided between times for quarreling and times for making love, leaving her either exhausted or exhilarated. She shows by the frequency with which she declares, without reference to her lover, her days or nights to be "horrid," "beastly," "hideous," or other similar epithets that she is finding living itself intensely unpleasant. In her diary she describes suffering a great number of unnamed illnesses during this short period that keep her in bed for hours or days at a time, one of which had to do with abnormal menstruation. Indeed, she seems to have been, whether hypochondriacal or not, quite unstable emotionally. The affair came to a conclusion when Buckle enlisted in the Army and went off to fight in the war (Eliot, Vivien, UD, February–September 1914). The diary reveals an immature woman who, whatever physical illnesses she had, was self-centered and mentally unstable.

Vivien's mother had already spoken in opposition to her marriage to Buckle, for she believed that Vivien suffered from the then frequently diagnosed "moral insanity" and thus was unfit to marry or have children. Seymour-Jones states: "'Moral insanity,' a term more usually applied to women than men, was short-hand for a precocious sexual awareness leading to promiscuity" (Seymour-Jones, 14). There is no doubt that Vivien had suffered from real tuberculosis, requiring many surgeries, irregular and painful menstruations, and was given drugs for hysteria and anxiety at an early age. The wonder is that she excelled in swimming and the dance. And she would go on to marry despite her mother's concerns. Perhaps, as Seymour-Jones notes, "For Vivien, marriage was a revenge upon Rose Haigh-Wood as much as it was—for Tom—upon Charlotte Eliot," another strong-willed mother (8–14, 78).

After the marriage, the bride and groom notified their parents. Vivien sent a telegram to hers; Eliot no doubt at the same time cabled his parents. In his July 2 letter to his brother, written only some six days after his marriage, he assumed that his brother knew about his marriage ("changes in my plans").

Although we do not know explicitly what his father said in his return cable, there can be little doubt that he made it clear to his son that he must return to America to discuss his future, both personal and financial, in the light of his unexpected marriage.

But in the month before Eliot departed for America, much had happened in his marriage. Although Vivien supported his commitment to writing poetry and helped him with her stenographic skills, deep down he seems to have been unhappy. His family was displeased with the marriage, and Eliot was still dependent on them for his living expenses abroad. And he no doubt feared the wrath of his father. But the unhappiness, or disillusion, was surely in some sense sexual, and this was connected with Vivien's chronic illnesses. It seems likely that the marriage was never consummated, because of his, not her, failure. Eliot's early poems showed him to be distrustful of women, and one who referred to sexual intercourse as the "coupling of animals." Apparently, the primary purpose of the marriage, as Eliot explained to Valerie Eliot years later, was to enable him to undermine his father's strong determination that Eliot return from England and become a philosophy professor in America. He would often observe that he owed much to Vivien because in the final analysis it was she who enabled him to stay in London and to become the poet he wanted to become.

3. A Flurry of Correspondence, a Day of Decision

In what seems the longest letter (five pages) included in the first volume of Eliot's *Letters,* Ezra Pound wrote on June 28, 1915, two days after Eliot's marriage, to Tom's father Henry Ware Eliot: "Your son asked me to write this letter, I think he expects me to send you some sort of apologia for the literary life in general, and for London literary life in particular." Pound cited himself as the best example: "I am as well off as various of my friends who had plugged away at law, medicine, and preaching. At any rate I have had an infinitely more interesting life." In placing the young Eliot in the literary scene of the time, Pound assumed a literary knowledge on the part of the father that was probably warranted and compared his son briefly with any number of other poets past and present, notably Edgar Lee Masters, Robert Browning, Robert Frost, and of course Ezra Pound. He encapsulated modernist poetics when he concluded: "T. S E. has gone farther and, begun with the much more difficult job of setting his 'personae' in modern life, with the discouragingly 'unpoetic' modern surroundings." Moreover, T. S. E. is, as had been said of Pound, "that rare thing among modern poets, a scholar."

This trait, the learned scholar Ezra Pound asserted, meant "having matter and volume enough in one to keep on writing more and more interestingly, with increasing precision and development" (*LTSE1*, 99–101).

So much for Eliot's poetic talent. Why does he need to stay in London? Primarily for "an international hearing." And then, alluding to George Moore, Pound wrote: "The situation has been very well summed up in the sentence: 'Henry James stayed in Paris and read Turgenev and Flaubert, Mr. Howells returned to America and read Henry James." In addition there is, on the practical side, the lower cost of living in England, availability of the British Museum for the scholarly inclined, access to both American and English publications in London, and so forth: "If a man is doing the fine thing and the rare thing, London is the only possible place for him to exist. Only here is there a disciplinary body of fine taste, of powerful writers who 'keep the editors under,' who make it imperative that a publisher act in accordance, occasionally, with some dictates other than those of sheer commercialism." Of course he urged Eliot to cultivate American editors, assuring Eliot's father that Pound would use his influence to get his work recognized in London (102–3).

Although Pound did not refer to Eliot's marriage, he wrote with the knowledge that Eliot's father had demanded his return to America for consultation. As he closed his lengthy letter, Pound turned more and more to a discussion of money, specifying that for a decent start a man needs "five hundred dollars for the first year and two hundred and fifty for the second" (103–4). Pound was clearly aware here that Eliot's father held important cards in his hand: he could increase, continue, or eliminate the small allowance that he provided Eliot to supplement his fellowship from Harvard.

The rather penniless newlyweds were living with her parents in Hampstead at this time, as the return address on Eliot's correspondence up to his July 24 departure for America shows. In his letter of July 2 to his brother, Eliot revealed Henry to have been a co-conspirator: "You know, however, what I have always wanted, and I am sure that it will seem natural enough to you. The only really surprising thing is that I should have had the force to attempt it, and when you know Vivien, I am sure that you will not be surprised at that either."

The word "either" here makes it clear that what he "has always wanted" (which Henry has always known) was to locate permanently abroad. When Eliot stated that the "only really surprising thing is that I should have had the force to attempt it" he reveals that his motive for marriage was to assure his residence abroad. He tells his brother, not that his love was so strong that it justified his action, but rather: "I know that you will agree that the responsibility and independent action has been and will be just what I needed." In short, the break with his father (and mother) was the supreme feature for him in what he has done. But though Vivien did not come first in his thinking, he realized that she was of considerable importance and he had a considerable responsibility: "Now my only concern is how I can make her perfectly happy, and I think I can do that by being myself infinitely more fully than I ever have been. I am much less suppressed, and more confident, than I ever have been" (104). Note Eliot's use of the word "suppressed" as defining his emotional/mental state before marriage (it bears a probable if indirect relation to his poem "Suppressed Complex," discussed above).

The bulk of Eliot's letter to Henry was taken up with suggestions as to how his brother might contact various American magazines to publish his reviews, articles, or even "letters from abroad" covering literary events in England or France. After many specific suggestions—the *Atlantic Monthly, The Smart Set, Century, Harper's,* the *New Republic*—Eliot draws himself up sharply: "Forgive the exclusively practical tone of this letter. I feel more alive than I ever have before. We are anxious that mother and father should come over to see us, and I hope you will use your influence, as I do not want *anything* but possibly his business to interfere." At moments in this letter, Eliot seems downright giddy. At the close, he comes back to his new wife to mention that he wants to send Henry her picture soon: "Vivien is not very well at present, and this has knocked her out completely, so I do not want one taken yet." The only reasonable antecedent to "this" is the marriage: in other words, the marriage has "knocked her out completely" (104–6). A reference to her being in one state of illness or another became a refrain in almost every letter Eliot wrote to family members and friends during their marriage. Vivien appended her own note, sure that they can depend on Henry for help, feeling that she knows him, and hoping he will write to her. (This was the beginning of a correspondence between them which would have her tellingly close her letter of August 23, 1921: "Good-bye Henry. And *be personal,* you must be personal, or else it's no good period. Nothing's any good" [466].)

One acquaintance, Bertrand Russell, was not only informed of the marriage but was invited to dinner in order to meet the bride. The dinner took place on July 9, 1915, only two weeks after the event. Russell was impressed by Vivien and would figure in important if ambiguous ways in the life of the Eliots during the first years of their marriage. He gave one of the most vivid accounts of the Eliots at this period in a letter to his intimate friend and sometime lover, Ottoline Morrell: "Friday evg. I dined with my Harvard pupil, Eliot, and his bride. I expected her to be terrible, from his mysteriousness;

but she was not so bad. She is light, a little vulgar, adventurous, full of life—an artist I think he said, but I should have thought her an actress. He is exquisite & listless." So far the account is descriptive, but it suddenly purports to quote Vivien in remarks that would hardly have been spoken aloud at the dinner table: "She says she married him to stimulate him, but finds she can't do it. Obviously he married in order to be stimulated. I think she will soon be tired of him. She refuses to go to America to see his people, for fear of submarines. He is ashamed of his marriage, and very grateful if one is kind to her. He is the Miss Sands type of American" (Russell, *A*, 278). Ethel Sands was an American and, as a lesbian, lived abroad and became friends with many of the Bloomsberries. Since this letter was written some days after the dinner, it is possible that Russell would have found an occasion, given his aroused interest, to talk with Vivien. He later came to the financial rescue of the Eliots by letting them live in a room of his London flat.

Eliot apparently spent July 10, 1915—a day of decision—writing a number of letters, some having to do with business, others with his plans for the future. In a brief letter to the editor of *Poetry* magazine in Chicago, Harriet Monroe, he acknowledged receipt of payment for "The Love Song of J. Alfred Prufrock," which she had published in the June issue of her magazine (*LTSE1*, 106). The sum, eight guineas, though not extraordinarily high, would have helped convince Eliot that he could somehow stake out a living while continuing on a writing career.

A second letter addressed to Mrs. Jack Gardner was in answer to his inquiries about their mutual friend, Matthew Prichard. Eliot wrote that he was glad to hear of Prichard's whereabouts, that he had been in touch with Henry Furst (who had inspired his previous letter to Mrs. Jack), and that he has seen another mutual friend recently, Richard Fisher. From this growing list of mutual acquaintances, it is clear that Eliot's involvement while he was at Harvard with Mrs. Jack's large circle of unconventional, tradition-defying friends was much deeper than heretofore realized. He broke the news of his marriage: "You said once that marriage is the greatest test in the world. I know now that you were right, but now I welcome the test instead of dreading it. It is much more than a test of sweetness of temper, as people sometimes think; it is a test of the whole character and every action. This is what I have discovered." To this ambiguous statement Eliot added: "I know that saying this, more than anything I can tell you about Vivien, and about my happiness, will show you that I have done the best thing." Ambiguity seems added to ambiguity. He announced that he has "changed [his] plans," that he wants "to live in London" primarily because London "is the best place to be" for anyone bent on a literary career (107–8).

Eliot wrote yet two more letters this same day, July 10, to two of his professors at Harvard, J. H. Woods and L. B. R. Briggs. He informed Professor Woods that he was withdrawing his application for an assistantship at Harvard for the coming academic year. He explained: "My reason for resigning is that I wish now to remain in London and engage in literary work. This may perhaps seem a surprising choice and is admittedly a great risk— still it is much worse to be deterred from anything by fear, and I shall try it out. It is what I wanted to do before." Eliot added that he has already made a beginning: "Now I have made a few professional connections and am anxious to start the battle, with an initial literary capital of eight guineas from *Poetry* in Chicago." Eliot's choice of metaphor—war—reveals his fierce determination in a "battle" in which there are winners and losers, and in which propaganda (in the journals and little magazines) plays a part. Finally, almost as an afterthought, Eliot mentioned the change in his situation: "I wish also to tell you that on the 26th June I was married quite privately to Miss Vivien Haigh-Wood of London. Our marriage was hastened by events connected with the war" (108–9).

Eliot's letter to Professor Briggs was a bit more formal, a "final report" on his work at Oxford. But he added at the end that he would not continue his work at Harvard but would remain in England to pursue a literary career. And in a curt last paragraph he announced his marriage and the name of the bride, indicating that the "marriage was accelerated by events connected with the war" (109–10). This vague explanation may well have satisfied Eliot's professors, but it was not an explanation that his family would have accepted.

On the night before he was to sail alone to America, July 23, Eliot wrote a letter to his father and gave it to Vivien to be sent should anything happen to the ship on which Eliot was traveling. Transatlantic travel was, of course, dangerous during the war. In it, he asked his father to give his wife the $5,000 insurance taken out for him: "She will need it. . . . Her own family are in very straitened circumstances owing to the war, and I know that her pride would make her want to earn her own living." Eliot affirmed his love of Vivien: "Now that we have been married a month, I am *convinced* that she has been the one person for me. She has everything to give that I want, and she gives it. I owe her everything. I have married her on nothing, and she knew it and was willing, for my sake. She had nothing to gain by marrying me." At the end of the letter Eliot noted: "She has not seen this. I will seal it and give it her to keep in case of emergency" (110–11). The letter was found unopened in Vivien's papers (Seymour-Jones, 593).

4. An Unhappy Visit Home (Gloucester, July 24–September 4), a Disastrous Honeymoon (Eastbourne, September 4–10)

Eliot's ship embarked on its voyage on July 24 and fortunately did not encounter enemy submarines. By August 5 Eliot was writing Conrad Aiken a letter from Eastern Point, Gloucester, Massachusetts, telling him all the news—including his marriage "on June 26 to Miss Vivien Haigh-Wood of London England." He had already talked with his family about his plans for the future, and seems to have made some concessions; but in spite of any promises he had made to them, his determination to stay in England as revealed in this letter seems unshaken (no doubt unbeknownst to them): "I mean to try to go back there to live, and have a job in a school for next year in point of fact; but I have agreed to my family's wish that I should complete my work and take my Ph.D., so it's not yet certain whether I stay this winter or return for it later." The teaching job Eliot referred to in his letter was at a primary school, High Wycombe, outside London. Near the end of his letter to Aiken, Eliot turned abruptly to his fundamental problem: "What I want is MONEY! $! £!! We are hard up! War!" The remark is half-serious, half frivolous, as it is followed by exclamatory nonsense: his concocted list of what he wanted to "BLAST" (the Kaiser, American ambassadors, the Democrats) and what he wanted to "BLESS" (Constantinople, T. S. Eliot, Harriet [Monroe]) (*LTSE1*, 111).

During his brief time in Gloucester Eliot wrote to his old classmate Scofield Thayer, on August 9, responding to a communication from Thayer—barely able to control his temper. In it Eliot scolded Thayer for apparently accusing him of marrying the woman Thayer had chosen for himself. Of course it was through his acquaintance with Thayer, and in Thayer's rooms at Oxford, that Eliot had first met Vivien. Eliot said that he could not understand why Thayer was "nettled" because he had never given Eliot—nor even Vivien—the impression that he was "in the slightest degree" in pursuit of her: "I presumed that I had wounded your vanity rather than thwarted your passion. If I was in error, at least Time (let us say) is the anodyne of disappointment rather than the separation of friends" (112).

Evidently Thayer wrote back telling Eliot that he was entirely wrong in his assumption about Thayer's feelings for Vivien. Eliot replied in a September 4 letter written while on his honeymoon at Eastbourne, apologizing for his "shabby letter" and asking Thayer to accept his "regrets for a petty irritation which should have evaporated long" before he wrote it. In this letter Eliot took care to give Thayer his future address so that they could keep in touch (phrasing the information in such a way as to suggest the intimacy he had developed with the distinguished British philosopher):"My address (anyhow till Christmas) will be care of Bertie Russell, 34 Russell Chambers, Bury Street, W. C. He is lending us his flat for a time" (113). Son of a wealthy family, Thayer would later become owner of the *Dial* and figure importantly in Eliot's poetic career.

Early in his command appearance at Gloucester, Eliot had gone to nearby Harvard and met with two of his professors, Herbert Palmer and Ralph Barton Perry, and had told them of his plans not only to complete his Ph.D., but also to teach at a primary school in England. In an August 16 letter from Gloucester to Professor J. H. Woods, Eliot reported that Palmer and Perry had thought there would be difficulties in the academic year ahead for him to both teach and attempt to complete his dissertation and prepare for his final orals—but that he thought he had no other choice. The alternate plan, proposed by his professors, was for Eliot to return to America in September and finish all the work on his degree at Harvard—perhaps with some kind of assistantship, probably at Wellesley (which had been discussed in earlier correspondence). But Eliot pointed out two objections to the alternate plan: he had made a commitment to the English school's headmaster that he could not easily abrogate; and the condition of his wife needed his attention: "Unfortunately I have just had word that my wife is very ill in London, so I must go at once, sailing Saturday. I do not anticipate that her illness will prevent my return before the opening of college; but if it is serious enough to detain me I will cable to you" (112–13).

It seems likely that Eliot had already made up his mind—in spite of his assurances to his father and mother—that (as he had told Aiken) his return to England would be permanent. In any event, his August 16 letter to Woods was the last of the letters written by him from Gloucester. In the latter part of August he sailed for England and arrived there in early September. Although he could not have known it at the time, this was the last visit Eliot would make to America for some eighteen years, and the last time ever he would see his father.

The most revealing source of the state of the relationship between Eliot and his parents at the time of his visit home is in a letter written after his return to England, dated September 10, 1915. His parents would have no doubt believed that they had persuaded him to return to Harvard. But Eliot wrote to his father that he had made a "great mistake" in hurrying home before receiving their letters to him and thus "failing to get a balanced view of the situation" and "blundering into a change of plan . . . unjustified and unnecessary" (113–14). This brusque sentence must have been like a blow in the face to the father.

But of course, Eliot would not have intended to break with his parents for the very practical reason that he needed his father's financial help. Despite a teaching job and "a very economical mode of life, and Vivien's resourcefulness and forethought," they would be in "urgent need of funds . . . very soon." And then, the poignant plea: "We are not planning how to make living easier: the question is how to live at all." In his final paragraph Eliot adopted a conciliatory tone: "I know that I have made matters hard for you by the blunders of which I spoke. Had I avoided them, I am sure that you would have felt at ease. Nevertheless, I feel that I shall make matters right by returning to my original course." In two postscripts, Eliot promised to "write again in a few days," and he asked his father to remind his mother to send his clothes "as soon as she can" (113–14). There can be little doubt that this letter expressed the strongest of Eliot's feelings that he could never have found the courage to express directly.

Some time shortly after Eliot's return from America, he and Vivien headed for Eastbourne in Sussex on the English Channel, booking rooms at Lansdowne for a two-week honeymoon, but their money was gone after six days. What happened during this honeymoon is the subject of a scene in Michael Hastings's play, *Tom and Viv*, and although the drama is an "imaginative" work, Hastings clearly did an enormous amount of scholarly research in writing it. A major source for him seems unimpeachable: Vivien's brother, Colonel Maurice Haigh-Wood, who spent over five months being interviewed by Hastings in 1980 before his death later that year. Maurice, six years younger than Vivien, would have been eighty-six years old in 1980.

In an early scene of act 1, set at the Haigh-Woods' home in Hampstead (at 3 Compayne Gardens), Hastings dramatized Tom and Vivienne's (spelled thus in the play) return from their honeymoon, dropping off clothes (and bedding, soiled by her uncontrollable menstruations). Vivienne enters first and finds at home only her brother—her tightly wound, wisecracking, soldier sibling. When he mentions the honeymoon, Vivienne responds only that she "set light to the hotel curtains." When Maurice persists, assuming that she and Tom had "seen all the sights and stuff," her reply is brief: "I lay in bed all day with the blinds closed. And I bolted the door." Maurice comments: "Oh rather—got stuck into the dreaded sex business." Vivienne: "Every night Tom took a rug and slept in a deckchair under the pier. With a bottle of gin" (Hastings, 61).

We might assume that Maurice the old soldier had, in 1980, revealed these remembered "facts" of the honeymoon to Hastings. Later in the same scene, after Tom enters, Maurice says to him: "I've just been hearing about the honeymoon." Tom answers, putting his arm around Vivienne: "Yes. We're enormously happy. I'm a very proud man." Maurice then says: "I gather you're going to be the poet in the family," and then wonders out loud whether Tom's poems rhyme. Tom answers "Massively," and then cites some lines from his bawdy verses to show how: "King Bolo and his big black hairy kween / whose bum is as big as a soup tureen." On hearing Maurice's pleased reaction, Tom offers more: "King Bolo's big black bastard kween / That airy fairy hairy 'un, / She led the dance on Golders Green / With half a jew boy's knickers on—" After more such bantering, with Maurice offering to quote from his favorite poet, Robert Service, the scene comes to a sudden halt with the rapid departure of Tom and Viv, and with Viv refusing to drink Maurice's toast to their honeymoon. Though he has departed the immediate scene, Tom has the final lines of the episode spoken directly to the audience. He affirms Vivienne's earlier statement as to where he slept on the honeymoon: "At night, Eastbourne pier possesses one hundred and fourteen uprights which stand clear of the sea. The tide comes in at dawn, thus reducing this number to twenty-eight" (61–63).

A following scene shows Vivienne buying medicines at her "chemist" shop, both an "anodyne" and a "bromide." When the clerk wonders aloud how the prescription could be signed by the King's personal physician, Vivienne says: "He's also mine." Whereupon the "chemist" reveals what is actually in the medicines Vivienne is buying: the "anodyne is sixty per cent spirit of ether. And the bromide is ninety per cent alcohol." When Vivienne retorts, "Well, what about it?" the chemist responds: "Hope you won't think I'm too keen but—when taken together these compounds have a dangerous effect." Vivienne replies with some irritation: "You think the King's personal physician erred in some way?" The chemist quickly backs down and apologizes. This brief scene ends and the stage dims, after which Rose Haigh-Wood, Vivienne's mother, steps forward to describe to the audience her family's wealthy background, mentioning their summer home in Anglesey and their properties in Dublin. She then describes how, only a short time before, Vivie had met Tom while staying with friends at Oxford: "Out of the blue came a telegram. Tom and Viv had run off and married in a registry place. Vivie had contrived it to spite me. With her medical history she knew I would have to put a stop to it. And I was especially afraid for young Tom" (63–64).

Tom and Viv goes on to portray Vivien's tragic life with Eliot and his final separation from her. But that story lies ahead. For now, "young Tom" found aid in another quarter.

5. "Bertie" Russell's "Friendship"

We have seen that one of the first of Eliot's friends to meet his new wife was Bertrand Russell, whose classes at Harvard Eliot had attended. Russell was caught in a failed marriage and, at the time he met Vivien Eliot, he was in the middle of a fairly long affair with Ottoline Morrell. How was it that Russell had become such a friend of the Eliots? One answer to this question is provided by Eliot's first biographer, Robert Sencourt, who had been Eliot's friend for twenty years before Eliot's death and had met Lady Ottoline with the Eliots. Sencourt writes: "[Ottoline Morrell] was the wife of a member of Parliament and the half-sister of a duke. Her husband, Philip Morrell, was a man of considerable fortune, who had entered the House of Commons as a Liberal in 1906 and shared Russell's pacifist attitude towards the War. Her half-brother, the sixth Duke of Portland, reigned at Welbeck Abbey, where he entertained kings." When Sencourt met Ottoline, he reports that he "was impressed by her combination of sympathy, generosity and high breeding. Her distinguished bearing was set off by dress unconventionally elaborate" (Sencourt, 58).

Obviously Sencourt was impressed by Ottoline Morrell. She would, of course, have been much younger when she was carrying on her affair with Bertrand Russell. And she was indeed younger still when she married Philip Morrell in February 1902. Born in 1873, Ottoline would have been almost thirty at the time of her marriage. Philip Morrell came from a wealthy, aristocratic family and had spent the ten years of his bachelorhood before marriage as an associate (or partner) in an antique business. One of his associates, who became his "best friend," was Logan Pearsall Smith, whose brother-in-law was the American Bernard Berenson (a friend and professional advisor of Mrs. Jack in Boston). The Pearsall Smiths came from America, where they had known Walt Whitman, and in England had come to know Henry James.

Philip Morrell's mother, Harriette, is said to have been the model for Mrs. Gereth in James's *The Spoils of Poynton*. Although Harriette Morrell was concerned about the woman her son Philip was wooing (and eventually married), she had never been concerned about his long relationship with his longtime partner Logan. As her biographer Miranda Seymour writes, "Logan's friendship offered no threat to her and, obvious though his homosexuality was, she had never chosen to worry about his devotion to her good-looking son" (Seymour, 44).

As for Ottoline Morrell's relationship with her husband Philip, her biographer explains: "Tall and unusually handsome with curling brown hair, a long sensual mouth and soft blue eyes, [Philip] was made still more attractive to

[Ottoline] by his unhappiness. . . . It was as a brother rather than as a poten-
tial husband that she soon began to look on him" (43). On their honeymoon
in Italy, they discovered that they did not find each other sexually attractive:
"Sexual relations did exist between them, but they were not of a particularly
satisfactory kind. It was not passion which bound them to each other, but
loyalty, affection, and need. The need was far stronger in Philip than in his
wife; the more aware she became of his dependence on her, the more deter-
mined Ottoline grew to protect and defend him" (51–52). Thus it was that
they grew into a quite satisfactory union, if not a passionate one, and they
both engaged in extramarital affairs. Bertrand Russell was the second for
Ottoline, and there would be others after Russell.

Russell's wife was born Alys Pearsall Smith, daughter of Hannah and sis-
ter of Logan, Philip's "friend." His marriage took place on December 13,
1894, against the wishes of his mother, Lady Russell. Bertrand and Alys were
married in a Quaker meeting house in London without any of the Russell
family present. While the first five years of the marriage seemed to be proof
of its success, there was something missing for Russell, as he came to recog-
nize with the passage of time. And Ottoline was only one of many mistresses.

Russell's biographer, Ray Monk, assumes that Eliot probably asked Russell
to look after Vivien during his six-week absence from England to visit his
parents in America. He writes: "By the time Eliot returned, around 3 Sep-
tember, Russell and Vivien had become intimate friends, sharing confidences
and making joint plans" (Monk, 439). Before the Eliots went off on their
"honeymoon," Russell must have offered them the use of a spare bedroom
in his London flat on their return to London, as Eliot gave his Eastbourne
correspondents Russell's London address as the place to send letters to him
until Christmas. In a "draft letter" (September 7 or 8, 1915) to Ottoline Mor-
rell, Russell wrote that he was "worried about these Eliots": "It seems their
sort of pseudo-honeymoon at Eastbourne is . . . a ghastly failure. She is quite
tired of him, & when I got here [from his rooms at Garsington to his Lon-
don apartment] I found a desperate letter from her, in the lowest depths of
despair & not far removed from suicide." Russell said he had given her "good
advice," and she seemed to rely on him: "I have so much taken them both
in hand that I dare not let them be. I think she will fall more or less in love
with me, but that can't be helped. I am interested by the attempt to pull her
straight. She is half-Irish, & wholly Irish in character—with a great deal of
mental passion & *no* physical passion, a universal vanity, that makes her desire
every man's devotion, & a fastidiousness that makes any expression of their
devotion disgusting to her" (440).

Russell knew of incidents in her past that he could have learned only from her: "She has suffered humiliation in two successive love-affairs, & that has made her vanity morbid. She has boundless ambition (far beyond her powers), but it is diffuse & useless. What she needs is some kind of religion, or at least some discipline, of which she seems never to have had any." Although she appeared to be the loser, Russell saw her as "punishing my poor friend for having tricked her imagination. . . . I want to give her some other outlet than destroying him. I shan't fall in love with her, nor give her any more show of affection than seems necessary to rehabilitate her. But she really has *some* value in herself, all twisted and battered by life, lack of discipline, lack of purpose, & lack of religion." Indeed, Russell seemed bent on performing for the Eliots the assistance or the support of a psychoanalyst. Either that, or he was writing deliberately to mislead Ottoline Morrell as to a deeper (and sexual) interest in Vivien than he admitted. In a reply to this letter, she said: "I feel *very* strongly that in getting her confidence, you are rather separating her from Eliot" (440).

Shortly before the Eliots left Eastbourne for London to stay at the Russell flat, Russell wrote to Eliot inquiring whether it would be all right for him to occupy his London apartment those nights that Eliot would be away because of his teaching duties at High Wycombe (441). In his reply of September 11, Eliot wrote: "As to your coming to stay the night at the flat when I am not there, it would never have occurred to me to accept it under any other conditions. Such a concession to conventions never entered my head; it seems to me not only totally unnecessary, but also would destroy for me all the pleasure we take in the informality of the arrangement" (*LTSE1*, 115). The use of his London flat was not the only gift Russell gave the Eliots: he gave £3,000 worth of engineering debentures to help them meet their living expenses. Ottoline observed that Russell also paid for Vivien's dancing lessons and gave her expensive silken underwear (Morrell, *M*, 120).

Thus after the Eliots returned to London from Eastbourne on September 15, it became customary for Russell to move into his London apartment with Vivien whenever Eliot moved out weekly to accommodations at Sydney Cottage, Conegra Road, near his teaching job at High Wycombe Grammar School. When Russell discovered Vivien's typing skills, he used her as a secretary to type his manuscripts (Monk, 442). In a letter to Ottoline dated November 10, Russell wrote: "Eliot had a half holiday yesterday and got home at 3:30. It is quite funny how I have come to love him, as if he were my son. He is becoming much more of a man. He has a profound and quite unselfish devotion to his wife, and she is really very fond of him, but has impulses of cruelty to him from time to time." It is clear as Russell continues his report on the Eliots that his interest has been most fully aroused by

Vivien's behavior: "It is a Dostojevsky type of cruelty, not a straightforward every-day kind. I am every day getting things more right between them, but I can't let them alone at present, and of course I myself get very much interested. She is a person who lives on a knife-edge, and will end as a criminal or a saint—I don't know which yet. She has a perfect capacity for both" (Russell, *A*, 280).

What might be called the climax of Russell's relationship with Vivien took place shortly after they had moved out of his flat on December 20. He took Vivien on a holiday at Torquay in Devon in January 1916, leaving Eliot in London working on his thesis. In a letter to Ottoline Morrell of January 1, 1916, Russell wrote that had he not gone with Vivien he would "have hurt her feelings." He assured Ottoline they would be "quite proper": "There is no tendency to develop beyond friendship, quite the opposite. I have really now done all I meant to do for them, they are perfectly happy in each other, & I shall begin to fade away out of their lives as soon as this week is over" (Monk, 449). Russell confessed in another to Ottoline that he detested Torquay but that Vivien seemed to like it, reiterating: "I have been quite fantastically unselfish towards her, & have never dreamt of making any kind of demands, so it has nothing to do with that." The ambiguity as well as the exaggeration of this claim may in themselves call the claim into question (449–50). After five days, Russell left and paid for Eliot to join his wife.

Upon receipt of Russell's invitation to come to Torquay, Eliot wrote to Russell from London on January 11, 1916, a letter of extraordinary appreciation: "This is wonderfully kind of you—really the last straw (so to speak) of generosity, I am very sorry you have to come back—and Vivien says you have been an angel to her—but of course I shall jump at the opportunity with the utmost gratitude. I am sure you have done *everything* possible and handled her in the very best way—better than I. I often wonder how things would have turned out but for you—I believe we shall owe her life to you, even" (*LTSE1*, 127). Eliot's enthusiastic response to Russell's questionable behavior is remarkable, either wholly trusting or masking more troubling and complicated feelings.

Russell's recent biographer, Ray Monk, who has provided the fullest account of the relationship between Russell and Ottoline Morrell, believes that Russell's affair with Vivien was in fact consummated. Indeed, Monk interprets one of Russell's short stories, "Satan in the Suburbs," written some five years after Vivien Eliot's death, to be based on his affair with her in 1915–18. The main character is a Mrs. Ellerker, based (according to Monk) on Vivien: "In the story Mrs. Ellerker betrays her rather dull husband to embark on an affair with Mr. Quantox, described by Russell as 'sparkling and witty, a man of education and wide culture, a man who could amuse any company by observations which combined wit with penetrating analysis.'" After Mr. Quantox (clearly Russell's self-portrait) has had his affair, he deserts Mrs. Ellerker and she deteriorates and is confined for the rest of her life to an asylum. Monk poses the question: "Did Russell suspect that he was in some way responsible for Vivien's fate? Certainly others have reached that conclusion" (Monk, 431–33).

Like Monk, Michael Hastings, in *Tom and Viv,* implies that Russell consummated his affair with Vivien. In a soliloquy addressed to the audience, Mrs. Rose Haigh-Wood, Vivien's mother, says at the end of a scene in act 1: "The Honourable Bertie bought her dresses and pressed her with jewels which were family heirlooms. She was swept off her feet. He took her to the Torbay Hotel for a holiday. What were we to believe? She wanted the affair" (Hastings, 71). Still in another scene with only Maurice (Vivien's brother) and Tom on stage, the dialogue reveals that Eliot never consummated his marriage with Vivien. In one episode in act 1, Maurice asks Tom: "Is there something beastly and quite bloody awful between you and Viv?" Eliot replies: "*Nothing. Nothing at all.*" Maurice responds: "Well done, sir" (74). Later, Maurice again asks Tom, "man-to-man," about his intimate relation with Vivie: "The old sort of thing under the sheets? . . . I mean there must have been a good moment. A single second." Eliot replies, "I can't say that there was." Maurice prods him: "When you think back?" Tom: "Not one" (112–13).

The letters written by Eliot from the Torbay Hotel in Torquay—one to his father and three to Russell—reveal a holiday alternating between bliss and anxiety, as well as their dependence on Russell, "Dear Bertie." To his father on Friday, January 14, Eliot, showing his Gloucester upbringing, described the "very towny seaside place," with a bay and a harbor in front of the hotel, and his impulse "to seize a boat and put to sea—except that Vivien couldn't come with me." He apologized for the "scrawly" writing for "Vivien is massaging my head." Even in the remote west country, there were signs of war: a torpedo boat and a naval officer who left the hotel to search for submarines. Vivien added a note, hoping her gifts had been received, thanking Mrs. Eliot for her "nice letters," and describing their flat. She closed with gratitude to Mr. Russell for giving them "this wonderful holiday." It was apparently a working holiday for Vivien, for in Eliot's letter to Russell on the same day he noted that the "MS is here, and Vivien will have it ready for you." Despite her having had a "bad night, and stomach and headache today," they took a taxi along "one of the loveliest bits of shore." Eliot was moved by the "perfect peace" of the ocean, and grateful to have left the town to be "bathed in this purity." But even under the "*perfect*" conditions provided by Russell,

Vivien was weak and fatigued. Eliot wrote: "I am convinced that no one could have been so wise and understanding with her as you. She was very happy. I have felt happier, these three days, than ever in my life" (*LTSE1*, 128–29).

Two days later, on Sunday, January 16, Eliot wrote to Russell that Vivien was "wretched today," although the day before they had "walked along the shore for over half an hour." He closed, looking forward to attending Russell's Tuesday lecture. But as the letter of Monday, January 17, reveals, he wouldn't be able to make the lecture, for Vivien's health caused them to postpone their return one day—the extra night at their "own expense." Eliot took the blame for her condition, having "let her do rather too much on Saturday." Eliot's prescription: "A very strict regimen, with very clear limits of exertion . . . for the rest of the winter" (130). Among his other duties, scrambling to make a living, Eliot had clearly taken over the care of the chronically ill Vivien.

Some two months later, the letter of March 6, 1916, is totally given over to Vivien's condition ("in very great pain, both neuralgia and stomach") and their trip to the dentist. The interview had shaken Vivien, who was told that in addition to decay, "there was a possibility of an abscess." What is telling in the letter is Eliot's criticism of the dentist—he had "quite failed in tact, and did not understand what was required." The dentist thought that Eliot was the fearful one in need of calming and "evidently had not understood what I had told him." What had Eliot told him? Eliot was taking great care to shield Vivien from even such a routine thing as a visit to the dentist: "She is very ill tonight, and I am very very sorry that she went through this. It has been too great a strain on her will." In a puzzling postscript, Eliot's report that she had finished the typing for Russell before going to the dentist is in jarring juxtaposition with Eliot's account of what the mistaken visit to the dentist had cost her—"the effort and the anticipation during the last weeks—which she didn't say anything about, and which had taken every ounce of strength out of her," such that Russell was not to expect her for their scheduled lunch or dinner for some days (133–34).

6. "What I Want Is MONEY!$!£!! We are hard up! War!"

Eliot's financial affairs were his main concern, especially now that he was married. His job at High Wycombe Grammar School paid a salary of £140 plus one meal per day. After one term he quit that job for one at Highgate Junior School in North London, which paid £160 plus dinner and tea. At the same time of his teaching, Eliot launched a career writing reviews and essays for various publications, particularly philosophical journals. His friend Bertrand Russell was instrumental in introducing him to the editors of many of the journals for which Eliot would write. But of course, an important job left to do, one he had promised his parents he would do, was the completion of his Harvard doctoral thesis. One of the first letters he wrote when he got back to London, of September 11, 1915, was to J. H. Woods informing him that he had decided not to return to America for the academic year but to remain in England. He promised to forward chapters of his thesis as he finished them and to return in the spring or the fall in order to take his final orals (*LTSE1*, 116–17).

In a letter written to his father only a week later, September 27, 1915, Eliot reported that he had taught for a full week at High Wycombe and was beginning "to get into the routine." His two upper classes, he reported, were "quite good at French, the middle boys indifferent at history" and "the small boys capable of being interested." He assured his father that he would have enough time to work on his thesis and prepare for the exams. But there remained a major problem—he was "harassed by the question of money." He wrote to his father in a language unusually forceful: "If no money comes from you at the end of a fortnight I shall be forced to cable, as I shall be reduced to the last pound by the time you get this. . . . You know that I should but for the degree have devoted my spare time to writing, which would have pieced out my income. So I must make it clear to you exactly how I am placed now, without waiting for your letter" (117–18).

Sometime during this period Eliot called on Bertrand Russell to write a letter to his mother, supporting Eliot's plan to remain in England rather than return to America for a career in philosophy. In his letter dated October 3, 1915, Russell used a common-sense argument, pointing out that since England was at war (as America then was not), all young men of military age were being called up to serve in the armed forces. Thus there were many opportunities in jobs for young men like Eliot who, not being English, would not be called up. Russell wrote: "I think he may rely with considerable confidence upon obtaining suitable work when he has taken his Ph.D." Russell reassured Eliot's mother that the school where Eliot was teaching would give him the time he needed to complete his dissertation, and that he was "no longer attracted by the people who call themselves 'vorticists.' . . . He seems to me to have considerable literary gifts, and I have hopes of his doing work which will bring him reputation as soon as he is free from worry as to ways and means" (118–19).

In a second letter from Russell to Eliot's mother, December 3, 1915, we discover that she had sent him a copy of her biography of Eliot's grandfather;

he tells her that he is sending her a copy of his *Philosophical Essays,* commenting "though I fear most of them are rather uninteresting." In both of his letters to "Mrs. Eliot," Russell referred quite favorably to Vivien, emphasizing how compatible she and Eliot were and how she would be of great assistance to him. In this last letter, he wrote that he has come to know Vivien well: "She has a good mind, and is able to be a real help to a literary career, besides having a rare strength and charm of character" (122–23). Given how he described Vivien to Ottoline, Russell's portrayal of her to Eliot's mother shows his genius at tailoring his prose to a shrewdly sized-up and particular audience.

In an October 11, 1915, letter to Russell, Eliot thanked his benefactor profusely for mentioning him as a potential reviewer to Sydney Waterlow, on the editorial committee of the *International Journal of Ethics.* Waterlow invited Eliot to dinner and, after sounding him out, asked him to review two important books for the journal—payment for which would help the Eliots out economically. The two books were A. J. Balfour's *Theism and Humanism* and A. Wolf's *The Philosophy of Nietzsche.* The two reviews did not appear until January and April 1916, but Eliot wanted them to represent himself at his best in order to be assigned more books to review. He wrote to Russell: "I think it is worth while to put in all my time on this reviewing until I have got these two books, at the expense of the thesis. Do you not agree with me? It is not worth doing at all unless I do my best: if I do a good review I can afford to do no more for some time. . . . Besides, it will (if good) impress people at Harvard much more than the same amount of work added to put in upon the thesis" (119–20). In the next three years or so, Eliot would become a frequent reviewer, especially of philosophical works. The pay was small, but not so small as to be pointless for the money-starved Eliots.

Although Eliot assumed that his mother and father would share the letters he sent to them individually, he never addressed them jointly. His prose to his father tended to be condensed or lean, to his mother expansive or chatty. Moreover, Eliot's salutations to his two parents differed markedly: his father he addressed as "My dear Father," while he addressed his mother as "Dearest Mother" or "My Dearest Mother"; or—as in his letter of November 18, 1915—"Darling Mother." He opened the letter by telling her about the two philosophical reviews he had written—and revealingly confessed that in preparation for writing the review of the book on Nietzsche he had to read some of Nietzsche's works that he had not read before (but would have had to read for his forthcoming final orals at Harvard). As for Balfour's book, *Theism and Humanism,* Eliot wrote proudly: "Russell was in town just before I sent the review away, so I showed it to him, and he liked it very much" (120).

The remainder of this letter to his mother gives some glimpses into the life in England during the Great War of 1914–18—a war that America would not enter for many months (declaring war in April 1917 but not massing troops in France until early 1918). Vivien's younger brother was in the British army and had been home on a five-day leave from France just before Eliot wrote this letter. Eliot mentioned that Maurice had left for France on the very day that Eliot had married Vivien, but that he had gotten to know him during his leave: "I was awfully pleased with him, and feel a strong affection for him now. . . . He is a very handsome boy, with a great deal of breeding— very aristocratic, and very simple too. It seems strange that a boy of nineteen should have such experiences." As relayed by Eliot, the experiences were indeed extraordinary. He was "often twelve hours alone in his 'dug-out' in the trenches" and spent most of his time shooting his revolver at the rats: "What he tells about rats and vermin is incredible—Northern France is swarming, and the rats are as big as cats. His dug-out, where he sleeps, is underground, and gets no sunlight" (121).

Eliot described for his mother the November Christmas the Haigh-Wood family had for their soldier son on leave: "It was awfully touching, and a bit melancholy—every one trying to be gay and cheerful—the immediate family and a few aunts. But every one was at their best and kindliest, and kept up the usual Christmas diversions." The Haigh-Woods paid the new American member of their family some attention also. They served cranberry sauce in Eliot's honor, but instead of serving it with the turkey, served it as a dessert. And they put an American flag on a "blazing" pudding they served. Indeed, the Haigh-Wood family did everything it could, according to Eliot, to make him feel at home and with family. Eliot was glad to have escaped the pain of seeing Maurice off at the station, but Vivien "was pretty well knocked out by it, and has had neuralgia in consequence."

Eliot ended his letter, declaring his love for London and the many different kinds of people he was beginning to know—"political and social as well as literary and philosophical." Eliot's closing sentences have a slight suggestion of eagerness for the future, but also (paradoxically) home-sickness. The final sentence reveals a touching nostalgia: "You will be having Thanksgiving dinner soon—I shall think of you on that day—it is next Thursday" (121–22).

On December 28, 1915, Eliot wrote to his Harvard professor J. H. Woods about his final orals. He thought he might be able to come in April during his month's holiday, but the schedule would be chancy and tight. He also wanted to know whether he might take the exam in the summer; he could get there for the first week in August. And he again went over the list of fields on which he would be questioned during his exam. Nowhere did Eliot suggest, as he had previously, that he might come back to stay in America. What Eliot did not realize at this juncture was that he would never return to take the examination he seems so concerned about in this letter. And indeed, he would not return to America for some eighteen years—in 1933, after both his mother and father had died, and when he was finally planning his permanent separation from the woman he had married in 1915.

7. Hallucinations, Heavenly and Hellish Poetic Visions: "St. Sebastian" and "St. Narcissus"

Eliot was very productive during this period (mid-1914 to 1915), writing a total of seventeen poems, his personal problems perhaps inspiring the most effective of them. At the end of this chapter is a list of the poems, followed by dates of composition (when known) and places of publication.

The year 1915 was a signal one for Eliot as a poet: for the first time in his career, several of his most important poems saw publication in the little magazines. *Poetry: A Magazine of Verse,* the Chicago publication for which Ezra Pound served as a grumpy foreign correspondent and editor, was the first to offer Eliot's work to a relatively large public. The word "large" should be read here in a very special sense, in that there was never and has never been a wide audience for poetry. But *Poetry* made a point of paying all contributors and was read by a public intensely interested in poetry—a public whose opinions made a difference. Eliot was pleased to receive the copy of *Poetry* that contained "The Love Song of J. Alfred Prufrock"—the June 1915 issue. The second and final issue of Wyndham Lewis's *Blast* appeared in July with two Eliot poems: "Preludes (I–IV)" and "Rhapsody on a Windy Night." The September issue of *Others* printed "Portrait of a Lady." The October issue of *Poetry* contained three Eliot poems: "The Boston Evening Transcript," "Aunt Helen," and "Cousin Nancy." And in November, Ezra Pound's *Catholic Anthology* came out with five Eliot poems in the opening pages: "The Love Song of J. Alfred Prufrock," "Portrait of a Lady," "The Boston Evening Transcript," "Miss Helen Slingsby [Aunt Helen]," and "Hysteria." Pound had decided that since Eliot had not yet produced enough poems to fill a volume, he would bring out an anthology featuring Eliot. In response to protests that the poets in the anthology were not Catholic, nor were the poems religious, Pound explained that the title meant simply "universal."

"The Love Song of St. Sebastian" and "The Death of Saint Narcissus" are two of the most puzzling poems in all of Eliot's poetry. Eliot himself seemed unsure about the two poems and did not place either of them in his *Collected Poems.* "The Love Song of St. Sebastian" first appeared in *The Letters of T. S. Eliot* (1988) in the July 25, 1914, letter from Eliot to Aiken; and it was republished with manuscript variations in *Inventions of the March Hare* in 1996. Eliot wrote to Aiken: "The S. Sebastian title I feel almost sure of; I have studied S. Sebastians—why should anyone paint a beautiful youth and stick him full of pins (or arrows) unless he felt a little as the hero of my verse? Only there's nothing homosexual about this—rather an important difference perhaps—but no one ever painted a female Sebastian, did they? So I give this title *faute de mieux* [for want of anything better]" (*LTSE1,* 44).

In an earlier letter to Aiken (July 19, 1914), Eliot had written about his visit to art galleries in Europe (see Chapter 7, Section 1), concluding: "There are *three* great *St. Sebastians* (so far as I know): 1) Mantegna (ca d'Oro [Venice]), 2) Antonello of Messina (Bergamo [Lombardy, Italy]), 3) Memling (Brussels)" (41). There seems to be some consensus among Eliot critics that Eliot listed the paintings in the order (in his view) of their greatness, the Mantegna thus being the greatest. Lyndall Gordon reproduced the Mantegna in her 1977 *Eliot's Early Years* (Gordon, EEY, 80), as did Harvey Gross with his important 1985 article on Eliot's poem ("The Figure of St. Sebastian"), reprinted in *T. S. Eliot: Essays from "The Southern Review"* (Gross, 103–14). In Mantegna's painting, St. Sebastian fills the frame of the picture as he stands almost fully naked before the onlooker, with what seems to be a torn piece of sheet wrapped around his middle; he is pierced with more than a dozen arrows, one seemingly aimed at his groin. Below a vague halo is a copious head of hair and a face turned slightly upward, with eyes and mouth open and lips turned up at the corners in what seems to be a combination of pain and pleasure.

Eliot's casual comment to Aiken ("There is nothing homosexual about this") is a little vague as to the antecedent of "this"; but the statement reveals that Eliot was aware of the homoerotic tradition surrounding St. Sebastian, in both photography and literature, during the latter nineteenth and early twentieth centuries. Indeed, in Boston at the time that the two Eliot boys attended Harvard, the famous photographer Fred Holland Day posed nude young men as St. Sebastians, with arrows positioned as though piercing their bodies. A number of these were done in 1906 and are reprinted in *F. Holland Day: Suffering the Ideal* (1995, plates 51–53). And Eliot could have seen them exhibited in Boston when he was attending Harvard (Day, plates 3–81). Day's publishing firm, Copeland and Day, was the "chief thrust of the aesthetic-decadent in America," publishing among others Oscar Wilde, Francis Thompson, Yeats, Aubrey Beardsley, and *The Yellow Book,* the "controversial journal of the Decadence" (Shand-Tucci, BB, 341, 356).

Day himself posed nude for his camera in a number of pictures as the crucified Christ. Whatever their religious content, the photographs were clearly homoerotic. One critic has written: "Day's photographs of young men *were* erotic. . . . It was, to be sure, quite a shocker the night of November 16, 1898, when Cram and Guiney [friends of Day] and doubtless most of the rest of [Boston] Bohemia trooped up to 9 Pinkney Street to see Day exhibit the first photographic frontal nudity seen in Boston (perhaps the most shocking of all was the fact that the exhibit features a very well-built and genitally well-endowed young man in a crucifixion study)." Although this was a private viewing, "Day's photographs were sufficiently admired that by 1900 he was one of the most famous photographers in the world" (43, 45).

In his wide reading of contemporary poetry, Eliot would no doubt have become familiar with the homoerotic portrayals of St. Sebastian, who was a frequent subject of many poets, among them the British aesthete writer and artist Frederick William Rolfe, known as Baron Corvo. Shand-Tucci calls him the "notorious homosexual outlaw of this era," whose work could be found in Isabella Gardner's library (184). Inspired by a painting by Guido Reni, he wrote "Two Sonnets for a Picture of Saint Sebastian the Martyr in the Capitoline Gallery, Rome." Here, as a sample of such works, is the second of the two sonnets:

> A Roman soldier-boy, bound to a tree,
>> His strong arms lifted up for sacrifice,
>> His gracious form all stripped of earthly guise
> Naked, but brave as a young lion can be,
> Transfixed by arrows he gains the victory;
>> And angels bear before his bright sweet eyes
>> The wreath of amaranth in Paradise,
> Where he shall put on immortality.
> And all unashamed because the saints are there,
>> Where God's eternal gardens gleam and glow
>> Sebastian's stainless soul no soil doth know
> The glorious beauty of the youth to bare,
>> And light the Land where fadeless lilies blow
> With his limbs of flaming whiteness and rayed hair.
>> (in Smith, Timothy, 182–83)

There is a reverential tone throughout Rolfe's sonnet that is entirely foreign to Eliot's "The Love Song of St. Sebastian," beginning with the title. Like "The Love Song of J. Alfred Prufrock," the title of Eliot's Sebastian appears ironic: neither seems to be a love song in the tradition of such lyric poems.

What is Eliot's poem about? Tradition tells us that the saint, although he suffered persecution and martyrdom under Diocletian, did not die of the wounds inflicted by the archers. He was rescued by a devout woman who had come to bury him, but, finding him alive, dressed his wounds. Upon recovery he confronted the emperor and was beaten to death. His body was found by another woman to whom Sebastian had appeared in a dream, ordering him to bury him.

Eliot's poem, however, bears no relation to this myth. St. Sebastian speaks in his own person and always in the ambiguous conditional "would." In the first of two stanzas, he seems to be a determined masochist bent on killing himself, inspired by his passion for a woman in white. He succeeds (in imagination) in "flogging" himself until he bleeds; in "prayer / And torture and delight," he "should arise [her] neophyte." And "Then you would take me in / Because I was hideous in your sight / You would take me in without shame / Because I should be dead / And when the morning came / Between your breasts should lie my head" (*IOMH*, 78, lines 4–6, 9, 16–21). Since the conditional is used throughout, we might assume that nothing at all has happened (yet) between the speaker and the hallowed woman; instead, the speaker is meditating on what he *might* do and what *might* happen if he did. Even so, most critics summarize the poem's "action."

In the second stanza, the speaker continues to speak in the conditional, imagining another encounter with the beloved woman in which he, in short, strangles her to death: "I would come with a towel in my hand / And bend your head beneath my knees; / . . . / I think that at last you would understand. / There would be nothing more to say. / You would love me because I should have strangled you / And because of my infamy; / And I should love you the more because I had mangled you / And because you were no longer beautiful / To anyone but me" (78–79, lines 22–23, 32–38).

It seems clear that the two stanzas do not portray a sustained sequence of actions, but rather two quite different actions, the first in which the speaker imagines killing himself through his self-laceration and thus dying in the lady's bed (his head between her breasts), the second in which he imagines himself gradually strangling the woman and thus inspiring her love for him. Gross sees this as "a case history in aberrant sexuality"—masochism followed by sadism (Gross, 109).

There is a fundamental absurdity in either of these imagined actions: one is incompatible with the other (the dead cannot rise and kill) and neither act could have succeeded the other in fact—only in imagination. What seems bizarre is the reasoning of the speaker in both of the imagined actions. Why did Eliot call it "The Love Song of St. Sebastian" and then claim to Aiken that it was not homosexual, knowing as he obviously did of the homoerotic cult-worship of the Roman Saint?

If we try to psychoanalyze the speaker in the poem, we might assume that he is, like Prufrock, a man who cannot love women in any normal sense; and beyond Prufrock, he is, like Sweeney (discussed in Chapter 10, Section 7), a man who despises women for their sexuality and wants to do them in. His self-inflicted wounds in the first stanza show that he is masochistic; his murderous action in the second stanza shows that he is also sadistic. Thus he is sadomasochistic, enjoying the pain that he inflicts on himself and on others. In short, he is sick. And lying beyond or beneath his sickness is, perhaps, a repressed homoeroticism that he refuses to admit. As we have seen in his earlier poems, Eliot views women sometimes as pure and saintly; more often, he views them with contempt, condemning them especially for their sexuality.

The question that arises is why Eliot wrote about St. Sebastian at all. Harvey Gross may have found the answer. While Eliot was in France in 1910–11 living along with Jean Verdenal in his Paris pension, the Ballets Russes presented a new ballet written in French by the Italian poet Gabriele d'Annunzio, entitled *Le Martyre de Saint Sébastien*. The dancer who took the part of the Saint was a famous female ballet dancer, Ida Rubenstein. (Recall that Eliot asked Aiken, "No one ever painted a female Sebastian, did they?") In the ballet, as the arrows begin to pierce Sebastian's body, he only calls for more: "Encore! Encore! Amour Éternel!" And at a critical moment, Sebastian says to the archers: "Il faut que chacun / tue son amour" (108). This is the French rendering of Oscar Wilde's famous line in "The Ballad of Reading Gaol": "Yet each man kills the thing he loves."

By selecting a woman to take the part of Sebastian, and by putting Wilde's words in Sebastian's mouth, d'Annunzio was perceived by his audience as identifying the saint with the most notorious homosexual of the time (the Wilde trial had taken place in 1895, and he died in 1900). If Eliot did not attend a performance of the ballet, performed from May 29 to June 19, 1911, he certainly would have read about the scandal in the paper: "The archbishop of Paris issued a pastoral letter forbidding Catholics to attend. The pro fascist *Action Française* denounced the play for its unmanly decadence and jeered at d'Annunzio for being an impudent foreigner" (108). In her study of Eliot's year in France, Nancy Hargrove agrees that Eliot may have seen the production. In a May 23 *Le Figaro* review, three paragraphs are devoted to the fact that the play is written in verse, something that would have interested Eliot.

And in the May 25 issue, a cartoon depicts a woman confessing she had seen the work to a priest who asked "How many times?" (Hargrove, 52). Ultimately, of course, Eliot chose not to publish his Sebastian poem, perhaps because he found it to be revelatory, or perhaps because he was unsure himself of its meaning.

Richard A. Kaye, in a comprehensive study entitled "'A Splendid Readiness for Death': T. S. Eliot, the Homosexual Cult of St. Sebastian, and World War I," argues that Eliot rejected "the sentimentalized Christian athlete" found in the homoerotic St. Sebastian poems by such poets as Frederick Rolfe, John Gray, and Cocteau, and instead "refigured the Roman martyr as a stark Symbolist icon of a *heterosexual* perversity" (Kaye, 112). Kaye believes that Eliot emptied the homoerotic content by refashioning the poem into a cautionary legend of a female who inspires sexual mayhem and by linking the poem to two heterosexual narratives. The lamp, bed, braided hair, and the lover relate to the myth of Eros and Psyche, but Eliot's poem ends with "a deadly blood-bath for the two lovers" (120–21). "And then put out the light" in Eliot's poem is an allusion to Othello's line "Put out the light, and then put out the light" after he murders Desdemona, and thus is an expression of heterosexual jealousy. But Kaye concedes that given "Iago's obsessive relation to Othello, Eliot has reinserted a homosexual subtext into his poem" (121).

But Kaye weakens his case by admitting a homosexual subtext. And in the face of a myth loaded with such homosexual freight, why should Eliot have chosen the myth at all? Kaye writes that "Eliot's masochistic and murderous saint is transformed *mutatis mutandis,* into the paradigmatic modernist sufferer Prufrock, as self-punishing as the poet's Sebastian, but now not only passive but too paralyzed to commit any act" (109). It may be reasonably argued that both Eliot's Sebastian and Prufrock are related in the underlying homoeroticism of their personalities; see the discussion of the original "Prufrock" in Chapter 5, Section 6.

Kaye is more convincing when he sees the poem as shaped by the violence of its time: "Eliot's 'Love Song of St. Sebastian' presages the tone of much of the verse of World War I, in which poets such as Wilfred Owen . . . and Siegfried Sassoon, eschewing the balanced felicities of Georgian verse capitalized on the shocking topics provided by the conditions of trench warfare" (109). Kaye's discussion of the poem as "one of the earliest poetic documents of the spiritual despair before the start of World War I" traces St. Sebastian as passing "from the self-enclosed cenacles of 'decadent' art into the larger contours of social history" (128).

The history of Eliot's other "Saint" poem is even more puzzling than that of his St. Sebastian poem. "The Death of Saint Narcissus" was set up in type for publication in *Poetry* but, as Harriet Monroe's annotation on the proof indicates, was never published. It is possible that Pound had submitted it to Monroe in August 1915, along with three other poems, while Eliot was in America. This was apparently against Eliot's wishes, for it was withdrawn by the author. Eliot later said that he did not care to have the poem printed in his lifetime, but he did supervise the privately printed *Poems Written in Early Youth,* edited by his friend John P. Hayward and published in Stockholm in 1950 in an edition "limited to twelve copies." *Poetry's* cancelled proof provided the text for this first publication of the poem (*PMC,* 1980). Eliot's widow Valerie Eliot brought out the volume again in 1967 because, she said in an introductory note, she wanted to make it "generally available as a corrective to the inaccurate, pirated editions" (*PWEY,* v).

When the lost *Waste Land* manuscripts were discovered in 1968, after Eliot's death, and published in a 1971 facsimile edition by Valerie Eliot, two versions of "The Death of St. Narcissus" in Eliot's hand came to light, with variants from the *Poetry* typescript. Thus Eliot had included it in the mass of manuscripts of *The Waste Land* that he turned over to Pound for his editing in 1922. In the discussion of the poem that follows, I will be using the version printed in *Poems Written in Early Youth,* with reference to variants in the *Waste Land* drafts when relevant. The opening lines of "Narcissus" were incorporated almost exactly in Part 1 of *The Waste Land:* "Come under the shadow of this gray rock— / Come in under the shadow of this gray rock / And I will show you something different from either / Your shadow sprawling over the sand at daybreak, or / Your shadow leaping behind the fire against the red rock: / I will show you his bloody cloth and limbs / And the gray shadow on his lips" (28). Compare these lines with lines 25–30 from *The Waste Land:* "There is shadow under this red rock, / (Come in under the shadow of this red rock), / And I will show you something different from either / Your shadow at morning striding behind you / Or your shadow at evening rising to meet you; / I will show you fear in a handful of dust" (*CPP,* 38). Of course, the speaker in the first passage is speaking directly to "you" (the reader?) as a possible companion, asking you to join him so that he can show you a third person, presumably dead: he has "bloody cloth and limbs" and has a "gray shadow on his lips"—presumably Saint Narcissus, the central figure in Eliot's poem. In *The Waste Land* lines, the "you" *is* what he'll show you—that is "you" and "your shadow," and—primarily—"*fear* in a handful of dust" (i.e., death).

How should these lines be read when used as the introduction of "The Death of Saint Narcissus"? They paint a somewhat desolate desert scene, and we might assume that they portray the place where the poem's title character has exiled himself from Jerusalem (where he occupied the Episcopal See) after charges of committing some infamous deed were brought against him (Englebert, 410). There are in fact four saints with the name of Narcissus, but Eliot critics have tended to agree that Eliot must have had in mind the Saint Narcissus of Jerusalem, who died about 212. The problem is that just as Eliot portrayed a Saint Sebastian who was not (as all the great artists portray him) pierced by arrows, he portrayed a Saint Narcissus as pierced by arrows in an event that never took place. In fact, Saint Narcissus of Jerusalem eventually returned from exile and was warmly welcomed back to his old position and status. Most readers assume that Eliot's Saint Narcissus is dead or dying in his desert "home" by the end of the poem.

The truth is that in Eliot's poem, there is more of the Narcissus of Greek mythology than of the Saint of Jerusalem. This Narcissus was a beautiful boy loved by the nymph Echo. He, however, repelled her. As related in Ovid, Narcissus ultimately fell in love with his own image as he gazed into the water of a well and eventually died in the attempt to embrace his own reflection. Eliot's poem is devoted to Narcissus's falling in love with his own body. As he walked "between the sea and the high cliffs," the wind made him "aware of his limbs smoothly passing each other / And of his arms crossed over his breast." Whenever he walked through the meadows, he "was stifled and soothed by his own rhythm," and along the river, his "eyes were aware of the pointed corners of his eyes / And his hands aware of the pointed tips of his fingers." With this deepening knowledge of the pleasures of his own body, he concluded that he "could not live men's ways, but became a dancer before God." His transformation was profound; walking in "city streets," he "seemed to tread on faces, convulsive thighs and knees." This consuming vision of "trampling" on multitudes of couples having sexual intercourse, presumably between the sexes, caused him to retreat where we encountered him at the beginning of the poem: "So he came out under the rock" (*PWEY,* 28–29, lines 8–10, 12, 14–15, 17–20).

The next three stanzas of the poem portray Narcissus reviewing the identities he assumed throughout his life before retiring under the "gray rock." "First he was sure that he had been a tree / Twisting its branches among each other / And tangling its roots among each other." If we take the tree as metaphor for the body, with the "branches" the upper part (arms etc.) and the roots the male genitalia, we discover an obscure image of youthful narcissistic love of one's own sex—or the longing for such love. Next, Narcissus "knew that he had been a fish / With slippery white belly held tight in his own fingers, / Writhing in his own clutch, his ancient beauty / Caught fast in the pink tips of his new beauty" (29, lines 21–27). Narcissus is making love to himself by masturbating, his root clutched in the sensitized tips of his own fingers. His "ancient beauty"—perhaps that beauty of looks noticed in the water—has faded in the discovery of his "new beauty"—the discovery, in short, of the "beauty" in self-induced orgasm.

Next, Narcissus sees himself as "a young girl / Caught in the woods by a drunken old man / Knowing at the end the taste of his own whiteness / The horror of his own smoothness / And he felt drunken and old" (30, lines 28–32). In the *Waste Land* drafts of "Narcissus," the possessive adjective is "her," not "his" (*WLF,* 93, 97). One persuasive interpretation of these ambiguous lines is that this is Narcissus's memory of his first homosexual encounter, with an older man who, in assuming the dominant (or male) role, places Narcissus in the compliant female role. This encounter brought its own knowledge to Narcissus—in this role he/she came to know the "taste of his/her own whiteness" (semen) and the "horror of his/her own smoothness" (the beauty of youth that attracted the "drunken old man"). At the end, Narcissus feels "drunken and old"—he identifies with his aggressive sexual partner and makes his decision to withdraw into isolation.

"So he became a dancer to God" (*PWEY,* 30, line 31). The "before God" of the first *Waste Land* draft (*WLF,* 95) has become "to God"—and Narcissus seems to have learned from experience that orgasmic sex can bestow bliss (if self-induced) as well as despair (if by "coupling"). At this point in the poem, Eliot's Narcissus takes on the role of the St. Sebastian of the art masterpieces: "Because his flesh was in love with the burning arrows / He danced on the hot sand / Until the arrows came" (*PWEY,* 30, lines 34–37). The use of "came" in this climactic position suggests the role of the arrows universally assumed by the homoerotic cult surrounding the traditional St. Sebastian. It is significant that in the first *Waste Land* draft, the adjective is phallic—"penetrant" not "burning" (*WLF,* 93). "As he embraced them [the arrows] his white skin surrendered itself to the redness of blood, and satisfied him" (*PWEY,* 30, line 37). Notice the use of the sexually suggestive language—"embraced," "surrendered": penetration (of the arrows) brings what seems like sexual "satisfaction." The traditional St. Sebastian is often portrayed in paintings as expressing both pain and pleasure as he is pierced by the soldier's arrows. The poem concludes: "Now he is green, dry and stained / With the shadow in his mouth" (30, lines 38–39). The original St. Sebastian was not killed by arrows, but was left for dead and, on trying to escape, was caught, bludgeoned, and thrown into a sewer. There is no tradition of Saint Narcissus of Jerusalem being pierced by arrows. Although Eliot's last line does not assign his Saint Narcissus to death, he appears—"green, dry and stained"—to be near death from starvation and dehydration, not to say total isolation. Indeed, two rejected lines that preceded the two final lines in the first draft, indicate that Narcissus faces death: "We each have the sort of life we want, but his / life went straight to the death he wanted" (*WLF*, 93). The lines are unimpressive as poetry and out of character for the voice that has been established for the speaker. Eliot might have eliminated them for these reasons—or he may have wanted to end the poem with some ambiguity as to Narcissus's final state.

"Narcissism" became a psychological term about the time Eliot was attending school and college. His study of philosophy at Harvard, as we have seen, included the study of psychology, including psychological aberrations. One of the important studies we know Eliot read (see Chapter 4, Section 8) was Havelock Ellis's "Sexual Inversion," part 2 of volume 2 of Ellis's influential *Studies in the Psychology of Sex* (1897–1910). In a summary passage, Ellis presents Freud's view that young males as they grow up go through an "intense but brief fixation on a woman," usually the mother but perhaps a sister: "Then [experiencing] an intense censure inhibiting this incestuous impulse, they overcome it by identifying themselves with women and taking refuge in Narcissism, the self becoming the sexual object. Finally they look for youthful males resembling themselves, whom they love as their mothers loved them. Their pursuit of men is thus determined by their flight from women." Ellis goes on to point out that this view was held not only by Freud, but also "Sadger, Stoken, and many others" (Ellis, si, 304). The passage might well have been a shaping influence on Eliot's imagination as he wrote "The Death of Saint Narcissus."

But there is another source that might also have helped shape Eliot's poem. David Bernstein, in a 1976 article about Eliot's poem and the ballet dancer Vaslav Nijinksy, points out that at the time Eliot was in Paris in 1911, the Ballets Russes, under the directorship of Sergei Pavlovich Diaghileff, was continuing a successful run of several of its ballets, one of them being Fokine's "Narcisse," danced by Nijinsky. At the time, the bisexual Nijinsky was having an affair with Diaghileff (Bernstein, 76–77). Bernstein points out Herbert Howarth's observation in his *Notes on Some Figures Behind T. S. Eliot* that Eliot's passion for the Russian ballet exceeded his passion for the London music hall, and he saw works performed by it both in Paris during his 1910–11 year there, and later in London, beginning in 1914 (98). Thus Bernstein attempts to make a case for Eliot's modeling his life of St. Narcissus after Nijinsky's life. But this would mean the poem would have had to have been written some time between early 1919 (after Nijinsky's mental collapse) and late 1922 (when the *Waste Land* drafts went to John Quinn). Although many of the events in both lives have striking similarities, and even though Nijinsky had that self-awareness of his own beauty, felt a strong self-love, and executed dance movements that struck many viewers as quite feminine, the evidence for Eliot's writing the poem earlier is too fully documented to support Bernstein's thesis. Bernstein does admit that "no fewer than three highly qualified authorities" date the poem at 1915 (102).

Nancy R. Comley, however, makes a good case for taking Eliot's Saint Narcissus as a forerunner of his Tiresias in *The Waste Land* in her 1979 article, "From Narcissus to Tiresias: T. S. Eliot's Use of Metamorphosis." She writes: "it is knowledge . . . of the extremes of sensuality and the impossibility of transcending the body and its insistent desires, that Eliot's Narcissus finds unbearable, and which leads to this ascetic retreat to the desert (a Waste Land in embryo)" (Comley, 284).

A challenging and elusive treatment of the relationship of Eliot's poem and *The Waste Land* is found in Merrill Cole's 1997 essay "Empire of the Closet." Focusing on "The Death of Saint Narcissus" as the primary forerunner of *The Waste Land,* Cole writes, for example, such provocative sentences as the following: "Without becoming our interpretive salvation, the closet's pull of secrecy must itself come under analysis: beyond the sexually-charged erasure of the homosexual, the poem proceeds to construct its closet walls out of literary allusion, traditional authority, and, ultimately, the ideology of empire. Eliot's closet enables the assumption of a panoptical overview of society, with impersonality functioning as the guarantee of objectivity. Such a perspective links Eliot to other presumptively 'objective' forms of imperialist discourse, like news reportage, the realist novel, and historical writing, all of which depend on the myth of the neutral and encompassing Western gaze" (Cole, 71). Most readers would agree that Cole's sentences do not become an "interpretive salvation" in approaching Eliot's poem.

One distinguished critic of "The Death of Saint Narcissus" cannot go unmentioned here: Ted Hughes. He was one of "Eliot's poets" published at Faber and Faber, and until his recent death, poet laureate of England. And he has had some fame in America for being the divorced husband of the American poet Sylvia Plath, who committed suicide. Hughes gathered three of his tributes to Eliot in one volume, *A Dancer to God* (1992). The title essay in abbreviated form was given as a toast to Eliot at a centenary dinner that coincided with publication of *The Letters of T. S. Eliot* on September 26, 1988. Valerie Eliot was in the audience and, later, Hughes dedicated his volume to her. Hughes, in one of the highest tributes one poet could pay to another—almost an apotheosis of Eliot—singles out "The Death of Saint Narcissus" as a poem that stands "very oddly alone, in an odd position, at the threshold of the *Collected Poems* yet not within," as "the first portrait, perhaps the only full-face portrait, of Eliot's genius" (Hughes, 33).

Hughes sees the "holy figure" of the poem as "some form of Eros/Diony-sus, the androgynous, protean daemon of biological existence in the repro-ductive cycle." Having lived the sexual life of both male and female, having become the god who was a fish and the god in the tree, he becomes "the elemental and timeless incarnation of all the dying gods of the birth, copu-lation and death mythos . . . the tragic, sacrificed form of Eros, simply the god of love." Thus, for Hughes, the poem "reclaims the sanctity of biologi-cal and primitive feeling, and fuses it with a covert . . . variant of the life and death of Christ" (35–36). Just as the poem is an "objective correlative" for Eliot's poetic self, so does the poem lay down a "life-plan" for the entire drama that is Eliot's poetic works. Prufrock, the "diffident John the Bap-tist," precedes the death and "sacrificial dismemberment and scattering of the parts" that is *The Waste Land* and *The Hollow Men*. "In a harrowing rebirth, out of the nadir, the Christ soul emerges, surrounded by 'Journey of the Magi,' 'Animula,' 'Marina,' 'A Song for Simeon.'" Now the new soul, the energies of Eros refocused within the Christian ethos, moves through *Ash Wednesday,* through *Murder in the Cathedral,* to "the rose-window, many-petalled choreography of the dance before God in an English chapel, which is the pattern of the *Four Quartets*" (43–44).

But why is such a poem, this "life-plan," so oddly alone, at the threshold, not within the *Collected Poems*? Hughes recognizes the "self-exposure" that may have played a part in Eliot's withdrawal of the poem from publication: "The physical details and the subjective feeling attached to them are experi-enced with such first-hand intensity they reduce the mythic/historic context to nothing more than a theatre backdrop, while this dance in the foreground is suffered through like a biological transformation, so nakedly that it is shocking." In "a sort of alternative current of voluptuous horror and mysti-cal rapture," the poem transmits "a supercharge . . . of the richest erotic feel-ing going through a very bizarre transmutation" (36). Eliot may indeed have recoiled from exposing such raw emotion at a time in his life when he was experiencing it.

8. Poems Written 1914–1915

The poems of 1914 through 1915 are divided into four roughly interrelated groups. Titles of poems are followed by dates of composition (when known) and dates of first publication in journals and books. "Leyris" refers to Pierre Leyris, French translator of Eliot's work *T. S. Eliot's Poèmes, 1910–1930* (1947), for which John Hayward (Eliot's British friend and longtime apartment mate) provided notes and dates of composition. *POO: Prufrock and Other Observations* (1917); *PWEY: Poems Written in Early Youth* (1967); *WLF: The Waste Land: A Facsimile and Transcript of the Original Drafts* (1971); *LTSE1: The Letters of T. S. Eliot* (vol. 1, 1988); *IOMH: Inventions of the March Hare* (1996).

Derangements, Hallucinations, Hellish and Heavenly Visions: Fragments for
    The Waste Land
  "So Through the Evening" (1914?); *WLF*
  "After the Turning" (1914?); *WLF*
  "I am the Resurrection" (1914?); *WLF*
Descent from the Cross
  "The Burnt Dancer" (June 1914); *IOMH*
  "Oh Little Voices" (July 1914); *WLF; LTSE1; IOMH*
  "The Love Song of St. Sebastian" (1914); *LTSE1; IOMH*
  "The Death of St. Narcissus" (early 1915); *PWEY; WLF*
Miniature Scenes, Sketches, Portraits
  "In the Department Store" (1915?); *IOMH*
  "Afternoon" (1914?); *LTSE1; IOMH*
  "Morning at the Window" (1914; 1915, Leyris); *Poetry*, September 1916;
    POO; LTSE1; IOMH
  "The Boston Evening Transcript" (1915); *Poetry*, October 1915; *POO*
  "Aunt Helen" (1915); *Poetry*, October 1915; *POO*
  "Cousin Nancy" (1915); *Poetry*, October 1915; *POO*
  "Mr. Apollinax" (1915); *Poetry*, September 1916; *POO*
I/She: Complexes and Hysteria
  "Suppressed Complex" (1914?); *LTSE1; IOMH*
  "Paysage Triste" (1914?); *IOMH*
  "Hysteria" (1915); *POO*

[9]

1916

MAKING DO, FINDING MEANS, EXPANDING CONNECTIONS

(1) *"The Most Awful Nightmare of Anxiety"; "Pegasus in Harness,"* 255; (2) *The Triumph of Poetry over Philosophy,* 257; (3) *Reviews and Essays, Teaching and Lecturing: Total Immersion,* 260; (4) *A Widening Circle of Friends and Associates, Writers and Artists,* 269

1. "The Most Awful Nightmare of Anxiety"; "Pegasus in Harness"

One of the first letters Eliot wrote at the beginning of the new year, 1916, and one so important I have quoted it again and again, was to his friend Conrad Aiken on January 10, and seemed to present an overview of the crisis-state of every side of his life: "That I am to be at Highgate School . . . that I am starting to rewrite my thesis, that my wife has been very ill, that I have been taken up with the worries of finance and Vivien's health, that my friend Jean Verdenal has been killed . . . that compulsion [draft] is coming in, that my putative publisher will probably be conscripted, that we are very blue about the war, that living is going up" (*LTSE1,* 125). After lapsing into four stanzas of the bawdy King Bolo verses, which served, perhaps, as a psychological safety-valve in the face of his problems, Eliot continued: "I *hope* to write when I have more detachment. But I am having a wonderful life nevertheless. I have *lived* through material for a score of long poems in the last six months" (126). As we noted in the opening pages of Chapter 5 and in the introduction, this claim deserves attention, particularly in the light of Eliot's discussion later of something he is to call an "impersonal theory of poetry" (in the essay "Tradition and the Individual Talent," 1919). At this point in his career, he saw the material for his poetry as coming directly out of the experiences he has "*lived* through"—obviously those that are emotionally powerful.

Eight months later, on September 6, 1916, Eliot confessed to his brother Henry his fears that "'J.A.P.' is a swan song." He could not speak of this to Vivien because she was "exceedingly anxious" that he should "equal it, and would be bitterly disappointed" if he did not. He confided that the "present year has been, in some respects, the most awful nightmare of anxiety that the mind of man could conceive, but at least it is not dull, and it has its compensations" (151). It is hard to conceive of a "nightmare" that has its compensations, but in the context we might assume that those "compensations" lie in the possibilities the terrible year offers in the way of raw material for the writing of new poems reaching beyond "The Love Song of J. Alfred Prufrock." Vivien dominated Eliot's thoughts as he wrote this letter—as she had in almost everything else he had done since their marriage.

Vivien's chatty letter to Henry a month later, on October 11, is significant in several respects: it shows something of her character as well as the state of her health; it speaks to their financial condition; and it reveals her views of her husband as a poet. Vivien wrote en route by train on a dreaded visit to Lancashire to visit "*old*" friends, "dreadful . . . very *very* rich manufacturing people—*so provincial*" that her American friends, including her husband, say they are "very much like Americans!!" Having been this friend's bridesmaid two years earlier, Vivien seems both disloyal and hypocritical in her comment. That she and Eliot would link rich manufacturing people with provincial Americans indicates that they think they are in a superior class. Vivien's description to Henry of her "rare" migraine headaches—which "*no drug touches*"—as "nerve storms" lasting fifteen to twenty-four hours, making her "rise up weak and white," foreshadows the lady in *The Waste Land* whose "nerves are bad to-night. Yes, bad." She thanked Henry for his "constant five poundses," for they had only "twenty two pounds in the bank" and Tom would not be paid until Christmas, thus causing them to write to his father for help. Despite her protestation that she couldn't "bear to do that," she then tellingly admitted that she shouldn't have made this visit at all for it meant "getting more clothes."

Finally, as an indication that Henry must have tried to reassure Eliot about his writing fears, Vivien confessed that she had read Henry's last letter before Tom had come home. And she declared that "of the two," she worried most: "I look upon Tom's poetry as real genius—I *do* think he is made to be a great writer—*a* poet. His prose is very good—but I think it will never be so good as his poetry." Whereas Eliot had confided to his brother that Vivien was anxious that he should equal "Prufrock," Vivien admitted another reason for her concerns. It was "a *constant* canker" with her when she saw that he was not writing poetry and that his feeling of being "*dried up*" was independent of either time or money constraints. Furthermore, she felt "*very* strongly" that journalism was bad for him and would be "the *ruin* of his poetry." At the end of the letter Vivien urged Henry to join them in London to pursue his own journalistic career. Since he was unattached, she said, he should risk it. Tom had taken a much larger risk a year ago and she "can swear that he has never regretted it." Of course he had her to "shove him—I supply the motive power, and I *do* shove" (154–57). In spite of all her handicaps at this time, Vivien was a crucial support, one of the forces, along with Pound, that made it possible for Eliot to write poetry.

2. The Triumph of Poetry over Philosophy

Eliot was immersed in a plethora of details—his search for income, for ways of getting and earning money. Weighing most heavily was the promise he had made to his parents that he would finish his thesis and return to America for his final oral examination. As we have seen, Eliot had some of his prominent friends (Ezra Pound, Bertrand Russell) write to his parents to assure them of his abilities, both philosophical and literary—and of his need for money. In a letter of January 18, 1916, sent by Eliot's mother to Bertrand Russell in their ongoing correspondence, she revealed what the family expectations were for his future: "I do not see any reason why if my son makes Philosophy his life work he should not write all the poetry he desires, if not too much of the ephemeral 'vers libre.'" She was most concerned that Tom would come to take the degree in May, for the Ph.D. was essential for an academic position in America. Men teaching in secondary schools, she wrote, were "as a rule inferior" to women, "with little social position or distinction." And she hoped he would not have to continue in such work another year—"it is like putting Pegasus in harness" (*LTSE1*, 131).

As for Tom's need for money, Charlotte Eliot assured Russell that his father would "do for him all he can as soon as he can," mentioning in passing that both she and her husband were hoping "for a return to power of the Republican party, and a consequent revision of the tariff"—to keep America after the war from being "flooded with cheap German goods" (131). In this letter Charlotte Eliot came around again to the question of poetry, mentioning that she had seen Ezra Pound's praise of Tom in the *Fortnightly Review* as "one of two of the most intelligent writers." She herself was critical of Pound's articles as "over-strained, unnatural." And when Mr. Eliot saw *Blast,* he remarked that "he did not know there were enough lunatics in the world to support such a magazine" (131). Such cultural and literary views in the Eliot household in St. Louis help us understand why Eliot had decided to settle in England.

Bertrand Russell wrote to Eliot's Harvard professor J. H. Woods on March 4, 1916, about arrangements for the lectures he had been invited to deliver at Harvard the following year, and devoted much of his letter to T. S. Eliot. He hoped all was well with his work on the thesis for he feared that his efforts at making a living and the time spent caring for his wife may have caused him to grow "rusty in his work." In "despair" at seeing his "fine talents wasting," Russell explained that Eliot had genuine talent as a poet with "a very considerable reputation for his poetry.... My view is that he is right to live in Europe because the atmosphere ... is better for that sort of work; and that is the sort of work he ought to aim at doing." Russell took it upon himself to speak for Eliot who, he believed, was too "reserved and modest" to reveal "something of the struggle he has had" (132–33).

Eliot himself wrote to Professor Woods on March 6, 1916, telling him that he would be sending off his revised thesis (entitled *The Nature of Objects, with Reference to the Philosophy of F. H. Bradley*) "in a few days," and that if all went well, he would board ship for America on April 1 and could therefore be in Boston for the final examination "the week of April 10." Eliot cautioned that this plan would work only if there were "no international developments" that would "prevent my sailing" (134). As it turned out, Eliot had to send a cable to Woods that he had cancelled his reservation because of the war-related danger involved. And it appears that he asked Bertrand Russell to cable his father in support of the cancellation, for Henry Ware Eliot sent a copy of the cable in a letter to Woods bearing the impressive (if somewhat incongruous) letter-head of his company: "Hydraulic-Press Brick Company, / Central National Bank Building, / St. Louis, Mo." He was not pleased with Russell's language—no doubt the injunction to cable Tom "AGAINST SAILING . . . UNLESS IMMEDIATE DEGREE IS WORTH RISK-ING LIFE" (136).

T. S. Eliot wrote to "Dr. Woods" on May 3, reporting that the ship on which he had booked passage had been "postponed" and that he would come "*at the first opportunity.* I hope that the war will be over, as naturally I do not like to leave my wife here, or venture the waves myself, while it is still on" (136–37). While Eliot was stranded on the other side of the ocean, his mother was anxiously awaiting news of his progress toward the completion of his degree. She wrote a letter on May 23 to Russell, in which she made what appears to have been a last appeal to obtain his aid in discouraging her son from abandoning philosophy, which she has "absolute faith in . . . but not in the vers libre" (138–39).

One month later, on June 23, 1916, Professor Woods wrote to Eliot: "The Division of Philosophy has accepted your thesis without the least hesitation. Prof. Royce regards it as the work of an expert. . . . Please let us be reassured that your interest in Philosophy is as strong as before" (142–43). This last remark implied that Woods himself had developed some doubts about Eliot's commitment to philosophy. Eliot took his time about replying, and his letter on September 7, 1916, seemed designed to suggest implicitly that his interest in philosophy was not as "strong as it was before." He thanked the department and hoped "to justify its acceptance by passing a good examination" when he came to America, but he could not make plans for that yet with "so much on foot" (152).

The rest of Eliot's letter was devoted to what was "on foot." He was "to give a course of six lectures in Yorkshire on Social, Philosophical and Religious Problems in Contemporary France" under the Oxford Extension Lecturing program so that he could give up teaching and "also have a clear six months a year for whatever else" he wanted to do. So much for teaching and lecturing; what else? Eliot spoke of being "very busy in Fleet Street journalism as well." Among other things, his projects included reviewing books for the *Westminster Gazette* and writing articles for the *Monist:* "one on Leibniz and Bradley, the other on Leibniz and Aristotle." After this summary of his activities, Eliot wrote that his duties and his wife's health prevented him from attending the Aristotelian Society meetings but he hoped to do better in the future. Near the end of the letter Eliot mentioned a recent holiday that he and his wife had at a little village near Portsmouth, on the coast. Their "delightful month" was somewhat ruined, at the end, by Vivien's "attack of neuralgia" (152–53). Just as Eliot's marriage to Vivien had enabled him to remain in England, so it was Vivien's constantly recurring illnesses that ensured that he would stay there.

Thus Mrs. Eliot's wishes were partially answered. Eliot had completed his thesis in philosophy, but war and his duties as a teacher, lecturer, and reviewer, as well as the demands imposed on him by Vivien's health, prevented him from returning to America to take his exams. And by the end of the year, as Eliot wrote in a letter of November 5 to his brother, he would give up teaching, "as I find that I am losing in every way. . . . I do think that if one makes up one's mind what one wants, then sooner or later an occasion will come when it is possible to seize it, for I think everybody gets the kind of life he wants" (157). Pegasus, still in harness, was gradually loosening the constraints that bound him.

3. Reviews and Essays, Teaching and Lecturing: Total Immersion

In late March 1916, the Eliots had moved to 18 Crawford Mansions into the "tiniest" of flats, with the "*luxury*" of "constant hot water," described by Vivien in a June 1 letter to Henry. She had chosen "*orange*" paper for the dining room, which was "also Tom's dressing room and study!" Tom, she wrote, was "wonderful," getting "so much pushing and helping" because people could see that he was "*worth* helping." But the problem was that teaching, "for which he is *too* good, and *not* fitted," meant throwing away "innumerable chances and openings for writing" and making "do the little scraps that he has time, and energy, for" (*LTSE1*, 139–40).

During these scraps of time, Eliot was systematically developing his skills as a reviewer of books for various periodicals and increasing his reputation as a writer of significant articles for philosophical journals. His main concern was to turn out good material for journals that paid the cash he so desperately needed. In a letter of August 21, 1916, to Conrad Aiken, Eliot outlined the writing he was able to do once freed from the school day: "philosophy for the *Monist* and the *International Journal of Ethics,* reviews for the *New Statesman,* the *Manchester Guardian* and the *Westminster Gazette.* . . . I am now trying to get an introduction to the *Nation.*" Eliot was enthusiastic about his labors and mindful of its effect on his style: "Composing on the typewriter, I find that I am sloughing off all my long sentences which I used to dote upon. Short, staccato, like modern French prose. The typewriter makes for lucidity, but I am not sure that it encourages subtlety" (143–44).

Eliot revealed to Aiken that, in addition to teaching, reviewing, and writing articles, he was planning a sequence of lectures on "contemporary intellectual movements in France to deliver . . . to the general public—mostly, I believe, ladies. If they come off, I ought to be able to secure plenty of lecturing, at least enough to keep us." Eliot mentioned that he had "distinguished predecessors on the Oxford lecturing circuit—Belloc and F. E. Smith, for instance." The one thing Eliot wanted desperately to do—write more poetry—seemed to be the only activity not on his agenda: "You will see that I have been very busy grinding axes. Of poetry I have not written a line; I have been too worried and nervous" (144–45).

It was to take more than a year of spreading his attention and energies over all these money-making activities before Eliot was able to devote a significant part of his time to the writing of poetry. This does not mean that what he did do during this period was a waste of his time. Indeed, except for teaching young pupils (and his stint of teaching at Highgate was to be his last), most of his activities were calculated to hone his skills in writing—

mainly in prose, but prose often related to poets and poetry. Of course his fame was ultimately to be in both. Few readers of Eliot have focused exclusively on his poetry, but have inevitably been attracted to and influenced by his essays.

Eliot's hopes that his first series of lectures would lead to others were realized. He became an "extension lecturer" beginning in 1916 and continued lecturing into 1919—even after he obtained a full-time job in 1917. The various syllabi that Eliot prepared for his five courses of lectures and that were distributed to potential students were published as booklets at the time and they have been reprinted along with explanatory commentary by Ronald Schuchard as the first chapter, "In the Lecture Halls" (25–51), of his book *Eliot's Dark Angel: Intersections of Life and Art* (1999), from which I have drawn the following account.

1916–1917: The first series of lectures, *Modern French Literature,* was delivered under the auspices of the Oxford University Extension Delegacy on afternoons from October 3 to December 12, 1916, at Ilkley, in Yorkshire. Another series of lectures, *Modern English Literature,* was sponsored by the University of London Extension Board, and was initiated in October 1916 in Southall (in Middlesex, west of London) concurrently with his teaching at Highgate and his Yorkshire lecture series. The Southall lectures were delivered on Monday evenings for a total of twenty-four weeks during the autumn and winter (and repeated with shifts in subjects for the next two academic years) (Schuchard, 26, 32).

1917–1918: The Southall lecture series, *Modern English Literature,* had a completely different list of authors in its second year. And Eliot was sponsored during this same period (autumn–winter) in a course of lectures on Victorian literature by the London County Council, including many of the authors he had included in his modern English literature series. Twenty-five weekly lectures were given Friday evenings at the County Secondary School, High Street Sydenham (39).

1918–1919: The Southall lectures continued, autumn through winter, and were devoted, at the request of the students, to Elizabethan literature (45).

Eliot delivered these lecture series at the same time that he was doing extensive writing of articles and reviews for various publications (especially philosophical). Moreover, beginning in March 1917, he was appointed to a full-time job working in the Colonial and Foreign Department of Lloyds Bank (a post he would hold for several years), and, beginning in June 1917, he assumed the duties (replacing Richard Aldington) of assistant editor of the *Egoist,* a position he held until the little magazine ceased publication in December 1919. Eliot's five lecture courses all required extensive planning and preparation, his duties as assistant editor required much reading and eval-uation (as well as writing), and his obligations to his regular job at Lloyds required his full attention. Can it be any wonder that Eliot found little time to devote to the writing of poetry?

The lecture series, along with the lecture titles and reading lists, are extraordinarily illuminating as to Eliot's interests, background, and views or opinions at this stage of his life, in his late twenties. Ronald Schuchard, who first made the syllabi for the extension courses widely available, has assessed the value of Eliot's experience persuasively: "The necessities that forced him to lecture from 1916 to 1919 also forced him into a three-year period of intensive reading and selective organizing. His courses required him to artic-ulate his developing critical concepts, to exercise his taste, and to reorder the poems of the English tradition into his own aesthetic and moral hierarchy when he would not otherwise have done so." Schuchard also finds the ori-gin of Eliot's extraordinarily allusive style in his extension-course experi-ence: "His preparations expanded the obvious erudition that he brought to his first critical efforts, and they provided a tremendous personal storehouse of allusions for his poetry" (50).

Eliot's lectures on modern French literature attracted almost sixty stu-dents, but attendance at the discussion sessions dropped to around fifteen; because of the war, these students were mainly female. Eliot's evaluation of the course suggests a good deal of frustration on his part. He wrote: "The audience seemed extremely intelligent, but somewhat passive; it seemed to consider the subject rather as interesting information than as matter to pro-voke original thought. It did not wish mere entertainment, but was not pre-pared for study" (quoted in Schuchard, 31–32). This seems to be damning with faint praise. Of course Eliot would not have suggested that the classes were a failure because that might have jeopardized his chances of receiving future lecture assignments. A "Local Secretary" for the extension lectures wrote of Eliot's classes: "The hour of the lectures was unpopular—It also made it impossible for most teachers to attend the course—The subject was difficult, and it was all new ground—Lectures much appreciated by the better educated members of the audience, who used the Library hard— The war has affected the centre adversely—Many of our members are away nursing and so on—others are too busy or tired to attend regularly or to read" (32).

Eliot's first series of lectures, *Modern French Literature,* is the most un-usual and interesting. The six lectures were entitled: I. The Origins: What is Romanticism?; II. The Reaction against Romanticism; III. Maurice Barrès and the Romance of Nationalism; IV. Royalism and Socialism; V. The

Return to the Catholic Church; VI. Before and After the War: Questions for the Future. What Eliot's syllabus makes clear is that his baldly stated rightist or reactionary positions might well have had an effect on the reaction of his students. Instead of setting forth topics or subjects that were to be explored from several perspectives, the syllabus set forth conclusions that Eliot had already come to on the matters under examination. Eliot might have called the series "The Defeat of a Tawdry and Poisonous Romanticism by a Valid and Sound Classicism in Modern French Literature." In the first lecture on romanticism he wrote that its "germs" were all to be "found in Rousseau," whose "great faults were (1) Intense egotism [and] (2) Insincerity." At the end of his description, Eliot revealed the truth the students would be learning from him: "Romanticism stands for *excess* in any direction. It splits up into two directions: escape from the world of fact, and devotion to brute fact. The two great currents of the nineteenth century—vague emotionality and the apotheosis of science (realism) alike spring from Rousseau" (27–30). It is somewhat astonishing to find such a questionable proposition presented as an unquestionable truth.

When Eliot turns to comments on classicism in his second lecture, "The Reaction against Romanticism," his tone shifts radically—suggesting that he is revealing an almost divine truth: "The beginning of the twentieth century has witnessed a return to the ideals of classicism. These may roughly be characterized as *form* and *restraint* in art, *discipline* and *authority* in religion, *centralization* in government (either as socialism or monarchy). The classicist point of view has been defined as essentially a belief in Original Sin—the necessity for austere discipline" (Schuchard, 27–28). This passage was clearly shaped by Eliot's reading of T. E. Hulme's philosophical speculations, which were appearing during 1914–15 in the *New Age*—emphasizing the centrality of original sin to the "classical point of view." When T. E. Hulme's *Speculations* was published posthumously in 1924, Eliot wrote "[Hulme] appears as a forerunner of a new attitude of mind, which should be the twentieth-century mind, if the twentieth century is to have a mind of its own. Hulme is classical, reactionary, and revolutionary; he is the antipodes of the eclectic, tolerant, and democratic mind of the last century" (ACTEH, 231). But of course Eliot had been moving almost all his life toward these views—influenced by his professors at Harvard such as Babbitt and by his reading of Maurras and other members of the Action Française during his year in Paris. Eliot himself paid homage to the three in 1961: "The influence of Babbitt (with an infusion later of T. E. Hulme and of the more literary essays of Charles Maurras) is apparent in my recurrent theme of Classicism versus Romanticism" (*TCTC,* 17).

Eliot's definition of classicism will remind readers of his famous statement of 1928 in his introduction to *For Lancelot Andrewes: Essays on Style and Order,* published shortly after his "conversion" to Anglo-Catholicism and baptism in 1927: "The general point of view [of the book] may be described as classicist in literature, royalist in politics, and anglo-catholic in religion" (FLA, 7). (But of course in making such a statement, Eliot reaches back further than 1915 to his year in Paris.)

The twentieth century has raised questions about the accuracy of Eliot's diagnosis of the problems and hopes for the future. It would seem, looking back from the end of the twentieth century, extremely difficult to speak of its art—whether literary or visual—as characterized by either form or restraint. We need only think of Allen Ginsberg, John Ashbury, Vladimir Nabokov, or Joseph Heller; free verse, rap, theater of the absurd, fantasies of (or in) fiction, abstract expressionism, or pop art—the list goes on. As for the century's religion, the truth seems to be that the authority of leaders, whether pope or pastor, has been weakened, and rebellion has dominated discipline; the relation of church and state has weakened worldwide. And the "centralization" in government that Eliot seemed to welcome resulted in a Stalinist Russia, a Hitlerian Germany, a fascist Italy, and an imperial Japan bent on ruling as much of the world as they could conquer. As to the unquestioning belief in any religious dogmas of the multitude of existent religions, such belief has tended to result in social repression and violence more than harmony and peace.

In his first course on modern English literature, Eliot's choice of authors is noteworthy, and his assigned reading somewhat staggering. There is no reason to believe that when he wrote the syllabus for this first course on the subject, he would be asked to teach another—and yet different—course the following year. For this first course he lists his authors: I. Tennyson; II. Browning; III. Elizabeth Barrett Browning; IV. Carlyle; V. John Henry Newman; VI. Dickens; VII. Thackeray; VIII. George Eliot; IX. Matthew Arnold; X. Minor Novelists (Disraeli, Peacock, Reade, Trollope); XI. The Brontës; XII. George Borrow; XIII. Ruskin; XIV. Edward Fitzgerald; XV. George Meredith; XVI. Retrospect (32–35).

For Tennyson, Eliot's syllabus instructs for the "early verse," "Read: *Lady of Shalott, Lotos-Eaters, Morte d'Arthur, Ulysses, Locksley Hall, The Two Voices, The Palace of Art.*" For the "longer poems," "Read: *Maud, In Memoriam, Idylls of the King.*" Such heavy reading assignments are common throughout the syllabus, as, for instance, that for Edward Fitzgerald. He writes: "Comparison of the two versions of Omar Khayyám. His prose works. Letters. Read: *The Rubáiyát of Omar Khayyám, Euphranor.*" The Fitzgerald assignment is interesting in view of Eliot's longtime passion for the poem, and its extra-ordinary influence on a poem yet to be written, "Gerontion." There is at the end of the syllabus a long list of "Supplementary Reading" in secondary sources. For example, for Tennyson, Eliot lists A. C. Bradley's *A Commentary on Tennyson's In Memoriam*. And for Fitzgerald, he lists editor W. A. Wright's *A Collection of the Letters of Edward Fitzgerald*. At the end of the list, Eliot writes, "*The English Men of Letters* is the best series of biography" (32–39). It is to this series that A. C. Benson contributed in 1905 his biography, *Edward Fitzgerald*.

Anyone glancing at the number of literary, critical, and biographical works Eliot listed in his syllabus would assume that his adult students, busy with jobs, families, and so forth, would not find the time to do the necessary reading. Indeed, Eliot's report on the class confirms this view: "I ask the students *all* to read some particular work on the current author, in order that there may always be a common basis for discussion; but when (as is usually the case), a student has very little time, I recommend further reading of one author in whom the student is interested, rather than a smattering of all." Eliot's course was scheduled for one meeting a week for a period of twenty-four weeks. In fact, the amount of material listed in the syllabus would have been difficult to cover in a full academic year of single weekly meetings. Eliot wrote: "Because of the students' lack of time . . . it seems to me on the whole desirable to devote more time to fewer authors, even if it is necessary to sacrifice altogether some of those named in the syllabus." Students were also expected to submit "fortnightly essays" during the course: "By the end of the year only three students had satisfied the writing requirements, and one of his best students had been summoned to the war" (37–38).

Eliot's classes for his first presentation of his modern English literature series were over in March 1917, and he would present another series under the same title with different authors beginning in the fall of 1917. Since he was desperate to increase his income, and since he preferred lecturing to teaching in lower-level schools, Eliot prepared another syllabus for the London County Council for a series on Victorian literature to be given on Friday evenings over a period of twenty-five weeks, beginning in the fall and continuing into the winter (parallel with the second series on modern English literature). His classes were to be held at the County Secondary School, High Street, Sydenham, beginning in late September (39).

The syllabus that survives lists an introductory lecture (I. The Social Framework) followed by four groups of lectures. The first of these is enti-tled "The Makers of Nineteenth-Century Ideas," and includes "2. History and Criticism—Thomas Carlyle; 3. A Contrast in Ideas: John Stuart Mill and

Matthew Arnold; 4. The Influence of Science—Darwinism in T. H. Huxley and Herbert Spencer; 5. Art and Economics—John Ruskin and William Morris." The second category was entitled "The Development of English Poetry" (nos. 6–14) and the third "The Development of English Fiction" (nos. 15–22). The last and smallest group of lectures was entitled "Byways of Victorian Literature" and seems in some way the most eccentric. There were three groups of writers discussed: "23. The Gipsy Pateran—George Borrow, Richard Jefferies and others; 24. Aestheticism—Walter Pater and Oscar Wilde; 25. The Laureates of Nonsense—Edward Lear, Lewis Carroll, and the Makers of Light Verse." The syllabus for this course does not contain reading assignments, and apparently no evaluation of the course survives, but we might conclude from the organization of the material and the listing of the writers that Eliot had learned a great deal from the shortcomings of his first course the year before (39–40).

For his second course in modern English literature, given during the same months of 1917–18 as his course on Victorian literature, Eliot presented ten groupings of lectures: I. Emerson; II. William Morris; III. Dante Gabriel Rossetti; IV. Swinburne; V. Walter Pater; VI. Samuel Butler; VII. Robert Louis Stevenson; VIII. The "Nineties"; IX. Thomas Hardy; X. Conclusion (41–43). Perhaps the most surprising inclusion in this series of writers is Ralph Waldo Emerson, and the question arises as to why Eliot included him—and put him first. The answer seems to be simple. In a letter to his mother of September 12, 1917, Eliot wrote, "they want me to start with Emerson." The "they" must be the University of London Extension Board, sponsor of the series. It seems that Eliot had never read Emerson before—at least from what he wrote to his mother a week later, on September 19: "I am busy reading Emerson. He strikes me as very wordy. He has something to say often, but he spreads it out and uses very general terms; it seems more oratory than literature. His biography is interesting and contains many familiar names" (*LTSE1*, 194–96).

It is unfortunate that Eliot's lecture on Emerson has not survived. But we can get some inkling of his presentation from his comments in the syllabus. In the first of three paragraphs, Eliot puts Emerson "in his place": "Characteristics of New England literature of the time. Emerson's relation to English men of letters. The society in which he lived. Religious and philosophical environment: Unitarianism and Transcendentalism." And in his second paragraph Eliot reveals something of his opinion: "Emerson style as an essayist. His aloofness; contrast with Carlyle, Arnold, and Ruskin. Quality of his thought. Read: *Essays, Nature,* and *The Conduct of Life*" (Schuchard, 41). Both of the titles here are extraordinarily long works (for Emerson), one early, the other late, and are not the best as an introduction to Emerson. Far better would have been "The American Scholar" and "Self-Reliance," which are indispensable for an understanding of both Emerson and America—its literature and its people.

In his third and final paragraph, Eliot wrote: "Emerson as a poet. Read: *Selected Poems.* Suggested Reading: "Thoreau, *Walden;* Hawthorne, *The Scarlet Letter;* chapter in *Great Writers of America,* in the 'Home University Library.'" The American writers conspicuous by their absence are Walt Whitman and Herman Melville. (Melville would remain the great unread American novelist for Eliot.) In the "Supplementary Reading" section of his syllabus, Eliot recommends other Emerson items: "On Emerson: Oliver Wendell Holmes, *Ralph Waldo Emerson;* Charles E. Norton, ed., *The Correspondence of Thomas Carlyle and Ralph Waldo Emerson, 1834–72;* Emerson's *Journal* (10 vols.) is well worth reading parts of, to obtain a more intimate knowledge of the man." Among the "Suggestions for Papers" (following "Supplementary Reading"), we find "Emerson and His Circle (the point of view of Emerson, Thoreau, Hawthorne, etc." (41, 43–44). While the additional reading suggested is useful (especially the remark about Emerson's *Journal*), the suggested topic seems perfunctory and quite uninspired.

Probably Eliot's most sensational set of lectures was that on "The 'Nineties,'" described in one long paragraph: "Characteristics of the group of the 'Yellow Book.' Influence of Walter Pater. Their attitude toward life. Some personalities: Wilde, Ernest Dowson, Lionel Johnson, Aubrey Beardsley, Francis Thompson, W. B. Yeats, and Bernard Shaw (in his earlier phase). The 'Celtic Movement': Yeats, Synge, A.E., Fiona Macleod. Read: Oscar Wilde: *Intentions; The Importance of Being Earnest; The Ballad of Reading Gaol;* Selected poems of Dowson, Johnson, Thompson, Symons, Yeats, Davidson; Synge: *The Playboy of the Western World.*" It would be most interesting to know what Eliot said in his lectures about all these personalities, and especially Oscar Wilde and the works he lists for his students to read, including *The Ballad of Reading Gaol* and *Intentions* (1891), a collection of Wilde's essays on the theory of literature and criticism. Under "Supplementary Reading," Eliot listed one book for Wilde: A. Ransome, *Oscar Wilde: A Critical Study* (1912) (43–44).

Some insight into Eliot's feelings and thoughts when he was preparing the two sets of his 1917–18 lectures (on Victorian and modern English literature) is found in a letter to his mother written September 2, 1917, describing his state of mind. After explaining that he had done two articles for the *Egoist* and two for the *New Statesman,* and was finishing a longer one, he wrote about his lecture preparations, "which will involve reading a number of authors of whom I know very little: Brontë, George Eliot, Emerson, Charles Reade, Kingsley, Huxley, Spencer, Samuel Butler" (*LTSE1,* 193). For readers used to thinking that Eliot had read everything in every language, his confession to his mother is surely something of a shock.

And he confessed no doubt his deepest feelings to his mother when he wrote that, though he enjoyed the lectures, he would be glad when he could give them up for "work of a more permanent nature." And though they contributed to his income, he looked forward to spending "*all* my spare time exactly as I please." But of course Eliot is shading his prose to his audience. He knew what he says to his mother will be passed on to his father, from whom he would appreciate more financial help. He continued: "When I can earn all the money I need out of one thing, and be able to read and write in the rest of my time without thinking of the financial reward for what I do, then I shall be satisfied. The lecturing really takes more out of me than the bank work during the day" (193).

Eliot's last series of lectures, devoted to Elizabethan literature, was given in the autumn and winter of 1918–19. On May 10, 1918, Eliot wrote to his mother that these lectures "would interest me more than what we have done before, and would be of some use to me too, as I want to write some essays on the dramatists, who have never been properly criticized" (231). This series of lectures enabled Eliot to draw on his previous academic training more than any of the other lecture series he presented—and, as he acknowledged, the subjects were closer to his own interests. In another letter to his mother the following month (June 2, 1918), Eliot wrote that he was preparing for next year's Southall class by "rereading the poets and dramatists of the time of Shakespeare and immediately after," a period that he preferred "infinitely to the 19th Century—to any periods in English literature" (233). In actuality, the enrollment for Eliot's classes at Southall was so small that it was almost cancelled, but he was so intent on teaching the subject so dear to his heart that he offered to give his course for a reduced fee if necessary. In the end, he was allowed to present his lectures as planned.

The titles for the eighteen subdivisions of the lecture series not only show the extent of Eliot's coverage of the Elizabethan period, but also serve as a Who's Who of the many authors and titles that turn up in the footnotes of Eliot's poetry: I. The Earliest Forms of Drama; II. The Revival of Learning; III. The Elizabethan Stage; IV. Kyd: The First Important Dramatist; V. Christopher Marlowe [The greatest poet since Chaucer and the greatest dramatist before Shakespeare]; VI. The Chronicle Play; VII. Euphuism [John Lyly]; VIII. Shakespeare [The early Shakespeare . . . The mature Shakespeare . . . The later Shakespeare . . . Shakespeare's relation to his time]; IX. Non-Dramatic Poetry; X. Spenser; XI. The Lyric and the Sonnet; XII. The Beginnings of Prose; XIII. Sidney and Raleigh; XIV. The Elizabethan Romance;

xv. Montaigne; xvi. Bacon; xvii. Ben Jonson; xviii. The Later Drama [Chapman, Dekker, Heywood, and Middleton, Beaumont and Fletcher, John Webster, Ford] (Schuchard, 45–48). The syllabus concluded with three longish reading lists for drama, poetry, and prose. Eliot's brief characterizations of items on the reading list exudes self-confidence: "There is very little good criticism of Elizabethan and Jacobean drama, but J. A. Symonds: *Predecessors of Shakespeare* is useful, and Swinburne: *Age of Shakespeare* and *Study of Ben Jonson,* as well as Rupert Brooke: *John Webster,* are interesting, though misleading" (49–51).

Of his experience as an extension lecturer, Eliot himself wrote, in "The Function of Criticism" (1923): "I have had some experience of Extension lecturing, and I have found only two ways of leading any pupils to like anything with the right liking: to present them with a selection of the simpler kind of facts about a work—its conditions, its setting, its genesis—or else to spring the work on them in such a way that they were not prepared to be prejudiced against it. There were many facts to help them with Elizabethan drama: the poems of T. E. Hulme only needed to be read aloud to have immediate effect" (SE, 20–21). It is clear from these comments that Eliot had learned to teach from his experience and experiments in the classroom—as most good teachers do.

A glance at the table of contents for Eliot's *Selected Essays* reveals some dozen essays that are dated by Eliot from 1919–22, all of which are related in one way or another to subjects of his extension lectures, including "Tradition and the Individual Talent," "A Dialogue on Dramatic Poetry," "Christopher Marlowe," "Hamlet and His Problems," "Ben Jonson," "The Metaphysical Poets," "Andrew Marvell," "John Dryden," "William Blake," and "Swinburne as a Poet." Although Eliot suffered from his "overload" during this period— his teaching, his writing, his reviewing, his lecturing, his daily job at the bank—he was shaped by this experience into the poet who would write *The Waste Land* and, much later, *Four Quartets.* Given Vivien's various illnesses, Eliot was probably fortunate to be so consumed every day of the week, compelled as he was to concentrate on literature—reading, writing, teaching— and thus deprived of the leisure to worry about matters that could find no lasting remedy.

4. A Widening Circle of Friends and Associates, Writers and Artists

Eliot was lucky in his relatively small circle of friends in London, a circle that included Ezra Pound and Bertrand Russell. Pound was his literary mentor, not only advising Eliot on his poetry but actually editing his manuscripts and then getting them placed in various publications for which he served as adviser or assistant editor. Russell, on the other hand, looked on Eliot as his son, and provided (as we have seen) the means for food and shelter; and saw that he was introduced to other artists and writers who shared his interests. Through Pound and Russell, Eliot was gradually introduced to an ever widening circle of people, some of whom played key roles in his career. We have already discussed Pound's role as foreign editor, beginning in 1912, of Harriet Monroe's newly established Chicago magazine, *Poetry*. And in 1913 Pound assumed a similar role for the British little magazine the *Egoist* (originally the *New Freewoman*), edited by Harriet Shaw Weaver. Pound became recognized as a kind of poetry entrepreneur, leaving behind the old, courting the new. Indeed, he had been the center, organizer, and chief theorist of two literary "movements" that attracted the attention of other writers, poets, and artists: Imagism and Vorticism.

No doubt the more important of these was Imagism, the chief inventors of which were T. E. Hulme and Ezra Pound. Pound, however, was the primary theorist. The main principle involved, modeled in part on the Japanese haiku, was that the image was not to be "described" but created with precision and brevity. In "A Few Don'ts by an Imagiste," published in *Poetry* in March 1913, Pound defined the "Image" as "that which presents an intellectual and emotional complex in an instant of time." Pound's three principles "demanding direct treatment, economy of words, and [composition in] the sequence of the musical phrase" stirred the new movement in poetry (Pound, *LE,* 4). Pound included Hulme's poems along with his own in *Riposte*s (1912) and, to ensure an audience for poets he admired, brought out *Des Imagiste*s (1914), representing the movement at its peak. Among the contributors was an American poet, perhaps the quintessential imagist—Hilda Doolittle, known as H.D.—whom Pound had met when they both attended the University of Pennsylvania in Philadelphia early in the 1900s. She was married to the British writer Richard Aldington (who was to become an assistant editor for the *Egoist*). When Imagism became so exciting as to attract such conventional poets as the American Amy Lowell, who began to propound (and distort, Pound believed) Imagistic theory, Pound abandoned the movement and contemptuously called it "Amygism."

In 1914 Pound joined with Wyndham Lewis to promote the Vorticist movement, focusing on the visual image of the "vortex," a whirlpool of imaginative energy resulting in creative works that included elements of abstraction in art and symbolism in poetry. Definitions of Vorticism were so studded with seemingly irreconcilable opposites and contraries as to make the movement incomprehensible to many potential followers. As already noted, Lewis founded the little magazine called *Blast* to publish Vorticist works, but only two issues were published, one in 1914 and the other in 1915, the war making it difficult to find money for such avant-garde artistic enterprises.

Others in Pound's circle were Ford Madox Ford (formerly Hueffer) and William Butler Yeats. Ford was a novelist and the astute editor of the *English Review* and Yeats was the preeminent Irish poet, for whom Pound had served as "secretary" (answering business letters) during the winter of 1913–14. By 1915 Pound was meeting with these and other friends at one restaurant or another for literary discussion. You can see them in the famous William Roberts portrait *The Vorticists at the Restaurant de la Tour Eiffel: Spring 1915* in the Tate Gallery, London. Eliot often joined these informal gatherings. And no doubt at some point in the discussions, the name of James Joyce came up. When Pound asked Yeats about possible Irish imagists to be included in his imagist volume, Yeats referred him to Joyce's first book, a volume of poems entitled *Chamber Music*. Pound wrote to Joyce, then living in Trieste, and found out about his works in progress, including the book of short stories, *Dubliners*, and a novel, *A Portrait of the Artist as a Young Man*. On receiving copies of manuscripts from Joyce, Pound began aggressively to promote Joyce's fiction, and soon the novel was being serialized in the *Egoist* (Carpenter, 224–27). So began the making of Joyce's remarkable reputation. Eliot echoed Pound's enthusiasm for Joyce's work, seeing Joyce as doing in fiction what he was doing in poetry.

We have already spoken of the direct assistance, financial and otherwise, that Bertrand Russell provided the Eliots. But he was of more lasting and vital help to them in introducing them to his own friends and acquaintances in London. In his memoir, *Old Friends, Personal Recollections* (1956), Clive Bell, art critic and husband of Virginia Woolf's sister Vanessa and one of the principals of the Bloomsbury Group, devotes an entire chapter to T. S. Eliot: "So far as I can remember, it was in the summer of 1916 that first we met. Bertrand Russell asked me to look out for a man called 'Eliot' who had just come, or was just coming, to England, and had been his best pupil at Harvard: he may have said 'My only good pupil,' but if so, doubtless he exaggerated as philosophers will." Bell reports that at the time, he was living with Maynard Keynes but was alone the night he invited Eliot to dine: "After dinner the poet and I sat in my room at the top of the house and talked about books. . . . For my part I liked him so much that I determined, there and then, to make him acquainted with some of my friends. Soon afterwards I introduced him to Roger Fry and Virginia Woolf, both of whom were to play parts in later encounters" (Bell, 119).

Virginia Woolf was to become one of the most important and closest of Eliot's friends among the Bloomsbury Group. Clive Bell describes Woolf's reaction to Eliot, which he shared: "Between Virginia and myself somehow the poet became a sort of 'family joke': it is not easy to say why. To some people the combination of human frailties with supernatural powers will always appear preposterous, which is, I suppose a roundabout way of saying that a poet is an oddity." Bell goes on to describe that oddity in terms that seem to echo other descriptions of Eliot: "To us at any rate this mixture, talent in his rarest form, combined with studied primness of manner and speech, seemed deliciously comic. Besides, Virginia was a born and infectious mocker." As an example of her mockery, Bell quotes an invitation he received from her: "Come to lunch on Sunday. Tom is coming, and, what is more, is coming with a four-piece suit" (120).

Bell took Russell's request seriously; witness the guest list at one of the events he describes in his memoir. The event was the 1917 Easter party at Lady Ottoline Morrell's country house, Garsington. Although Bell seems not to have brought Eliot to the party, he did bring "ten or a dozen copies" of Eliot's first book, the just-published *Prufrock and Other Observations*. Indeed, the presence of Eliot's first book was presence enough for the poet. It had been published by the Egoist Press, but it was Ezra Pound who supplied the money for publication. Bell writes that he "distributed . . . copies hot from the press like so many Good Friday buns." He then gives the guest list: "Our host and hostess, Philip and Lady Ottoline Morrell, of course. Mrs. St. John Hutchinson, Katherine Mansfield, Aldous Huxley, Middleton Murry, Lytton Strachey perhaps, and, I think [Mark] Gertler. Were there others? Maria Balthus for instance (later Mrs. Aldous Huxley). I cannot tell: but of this I am sure, it was Katherine Mansfield who read the poem ["The Love Song of J. Alfred Prufrock"] aloud." The reaction to the poem, Bell reports, was lively: "As you might suppose, it caused a stir, much discussion, some perplexity" (121–24).

Most of those present at this reading of "Prufrock" were already—or were to become—well-known writers or artists. The one exception is Mrs. St. John Hutchinson. Although a volume of her short stories was published in 1927, as wife of a distinguished Barrister and cousin of the Stracheys, Mary Hutchinson was prominent as a hostess in her own right and became a close friend of both Eliots. And as the mistress of Clive Bell himself, she was certainly a "member" of the Bloomsbury Group. It should be emphasized that the very term "Bloomsbury Group" has no fixed definition; indeed it seems to be a floating term that users may define for themselves. Even Clive Bell, in a chapter entitled simply "Bloomsbury," goes to great length to point out how vague the word is: "Let everyone have his or her notion of 'Bloomsbury'; but let everyone who uses the name in public speech or writing do his or her best to say exactly what he or she intends by it. Thus, even should it turn out that in fact there never was such a thing, the word might come to have significance independent of the facts and acquire value as a label" (128).

Leon Edel, in his history *Bloomsbury: A House of Lions* (1979), sums up "the public legend" that "made them out to be rude busybodies in painting, politics, economics, the novel. They espoused 'the new,' it was alleged, more for oddity and sensationalism than anything else. They were always against the Establishment. They were bad-mannered egotists. They were self-indulgent. They were homosexuals or lesbians. They practiced free love" (Edel, *B*, 286). Indeed, the paperback edition of Edel's book lists on the back cover the subjects of his study: "Virginia Woolf, Maynard Keynes, Leonard Woolf, Clive Bell, Duncan Grant, Lytton Strachey, Roger Fry, Vanessa Bell, Desmond MacCarthy" and follows their names with these labels: "A Novelist, A Homosexual, A Publisher, A Hedonist, A Painter, A Pederast, A Critic, A Feminist, A Knight, A Bisexual, A Theorist, A Snob." One can play a game and apply the labels to one or more of the names. Edel's book traces the complexities of his "Eminent Bloomsberries" through successive manifestations and memberships. As Clive Bell notes, they began in 1899 as a "reading society" in Cambridge and moved to the houses in Gordon and Fitzroy Squares between 1904–14 and beyond, with Virginia and Vanessa at "the heart" of the group. Throughout they were "loving friends," and for some G. E. Moore was "the binding influence" (Bell, 129–33). Moore was a professor of philosophy at Cambridge, and his book *Principia Ethica* (1903) and other works earned him the title, father of analytic philosophy.

Edel gives an amusing instance of what their unconventional lifestyle entailed: "[The artist] Duncan Grant was fond of his cousin [Lytton Strachey], but he found Lytton's hysterical proclamations of love more than he could bear. Lytton was too possessive, too oppressive. Duncan was unaccustomed to his kind of operatic style; and so he distanced himself. 'Duncan tortures me,' complained Lytton. And then it all became a Restoration comedy, because Duncan met Maynard Keynes in Paris and they became lovers even while Lytton still confided in Keynes and extolled Duncan's virtues" (Edel, *B*, 155).

Edel distinguishes Bloomsbury from the "celebrity salon" run by Lady Ottoline Morrell, whose "lions were D. H. Lawrence, Aldous Huxley, Bertrand Russell, painters such as Mark Gertler and, briefly, dancers such as Nijinsky." In their inclusion of artists and writers, and in their acceptance of unconventional lifestyles, both Bloomsbury and Lady Ottoline's salon were similar to the circle surrounding Mrs. Jack in Boston. There the central figure was Isabella Stewart Gardner; in Bloomsbury, Virginia Woolf and a bit beyond the Bloomsbury circle, Ottoline Morrell. Both in Boston and Bloomsbury, heterosexuality and homosexuality existed side by side, with frequent changes in sexual partners.

By the spring of 1919, Eliot was entangled in all of the intricacies and intrigues of Bloomsbury. As Hermione Lee writes in her biography of Virginia Woolf, there was a "'Bloomsbury' imbroglio, arising from Clive's jealous intuition of a new powerful influence on Mary. . . . There was a spate of 'telling.' Clive told Virginia that Tom Eliot had told Mary he didn't like her; Mary told Virginia it wasn't true; Virginia told Vanessa what Mary had told her; the Murrys told Virginia that Tom had told them how much he liked her" (Lee, 434). In a June 19 letter to his cousin Eleanor Hinkley, Eliot wrote to "show what social life entails." In his comic tour de force, Eliot only thinly disguises the participants in this social drama by using capital letters instead of names (supplied by the editor):

> I happen to make to a lady I know pretty well named A. [Mary Hutchinson] some flippant remarks about a lady B. [Virginia Woolf]. Later I get to know B. and get on with her quite well. B. repeats to others the compliments I paid her on one of her books. Then sudden coolness. Next C. [Murry] a mutual friend asks me if I ever said that I disliked B. and thought her book rubbish because B. has been told that I said it, and was much upset. I may remark that B. has occasionally suffered from melancholia. I deny the remarks, but say that some time ago I had made some light comments which might have been twisted that way. C. promises to report to B. Meanwhile A. gets in a funk lest I hear of this and trace it to her, and anxiously confides in Vivien. A. you see hates B. and also is jealous of her. She therefore repeats my remarks to D. [Clive Bell] a man friend of hers (A.'s) who dislikes me because A. likes me. D. is a connection of B. and when he hears her repeat my compliments, is irritated, and tells her, with alterations, what I said elsewhere. (*LTSE1*, 304–5)

Eliot went on like this for two more paragraphs of innumerable permutations and then commented: "This is an illustration. It will seem to you foolish. But think of this sort of thing as going on continually in a society where everyone is very sensitive, very perceptive and very quick. . . . The first thing one tries to notice in entering a room is everyone's frame of mind and the attitude towards everyone else, individually, which may have changed in twenty-four hours!" (305). Although Eliot is making fun of this situation, his wife Vivien wrote about the same matter to her friend Mary Hutchinson and commented that Eliot "hates and loathes all sordid quarreling and gossiping and intrigue and jealousy, *so much,* that I have seen him go white and *be ill* at any manifestation of it" (288). In the midst of these intrigues, Eliot had spent the Whitsun holiday with Mary Hutchinson at her home without Vivien. And his letter to Hutchinson, on June 15, expressing the pleasure with which he is "still looking back on the two days at Wittering" is suggestive of a growing intimacy. He continued: "I preserve—at least the illusion—that it was not a drifting fog but was rather only something interrupted or suspended" (302).

What Pound thought of the Bloomsbury Group, however, was another matter. Wyndham Lewis had quarreled with Roger Fry, and Pound gave his support to Lewis: "This quarrel was certainly one to draw Ezra's sympathy; in 1917 he wrote to his father: 'I may have met Clive Bell, but there are a lot of those washed-out Fry-ites, and I cant tell one from the other. A sort of male Dorcas-society.' 'The 'Bloomsbuggars,' as he liked to call them, never attracted the faintest admiration from [Pound]" (Carpenter, 243–44). Eliot was able to negotiate successfully between the two groups, the Poundians as well as the Bloomsberries.

Eliot was pleased to enter the houses, to lean against the eighteenth-century marble fireplaces, to join the society that both attracted him and filled him with anxiety and fear of humiliation. In a letter of July 1919, shortly after the Whitsun holiday, Eliot wrote a long letter to Mary Hutchinson in which he expounded on the differences between "civilization" and "culture." "Culture, if it means anything decent, means something personal: one book or painter made one's own rather than a thousand read or looked at." He went on to discuss what he felt about contemporary taste; what those tastes were; the two ways of reading: "because of particular and personal interest" or "because it is something one 'ought to have read'"; the "kinds of intelligence: the intellectual and the sensitive"; the books he was presently reading—in short, just the sort of "conversation" that attracted others to Eliot and the sort of conversation we might hear him speaking in the drawing rooms of Bloomsbury.

Eliot could write this way to Mary Hutchinson, whose opinion he sought when he shared his poetry with her, because she was a valued friend and confidante—to both Eliots. At the end of the letter Eliot cautioned her: "But remember that I am a *metic*—a foreigner, and that I *want* to understand you, and all the background and tradition of you. I shall try to be frank—because the attempt is so very much worth while with you—it is very difficult with me—both by inheritance and because of my very suspicious and cowardly disposition. But I may simply prove to be a savage" (*LTSE1*, 316–18). Eliot here reveals the attraction that English upper-class society—in the person of Mary Hutchinson—had for him.

[10]

1917–1918

T. S. ELIOT: BANKER, LECTURER, EDITOR, POET, ALMOST SOLDIER

1. Eliot the Banker: March 19, 1917–November 1925

As we have seen, once Eliot had made his decision to stay in England and earn enough money to support himself and his wife, he devoted all his mental and physical energies to writing reviews and essays, teaching school, and delivering a mind-boggling series of lectures. Little time was left for the newlyweds to spend together, and even when they were together, almost inevitably one or the other was sick. As Vivien wrote to Charlotte on April 8, 1917, she was suffering from migraines and he the "influenza for *weeks*"—he "felt that life was simply not worth going on with," each day "the screw turned a little tighter" (*LTSE1,* 161). Eliot's activities in earning a living were so frenzied that he frequently found himself running short of energy or compelled to slow down and get some rest. Little or no time was left to write poems.

It is useful to review just how much of Eliot's time was consumed earning money. The pay was minuscule for the reviews and essays he wrote and not much better for the full-time teaching he began in September 1915 and continued until December 1916. Eliot taught first at High Wycombe Grammar School for a term, September through December 1915; the salary:

£140. During this period he lived at Sidney Cottage, Conegra Road, High Wycombe (a municipal borough in South Bucks, on the River Wye). Next he taught at Highgate Junior School, north London, January through December of 1916; the salary: £160, with dinner and tea. (One of his students there was the future poet laureate John Betjeman.) Although Eliot preferred the older students at Highgate Junior School, he was quite happy to end his school-teaching career at the end of 1916.

By that time he was embarked on a three-year career, 1916–19, delivering a total of five different extension lecture courses at the college level, all of them requiring different (and extensive) preparations. In 1916–17, Eliot taught two such courses (one on Friday afternoons, the other on Monday evenings); the meetings lasted for at least two hours, one hour for the lecture, another for discussion and questions. In 1917–18, Eliot again taught two courses but in 1918–19, he taught only one course. In effect, Eliot's college-level teaching career was full-time, while he was also devoting much time to publishing prose pieces, including reviews. Then, on March 19, 1917 (only three months after giving up his "full-time" grammar-school job), Eliot began working at London's Lloyds Bank, in the Colonial and Foreign Department— a full-time job in itself.

In fact, Eliot quickly found that he liked his bank job and he remained a banker until November 25, 1925, when he became a "director" of the publishing firm, Faber & Gwyer (later Faber and Faber). Within two days of his appointment, Eliot wrote to his mother describing his great good fortune, for after spending much time "hunting for work to stop the gap," he has found work and is "in much better spirits. . . . A friend of the Haigh-Woods is a very successful banker, and he gave me an introduction to Lloyds Bank, one of the biggest banks in London." Eliot's tone exudes excitement: "I am now earning two pounds ten shillings a week for sitting in an office from 9:15 to 5 with an hour for lunch, and tea served in the office. This of course is not a princely salary, but there are good prospects of a rise as I become more useful." Eliot would later write in his biography for the "Harvard College Class of 1910" (as the editor of the *Letters* informs us in a note) that he was appointed at Lloyds Bank for "£120 a year and no food . . . on the false pretense of being a linguist" (*LTSE1*, 163–64).

Most unexpected was Eliot's attitude toward his job: "Perhaps it will surprise you to hear that I enjoy the work. It is not nearly so fatiguing as school teaching, and is more interesting. . . . The filing cabinet is my province, for it contains balance sheets of all the foreign banks with which Lloyds does business. These balances I file and tabulate in such a way as to show the progress or decline of every bank from year to year." Eliot owed his job in part to the

Great War having cleared London of many employees who were now in the trenches in France. Eliot's gift for languages came into play: "French and Italian I find useful, and shall have to pick up a little Spanish, Danish, Swedish, and Norwegian as well." Eliot found the new job "very interesting" but was ready at the end of the day to "think about writing for Jourdain [editor of the *Monist*], or the *New Statesman*, or my class" (164).

He was always looking to add "more evening work" and to get his "name known" through articles—his "Reflections on *vers libre*" for the *New Statesman* "was a great success." The editor of the *New Statesman* urged him to write for American periodicals and offered to introduce him to the *Century* and the *Dial*. And the *Monist's* editor, Philip E. B. Jourdain, gave him more work, in view of the shortage of qualified reviewers, with Eliot doing "philosophy, theology, biology and anthropology" (164).

Inevitably, Eliot came around to the problem of his wife's health. Her laryngitis lingered and Eliot refused to let her give up the charwoman even with warmer weather coming. He worried that the work "would take all her time and the strength which should go to building up; and I am afraid she cannot have as good a holiday as last summer." Eliot wanted her to go away in July and August with another girl; he would possibly join her on a short vacation: "I think we could live almost as cheaply, she in the country I here, during the hottest period, as we do now. Besides, for the present, I do not feel comfortable for her never to have anyone in the flat while I am out all day" (164–65). For several summers during August and September, beginning in 1916, the Eliots took a cottage for the "holidays" at Bosham, a harbor near Chichester in Sussex. Thus the pattern of the lives of the Eliots had become established during these early years after the marriage: his energies consumed by a multitude of money-making enterprises and her energies consumed by one debilitating illness after another, making it impossible for them to live together for any long period of time.

Ever the dutiful correspondent, on March 23 Eliot let his cousin Eleanor Hinkley know about his new life: "Not that I know anything about banking, but the business is so huge that I don't suppose more than half a dozen men in the bank know more than their own little corner of it." His office mate was "Mr. McKnight, who lives in a suburb, cultivates a kitchen garden out of hours, polishes his silk hat with great care when he goes out, and talks about his eldest boy." A footnote informs us that Mr. McKnight is the person "on whom Eggerson in *The Confidential Clerk* [Eliot's play of 1954] was based" (168). But we also note that in Eliot's 1917 short story "Eeldrop and Appleplex," Eeldrop is a "bank-clerk" who lives in a suburb and has a vegetable garden.

Banking seemed to agree with Eliot, as evidenced by two of Vivien's letters. On Easter Sunday, April 8, 1917, Vivien wrote to her mother-in-law about Tom's "*much* improved" health since going to the bank. "His nerves are so much better—he does not have those black silent moods, and the irritability. . . . He *writes* better," and feels better when he knows money is "*assured*." Then on April 30, she wrote that Tom was considering banking as his "*money-making* career!" His friends had noticed the great change in his "health, appearance, spirits, and literary productiveness." The bank seemed to be the means for him to be able to devote time to writing without having to depend on writing for money. Both Vivien's and Pound's fears about the new job were allayed when he wrote "*five,* most *excellent* poems in the course of one week" (173, 177–78).

2. Eliot the Extension Lecturer

On the same day that he wrote to his mother, March 21, 1917, Eliot wrote to his sister, Charlotte Eliot Smith, and in an interesting description of his extension lecture he revealed his feelings about education, the working class, and his adopted and native countries: "My literature (working people's) class has been a great success, and I am enthusiastic about the work. These people, who meet once a week for my lecture and discussion, and write papers, are very anxious to improve themselves, though there is not the slightest chance of its helping them to make a better living." As was his inclination, Eliot then made a comparison of the English system with that of America, to the latter's discredit: "In America there would, I think, be less chance for this sort of class. Education is so diffused, and it is so easy for almost anyone to get a so-called 'college education,' that education is less prized. A young man who will work himself to death to 'go through college' usually works himself to death making money afterwards. The idea of people studying all their lives is unknown, as also among the more prosperous classes in England. But my class is entirely *disinterested* in its devotion to study and thought" (*LTSE1,* 165–66). Most readers, American especially, will sense the oversimplification of Eliot's broad generalizations: such extension (adult) education courses have long been offered in the United States; the University of Chicago, for instance, was a pioneer in offering such courses, beginning shortly after its founding in the 1890s.

In the March 23 letter to his cousin, Eliot revealed a bit more about his experience teaching his "workingmen's class on Monday evenings," which was his "greatest pleasure." He had "steered them" through Browning, Carlyle, Meredith, Arnold, and Ruskin: "There are not many working *men* at the present, except one very intelligent grocer who reads Ruskin behind his counter." Most were female elementary schoolteachers, who "come with unabated eagerness to get culture . . . stimulated" by Eliot's "personal magnetism." Two are mad, some clever, but "this class of person is really the most attractive in England . . . not so petrified in snobbism and prejudice as the middle classes. . . . To an American, the English working classes are impressive because of their fundamental conservatism; they are not, as a whole, aggressive and insolent like the same people in America" (168–69). In these remarks, Eliot betrays condescension toward the American working class, which, because of his privileged background, he never encountered in America in quite the same way as he did these English students. It is to his credit, however, that he shows such enthusiasm about teaching the "class" beneath him.

Eliot was gradually perfecting his skills as a lecturer. In letters to his mother and father written in October 1917, he noted that he no longer wrote his lectures but rather spoke from notes. The "lectures cost . . . less in effort and time than they used to . . . I can talk away for an hour or more" and "press a few simple ideas without many qualifications, and my audience keeps awake. I never thought I should ever be a passable public speaker, but now . . . I could almost speak extempore. The feeling of power which you get by speaking from very brief notes is pleasant" (203–4).

In letters that Vivien wrote to her husband's mother a few months after he had been on the job at the bank, we catch glimpses of the effect on their lives of the many money-making enterprises claiming so much of Eliot's waking hours. Vivien wrote to Charlotte C. Eliot on June 28, 1917, using the address of her family's Hampstead home, which the Eliots were temporarily using: "Tom enjoys and revels in the *large* and airy rooms in this house, the peace and quiet of the neighborhood, and the green-ness of the open square behind the creeper-covered houses in front." In spite of these attractions, Vivien went on to explain a major drawback: even though her father charged no rent and paid for their servants' food, it cost more for Tom and her to live there "free" than it did to rent their own apartment.

Vivien's letter offers a rare glimpse into her feelings about what her marriage had brought her: "It seems strange to me, very strange, to be back here in this home of mine, with Tom, *living* here, after 2 years of noisy struggle. I had almost forgotten that life could be so pleasant, so smooth. It is the old tale, I suppose, of no-one's ever appreciating anything until they have lost it." Vivien went on to describe the Eliots' flat: "Living where *we* do

(Crawford Mansions) in a little noisy corner, with slums and low streets and poor shops close around us—(and *yet* within a stone's throw of great squares with big houses and one of the most expensive residential districts) it is like being in a wilderness, we are just 2 waifs who live perched up in our little flat—no-one around us knows us, or sees us, or bothers to care how we live or what we do, or whether we live or not" (185–86). It is likely that Vivien's description, however melodramatic it may seem, was very close to the actual truth of their daily lives. No doubt the note of isolation, loneliness, and even desperation Vivien sounded was genuine, and it served her underlying purpose to get more cash from the Eliots.

And it did bring help, as Vivien noted in the opening of a follow-up letter to Tom's mother of October 22, 1917, with the unusual return address of "Senhurst Farm, Abinger Common, Surrey." Opening with a reminder that she had sent just the previous week a brief note of thanks for the money for "Tom's underwear," Vivien went on to write a letter most revealing of the hardships she and Tom faced in being so nearly destitute in war-torn London. She had been assigned the task of finding an inexpensive "tiny cottage" within easy reach of London so that Tom could comfortably commute. She had finally found a possibility—but because it was six "miles from the nearest station," it meant "that Tom can only be here at weekends." She went on to describe in lyrical terms where they stayed, "a sort of fairy tale farm. An old house . . . on the steep side of a high hill—surrounded by pine trees." She and Tom thought it "the most beautiful country in England. It is all hills and miles and miles of pine forests—with stretches of heath—heather and bracken and bushes—in between."

In the middle of her letter, Vivien got around to explaining that though they may appear to have moved to the country, they have maintained the flat at Crawford Mansions: "You see we are bound to keep on the flat, for several reasons. If it were not that Tom considers it absolutely necessary to have all his books about him (and it *is* necessary) we could wander about and not be so fixed. But we can't wander with 50 or 100 books—to say nothing of papers—typewriters, and all the other business!" At this point Vivien became explicit about the demands of her husband's weekly schedule. Eliot was giving two lectures a week, at opposite ends of London, necessitating that he stay at least two nights in London while Vivien was in the country. Vivien confided her worries about him being alone in the empty flat, but "he could not work any where else." She was pleased to have found "a hard working . . . excellent cook" with "common sense" so that she now felt confident that when Tom was at home he was "well looked after and fed" (200–202).

3. Eliot as Eeldrop

In the May and September 1917 issues of Margaret Anderson's *Little Review*, Eliot published his only short story (if indeed it is a short story), entitled "Eeldrop and Appleplex." Ezra Pound had just become "foreign editor" of the avant-garde magazine and was responsible for Eliot's first appearance there. In a letter to his mother on April 11, 1917, Eliot referred to the work as "a sort of dialogue serial (prose)," suggesting that he did not exactly consider it a "story" (*LTSE1, 175*). And in a letter to Ezra Pound on September 23, 1917, Eliot referred to the characters of the dialogue in a way that suggested obliquely that Pound was Appleplex and he, Eeldrop. Eliot had a "Lecture Friday & Appleplex on the brain" and was irritated at the number of women in the gathering on Thursday and suggested a "special evening for males only"—"Eeldrop on the feminization of modern society" (197–98). At one point Eliot included the dialogue in a volume of his poems and essays to be submitted for publication in America by the friend and patron, lawyer John Quinn. In a letter to Quinn of July 9, 1919, discussing this volume (never published), Eliot suggested that "Eeldrop and Appleplex," included with his essays, might be withdrawn as "crude stuff," revealing his uncertainty about the success of the piece (313). In fact, Eliot never included the dialogue in any of his many collections, but Margaret Anderson included it in *The Little Review Anthology*, published in 1953.

It is possible to read "Eeldrop and Appleplex" as quite revelatory of Eliot's psyche at the time of its composition. The first challenge is to discover what is lurking in the strange names of his two "characters," Eeldrop and Appleplex. There are two elements of the first name, "eel" and "drop." Eliot may have chosen "eel" because of Pound's fondness for using animal features in characterizing Eliot—"possum" and "serpentine." In its association with snakes, the eel is suggestive of a treasure house of both religious and sexual symbolism. By adding the unusual "drop" to the word, Eliot suggests the opposite of what he would have suggested had he written "Eelerect." Perhaps not impotent, but understimulated by the traditional stimulants. "Appleplex" is equally suggestive of something opposite to "Eeldrop": "Apple[com]plex," overstimulated by what the apple has stood for beginning with Adam and Eve: sex.

We learn little about the two main characters except that they are both male, they have chosen to come together at night, sometimes sleeping overnight, in "two small rooms in a disreputable part of town." They remain virtual strangers to each other: when they do stay overnight and then depart the next morning, they set out for destinations "unknown to each other." We learn nothing of how they met, but we do learn that they have taken great care to choose an evil neighborhood "of silence"—because, they agree, such neighborhoods are "more evil" than those of "noise" (E&A, 102). Across the street from their rooms is a police station, and their windows look directly out on the station, enabling them to observe the various malefactors that are frequently brought to be booked. And from their windows they could observe, too, the crowds of people watching the police at work, many coming from the buildings dressed in their sleep clothing—but also the street people wearing street clothes and caps.

Moreover, Eeldrop and Appleplex could, when they wished, rush out into the streets "to mingle with the mob." Appleplex "had the gift of an extraordinary address with the lower classes of both sexes, questioned the onlookers, and usually extracted full and inconsistent histories." Eeldrop, on the other hand was "more passive," and listened to the conversations and observed "their redundance of phrase" and "their various manners of spitting." On returning to their rooms, Appleplex "entered the results of his inquiries into large notebooks, filed according to the nature of the case, from A (adultery) to Y (yeggman [safecracker])." In contrast, Eeldrop "smoked reflectively": "It may be added that Eeldrop was a sceptic, with a taste for mysticism, and Appleplex a materialist with a leaning toward scepticism; that Eeldrop was learned in theology, and that Appleplex studied the physical and biological sciences" (102–23). At this point, the narrator, who seemed earlier unable to sketch the everyday lives of his characters, is suddenly endowed with the ability to characterize definitively their inner natures.

Eeldrop's description, that he was a "sceptic, with a taste for mysticism" and "learned in theology," seems to fit Eliot better than Appleplex's description fits Pound, who might have been "materialist with a leaning toward scepticism," but certainly had not devoted himself to the study of the sciences. At this point, it would seem that Appleplex was created to fit roughly the character of two of Eliot's closest associates, Pound and Bertrand Russell. In particular, Appleplex's plans to visit "Mrs. Howexden" at the conclusion of each of the two parts of the dialogue suggests something of the nature of Russell's relationship with the married Lady Ottoline Morrell.

Whereas we might have suspicions early on as to the deeper motives of Eeldrop and Appleplex in seeking out "evil neighborhoods," much in the way Eliot himself (as he revealed in his letters) sought out such neighborhoods in Boston, Paris, and London, we are told in the third paragraph that they shared a "common motive": "Both were endeavoring to escape not the commonplace, respectable or even the domestic, but the too well pigeonholed, too taken-for-granted, too highly systematized areas, and,—in the language of those whom they sought to avoid—they wished 'to apprehend the human soul in its concrete individuality'" (103). It might well seem incomprehensible for the reader to understand why the two "loners" would adopt the language of "those whom they sought to avoid" (their families, friends, associates) to define their innermost motive: "to apprehend the human soul in its concrete individuality." Is it indeed only in the environment of the "evil neighborhoods of silence" that the human soul can be apprehended in its "concrete individuality"? And what does this last phrase really mean?

In its fourth paragraph, the dialogue seems bent on finding an explanation of this phrase, which is in effect a page-long monologue by Eeldrop. He introduces three examples for his "argument": the vulgar "fat Spaniard" who ate at the same table with them that evening; one "young Bistwick, who three months ago married his mother's housemaid" and suffered mightily; and "in Gopsum Street a man [who] murders his mistress" and suffers even more. All of these "examples" are concerned with male-female relationships of various kinds, but all of them ending in one kind of disaster or another. The "fat Spaniard" ("oppressively gross and vulgar") overhears his tablemates discussing marriage, and suddenly intervenes with the single exclamation: "I was married once myself." Although the scene seems to be comic in tone, Eeldrop comments that the exclamation at once identified him as a "unique being, a soul, however insignificant, with a history all of its own. . . . the essential is unique" (103).

Young Bistwick, Eeldrop continued, became aware only after his marriage of the fact that his bride was his "mother's housemaid." There followed the family's "collective feeling . . . of disgrace." Bistwick is "classed among the unhappily married": "But what Bistwick feels when he wakes up in the morning, which is the great important fact, no detached outsider conceives. The awful importance of the ruin of a life is overlooked. Men are allowed to be happy or miserable in classes." As for the man in Gopsum Street who has murdered his mistress, his "act is eternal . . . for the brief space he has to live, he is already dead. He is already in a different world from ours. He has crossed the frontier. The important fact is that something is done which can not be undone—a possibility which none of us realize until we face it ourselves." The words from *Macbeth* lend gravity to Eeldrop's statement. In presenting the murderer in his unique individuality, Eeldrop differs from others who, Eeldrop says, retreat into generalizations, raising such matters as "the Drink question" or "Unemployment, or some other category of things to be reformed" (104).

Given the disastrous state of Eliot's marriage to Vivien Haigh-Wood, it is impossible to read this dialogue without glimpsing autobiographical implications. There is a sense in which you might see Eliot examining his own misery in the guise of the "fat Spaniard," the young Bistwick, and the un-named Gopsum Street murderer. What are the options for a man unhappily married? One solution is to end the marriage and leave it behind as part of one's past. But the "fat Spaniard" reveals that this is no solution, as the impact of the unhappy marriage endures for years, probably forever after, even if one is "gross and vulgar." Young Bistwick's situation is closest to Eliot's, even though Vivien was not his mother's servant. Eliot's Bloomsbury acquaintances, in many instances, found her incompatible with their views and values, and unsuitable as the wife of Eliot. Yet Eliot endured his marriage for many years, no doubt feeling as Bistwick himself did, waking up each morning with a sense of the "awful importance" that the marriage has bestowed on him the "ruin" of his life. Could Eliot ever have considered, even fleetingly, bringing about the death of his wife, as the Gopsum Street murderer did his mistress? It is doubtful, precisely because he knew that such a terrible act would bring immediately his own death in life: and clearly—what is done "can not be undone."

Although the dialogue directs attention to the subtleties of argument presented by Eeldrop and Appleplex, the substance seems to lie elsewhere, in the examples cited or the philosophers quoted. At one point in answering Appleplex's comment against classification ("When a man is classified something is lost"), Eeldrop cites still another example of a marriage, this time apparently "successful": "When Wolstrip married, I am sure he said to himself: 'Now I am consummating the union of two of the best families in Philadelphia.'" Wolstrip, in short, cannot see himself as any other than the "generalized man." Appleplex poses the question as to what their philosophy should be, and adds: "Mrs. Howexden recommends me to read Bergson" (105).

Eeldrop immediately disagrees about the need for a "philosophy," saying: "The essential is, that our philosophy should spring from our point of view and not return upon itself to explain our point of view." And Eeldrop refuses the possibility of identifying himself and his companion as "individualists" or "anti-intellectualists," both being members of mobs: "Nietzsche [author of *Superman*] was a mob-man, just as Bergson [author of *Creative Evolution*] is an intellectualist. We cannot escape the label, but let it be one which carries no distinction, and arouses no self-consciousness." He goes on to "confess" that "in private life," he is a "bank-clerk." Appleplex immediately replies (or "generalizes") that as such, he should "according to your own view, have a wife, three children, and a vegetable garden in a suburb." Eeldrop confesses that the description of him is apt, and that, since it is Saturday, he is going to return to "his suburb" and spend the next day "in that garden." Appleplex's reply is "murmured": "I shall pay my call on Mrs. Howexden" (105). We may assume that Eeldrop is a conventional "family man" (which Eliot was not) and that Appleplex had a mistress waiting for him (as, for example, Bertrand Russell had his Lady Ottoline). Thus concludes Part I of the dialogue.

The second dialogue opens with a brief paragraph informing us that "the suburban evening was grey and yellow on Sunday . . . the tropical South London verdure was dusty above and mouldy below; the tepid air swarmed with flies." Eeldrop is portrayed at the window welcoming the "smoky smell of lilac, the gramophones, the choir of the Baptist chapel, and the sight of three small girls playing cards on the steps of the police station" (105). This is a familiar Eliot urban scene, with a touch of the unhealthy or evil lurking just beneath the superficial surface of the ordinary. Surprisingly, the "evil neighborhood of silence" is relegated to the background and Part II shifts the focus in such a way as to suggest that Eliot might have had in mind an entire series of somewhat "independent" dialogues for the *Little Review*. But although the focus clearly shifts, it is apparent that at the core of the discussion is a fascination with human relationships, especially sexual, in all their possible mutations: male-female, female-female, male-male.

Again surprisingly, the center of concern is one Scheherazade, whose "real" name is "Edith" (106). In fact, it is not at all difficult to conclude that among Eliot's acquaintances of this time, only Katherine Mansfield could have provided the basis for Edith/Scheherazade. Indeed, Eliot himself revealed—or confirmed—this identification in a letter of August 13, 1935, to Ezra Pound (Gordon, EIL, 577). We noted in Chapter 9, Section 4, that in 1917 Clive Bell took advance copies of Eliot's *Prufrock and Other Observations* to an Easter party given by the Morrells at Garsington and that it was Katherine Mansfield who read the title poem aloud to the assembled Bloomsbury Group. Since Eliot's poem is written for a male voice, it seems strange that Mansfield would recite the poem: there were several males in attendance, including Philip Morrell himself and Aldous Huxley, Middleton Murry, and perhaps Lytton Strachey (the latter's voice surely more suitable for the poem than Mansfield's).

Other than this event, not much is known about the relationship between Eliot and Mansfield during the early years that might explain his choice of her as the main character of Part II of the dialogue. Why did Eliot choose Scheherazade as her "pseudonym" or "nickname"? Of course, there is the fact that Scheherazade, in *The Thousand and One Nights*, is a gifted storyteller (as was Mansfield), but Scheherazade's stories all had to be cliffhangers: their main purpose was to keep her husband the king from killing her as he had innumerable wives-for-a-day from the moment he found his first wife so flagrantly sexually unfaithful to him. Mansfield's short stories were, on the other hand, considered to be essentially plotless, of the *New Yorker* type, but revealing of social and psychological situations so as to provide glimpses into "the way things are."

But of course the Scheherazade of the dialogue, whose "real" name is "Edith," aspires to be a poet, and Eeldrop, after reading her poem, does not believe she has the talent to succeed. One of her poems, "written on a restaurant bill," is entitled "To Atthis." "Atthis" is defined in classical dictionaries as not a person but a type of literature concerned with the history of Attica, a specific part of Greece. Is it, however, possible that Eliot (or Edith) meant to title the poem "To Attis," thus invoking a Phrygian deity who was spawned by the daughter of a river god? He grew up and wanted to marry, but he was loved by the goddess Cybele, or "Great Mother," who drove him mad; he castrated himself and died. Zeus revived his spirit in a pine tree and violets sprang from his blood, thus symbolizing the death and rebirth of plant life. The conventionality of such a poem, tending to romantic meaninglessness, may well have been Eliot's purpose in inventing such a title and never revealing the nature of the poem itself.

Eliot makes Edith the "daughter of a piano tuner in Honolulu" and a graduate of the University of California (where she took "Honors in Social Ethics"). She "married a celebrated billiard professional in San Francisco, after an acquaintance of twelve hours, lived with him for two days, joined a musical comedy chorus, and was divorced in Nevada." She "turned up . . . later in Paris . . . as Mrs. Short" and "reappeared in London as Mrs. Griffiths." By this time she had published a "small volume of verse." She then, according to Eeldrop, turned up in "several circles known to us" (E&A, 107). In contrast, Mansfield was the daughter of a wealthy banker in Wellington, New Zealand, and she went first to Wellington College, where she became fascinated with the literature of the end-of-the-century decadents, including Wilde, Pater, Huysmans, and Verlaine. She studied music briefly at Queen's College in London's Harley Street.

Mansfield's first love (Arnold Trowell) was over too soon for marriage; a first marriage (to George Bowden in 1910) was over too soon for consummation (she moved out before her wedding night was over). Her biographers have dealt openly with her bisexuality (see especially Claire Tomlin's *Katherine Mansfield: A Secret Life,* 1987), and have described her various crushes and affairs. In 1912 she met John Middleton Murry and after living together for some years they married in 1918. Murry himself was complicated sexually. For example, in his and his wife's relationship with D. H. and Frieda Lawrence the sexual feelings tended to flow in several directions (see especially Mark Kinkead-Weekes's *D. H. Lawrence: Triumph to Exile 1912–1922*

[1996]). Given their sexual makeup and their serious interest in literature, it is no wonder that they seemed to feel comfortable in mingling with the Bloomsbury Group.

There is no need here to go into a detailed sexual history of Mansfield, but it seems clear from "Eeldrop and Appleplex" that Eliot was, in writing his dialogue, essentially aware of her ambiguous sexuality even though he does not deal with it directly. Early in his discussion with Appleplex, Eeldrop remarks: "I wonder what has become of her [Edith]. 'Not pleasure, but fulness of life . . . to burn ever with a hard gem-like flame,' those were her words. What curiosity and passion for experience! Perhaps that flame has burnt itself out by now" (E&A, 106). The words were not hers, of course, but those of Walter Pater at the end of his *Studies in the History of the Renaissance* (1873), words that Oscar Wilde proclaimed "the holy writ of beauty."

At one point in the dialogue, Appleplex introduces into the conversation two unexplained words in reference to Edith: "Marius, des Esseintes." Two "decadent" novels are invoked: Pater's *Marius the Epicurean* (1885) and J.-K. Huysmans's *À Rebours* (1884), the latter translated variously as *Against the Grain* or *Against Nature* (perhaps more apt): the main character is Jean Des Esseintes. The heroes of both novels might be described as sophisticated or complicated versions of J. Alfred Prufrock, the man who cannot love women: they too cannot, or discover that they cannot, love women. (It is interesting to observe that in Des Esseintes's study of Latin writers, the one that delighted him most was Petronius, a favorite of Eliot's [see Chapter 4, Section 6].) *À Rebours* was lavishly praised by a character in Oscar Wilde's *The Picture of Dorian Gray* (1891), and was introduced at Wilde's infamous trial in 1895: Wilde refused to proclaim whether the book was moral or immoral, his refusal contributing to his own conviction. It is of some importance to observe that Huysmans and Oscar Wilde were authors Eliot treated in his extension course on modern French literature in the last three months of 1916; and Walter Pater and Oscar Wilde were not only read in his extension course in Victorian literature, in the last three months of 1917, but also in his course in modern English literature during the same period.

There appear to be some interesting and perhaps telling differences between Eeldrop and Appleplex. Appleplex is committed to finding and attending to details and to the preservation of those details in elaborate notebooks and files. Eeldrop is, on the other hand, committed to the use of his imagination, depending on his instinct to gather in enough of reality to inspire the imagination and send it off in the right direction. At the end, the conversation comes around to what it is that people do to "provide material for the artist." Eeldrop appears to conclude that Edith provides nothing:

"Edith, in spite of what is called her impenetrable mask, presents herself too well. I cannot use her; she uses herself too fully. Partly for the same reason I think, she fails to be an artist: she does not live at all upon instinct. The artist is part of him a drifter, at the mercy of impressions, and another part of him allows this to happen for the sake of making use of the unhappy creature" (E&A, 108).

This generalization he applies to Scheherazade: "But in Edith the division is merely the rational, the cold and detached part of the artist, itself divided. Her material, her experience that is, is already a mental product, already digested by reason. Hence Edith (I only at this moment arrive at understanding) is really the most orderly person in existence, and the most rational. Nothing ever happens to her; everything that happens is her own doing." The dialogue draws to a close with Eeldrop wondering what Edith, who sometimes dines with Mrs. Howexden, has in common with her, saying that the subject "invites the consideration . . . of Sets and Society," a subject he proposes that they pursue the following night. Appleplex, looking "a little embarrassed," replies: "I am dining with Mrs. Howexden. . . . But I will reflect upon the topic before I see you again" (108–9). Thus the dialogue concludes, and the dialogue on "Sets and Society" never takes place. Although this short story has regrettably been forgotten, it is of interest for the light it sheds on Eliot's life.

4. Eliot the Assistant Editor: June 1917–December 1919

In June 1917, Eliot was appointed assistant editor of the *Egoist*. Eliot had his friend, Ezra Pound, to thank for his appointment. As with so many little magazines at the time—*Poetry*, the *Little Review*, *Blast*, the *Egoist*—Pound was influential in educating public taste, in searching out the new, and in finding publishers—in part because of the force of his personality and in part because of his connections with wealthy backers of the arts, such as his friend the New York lawyer John Quinn.

The forerunner of the *Egoist* was founded as the *Freewoman* in 1911 by Dora Marsden, an activist in the suffragist movement. The name was changed to the *New Freewoman* in 1913, the same year Marsden appointed Ezra Pound as literary editor on the recommendation of Ford Madox Ford and Rebecca West. Although there was no salary for the position, Pound was anxious to see the birth of a little magazine where he could publish not only his own work but also the poetry and prose of young writers he had been encouraging, and could not only publish poems and related essays but pay poets and critics for their contributions (Carpenter, 206). After publication of only some thirteen issues, the *New Freewoman* became *Egoist: An Individualist Review* in 1914, partly at the instigation of Ezra Pound. At the same time that the new magazine was born, the Egoist Press was brought into being, under the same management. After the magazine changed names in 1914, Marsden served only a few months and, in order to devote her full time to writing philosophical articles, resigned her editorship, leaving Harriet Shaw Weaver, Joyce's "fairy godmother," as the editor (Hoffman et al., 244–45). Weaver was an unassuming but very intelligent woman who, with a modest amount of money and under Pound's guidance, was to play a central role in the publication of some of the key texts that defined "modernism," such as the early books of Eliot and James Joyce.

Pound continued as literary editor of the *Egoist,* and two poets, Richard Aldington and his wife H.D. (Hilda Doolittle), also served as assistant editors (244). Pound knew both of them well. He had come to know H.D. when he was a freshman at the University of Pennsylvania in Philadelphia and she was the daughter of a professor there; their paths crossed later and, though he seems to have fallen in love with her (and she with him), they were never to marry. He had met Aldington, some seven years his junior, during his early years in London. It was through Pound that the British Aldington met H.D., and they were married in 1913. Pound himself was married the following year (1914) to an Englishwoman, Dorothy Shakespear; her family was wealthy and her annuity of £150 a year and other resources became a means of support for Pound and his various enterprises (Carpenter, 233–35). From the beginning of his appointment, Pound dominated the *Egoist,* as he tended to dominate other little magazines with which he became associated. But assistant editor Aldington "was often touchy and Ezra Pound, who was happiest in master-pupil or patron-protégé relationship, was apt to be irascible or bored when he felt that his authority was waning" (Lidderdale and Nicholson, 78). Pound celebrated Aldington's departure from the magazine when he left for service in the British Army in 1916, but Pound also wanted his job "kept open for him" (Doyle, 51). Following the advice of Pound, Harriet Weaver appointed T. S. Eliot to replace Aldington. Eliot had already contributed a number of reviews to the *Egoist,* but as an assistant editor he was in a position to help determine what would be accepted for publication.

In a letter to his mother on May 13, 1917, Eliot revealed his motive in accepting his new (and time-demanding) job: "I am going to undertake a 'contributing editor' job with a monthly paper called *The Egoist*—the same which is publishing my [first book of] poems (next week, I hope). It will not take much time, and accordingly will not bring in much money—not more than a pound a month, but it will add to my notoriety. At present it is run mostly by old maids, and I may be a beneficial influence. This is due to Ezra Pound" (*LTSE1*, 179–80). Eliot's reference to "old maids" suggests something of his attitude toward women working in what he considered a man's world. In a letter of October 31, 1917, he had complained to his father that he struggled "to keep the writing [in the *Egoist*] as much as possible in Male hands, as I distrust the Feminine in literature. . . . It is bad enough in a bank," where in some cases women don't have to work and "are rather *in*dependent" (204). Eliot came to think well of Weaver, but he found Miss Marsden, the single time he met her, so repugnant that he confided in a July 9, 1919, letter to John Quinn that he "frothed at the mouth with antipathy" (315).

Although Eliot described himself to his mother as a "contributing editor" instead of the "assistant editor" he in fact had been appointed, he did not distort his role with the *Egoist*. He did indeed contribute his own work for publication. He published essays on contemporary poetry and reviewed many books in the little magazine. And what has often been labeled his most famous or influential essay, "Tradition and the Individual Talent," appeared there in the September and December issues of 1919. Moreover, his first book, *Prufrock and Other Observations*, was published in 1917 by the Egoist Press (discussed below).

During his two and a half years as assistant editor of the *Egoist*, Eliot's most ambitious project was to assemble a Henry James memorial issue, James having died in England in 1916. Three of James's volumes were published posthumously, thus keeping his name before the reading public: the last of his three autobiographical volumes, *The Middle Years* (1917), and two novels that James had completed but had not fully finished (he was an obsessive reviser), *The Sense of the Past* (1917) and *The Ivory Tower* (1917). Although James had lived most of his life abroad, he did not give up his American citizenship and become a British subject until 1915, when he became incensed that America had not entered the war on the side of the Allies against the Germans.

The first mention of the *Egoist's* Henry James issue is to be found in an October 31, 1917, letter from Eliot to his cousin Eleanor Hinkley: "I have not time to write much at present, and my regular work for *The Egoist* takes up most of that. I am trying to make up a Henry James number at present, as three of his posthumous works have just appeared. But there are very few people to write nowadays; all the old lot is broken up, and only drivellers left. I am just writing to ask May Sinclair for something, but I don't believe she will" (205). Eliot's James issue appeared in January 1918, and he wrote again to his cousin on December 31, 1917, with some obvious pride for the issue and deep appreciation of James, but also anxious as always to advise Eleanor (three years his junior) about what volumes she should add to her reading list: "I will send you a copy of the Henry James number of *The Egoist* when it appears. The idea is mine, and I have a great admiration for him. Not so much the later stuff, but read *The Europeans* and *The American*, and *Washington Square*, and *Daisy Miller*. The first is especially a wonderful criticism of New England" (217). This last remark, with the quick dismissal of James's "later stuff," may surprise James enthusiasts of recent decades who deem such "stuff" (*The Wings of the Dove*, 1902; *The Ambassadors*, 1903; *The Golden Bowl*, 1904) his greatest work.

On opening Eliot's January 1918 James issue of the *Egoist*, Eleanor would have found, in the crowded total of sixteen pages, only four articles on the master filling not quite four pages. Eliot's own "In Memory of Henry James" opened the issue, followed by Ezra Pound's brief review of *The Middle Years* and Enrique Gomez's even briefer review, "Two Unfinished Novels." The fourth essay, by Arthur Waley, was a slight piece on "The Turn of the Screw" exploring the text's relationship to James's preface. In the remaining dozen pages of the issue, there is no mention of James. Eliot's short essay is highly laudatory, but it is slyly dominated by sentences that, isolated, seem to be ambiguously deprecatory: "The 'influence' of James hardly matters . . . ; there will always be a few intelligent people to understand James. . . . I do not suppose that any one who is not an American can *properly* appreciate James. . . . For the English reader, much of James's criticism of America must merely be something taken for granted. . . . James was emphatically not a successful *literary* critic. His criticism of books and writers is feeble. . . . The rest is charming talk, or gentle commendation. . . . He was a critic who preyed not upon ideas, but upon living beings. It is a criticism which is in a very high sense creative. . . . James's critical genius comes out most tellingly in his mastery over, his baffling escape from, Ideas; a mastery and an escape which are perhaps the last test of a superior intelligence. He had a mind so fine that no idea could violate it" (IMHJ, 1–2). Stepping through sentences such as these is like treading in quicksand. Beware the reader who does not take into careful account the signals sent by significant *italics*. This style, incidentally, is not confined by any means to this one essay.

The remaining twelve pages plus of this January issue of the *Egoist* are filled with generally unmemorable items of little note—a longish short story by "J." entitled (appropriately) "A Sordid Story," involving a Cambridge student's loss of chastity with a loathsome and partially unwilling woman of the streets, with the only interesting scene occurring offstage; a similarly longish piece entitled "Passing Paris," by one "M. C.," bringing Londoners up to date on the goings-on in the other world capital; another piece, somewhat obscure, by Ezra Pound entitled "Elizabethan Classicists-v"; a series of unremarkable poems by Leigh Henry; two anonymous reviews of novels, one of Edith Wharton's *Summer,* in which the reviewer (perhaps Eliot) surmised that "this novel will certainly be considered 'disgusting' in America" (*Egoist* 5 (1): 10); and an endless piece assembled by one Madame Muriel Ciolkowska entitled "Alfred de Vigny on the Art of the Stage" (10–15), the bulk of which is devoted to "Letter to Lord ———— on the Performance of October 29, 1829, and on a Dramatic System." Under Announcements we find: "A new novel by Mr. James Joyce, *Ulysses,* will start in the March issue." One of the most interesting pages of this issue is the back page (16), full of advertisements, the biggest devoted to "*PRUFROCK* / By T. S. Eliot, published by The Egoist Ltd.," with quotations from reviews in the *Westminster Gazette, New Statesman, Daily News, Southport Guardian,* and *Literary World.*

If we take Eliot's word to Eleanor at face value—that the idea for a James issue of the *Egoist* was his own—we must assume that it is one of his ideas that he shared with his principal tutor and promoter, Ezra Pound. Pound was a great admirer of James and was himself to edit a James issue for one of the American magazines for which he served as "foreign editor," the *Little Review.* This issue appeared in August 1918 (some seven months after Eliot's issue) and contained pieces by Pound and Eliot, as well as several others. Indeed, in 1912, Pound had, through a mutual friend (Ford Madox Ford) met James and liked him—and was to give him a memorable step-on appearance in his Canto 7: "And the great domed head, *con gli occhi onesti e tardi* [with eyes honest and slow] / Moves before me, phantom with weighted motion, / *Grave incessu,* drinking the tone of things, / And the old voice lifts itself / weaving an endless sentence" (Pound, *C,* 24).

The reverence in these lines suggests that Pound's appreciation of James was deep and long-lived, and it extended not only to James's body of fiction but also to James's life lived not as an American but as a "European." Pound's memorial issue of the *Little Review,* dedicated to "Henry James, 1843–1916," reveals in its sixty-four pages of text the extraordinary depth of Pound's reverence, a reverence that is remarkable for one who played his self-appointed role as master to innumerable younger poets and critics, both American and British. Although there are a total of six authors who wrote pieces for this issue, Pound's several interrelated pieces take up over half (thirty-six plus) of those pages. T. S. Eliot's contribution takes up another ten pages, and includes, in addition to his "In Memory" reprinted from the *Egoist,* a piece entitled "The Hawthorne Aspect." The remaining eighteen pages contain essays by Ethel Coburn Mayne ("Henry James [As seen from the 'Yellow Book'])," A. R. Orage ("Henry James and the Ghostly"), John Rodker ("The Notes on Novelists"), and Theodora Bosanquet ("The Revised Version").

Out of Pound's five contributions, one so dominates the others as to make them seem merely notes. His "A Shake Down" takes up some thirty pages of the thirty-six he assigned himself, and it is an astonishing survey, written in Pound's very personal language, of the total body of James's work from beginning to end. It is, his biographer tells us, "the most substantial piece" Pound "ever produced on any prose writer" (Carpenter, 168). And it is also surely one of the most vigorously argued of all the cases that have been made for Henry James as a (the) master "American" novelist whose "great labour" was the "labour of translation, of making America intelligible, of making it possible for individuals to meet across national borders." Pound saw James's achievement as immense: "I think half the American idiom is recorded in Henry James's writing, and whole decades of American life that otherwise would have been utterly lost, wasted, rotting in the unhermetic jars of bad writing, of inaccurate writing. No English reader will ever know how good are his New York and his New England; no one who does not see his grandmother's friends in the pages of the American books. The whole great assaying and weighing, the research for the significance of nationality, French, English, American. No one seems to talk of these things" (Pound, BN, 7).

Most emphatically, Pound saw James as his predecessor in the role of a displaced American whose "country" became in some vague way the whole of "Europe." Pound's biographer writes, "James mattered to Ezra as the great example of the American exile sitting in judgment on two continents" (Carpenter, 168). As Pound helped to shape Eliot's views of poetry, so he also was influential in shaping Eliot's view of Henry James. Of course, Eliot had studied at Harvard when Henry's brother William James was a prominent professor of philosophy there. Eliot would no doubt have had, early on in his life, encounters with the older brother's works of fiction. But it is striking that, although Eliot included works of Emerson, Thoreau, and Hawthorne in one of his extension lecture series (*Modern English Literature*), he did not include any of James's volumes of fiction or critical essays.

If Pound's "A Shake Down" tried to encompass and convey the essence of the whole of James's writing, Eliot in "The Hawthorne Aspect" set himself the task of "merely" providing a "note." Central to Eliot's note is James's short volume, *Hawthorne,* published in 1879, a book he probably read when he taught *The Scarlet Letter* (along with Emerson and Thoreau) in his extension course on modern English literature. He wrote of James's biography:

"The first conspicuous quality in it is tenderness, the tenderness of a man who escaped too early from an environment [America] to be warped or thwarted by it, who had escaped so effectually that he could afford the gift of affection. At the same time he places his finger now and then, very gently, on some of Hawthorne's more serious defects as well as his limitations. . . . But gentleness is needed in criticizing Hawthorne, a necessary thing to remember about whom is precisely the difficult fact that the soil which produced him with his essential flavour is the soil which produced, just as inevitably, the environment which stunted him." Eliot identifies Hawthorne's works set in the past, among them *The House of the Seven Gables* ("Hawthorne's best novel after all"), as his finest works, observing: "The only dimension in which Hawthorne could expand was the past, his present being so narrowly barren. It is a great pity, with his remarkable gift of observation, that the present did not offer him more to observe" (HAHJ, 49–53).

It is extraordinary how Pound and Eliot, with their differing approaches to his work, both found in James their predecessor and pattern-setter as expatriate American authors. Like James, they went in search of the richer artistic material offered by a Europe that, they believed, only expatriate Americans could discover and exploit. James had been there first, but he was now dead, leaving them to follow in their careers the pattern he had set. There seems no doubt that Eliot believed what he was saying about the "thinness" (James's word in *Hawthorne*) of American culture; but of course he was still under the pressure from his family back in Boston to explain or justify his abandonment of his native country. And in all probability he was still searching within himself for the motive that led him to leave America permanently and settle in England.

But if Eliot's generalizations, adapted from James's example and writing, were to be accepted as truths grounded in universal reality, at some point other American authors, unmentioned by Eliot, must be taken into account. Examples: Herman Melville and his several enduring novels; Emily Dickinson and her multitude of sculpted poems. Of course Melville at seventeen sailed to the South Seas—where he certainly found nothing comparable to European culture, but rather the material for *Moby Dick;* and Dickinson stayed at home (and mainly in her room) in Amherst, Massachusetts, and found the material of her poems both without and within. Three other American writers—Edgar Allan Poe, Walt Whitman, and Mark Twain—had found acclaim both at home and abroad: Poe as both a short story writer and poet; Whitman as a free-verse epic poet, who found the material for his poems in the very American ideals that Eliot abhorred; and Twain in biography and fiction, introducing American everyday life and the Mighty Mississippi. Throughout his life Eliot remained puzzlingly silent about Melville and Dickinson. And he ridiculed Poe, rejected Whitman until late in his own life, and confessed his love for Twain's *Huckleberry Finn* only in his sixties, in an introduction to a reprinting of the novel in England (1950). As we have observed in Chapter 1, Section 3, he had not been permitted to read it as a boy.

In *Three Voyagers in Search of Europe: A Study of Henry James, Ezra Pound, and T. S. Eliot* (1966), Alan Holder devotes nearly four hundred pages to the three most famous expatriate Americans, exploring their beliefs, attitudes, and motives in depth. The opening chapter, entitled "The Quarrel with America," begins: "In choosing to live abroad, James, Pound, and Eliot registered in the most acute way possible both the pull they felt toward Europe and the distaste induced in them by America. The attraction and repulsion were, of course, complementary—Europe seemed to promise them what America lacked and offered refuge from what they found undesirable in American life" (Holder, 19). It is clear that this "expatriate period" in American intellectual life played itself out in a time dating from the late nineteenth century to the mid-twentieth century. Since the end of World War II, there have been no notable American literary expatriates with the exception of Richard Wright and James Baldwin. And it is interesting to note that before Eliot died in 1965, he began to look upon himself as essentially an American writer (discussed in Chapter 14, Section 2), changing radically his dismissive attitude, for example, toward one of his major predecessors, Walt Whitman.

5. Eliot the Poet

Major moments in a poet's career: his poetry and prose for the first time published in books—*The Catholic Anthology 1914–15,* in November 1915; *Prufrock and Other Observations,* June 1917; and *Ezra Pound: His Metric and Poetry,* January 1918. T. S. Eliot the author, Ezra Pound making it happen.

Because Eliot had not yet written enough poetry to fill a book, and in order to bring his poetry to the attention of British readers, Pound included a selection of the best in an anthology. He turned to Elkin Mathews, "a key figure in the 1890s," whose bookshop was popular with poets and who had published, among others, Wilde, Yeats, Pound, and "young unknowns," having brought out Joyce's first collection of verse, *Chamber Music* (1907). Pound chose the following Eliot poems to lead off *The Catholic Anthology*'s contents: "The Love Song of J. Alfred Prufrock," "Portrait of a Lady," "The Boston Evening Transcript," "Hysteria," and "Aunt Helen" (here entitled "Miss Helen Slingsby"). Other poets included were William Butler Yeats,

William Carlos Williams, and Pound himself. There also appeared an essay by the editor of *Poetry* magazine entitled "Letter from Peking." Pound christened the book *The Catholic Anthology*, explaining he used the term in its nonreligious sense to indicate that it contained poems of no single school but was, rather, universal in nature. Prominent Catholic leaders protested to the publisher, Elkin Mathews, and as a result he did not send out copies for review. Thus the book did not achieve Pound's purpose, to develop a larger readership for Eliot's poetry (Carpenter, 98, 282).

Although *The Catholic Anthology* was not reviewed, it caught the attention of Arthur Waugh, father of novelists Alec and Evelyn Waugh, who published his comments in a piece called "The New Poetry," in the *Quarterly Review* for October 1916. A devotee of the old poetry ("the first essence of poetry is beauty"), Waugh found nothing to like—and much to despise—in the new. He wrote: "This strange little volume bears upon its cover a geometrical device [by Dorothy Shakespear Pound], suggesting that the material within holds the same relation to the art of poetry as the work of the Cubist school holds to the art of painting and design. The product of the volume is mainly American in origin, only one or two of the contributors being of indisputably English birth." He went on to point out that the publisher is "associated with some of the best poetry of the younger generation, and [the book] is prefaced by a short lyric by Mr. W. B. Yeats." But, he continued, the reader quickly found himself "in the very stronghold of literary rebellion, if not anarchy." After quoting several lines from individual poets (Orrick Johns, Ezra Pound, and Eliot's "Prufrock"), he wrote: "If the fruits of emancipation are to be recognized in the unmetrical, incoherent banalities of these literary 'Cubists,' the state of Poetry is indeed threatened with anarchy which will end in something worse even than 'red ruin and the breaking up of laws'" (quoted in Grant, 67–69).

To illustrate the threat to poetry posed by these "literary 'Cubists,'" Waugh cited an example from classical history: "It was a classic custom in the family hall, when the feast was at its height, to display a drunken slave among the sons of the household, to the end that they, being ashamed at the ignominious folly of his gesticulations, might determine never to be tempted into such a pitiable condition themselves" (69). It is this image that Ezra Pound seized upon to defend his *Catholic Anthology*, and especially Eliot, in an essay entitled "Drunken Helots and Mr. Eliot," published in the June 1917 issue of the *Egoist:* Mr. Waugh "calls Mr. Eliot a 'drunken helot'. . . . I shall call my next anthology 'Drunken Helots' if I can find a dozen poems written half so well as the following." Here Pound quoted the whole of Eliot's "Conversation Galante," which did not appear in *The Catholic Anthology.* Pound's essay was as much an attack on Waugh and company as a defense of Eliot: "They [the defenders of the 'old poetry'] are all for an aristocracy made up of, possibly, Tennyson, Southey and Wordsworth, the flunkey, the dull and the duller. Let us sup with the helots. Or perhaps the good Waugh is a wag, perhaps he hears with the haspirate and wishes to pun on Mr. Heliot's name: a bright bit of syzygy" (quoted in Grant, 71).

Pound was more determined than ever to bring out a volume devoted solely to Eliot's poetry. After finding Elkin Mathews unenthusiastic and demanding an advance payment for producing such a volume, Pound decided to raise the money to publish it himself, giving it the imprint, with Harriet Weaver's approval, of The Egoist Ltd. John Quinn offered money, but Pound found his wife Dorothy willing to loan five pounds, "later repaid." Eliot never knew anything of these arrangements. Some five hundred copies of *Prufrock and Other Observations* were printed in June 1917, selling at a shilling each. The volume contained all of Eliot's poems in *The Catholic Anthology* plus "Preludes," "Rhapsody on a Windy Night," "Morning at the Window," "Cousin Nancy," "Mr. Apollinax," "Conversation Galante," and "La Figlia Che Piange." The first review of the book was written by Ezra Pound himself and published in the *Egoist* in the same month as the book's publication: "Mr. Eliot has made an advance on Browning. He has also made his dramatis personae contemporary and convincing. He has been an individual in his poems. . . . Mr. Eliot at once takes rank with the five or six living poets whose English one can read with enjoyment" (Carpenter, 312).

If Pound hoped other reviewers might be influenced by his high praise, he must indeed have been disappointed. In quick succession three dismissive reviews appeared in British publications presumably written by British reviewers. On June 21, 1917, the anonymous reviewer for the *Times Literary Supplement* wrote: "Mr. Eliot's notion of poetry—he calls the 'observations' poems—seems to be a purely analytical treatment, verging sometimes on the catalogue, of personal relations and environments, uninspired by any glimpse beyond them and untouched by any genuine rush of feeling. As, even on this basis, he remains frequently inarticulate, his 'poems' will hardly be read by many with enjoyment" (quoted in Grant, 73). Thanks to Derwent May's publication in 2001 of his *Critical Times: The History of "The Times Literary Supplement,"* we now know that the review was by F. T. Dalton, who helped to found the *TLS* in the early years of the twentieth century (May, 115–16).

Two other negative reviews of Eliot's book appeared, one in the July 5, 1917, issue of *Literary World*: "Mr. Eliot has not the wisdom of youth. If the 'Love Song' is neither witty nor amusing, the other poems are interesting experiments in the bizarre and violent. The subjects of the poems, the imagery, the rhythms have the wilful outlandishness of the young revolutionary idea. We do not wish to appear patronizing, but we are certain that Mr. Eliot could do finer work on traditional lines" (quoted in Grant, 74). And another in the August 18, 1917, issue of the *New Statesman:* "Mr. Eliot may possibly give us the quintessence of twenty-first century poetry. Certainly much of what he writes is unrecognizable as poetry at present, but it is all decidedly amusing, and it is only fair to say that he does not call these pieces poems. He calls them 'observations'" (quoted in Grant, 75).

Pound's second review of Eliot's book, entitled "Versification," appeared in the August 1917 issue of Chicago's *Poetry* magazine and was full of praise, but seems somehow scattered: it began with a sentence from Rémy de Gourment about Flaubert and it ended with a discussion of vers libre and Eliot (75–80). Pound's biographer, Humphrey Carpenter, wrote of the review: "It was a generous review, but it left the faint impression that [Pound] still did not understand or enjoy Eliot's poetry. He said nothing about individual poems, and anyone not already familiar with Eliot's work would scarcely have gained any idea of its nature from the review" (Carpenter, 313). In contrast, the novelist May Sinclair's essay in the December 1917 issue of the *Little Review* did precisely what Pound had not done: she talked about individual poems and conveyed throughout a vivid sense of Eliot's poetry. Taking on Waugh and the anonymous *New Statesman* reviewer, she wrote: "For 'The Love Song of J. Alfred Prufrock,' and the 'Portrait of a Lady' are masterpieces in the same sense and in the same degree as Browning's 'Romances' and 'Men and Women'; the 'Preludes' and 'Rhapsody on a Windy Night' are masterpieces in a profounder sense and a greater degree than Henley's 'London Voluntaries'; 'La Figlia Che Piange' is a masterpiece in its own sense and its own degree. It is a unique masterpiece." She went on to quote and discuss key passages from the poems, delineating his modern tendencies, his technique, his method—in effect giving brief and vivid "readings" in such a way as to send readers off in search of the poems themselves (quoted in Grant, 83–88).

Two American women poets also provided, in their brief reviews of Eliot's book, antidotes for those three British anonymous reviewers we have already noted. Babette Deutsch was in her early twenties when she wrote her review, "Another Impressionist," for the February 16, 1918, issue of the *New Republic.* She wrote: "Mr. Prufrock, as he explains in his amorous discursions, is no longer young; his hair has perceptibly thinned, his figure has lost what Apollonian contours it may have possessed. He is self-conscious, introspective, timid. In a-metrical but fluent lines, embroidered with unique metaphor, he draws himself; his desires, his memories, his fears. 'Do I dare,' he asks. . . . In the end, he does not presume" (quoted in Grant, 88–89). Marianne Moore, more nearly Eliot's age, began her review (a "Note") in the April 1918 issue of *Poetry* by suggesting that Eliot had made a mistake in putting "Prufrock" first. She suggested that a "fangless" edition of the book, for the "gentle reader who likes his literature . . . sweetened," might begin with "La Figlia Che Piange," followed by "Portrait of a Lady," but she cursed the poet for the "ungallantry," the "youthful cruelty" of "Portrait," with its ending that "wrenches a piece of life at the roots." She concluded: "But Eliot deals with life, and with beings and things who live and move almost nakedly before his individual mind's eye—in the darkness, in the early sunlight, and in the fog. Whatever one may feel about sweetness in literature, there is also the word honesty, and this man is a faithful friend of the objects he portrays; altogether unlike the sentimentalist who really stabs them treacherously in the back while pretending affection" (quoted in Grant, 90).

This sampling of response to Eliot's first volume of poetry in the reviews reflects in some measure the literary wars of the time, especially between the new and the old poetry. What of the response of ordinary readers? An important aspect of the two leading poems of Eliot's volume, "The Love Song of J. Alfred Prufrock" and "Portrait of a Lady," is that both betray their titles: the first by no means a "love song," and the second hardly a picture of a "lady." Prufrock is incapable of loving a woman; the "lady" is, in the most sophisticated sense, "on the make," and in some sense provokes her rejection by the man. In a way the men of the two poems are one in their inability to "love" women. It is revealing to relate here the response of the American poet, Hart Crane (1899–1932), to Eliot's poetry. Crane was a homosexual and, after writing his masterpiece, "The Bridge," committed suicide. He began to read Eliot's poetry in his teens, finding it in many of the little magazines he pored through. He was in a sense overwhelmed by it, and at the same time rejected its negativism.

Crane struck up a correspondence with Allen Tate when both were beginning poets. Many years later Tate was interviewed by Crane's biographer, John Unterecker. Asked about his early relationships, Tate reported receiving a letter from Crane in May 1922, after one of Tate's first poems, "Euthanasia," appeared in a little magazine. Crane wrote that he was sure that Tate "had been reading Eliot." Tate commented: "And he gave me some 'signals,' which I didn't understand at that time. He said, 'I admire Eliot very much too. I've had to work through him, but he's the prime ram of our flock,' which meant that in those days a lot of people like Hart had the delusions that Eliot was homosexual. 'Ram of our flock' I didn't get onto until later, and when I knew Hart, much later, we joked about it" (Unterecker, 239–400). Crane's view of Eliot as a homosexual could have been shared by others in both America and Great Britain and might well have provoked much of the negativism in the important anti-Prufrock reviews. As we have seen in Chapter 5, Section 6, the manuscript of "Prufrock" provides many hints of homosexuality in the poem (particularly in the epigraph); and there is the confession by the older poet that the poem was "partly an expression of feelings of my own."

Eliot's next book, published in January 1918, was entitled *Ezra Pound: His Metric and Poetry,* and it does not reveal the name of the author. It was written at Pound's request, a favor Eliot could not refuse, given all that Pound had done for Eliot, to help publicize Pound's latest collection of poems, *Lustra,* published by Knopf and subsidized by Quinn in America. Pound figured that it would not be wise to reveal the author because of the quite visible promotion of Eliot's work by Pound. Eliot himself wrote of the book: "There was a time when it did not seem unfitting for me to write a pamphlet, *Ezra Pound: His Poetry and Metric* [sic], but Ezra was then known only to a few and I was so completely unknown that it seemed more decent that the pamphlet appear anonymously" (quoted in Gallup, TSEB, 24). The essay was not published under Eliot's name until 1965, when Valerie Eliot included it in *To Criticize the Critic and Other Writings.*

After Eliot finished his essay on Pound, he turned the manuscript over to him. Pound's biographer writes that before Pound passed the manuscript on to John Quinn for publication in America, Pound "had made a few alterations in it where he thought necessary; indeed, were it not for Eliot's own testimony that he 'wrote it under considerable pressure of time' and the existence of the manuscript (at Harvard), one might suppose Ezra himself to have been the author, so Poundian are many of its cadences—or was this meant by Eliot as a subtle parody?" (Carpenter, 305–6). In his little book, Eliot set forth his purpose: "The present essay . . . is not intended to be either a biographical or a critical study. It will not dilate upon 'beauties'; it is a summary account of ten years' work in poetry. The citations from reviews will perhaps stimulate the reader to form his own opinion. We do not wish to form it for him" (TCTC, 165).

Eliot quoted many favorable reviews of Pound, but he was certainly not sparing in quoting from unfavorable ones. After mentioning that Pound had become "known as the inventor of 'Imagism,' and later, as the 'High Priest of Vorticism,'" he wrote: "The impression which his personality made, however, is suggested by the following note in *Punch,* which is always a pretty reliable barometer of the English middle-class Grin." The note is worthy of quotation in its entirety in revealing the deadly humor of British anti-Americanism: "Mr. Welkin Mark (exactly opposite Long Jane's) begs to announce that he has secured for the English market the palpitating works of the new Montana (U.S.A.) poet, Mr Ezekiel Ton, who is the most remarkable thing in poetry since Robert Browning. Mr. Ton, who has left America to reside for a while in London and impress his personality on English editors, publishers and readers, is by far the newest poet going, whatever other advertisements may say. He has succeeded, where all others have failed, in evolving a blend of the imagery of the unfettered West, the vocabulary of Wardour Street, the sinister abandon of Borgiac Italy" (174).

Since Eliot's essay is so limited in scope and purpose, it is not in the first rank of his works; indeed later essays and commentaries on Pound by Eliot render this essay "dated." But it provides occasional insights into Eliot himself that are worth noting. For example, Eliot found it necessary to emphasize that Walt Whitman had no influence on Pound. Early in the essay, with respect to the "unfamiliar" "meters and the use of language," he wrote: "There are certain traces of modern influence. We cannot agree with Mr. Scott James that among these are 'W. E. Henley, Kipling, Chatterton, and especially Walt Whitman.'—least of all Walt Whitman. Probably there are only two: Yeats and Browning" (167). Later in the essay, Eliot came back to the subject: "There are influences, but deviously. . . . There is Catullus and Martial, Gautier, Laforgue and Tristan Corbière. Whitman is certainly not an influence; there is not a trace of him anywhere; Whitman and Mr. Pound are antipodean to each other" (177). Clearly Eliot had not seen Pound's early essay on Whitman entitled "What I Feel about Walt Whitman" (written in 1909, published in 1955), in which Pound "reluctantly" confessed his debt to the Good Gray Poet (Pound, SP, 145–46). But Eliot might have seen the April 1913 issue of Poetry where Pound made "A Pact" with Walt Whitman: "We have one sap and one root" (Pound, SPEP, 27).

The following passage from Eliot's essay on Pound appears to reveal Eliot's own notions of the nature of a poet's development: "When a poet alters or develops, many of his admirers are sure to drop off. Any poet, if he is to survive as a writer beyond his twenty-fifth year, must alter; he must seek new literary influences; he will have different emotions to express. This is disconcerting to that public which likes a poet to spin his whole work out of the feelings of his youth; which likes to be able to open a new volume of poems with the assurance that they will be able to approach it exactly as they approached the preceding. They do not like that constant readjustment which the following of Mr. Pound's work demands" (TCTC, 177–78). Indeed, Eliot describes his own development here, even before he has actually "developed." Eliot would develop from a skeptic to a religious poet in the latter twenties, and Pound would turn out to be the kind of dismayed reader here described by Eliot.

6. America Enters War: April 6, 1917–Armistice Day, November 11, 1918

Life in England, and especially in London, during this period of the Eliots' existence was hard and getting harder because of the seeming endlessness of the Great War. On Good Friday, April 6, 1917, America declared war on Germany, but it would be some time before the country became engaged in the fighting. On Easter Sunday, April 8, only two days after the United States had officially joined the Allies, Vivien wrote to her mother-in-law, longing for the end of the war, finding it "rather terrible" that "America has declared war," dreading that "Tom might have, some day, to fight." She expressed her anguish: "You, over there, do not realize the bad and dreadful effect war has on the characters of young men (and old men), if they are nervous and highly strung (as Tom is, and also my brother), they become quite changed. A sort of desperation, and demoralization of their minds, brains, and character. I have seen it so, so often. It is one of the most dreadful things. But how can they help it?" (*LTSE1*, 173).

America's declaration of war in April did not mean that American troops were sent to the French trenches immediately. There was first mobilization with a selective service act for the purpose of developing an army of regulars and draftees. A token force under the command of General John J. Pershing was sent in June to the Western front. Because the Allies seemed on the verge of losing the war near the end of 1917, America began to rush men over to the front and by July 1918, some one million American soldiers were in France; and by the time of the armistice in November, two million were serving in France. Eliot wrote to his mother on April 11, 1917, full of concern about what America's entry meant for him. Since he remained an American citizen, he could be caught up in the draft; and he knew that many of his Harvard classmates had already been called to war. He thought the war would be over before he would be called: "I should go then, but not till then" (174).

In a letter of June 13, 1917, to his father, Eliot tried to describe his complicated feelings about the war, which was absorbing the attention and energies of all those about him in England: "To me all this war *enthusiasm* seems a bit unreal, because of the mixture of motives. But I see the war partly through the eyes of men who have been and returned, and who view it, even when convinced of the rightness of the cause, in a very different way: as something very sordid and disagreeable which must be put through. That would by my spirit" (183). About a month later, in a letter on July 23, 1917, to his cousin Eleanor Hinkley, he wrote: "Life moves so rapidly over here that one never hears twice of the same person as being in the same place or doing quite the same thing. It is either killed or wounded, or fever, or going to gaol, or being let out of gaol, or being tried, or summoned before a tribunal of some kind. I have been living in one of Dostoevsky's novels, you see, not in one of Jane Austen's." Eliot's life, in short, has been filled with unreal events: "If I have not seen the battle field, I have seen other strange things, and I have signed a cheque for two hundred thousand pounds while bombs fell about me. I have dined with a princess and with a man who expected two years hard labour; and it all seems like a dream. The most real thing was a little dance we went to a few days ago, something like yours used to be, in a studio with a gramophone; I am sure you would have liked it and the people there" (189). Echoes of this wartime life in London, this "Unreal City," would reverberate in *The Waste Land*.

Having read about the war in American newspapers, Eliot wrote to his mother on April 28, 1918, and struggled to explain the difference between the war's effect in America and in England. He foreshadowed the cynical sentiments that would be expressed in the poetry and novels of the "lost generation" when he wrote that the war for America is "not the obsessing nightmare that it is to Europe. . . . Your papers talk about the 'fight for civilization'; do they realize either what civilization means or what the fight for it means? We are all immeasurably and irremediably altered over here by the last three years" (230).

During the last months, up to the signing of the armistice on November 11, 1918, Eliot was preoccupied with avoiding the draft in the United States by getting some special position in one of the American services based in England. In a letter to his brother on August 25, 1918, thanking him for Henry's report on Eliot's draft status back in America, Eliot wrote: "It would appear . . . that I have as good a chance [of getting a commission] over here. Since the end of July I have tried several things." He first looked into the possibility of obtaining a commission in the navy, which seemed receptive to taking him in for service in the Intelligence Department—or perhaps an even better job "directly under the Admiral" (241). But he was soon informed that the Navy Office in London had received a cable from Washington that no more commissions would be given in England.

After this dead end, Eliot applied for a commission in the Quartermasters' or Interpreters' Corps. He had a medical examination, and was passed for "*limited* service (hernia)." To get this position he needed several "testimonials." He summarized his feelings to his brother: "Not being fit for active service, I am much more useful in my present occupation than in any limited service job for which I could be conscripted as a private, and with an invalid dependent wife it is obvious that I should suffer badly on a private's pay"

(241). Eliot feared being drafted as a private—a feeling not unusual among those who faced forced military service. In a letter to his father on September 8, 1918, Eliot revealed that he was on an inside track for appointment in the Intelligence Service. He had met "a Major Turner of the Intelligence Service" from St. Louis who might get Eliot in—but Eliot "*must* have 3 *American* testimonials. . . . This is *just* the work for a man of my qualifications and I am the sort of man wanted for it, and my physical disabilities (hernia and tachycardia [rapid heart action]) would not disqualify me" (243). In Valerie Eliot's "Biographical Commentary" in *The Letters* she points to one American, Ezra Pound, who provided a testimonial of sorts; Pound wrote to Quinn on September 11 "that he went to the Embassy 'to point out that if it was a war for civilization (not merely for democracy) it was folly to shoot or to have shot one of the six or seven Americans capable of contributing to civilization or understanding the word'" (xxiv). Pound's lines come to mind: "There died a myriad, / And of the best, among them, / For an old bitch gone in the teeth, / For a botched civilization / . . ." (from "Hugh Selwyn Mauberly," v, SPEP, 64).

Again and again Eliot encountered situations that would be called in the next world war SNAFU (situation normal, all fouled up; the fourth word had a well-known substitute among the troops). All this Eliot reported to his father in the long letter of November 4, 1918, seven days before the armistice. First there were his encounters with Naval Intelligence, then Political Intelligence, by which time Eliot had mustered sixteen "excellent recommendations from prominent British citizens. The doors opened, and then the doors shut. Then came the possibility of Army Intelligence, but there must be three *American* letters of recommendation." Eliot cabled for them, but there were delays and difficulties. When he had just about assembled these documents, Navy Intelligence sent for Eliot and told him he was badly needed and, though they could not commission him "straight off," they could make him a Chief Yeoman to work in London with good pay and promising him a commission in a "few months' time" (246–49).

Eliot arranged to train his temporary replacement at the bank for two weeks and then to go into the Navy Intelligence job, but this was postponed for two weeks. After receiving the cable approving his appointment, Eliot rushed over to Navy Intelligence, only to find out approval was conditioned on his not being registered for selective service. Eliot explained that "*every* American of draft age is registered in England, and that Americans who had failed to register are automatically *liable for service in the British Army.*" Eliot complained bitterly, and Navy Intelligence cabled "very urgently" to Washington. A reply indicated that the matter had to be referred to the

"Provost Marshall General in Washington," requesting at the same time Eliot's registration number. At this point Eliot, out of his job at the bank, cabled his father hoping to "get an introduction to the Admiral to lay the matter before him personally and explain the injustice," but this too failed (247–49).

Eliot enumerated his "losses": "At least two weeks pay," no "army commission," and the inability to apply to the St. Louis Board because of not knowing if he was to "be in the navy or not," and besides it was unlikely the local board would call him up since his physical examiner had recommended him "for six months exemption straight off." In the final lines, Eliot revealed his exhaustion as well as his frustration: "This constant deferment for three months has told on me very much; I feel years older than I did in July! I feel now that perhaps I am much more useful in the bank than in the army, and that I would have done better not to have bothered about it" (246–49). Eliot was more succinct with his brother in a letter written the same day, recounting the "three months of trying for a job": "I can't help feeling, after seeing more of my countrymen lately than I have for four years—that I get on very much better with [the] English. . . . Americans now impress me . . . as very immature" (25).

In a letter to Mrs. Jack Gardner on November 7, 1918, Eliot, unaware, of course, that the war would end in four days, briefly summarized his troubles with the armed services and then reviewed his literary activities. He cited articles that he had done "in the spring" for the *Little Review* before he got embroiled with the military, and then he surveyed his current "civilian" responsibilities. Besides his editing and lecturing, he mentioned his "daily work in the Foreign Department of Lloyds Bank. The latter will sound odd to you, but it is the most interesting business work there is, and offers a secure livelihood, and enables me to live in London and pursue my interests and see my friends." Among the friends he listed were Ezra Pound and Wyndham Lewis ("the ablest literary men in London"), the latter caught up in military service. And then the interesting literary news: "I . . . think that a younger friend of mine named Sacheverell Sitwell has unusual poetic merit. What do you think of Joyce? I admire *Ulysses* immensely. Lytton Strachey has suddenly become a social lion on the strength of his *Eminent Victorians,* which is really very entertaining" (250–51).

After the armistice was signed and peace presumably reigned, the Eliots seemed to have felt only intense exhaustion. Vivien wrote to Eliot's brother Henry on November 22, 1918, thanking him for sending money (as noted, a frequent act on Henry's part), and mentioned the armistice: "I really have not been able to rejoice much over Peace! In the abstract I do, and I try to make myself *realize* it. But conditions here will be so hard, harder than *ever,* perhaps, for a long long time, and I must say it *is* difficult to feel anything at all. One is too stunned altogether" (258). With somewhat the same tone, Eliot wrote to his mother on December 8, 1918, reporting the illnesses both Vivien and he had suffered, a devastating influenza, probably the same World War I "flu" that ultimately caused more deaths than the war itself. He concluded his brief letter, "At present I am very tired from a most exhausting year, alarms, illness, movings and military difficulties. I want first a rest. So I am not going to write for several months" (159–60). Vivien wrote to Charlotte a week later saying that she felt Tom needed "a complete *mental* rest" and she "got him to sign a contract"—for three months, except for that required by his lecture, there was to be "no writing of any kind . . . no reading, except poetry and novels. . . . When one's brain is very fatigued, the only thing to do, I think, is to *give up* the attempt to use it" (261–62).

In an end-of-year letter to his mother, Eliot described his and Vivien's celebration of Christmas, a kind of American Christmas abroad, with "a small Christmas tree," and "our stockings as usual with nuts and oranges and such candies as were obtainable. . . . I gave her a coal-scuttle for the drawing room and she gave me some books. Her aunt presented a turkey, and we had Mr. and Mrs. Haigh-Wood to dinner." On Boxing Day, the holiday when gifts, or boxes, are given to errand boys, postmen, and so forth, the Eliots went to "see President Wilson arrive and drive to Buckingham Palace. There was a huge crowd, and the streets were all hung with American flags. It was really an extraordinary and inspiring occasion. I do not believe that people in America realize how much Wilson's policy has done to inspire respect for America abroad." Of course, as the Eliots (including T. S.) were conservative Republicans, it was unusual for T. S. E. to comment so favorably on a Democratic president. Eliot explained: "I don't think much of the Democratic party, but I hope it will survive long enough to see the satisfaction of the peace negotiations along Wilson lines. America certainly has a more disinterested record of foreign policy . . . than any other country" (264). Such commendation of America's liberal party was most unusual indeed, coming, as it did, from such a determined expatriate who, like James before him, would a few years later become a British citizen.

Vivien's letter to Tom's mother, written on the same date, gave her report of the Wilson visit—the first visit ever of an American president to England—and is worth placing beside her husband's: "We had lovely weather . . . 'Wilson weather,'" and London looked "its *most* beautiful when Wilson drove through the streets. Although very tired . . . Tom and I went early and stood in the best place we could find, for over 2 hours. Even then we had quite

30 *rows* deep of people in front of us—and I should have seen nothing at all if Tom had not lifted me up just as they passed. It was a most moving and wonderful sight to see him sitting next the King, and having such a glorious welcome. We all follow American politics now, although before the war I suppose no ordinary English person knew anything about them." Vivien concluded her letter with a description of England's revived capitol: "London has never been so full. The crowds are so enormous, everywhere, in the streets and public places, theatres, restaurants, you cannot possibly imagine. Of course one sees Americans at every turn" (265). So ended the Great War and the remarkable year 1918.

7. "Writing . . . Again": The French and Quatrain Poems

We have seen that Eliot felt the pressures of having so little time to write, and when he did find time, feared that he could not repeat the success of his early poems like "Prufrock" that had so impressed Pound and other critics. To Mary Hutchinson he wrote, "They are growing tired of waiting for something better from me" (*LTSE1*, 188). It is noteworthy, therefore, that in a letter to his mother of April 11, 1917, Eliot confided that he "felt more creative lately. . . . I have been doing some writing—mostly in French, curiously enough it has taken me that way—and some poems in French which will come out in the *Little Review* in Chicago." Some forty years later in his *Paris Review* interview, first published in the Spring/Summer issue of 1959, when Eliot was asked about his early French poems and whether he had written poetry in French since, he replied: "No, and I never shall. That was a very curious thing which I can't altogether explain. At that period I thought I'd dried up completely. I hadn't written anything for some time and was rather desperate. I started writing a few things in French and found I *could,* at that period" (INT, 98).

Composing poems in French freed him from taking "the poems so seriously, and . . . not taking them seriously, I wasn't so worried about not being able to write. I did these things as a sort of *tour de force* to see what I could do. That went on for some months. The best of them have been printed." After Eliot's "French period" ended, he "suddenly began writing in English again and lost all desire to go on with French." Eliot wrote more poems in French than the six that survived, but they, Eliot said, "disappeared completely" (98).

Asked in this same interview if he had thought he might become a French symbolist poet, Eliot replied: "I only did that during the romantic year I spent in Paris after Harvard. I had at that time the idea of giving up English and trying to settle down and scrape along in Paris and gradually write French. But it would have been a foolish idea even if I'd been much more bilingual than I ever was, because, for one thing, I don't think that one can be a bilingual poet." Eliot added that he could not think of a single poet who could write equally well in two languages. Moreover, he said, he thought that "the English language really has more resources in some respects than the French," adding: "I've probably done better in English than I ever would have in French even if I'd become . . . proficient in French" (98–99). Ezra Pound found the French poems to be not among Eliot's best poetry. In a letter to James Joyce of April 19, 1917, he wrote: "I hope to send you Eliot's poems in a few weeks. He has burst out into scurrilous French during the past few weeks, too late for his book, which is in press, but the gallicism should enrich the review [*Little Review*]" (Pound, *LPJ*, 112).

In the 1959 *Paris Review* interview, Donald Hall asked Eliot about his and Pound's decision "to write quatrains, in the late teens, because *vers libre* had gone far enough." Eliot answered: "I think that's something Pound said. And the suggestion of writing quatrains was his. He put me onto [Théophile Gautier's] *Emaux et Camées* [*Enamels and Cameos*, 1852]." Raising "the relation of form to subject," Hall then asked: "Would . . . you have chosen the form before you knew quite what you were going to write in it?" Eliot replied: "Yes, in a way. One studied originals. We studied Gautier's poems and then we thought, 'Have I anything to say in which this form will be useful?' And we experimented. The form gave the impetus to the content" (INT, 97). Thus, Eliot moved from writing poems in French to writing poems in quatrains: four line stanzas with various rhyme schemes, a more "compressed and disciplined form," in George Williamson's words, whose "gain in incisiveness was offset by a loss in musical utterance." Williamson notes another influence as well: "Both the French and the English poems probably owe something to the scoffing realism of Corbière. At least they seem to extend the irony of Laforgue into the sardonic humor of Corbière" (Williamson, *TTSE*, 89).

One of Eliot's important French poems is "Dans le Restaurant," some of the lines of which ended up in "The Waste Land." Having discussed it in my earlier book on Eliot (Miller, *TSEPWL*, 110–12), I have chosen another French poem, "Petit Epître" ("Little Epistle"), to discuss here, primarily because I find it to be rather autobiographical. And I have chosen for explication Eliot's quatrain poem "Sweeney Erect," primarily because it introduces a character who enters several of Eliot's works.

There is no way of knowing in what order Eliot wrote the French poems. The arrangement listed at the end of this chapter is somewhat arbitrary.

Of the six surviving poems, I have put the four poems that were published during Eliot's lifetime first, and the two published only after his death last. As Christopher Ricks has observed in his edition of *Inventions of the March Hare*, Eliot often made mistakes in writing the French poems and he has not corrected Eliot's French. The reader should keep in mind that in dealing with the French poems we are often dealing with somewhat unreliable texts.

The French poem "Petit Epître" is found in *Inventions of the March Hare* (*IOMH*, 86–87). My discussion of the poem "Little Epistle" is based on my English translation of Eliot's French text, with the assistance of Professor Gerald Honigsblum of Boston University. An attempt has been made to stress the literal meaning rather than literary style, and thus much of the poem's music is lost in translation.

"Petit Epître" (1917?; IOMH, 86–87)

"Petit Epître" and "Tristan Corbière" are the two French poems that have survived that were not printed until 1996 with the publication of Ricks's *Inventions of the March Hare*. Ricks has pointed out that both were influenced by a number of Corbière's poems, including his "sardonic self-portrait, *Le Poète contumace* (1873) . . . with its aggressive officials and gossips" (*IOMH*, 292). Like some of Eliot's other French poems, it appears to be written directly out of Eliot's emotions aroused by the public response to his work. By 1917 Eliot had published one of the greatest poems of the twentieth century, "The Love Song of J. Alfred Prufrock," in three important places, in *Poetry* magazine in Chicago and in *The Catholic Anthology*, both in 1915, and in his book entitled *Prufrock and Other Observations* in 1917. Yet he was still largely unrecognized as a poet, and, indeed, excoriated by reviews in many major publications such as the *Times Literary Supplement,* the *Quarterly Review, Literary World,* and the *New Statesman.* We have seen above, in Section 5, something of the reception of Eliot's first book, *Prufrock and Other Observations;* of course, there had been reactions to his poems, reviews, and essays from the time of their publication in the little magazines, especially with *Poetry's* publication of "The Love Song of J. Alfred Prufrock" in 1915. We have already seen how the editor Harriet Monroe resisted publishing the poem, and even suggested revisions which would change its meaning. But Ezra Pound prevailed and the work appeared as Eliot wrote it.

Pound expected Eliot's "Prufrock" to win one of *Poetry's* prizes for best poems of the year, and he was outraged when he learned that the Levinson Prize for 1914–15 was awarded to Vachel Lindsay (one of Monroe's favorites because he was "more American") for "The Chinese Nightingale" over

Eliot's "Prufrock." The slight to Eliot was all the greater because Lindsay had already been given another award that made him seemingly ineligible for further awards. Ellen Williams writes: "Eliot was also passed over in 1915 for a hundred-dollar second prize, which went to Constance Lindsay Skinner for her West Coast Indian songs, and for a special prize for a lyric poem, which went to H.D. 'Prufrock' got third honorable mention." Since Pound had handled all matters with Harriet Monroe, Eliot remained silent and left Pound to complain. Williams reports that Pound wrote on December 1, 1915: "Yes the prizes were peculiarly filthy and disgusting, the £10 to H.D. being a sop to the intelligent, however I knew it would happen, I know just what your damn committee *wants*" (Williams, 158–59).

Eliot's "Little Epistle" is directed to all those reviewers, critics, and commentators who found him to be not only a bad poet and a wrong-headed essayist, but also a wicked human being. It might have been entitled "Portrait of a Paranoid Poet," but that might suggest that the poem is confessional, which it is not. Still, in certain respects, the poem seems to correspond to the life.

The fifty-line poem consists of four stanzas of irregular lengths, with a predominant aa, bb rhyme scheme, with variations. In each of the stanzas the speaker characterizes his verse, his motives for writing, his subject matter, and his critics. The "I" of the poem (which he calls in line 2 his "foul-tasting ego") does not admit to being paranoid, but he clearly perceives wicked enemies attacking him and his verses (which he says in line 4 "smell a bit too much like sauerkraut"). He would not admit to painting a negative portrait of himself, but does of the literary scene generally, in which many commentators and critics are prejudiced and bent on denying him his fame as a literary figure. There is considerable venom, for example, in the poet's characterization of his literary "enemies." In line 6, they are "'jackals' unleashed"; in line 17 "crab-lice"; in lines 48–49, their criticism is characterized as the "gibberish" of "squirrel monkeys." In short, their intellects are subhuman, comparable to that of annoying, incomprehensible animals.

Twice in his poem (lines 5 and 16), the speaker asserts that whatever it is he has done (or written) has been "for the sake of fame." In his letters Eliot had repeatedly revealed that his motive for accepting writing assignments was for the enhancement of his reputation. The first criticism the poet addresses in the first stanza concerns his reference to male and female odors, that they are "not the same," above all "in the season of rutting"—a term applied usually to animals during their periods of sexual excitement. The poet does not deny that he has introduced this image in his poetry (and readers of Eliot's poetry would agree; see *IOMH*, 292, where Ricks gives other Eliot examples from such poems as "Rhapsody on a Windy Night," "Lune de Miel," "Dans le Restaurant," and the excised Fresca passage in the facsimile *Waste Land*). He merely reaffirms the assertion, pointing out that he just recently noticed it at Mid Lent, on "such and such a woman." He does not, of course, address the question as to why he uses terms that classify females and animals together (both have "rutting" periods, human males do not). He cites an instance in which an unspecified woman made such a "ruckus" during the "season of rutting" that "they kicked in" his windows—an incident hard to imagine.

In stanza 2, in responding to his critics, the speaker answers "I conceived a paradise"—surely incongruous in this poem—"Where one would share his worldly goods." This Christian/Marxist ideal is immediately undercut by "(I would also have yours)." Next, in lines 22–27, the speaker cites a baffling episode, inasmuch as he seems to be recalling a time in which he was arrested and called before the "prefect of police." Although, the poet claims, the prefect had many vices of his own, he found the poet guilty of "promiscuity" and fined him five hundred dollars ("cinq cents balles"). There seems to be no record in any of the biographies that Eliot had to appear before the police and pay a fine for some kind of sexual misconduct. It is tempting, however, since the poet uses the French term "prefect" for the police authority before which he appeared, to think that he is recalling some incident during his year in Paris. During that year, as Eliot has affirmed, he and Verdenal (in some ways like Eeldrop and Appleplex) frequented the red-light districts of Paris, where both male and female prostitutes were available (see Chapter 5, and especially the discussion in Section 1 of Eliot's introduction to the French novel, Charles-Louis Philippe's *Bubu of Montparnasse*).

The third stanza, lines 28–46, is perhaps the most interesting and revealing part of the poem. In dripping sarcasm, the speaker addresses the "honorable editors," "master singers," "the titled people" who have presented him with questions, in the form of charges. The speaker answers in a back and forth pairing that echoes some of the charges that were made and are still being made about Eliot's work. He is accused of "mocking equality" and thus of being a "reactionary." An early target of Eliot's essays was "democracy," and thus this charge is true. He is accused of criticizing clergymen, and thus is "a saboteur, a cad." Eliot's criticism is full of comments on the antireligious thrust of several of the early poems—in stark contrast with the poetry that followed his "conversion" in 1927. He is criticized for citing a "German," probably on some literary matter, this at a time when the world was at war with Germany, and is thus "an agent of the devil." He doubts "a future life," therefore he is "a man of impure morals." Because he does not believe in the "existence of God," he is "superstitious." And as he "does not have children," he is a "eunuch, that is understood." This could be read as an oblique reference to the sexual problems and possible lack of consummation of Eliot's marriage. Recall Vivien's addition to *The Waste Land,* the telling line "What you get married for if you don't want children?" (Part II, "A Game of Chess," line 164; see WLF, 20). Immediately after the word "eunuch" is dropped into the poem, the speaker's misogyny comes to the fore in the next and final charge: "For women / He does not demand / The right to vote? / He is a pederast, without doubt." The vulgarities in the poem align it with Eliot's bawdy King Bolo verses, which, as we have seen, include pederasty. In the last stanza, only four lines, the poem concludes with the critic's judgment: "As for his book, it is not worth a damn!" The speaker calls this "gibberish / Of the squirrel monkeys" which he listens to "on the road."

Most critics, even those hailing Eliot as one of the great poets of the twentieth century, have concluded that he was at the core a misogynist throughout his entire career. For some of these critics, but not all, the immediate question arises: if Eliot was not sexually aroused by women, what about men? And some have concluded he was "Uranian" (Pound's term for him), or "homosexual," without going so far as to label him specifically a "pederast" (the word he amazingly writes in this poem). Although the term pederasty is usually defined as homosexual relations between men and boys, it is often used as a general term for sexual relations between males—of whatever age.

"Sweeney Erect" (1918?; IOMH, *355–56)*

The character Sweeney entered Eliot's poetry in the quatrain poems and reappeared in a number of his later works. William Arrowsmith depicts the "*evolving persona*" of Sweeney in his 1981 essay, "The Poem as Palimpsest: A Dialogue on Eliot's 'Sweeney Erect'": "Sweeney is Eliot's recurrent type of carnal or natural man, *l'homme moyen sensual.* In 'Mr. Eliot's Sunday Morning Service' we find him shifting from ham to ham, like a baby in the bath, while the sterile theologians . . . conjugate the abstract Word; or, in *The Waste Land,* announced by the sound of horns and motors which bring him to Mrs. Porter in the spring. . . . Even in the early poems, whether we meet him as orang-outange or the apeneck among the nightingales, he already possesses an implicit tragic nature linking him to Theseus, Agamemnon, Dionysus, Christ and later, to the Fury-hounded Orestes of 'Sweeney Agonistes'" (Arrowsmith, PP, 23–24).

Sweeney here looms large in mythic dimensions. But there has been speculation as to the identity of the real person who inspired his portrayal. We have no definitive answer, but there have been guesses.

One was made by Conrad Aiken, Eliot's fellow student at Harvard. In his brief memoir "King Bolo and Others," Aiken wrote that after his year at the Sorbonne, Eliot started taking boxing lessons upon his return to Harvard for graduate work: "The boxing lessons . . . took place at a toughish gymnasium in Boston's South End, where, under the tutelage of an ex-pugilist with some such moniker as Steve O'Donnell, he learned not only the rudiments of boxing but also, as he put it, 'how to swarm with passion up a rope'-his delight at this attainment was manifest. Was Steve O'Donnell the prototype of Sweeney, as some have suggested?" Aiken goes on to relate that on one occasion, Eliot showed up late for dinner exhibiting a "magnificent black eye," given him by Steve because he had accidentally hit Steve "too hard" (Aiken KB, 21). When asked by one of his serious Oxford readers (Nevill Coghill) as to who Sweeney was, Eliot answered: "I think of him as a man who in younger days was perhaps a professional pugilist, mildly successful; who then grew older and retired to keep a pub" (in March and Tambimuttu, 86). The answer as to Sweeney's identity is unlikely ever to be found. As with other figures in Eliot's life, he has suffered a sea-change, transfigured by art.

The poem "Sweeney Erect" appeared in the 1919 summer issue of *Art and Letters*, where it, along with "Burbank with a Baedeker: Bleistein with a Cigar," was seen and praised by the British novelist Edgar Jepson. Eliot wrote, thanking him (*LTSEI*, 332). And, in a letter to his brother of February 15, 1920, Eliot asked of his mother: "Do you think that 'Sweeney Erect' will shock her? . . . Some of [my] new poems, the Sweeney ones . . . are intensely serious. . . . But even here I am considered by the ordinary Newspaper critic as a Wit or satirist" (363). For its time, the poem's very title was no doubt shocking to many people. There is the sexual connotation as well as the anthropological one—*homo erectus*.

An original typescript of the poem exists as well as a carbon typescript of another version. Before discussing the poem we might keep in mind what Arrowsmith has said in another essay, "Eliot's Learning": "It takes a university to read Eliot, and no single critic can do the job" (Arrowsmith, EL, 170). But in Arrowsmith's erudite explication of this poem, Eliot has found his reader. As Arrowsmith puts it, the poem "engages a set of texts which in turn engage a myth; myth and text engage different cultural and temporal situations. In their *re*combination—in the way in which the past issues into the present, and the present resumes, without repeating, the past—there is the irony of incongruous juxtaposition, but also a recurrent pattern, a rhythm." The reader can consult his essay for his extensive analysis. A partial list of the texts he has isolated includes those of Catullus 64, Beaumont and Fletcher, Ovid, Poe, Shelley, Rousseau, Voltaire, and so on (Arrowsmith, PP, 17–68).

On the second version of "Sweeney Erect" appeared an epigraph never published: "*Voici ton cierge, / C'est deux livres qu'il a coûté.*" No attribution is cited, but as Ricks notes, the lines come from Corbière's *La Rhapsodie foraine et le Pardon de Sainte-Anne* ("The Travelling Minstrel and the Pardon of Saint Anne," lines 113–14) (*IOMH*, 356). The lines are found in the middle of the long poem, translated by Val Warner, a poem she calls "ironical at the expense of religion"; the complete quatrain reads: "—*Here's your taper.—To next year! / (Two pounds, that dear) / . . . Respects to Madam the Virgin Mary, / Not forgetting the Trinity*" (Warner, xxviii; Corbière, 87). George Williamson points to the "scoffing realism" and "the sardonic humor of Corbière," which appealed to Eliot (Williamson, RGTSE, 89).

Another epigraph appeared in the first book publication, without attribution: "And the trees about me, / Let them be dry and leafless, let the rocks / Groan with continual surges; and behind me / Make all a desolation. Look, look, wenches!" The quotation comes from *The Maid's Tragedy* (ca. 1610) by Francis Beaumont and John Fletcher and is spoken by Aspatia, the central character. She has been betrayed by the man who had promised himself to her, but who receives from the king the gift of a woman of the court in marriage, who turns out to be the king's mistress. The lines of Aspatia are spoken in a scene in which her attendants are weaving a tapestry telling the story of Ariadne who, like Aspatia, lost her beloved Theseus when he abandoned her.

The opening stanzas of "Sweeney Erect" introduce still other mythological characters: "Paint me a cavernous waste shore," the speaker commands, "by the snarled and yelping seas" where the winds "tangle Ariadne's hair" and hasten "the perjured sails." We assume that Eliot is not, in his direct address, appealing to his readers but to his muse. But the reader is left on his own to reconstruct the scenes that Eliot's lines attempt to evoke. Here is one version of the story of Ariadne: she falls in love with Theseus and accompanies him to slay the Minotaur, half-bull, half-man, to whom King Minos of Crete sacrificed captured Greeks. But Theseus abandons her (accidentally?) on Naxos, where she hangs herself. In poetic justice, as Theseus approaches home and displays the wrong (black) flag, indicating failure on his mission, his father—believing his son dead—throws himself into the sea (Gayley, 252–57).

After the opening line of stanza 3, "Morning stirs the feet and hands," two additional mythological characters are mentioned parenthetically: Nausicaa and Polypheme. Their tales are told in Homer's *Odyssey*, and they relate to this opening line because of important events that take place at the time of awakening in the morning. Shipwrecked and nude, Odysseus wakes up to discover himself on an island, a beautiful maiden nearby playing ball with her attendants. He improvises a loin cloth and emerges, to find all the attendants fleeing but Nausicaa remaining—and willing to help him with food, drink, and directions. She then shows him the way to the city, and accompanies him part way. In another episode in the *Odyssey,* Odysseus and his men fall into the hands of the one-eyed cyclops, Polyphemus, who imprisons them in his cave. But during the night they blind his single eye, and the next morning hang underneath his sheep that he drives out to pasture, and thus escape (332–38).

Stanza three finally introduces the erect Sweeney. He clearly is "erect" in two senses: although having all the attributes of an Orang-outang (a large anthropoid ape), he differs only in that he is erect, i.e., walks upright; he is also erect in that he is clearly engaged in copulation in stanzas 3–5: "This withered root of knots of hair / Slitted below and gashed with eyes / This oval O cropped out with teeth: / The sickle-motion from the thighs / Jacknifes upward at the knees / Then straightens down from heel to hip / Pushing the framework of the bed / And clawing at the pillow-slip." This surely is one of the frankest descriptions of sexual intercourse in all of literature, rendered repugnant because of the vividly portrayed animal attributes of Sweeney. His "clawing at the pillow-slip" signals his reaching sexual climax, and the next stanza portrays him out of bed and readying his morning shave. Having seen the pure physicality of his head in stanza 4, inspiring doubt as to whether there could be a brain in such a head, in stanza 6 we see Sweeney in the nude, suds on his face, and knowing "the female temperament." The text alluded to here is Edgar Allan Poe's "The Murders in the Rue Morgue," in which "razor in hand, and fully lathered," an "Ourang-Outang" attempts the "operation of shaving," is surprised by his master and runs out on a murdering rampage (Poe, 166).

At this critical moment, we find a parenthetical stanza aimed at the American essayist Ralph Waldo Emerson: "(The lengthened shadow of a man / Is history, says Emerson / Who had not seen the silhouette / Of Sweeney straddled in the sun)." As already discussed, Eliot had, in fact, been asked to include Emerson in his 1917 extension course on Victorian literature, and had read him in depth apparently for the first time then in preparation for his teaching (see Chapter 9, Section 3). In one of his most popular essays, "Self-Reliance," Emerson wrote the line that Eliot quotes, but it must be placed in context for the meaning to be understood.

The passage Eliot quoted shows that Emerson was expanding on his friend Thomas Carlyle's "great man" theory of history: "A man Caesar is born, and for ages after, we have a Roman Empire. Christ is born, and millions of minds so grow and cleave to his genius, that he is confounded with virtue and the possible of man. An institution is the lengthened shadow of one man; as . . . the Reformation, of Luther; Quakerism, of Fox; Methodism, of Wesley; Abolition, of Clarkson. . . . and all history resolves itself very easily into the biography of a few stout and earnest persons." It is in "Self-Reliance" that Emerson also wrote: "Who so would be a man must be a nonconformist." And: "A foolish consistency is the hobgoblin of little minds, adored by little statesmen and philosophers and divines." And: "Insist on yourself; never imitate" (Emerson, SR, 265, 263, 260). We must conclude that had Emerson seen "Sweeney straddled in the sun," he would have shaded his eyes and passed him by. Is Eliot implying that Emerson would put the Orang-outang Sweeney alongside Caesar? Christ? Luther? Surely Sweeney, had Eliot not memorialized him in his poetry, would have passed out of historical notice, supporting Emerson's (and Carlyle's) "great man" theory. Eliot's distortion of Emerson's thinking raises questions about how much he understood Emerson after his rapid preparation for his lectures!

Sweeney prepares to shave, testing the razor first "on his leg," but he waits "until the shriek subsides; / The epileptic on the bed / Curves backward, clutching at her sides." Contrary to most critics, I take the word "epileptic" as metaphoric: this is her sexual reaction to the copulation with Sweeney, perhaps delayed but no less delirious. The sounds she and Sweeney have made in the bed have disturbed the delicate sensibilities of the inhabitants of the whore-house, here called "ladies." And Mrs. Turner, the madame in charge, complains to Sweeney of the identifiable noises emanating from the room. There is, however, one sympathetic member of Mrs. Turner's "ladies": Doris, wrapped in a towel and barefoot enters with "a glass of brandy neat." No doubt Sweeney sizes her up, and plans a future with her rather than his recent partner still in bed. And indeed she turns up later in Eliot's drama, "Sweeney Agonistes."

Beyond the mythic and impersonal dimensions, "Sweeney Erect" is, as Arrowsmith concludes in his essay, "like all of Eliot's poetry, intensely personal. Why, we may reasonably ask, did Eliot choose . . . the tale of Theseus and Ariadne? Because, I suppose, it engaged two of the most obsessive themes of his poetry." We might argue whether the themes identified by Arrowsmith—"the seduction and abandonment (death, whether metaphorical or real) of a young girl" and "the death of a father"—are the "most obsessive" of Eliot's poetry. However, we can agree that the "Sweeney he shows *us,* the Sweeney the poem asks us to recognize as a part of *us,* is a part of the poet too. . . . The story of Theseus engages the poet's 'private agonies'" (Arrowsmith, PP, 67–68).

8. Poems Written 1917–1918

The poems of 1917 through 1918 are divided into two groups, the French poems and the quatrain poems, and the latter are divided into two roughly related groups. Titles of poems are followed by dates of composition (when known) and dates of first publication in journals and books. "Leyris" refers to Pierre Leyris, French translator of Eliot's work, *T. S. Eliot's Poèmes, 1910–1930* (1947), for which John Hayward (Eliot's British friend and longtime apartment mate) provided notes and dates of composition. *AVP: Ara Vos Prec* (1920 in England); *P: Poems* (1920 in America); *WLF: The Waste Land Facsimile and Transcript of the Original Drafts* (1971); *IOMH: Inventions of the March Hare* (1996). Not included is the pamphlet, *Poems*, published in 1919 by the Woolfs' Hogarth Press in a very limited edition, whose contents are included in *Poems* (1920) above.

The French Poems
  "Le Directeur" (1917); *Little Review*, July 1917; *AVP* [as "Le Spectateur"]; *P*
  "Mélange Adultère de Tout" (1917); *Little Review*, July 1917; *AVP; P; IOMH*
  "Lune de Miel" (1917?); *Little Review*, July 1917; *AVP; P; IOMH*
  "Dans le Restaurant" (1917, Leyris); *Little Review*, September 1918; *AVP; P; IOMH*
  "Petit Epître" (1917?); *IOMH*
  "Tristan Corbière" (1917); *IOMH*
The Quatrain Poems I: Animals, the Past, the Future, and Airs of the Earth
  "The Hippopotamus" (1917?); *Little Review*, July 1917; *AVP; P*
  "A Cooking Egg" (1917?); *Coterie*, May 1919; *AVP; P; IOMH*
  "Airs of Palestine, No. 2" (1917?, 1918); *IOMH*
  "Whispers of Immortality" (1918); *Little Review*, September 1918; *AVP; P; IOMH*
The Quatrain Poems II: Eliot, Sweeney, Burbank and Bleistein
  "Mr. Eliot's Sunday Morning Service" (1918); *Little Review*, September, 1918; *AVP; P; IOMH*
  "Sweeney Among the Nightingales" (1918?); *Little Review*, September 1918; *AVP; P; IOMH*
  "Sweeney Erect" (1918); *Art and Letters*, Summer 1919; *AVP; P; IOMH*
  "Burbank with a Baedeker: Bleistein with a Cigar" (1918); *Art and Letters*, Summer 1919; *AVP; P; IOMH*
  "Dirge ('Full fathom five your Bleistein lies')" (1919); *WLF* (1918)
  "Ode" ("Ode on Independence Day, July 4th 1918") *AVP* (never collected by TSE); *IOMH*

1919–1920
UP THE LADDER, GLIMPSING THE TOP

1. Death of a Father

The American lawyer and art patron John Quinn had been enlisted by Ezra Pound to help Eliot get his books published in America. In 1918, Quinn had attracted the interest of the New York publisher Alfred Knopf in publishing a book of Eliot's poetry and prose and Eliot had submitted a hastily assembled manuscript. In a letter to Quinn of January 6, 1919, Eliot wrote that even though Knopf had had the manuscript in hand for two months or so, he had not heard from him; and indeed Knopf had not responded to a cable Pound had sent a week earlier. Eliot confessed to Quinn that he was "not at all proud of the book" because the essays consisted "of articles written under high pressure in the overworked, distracted existence of the last two years, and very rough in form."

Nevertheless, he said, it was important to him that it appear in America before he visited his family there later in the year. He hoped, in short, that the book would repair the deterioration in his relationship with his parents, especially his father: "You see I settled over here in the face of strong family opposition, on the claim that I found the environment more favorable to the production of literature. This book is all I have to show for my claim—it would go toward making my parents contented with conditions—and towards satisfying them that I have not made a mess of my life, as they are inclined to believe" (*LTSE1*, 266). Eliot was evidently not aware that his father's impatience with him had somewhat abated. The elder Eliot had written a letter to his brother in the West (January 3, 1919) that Tom Eliot was "getting along now and has been advanced at the bank so that he is independent of me" (xxiv). It is likely that the appearance of the book would have unsettled his father, who obviously believed his son was working his way up in the banking business.

Henry Ware Eliot died January 7 of a heart attack, the day after Eliot wrote his letter to Quinn, and Eliot himself, though he knew his father had been ill, did not learn of his death until he received a cable from his mother sent on the same day. The cable arrived on the morning of January 8, and Vivien held it back until Eliot returned to the apartment in the evening. Vivien described the day and evening in her diary as "fearful" (Eliot, Vivien, UD, 8). Eliot cabled his brother offering to come to St. Louis immediately. His brother cabled on January 11: "Do not come now plans uncertain mother well." Eliot wrote back about his "restless feeling that I shall wake up and find the pain intolerable." To his mother he wrote poignantly, remembering a childhood song: "You have not been long out of my thoughts since then [hearing of the death], I have been over all my childhood. I don't feel like writing anything in this first letter except to say again how much I love you—if only I could have been with you these last few days. I do long for you, I wanted you more for my sake than yours—to sing the Little Tailor to me" (*LTSE1*, 267).

Eliot's subsequent letters to his mother are filled with his feelings of both loss and guilt for a father who would now never know his son's success as a poet and critic. This pain was added to that he had already suffered in the loss of close friends in the war. In a letter to his mother of January 19, 1919, he told her how the loss had led him to think of "little things," among them his father's comic drawings—one was "a wonderful set of comic animals that he drew long ago, and were kept in an album." Other things he remembered were scrapbooks, a genealogy, many books, one of which ("perhaps one of his Latin texts") he would be pleased to have as a keepsake. He added: "If I can think at the end of my life that I have been worthy to be his son I shall be happy." He also explained that he must put off a visit in the near future because his bank had taken over another bank, and was still short of the men who had gone into the armed services. Indeed, his service had become so important to the bank that he was expecting a pay increase in June. He would come later, he promised, when he could stay longer—and after that "*often*" (268).

As we have seen, Eliot's relationship with his older brother Henry was in some ways closer than that with his parents—he could express more of his feelings and thoughts to him than to them. His letter to Henry on February 27, 1919, reveals Eliot's sharpest insights into his father's life: "I wished . . . that father could have had more satisfaction out of his children, yet I cannot think (so far as I know) that his life was a very unhappy one, and after all none of his children was made for the kinds of success that he could have appreciated. I don't think Ada's distinction ever meant very much to him." This seems a kind of critical assessment of the father's sensibility and acumen, a rejection indeed of the nature of the "success that he could have appreciated" (273). The reference to Ada, the oldest of four sisters and married to a Cambridge professor, and her "distinction" (under her mother's tutelage) was to the many social service positions she held in Cambridge and New York City, becoming known in the latter as "the angel of the Tombs," a New York City jail (Anon., EFSL, 42). As for himself, Eliot wrote that he "always tried to give as powerful an impression" as he could of his "position here [in England] but it was a prominence essentially too esoteric to be of much use in that way" (LTSE1, 273). Recall, for example, Eliot's hope to publish a volume of his work in America before his scheduled visit.

In the end Eliot came to focus on the realities of his father's life: "Now, I find that I think more of his own youthful possibilities that never came to anything: and yet with a great deal of satisfaction; his old-fashioned scholarship! his flute-playing, his drawing. Two of the Cats that I have seem to me quite remarkable." And then a rather sad realization: "I feel that both he and mother in spite of the strength of their affection were lonely people, and that he was the more lonely of the two, that he hardly knew himself what he was like. In my experience everyone except the fools seem to me warped or stunted" (273). His father was apparently one or both. Did Eliot include himself in his generalization? They apply, after all, to everybody "except the fools"—and he would not include himself in the latter category.

Charlotte Eliot spent the months after her husband's death sorting through the family's belongings to see what should be saved and moved, what should be sent to the children, and what should be gotten rid of. In writing to his mother in a May 4 letter Eliot thanked her for everything she had sent, requested his father's bathrobe, and listed what he wanted: "1. Things I value and others don't; 2. Things (i.e., certain books) which I could make better use of than anyone else. There it is in brief" (289). A July letter thanked her for "the set of Dickens . . . and the beloved Rollo books," pictures and other mementos (315). And in an August 1920 letter from his mother can be found a list of books sent to Eliot, an impressive reminder of the astonishing range of books in the Eliot house (398–99).

Aside from distributing the personal belongings, Eliot's mother had made the decision to sell the two Eliot houses, the one in St. Louis and the one on the Atlantic seacoast in Gloucester. Eliot wrote: "I am very sorry you have had so much trouble in disposing of the houses: I should think that E. Point at least ought to realize very handsomely. It will be very valuable property in time if not too many cheap houses are built" (290). Filled as the houses were with memories that would remain vividly with Eliot until his death, their sale was in some sense bringing an abrupt end to his American past.

In part, selling the houses was a financial necessity in that Charlotte Eliot would need money to buy a home in Cambridge, and she still had with her two unmarried daughters, Charlotte Chauncey and Marian Cushing. She had the help of her eldest son Henry, who not only continued to send Eliot money but kept him informed of his mother's health and family finances (406). Although Henry Ware Eliot's will provided money for each of the six children, Eliot's share was put in a trust that was to revert to the estate on Eliot's death. This was the means by which Eliot's father made sure that Vivien, of whom he disapproved even in death, would never receive the money.

2. Banking, Teaching, Editing, Writing: Money and Power

"The money trouble is always cropping up." Vivien's complaint to her friend Mary Hutchinson in a letter of July 16, 1919, was the dominant leitmotif during this period (*LTSE1,* 320). Eliot had a full-time job at the bank, he was assistant editor at the *Egoist,* he continued to teach an extension course, and he wrote many essays for various magazines and journals. As Vivien said, it was "V. bad for his work," but he did find time to write poetry—with some measure of success. We have seen above how pleased Eliot seemed to have been with his job at the bank, and his feeling of success in it, especially when he mentioned to his mother the "rise in salary" he was expecting in June. In March 1919, he was offered a two-year appointment as assistant editor of the weekly literary magazine *Athenaeum* for £500 a year, a salary somewhat higher than his bank salary. He wrote to his mother (12 March) discussing the pros and cons of his accepting the position. "The chief fact militating against the acceptance is the insecurity after two years, and the fact that there would be a lot of drudgery in journalism which would be fatiguing. There is of course as much difference between journalism and literature as between teaching and literature" (276).

On March 29, Eliot was able to tell his mother that he would stay at the bank in a new position, "not ordinary bank work at all but economic work," offering "opportunity for initiative . . . more responsibility, and therefore more freedom." His expectations for a salary increase were high, "and in a few years ought to be beyond the £500 offered by the *Athenaeum*." The work "gives opportunity for initiative and is work for which they wish men of higher education. It will give much more responsibility, and therefore more freedom" (279–80).

Some indication of Eliot's new and more important position with his bank may be found in correspondence with Lytton Strachey. In declining Strachey's suggestion that they get together for dinner, Eliot explained that he would be gone for a few weeks on bank business. Strachey apparently showed some curiosity as to what Eliot would be doing for his bank "on a tour of the provinces" (295). Some sense of Eliot's advanced position at the bank is suggested by Eliot's June 1 reply: "You are very—ingenuous—if you can conceive me conversing with rural deans in the cathedral close. I do not go to cathedral towns but to centres of industry. My thoughts are absorbed in questions more important than ever enter the heads of deans—as *why* it is cheaper to buy steel bars from America than from Middlesborough, and the probable effect—the exchange difficulties with Poland—and the appreciation of the rupee" (299).

The latter part of Eliot's letter was somewhat ambiguous. He wrote: "My evenings in Bridge. The effect is to make me regard London with disdain, and divide mankind into supermen, termites and wireworms. I am sojourning among the termites. At any rate that coheres. I feel sufficiently specialized, at present, to inspect or hear any ideas with impunity" (299). Obviously Eliot is writing somewhat jokingly. Do we assume that the "supermen" are in London, while the "termites" and "wireworms" (larva that feed on roots of crops) are found in the provinces? If so, why does Eliot feel disdain for London? Perhaps he is contrasting the chaotic getting and spending of urban life with the coherence of small-town life. In a more serious vein, Eliot wrote to his brother one month later, on July 2, about the difficulties of living as a foreigner—"only the lower classes can assimilate." Society was harder: "It is like being always on dress parade—one can never relax. It is a great strain." One was made to "feel humiliated and lonely." People are "critical," "always intriguing and caballing. . . . London is something one has to fight very hard in order to survive." Of course this was preferable to living in "barbarous" America where there was no "respect for the individual." In contrast, English country hosts would allow one solitude "to write or read or sit in the garden alone," expecting only that one be "as brilliant as possible in the evenings"

(310). Perhaps something of this ambivalence toward life and society lay behind his remarks to Strachey.

Eliot provided another glimpse of his activities for the bank in a letter to his mother of February 22, 1920, when he described his demanding "work on German Debts," requiring the help of "an assistant and a typist to write . . . letters and do card indexing." The "chaos" involved "receiving hundreds of reports from Branches of the bank, classifying them, picking out the points that needed immediate attention, interviewing other banks and Government Departments and trying to elucidate knotty points in that appalling document the Peace Treaty" (368). The peace treaty of Versailles was signed in June 1919, and it not only concluded the war between the Allies (including England, France, Italy, the United States) and Germany, but also imposed on Germany immense reparations for damages done in the war. Germany was in essence penniless, and had no way of making such payments. Many historical scholars believe that the severe terms of the Treaty of Versailles laid the groundwork for World War II.

In addition to working at the bank, Eliot spent the first half of 1919, January through May, delivering twenty-four lectures on Monday evenings for his University of London extension course on Elizabethan literature. This was to be the last of his extension lectures. Even though it demanded an enormous amount of preparation on his part, it enabled him to deal with his favorite period of literature and to review texts most of which he had encountered at Harvard and on which he wanted in the future to publish essays of criticism. After he had finished the course and had delivered his last lecture, Eliot's students "presented him with several books to mark the completion of their three-year course, including a copy of the *Oxford Book of English Verse,* inscribed 'with the gratitude and appreciation of the students of the Southall Tutorial Literature Class May 1919'" (Schuchard, 51). In a May 25, 1919, letter, Eliot told his mother about the gift and added: "I don't know whether it will be desirable for me to continue [teaching]. . . . I can make more money as well as more reputation from [writing for] the *Athenaeum*" (*LTSE1*, 295).

Eliot remained assistant editor of the *Egoist* throughout 1919 until its "suspension" at the end of the year. It turned out that the suspension was permanent. A large amount of the editors' time during 1919 was spent attempting to publish a sequence of chapters from James Joyce's *Ulysses*. Joyce's *Portrait of the Artist as a Young Man* had made its first serial appearance in the magazine in 1914 and 1915, and by 1919 editor Harriet Weaver as well as assistant editor T. S. Eliot and "adviser" and supporter Ezra Pound had become enthusiastic supporters of Joyce. *Ulysses* was to appear in installments in the *Little*

Review in America at the same time that it was to appear in the *Egoist* in England. But Weaver found many problems, chiefly economic, in getting her issues out. *Ulysses* was much longer than Joyce's *Portrait*. She found difficulty fitting the sections she received from Joyce into the pages of her magazine; in wartime England there had developed a shortage of paper. Moreover, Joyce's book was considered "obscene" by the printers who set the *Egoist* in type (printers in England could be held liable for printing obscene material); in America, the *Little Review* was brought to trial for printing the book—and lost. The post office had stopped the May issue of the *Review*, containing the "Scylla and Charybdis" chapter, which Eliot called "almost the finest I have read: I have lived on it ever since." Its suppression in America was "one more episode in a national scandal" (314). Eliot proposed that the sections of *Ulysses* be published in a series of supplements to the *Egoist*. Though much time was consumed on the proposition, nothing came of it. And in the end, the matter was instrumental in the demise of the *Egoist*.

Weaver had charge of the book publication of *Ulysses*, and she decided to spend all of her time on that challenging task. The Woolfs turned it down for their press. And it was finally published in 1922 in Paris by Shakespeare & Company, the bookstore and sometime publisher, headed then by the American Sylvia Beach. Weaver continued to pursue publication of the book in England and was successful in getting copies printed in France under her Egoist Press imprint: "Published for The Egoist Press, London, by John Rodker, Paris 1922" (Lidderdale and Nicholson, 205–6). The first shipment to England of one hundred copies sold out almost immediately. Charges of the book's obscenity held up publication in America until 1933.

Thus it was that the last year of the *Egoist* was somewhat hectic, and Eliot himself, although he was enthusiastic about the publication of Joyce's *Ulysses*, did not get caught up in the intricacies of its book publication. Whereas he had published some fourteen pieces in the *Egoist* in 1918, he published only two pieces during the whole of 1919. The first was a very brief review ("Reflections on Contemporary Poetry") of Herbert Read's *Naked Warriors*, Tristan Tzara's *Manifeste Dada*, and Conrad Aiken's *The Charnel Rose and Other Poems* (July 1919). The second was "Tradition and the Individual Talent"— published in two parts, in the September and December issues. In his review, Eliot devoted one paragraph to each of the books he reviewed, indicating strengths and weaknesses of each of the poets. But his most interesting comment was what he had to say about his Harvard classmate, Conrad Aiken. He wrote of Aiken's "Senlin: a Biography": "Mr. Aiken has gone in for psycho-analysis with a Swinburnian equipment; and he does not escape the fatal American introspectiveness; he is oversensitive and worried. He is tangled in himself. The effect is of immaturity of feeling, not at all of any lack of it" (RCP, 39–40). The word "immaturity" was sure to cause pain to the fellow poet. "*Immaturity of feeling*"—Eliot had used the same phrase about Americans in his July 2 letter to his brother (discussed above) followed by the word "childishness" (*LTSE1*, 311). After offering these observations, Eliot turned to what he believed to be the cause of Aiken's shortcomings as a poet. "It is difficult for a writer to mature in America. This is a pity; if Mr. Aiken were not so isolated, if he was in contact with European civilization, he might go so very much farther; his attempt is more impressive than many English successes" (RCP, 39–40). Of course, Eliot's assumption is that Aiken should have patterned his career after Eliot's own, i.e., that he should have settled in England and have turned himself into a European poet. Eliot's comments were bound to become a factor in the relationship of these two friends and ambitious poets, guaranteeing some rough stretches ahead.

Although Eliot turned down the position of assistant editor of the literary weekly the *Athenaeum,* he nevertheless continued to publish his essays in it. Indeed, it is quite astonishing to see the list of review-essays Eliot published in that magazine during 1919 and 1920—a total of some thirty. And out of these, a number were chosen to be reprinted, with revision and nearly always under a different title, in Eliot's first book of essays, *The Sacred Wood* (1920). For example, "Hamlet and His Problems" (September 26, 1919), a review of the Rt. Hon. J. M. Robertson's *The Problem of 'Hamlet'* became simply "Hamlet" in the book. "Dante as a 'Spiritual Leader'" (April 2, 1920), a review of Henry Dwight Sidgwick's *Dante,* became simply "Dante." It is quite clear that Eliot was writing his reviews with an eye to turning them, in the end, into his first volume of essays. It is possible, even probable, that during this period, Eliot's reputation as a critical essayist was greater (certainly less controversial) than his reputation as a poet. The *Athenaeum* merged in 1921 with the *Nation* and the new publication was known as the *Nation & Athenaeum.*

Eliot's correspondence, especially with his mother, reveals the extent to which he was concerned that his reputation as both critic and poet rise to the very highest levels in England. In a letter of March 29, 1919, Eliot wrote to his mother about his "privileged position," above the "intrigues of journalism." Respected for his bank work, writing only what he wants to, and because all concede that his writing is "good" and he is "disinterested," he "can influence London opinion and English literature in a better way." Eliot sees even his position as assistant editor of the *Egoist* as bolstering his reputation beyond the reputation of those "far better known." And then he wrote: "There is a small and select public which regards me as the best living critic, as well as the best living poet, in England." The reviews he writes for give him "more than enough power to satisfy [him]." Indeed, Eliot sees himself competing with the most famous of America's expatriate writers: "I really think that I have far more *influence* on English letters than any other American has ever had, unless it be Henry James." At the end of this soaring self-description, Eliot added: "All this sounds very conceited, but I am sure it is true, and as there is no outsider from whom you would hear it, and America really knows very little of what goes on in London, I must say it myself. Because it will give you pleasure if you believe it, and it will help to explain my point of view" (*LTSE1*, 280–81). These lines reveal a genuine pride, but it is a pride verging on conceit. In some ways Eliot doesn't fully understand that he was addressing not only his mother, but also his dead father.

But Eliot's "bragging" was not limited to family correspondence. In writing to his Harvard professor, J. H. Woods, Eliot wanted to explain and justify his moving out of philosophy as an academic career. In a letter of April 21, 1919, Eliot wrote about his turning down the assistant editorship at the *Athenaeum* at a very high salary, and he discussed at length his growing reputation. In effect he became the professor explaining the facts of literary life to his former professor: "There are only two ways in which a writer can become important—to write a great deal, and have his writings appear everywhere, or to write very little. It is a question of temperament. I write very little, and I should not become more powerful by increasing my output." Eliot noted that his reputation in London is built upon "one small volume of verse, and . . . two or three more poems in a year," stressing that "these should be perfect in their kind, so that each should be an event." He then explained the basic reasons for his remaining abroad: "I am a much more important person here than I should be at home. I am getting to know and be known by all the intelligent or important people in letters, and I am convinced that I am more useful in the long run by being here. Finally, one changes. I have acquired the habit of a society so different that it is difficult to find common terms to define the difference" (285). Eliot seems brimming here with self-confidence, with no hint of doubt or uncertainty. Such moments tend to have their limits—and their opposites.

Another recognition came to Eliot in the latter part of 1919. He was chosen to write front page reviews (or leaders) for what was regarded by most literary figures as the preeminent critical pages, the *Times Literary Supplement*. During this time, and for a long time into the future, the authors of reviews in the weekly remained anonymous. It was not until January 7, 1975, that all *TLS* reviews were signed (May, 421). Richard Aldington, who was a *TLS* contributor, heard that the editor, Bruce Richmond, was seeking reviewers and explained his motive for suggesting Eliot in his autobiography, *Life for Life's Sake* (1941):"I knew when it was whispered around that Eliot was writing *Times* literary leaders, it would shut up a lot of the opposition writers who were panning his work. Unfortunately, some of these people had Richmond's ear, and he was accordingly prejudiced." Aldington finally persuaded Richmond to have lunch with Eliot upon Eliot's return from the continent. Aldington arrived early in the office and at last, "in came Tom—wearing, if you please, a derby hat and an Uncle Sam beard he had cultivated in Switzerland. I had always thought of him as handsome, certainly very distinguished in appearance; but with the combination of that hat and beard he looked perfectly awful, like one of those comic-strip caricatures of Southern hicks. Richmond shook his head and blinked; I shook my head and blinked; Tom smiled urbanely, and looked more awful than ever." But Aldington's despair soon disappeared after Eliot began to talk: "In five minutes he had completely captivated Richmond, as he can captivate any intelligent person. Afterwards Richmond made a discreet Oxonian jest about the beard, but when we next met Tom it had vanished; and all was forgotten and forgiven" (Aldington, LLS, 268–69).

It was not long after the meeting that Eliot amended his résumé for his mother. In an October 2, 1919, letter to her he told her about his new position, describing it as "the highest honour possible in the critical world of literature." And he mentioned the books to appear in the coming year—"three and possibly four," one or two of essays, "a new edition of poems." He enclosed John Quinn's letter offering a New York edition to show Quinn's "kindness." Quinn had problems in dealing with two publishers and finally ended up with Knopf, who was "willing and anxious" to publish Eliot's *Poems* in America (LTSE1, 335, 337).

In this letter to his mother, Eliot revealed his intense feelings about an important international event of the time, the Versailles Conference at the end of the Great War: "It is certain that at the Peace Conference the one strong figure was Clemenceau, who knew just what he wanted, and that Wilson went down utterly before European diplomacy. It is obviously a bad peace, in which the major European powers tried to get as much as they could, and appease and ingratiate as far as possible the various puppet nationalities which they have constituted and will try to dominate. That is exactly what we expected. And I believe that Wilson made a grave mistake in coming to Europe" (337). On December 18, again to his mother, Eliot expressed his concern about the lack of progress on the peace treaty. "I hope it will not prevent America from helping in central Europe; the destitution, especially the starvation in Vienna, appears to be unspeakable. I suppose Americans realize now what a fiasco the reorganization of nationalities has been: the 'Balkanization' of Europe" (351). The U.S. Senate refused to ratify it, necessitating a separate treaty completed at Berlin, August 25, 1921. Bulgaria, Romania, Serbia, and so forth make up the Balkan states, called "the powder keg of Europe," whose complex politics resulted in the Balkan Wars (1912–13) preceding the Great War.

One final note on Eliot's résumé, which he made in another letter to his mother (November 10, 1919) about his October 28 lecture on poetry to the Arts League of Service at the Conference Hall, Westminster. He lectured to "about three hundred," and a "good many poets etc. came prepared to ask questions." He had "both a hostile chairman and a hostile audience. The chairman, [Laurence] Binyon, is a middle aged poetic celebrity who evidently knew nothing about me except that I was supposed to be the latest rage and he didn't understand it and didn't like it." Eliot had become so adept in lecturing that he managed to escape all of the traps that lay in wait: "He did his best, but thought it his duty in his introductory speech to refute—or at least to deny—everything he thought I would say. I carefully avoided mentioning any living poet by name, which disappointed the people who had come to hear me praise Pound or condemn Rupert Brooke, or put my foot into it in any of the ways in which I might bring popular fury onto myself. There was a heavy fire of heckling afterward, out of which I managed to escape by the philosophic method of replying to any question by another question" (346). Eliot gave the Secretary of the Arts League of Service permission to publish the essay under the title "Modern Tendencies in Poetry" in *Shama's* (Urur, Adjar, India), where it appeared in the April 1920 issue. Eliot told his mother: "It took me a long time to prepare the lecture. . . . I am going to develop the various parts of it, divide it into separate essays or chapters, and make a small book of it" (346). It is likely that the substance of the lecture ended up in Eliot's most famous essay, "Tradition and the Individual Talent," which ultimately was placed at the beginning of his collection, *Selected Essays.*

3. Friendships and Relationships: Deeper and Wider

Eliot's closest friend in England was undoubtedly Ezra Pound—not just a friend, but also a mentor and promoter. Long before he took over revising and revamping Eliot's *Waste Land,* he had suggested revisions for poems and often determined which poems should be published and which not. Eliot rarely turned down his advice. His was a presence keenly felt during 1919 and 1920, but by the end of 1920 he had left England for good, living first in Paris, later in Italy. Of course the move did not decrease Eliot's reliance on his literary judgment, as witness his effect in remaking *The Waste Land*, and Eliot's dedication of the poem to him: "For Ezra Pound / *il miglior fabbro* [The Better Craftsman]."

By this time Eliot and Pound were in such a close relationship that they joked with each other and also spoke their minds and revealed their private opinions in their correspondence. Eliot's letter to Pound, dated 30 Maggio 1920, is typical. It opens: "Cher E., Tengo en mi poder su honrada del 13 cnte." Giving the date in Italian, the salutation in French, the first sentence in Spanish, Eliot played on their multilingual backgrounds. "I have in my possession your honored letter of the 13th inst." Eliot had acquired Spanish because of the linguistic demands of the bank. He dwelt briefly on his exhaustion from "flathunting," finding the places available charging some 250 percent above their present rent.

Eliot next turned to describing the new Americans then coming to England: "Conrad Aiken is here; stupider than I remember him; in fact, stupid. Also [Maxwell] Bodenheim, the American Max, who arrived in the steerage on Monday with a wife and a baby which will see the light in a few weeks. . . . He is not unintelligent, anyhow better than Aiken, and being Semites I suppose they will survive somehow. He reports that [Ben] Hecht has decided to make a million dollars in a year, and has become press agent for the Baptist Church. When asked could not recall anyone else of intelligence in America" (*LTSE1*, 383–84). Both Bodenheim and Hecht were writers of some note in America: both had early connections with Chicago in something once called the Chicago Group, and the two had collaborated on a series of plays early in their career, notably *The Master Poisoner* (1918). Both were iconoclastic, bohemian Americans of the sort that inspired Eliot's amusement and contempt.

Something more is to be seen of Eliot's temperament in a postscript in his letter to Pound of July 3, 1920. It involved John Middleton Murry, whose offer of the lucrative job of assistant editor to the *Athenaeum* Eliot had turned down, but for which he became a prolific reviewer during this period. Murry's wife was Katherine Mansfield, and she played an important role in the editing of Murry's *Athenaeum*. Eliot wrote: "I meant to begin with this: I have seen Murry and secured a vague understanding that he would print a few of the poems (I said *not more* than five) but he has not read them yet. I must say that he is much more difficult to deal with when K. M. is about, and I have an impression that she terrorizes him. He told Ottoline [Morrell] that K. M.

was the only living writer of English prose (this is as Ott. reports it). I believe her to be a dangerous WOMAN; and of course two sentimentalists together are more than 2 times as noxious as one. She is going back to San Remo for the winter, in September" (389). By this time, Mansfield was plagued by tuberculosis (she would die in 1923), and her retreat to San Remo on the Italian Riviera was undoubtedly for her health.

In August of 1919, Eliot and Pound went on a walking tour in the Dordogne in southern France. Pound knew the area well, having made a walking tour there in the summer of 1912, taking copious notes in a small notebook. The notebook was published in 1992, edited by Richard Sieburth, under the title *A Walking Tour in Southern France: Ezra Pound among the Troubadours.* Eliot joined Ezra and Dorothy Pound in the Dordogne: "Together, he and Ezra examined the castle of Excideuil, associated with the troubadour Giraut de Bornelh, where, according to Canto 29, Eliot told Ezra: 'I am afraid of the life after death.'—and, after a pause, 'Now, at last, I have shocked him.'" As we have seen (Section 2 of this chapter), Eliot was relaxed and even grew a beard. Leaving Dorothy to sketch, the men hiked to Thiviers and Brantôm, with Eliot acquiring "7 blisters." After he left the Pounds, Eliot visited the "Dordogne prehistoric cave paintings by himself before returning to London" (Carpenter, 349).

Vivien wrote in her diary on August 31 that when Tom came home he was "very nice at first," and then "depressed" (Eliot, Vivien, UD). While on holiday, Eliot had written cards only to Vivien, so Eliot tried to capture the trip to France for his mother in a series of letters, the fullest account written on September 3, 1919. There he described the overnight trip to Havre, the steamer to Trouville, crowded with "men with violins and singers passing their hats . . . all so French and so sudden," the train to Paris, the dash by taxi to another station to catch the train to Limoges, where he found himself in "the company of two young soldiers . . . who played the accordion the whole way." Eventually "it began to be light, and I could see the beautiful landscape of Perigord, hilly and wooded, very different from Northern France. . . . You feel at once that you are in a different country, more exciting, very southern, more like Italy. . . . Finally . . . I reached Perigueux . . . where I was last in January 1911. And there Pound met me at the station" (*LTSE1*, 328).

Like most people, Eliot got caught up in the dailiness of his life and could only promise his mother that he would continue his account in his next letter. That never happened, as seen in letters of September 9 and October 2, but an unfinished letter to his mother, dated October 14, begins: "11— Perigueux is a town that I like. . . . It had taken me thirty-six hours to get there, but I felt that I had left London—the London of four years of war—

and reached the South at one instant—suddenly Roman ruins, and tall white houses, and gorgeous southern shrubs, and warm smells of garlic—donkeys—ox carts" (339). In a later letter (November 10, 1919), Eliot explained that he had always wanted to write "a really *good* letter," and thus postponed it until another night—and then time flew by:"The trouble is . . . that I want to write you several letters at once: one about my and our personal affairs, one about literature, one about your affairs, and one just affection" (345). In the meantime, southern France faded into the background.

By early 1920, Ezra Pound's powerful position on the literary scene in London was waning, and Eliot was alert to the increasing problems that Pound would be facing. He turned to one of Pound's most diligent backers, John Quinn, and explained to Quinn, in a letter of January 25, 1920, that he saw the London literary scene as divided into two warring camps. At the center of the most powerful camp was the *London Mercury,* started in 1919 "with a great deal of advertisment" and run "by a small clique of bad writers." It was edited by one J. C. Squire, who, Eliot observed, "knows nothing about poetry; but he is the cleverest journalist in London. If he succeeds, it will be impossible to get anything good published. His influence controls or affects the literary contents and criticism of five or six periodicals already." The second camp was smaller and included the *Times Literary Supplement* ("always more or less apart"), the *Athenaeum,* and *Art and Letters* ("of less influence"). But even the *Athenaeum* was problematic because "a majority of the . . . contributors belong to a small set that dislikes Pound" (358).

Eliot summed up Pound's situation: there was "no organ of any importance" that would review him or allow him to "express himself, and he is becoming forgotten." A first volume "may always attract attention," but when one has enemies "it is essential that he should establish solid connections with at least one important paper." From the start, Pound seemed to be everywhere, on both sides of the Atlantic, exerting his influence in such little magazines as *Poetry* (1912), the *Little Review* (1917), the *Dial* (1920), and the *Egoist* (1914), to name only those touched on in this book. Eliot wound up his confidential report to Quinn: "I know that Pound's lack of tact has done him great harm. But I am worried as to what is to become of him. I should at some time—when you have time, if you ever have any time—like very much to know your candid and confidential opinion about Pound and his future, if you have enough confidence in my discretion to express it" (358).

In September, Pound wrote to William Carlos Williams: "There is no longer any intellectual *life* in England save what centres in this eight by ten pentagonal room [of his apartment] . . . ; and NO literary publication whatever extant in England save what 'we' print (*Egoist* and Ovid Press)" (Pound, *L*, 158). Pound kept his apartment in London and left for France at the end of 1920 (Carpenter, 378). He headed first for the south for a time, with plans to return to Paris. He wrote a letter to Eliot, who found it "extremely obscure." Was it a farewell? Eliot called it "a blow. Please write and explain lucidly what your plans are and for how long. What happens to the *Dial*? Am I expected to receive books for review, in your absence? I will deal with them as directed. I have the opuscule this evening, and observe that you have commenced operation on it. If no more, Farewell and Pleasure" (*LTSE1*, 426–27). No doubt Eliot referred to one of his poems—"opuscule: a small, ordinary art work"—on which Pound had penned his usual terse suggestions, recommendations, or exclamations. Of course it would not be many months before Pound would have before him, in Paris, Eliot's poem that could only be labeled the exact opposite of an "opuscule." Pound realized that he had already made his decision to leave London for good after only a few months in France.

Although Bertrand Russell had been a key figure in Eliot's early years in England, by this time his role in Eliot's life had diminished, and others had come to the fore. It was Virginia Woolf and her circle of friends who took Eliot in and gave him a feeling of belonging. At their first meeting on November 15, 1918, however, it was not at all clear that Virginia would take to him. She wrote in her diary: "I was interrupted somewhere on this page by the arrival of Mr. Eliot. Mr. Eliot is well expressed by his name—a polished, cultivated, elaborate young American, talking so slow, that each word seems to have special finish allotted to it. But beneath the surface, it is fairly evident that he is very intellectual, intolerant, with strong views of his own, & a poetic creed." They disagreed about the merits of Pound, Lewis, and Joyce, whom Eliot "admires . . . immensely." She characterized the poems he brought as "the fruit of two years, since he works all day in a Bank, & in his reasonable way thinks regular work good for people of nervous constitutions" (Woolf, *D1, 218–19*).

That Eliot interested her is attested to by her perceptive comment on him: "I became more or less conscious of a very intricate & highly organized framework of poetic belief; owing to his caution, & his excessive care in the use of language we did not discover much about it. I think he believes in 'living phrases' & their difference from dead ones; in writing with extreme care, in observing all syntax & grammar; & so making this new poetry flower on the stem of the oldest." To "illustrate" her portrait of Eliot, she added something that Desmond MacCarthy (a family friend and writer) told her. He had asked Eliot how he had come to add "at the end of a poem on his

Aunt & the *Boston Evening Transcript* that phrase about an infinitely long street, & 'I like La Rochefoucauld saying good-bye.'" (Eliot's "The Boston Evening Transcript" concludes: "I mount the steps and ring the bell, turning / Wearily, as one would turn to nod good-bye to Rochefoucauld, / If the street were time and he at the end of the street, / And I say, 'Cousin Harriet, here is the *Boston Evening Transcript.*'") Eliot replied, MacCarthy reported, that the lines "were a recollection of Dante's 'Purgatorio'!" (218–19). Her exclamation point surely does not indicate that Woolf had not detected Eliot's conversational irony.

The Woolfs had established the Hogarth Press, named after their home, Hogarth House, Richmond, and undertook to publish experimental or unconventional works. Eliot had given them seven poems, three of which were in French. They were enough to make a small pamphlet, which was brought out in May 1919, and thus became his fourth "book publication." Only 250 volumes were issued, but they were hand-printed and hand-bound. The poems included were: "Sweeney among the Nightingales," "The Hippopotamus," "Mr. Eliot's Sunday Morning Service," "Whispers of Immortality," "Le spectateur ['Le directeur']," "Mélange adultère de tout," and "Lune de miel." At the same time that Hogarth Press published Eliot's *Poems* it also published John Middleton Murry's *The Critic in Judgment*. In her diary entry for December 3, 1918, Virginia compared the two: she found that both were hard to read, but Murry "does his thinking aloud; not making you fetch it from the depths of silence as Eliot does" (223).

An anonymous review of the two volumes, entitled "Not Here, O Apollo," appeared in the *Times Literary Supplement* on June 12, 1919, and was highly critical of Eliot's poetry. A sample: "Mr. Eliot's . . . composition is an incessant process of refusing all that offers itself, for fear that it should not be his own. The consequence is that his verse, novel and ingenious, original as it is, is fatally impoverished of subject matter. He seems to have a 'phobia' of sentimentality, like a small schoolboy who would die rather than kiss his sister in public" (quoted in Grant, 98). The reviewer was Arthur Clutton-Brock, author of several books including *Shelley: The Man and the Poet* (May, 127). Most interesting was the unsigned review "Is This Poetry?" in the *Athenaeum* on June 20, 1919, written by Leonard and Virginia Woolf. As Virginia explained to Eliot: "We felt awkward reviewing our own publications, and agreed to share the guilt: he reviewed you, and I reviewed Murry" (quoted in *LTSE1*, 309). In his review Leonard Woolf observed that Eliot was attempting "something which has grown out of and developed beyond all the poems of all the dead poets. . . . The poetry of the dead is in his bones and at the tips of his fingers: he has the rare gift of being able to weave, delicately and delightfully, an echo or even a line of the past into the pattern of his own poem" (quoted in Grant, 100).

Virginia Woolf continued to amend, expand, and puzzle over Eliot, providing insights into both writers and their art. Eliot visited the Woolfs at their summer home, Monk's House, Rodmell, located in Lewes, East Sussex, near Brighton, without Vivien on Saturday, September 18, and left right after supper on Sunday the 19th. Virginia's diary reveals in several entries an almost obsessive concern for penetrating the various mysteries of personality that Eliot presented for her. The first entry, written early Sunday morning, opens: "Eliot is separated only by the floor from me. Nothing in mans or womans shape is any longer capable of upsetting me. The odd thing about Eliot is that his eyes are lively & youthful when the cast of his face & the shape of his sentences is formal & even heavy. Rather like a s[c]ulpted face—no upper lip: formidable, powerful; pale. Then those hazel eyes seemed to escape from the rest of him." He seems here to have become a candidate for a character in one of her novels, one part of him (his eyes) out of the disciplined control of the other, rigid part of him. In recounting the previous evening's discussion, she repeated a remark Eliot had made about himself about his stay at Garsington: "And I behaved like a priggish pompous little ass." That Eliot would speak about himself in this way shows a disarming attempt to become one of them. Virginia found Eliot to be one of the younger generation, although, she added, "I dare say superior" (Woolf, *D2,* 67).

On the next day, Monday, September 20, Virginia revealed her insecurities: "he completely neglected my claims to be a writer, & had I been meek, I suppose I should have gone under—felt him & his views dominant & subversive." About his writing, she suspected "him of a good deal of concealed vanity & even anxiety." At this point, Virginia went—mildly—on the attack: "I taxed him with willfully concealing his transitions," to which he responded that "If you put it in, you dilute the facts. You should feel these without explanation." To her charge that "a rich & original mind is needed to make such psychological writing of value," he replied "he was more interested in people than in anything. He cant read Wordsworth when Wordsworth deals with nature. His turn is for caricature. In trying to define his meaning ('I don't mean satire') we foundered." Virginia was able in the conversation to lead Eliot to reveal his private thoughts about his career: "He wants to write a verse play in which the 4 characters of Sween[e]y act the parts. A personal upheaval of some kind came after Prufrock, & turned him aside from his inclination—to develop in the manner of Henry James. Now he wants to describe externals. Joyce gives internals. His novel *Ulysses,* presents the life of man in 16 incidents, all taking place (I think) in one day. This, so far as he has seen it, is extremely brilliant." On the following Sunday, Woolf confided to her diary that Eliot's visit "cast shade" upon her, that although he said nothing, she felt that what she was doing was "probably being better done by Mr. Joyce" (Woolf, *D2,* 67–69). This spurred a self-examination that would recur in her future encounters with Eliot.

A notable evening occurred a year later, during a particularly bad period, when Vivien's health required that she be put in a nursing home. On Sunday, March 20, 1921, Eliot dined with the Woolfs and went to see Congreve's *Love for Love* at the Lyric Theatre, Hammersmith. Virginia was to review it for the *New Statesman,* so Leonard sat upstairs with that ticket and she and Eliot sat in the pit. She and Eliot missed the train and drove to the theatre by taxi—"through dark market gardens." In her diary entry for March 22 she recounted their dialogue in which Eliot agreed that "Missing trains is awful," but "humiliation is the worst thing in life." She asked if he was "as full of vices" as she. His answer: "Full. Riddled with them." She feared they were "not as good as Keats," but he said, "Yes we are. . . . We're trying something harder." In this Virginia thought her work, compared with the classics, was "futile. Negligible. One goes on because of an illusion." In this exchange between two of the pioneers of modernism, Virginia betrayed more doubts. But in the performance of their art, both would go on to suffer nervous breakdowns, and of course, Woolf would commit suicide. Virginia thought "one could probably become very intimate with Eliot because of our damned self conscious susceptibility: but I plunge more than he does: perhaps I could learn him to be a frog" (103–4). Intimacy would grow, and Eliot would find himself able to reveal feelings and thoughts with her, if not as a frog, at least as a friend.

Eliot grew closer as well to a number of individuals who had some involvement, large or small, with members of the Bloomsbury Group, including Mary and Jack Hutchinson; Sydney and Violet Schiff—she, an accomplished musician and he, the wealthy patron, friend, and translator of Proust, who wrote novels under the name of Stephen Hudson, and who financed the quarterly *Art and Letters* (editor Frank Rutter, sometime assistant editor Osbert Sitwell); and the three Sitwells, Edith, Osbert, and Sacheverell, who all wrote poetry but many prose works as well. Sydney Schiff, curiously omitted from textbooks of literary history, is "one of the great casualties of English letters," according to Proust's biographer Jean-Yves Tadié. Tadié notes that "apart from Proust, there were only two people with whom the two Schiffs wished to exchange views, Eliot and Wyndham Lewis." Inviting Proust to his home, Schiff wrote: "There will be twenty or so people, homogeneous and homosexual," and he named among them Lewis and the Sitwells (Tadié, 692). The Sacheverell Sitwells accompanied the Eliots to the opening night of Manuel de Falla's ballet, *Three-Cornered Hat,* performed by Léonide Massine and the Ballets Russes. The Eliots often took part in private theatricals with the Schiffs at their homes in Cambridge Square and Eastbourne (Gordon, *EIL,* 128). But none of these relationships in Eliot's life matched the particular closeness that developed between him and Virginia Woolf.

4. A Voice from the Past; "An Encounter of Titans"; Moving Again

A voice from the past was heard in one of the strangest letters Eliot received during this period—from a third cousin once removed of his grandfather by the name of Charles W. Eliot, President of Harvard University from 1869 until 1909. While a student at Harvard, T. S. Eliot had joined other students and members of the faculty who criticized President Eliot for opting for the elective system of undergraduate education, thus allowing students to choose what courses to take (see Chapter 4, Section 1). From the opening of the letter, we learn that Charles Eliot had written previously on January 4, 1919, only a few days before Eliot's father died of a heart attack. Is it possible that Eliot's father had asked President Eliot to write? In any event, he wrote his July 25 letter in response to one received from Eliot dated July 9. This July 9 letter is not in the collected *Letters,* but we can infer what Eliot might have said from Charles Eliot's comments.

President Eliot explained that he wrote because he "felt interest in the career of a member of the Eliot clan," and "in an exceptional or peculiar career of a well-trained Harvard graduate,—especially if that career be literary or scientific." The younger Eliot must have said that he wanted to support himself, that he worked in a bank, that he wanted to gain a literary reputation, and that to do this he must live in London, because in his reply, the senior Eliot cited precedents of people who work for their "livelihood" and yet are "fresh" for "literary or scientific labors," and agreed that London, as the younger Eliot wrote him, "is good for you spiritually and . . . leads quicker . . . to established success in literature." But President Eliot went on to explain why he thought Eliot had made the wrong decision to live permanently abroad: "It is quite unintelligible to me how you or any other young American scholar can forego the privilege of living in the genuine American atmosphere—a bright atmosphere of freedom and hope" or get used to "the manners or customs of any class of English society, high, middle, or low." There was also, he pointed out, the positive contribution that could be made by an American man of letters to his own country; how is it possible for such an individual "to forego the privilege of being of use primarily to Americans of the present and future generations, as Emerson, Bryant, Lowell, and Whittier were?" (*LTSE1*, 322–23).

The younger Eliot had "mentioned the name of Henry James," and President Eliot noted that he knew well both his father and brother William, who had spent his career teaching at Harvard, and reported that he had told Henry "that his English residence for so many years contributed neither to the happy development of his art nor to his personal happiness." President Eliot's "last word": "if you wish to speak through your own work to people of the 'finest New England spirit' you had better not live much longer in the English atmosphere" (323). One can imagine TSE smiling at the American poets President Eliot listed in his letter: Emerson, Bryant, Lowell, and Whittier, whose poetry embodied everything he found wrong with American literature. As for Henry James, the expatriate model par excellence, Eliot, was, as we have seen, a firm believer in James's accomplishment in finding and mining his material out of his specifically European experience. It is likely the dutiful Eliot answered this letter, but if so it, like the July 9 letter, was somehow not saved. His answer would most likely echo that of any number of letters written to his father, since it raised all of the old questions.

On August 15, 1920, Eliot went on holiday with Wyndham Lewis in France, leaving Vivien in the care of his friends, Sydney and Violet Schiff. Lewis and Eliot went first to Paris and then on a walking and cycling tour of northern France. By train, by boat, and again by train, they carried a large, mysterious package for Joyce from Pound. Eliot had written Joyce in advance inviting him to dinner the evening of their arrival. Looking forward to meeting Joyce "at last," Eliot asked him to meet at the Hôtel l'Élysée where he "can take the parcel." As Ellmann notes in his biography of Joyce, "The meeting proceeded with a dignity befitting an encounter of Titans, but undercut by Pound's gift" (Ellmann, 507). Lewis's account captures the scene: "Joyce lay back in the stiff chair . . . crossed his leg, . . . an arm flung back. . . . He dangled negligently his straw hat, a regulation 'boater.' We were on either side of the table . . . upon which stood the enigmatical parcel. Eliot now rose to his feet . . . and he formally delivered it, thus acquitting himself of his commission." Eliot sat down and Joyce "was by now attempting to untie the crafty housewifely knots of the cunning old Ezra." Joyce turned to his son, whom he had brought and asked "crossly in Italian for a penknife. Still more crossly his son" said no (Lewis, *BB*, 269).

"At last the strings were cut. A little gingerly Joyce unrolled the slovenly swaddlings of damp British brown paper in which the good-hearted American had packed up what he had put inside. Thereupon, along with some nondescript garments for the trunk—there were no trousers I believe—a fairly presentable pair of *old brown shoes* stood revealed, in the center of the bourgeois French table." Then Joyce took over the evening, chose an expensive restaurant, and insisted on paying for it as well as the taxis and, for the remainder of their stay, everything was always paid by the "eminent recipient of the parcel of old shoes." Lewis attributed this to Joyce's "Irish pride" (269–70, 290–91).

The most astonishing matter in the encounter with Joyce was his treatment of Eliot. Joyce, Lewis wrote, "maintained a punctilious reserve. In alluding to him, with me, he would say 'Your friend Mr. Eliot,' as if Eliot had been an obscure family friend . . . who . . . must be suffered. . . . As to mentioning his writings, or as to ever a passing reference to him as *a poet*—that was the last thing that it ever occurred to Joyce to do" (291). But during their time together in Paris, Joyce once did "allow himself to say [to Eliot], 'I was at the Jardin des Plantes today and paid my respects to your friend the hippopotamus'" (quoted in Ellmann, 509). In conversation with Lewis, Eliot labeled Joyce "definitely burdensome, and *arrogant*" (Lewis, *BB*, 297). In a letter to Sydney Schiff on August 22, from Saumur, he described dining with Joyce in Paris, calling him "a quiet but rather dogmatic man," who "has (as I am convinced most superior persons have) a sense of his own importance. He has a source of gravity which seems more protestant than Catholic." And Eliot enclosed a charming sketch of the dinner party, mostly their heads, and identified by initials: F. V., Fritz Vanderpyl (a Belgian poet); W. L., Lewis; J. J., Joyce (with large glasses and a goatee); and T. S. E. in profile—all wearing various hats of the day. A bemused waiter with large mustaches stands looking down on the group (*LTSE1*, 402–3).

Eliot continued in his admiration for Joyce, and Joyce would come to respect Eliot as a poet. Ellmann recounts that after reading *The Waste Land,* years after this Paris meeting, Joyce told a friend he hadn't "realized that Eliot was a poet." To her comment that she couldn't understand it, Joyce "retorted . . . 'Do you have to understand it?'" (Ellmann, 509). The following May Eliot wrote to Quinn that the "latter part of *Ulysses*" was "truly magnificent," and to Joyce he returned portions of the manuscript, finding them "superb—especially the Descent into Hell, which is stupendous" (*LTSE1*, 452, 455). In reply to Aldington's attack on Joyce, Eliot wrote an important article entitled "Ulysses, Order and Myth," published in the November 1923 *Dial*. There he notes that "Joyce's parallel use of the *Odyssey* . . . has the importance of a scientific discovery. . . . In using the myth, in manipulating a continuous parallel between contemporaneity and antiquity, Mr. Joyce is pursuing a method which others must pursue after him." This "mythical method" is "a step toward making the modern world possible for art" (*SP*, 177–78). Critics have applied Eliot's astute analysis of *Ulysses* to Eliot's own *Waste Land*. With these two works, published in 1922, the modernist movement was born.

The Eliots had been living in their flat at 18 Crawford Mansions since late March 1916. What was described in Vivien's letters as "the tiniest place imaginable"—with the dining room serving as "Tom's dressing room and study"—on June 1, 1916, became "a little noisy corner, with slums and low streets and poor shops" on June 28, 1917. So Vivien signed a five-year lease for a house in Buckinghamshire, with financial support (and furniture) from Russell. Thus it was that on June 9, 1918, Eliot could write his mother from 31 West Street, Marlow, Bucks, that "we have finally (like all our friends) come out of London" into "a charming old little town," located "on the Thames . . . in the street where Shelley used to live." Tom commuted by train and both benefited "mentally and physically" from being out of London. Vivien became quite attached to the gardens, "brilliant with hollyhocks . . . which start after the foxgloves and lupins and larkspur." They had to let the house in the fall and eventually had to give it up when Russell pulled out of the deal and they could no longer manage it financially. They gave up the lease on November 15, 1920. They could no longer afford to keep it when they were finally able to leave Crawford Mansions, which, by July 3, 1920, they had come to "loathe" for its "noise and sordidness" (*LTSE1*, 139–40, 186, 233–34, 239, 270, 284, 390).

Eliot had been hunting for a flat since June and was able to write his mother on September 20, 1920, that he had found one in a "better neighborhood in which not so many people are arrested," "free from the neighborhood of prostitution" (408). (Recall that Eeldrop and Appleplex lived across from the police station where they watched malefactors apprehended [see Chapter 10, Section 3].) Osbert Sitwell reported that from their windows the Eliots could look out on a pub across the street, while above two "actresses" shouted to friends below and played the phonograph very loudly (quoted in Ackroyd, 94–95). Although the Eliots entertained their friends in the flat, no wonder Tom and Vivien took every opportunity to leave, staying at cottages in Marlow, Bosham; visiting the great houses at Wittering, Eastbourne, Garsington, together or, more often, alone. Eliot tried to escape the misery of the marriage as often as possible. The atmosphere within the marriage, within Crawford Mansions, was oppressive.

Despite the efforts of the "insanely suspicious grasping old spinster" who set up every obstacle, they were finally able to take over the new flat by October 31, when Eliot wrote his mother that with an extra room and "rather bigger" rooms, "one flight up," equipped with a "lift," "anthracite stoves," and "constant hot water": "It will do beautifully for you when you come" (*LTSE1, 418*). The new address was 9 Clarence Gate Gardens, not far from their old flat, near Regents Park, in a large block of apartments. The Eliots would live in one or another of the flats there until 1932, when Eliot left Vivien to lecture for a year at Harvard. He would return to England but not to her. Except for a brief flurry of hotel stays at the end, Vivien would stay on until July 1938, when she was committed to a private mental asylum, Northumberland House, where she died January 22, 1947, at the age of 58 (Seymour-Jones, 557–58, 568).

5. Three New Books: Poetry and Prose

In 1920, the publication of three important books marked the close of Eliot's period of anonymity, poverty, and uncertainty about his career. In early February, John Rodker's Ovid Press published a volume of poems entitled *Ara Vus Prec* (later the title was corrected to *Ara Vos Prec*). In late February, Knopf published *Poems* in New York. The contents of these two books were almost— but not quite—the same. In the American edition, the poems appeared in a slightly different order, and one poem found in the Ovid publication, "Ode on Independence Day, July 4th 1918," was replaced by a prose poem, "Hysteria." In early November Methuen published a book of prose, *The Sacred Wood;* it was published the following year in America, February 1921, by Knopf, Eliot's first commercial publisher.

The most puzzling of all Eliot's choice of titles, *Ara Vos Prec* ("Now I pray you"), is a phrase that appears in Dante's *Purgatorio,* Canto XXVI, lines 142–48, spoken by Arnaut Daniel, assigned to the circle of "The Lustful," including hermaphrodites and sodomites. His plea concludes, "be mindful in due time of my pain." We have already encountered this passage in the manuscript version of "The Love Song of J. Alfred Prufrock," analyzed in Chapter 5, Section 6. And we'll encounter it again in Eliot's work. A first question that arises here is Eliot's error in the title as it first appeared, *Ara Vus Prec.* The matter is cleared up by Donald Gallup in his Eliot *Bibliography.* He writes that Eliot told him: "The current title of the book is *Ara Vos Prec.* It only happened to be *Vus* on the title page because I don't know Provençal, and I was quoting from an Italian edition of Dante the editor of which apparently did not know Provençal either" (Gallup, *TSEB,* 26).

The second question is: Why did Eliot give such a title to a volume of the poems in 1920? In a postcard of October 3, 1919, to his publisher John

Rodker, he said that the "title *Ara Vus Prec* would do. For it is non-committal about the newness of the contents, and unintelligible to most people" (*LTSE1*, 338). The implication is that enlightened people who recognized the phrase as Dante's would learn something about his poems in the book. It should be noted that Eliot's poems in this volume (as well as in *Poems*, published in America only a few weeks later) were not arranged as they would be in the series of *Collected Poems* that were to be published later and throughout the remainder of Eliot's career: whereas in these later volumes the poems appear chronologically as they first appeared in published books, with the 1917 *Prufrock and Other Observations* leading the volume, in *Ara Vos Prec* Eliot's latest poems appear first, beginning with "Gerontion," continuing with the quatrain and French poems, and ending with the poems from the earliest *Prufrock* volume. Thus, the question arises as to if (or how) the title of the volume relates to the poem to which it is nearest, "Gerontion," a question that will be fully explored—and answered in the affirmative below (Section 6).

On the whole, the reviews of *Ara Vos Prec* were more positive than were those of Eliot's previous book. But some of the reviewers found his later work, leading off in the book, somewhat less interesting, and certainly more difficult, than his earlier work, especially "The Love Song of J. Alfred Prufrock" and "Portrait of a Lady." The names of the reviewers were recognizable, and included John Middleton Murry, Desmond MacCarthy, and Clive Bell.

One of the most negative reviews, "A New Byronism," appeared anonymously in the *Times Literary Supplement*. In fact, the reviewer was Arthur Clutton-Brock (May, 127), who had reviewed Eliot's Hogarth Press volume of poetry (see Section 3 of this chapter). In this review, he was harsh in his criticism of *Ara Vos Prec* and other Eliot works, concluding: "Art means the acceptance of a medium as of life; and Mr. Eliot does not convince us that his weariness is anything but a habit, an anti-romantic reaction, a new Byronism which he must throw off if he is not to become a recurring decimal in his fear of being a mere vulgar fraction" (quoted in Grant, 108). John Middleton Murry entitled his review in the *Athenaeum* "The Eternal Footman," and used this metaphor to express his concern for Eliot's new poetry: "At a crucial moment in his beautiful—we insist, precisely beautiful—'Love Song of J. Alfred Prufrock,'—'The Eternal Footman snickers.' Since that day Mr. Eliot has fallen deeper and deeper into the clutches of the Footman, who has come to preside over his goings out and his comings in. The Footman has grown into a monstrous Moloch. All that Mr. Eliot most deeply feels is cast into his burning belly—or almost all" (103). Yet Desmond MacCarthy in the *New Statesman* concluded: Eliot "is, to my mind, the most interesting of 'the new poets.'" (117). And Clive Bell in a long essay "on jazz and its influence on modern art," in the *New Republic,* included Eliot, calling him "about the best of our living poets, and, like Stravinsky, he is as much a product of the Jazz movement as so good an artist can be of any" (118).

To this account of reviewers' responses to *Ara Vos Prec,* we might add that of an important reader, I. A. Richards, a Cambridge don, who purchased a copy of the book and recalled in a talk "On TSE": "I remember sunlight on those large, fine pages and a breathless exhilaration . . . —unable NOT to read in the Market Place . . . —spreading the resplendent thing open: lost in wonder and strangeness and delight." Richards tried (unsuccessfully) to "winkle" Eliot out of his bank and "annex" him to Cambridge for the new English studies course Richards was establishing. He provided an unforgettable portrait of Eliot when he visited him at his office, where he saw "a figure stooping, very like a dark bird in a feeder, over a big table covered with all sorts and sizes of foreign correspondence. The big table almost filled a little room under the street. Within a foot of our heads when we stood were the thick, green glass squares of the pavement on which hammered all but incessantly the heels of the passers-by" (Richards, TSE, 2–4). An enthusiastic promoter of Eliot, Richards became a friend and perceptive critic of his work. (See Chapter 4, Section 5 for his account of the relevance of Dante's Canto XXVI of the *Purgatorio* to *The Waste Land.*)

In America, Eliot's *Poems* were reviewed by widely recognized critics or poets, including E. E. Cummings, Mark Van Doren, Louis Untermeyer, and Padraic Colum. Marion Strobel (in *Poetry*) echoed many other reviewers in finding the earlier poetry "far superior" to the later, calling "Prufrock" and "Portrait" the best in the volume (quoted in Grant, 120). Mark Van Doren was enthusiastic in his review (in the *Nation*): "Whatever happens [to Eliot, whether he comes back to America from England where he "set up as a critic" or not], it is hoped that he keeps somehow to poetry. For he is the most proficient satirist now writing in verse, the uncanniest clown, the devoutest monkey, the most picturesque ironist; and aesthetically considered, he is one of the profoundest symbolists" (125–26). Louis Untermeyer (in the *Freeman*) found little to like in Eliot: "His contribution is related to poetry only at rare intervals. His lines, for the most part, are written in a new *genre* or, to be more accurate, in a modernization of a surprisingly old one. They are, primarily, a species of mordant light verse; complex and disillusioned *vers de société*" (130). Padraic Colum concluded (in the *New Republic*): "The poetry of Mr. Eliot, in spite of its being so well exercised and so well disinfected, belongs after all to Byzantium; the shadows of a long decay are upon it all" (133).

Eliot's book of prose, *The Sacred Wood: Essays on Poetry and Criticism,* was published in England in early November 1920, and later in America in early 1921. All of the pieces had already appeared in magazines, most of them in the *Athenaeum* during 1919 and 1920. Many of them were reviews and had slightly different titles in the magazines. But it is fairly clear that Eliot wrote them with the intention of ultimately seeing them in book form. In all, seventeen essays were included, some nine of which found their way into Eliot's *Selected Essays,* the first volume of which appeared in 1932. *The Sacred Wood* has been repeatedly reissued in paperback, as recently as 1989.

Eliot had dedicated his first book, *Prufrock and Other Observations,* "To Jean Verdenal 1889–1915," so he dedicated *The Sacred Wood* to his father: "For H. W. E. / *'Tacuit et fecit.'*" The Latin phrase, the family motto, literally reads: "He has been silent and he has performed [accomplished]." As we have seen above, Eliot had rushed to get his work published in 1920 because he had planned a visit to America and he thought his father would be reassured by seeing his poetry and criticism in print—and no doubt he hoped for some kind of reconciliation with his family. As it turned out, his dedication was a substitute for his original plan, and by using only initials that few could identify and a phrase in Latin that many would not understand, he privately said his farewell to the father he wanted so much to please.

In naming his book *The Sacred Wood,* Eliot is invoking the monumental work of Sir James Frazer, *The Golden Bough,* which first appeared in thirteen volumes, 1890–1915, and later in a condensed volume in 1923 (after the appearance of Eliot's book). An anthropological work on comparative religion and mythology, the title refers to the bough Aeneas broke from a sacred tree before his entrance into the underworld; of course the tree was in the sacred grove, which Eliot adapted for his book as *The Sacred Wood.* Frazer sifted through all religions and myths to identify the archetypal patterns that bind them together. At the center he described the Sacred Grove (or Wood), in which one particular tree with its precious bough was guarded by "a priest[-king] and a murderer" and he was deposed only when he was murdered and succeeded by the new priest-king. The priest-king was the guardian of the goddess, Diana of the Grove (Diana Nemorensis). Later religions and mythologies followed with variations of this basic pattern, i.e., death followed by a rebirth. What is the meaning, then, of Eliot's title? Elizabeth Drew believed that Eliot employed the title "as a symbol for the immortal poetic tradition, always dying and being reborn" (Drew, 43).

John B. Vickery, in his valuable work *The Literary Impact of "The Golden Bough"* (1973), agrees with Drew and adds: "But the nature of the ritual itself may further illuminate Eliot's choice of titles. The priest-king who guards the sacred grove ruled so long as he could defeat in ritual combat anyone who chose to oppose him. When we remember that the volume is subtitled 'Essays in Poetry and Criticism,' and when we regard the composition of the volume—beginning with 'The Perfect Critic' and ending with Dante, the perfect poet—it seems clear that if poetry is the sacred goddess, then criticism is her warrior-priest who defends her honor and sanctity, and whose function is to prevent inferior poetry and criticism alike from usurping unworthily the role of deity or of priest and attendant" (Vickery, 234).

As we have seen in Chapter 4, Section 6, one of Eliot's favorite classical texts was Petronius's *The Satyricon*. It might seem puzzling for Eliot to select a passage from this bawdy tale as one of the two epigraphs for *The Sacred Wood*. Here is the text of the passage in English as translated by W. C. Firebaugh that appeared first in 1922 (an edition introduced by Charles Whibley's essay on *Petronius*, much admired by Eliot): "a white-haired old man entered the picture gallery; his face was care-worn, and he seemed, I know not why, to give promise of something great, although he bestowed so little care upon his dress, that it was easily apparent that he belonged to that class of literati which the wealthy hold in contempt. 'I am a poet,' he remarked, '. . . and one of no mean ability, I hope, that is, if anything is to be inferred from the crowns which gratitude can place even upon the heads of the unworthy!'" (Petronius, 152). Clearly the poet of Petronius plays the role in society that Eliot the poet sees himself playing in writing the critical essays in his book.

A second epigraph is set below the Petronius passage: "I also like to dine on Becaficas." Eliot does not deign to indicate that these puzzling words constitute the opening line of Stanza 43 of Byron's poem "Beppo." Most readers would be baffled by "becaficas." The Oxford English Dictionary reveals that "becafica" is a variant for "beccafico" (derived from Italian: "a pecker of figs"): small migratory birds of the genus *Sylvia*, "most esteemed as dainties in the autumn" after the birds have been "fattened on figs and grapes." The solemnity of the poet speaking in the first epigraph is broken by the oddity of someone saying out of the blue that he "also" likes to dine on some extraordinarily obscure "migratory bird." Is this line meant to humanize somewhat the Petronius poet's elevated self-reference? Or is there something of the nature of these extraordinary birds in the nature of extraordinary poetry? Both speculations seem plausible, even when we discover that Eliot's second epigraph, though from Byron, brings us back again to Petronius, to "Eliot's undergraduate copy of the *Satyricon*, a 1904 [Latin] edition of Bücheler" that Eliot had annotated. In their 1975 "T. S. Eliot and Petronius," Gareth L. Schmeling and David R. Rebmann point out: "At *Satyricon* 33, Eliot notes that the Latin word *ficedula* means ... 'fig-pecker' and refers to Ryan's translation (1905) which has a cross reference to the fact that the Italian word for *ficedula* is *beccafico*" (Schmeling and Rebmann, 400–401). Eliot may have had his learned annotation in mind when he selected the line from Byron for his second epigraph.

We can say that the two epigraphs are taken from somewhat bawdy works. One critic of Byron, Paul G. Trueblood, describes "Beppo" in this way: "The story of 'Beppo' is slight, a mere peg on which to hang the poet's digressions. ... Beppo, a Venetian merchant, reappears during the Carnival after years of Turkish captivity to find that his wife, Laura, has taken the Count as her lover. He discloses his identity, reunites with his wife, and befriends the Count." But this plot is not the substance of "Beppo": "The racy tale ... occupies very few of the ninety-nine stanzas. Around and in and out of this slender narrative fabric the narrator's whimsical digressions and ironic comment flash like summer heat lightning. With amused tolerance the poet allows his digressive comment to play over the vanities, trivialities, and immoralities of Venetian life" (Trueblood, 93).

Having found our way to the actual opening pages of *The Sacred Wood*, what do we find there? There are two essays in it that during much of the twentieth century were required reading for any student of literature: "Tradition and the Individual Talent" and "Hamlet and His Problems." The first was famous for its introduction of the "impersonal theory of poetry": "The business of the poet is not to find new emotions, but to use the ordinary ones and, in working them up into poetry, to express feelings which are not in actual emotions at all." And: "Poetry is not a turning loose of emotion, but an escape from emotion. It is not the expression of personality, but an escape from personality" (*SE*, 7, 10). In the "Hamlet" essay, Eliot introduced his notion of the "objective correlative": "The only way of expressing emotion in the form of art is by finding an 'objective correlative'; in other words, a set of objects, a situation, a chain of events which shall be the formula of that *particular* emotion; such that when the external facts, which must terminate in sensory experience, are given, the emotion is immediately evoked" (124–25).

A third famous principle of criticism paralleling these, conceived about this same time, Eliot included in an essay, "The Metaphysical Poets," published first as a review in the *Times Literary Supplement* (October 20, 1921) and included in his book of essays *Homage to John Dryden*, published in 1924: "In the seventeenth century a dissociation of sensibility set in, from which we have never recovered; and this dissociation, as is natural, was aggravated by the two most powerful poets of the century, Milton and Dryden. ... The sentimental age began early in the eighteenth century, and continued. The poets revolted against the ratiocinative, the descriptive; they thought and felt by fits, unbalanced; they reflected." How should contemporary poets cope with this situation? Eliot wrote: "We can only say that it appears likely that poets in our civilization, as it exists at present, must be *difficult*. . . . The poet must become more and more comprehensive, more allusive, more indirect, in order to force, to dislocate if necessary, language into his meaning" (247–48). Any reader who has attempted to read far into Eliot's collected poems will recognize here that Eliot wrote them in accord with his theory as expressed in these lines.

Reviews for Eliot's first book of prose were mixed, but a few were filled with high praise. One of the most enthusiastic was Richard Aldington's brief review ("A Critic of Poetry") in *Poetry* magazine in March 1921. In his opening paragraph he called *The Sacred Wood* the most "stimulating and thoughtful book of criticism of the year." His praise was indeed extraordinary, given that he was unsympathetic to Eliot's poetry: "It is perhaps an unique experience in the life of this generation, to find that we possess a critic of Mr. Eliot's intelligence; a critic with principles, not impressions; a critic whose perceptions have been stimulated by the best literature of the past; whose appreciation of the present is equally keen and just; a critic without fads, personal vanity, or affectation. A critic who has read the books he criticizes" (Aldington, ACP, 345–46).

It should be noted that Aldington's opinion turned out to be that of successive generations. One of the most influential critical works on Eliot, entitled *The Achievement of T. S. Eliot: An Essay on the Nature of Poetry*, was written by F. O. Matthiessen and first published in 1935. Matthiessen taught at Harvard and had come to know Eliot when he lectured there in the academic year 1932–33, and was able to have many discussions with him about his work. In his opening chapter, "Tradition and the Individual Talent," Matthiessen began with a discussion of Eliot's first book of prose, writing about the historical development of criticism since the death of Matthew Arnold (in 1888): "There was no detailed intensive re-examination of the quality and function of poetry until the publication of *The Sacred Wood* in 1920. It could not be wholly clear then, but it has become so now, that the ideas first arriving at their mature expression in that volume definitely placed their author in the main line of poet-critics that runs from Ben Jonson and Dryden through Samuel Johnson, Coleridge, and Arnold." But Matthiessen took care to explain that his praise was not limited to critical theory: "In fact, what has given the note of authority to Eliot's views of poetry is exactly what has made the criticism of the other writers just named the most enduring in English. They have not been merely theorists, but all craftsmen talking of what they knew at first hand" (Matthiessen, 2–3). Of course, Matthiessen was writing some fifteen years after Eliot's book appeared, but it is a view that came to prevail in the modernist movement. And Eliot's poetry and criticism would inform much of the New Criticism that dominated literary studies in the first part of the twentieth century.

6. "Gerontion": Return of Fitzgerald's Omar

At the end of four previous chapters (3, 5, 8, 10), I analyzed the personal dimensions of a select few of Eliot's poems in order of composition. Often the texts used in these chapters have been manuscript copies made available only with the publication in 1971 of Valerie Eliot's edition of *The Waste Land: A Facsimile and Transcript of the Original Drafts* and in 1996 of Christopher Ricks's edition of *Inventions of the March Hare,* providing a succession of texts for the early poems frequently revised. Sometimes the strict chronological order has been abandoned in favor of placing poems together (such as the French poems and the quatrain poems) because of their similarities in form or poetic intention. The poems ranging in date from 1918 to 1920 are listed at the end of this chapter. Out of the six poems written during this period, two are of extraordinary importance: "Ode," which was published only in *Ara Vos Prec* in 1920, but which appears in *Inventions of a March Hare* as "Ode on Independence Day, July 4th 1918"; and "Gerontion." My analysis and assessment of "Ode" may be found in chapter 5 ("A Suppressed 'Ode': A Confessional Poem," pp. 47–58) of my 1977 book *T. S. Eliot's Personal Wasteland.* My treatment of "Gerontion" appears below.

"Gerontion" (1919; IOMH, 349–52)

"Gerontion" (written largely in 1919) is generally considered to be the second of three major poems produced by Eliot during the early part of his career. The first is "The Love Song of J. Alfred Prufrock" (1911), and the third *The Waste Land,* completed in 1922. The character Gerontion appears to be in many ways a portrait of Prufrock grown older, as he seems also to foreshadow the speaker of *The Waste Land.* As for the latter, Eliot once proposed to Pound that "Gerontion" appear as a prologue to *The Waste Land* to be published after Pound's severe revisions. It could be argued that the three poems belong together as beginning ("Prufrock"), middle (*The Waste Land*'s speaker), and end ("Gerontion"). In effect, the pivotal center of all these characters is Eliot himself, and his biographical and psychological history is relevant to all three. But just as all human beings change over time, so the Eliots of 1911, 1919, and 1922 are not identical beings in their physical, spiritual, and psychological essences. Two early versions of "Gerontion" exist, an original typescript and a revised version on a carbon typescript with Pound's pencil suggestions, published in Ricks's edition of *Inventions of the March Hare,* from which I quote in the following discussion. On the original typescript, the title was "Gerousia," the name for the Council of Elders at Sparta, but it was changed to "Gerontion," Greek for "little old man," and thus not the actual name of the speaker of the poem. Eliot may have been influenced by John Henry Newman's *A Dream of Gerontius* (1866), a long poem in which the title character is taken by his guardian angel on his last journey to God.

For many years after Eliot's poems were first published, critics, influenced by his "impersonal theory of poetry" expounded in "Tradition and the Individual Talent," tried to render impersonal readings of individual poems but to little avail. Eliot himself, in a quotation cited at the beginning of the facsimile *Waste Land,* insisted that the poem was not the "bit of social criticism" that the critics asserted, but rather "only the relief of a *personal* and wholly insignificant grouse against life; it is just a piece of rhythmical grumbling" (my emphasis). Ronald Schuchard, in his recent book *Eliot's Dark Angel* (1999), is representative of most recent critics and scholars when he writes on his first page, "Eliot's dark angel was at once his fury and his muse, causing and conducting the internal drama of shadows and voices that inhabit his acutely personal poems and plays" (Schuchard, 1).

We have seen in Chapter 2, Section 1, that, at the age of fourteen, Eliot was overwhelmed by his finding and reading a copy of Edward Fitzgerald's "translation" of Omar Khayyám's *Rubáiyát.* The quotation marks around "translation" are to indicate that, in fact, there are many important differences between the original and the translation from the Persian—so many as to inspire some to label it an unfaithful or bad translation, yet it has nevertheless had a multitude of faithful readers. It first appeared in 1859, with revised versions issued in 1868, 1872, and 1879. Fitzgerald was not identified as the translator until the early 1870s, and as its enthusiastic readership grew in size in both England and America it became known as one of the masterpieces of nineteenth-century poetry. Ezra Pound, for example, in a letter of July 8, 1922, listed Fitzgerald's name alongside those of Homer, Dante, Villon, and Omar, remarking "Fitzgerald's trans. of Omar is the only good poem of the Vict. era" (Pound, *L,* 180).

One of the most important works on "Gerontion" is Vinnie-Marie D'Ambrosio's *Eliot Possessed: T. S. Eliot and Fitzgerald's Rubáiyát* (1989). Her use of the word "possessed" in her title seems exactly right. And her description of Eliot's state of mind and spirit cannot be improved upon: Eliot "was exhausted by the bank work begun in 1917 and by his wife's illnesses, for his marriage was physically and emotionally disastrous. . . . He had lived among frightened and repressed Londoners during the war, not allowed to take part in the action even with a letter of recommendation from Harvard's former president, C. W. Eliot; he had lost to battle three persons he cared about—T. E. Hulme, Karl Henry Culpin, and Jean Verdenal; his father had died disapproving of him." One might think that this was enough—but wait, there is more in this extraordinary summary of Eliot's problems: "Exhausted . . . [there was] added to his new demeanor . . . a not entirely contained air of self-involvement and *aboulie.* The torments, nonetheless, lay beneath, robbing the last shreds of vitality. The parallels to his own life that were to be found in a reading of Benson's *Fitzgerald* would intensify his anxiety about his present condition, would arouse even more fear as a prophecy of what could lie in store for him in an old age like Fitzgerald's" (D'Ambrosio, 159).

An important source for "Gerontion," as D'Ambrosio indicated, was a biography of Fitzgerald by A. C. Benson published in 1905 in the series "English Men of Letters." Eliot included Fitzgerald's book in his reading lists for his University of London Extension lectures in a course on modern English literature for the autumn and winter of 1916–17 and again in a course on Victorian Literature during the autumn and winter period of 1917–18. In the first of these lecture series, Fitzgerald was listed by himself along with the theme: "Isolation." Texts to be read were *The Rubáiyát of Omar Khayyám* and *Euphranor: A Dialogue on Youth,* along with the *Letters* and biographies. Special recommendation was made of the biographies in the English Men of Letters series—thus the biography written by A. C. Benson. In the 1917–18 syllabus, Fitzgerald's name appeared along with the names of two other poets (Matthew Arnold and James Thomson) as "Three Poets of Doubt."

It was noted as long ago as 1947, in the second edition of F. O. Matthiessen's seminal critical work, *The Achievement of T. S. Eliot,* that the opening of "Gerontion" as well as many other details and phrases in the poem were taken by Eliot from the A. C. Benson biography. Eliot's poem opens: "Here I am, an old man in a dry month, / Being read to by a boy, waiting for rain." Matthiessen credited Morton Zabel (an American literary scholar) with pointing this out to him in a letter: "The passage in Benson . . . occurs where he is weaving together some excerpts from Fitzgerald's letters, and making interpolations of his own: 'Here he sits, in a dry month, old and blind, being read to by a country boy, longing for rain:—"Last night . . . we heard a Splash of Rain, and I had the book shut up, and sat listening to the Shower by myself—till it blew over, I am sorry to say, and no more of the sort all night. But we are thankful for that small mercy.'"" Zabel also added that Benson's "whole book, with its picture of Fitzgerald in his pathetic, charming, and impotent old age, pondering on the pessimism of Omar, and beating out the futility of his final years, may have crystallized in Eliot's mind the situation . . . of 'Gerontion'" (Matthiessen, 73–74).

It is important to recall that "Gerontion" was positioned as the first poem in *Ara Vos Prec,* thus associating the poem with the book's title, words taken from the passage in *Purgatorio* (Canto XXVI, lines 145–48), which we first encountered as epigraph in Eliot's manuscript version of "Prufrock"—the passage in which the poet Arnaut Daniel, assigned to the circle of the lustful (along with hermaphrodites, sodomites, and so forth) cries out: "'*Now I pray you,* by that goodness which guideth you to the summit of the stairway, be mindful in due time of my pain.' Then he hid him in the fire which refines them." It also should be noted once again that *Ara Vos Prec,* although it contained no dedication, had instead in its opening pages the lines from Dante's *Purgatorio* (Canto XXI, lines 133–36), lines that were to appear eventually (not until 1925) on the dedication page alongside Jean Verdenal's name as part of the dedication: "Now canst thou comprehend the measure of love / which warms me toward thee / When I forget our nothingness / And treat shades as a solid thing." Thus Verdenal's name is silently invoked by these lines, connecting as does the book's title with "Gerontion." Contemporary readers of *Ara Vos Prec* could not have known this, but later readers should not ignore the silent linkage.

The original typescript of "Gerontion" has two epigraphs, the first the one that appeared in the published version from Shakespeare's comedy, *Measure for Measure* (act 3, scene 1, lines 32–34): "Thou hast nor youth nor age / But as it were an after dinner sleep / Dreaming of both." The words are spoken by the Duke, disguised as a friar, when he visits Claudio, under sentence of death in prison. The Duke urges him to wish for death because life is conflict, cowardice, insecurity. Of course, the happy ending of that play is unrelated to "Gerontion." The second epigraph, which appears only on the original typescript, is from Dante's *Inferno* (Canto XXXIII, lines 122–23): "Come il mi corpo stea / Nel mondo su, nulla scienza porto" ("How my body stands / in the world above, I have no knowledge"). It is revealed in this canto that sometimes after a dastardly deed, a soul is sent to the Inferno as the body remains on earth, inhabited by the devil. How this applies to "Gerontion" is left to the imagination, but it seems at times in the monologue that Gerontion is already deprived of his soul, sent down to hell.

In reading the details of Fitzgerald's life, Eliot would have found many that echoed his own fate. Fitzgerald seems to have been a misogynist but bonded closely with many male friends, including the famous (Tennyson, Carlyle, Thackeray) and many of the not so famous, one of whom, W. K. Browne, became the model for the principal character in *Euphranor: A Dialogue on Youth* (1851). Because of a misunderstanding, Fitzgerald found himself married to a woman with whom he could not live. Although the marriage was never consummated, the woman refused to give up her pursuit of him, as he continued pursuing male friends. In his later years he picked up friendships with several Suffolk fishermen, one of whom ("Posh") became his constant and steady mate. All of these relationships were treated with full detail in the Benson biography, and in them Eliot might have seen a kaleidoscope of his own life.

Moreover, as we have seen in Chapter 4, Section 3 (in our discussion of Santayana), while at Harvard Eliot read Havelock Ellis's *Sexual Inversion,* one of the volumes of his massive work, *Studies in the Psychology of Sex.* In the long introduction to *Sexual Inversion,* Ellis discussed the prevalence of homosexuals in various social groups such as soldiers and prisoners; in his short survey of artists and writers, he included Michelangelo, Oscar Wilde, and Edward Fitzgerald (1809–83). Here is what Eliot would have read Ellis saying about the writer he had "loved" from age fourteen to twenty-four: "In a writer of the first order, Edward Fitzgerald, to whom we owe the immortal and highly individualized version of *Omar Khayyám,* it is easy to trace an element of homosexuality, though it appears never to have reached full and conscious development" (Ellis, SI, 50).

It is not clear that Ellis knew about the ambiguities that Fitzgerald inserted in his translation of verse 12 (fifth edition), perhaps the most famous of his lines: "A book of Verses underneath the Bough, / A Jug of Wine, a Loaf of Bread—and Thou / Beside me singing in the Wilderness— / Oh, Wilderness were Paradise enow!" The ambiguity of most interest here is the use of "Thou" at the end of line two. Literally, it is "little sweetheart," but for "Persian poetic taste" the reference would be to a "pretty young boy" (Arberry, 22). Eliot was gifted in languages, infinitely curious, and a tireless reader, and it is entirely possible that in his preparation for teaching Fitzgerald in his extension lectures, he would have come across the literal meaning of the original. Indeed, he indicated in his syllabus that there would be a comparison of two translations of *Omar.*

Ellis wrote of Fitzgerald's marriage: "He felt himself called on to marry, very unhappily, a woman whom he had never been in love with and with whom he had nothing in common." And he wrote of his male bonding: "All his affections were for his male friends. In early life he was devoted to his friend W. K. Browne, whom he glorified in *Euphranor.* 'To him Browne was at once Jonathan, Gamaliel, Apollo,—the friend, the master, the God,—there was scarcely a limit to his devotion and admiration.' On Browne's premature death Fitzgerald's heart was empty" (Ellis, 51, 50). Would Eliot not have seen the outline of his own life in these lines—his marriage to Vivien, his loss of Verdenal? Thus he set out to paint himself as Fitzgerald/Gerontion, liberally using details, images, and phrases from the Benson biography.

A good example of such use by Eliot of Benson's biography is a long passage in which Benson quoted a Fitzgerald letter to Frederic Tennyson (older brother of Alfred) answering the charge by his friend Frederic that Fitzgerald's letters were "dull": "It is true; I really do like to sit in this doleful place with a good fire, a cat and dog on the rug, and an old woman in the kitchen. This is all my live-stock. The house is yet damp as last year; and the great event of this winter is my putting up a trough round the eaves to carry off the wet. There was discussion whether the trough should be of iron or of zinc: iron dear and lasting; zinc the reverse. It was decided for iron; and accordingly iron is put up" (Benson, 29). By comparing these lines with the opening lines of "Gerontion" (lines 1–16) one can find the source of most of the significant details. Some important elements are missing, of course. Early in this opening, Gerontion announces where he has not been, before launching forth on the "decayed house" where he is. He was *not* at the "hot gates," nor did he fight in the "warm rain," nor did he fight with a "cutlass" in the "salt marsh," "bitten by flies." These lines might remind the reader that Eliot had tried desperately to enter the American armed forces stationed in England during the Great War, but was frustrated at every turn (see Chapter 10, Section 6). Vinnie-Marie D'Ambrosio has pointed out that many elements in this passage relate to Sigismundo Malatesta, a Renaissance hero mentioned in the Benson biography and, more important, the subject of Ezra Pound's "Malatesta" Cantos. D'Ambrosio writes: "Pound used the same series of images—'marsh land,' 'salt heaps,' 'the dyke-gate,' and 'get the knife into him'" (D'Ambrosio, 176; Pound, C, 28–57). Of course, using such suggestive images of an authentic battle hero can only be ironic when related to Gerontion.

The astonishing lines 8–9 have given pause to many readers: "And the jew squats on the window sill, the owner, / Spawned in some estaminet of Antwerp." There seems no source for these lines in Benson. And it is not surprising that Anthony Julius, in *T. S. Eliot, Anti-Semitism, and Literary Form* (1995), devotes a chapter to a sustained attack on the poem: "The 'jew' is on the window sill both because he has been denied any more secure resting place and because he himself may thus deny his tenant peaceable possession of his house. He crouches because he is weak; Bleistein's 'saggy bending of the knees' betrays a similarly impaired posture. The faulty posture of Jews, and in particular their weak feet, is an anti-Semitic theme that became, according to Sander Gilman, 'part of the . . . discourse about Jewish difference in the latter half of the nineteenth century'" (Julius, 47–48).

The opening of the second part of the poem, lines 17–32, raises the question of the authenticity of religion—the religion that Fitzgerald's *Omar* rejected: "Signs are taken for wonders. 'We would see a sign': / The word within a word, unable to speak a word, / Swaddled with darkness. In the juve[ne]scence of the year / Came Christ the tiger / In depraved May, dogwood and chestnut, flowering judas, / To be eaten, to be divided, to be drunk / Among whispers." Before discussion of these lines, three of Eliot's sources must be placed beside them. The first is a Nativity Sermon by Lancelot Andrewes, delivered to the king on December 25, 1618, referred to in Eliot's essay on Andrewes: "Signs are taken for wonders. 'Master, we would fain see a sign,' that is a miracle. And in this sense it is a sign to wonder at. Indeed, every word here is a wonder. . . . *Verbum infans,* the Word without a word; the eternal Word not able to speak a word; a wonder sure. And . . . swaddled, a wonder too. He that takes the sea 'and rolls it about with the swaddling bands of darkness';—He to come thus into clouts, Himself!" (quoted in Williamson, *RGTSE,* 108).

This passage is quoted in part in Eliot's essay on "Lancelot Andrewes" in his *Selected Essays,* as is another sermon that contains the phrase, "Christ is no Wild-Cat." In a Nativity Sermon given in 1622, Andrewes describes the Magi as rushing to reach Bethlehem for the birth of Christ while others did not—but instead exclaimed: "Christ is no Wild-Cat. . . . What needs such haste?" (Southam, 71–72). It should be no surprise that Eliot substituted "Tiger" for "Wild-Cat." In *The Education of Henry Adams* (1918), which Eliot reviewed in the *Athenaeum,* May 23, 1919, is found a passage in which Adams, raised in Massachusetts, finds himself in Maryland and describes the strange Maryland spring: "Here and there a negro log cabin alone disturbed the dogwood and the judas-tree, the azalea and the laurel. The tulip and the chestnut gave no sign of struggle against a stingy nature. . . . The brooding heat of the profligate vegetation; the cool charm of the running water; the terrific splendor of the June thundergust in the deep and solitary woods, were all sensual, animal, elemental. No European spring had shown him the same intermixture of delicate grace and passionate depravity that marked the Maryland May. He loved it too much, as though it were Greek and half human" (72). We might note here parenthetically that I. A. Richards loaned his copy of *Ara Vos Prec,* with "Gerontion," the lead poem, to Benson, who commented: "Watch out! I hear the beat of the capripede hoof!" (Richards, TSE, 6).

All the sources of the allusions in lines 15–21 of this second part of "Gerontion" have religious meaning or suggestion, and they seem to be out of reach of the speaker of the poem: he does not "see a sign" and is unable to "speak a word": if the "word" is the infant Jesus, he is "swaddled with darkness"—beyond the sight of Gerontion. Religious beliefs or customs offer no comfort to his misery, as they could not to the author of the atheistic *Rubáiyát*. Indeed, the spring of the year, which signals rebirth, brings no comfort for Gerontion, who finds it (like the alienated Henry Adams) "depraved," and even sinister, as suggested by the "flowering judas"; spring's signs of life hide signs of betrayal and death. There seems to be in line 22 a reference to the Eucharist, the eating of the bread and drinking of the wine, symbols of the flesh and blood of Christ, but it is taken "among whispers."

The whispering individuals, apparently, are Mr. Silvero, Hakagawa, Madame de Tornquist, and Fräulein von Kulp. According to George Williamson, the "phrase 'among whispers' introduces further depravation. It is perverted by Mr. Silvero, whose devotion turns from the Lord's supper to his porcelain at Limoges; by Hakagawa, who worships painting; by the Madame, who turns 'medium'; and by the Fräulein, her client." After the appearance of these "characters," Gerontion's thoughts about his plight take over. As Williamson writes, "'Vacant shuttles / Weave the wind,' not spiritual reality. I have no haunting spirits, but I am a shuttle for the wind, 'An old man in a draughty house.' The meaning of 'A dull head among windy spaces' is beginning to unfold" (Williamson, *RGTSE*, 109–10).

The third part of "Gerontion," lines 33–47, is wholly a meditation on life, or history, by Gerontion, speaking from his own terrible and defeating experiences. He is in effect talking to himself, he is his own rapt audience. It opens: "After such knowledge, what forgiveness?" The word "knowledge" here is not the learning of books, but the learning of experience, full involvement with life in all its varied aspects, extraordinary relationships with people. Experience is constantly tempting, constantly deceiving, constantly refuting: ambiguities are rife, generalizations suspect, conclusions never final. The remainder of these lines constitutes in essence an ironic, or even cynical, exploration of that knowledge.

A signal is sent with the beginning word "Think," which occurs three times in these lines: "*Think now* / Nature has many cunning passages, contrived corridors / And issues; deceives with whispering ambitions, / Guides us with vanities." "Nature," then—human and other—is extraordinarily misleading, indeed a kind of villain: "*Think now* / She gives when our attention is distracted, / And what she gives, gives with such supple confusions / That the giving famishes the craving. Gives too late / What's not believed in, or if still believed, / In memory only, reconsidered passion. Gives too soon / Into weak hands, what's thought can be dispensed with / Till the refusal propagates a fear. *Think* / Neither fear nor courage saves us. *Unnatural vices* / Are fathered by our heroism. Virtues / Are forced upon us by our impudent crimes" (emphasis added). It is extraordinary that Gerontion in these last lines balances not vices and virtues, but rather "unnatural vices" and "virtues."

The question might be posed immediately: what are "unnatural vices," and how do they differ from natural vices? Most would agree, it seems, that when the term "unnatural vices" has been used, it has referred to deviant sexual behavior, such as homosexuality. When Gerontion muses earlier that "[Nature] Gives too late / What's not believed in, or if still believed, / In memory only, reconsidered passion," does the last phrase somehow refer to the "reconsidered passion" of "unnatural vices"? Is a "reconsidered passion" one whose moral validity the individual is utterly convinced of in the midst of surrendering to it; but then in retrospect, begins to have doubts about such validity? Is Gerontion here circling around another term that will later appear in the last section of *The Waste Land,* "The awful daring of a moment's surrender / Which an age of prudence can never retract"? Is this an oblique revision of "Unnatural vices / Are fathered by our heroism"? Is the "awful daring" a form of "heroism"? Part three of "Gerontion" ends: "These tears are shaken from the wrath-bearing tree." Is this the tree in the Garden of Eden that bestowed through its fruit the knowledge of good and evil, which invoked God's wrath? Gerontion's tears cannot, of course, gain him a return to the "innocence" of the Garden.

Part four of "Gerontion," lines 48–60, continues Gerontion's inner search of part three, but he for the first time introduces pronouns that can no longer be confined to the reader (as the "you" in part three) but conjures up a specific individual. The opening is indeed threatening: "The tiger springs in the new year. Us he devours." We may assume this is "Christ the tiger" of part two. As George Williamson puts it: "Having made the great refusal, Gerontion must abide by the natural order, in which time devours; only the supernatural contravenes this order, and he is committed to the order of death, not of life" (110). Gerontion next returns to the refrain he used in part three: "*Think at last* / We have not reached conclusion, when I / Stiffen in a rented house. *Think at last* / I have not made this show purposelessly / And it is not by any concitation / Of the backward devils" (emphasis added. "Concitation": stirring up, rousing [obsolete]). The "we" here can in no way be interpreted as the speaker and reader, but rather another being whose personal relation with the speaker cannot reach "conclusion" when the speaker is still alive, stiffening in something of a rented (borrowed?) life "in a rented house."

With Eliot in the guise of Gerontion/Fitzgerald, that individual can only be Jean Verdenal.

There follow the most personal—and lucid—lines of the poem: "I would meet you upon this honestly. / I that was in your heart was removed therefrom / To lose beauty in terror, terror in inquisition. / I have lost my passion: why should I need to keep it / Since what is kept must be adulterated? / I have lost my sight, smell, hearing, taste, and touch: / How should I use it for your closer contact." How was the speaker removed from the heart of the one addressed? There was first the parting, with Eliot's return to America after his year in Paris. There was the long separation. And finally, there was the violent end, a kind of inquisition, with Verdenal's death in the Dardanelles. The speaker has lost, through his lasting grief, his "passion" as well as all of the five senses.

Part five, the final section of the poem, portrays Gerontion as wondering about how what has happened, or is happening, to him will finally come to an end and how his fate will be reflected in the world about him. He seems to sense endless torture in a foreshortened future: "These with a thousand small deliberations / Protract the profit of their chilled delirium, / Excite the membrane, when the sense has cooled / With pungent sauces, multiply variety / In a wilderness of mirrors." Instead of sensing some conclusion, Gerontion senses an increase, not a decrease, in the seemingly infinite concerns that have undermined his life and sanity. And he poses impossible, perhaps pointless, questions: "What will the spider do, / Suspend its operation, will the weevil / Delay? De Bailhache, Fresca, Mrs Cammel, whirled / Beyond the circuit of the shuddering Bear / In fractured atoms. [We have saved a shilling against oblivion / Even oblivious]" (*IOMH*, 351, lines 69–70). These last words were omitted in the published version of the poem, and the following lines became lines 69–73 of the poem: "In fractured atoms. Gull against the wind, in the windy straits / Of Belle Isle, or running on the Horn, / White feathers in the snow, the Gulf claims, / And an old man driven by the Trades / To a sleepy corner."

Some of the details here may ring bells for those familiar with Eliot's poetry. For example, the spider of "Gerontion" may be related to the spider that appears in the closing lines of *The Waste Land*. There the speaker says that he and his friend are mutual participants in the "awful daring of a moment's surrender, / Which an age of prudence can never retract / By this, and this only, we have existed": that existence can not be found in their "obituaries / or in memories draped by the beneficent spider / Or under seals broken by the lean solicitor / In our empty rooms." And the Fresca of "Gerontion" bears the same name as the Fresca who played a prominent role in the manuscript of *The Waste Land* at the beginning of Part II ("A Game of Chess), a lengthy fragment that was excised by Ezra Pound.

The published poem ends with two lines set off from part five: "Tenants of the house, / Thoughts of a dry brain in a dry season." It seems to be the "thoughts" that have become the only "tenants" of the house, appropriate for a now invisible speaker who, at the end of his first section, portrayed himself in the lines: "I an old man, / A dull-head among windy spaces." Since they are the product of a "dry brain" and a "dry season," they are not likely to be fruitful and multiply for very much longer. Indeed, they seem to be on the verge of complete disappearance, as does Gerontion himself, having been reduced to them.

"Gerontion" has inspired mixed reviews by Eliot's critics, from virtual dismissal to high praise. Grover Smith, for example, concludes his discussion of the poem thus: "Because Gerontion, though primarily a symbol, is still dramatic enough to remain a person, the poem tends to split between the personality, which nevertheless is undefined, and the argument, which is not intimately enough related to the old man's feelings. One is inclined to apply Eliot's statement about Hamlet . . . and to say that Gerontion 'is dominated by an emotion which is inexpressible, because it is in excess of the facts as they appear'" (Smith, Grover, *PP*, 64–65). On the other hand, John T. Mayer concludes his discussion with praise: "In 'Gerontion,' Eliot returns to the main line of development of the psychic monologue and to the prophetic poetry that he sought from the sacred wood. 'Gerontion' is an important achievement, assuring Eliot that if he moved away from the satiric model developed in the recent quatrain poems, he might recover the power that produced his earlier triumphs. In spite of its complexity and literariness, the poem explores concerns rooted in Eliot's lived experience of the frustrations and contradictions of life" (Mayer, 236).

7. Poems Written 1918–1920

Titles of poems are followed by dates of composition (when known) and dates of first publication in journals and books. "Mayer" refers to John T. Mayer's *T. S. Eliot's Silent Voices* (1989), in which Mayer estimates dates of composition. *AVP: Ara Vos Prec* (1920 in England); *P: Poems* (1920 in America); *WLF: The Waste Land: A Facsimile and Transcript of the Original Drafts* (1971); *IOMH: Inventions of the March Hare* (1996).

"Ode" ("Ode on Independence Day, July 4th 1918") (1918); *AVP* (never collected by TSE); *IOMH*

"The Death of the Duchess" (1918, Mayer); *WLF*

"Elegy" (1918?, Mayer); *WLF*

"Exequy" (1918?, Mayer); *WLF*

"Gerontion" (1919); *AVP*; *P*; *IOMH*

"Song for the Opherion" (published pseudonymously in *The Tyro,* April 1921 by "Gus Krutzsch"); *WLF*

[12]

1. Prologue: Paris and the Pension Casaubon, Paris Again in the Spring

Eliot visited Paris alone in mid-December 1920. As he recounted the visit to his mother in January 1921, he stayed in the Pension Casaubon, the same place that he had lived when he met Jean Verdenal during his year in Paris, 1910–11. This trip has been left out of Eliot biographies and chronologies (although it is treated in Seymour-Jones's biography of Vivien, p. 269). What must have drawn Eliot to the Pension on the rue St. Jacques at a time when he was absorbed with "a poem" he had "in mind"? Was there a connection between Eliot's determination to begin writing a new work and the visit to Paris—and indeed his desire, unfulfilled, to return again to Paris in the spring of 1921?

As long ago as November 5, 1919, in a letter to John Quinn, we find the first reference to his plans: "I hope to get started on a poem I have in mind." His "New Year's Resolution," shared with his mother on December 18, 1919, was "to write a long poem I have had on my mind for a long time"—as long ago, perhaps, as January 1916, when he wrote to Aiken that he had "*lived* through material for a score of long poems" (*LTSE1*, 344, 351, 126). It is not surprising that, given his various commitments—not least his full-time job at the bank and readying for publication his first book of prose—Eliot did not find time to "get started." But although he had not begun work on the poem, it clearly remained at the front of his mind during 1920. In a letter to his mother on September 20, Eliot mentions the long poem to her for the first time: "I want a period of tranquility to do a poem that I have in mind." During this period, the Eliots were confronted with searching for a flat, moving, and the emergency surgery of Vivien's father. On December 2, Eliot wrote to his mother in considerable detail about all the matters that demanded his attention—including the serious illnesses of Vivien and her father, his own social and professional engagements, his preparation of the manuscript for a volume of his prose published by Alfred A. Knopf—and then he commented: "I am rather tired of the book now, as I am so anxious to get on to new work, and I should more enjoy being praised if I were engaged on something which I thought better or more important. I think I shall be able to do so, soon" (408, 424).

Eliot finally found the time. He wrote to Sydney Schiff on December 6 that he "may run over to Paris on Saturday [December 11]—I have a week's holiday due me—I have been trying to write a little and find my brain quite numb, and Vivien wants me to have a change." Vivien stayed behind to care for her father. Eliot's holiday lasted six days, according to a New Year's day letter he wrote to his friend Scofield Thayer (425–26, 428).

What transpired in Paris was related in a letter to his mother on January 22, 1921. Eliot first discussed his activities, articles, criticisms of other reviewers and editors, and his hope "to settle down to work now," clearly referring to the important new poem. Then he turned to the two people who had inspired and would be a part of it: his chronically ill wife Vivien, and his dead friend Jean Verdenal. Whereas in most of the letters of 1921, Vivien was the invalid, here she was the caregiver for her seriously ill father, who is "touchingly devoted" to her, "fonder of her than anyone else, though he does not know that."

As for Paris, Eliot wrote how "much better" he had been since his "week in Paris," where he "stayed at my old pension Casaubon, you know the old people are all dead, and the grandson is now proprietor." He was "mostly with old and new French friends and acquaintances, writers, painters (I got very cheap a drawing for Vivien of one of the best of the modern painters, Raoul Dufy) and the sort of French society that knows such people. I want to get over again in the spring just before you come [to England]." But, he wrote, "If I had not met such a number of new people there Paris would be desolate for me with pre-war memories of Jean Verdenal and the others." Eliot's hope to return again in the spring recalls Verdenal's return to St. Cloud alone, described poignantly in his letter of April 22, 1912, remembering the trip they shared there the year before (432–33). Eliot's wish to retrace that spring trip of 1910 to renew old memories may be related to his plans to write his long poem.

Eliot's return to the Pension Casaubon in Paris, only a few weeks or so before he would find the time to begin work on the new poem he had in mind, suggests the importance of place to memory in strong friendships. In 1936, Eliot wrote an introduction to a collection of Alfred Lord Tennyson's poems, reprinted both in *Essays Ancient and Modern* (1936) and in his *Selected Essays.* Eliot quotes the following three stanzas from *In Memoriam,* in which Tennyson describes his melancholy visit to the empty house of his now dead friend, Arthur Henry Hallam: "Dark house, by which once more I stand / Here in the long unlovely street, / Doors, where my heart was used to beat / So quickly, waiting for a hand, // A hand that can be clasp'd no more— / Behold me, for I cannot sleep, / And like a guilty thing I creep / At earliest morning to the door. // He is not here; but far away / The noise of life begins again, / And ghastly thro' the drizzling rain / On the bald street breaks the blank day." Eliot comments: "This is great poetry, economical of words, a universal emotion related to a particular place; and it gives me the shudder that I fail to get from anything in *Maud* [a poem just previously commented on by Eliot]. But such a passage, by itself, is not *In Memoriam: In Memoriam* is the whole poem. It is unique: it is a long poem made by putting together lyrics, which have only the unity and continuity of a diary, the concentrated diary of a man confessing himself. It is a diary of which we have to read every word" (*SE,* 291). The praise Eliot bestows on *In Memoriam* suggests in its extravagance that his response is shaped by his own similar experience in similar circumstances.

His response to the poem differed from that of Tennyson's contemporary readers, who, "once they had accepted *In Memoriam,* regarded it as a message of hope and reassurance to their rather fading Christian faith." For Eliot, *In Memoriam* reveals Tennyson as a "tragic" figure, deeply unsettled in his beliefs by the loss of his friend. Following the comment above, Eliot wrote his most revealing sentence: "It happens now and then that a poet by some strange accident expresses the mood of his generation, at the same time that he is expressing a mood of his own which is quite remote from that of his generation" (291). The language used here seems uncannily close to Eliot's comment placed as an epigraph to Valerie Eliot's edition of the *Waste Land* manuscripts: "Various critics have done me the honour to interpret the poem in terms of criticism of the contemporary world, have considered it, indeed, as an important bit of social criticism. To me it was only the relief of a personal and wholly insignificant grouse against life; it is just a piece of rhythmical grumbling" (*WLF*, 1).

Pension Casaubon in Paris was surely significant for Eliot in the way that Hallam's house was for Tennyson. Not only does he have the memories of the year 1910–11 when he lived there with Jean Verdenal. But his memories have been reinforced by his saving and rereading the letters from Jean Verdenal (explored in Chapter 5), in which his friend often sent vivid descriptions of the Pension and its garden—indeed, having written one of the letters while himself occupying the room that had been Eliot's. And it is of considerable significance that Eliot had plans, unfulfilled, to return to Pension Casaubon and Paris in the spring of 1921, when the writing of the long poem would be well underway.

2. "A Long Poem . . . on my Mind for a Long Time"

The year 1921 was spent by Eliot in planning and writing a poem eventually to be entitled *The Waste Land*. He had written, throughout his career, many lines that would eventually end up in his masterpiece some years before he had conceived such a work. These miscellaneous poems, or poem fragments, include "So through the evening," "After the turning," and "I am the Resurrection"; according to Valerie Eliot they were written by Eliot in 1914 (or earlier) when he was finishing his graduate work at Harvard. Other Eliot poems containing lines that would turn up in *The Waste Land* are "The Death of Saint Narcissus" and "The Death of the Duchess," neither published during Eliot's lifetime. "The Death of Saint Narcissus," as we discussed in Chapter 8, Section 7, had been submitted to *Poetry* and set in type, but was apparently withdrawn by Eliot because of its vivid autoerotic imagery. Valerie Eliot notes that Eliot later "remarked on the 'breathless tension'" of the bed-chamber scene and "the poignancy of the Duchess's words" in Webster's *Duchess of Malfi*, which may be evoked in Eliot's "The Death of the Duchess" (*WLF*, 107, 130).

In a letter of February 6, 1921, to Mrs. Sydney Schiff, Wyndham Lewis reported that he had seen Eliot at a production of Jonson's *Volpone*, and that "he seems to be engaged in some obscure & intricate task of late." On the day following, in another encounter with Eliot, Lewis queried him about his work and Eliot showed Lewis "a new long poem (in 4 parts) which I think will be not only very good, but a new departure for him" (quoted in Gordon, *EIL*, 168–69). Whatever it was that Eliot showed Lewis, it was certainly not the first four of the five parts of the published *Waste Land*.

We have a rather good record of Eliot's composition (see below), and it is certain that he did not complete Parts iv and v until later in 1921—and it seems unlikely that he would have completed Parts i, ii, and iii by early February.

A major problem Eliot faced in applying himself to the new poem was the debilitating illness of Vivien, which he discussed in a frank letter to Sydney Schiff (April 3, 1921): "after her father was out of danger she nearly collapsed. . . . So she has been in bed for the last five weeks, at first in a nursing home, and lately, on account of the expense, at home." She was being treated "for nervous exhaustion and for her stomach trouble" and would not be "really well for a year or two." Eliot wrote of having "some very anxious moments," and this most likely affected his work, for he explained to Schiff that his "poem has still so much revision to undergo that I do not want to let any one see it yet, and also I want to get more of it done—it should be much the longest I have ever written. I hope that by June it will be in something like final form. I have not had the freedom of mind" (*LTSE1*, 443–44). Vivien's condition was vividly described in a letter to Brigit Patmore of March 17, 1921: Eliot wrote of her "lying in the most dreadful agony with *neuritis* in every nerve, increasingly—arms, hands, legs, feet, back." And he asked, "Have you ever been in such incessant and extreme pain that you felt your sanity going, and that you no longer knew reality from delusion? That's the way she is. The doctors have never seen so bad a case, and hold out no definite hope, and have so far done her no good. Meanwhile, she is screaming in agony, and I fear the exhaustion might just snuff her out" (441). Exaggeration? Melodrama? Surely, not. Eliot speaks of *her* "sanity going," but her condition was taking its toll on him, as well.

When Vivien was sent away in May, Eliot was freed for a time from the burden of caring for her. He wrote to John Quinn on May 9 of "a moment's breathing space after a protracted series of private worries extending over some months—for one my wife has been ill and in bed for eight weeks, and has just gone to the seaside." The letter is a general report on his recent activities and encounters (he has met the young American, Robert McAlmon, whom he likes), but offers some revealing comments on his style in response to Quinn's "objection" to his punctuation: "I hold that the line itself punctuates, and the addition of a comma . . . seems to me to over-emphasize the arrest: That is because I always pause at the end of a line in reading verse, which perhaps you do not." Eliot complains only of "the lack of *continuous* time . . . which breaks the concentration required for turning out a poem of any length." Significantly, he notes, that he has "a long poem in mind and partly on paper which I am wishful to finish" (450–51).

Again, in a letter to Dorothy Pound in Paris of May 22, 1921, Eliot wrote that he expected to be in Paris in October: "I shall be ready for a little mountain air, after I have finished a little poem which I am at present engaged upon" (456). It would be Dorothy's husband, Ezra, to whom Eliot would turn over the "little poem" he was writing for his advice and help later in 1921. He would have to put his poem aside when his mother, his sister Marian, and his brother Henry came to England on June 10. He and Vivien gave up their flat and moved to a tiny one at 12 Wigmore Street until the family's departure on August 20. In fact, by the time his family left England, Eliot himself was beginning to show signs of a nervous breakdown.

Some controversy has arisen about the order in which Eliot wrote the five main parts of *The Waste Land*, based primarily on these parts as they appear in the 1971 publication entitled *The Waste Land: A Facsimile and Transcript of the Original Drafts*, edited by Valerie Eliot. Her edition contains photographs of the manuscripts that Eliot handed over to Pound for his comments and recommendations. We have, therefore, not only the texts but also the scribbled conversations between Eliot and Ezra Pound, as well as Vivien's contributions, as they discussed how to revise and reduce the poem to turn it into the version that would be first published in 1922. Of immense value are the introduction and chronology that Valerie Eliot placed at the opening of the edition, and the several pages of notes she provided at the end. On the left-hand pages we have the poem as it appeared in the manuscript and on the right-hand we have the text repeated in a less obscure, more readable version—but still faithful to the manuscript or the typescript, as written or typed by Eliot.

As we open the facsimile edition to the title (pages 2–3), we find the epigraph from Joseph Conrad's *Heart of Darkness:* "Did he live his life again in every detail of desire, temptation, and surrender during that supreme moment of complete knowledge? He cried in a whisper at some image, at some vision,—he cried out twice, a cry that was no more than a breath—'The horror! the horror!'" Eliot wrote "Conrad" beneath this typed epigraph, giving his readers more information about the source of an epigraph (or allusion) than he usually did. Conrad's climactic passage is revelatory of Eliot's own experience as it is to be rendered obliquely in his poem. Conrad's character Kurtz, who went to Africa to convert the natives from their savagery, in actuality was converted to their way of life. It is surely no coincidence that the language and tone in the Conrad passage is evocative of the climactic moment near the end of *The Waste Land*, in which the poet describes the "awful daring of a moment's *surrender*" (emphasis added), which seems to provide the key to understanding his mental and emotional state.

As we turn to Parts I and II, we find the titles we are familiar with from the 1922 published version ("The Burial of the Dead" and "A Game of Chess" [the latter's first title, "In the Cage," is cancelled]), but we see that the two parts also carry the titles "He Do the Police in Different Voices: Part I" and "He Do the Police in Different Voices: Part II" (*WLF*, 4, 10). These first two parts of the poem have been written with a typewriter whose keys are somewhat worn and misaligned—at least in comparison with the typewriter Eliot used to write Part III, "The Fire Sermon" (22), with a text easier to read and less labored in appearance. A second typed version of Part III, including many of the revisions indicated on the original typed version, is apparently typed on the same typewriter.

Part IV, "Death by Water" (54), is written first by hand, followed by a typewritten version: it appears thus that Eliot originally composed this part by hand and then typed it later in order to revise it. Part V (70) is also first written out by hand and in this version has no number and no title. The typed version following it is given the title "What the Thunder Said." Pound has written on both handwritten versions, expressing his dislike of Part IV and his strong approval of Part V, indicating that Eliot did not hesitate handing over his handwritten versions for Pound to read. But Pound says in his one important note near the beginning of Part IV: "Bad—but / cant attack / until I get / typescript." And he says in his one important note on Part V: "OK / OK from / here on / I think" (54, 70). As will be discussed later, Pound's suggestions were largely followed, and Part IV was severely cut, while Part V underwent little revision.

In Section 3 of this chapter (below), "A Family Visit," we find that Eliot's brother Henry brought a new typewriter with him from America, and when he departed with his mother and sister, he took Eliot's old machine with him and left behind his new machine. Thus we are able to date roughly the composition of the first three parts of *The Waste Land,* the first two typed on an old machine, and the third on a new machine. Eliot's family arrived on June 10 and departed on August 20. Since Eliot had no time to write during their visit, we should assume that Parts I and II were composed on Eliot's old machine some time before June 10, and that Part III ("A Game of Chess") was written on Henry's (by then Eliot's) new machine after August 20 and finished by the time Eliot, for reasons of health, left London for Margate on October 12.

It should probably not have been a surprise that Eliot, in struggling to keep up with his bank job and all his other undertakings—and in beginning the poem he was desperate to write—suffered a serious breakdown at the end of September. He consulted a doctor and reported to Richard Aldington

(October 3?, 1921): "I have seen the specialist (said to be the best in London) who made his tests and said that I must go away *at once* for three months, quite alone and away from anyone, not exert my mind at all, and follow strict rules for every hour of the day. So I have been given leave by the bank for that period, very generously—they continue to pay my salary. I am going in about a week, as soon as I have taught enough knowledge of my work to a substitute" (*LTSE1*, 473). In mid-October, Eliot left London for the seaside resort of Margate, where he was joined by Vivien only for a short part of the time. It was here, we may assume, that he was able to devote full time to the writing of Part IV of his long poem ("Death by Water") until his departure on November 12. The first draft of Part IV was written by hand because Eliot had no typewriter in Margate.

On the advice of friends Ottoline Morrell and Julian Huxley, Eliot decided to see a specialist in nerves (a "nerve man") at Lausanne, Switzerland, one Dr. Roger Vittoz, author of *Traitement des Psychonévroses par la Rééducation du Contrôle Cérébral* (Paris, 1911). Valerie Eliot's footnote continues: In his copy of the third French edition (1921), Eliot marked passages such as "'Aboulie,' want of will"; "There is, in fact, often an excessive excitability which makes the sufferer aware of the slightest noise and is frequently the cause of insomnia"; and "against 'The muscles are at first more or less contracted and sometimes painful,' TSE has penciled 'handwriting.'" (480). Before leaving Margate, Eliot again wrote to Aldington about his latest understanding of the illness he was suffering: "I am satisfied, since being here [at Margate], that my 'nerves' are a very mild affair, due, not to overwork, but to an *aboulie* and emotional derangement which has been a lifelong affliction. Nothing wrong with my mind—which should account, mon cher, for the fact that you like my prose and dislike my verse" (486). Eliot left Margate for London, where he stayed a week before leaving for Lausanne on November 22, going by way of Paris. He was accompanied by Vivien, who then stayed with the Pounds in Paris. Harry Trosman, of the Department of Psychiatry of the University of Chicago, has written of Roger Vittoz (and his treatment of Eliot): "[He] was the founder of a method of psychotherapy that enjoyed great prestige in the first quarter of this century but which is today almost forgotten." His method was based on "cerebral reeducation," and involved his determining the "workings of the cerebral hemispheres by feeling their vibrations through the patient's forehead with his hand." He monitored "the disordered vibrations" and gradually educated the patient "to master his brain functions" (Trosman, 713).

By late November Eliot had settled into Lausanne and put himself under the care of the celebrated "nerve man." He wrote to Ottoline Morrell on

November 30, 1921: "I like [Vittoz] very much personally, and he inspires me with confidence. . . . I never did believe in 'nerves,' at least for *myself!* He is putting me through the primary exercises very rapidly—so that I seem to have no time for any *continuous* application to anything else. . . . I can't tell *much* about the method yet, but at moments I feel more calm than I have for many many years—since childhood—that may be illusory—we shall see" (*LTSE1*, 490). In a letter to his brother Henry of December 13, Eliot explained that he was learning to conserve his "energy . . . to be *calm* . . . and to concentrate. . . . I hope that I shall place less strain upon Vivien, who has had to do so much thinking for me." And he was "certainly well enough to be working on a poem!" (493). Eliot was able to finish his "long poem," Part v, "What the Thunder Said," which contained the "29 lines of the water-dripping section," considered by Eliot the only "*good* lines" in *The Waste Land*. Valerie Eliot notes: "Eliot said that he was describing his own experience in writing this section in Lausanne when he wrote in *The 'Pensées' of Pascal* (1931): '. . . some forms of illness are extremely favorable . . . to artistic and literary composition. A piece of writing meditated, apparently without progress for months or years, may suddenly take shape and word; and in this state long passages may be produced which require little or no retouch.'" To Russell he said that "Part v is not only the best part, but the only part that justifies the whole at all" (*WLF*, 129). Eliot joined Vivien in Paris on January 2, 1922.

Several perceptive critics have postulated that the parts of *The Waste Land* were not composed in the order in which they were finally placed in the poem, among them Hugh Kenner, Grover Smith, and Lyndall Gordon (in her early book). The main thrust of these critics is to conclude that Part iii ("The Fire Sermon") was written first, and this remained a debatable position until the publication in 1988 of the first volume of *The Letters of T. S. Eliot*. (See Kenner, ua, 23–49; Smith, Grover, TWL, 48–52; Gordon, EEY, 144–46.) For those interested in this controversy, an interesting (but not definitive) account appears in C. K. Stead's *Pound, Yeats, Eliot, and the Modernist Movement* (1986), "Appendix: A Note on the Dating of the Drafts of *The Waste Land*" (Stead, 359–63). Here a summary of the dates of Eliot's composition of the five parts of *The Waste Land* should prove useful. As we have discussed, the typeface of these original manuscripts as published in Valerie Eliot's facsimile edition makes it obvious that Eliot wrote Parts i and ii on his old typewriter before his family arrived on their visit June 10, and Part iii on the new typewriter after their departure August 20. Part iv was composed after Eliot's breakdown, which brought about his stay at Margate with orders to rest; he remained at Margate from October 12 until November 12, with no typewriter—free to devote the whole of his time to writing, but by hand. And Part v was written in Lausanne, where Eliot went (via Paris) for special treatment, arriving there November 22. Without a typewriter, he wrote the whole of Part v by hand. He returned to Paris on January 2, where he joined Vivien. It must be understood that the five parts of *The Waste Land* that Eliot brought with him to Paris to show Ezra Pound were far different from the five parts that would be published in 1922. I have dealt with Pound's hand in revising Eliot's poem in my book *T. S. Eliot's Personal Waste Land* (1977).

3. A Family Visit: Mother, Brother, Sister—Wife

Since his father's death, Eliot had not had the desire to visit America again. But he was determined that his family, especially his mother and brother, visit him in England. Early in 1921, Eliot began urging his mother to make plans, writing in his letter of February 13: "You should now decide on the time at which you wish to come, and should *reserve a passage immediately*." He then made a list, asking when she was coming, how much she would pay for board and lodging (he advised "two bedrooms and a sitting room in a hotel"), whether she needed "specially prepared" food, and whether she would "consider a small furnished flat, if we get a reliable woman to come and cook for you." He added "P.S. IMPORTANT: Please let me know also whether it will be only you and Marian or whether there is any chance of Henry coming too. . . . The poor fellow has *never* been abroad; he ought sometime to get at least a peep far outside of the commercial life of Chicago among the people he has to mix with there. Do try to make him come, for his own sake" (*LTSE1,* 437). Henry Eliot had, since 1917, been working in Chicago for an advertising agency (he would remain there until 1929).

These plans would change. In March Eliot wrote: "Lucy Thayer, Vivien's American friend, has taken a small but comfortable flat not far away, and would be glad to take us in, as she could easily do. You could have our comfortable flat and servant. This is the best scheme for *everybody*." With this "scheme," Eliot's sister Marian would not have to do the cooking, but would need only to order meals. Moreover, Eliot would see more of his mother and "under better conditions": "We should often dine here, I should keep my books here and should often work here in the evenings, and should be dropping in of course all the time" (438).

Eliot reassured his mother that the flat had electricity, gas stoves in the bedrooms, anthracite stoves in the sitting room, an elevator, and even Baedekers.

To the list of what they should bring—"*hot water bottles . . . and heavy and light underwear*"—he added "as many of my books as possible. Especially the *Century Dictionary,* the heaviest of all!" The question of a visit to France had arisen, but Eliot was somewhat discouraging: "Paris is hot, dusty, unhealthy, and crowded in August, and I do not at all approve your going in that month" (442–43, 453).

By the time of his family's arrival on June 10, Tom and Vivien had moved into Lucy Thayer's place at 12 Wigmore Street, had found quarters for Henry, and had readied the Eliot flat at 9 Clarence Gate Gardens for his mother and sister. On June 23 he wrote to Richard Aldington that his mother—"whom I have not seen for six years"—and his brother had come: "These new and yet old relationships involve immense tact and innumerable adjustments. One sees lots of things that one never saw before etc. In addition my wife is here for their benefit against the express command of her specialist, who told her that it was very wrong for her to be in town at all this summer. So I shall not rest until I have got her away again." Most likely, Eliot saw his greatest problem to be the presence of Vivien, not only out of concern for her health but also because of the "adjustments" entailed by bringing her and his family together (458–59).

In a later letter to Aldington of July 6, 1921, Eliot reported that he was "just getting [Vivien] away to a place in the country on Chichester Harbour" and he hoped she would find it "agreeable enough to stay in till the end of July." Getting Vivien away, of course, was not for the sake of her health alone. Eliot was involved in sightseeing, taking his family to a place he had never been—Warwick (on the river Avon, with its fourteenth-century castle perched on rock above the river)—and then to Stratford (Shakespeare country) and Kenilworth (with its twelfth-century castle described in Sir Walter Scott's *Kenilworth*). His seventy-seven-year-old mother proved to be "terrifyingly energetic." At times he felt that he did not know them: "Anxieties of several kinds, and the strain of accommodating myself to people who in many ways are now strangers to me, have consumed my time and energy" (459–60). He, not they, became exhausted at the pace they set.

Ottoline Morrell proved to be a good listener, as countless letters attest, as well as a supportive friend to Eliot during his family's visit. She invited the family to Garsington, which pleased Eliot's mother, who looked forward to meeting her son's friends. Eliot was of course still working, and to Ottoline he wrote on July 14 "*in the strictest confidence*" the news of a project to begin a new quarterly—what would become the *Criterion,* to be financed by Lady Rothermere. Negotiations at this period were difficult and Eliot was "obliged" to call Vivien back to help. Vivien, Eliot wrote, was "*invaluable*" but she became "worn out" and was "going back to the country at once" (458, 461).

Vivien gave her story in a letter of July 20 to Scofield Thayer, who had brought about Lady Rothermere's involvement with Eliot. Vivien proved to be quite capable in her assessment of the negotiations concerning the new journal, and showed some humor at their plight. She explained that because Tom was "busy finishing off various things before he goes away for ten days of his holiday," she was "writing for him, altho' my mind has left me and I am becoming gradually insane. . . . You must excuse Tom for any dilatoriness in writing, he has had his family on his hands since early June. We have given up our at least cool and civilized flat to them, while we are encamped in an attic with a glass roof. So you see other people have troubles as well as yourself, and I believe you invited me to come and drown myself with you, once. I am ready at any moment." Three months later, on October 13, after the family had left, Vivien would write her friend Scofield announcing Tom's "serious breakdown," adding "I have not nearly finished my own nervous breakdown yet" (462, 478).

The Eliot family left on schedule, sailing for America on August 20. Three days later, Eliot wrote to remind his mother of what he had said about "keeping up and keeping strong" for her next visit. (She visited again for six weeks in 1924. She would die on September 10, 1929, and Eliot would not return to America until 1932.) He went on: "We do not move back till the end of the week. We both said we could hardly bear to go back there—the flat seems to belong to you now and is very strange and desolate without you in it." In a footnote the editor informs us that Eliot's mother wrote to Henry on October 14, 1921: "I am surprised at Tom saying that when we were in the flat it had a cosiness which it misses now. I think the poor boy misses the affection that makes no demands from him, but longs to help him. Vivien loves Tom, and he her, although I think he is afraid of her" (464).

Apparently Eliot did not succeed in keeping Vivien away from his family on their departure. In an August 23, 1921, letter to Henry, Vivien first thanked him for the money they had found in the typewriter and for the typewriter itself. She was effusive: "You are shown up as an angel. A bloody angel, as they say over here." And then: "Now I want you to tell me something truly. You are not to lie. Did your mother or sister show, think, say or intimate that I behaved like 'no lady,' just like a wild animal when [we] saw you off? I was perfectly stunned on that occasion. I had no idea what I was doing. I have been more or less stunned for many months now and when I come to, I suppose it seems dreadful, to an American. I have worried all the time since." Tom, she said, had reassured her, saying it was "perfectly allright, etc."

Then, going against the prevailing view of the English as less emotional than Americans, she went on, "I am sure he has lived here so long he hardly realizes how *very* much less English people mind showing their emotions than Americans—or perhaps he does realize it so perfectly. But I was extremely anxious to show no emotion before your family at any time, and then I ended in a fit!" (465).

Whatever Vivien's actions had been, it is apparent that her efforts to contain her emotions before the family had failed. Like a volcano about to erupt, she found "the emotionless condition a great strain, all the time. I used to think I should burst out and scream and dance. That's why I used to think you were so terribly failing me." Vivien is baring her soul to the one relative with whom she felt close. She next proceeded to talk about her marriage quite openly: "But I don't want to talk about that now, except to ask you if ever two people made *such* a fearful mess of their obvious possibilities. I don't understand, and I never shall. Twenty-four hours of contact out of two months. Both flats are equally unbearable to us, so we stay here morosely" (465). Vivien is highlighting what had become a commonplace in her marriage: for a variety of reasons, the two spent less and less time together.

She gives a picture of the two without any "spirit to buy wine, yet when the evening comes we curse and abuse each other for not having seen we want it all the more now. I believe we shall become pussyfeet. Your roses have lived till now, but are dying so miserably as I write. Sorry about having to scratch out so many words, but you should be flattered that I write to you at all" (465–66). There seem to be terrible flashes of insight in these last lines, suggesting that Vivien is aware as much as Tom of the disastrous situation of their marriage. One has to wonder how Henry reacted to this letter.

We know in part at least how Henry reacted to Vivien overall. In a letter he wrote to his mother after their return to America of October 30, 1921, he confides his "feeling that subconsciously (or unconsciously) she likes the role of invalid, and that, liking it as she does to be petted, 'made a fuss over,' condoled and consoled, she . . . encourages her breakdowns, instead of throwing them off by a sort of nervous resistance." He thought that whatever the cause, physical or mental, "if she had more of 'the Will to Be Well' she would have less suffering. . . . She needs something to take her mind off herself; something to absorb her entire attention" (quoted in Gordon, *EIL*, 171). What might Vivien have thought had she seen this analysis of her illness and behavior?

It is true that Vivien was self-absorbed but, as is evident in Eliot's letter to Ottoline, she was an invaluable help with the *Criterion,* both in its establishment and operation. Furthermore, under the names of F. M., Fanny Marlow,

Feiron Morris, and Felix Morrison, her short stories, poems, and reviews were published in 1924 and 1925 in the *Criterion,* with the encouragement of Eliot. Eliot wrote to Richard Aldington in April 1924 that she used assumed names because of her awareness of her "untrained" mind, but that he thought she had "an original mind . . . not at all a feminine one" (quoted in Seymour-Jones, 340). Critics have seen her character "Sibylla" as a self-portrait and have detected autobiographical elements in her treatment of the American in Europe (Johnson, 48–61). At times Vivien revealed awareness of both herself and her situation in these creative works as well as in her diaries and correspondence. In a letter written to Aldington on July 15, 1922, for example, Vivien returned again to the differences between Americans and the English. She wrote chastising Aldington for his unfriendly criticism of the title *Criterion* and Tom's article in the July *Dial.* She ended her letter with strong words: "Each person who gives a push now gives him a push out of England. And that will be damned England's loss." What she wrote in the body of the letter sheds light on her view of the marriage and her part in its failure: "I am English, and once I liked England—once I fought like mad to keep Tom here and stop his going back to America. I thought I could not marry him unless I was able to keep him here, in England. Now I hate it. . . . You know I am ill and an endless drag on him" (*LTSE1, 544*).

4. A Room of One's Own; Wearing Makeup; Confidante Virginia Woolf

Living together in the same flat was less and less common as more and more Eliot and Vivien found ways to live apart. Whether because of the job, the family visit, holidays, or the dictates of health, one can trace their complicated living arrangements by looking at the return addresses on their voluminous correspondence. The year 1921 goes from Clarence Gate Gardens to Wigmore Street and back again, punctuated by visits to friends and trips to seaside retreats, ending with Eliot's recuperative stays at Margate and Lausanne. The year 1922 begins in Paris at the Hôtel du Bon Lafontaine. By March Eliot is back at Wigmore, having let Clarence Gate Gardens for three months. Vivien returns to Wigmore from a Paris hotel (where "she stood no chance of getting well") by April. May 17 finds Eliot writing to Ottoline from the Castle Hotel in Tunbridge Wells, Kent (where they've gone "to get braced up"), that he looks forward to Italy, which will "save" him from "another breakdown." Eliot had accepted his father-in-law's invitation to Lugano, while Vivien was undecided whether "to come as far as Paris with [him] and stay there . . . or to go miserably to the seaside in further search of health" (*LTSE1*, 521, 522–24). On June 23, Eliot wrote to Mary Hutchinson from Clarence Gate Gardens, thanking her for the introduction to Massine, the Russian dancer, and explaining that he is "rather tired—I went out to a dinner and a dance last night, while Vivien starved [on her special diet— "a perfectly new and violent cure"]; and enjoyed myself, and got off with the Aga Khan, finished up the evening at Wigmore Street where I ended the vermouth and packed my clothes, rather fun." In August Vivien is at Bosham in a "four roomed laborer's cottage," as Eliot wrote to Schiff: "I think she gets more out of solitary country life than anyone I know" (529–30, 563).

The moves would culminate in 1923. While Vivien was at Eastbourne, beginning another health "experiment," Eliot wrote confidentially to Otto-line on January 5 that he had discovered a "'tiny suite' of two rooms, amaz-ingly cheap. . . . The idea, he said, was to use them as an office for the *Criterion* work, and when the lease of Clarence Gate Gardens was up, to give that flat up" (quoted in Seymour-Jones, 348). Eliot rented rooms at 38 Burleigh Mansions, off Charing Cross Road. Although Eliot's time in these rooms takes us out of our chronology, this most bizarre period of Eliot's life has grown out of the past. And as we did in Chapter 8, Section 4, we might turn to Michael Hastings's play, of which he has written: "Essentially every line of dialogue in *Tom and Viv* remains true to the nature of events; but not every scene observes the literal procession of the calendar" (Hastings, 47).

In act one, part two, in a scene set in 1921, Vivienne and Tom have brought her mother and brother Maurice to a costume party at the Schiffs' with many of the familiar Bloomsberries in attendance. The scene opens with Maurice (in uniform, wearing his dress sword) dancing with his mother and commenting: "Pretty difficult to persuade anyone here to dance. I went up to this ravishing thing just now. She said she didn't dance with soldiers. Then I found this other creature by the bar. And she said she didn't dance with men at all. Life is thin, mummy" (Hastings, 78). In a few words, the playwright has conveyed two of the unconventional aspects of the Blooms-bury members—their antiwar views, and their open acceptance of artists and intellectuals without regard to the nature of their sexuality.

As Vivienne enters the scene, joining her mother and brother, she explains that she had brought them to the party because she wanted to show them the kind of life she and Tom are living: "These are our friends. These are the sort of people we've come to know." Maurice asks her about her "get-up." She explains: "I'm Dr. Crippen's mistress." Rose remarks, "That is a perfectly horrible idea," and Vivienne comments: "Crippen's wife was a nightmare to live with. He couldn't bear to touch her. He poisoned her and cut her into pieces. I am the typist he fell in love with. We ran off to Canada and on the boat I dressed as a boy." Rose's response—"I'm so glad your father isn't here"—reveals her uneasiness. When Vivienne mentions that Tom is dressed as Dr. Crippen, and invites her mother to go to the other room and look at him, Rose replies: "I'd rather not" (Hastings, 78–79). The Crippen murder occurred in 1910 and was one of those crimes that became celebrated in both England and America. Later that year Crippen was put to death, in spite of a worldwide movement for clemency. The story is related in Tom Cullen's *The Mild Murderer: The True Story of the Dr. Crippen Case* (1977). Citing Virginia Woolf's diary for November 1934, Lyndall Gordon reports her characterization of Eliot as "a kind of Crippen in a mask." Gordon calls it "a shrewd, almost prophetic dart, for Eliot chose to go as Crippen, the murderer of his wife, to a fancy dress party . . . six months after Vivienne was put away for life" (Gordon, *EIL*, 288).

Vivienne seems not to comprehend her mother's reactions of dismay and disgust as she points out several of their friends: "Over there, in the black tights and the lemonade tutu, you remember, the most hated man in London?" Clearly he is the iconoclast Bertrand Russell. "Now that ostrich inside a bedquilt is Ottoline. She thinks I take away Tom's muse. Poor woman, I am his muse." "The woman there. With the Kaiser Bill helmet. You've heard of Miss Mansfield from New Zealand. Who writes stories." This is, of course, Katherine Mansfield, famed for her short stories, the mistress and wife of John Middleton Murry. "And that one there in the Mad March Hare suit. That's Mrs. Woolf. She meets Tom in secret. She wants him to leave me. She calls me a 'bag of ferrets'" (Hastings, 78–80). Virginia Woolf had written in her diary (November 8, 1930): "Oh—Vivienne! Was there ever such a torture since life began!—to bear her on one's shoulders, biting, wriggling, raving, scratching, unwholesome, powdered, insane, yet sane to the point of insanity, reading his letters, thrusting herself on us, coming in wavering trembling. . . . This bag of ferrets is what Tom wears round his neck" (Woolf, *D3*, 331).

"Those two boys," Vivienne next points out, "are the most promising writers of this day. Both went to Eton. Both went to Oxford. And they're renowned pederasts. In the summer they take youth parties to the Tyrol. And drink chocolate in very small tents." Vivienne then adds the rather startling information: "They have a flat in Charing Cross. Tom keeps a room there. When he wants to get away" (Hastings, 80).

In the introduction to his play, Hastings describes how, when he set out to get background information for the play, he encountered hostility from Dame Helen Gardner, from Valerie Eliot, and from Faber and Faber. In a tense conversation with Frank Morley, representing Faber and Faber and the Eliot estate, he was accused of being a "jerk, a twister, a scandalmonger." And he was asked sarcastically: "What do you know about 46 Broadhurst Gardens, the Hampstead episode? What do you know about 38 Burghley [Burleigh] Mansions, and those goings on?" Morley never explained these cryptic questions, but Hastings informs the reader in a footnote: "Viv's aunt Lillia lived at Broadhurst Gardens, directly behind the Haigh-Wood home. The house was a refuge for Viv during the breakdown of her first engagement. Unlike the rest of the family, Lillia Symes encouraged Tom and Viv to marry. Burghley Mansions, St. Martin's Lane, was shared by C. H. B. Kitchin (1895–1967), Roger Senhouse (1900–1970) and Philip Ritchie (1899–1927)" (Hastings, 17–18). What Hastings does not reveal—did he know?—is that all three of these individuals were homosexuals. Indeed he suggests that he did know when, later in his introduction, he writes: "Mercifully, the mystery which surrounds Tom's fascination with Burghley Mansions, St. Martin's Lane, does not come into the subject of this play" (47).

Part of the mystery is revealed in Virginia Woolf's diary for December 19, 1923, when she describes the evening of December 17. After dining out at the Commercio with Clive and Vanessa Bell and Mary Hutchinson, Woolf and her companions all went to visit Eliot in his private quarters at 38 Burleigh Mansions. Woolf writes: "I'd like to record poor Tom's getting drunk. . . . We went to a flat in an arcade, & asked for Captain Eliot. I noticed that his eyes were blurred. He cut the cake meticulously. He helped us to coffee—or was it tea? Then to liqueurs. He repeated, L[eonard] noticed, 'Mrs. Ricardo,' as L. told his story; he got things a little wrong." We do not find out what this story was about, but we are told in an editor's note that "LW's story has not been retrieved." Woolf continues: "There was a long pale squint eyed Oxford youth on the floor. We discussed the personal element in literature. Tom then quietly left the room. L. heard sounds of sickness. After a long time, he came back, sank into the corner, & I saw him, ghastly pale, with his eyes shut, apparently in a stupor. When we left he was only just able to stand on his legs. We heard a shuffling as we went, and Clive [Bell] went back" (Woolf, *D2*, 278).

The next day, Virginia Woolf spent ten minutes on the phone listening to Eliot's apologies: "how distressing, what could we all think? Could we forgive him—the first time—would we ever come again? no dinner, no lunch—then sudden collapse—how dreadful—what a miserable end to the evening—apologize please to Leonard, to your sister [Vanessa Bell]—& so on. One of those comedies which life sometimes does to perfection." We are informed in a footnote by the editor Anne Olivier Bell that on December 10, Eliot had invited Lytton Strachey to a small party at 38 Burleigh Mansions, "perhaps that which the Woolfs went to on 17 December" (278). The presence at the party of Strachey (well-known in privileged circles by then for his sexual preferences) and that of the unidentified Oxford student (Strachey's friend?) in itself raises no eyebrows in this Bloomsbury circle; it is Eliot's persona as "Captain" and his drunkenness that is strange. As mysteriously, when visiting, Mary Hutchinson was told "to ask the porter for a 'Captain Eliot' and then to knock at the door three times" (Ackroyd, 136).

Did Captain Eliot's visitors see what Virginia Woolf had noted in her diary of March 12, 1922? "Clive, via Mary, says he [Eliot] uses violet powder to make him look cadaverous." And on September 27: "Tom's head is all breadth & bone compared with Morgan's [E. M. Forster]. He still remains something of the schoolmaster, but I am not sure that he does not paint his lips" (Woolf, *D2*, 171, 203–4).

Others of Eliot's friends visited Eliot at 38 Burleigh Mansions. Of the three Sitwells, Edith, Osbert, and Sacheverell, Osbert (like Strachey, well-known for his sexual preferences) appeared to be closest to Eliot. According to John Pearson, in his 1978 biography of the Sitwells, *Façades*, "they genuinely liked each other, and Osbert was one of the few to whom Eliot" spoke "on the depressing subject of his marriage." Tom resented not having been told of Vivien's burdensome health problems. The Eliot marriage, Osbert noted, seemed to be lived out in "an ambiance permeated with tragedy, tinged with comedy, and exhaling at times an air of mystification." In the mid 1920s, Osbert found Eliot acting strangely. Pearson recounts a dinner that Osbert and Sacheverell had with Eliot in the same "top-floor flat" that the Woolfs had visited. According to Osbert's unpublished notes on Eliot: "Visitors on arrival had to inquire at the porter's lodge for 'The Captain,' which somehow invested the whole establishment with a nautical—for I cannot say why, I took the title to be naval rather than military—a gay, gallant feeling. . . . The room in which we dined was high up, at the back of the block, and looked down on St. Martin's Lane, being almost on a level with the revolving glass-ball lantern of the Coliseum music-hall" (Pearson, 238–39).

In describing his visit, Osbert confirms some of the same observations that the Woolfs had made: "I sat next to Tom on one side, Sacheverell on the other. Noticing how tired my host looked, I regarded him more closely, and was amazed to notice on his cheeks a dusting of green powder—pale but distinctly green, the colour of a forced lily-of-the-valley." Osbert sounds as though he could hardly believe his eyes: "I was all the more amazed at this discovery, because any deliberate dramatization of his appearance was so plainly out of keeping with his character, and with his desire never to call attention to himself, that I was hardly willing, any more than if I had seen a ghost, to credit the evidence of my senses." A few days later, Osbert reveals, he went to tea with Virginia Woolf: "She asked me, rather pointedly, if I had seen Tom lately, and when I said 'Yes' asked me—because she too was anxious for someone to confirm or rebut what she thought she had seen—whether I had observed the green powder on his face—so there was corroboration!" Neither of them could find any way of explaining "this extraordinary and fantastical pretense; except on the one basis that the great poet wished to stress his look of strain and that this must express a craving for sympathy in his unhappiness" (239).

"The strange appearance" of the American poet in Vivien's story "Fête Galante" comes to mind: "The heavy slumbering white face, thickly powdered; the hooded eyes, unseeing, leaden-heavy; . . . the lips a little reddened." The story, published in the July 1925 *Criterion* under Vivien's pen name Fanny Marlow, might have been drawn from any of the parties attended by Eliot and Vivien. In fact, Osbert Sitwell reported that St. John Hutchinson was outraged upon recognizing in it the "unflattering portrait" of himself and his wife Mary, as well as other Bloomsberries, at one of the glittering parties given at their River House (quoted in Seymour-Jones, 397–99). The poet/financier in Vivien's story is first spotted "leaning with exaggerated grace against the eighteenth-century marble fireplace." Sibylla likes him—"if only he would—What? What is wrong, what missing?" Among the guests at the party are "the little whispering, posing Cambridge undergraduate," "a Georgian poet," "a great art critic," and "the Macaw," an "extravagantly *mondaine* figure," who places "a paper cap with streamers" upon the poet, who is now speaking "in a muffled, pedantic, and slightly drunken voice." To her friend's declaration that "He is the most marvelous poet in the *whole world*," Sibylla dryly replies, "He might be if he ever wrote anything." Sibylla then proposes the reason for his not writing: "Because he wants to be everything at once. . . . Perhaps the devil took him up into a high mountain and showed him all the kingdoms of the world—unfortunately for him! . . . He's still up on the mountain, so far as I know." Sibylla deserts the party, runs out to the balcony, leans over the railing, the river beneath her, and looks at the "gibbous moon," which she loves "like that"—"so fat, so comforting and solid," not like "Shelley's moon . . . a wretched, dreary invalid escaped from an asylum" (Eliot, Vivien, FG, 557–63). Vivien's last image is unfortunately prophetic.

Although Virginia Woolf and Osbert Sitwell seemed to agree on Eliot's somewhat innocent purpose in using makeup, there is evidence that Virginia Woolf at least had deeper but unrevealed ideas for Eliot's "extraordinary and fantastical pretense." In a letter to her friend the French painter Jacques Raveret of January 24, 1925, she wrote: "Have you any views on loving one's own sex? All the young men are so inclined, and I can't help finding it mildly foolish; though I have no particular reason. For one thing, all the young men tend to the pretty, and ladylike, for some reason, at the moment. They paint and powder, which wasn't the style in our day at Cambridge. I think it does imply some clingingness—a tiny lap dog, called Sackville-West, came to see me the other day (a cousin of my aristocrat and will inherit Knole) and my cook said, Who was the lady in the drawing room? He has a voice like a girls, and a face like a Persian cats, all white and serious, with large violet eyes and fluffy cheeks. Well, you can't respect the amours of a creature like *that*. Then the ladies, either in self protection, or imitation or genuinely, are given to their sex too." She went on to recount the aborted February 1920 elopement of two "Sapphic" women, Sackville-West's wife Vita and her friend Violet Trefusis, closing: "I can't take either of these aberrations seriously. To tell you a secret, I want to incite my lady to elope with me next. Then I'll drop down on you and tell you all about it" (Woolf, *L3*, 155–56). Virginia's "secret" was really not so secret in the artistic milieu of Bloomsbury; thus it is not clear, in her tea-time chat with Osbert, why she did not discuss men wearing makeup as evidence for "loving one's own sex."

The concerns she discussed with Osbert about Eliot's happiness were sincere, however, for the two had grown much closer since she had written in her diary on March 21: "Will he become Tom? What happens with friendships undertaken at the age of forty? . . . I suppose a good mind endures, & one is drawn to it & sticks to it, owing to having a good mind myself. Not that Tom admires my writing, damn him." By March of the following year, 1922, she listed people she has seen: "Eliot, Clive, Violet. . . . Of these Eliot amuses me most—grown supple as an eel; yes, grown positively familiar & jocular & friendly" (Woolf, *D2*, 100, 170). He had indeed become "Tom": the intimacy between them increased as they began to discuss their works written and works in progress—as well as their personal lives—with each other. It is likely that Virginia Woolf was the only friend with whom Eliot could confide the depth of his feelings on the loss of Verdenal in the war, and the fact that he did so has been explored in depth in a 1983 essay by Erwin W. Steinberg entitled "*Mrs. Dalloway* and T. S. Eliot's Personal Waste Land."

Steinberg's essay argues persuasively that the character of Septimus Smith in Woolf's *Mrs. Dalloway* (1925) is based on Eliot. Smith suffers a nervous breakdown similar to the *aboulie* that Eliot suffered when completing *The Waste Land* and the primary cause is the grief Smith feels on the loss of his superior officer, Evans, killed "just before the armistice." Smith's marriage to the wife he didn't really love—Lucrezia—took place shortly after Evans's death, as did Eliot's marriage to Vivien, only months after the death of Verdenal. Septimus Smith is, like Eliot, a clerk and a poet, and he is, also like

Eliot, appreciated by his employer in his job (and promoted). Smith suffers hallucinations, finding Evans still alive in this or that encounter with strangers—and then discovering his "mistake" (Steinberg, 10–12). Ultimately Smith commits suicide.

The fact assumed here, and I think an indisputable one, is that Eliot's grief endured, however much he was able to come to terms with it by embodying it in *The Waste Land*. That he would share it with Virginia Woolf, in the wake of the writing and publishing of the poem, bears testimony to the depths in him in which it was lodged. And indeed, Eliot's remembrance of Jean Verdenal a decade later—in 1934—causing him to burst through the bounds of the *Criterion* essay on an unrelated subject to exclaim his seemingly fresh memory of Jean Verdenal—"coming across the Luxembourg Gardens in the late afternoon, carrying a branch of lilac"—signals a memory of such intensity as to last a lifetime.

5. Roommates, "Renowned Pederasts": Kitchin, Senhouse, Ritchie

Hastings, in the 1988 introduction to his play *Tom and Viv*, in response to Morley's question, "What do you know about 38 Burghley Mansions, and those goings on?" footnotes: "Burghley [Burleigh] Mansions, St. Martin's Lane, was shared by C. H. B. Kitchin (1895–1967), Roger Senhouse (1900–1970) and Philip Ritchie (1899–1927)" (Hastings, 17–18). Carole Seymour-Jones interviewed Hastings in April 2000, and received additional information: "The Hon. Philip Ritchie, eldest son of Lord Ritchie of Dundee, a beautiful and gay young man to whom Lytton Strachey was attracted, stayed on occasion at Burleigh Mansions with Eliot, so Frank Morley, a Faber director, admitted to playwright Michael Hastings" (Seymour-Jones, 362–63, 624 n. 13). We should not confuse these three with the 1933 trio with whom Eliot shared quarters on Great Ormond Street. It can be confusing, for the later group includes a Kenneth Ritchie and the same C. H. B. Kitchin who appears in this trio of the early twenties. One book gives considerable insight into the individuals of the original trio, particularly as they were related to the Bloomsbury group: Michael Holroyd's *Lytton Strachey: The New Biography* (1994), the final and expanded version of his biography which first appeared in two volumes in 1967 and 1968. It is one of the most forthcoming and sexually revealing books about the Bloomsbury group and Strachey.

Whereas the novelist C. H. B. Kitchin seemed not to have been accepted by the Bloomsbury group, Roger Senhouse and Philip Ritchie became members of it. Kitchin is mentioned only once in the text (Holroyd, 523), but a footnote points out that his novel *Crime at Christmas* (1935) is dedicated to Kenneth Ritchie (one of the Great Ormond Street friends), and that in it he writes: "It is my fate, in Bloomsbury, to be thought a Philistine, while in other circles I am regarded as a dilettante with too keen an aesthetic sense to be a responsible person." Kitchin wrote to Holroyd (July 5, 1965), admitting that the sentence "has certainly an autobiographical overtone and largely sums up my social situation during the twenties. I was introduced to Bloomsbury by Philip Ritchie, who was a close friend of mine, and met most of the leading lights in that circle, but being in those days a tiresome mixture of shyness and conceit, I never felt sufficiently at home in it to form intimate contacts with its members." Virginia Woolf proved friendly, however, and the Hogarth Press published his first two novels, *Streamers Waving* in 1925 and *Mr. Balcony* in 1927 (738).

Kitchin, educated at Oxford, would become an accomplished novelist. He was also a barrister who, in 1925, along with Philip Ritchie, would join the chambers of the brilliant barrister and expert on inheritance law, C. P. Sanger. Sanger was a friend of Russell, and one of the Cambridge Apostles (an exclusive, intellectual society of friends), as well as a longtime friend of Virginia Woolf, who would dedicate *Orlando* to him. According to *Who's Who in Bloomsbury* (1987), "Charles and Dora Sanger's first London home was near the Adelphi, south of Charing Cross, and during the halcyon years of Old Bloomsbury they entertained the Stracheys, Woolfs, and . . . [others] at weekly parties" (Palmer and Palmer, 146). Upon Sanger's death in 1930, Lytton remembered those days "when, at first, they lived in a little set of rooms at Charing Cross—and afterwards by a curious chance, Philip [Ritchie] became an added link between us. How he loved Philip" (quoted in Holroyd, 655–56). Lytton met Ritchie, then an Oxford undergraduate, in early 1923, "the one charming element" at that Sunday afternoon tea: "He told me shocking gossip about everyone, and in my gratitude I nearly flung my arms around his neck" (523).

Ritchie, in his twenties, became the new love of Lytton, in his forties. Frances Partridge, in her memoirs, *Love in Bloomsbury* (1981), recalls Philip Ritchie as "clever and amusing, a devotee of chamber music, and discussions on abstract subjects" (Partridge, 100). Ritchie, "with his irregular features and endearingly gauche manner," was inseparable from another Oxford undergraduate, Roger Senhouse, "a romantic creature 'with a melting smile and dark grey eyes.'" "Roger was a connoisseur of books—later to be the partner [in the publishing] firm of Secker and Warburg, and a friend of Genet, a translator of Collette" (Holroyd, 546, 577). By 1926, he would become, in Virginia Woolf's words, Lytton's "new pink boy" (Woolf, *L3*, 343).

But first Lytton was smitten with Ritchie, sending him love poems and entertaining him. Ritchie is mentioned in a November 1923 letter from Lytton's friend Dora Carrington to Lytton as having been present at an "amusing" party at Lytton's house (Carrington, 265). And we know that in December 1923 Eliot invited Lytton to a party at 38 Burleigh Mansions. It is possible that Ritchie was the "long pale squint eyed Oxford youth on the floor" described by Woolf in her diary on December 17, 1923, even though she didn't name him. On May 5, 1924, she records "a queer little party" they had, attended by Roger Frye and Philip Ritchie and joined afterwards by Vanessa, Duncan, Lytton Strachey, and Eliot. She writes: "the sinister & pedagogic Tom cut a queer figure." "Queer," a word used often by Woolf, is not used in the present sense of "homosexual," but rather in the sense of the 1924 book by Charles G. Harper, *Queer Things about London: Strange Nooks and Corners of the Greatest City in the World*. Woolf found Eliot strange that day and harbored "suspicions" about him, which "at the worst" amounted to calling him "a very vain man. . . . There's something hole & cornerish biting in the back, suspicious, elaborate, uneasy, about him" (Woolf, *D2*, 302). Woolf was upset about Eliot's hypocrisy with respect to a performance of *King Lear* at which they had both jeered and his later column in the *Criterion* where he solemnly rebuked those who jeered. The entry, while shedding light on Woolf's view of Eliot, is also of interest, for the purposes of this discussion, to show that at this time, Ritchie and Lytton appeared at the same social gatherings as Eliot. No more can be said, at this time, in support of the implications in Hastings's footnote.

Clifford H. B. Kitchin is a minor character in novelist Francis King's autobiography, *Yesterday Came Suddenly* (1993). As we have been introduced to Kitchin in the early 1920s, settled into quarters with men of similar sexual interests, so again in the early 1930s we find him sharing accommodations with similar men, but in different quarters. In a several-page summary of his friendship with Kitchin, King writes: "Clifford [Kitchin] had . . . for a brief period, been a friend of T. S. Eliot, he and two other homosexual men— Ken Ritchie, later chairman of the Stock Exchange, and the well-known bibliophile Richard Jennings—providing Eliot with sanctuary in the Great Ormond Street flat which they were sharing, when he and his first wife Vivienne split up." King asked Kitchin if Eliot had "shown any signs of homosexuality." Kitchin's reply: "Well, he would hardly have spent that period living with us if he had not had *some* leanings, now would he? After all, all three of us liked to bring back trade." To bolster his belief, Kitchin continued: "He then told me of how Eliot would often, as he put it, 'apply a bit of slap' [theatrical makeup] before venturing out of an evening" (King, 197).

Not surprisingly, King thought an Eliot biographer would be interested in this information. He writes: "But when I passed on the information to my friend Peter Ackroyd when he was working on his fine life of T. S. Eliot, he brushed it aside. Biographers soon form ideas of their subjects and from then on are reluctant to accept any evidence that might force them to modify them" (197). The first Eliot critic to call attention to this episode was James Loucks, in a 1996 issue of *ANQ*, presenting part of his valuable Eliot chronology. After quoting from the King autobiography, he quotes Ackroyd's assertion that "all the available evidence suggests that when [Eliot] allowed his sexuality free access, when he was not struggling with his own demons, it [his sexuality] was of a heterosexual kind." But Loucks goes on to state the obvious—that "these qualifications effectively invalidate Ackroyd's assertion by reminding the reader that TSE's poems and plays often mirror TSE's struggle with inner demons, including those of sexuality." Eliot's sexuality is only one of several elements in his complex personality that Loucks concludes "are overdue for fresh discussion" (Loucks, 31, 33–34).

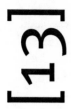

[13]

1922
OVER THE TOP

1. "The Uranian Muse," *The Waste Land*, and *"il miglior fabbro"*

From the beginning, Ezra Pound was an indispensable force in Eliot's career, nowhere more so than in the creation of *The Waste Land*. He would help to shape it at a time when Eliot was most dependent on him. To be sure, Eliot had been writing his long poem over a very long time and could be said to have finished it in Lausanne. He had shown a copy to Pound in Paris in November 1921, when he was en route to Switzerland, and he carried the completed manuscript back to Paris on January 2 when he joined Vivien there, leaving for London on January 16. Eliot, writing in 1946, remembered Pound's role: "It was in 1922 that I placed before him in Paris the manuscript of a sprawling chaotic poem . . . which left his hands, reduced to about half its size. . . . I should like to think that the manuscript, with the suppressed passages, had disappeared irrecoverably: yet, on the other hand, I should wish the blue penciling on it to be preserved as irrefutable evidence of Pound's critical genius" (EP, 28). As we know, Eliot got his wish, although he did not live to see the manuscript resurface to be published in the facsimile edition of 1971, where we can see Pound's penciling. Pound's "critical genius" was acknowledged earlier by Eliot with a meaningful, memorable epithet.

Upon the poem's book publication in America (1922), Eliot inscribed this dedication in one copy: "For Ezra Pound / *il miglior fabbro,*" but the dedication did not see print until 1925, with publication of *Poems 1909–1925.* The words ("the better craftsman") are spoken to Dante by Guido Guinicelli as a salute to the twelfth-century troubadour poet, Arnaut Daniel: "'O brother,' said he, 'this one whom I distinguish to thee / with my finger' (and he pointed to a spirit in front) / 'was a better craftsman of the mother tongue'" (*Purgatorio,* Canto XXVI, lines 115–17).

Pound's role in shaping *The Waste Land* is the focus of my 1977 book, *T. S. Eliot's Personal Waste Land: Exorcism of the Demons,* which made full use of the manuscripts in *The Waste Land: A Facsimile and Transcript of the Original Drafts.* I overlooked the relevance to my enterprise, however, of Pound's poem "Sage Homme," which was included in a letter Pound sent from Paris to Eliot in London. He wrote at the top, "24 Saturnus An I." It has been dated "24 December 1921" in brackets by D. D. Paige in Pound's *Letters* (1950) and by Valerie Eliot in *The Letters of T. S. Eliot* (1988). Both Peter Ackroyd and Lyndall Gordon believe January 1922 the more likely date. This is probably correct, based on the contents of the letter and Eliot's no doubt prompt reply, dated January 24?, 1922. However, for Pound, as he wrote to Mencken on March 22, 1922, "The Christian era ended at midnight on Oct. 29–30 of last year. You are now in the year I. p. s. U" (Pound, *L,* 174). Pound chose that date because Joyce finished *Ulysses* "on Mr. Pound's birthday [October 30, 1921]." Therefore, 1921 would still be part of "An I." But since Joyce was presented with the first published copy of *Ulysses* on *his* birthday, February 2, 1922, the year 1922 certainly qualifies (Ellmann, 538). In any event, "An I" is associated with the appearance of *Ulysses.* As Wayne Koestenbaum, in his study of male literary collaboration as "textual intercourse," has pointed out: "Pound dates his letter *24 Saturnus, An 1,* signifying that 1922, the year *Ulysses* was published, is the Year One of modernism, and that Joyce's epic gave birth to a new world. The Latin date *An 1,* spelled out, reads *An Unus.* Pound's playful reference to an(un)us as modernism's birthsite brings the poem's scene of gestation even closer to anal intercourse" (Koestenbaum, 122). "Saturnus" refers to the Roman god Saturn, protector of the sowers and the seed, later identified with the Greek Titan Cronus, father of Jupiter/Zeus. The festival in his honor, beginning on December 17, was traditionally the merriest of the year, with no war, the slaves freed, and presents exchanged, and commemorated the Golden Age, a time of peace and happiness. In addition to evoking the season, did Pound want to indicate the beginning of a new Golden Age?

In the letter containing "Sage Homme" from Pound to Eliot, Pound opens "Caro mio: MUCH improved," and comments on the poem, saying "The thing now runs from April . . . to shantih without [a] break. That is 19 pages, and let us say the longest poem in the English langwidge." He concludes: "Complimenti, you bitch. I am wracked by the seven jealousies, and cogitating an excuse for always exuding my deformative secretions in my own stuff, and never getting an outline. I go into nacre [Mother of pearl] and objets d'art. Some day I shall lose my temper, blaspheme Flaubert, lie like a shitarse and say 'Art shd. embellish the umbilicus'" (*LTSE1*, 497–98).

Beginning with his Italian plural ("complimenti"), Pound's vernacular speech becomes somewhat dense for the uninitiated. But what he seems to be saying is that Eliot has included, however covertly, the "personal" in his poetry in a way that Pound has never done: on the contrary Pound exudes his "deformative secretions" (misshaping semen) and includes banalities of the beautiful. But someday, he'll dare to change, blaspheming ensconced masters (Flaubert), tell tall tales, and follow Eliot's lead in his poetry, spotlighting the umbilical cord (and no doubt all below it).

At this point Pound "lapses" into verse, slyly picking up on the word "bitch," which he had used in addressing his male friend, and linking what would become *The Waste Land* with the theme of homosexuality. As between Eliot and Pound, Eliot is the "Sage Homme" (the Wise Man), whose poems are begotten by the "Uranian Muse" with a "Man" as "their Mother." In identifying Eliot's muse as "Uranian" (the "Sire") and Eliot as the Man-Mother of *The Waste Land,* Pound is locating the poem's origin in a homosexual union. Indeed, the term "Uranian" derives from Uranus, personification of the Heavens originating as the son of Ge, or earth (no female was involved in his birth), and later functioning as Ge's husband to sire the Titans. As we have discussed in Chapter 4, Section 8, "Uranian" was one of the candidates, along with "sexual inversion" and "homosexual," to signify same-sex love in the latter part of the nineteenth century; the latter term, of course ultimately triumphed. (For an account of Uranian poetry of the recent past, see Timothy d'Arch Smith's *Love in Earnest: Some Notes on the Lives and Writings of English "Uranian" Poets from 1889 to 1930.*) From the strange man-man nuptials that Pound describes, there resulted the "printed Infancies" that was the ur-*Waste Land* (the original manuscript) that Pound began with, and on which he performed his "caesarean Operation"—using the editorial knife to bring to birth the poem published in 1922. Most critics would agree that Pound's revision tended to obscure the poem's "Uranian" homosexual origins, diluting the personal dimensions and inflating its cultural and social themes. Certain it is that the ur-*Waste Land* reveals much more of Eliot's personal experience than did the 1922 version, shaped largely by Pound's revision. It was Pound who dubbed Eliot "Possum" not long after the appearance of *The Waste Land*. Is it possible that Pound, in his "caesarean Operation," pointed Eliot in the direction of obscuring the most personal elements of his poetry?

Pound's poem continues, characterizing (or obliquely satirizing) the contents of Eliot's poems: "Cauls [amniotic sack covering a child's head at birth] and grave clothes," "odour," and "rotting clothes" (*LTSE1*, 498–99). In effect, Pound suggests, Eliot's poems treat such repugnant subjects as birth and death, putrefaction, stupid and careless people, all levels of sexual congress (animals, humans, cannibals), and, "above all else," things that stink! It is instructive to recall here that in the excised Fresca passage of "The Fire Sermon," Eliot had written of the "good old hearty female stench." In her thoughtful and provocative essay, "Eliot's Grail Quest, or, The Lover, the Police, and *The Waste Land*," Christine Froula has argued that Fresca is "less a butt of misogynist ridicule than a counterphobic conduit for the poet's fear and hatred of his own deep female-identified self." Whether the Fresca passage is understood as an example of misogyny resulting from women-hating or, as Froula suggests, misogyny originating in "self-loathing," its existence cannot be denied nor can we deny the truth of Pound's characterization of Eliot's poetry in "Sage Homme." In addition, as Froula further reminds us: "When Conrad Aiken praised his poems in 1925, Eliot astounded him with a mute but eloquent demurral: a page torn from the *Midwife's Gazette* on which he had underlined the words 'blood,' 'mucus,' 'shreds of mucus,' 'purulent offensive discharge'" (Froula, EGQ, 244, 253). We might note here that in his letter of praise, Aiken had asked Eliot the following question: "How the devil did you manage to discover your identity so early?" (Aiken, *SL,* 109).

"Sage Homme" is followed by another poem (or perhaps part of the same poem; see Koestenbaum, 121), beginning "E. P. hopeless and unhelped," in which Pound addresses "venomously" his own poetry. The first two stanzas emphasize Pound's own avoidance or transfiguration of realities, his verse following "Yeats into the mists." He speaks of "Marmorean [marble] skies," "hands with mother of pearl" materializing on "the strapping servant girl," a satyr and "holy hosts of hellenists" (*LTSE1, 499*). In short, Pound describes himself (one should note unrealistically) as a romantic poet who, unlike Eliot, transfigures repugnant reality into beautiful unreality.

The last two stanzas of Pound's poem about his own work return to a sequence of sexual metaphors: "Balls and balls and balls again / Can not touch his fellow men. / His foaming and abundant cream / Has coated his world. The coat of a dream; / Or say that the upjut of his sperm / Has rendered his senses pachyderm [elephantine]. // Grudge not the oyster his stiff saliva / Envy not the diligent diver. et in aeternitate [and in eternity]" (499).

Pound is describing his creative process in terms of sexual climax however brought about (it would appear to be masturbatory). (Koestenbaum reads this as Pound impregnating Eliot: "Insemination depends on sperm that the expurgated verses supply" [Koestenbaum, 121].) Such a physical event begins with the balls and ends with the ejaculation of sperm (or "cream"). And it "is the upjut of his sperm" that has "coated his world," or hardened his senses, transforming reality into something it is not. The movement of the last two lines into the imperative—"grudge not," "envy not"—suggests that the reader should neither "grudge" nor "envy" Pound's creativity, which he thus likens to the oyster ejaculating "his stiff saliva" or the "diligent diver" plunging only into shallow waters. In trailing off into "and [so on] in[to] eternity," Pound seems to be suggesting that such (eternity) is not for him or his work.

Pound's letter ends with two lines that seem to present his only consolation: "It is after all a grrrreat litttterary period / Thanks for the Aggymemnon [Agamemnon, leader of Greeks in the siege of Troy; see Homer's *Iliad*]" (*LTSE1*, 499). In other words, Pound must accept his minor status in a period that Eliot's poem has rendered "great"—comparable to the greatness of Homer's great work.

Before we turn to Eliot's reply, we might look at Eliot's January 20 letter to Thayer, raising the possibility of publishing *The Waste Land* in the *Dial*. It demonstrates that the poem was still a work in progress: "I shall shortly have ready a poem of about four hundred and fifty lines, in four parts. . . . It could easily divide into four issues [of the *Dial*], if you like, but not more. It will have been three times through the sieve by Pound as well as myself so should be in a final form" (502). At this point Eliot thought of his poem as consisting of "four parts"—perhaps because he considered "He Do the Police in Different Voices" (containing both "Burial of the Dead" and "A Game of Chess") as a single "part."

Eliot answered Pound's letter in late January, addressing him "Cher maitre." It is notable for its brevity, asking questions about specific suggestions that Pound had made. For example, Eliot asked: "Do you advise printing Gerontion as prelude in book or pamphlet form?" Since Pound had suggested deleting the major part of *The Waste Land*'s Part IV ("Death by Water") as Eliot had originally written it, he asked: "Perhaps better omit Phlebas [the Phoenician] also???" (i.e., omit the whole of Part IV). On another matter, Eliot asks: "Do you mean not use Conrad quot. [as epigraph], or simply not put Conrad's name to it? It is much the most appropriate I can find, and somewhat elucidative." Eliot comments, uncharacteristically, about his own mental outlook: "Complimenti appreciated, as have been excessively depressed. V. sends her love and says that if she had realized how bloody England is she would not have returned [from Paris]" (504).

In his reply some three days later, January 27, Pound salutes, "Filio dilecto mihi" ("My charming son") and answers: On "Gerontion": "I do *not* advise printing Gerontion as preface. One don't miss it AT all as the thing now stands. To be more lucid still, let me say that I advise you NOT to print Gerontion as prelude." On "Phlebas": "I DO advise keeping Phlebas. In fact I more'n advise. Phlebas is an integral part of the poem; the card pack introduces him, the drowned phoen. sailor, and he is needed ABsoloootly where he is. Must stay in." In some cases, Pound was willing to bow to Eliot's wishes: "Do as you like about my obstetric effort. / Ditto re the Conrad; who am I to grudge him his laurel crown" (505). But even in his epigraph, Eliot gave up his use of the Conrad quotation from "The Heart of Darkness" (ending "The horror! the horror!")—a revision which most critics now think a mistake.

In his closing paragraphs Pound returned to the sexually explicit language he had used in his first letter on the *Waste Land* revisions: "Aristophanes probably depressing, and the native negro melodies of Dixee more calculated to lift the ball-encumbered phallus of man to the proper 8.30, 9.30, or even ten thirty level now counted as the crowning and alarse too often katachrestical [catachrestical: use of wrong word for the context] summit of human achievement" (505). Possible translation: Pound rejects Eliot's suggestion of using a quotation from Aristophanes as an epigraph and recommends the use of a "native Negro" melody of the American South that would be more stimulative of erections in his readers.

Finding his suggestion appealing, Pound continued: "I enclose further tracings of an inscription in the buildings (?) outworks of the city hall jo-house at Charlston S.C." Pound here is referring to out-houses of one kind or another; it was a common American custom for those using them while relieving themselves to inscribe sexually explicit slang or pictures on the walls. It seems in the next paragraph that Pound inscribed the "tracings" he had found: "May your erection never grow less." The paragraph continues, but in a comment directed at Eliot: "I had intended to speak to you seriously on the subject, but you seemed so mountainy gay while here in the midst of Paris that the matter slipped my foreskin" (505). ("Mountainy gay": recall Eliot to Dorothy Pound in Chapter 12, Section 2, where he equates Paris with "mountain air.") It is not difficult to detect beneath all the crudity of Pound's comments to Eliot a series of characterizations that have something of the ring of truth—characterizations based on his literal as well as in-depth reading of the *Waste Land* manuscripts: "bitch," "Uranian," "gay." The dictionary tells us that "gay" came into use to characterize homosexual behavior in the early 1900s, and became favored by homosexuals themselves some time after World War II (RHD, 792). Found in a context in which there are uses of other explicitly sexual words—"ball-encumbered phallus," "erection," "foreskin"—one has to wonder whether there were some times when Eliot squirmed as the butt of Pound's sexual "jokes."

For Pound, not only is the poem filled with complex themes of sexuality, but those themes have their roots in Eliot's own sexual nature. Pound has cloaked the names he has labeled Eliot—"bitch," "Uranian," "gay"—in a conversation filled with "Amurrican" humor, and thus has evoked not anger but appreciation, the appreciation of one who unconsciously assumes Eliot is the secret sharer, not the target, of the joke.

2. Publication of *The Waste Land*

Pound wrote on July 8, 1922, to Felix Schelling (his Shakespeare professor at the University of Pennsylvania) the much quoted sentence: "Eliot's *Waste Land* is I think the justification of the 'movement,' of our modern experiment, since 1900. It shd. be published this year" (Pound, *L*, 180). And indeed it was—royally. But not before some complicated maneuvers, detailed by Lawrence Rainey in "The Price of Modernism: Publishing *The Waste Land*." They involved Eliot, his mentor Pound, and his financial backer John Quinn. Eliot was so grateful to Quinn that he wrote on July 19 offering him *The Waste Land* manuscript: "When I say manuscript, I mean that it is partly manuscript and partly typescript, with Ezra's and my alterations scrawled all over it" (*LTSE1*, 548).

The poem, they knew, should be published in England and America, and in both places it should appear first in one of the distinguished little magazines and later as a book. Offering the poem to the public in this way would, if handled properly, guarantee maximum publicity and financial returns. The poem was in effect dangled before a number of little magazines and publishers before Eliot and Pound settled on the winners. Near the end of 1922, the poem was published without footnotes in England, in the first issue (October 16) of Eliot's own publication, the *Criterion*, and almost simultaneously in America (November) in Gilbert Seldes and Scofield Thayer's *The Dial*. It appeared in book form with Eliot's notes in a commercial edition in America, published by Boni & Liveright (1922), and in a limited edition in England, published by the Woolfs' Hogarth Press (1923).

In seeking publication of his new poem, Eliot at one point was corresponding with three little magazines, the *Little Review* and *Vanity Fair* as well as the *Dial;* and with four book publishers, two commercial (Alfred Knopf and Boni & Liveright) and two limited edition (Maurice Firuski and Hogarth Press). It would be somewhat tedious to go through all of the details of the negotiations leading to final decisions. But one aspect throws some light on the controversial subject of Eliot's adding footnotes to his poem. Conrad Aiken had recommended to Eliot the limited edition publisher, Maurice Firuski, of his new book of poems (*The Pool of Priapus,* 1922). Eliot wrote to Firuski (February 26) and described his book thus: "My poem is of 435 lines; with certain spacings essential to the sense, 475 book lines; furthermore, it consists of five parts, which would increase the space necessary; and with title pages, some notes I propose to add, etc., I guess that it would run to from 28 to 32 pages" (quoted in Rainey, 102–3).

In June Eliot wrote Quinn, "overjoyed" at his help negotiating with Horace Liveright, to whom Pound had introduced him in Paris. Unlike Knopf, Liveright offered autumn publication with a 15 percent royalty and $150 in advance. Eliot noted that to the long poem of about 450 lines he would add notes, making a book of thirty or forty pages (*LTSE1,* 530).

In reply to Quinn's letter informing him that he had a signed contract from Boni & Liveright, Eliot wrote a letter congratulating Quinn but subtly suggesting that he needed additional help. First Eliot assured Quinn that he was going to give him, gratis, those manuscripts of *The Waste Land* from which Pound had rescued the poem. Then he wrote that he had received "an attractive proposal from Mr. Watson of the *Dial,*" who was anxious to publish it, but wanted Liveright to postpone book publication, a "trouble" for both Liveright and Quinn that Eliot did not choose to pursue (564). The "attractive proposal" of the *Dial,* of course, was not only to give Eliot an advance of $150 for his book but also to agree to award Eliot the $2,000 annual *Dial* award for "services in the cause of letters" (Rainey, 83), thus violating their "rule" to wait until the end of the year to make the decision of the winner of the award. And of course, when Eliot wrote to Quinn that he did not want to "trouble Mr. Liveright or particularly yourself" to renegotiate the contract, it is clear he knew that was exactly what his remark, along with the gift to Quinn of the manuscripts, would lead Quinn to do.

At the end of August, Eliot wrote to Pound: "With most grateful thanks yours always sincerely, faithfully. I received a letter from your friend Watson most amiable in tone." There then followed two lines of one of Eliot's bawdy lyrics on "The Fall of Admiral Barry": "Far below a voice did answer, sweet in its youthful tone, / The sea-dog with difficulty descended, for he had a manly bone." After this "interruption," Eliot finished his incomplete sentence and stressed the proper way of referring to his poem: "offering $150 for the 'Waste Land' (not 'Waste Land,' please, but '*The* Waste Land,' and (in the strictest confidence) the award for virtue also." However, Eliot had already received Liveright's signed contract promising a November 1 publication and didn't see why they should postpone publication "to let the *Dial* kill the sale by printing it first." Eliot supposed that the offer of the *Dial* prize was due to Ezra's efforts, adding "Dam but why don't they give the prize to you?" And, as if to disguise his feelings, Eliot ended with another outburst of bawdy: "King Bolo's big black basstart kuwheen, / That plastic & elastic one, / Would frisk it on the village green, / Enjoying her fantastikon" (*LTSE1*, 567–68).

Quinn's September 7 letter to Eliot about a renegotiated contract with Boni & Liveright is summarized in a footnote to Eliot's "thank you" letter of September 21: Quinn had come to an arrangement with Gilbert Seldes and Liveright that "TSE would receive the annual *Dial* award of $2,000. The magazine would publish the poem without notes and buy 350 copies of the book; in return Liveright would allow them prior publication." In this letter, Quinn brought up the matter of Eliot's gift of *The Waste Land* manuscripts and notes, accepting "it not for what he had done for TSE but 'as a mark of friendship,' on condition that he was allowed to purchase the MSS of the early poems TSE had mentioned" (571).

Eliot was "overwhelmed" and effusive in his thanks, expressing only one regret: that he should receive the award before Pound, who deserved the "public testimony" more, "certainly 'for his services to Letters.'" Then Eliot provided an extraordinary description of the soon-to-be-lost masterpiece of modernism: "I have gathered together all of the manuscript in existence. The leather bound notebook is one which I started in 1909 and in which I entered all my work of that time as I wrote it, so that it is the only original manuscript barring of course rough scraps and notes, which were destroyed at the time, in existence. You will find a great many sets of verse which have never been printed and which I am sure you will agree never ought to be printed, and in putting them in your hands, I beg you fervently to keep them to yourself and see that they never are printed" (571–72). Quinn was to die in 1924, Eliot in 1965, and the manuscripts, after being discovered in the New York Public Library among Quinn's papers, would come to life in print in 1971.

Lawrence Rainey characterizes the publishing history: "The poem was important precisely for its representative quality, and publishing it was not necessarily a matter of appreciating its quality or sympathizing with its sub-stantive components—whatever those were—but of one's eagerness to posi-tion oneself as the spokesperson of a field of cultural production, the voice of an array of institutions ('the justification of the "movement," of our modern experiment, since 1900')" (Rainey, 81). The major irony that Rainey points out is that the representatives of the journals and publishers who made the critical decisions and offers in obtaining publication rights to *The Waste Land* had not read the work for which they lusted—and for which they paid high fees (including a handsome cash prize): the evidence for this is indisputable. Yet, says Rainey, "the dominant methodology of modern literary studies since roughly the end of World War II" has been to exhort "generations of students . . . to look closely at the poem, to examine only the text, to indulge in a scholastic scrutiny of linguistic minutiae" (105–6).

3. "Out into the World": *The Waste Land* Reviewed

The Waste Land would be the subject of endless "scholastic scrutiny" in the future, but members of its first audience responded more viscerally, in a deeply moving way. Virginia Woolf recalled Eliot reading his poem: "He sang it & chanted it [,] rhythmed it. It has great beauty & force of phrase: symmetry; & tensity. What connects it together, I'm not so sure. . . . One was left . . . with some strong emotion. The Waste Land, it is called; & Mary Hutch, who has heard it more quietly, interprets it to be Tom's autobiography—a melancholy one" (Woolf, *D2,* 178). Vivien, whose opinion Eliot always sought, wrote to Schiff on October 16, echoing Tom's thanks for his "real and true appreciation. . . . Perhaps not even you can imagine with what emotions I saw *The Waste Land* go out into the world. . . . It has become a part of me (or I of it) this last year. It was a terrible thing, somehow, when the time came at last for it to be published" (*LTSE1,* 584).

Pound's views of Eliot's poem, as we have seen, were delivered to Eliot as witty distortions or exaggerations in his letters, but were serious, particularly in what they divulged about Eliot's sexuality. He expressed them to the American poet John Peale Bishop, who, on behalf of Edmund Wilson, made a point of seeking out Pound on his honeymoon trip to Europe in November 1922. Wilson had been chosen by the *Dial* to write an essay about the poem after its appearance there that November. He had received an advance copy and had written to Bishop (September 5): "I am much excited about Eliot's *The Waste Land,* which I have just read. I will send you the proof I have if they will let me keep it. It will give you quite a thrill, I think; it is certainly his masterpiece so far" (Wilson, 94).

What Wilson wrote in this letter to Bishop was radically at odds with what he would soon write in his highly influential review of the poem, published in the December *Dial*. He admitted to Bishop that he had not read the footnotes that Eliot had by this time written to be published with the poem: "[Eliot] supplements [the poem] with a set of notes almost as long as the poem itself, explaining the literary, historic, anthropological, metaphysical, and religious significances to be found in it; but the poem, as it appears to me from two or three cursory readings, is nothing more or less than a most distressingly moving account of Eliot's own agonized state of mind during the years which preceded his nervous breakdown. Never have the sufferings of the sensitive man in the modern city chained to some work he hates and crucified on the vulgarity of his surroundings been so vividly set forth. It is certainly a cry *de profundis* if ever there was one—almost the cry of a man on the verge of insanity" (94). It surely is not by chance that Wilson's Latin phrase, "*de profundis* [From the Depths]" is the title Oscar Wilde gave to his 1895 essay written in prison and sent as a letter to his ex-lover, Lord Alfred Douglas, published in 1905. As it would turn out, Wilson did get around to reading Eliot's notes—and found them "clarifying" enough to turn him around radically on his initial view of the personal nature of the poem.

But before that happened, Bishop would connect with Pound in Europe and report on Eliot's poem. (Bishop had represented *Vanity Fair* in its bid for publication rights.) He later wrote to Wilson a full account starting with Ezra and Mrs. Pound's company at dinner, where "the great 'Amurcan' poet," in "his cups," poured out "a lot of his past" and "a few points about 'Tears' Eliot (as some Paris wit [E. E. Cummings] has recently christened him)." After speaking of Eliot's past (and poetic beginnings), Pound then moved on more or less to the present, giving an account of Eliot's wedding: "Eliot is tubercular and disposed toward epilepsy. On one occasion he decided to kill himself in Pound's house but funked at the final moment. '[Villanelle:] The Psychological Hour' in *Lustra* gives E. P.'s reaction to T. S. E.'s wedding which was substituted on the spur of the moment for a tea engagement at Pound's. It seems that Thomas and Vivienne arrived in the hallway and then turned back, went to the registrar's and were wed, to everybody's subsequent pain and misery. She is an English lady, daughter of a member of the Royal Academy and sister of an officer in the Guards. She, likewise, is an invalid and according to Muriel Draper, very dreary and washed out." These plentiful (and not entirely accurate) details are all a preparation for some *Waste Land* explication: "Eliot's version of her is contained in 'The Chair she sat in like a burnished throne . . .' and so forth. . . . By the way, do you know that the 'Hurry up please it's time' is what the bartenders all say when the English pubs are about to close? . . . according to E. P., [it] reflects the atmosphere outside their first flat in London. Eliot, it seems, is hopelessly caught in his own prudent temperament. As E. P. says, 'I am too low for any steam-roller to flatten me out. I can always creep out of the way.' But Eliot is incapable of taking the least chance, as one would have surmised" (quoted in Spindler, 79–80).

Bishop's report that Pound referred him to Pound's poem "Villanelle: The Psychological Hour" (in *Lustra*) is intriguing. The poem, in three parts, opens, "I had over-prepared the event" (the poem's "middle-ageing" speaker reveals that he has nervously prepared his flat for "two friends"): he "had laid out just the right books," he watched "from the window" (but nobody came), "Youth would awhile forget." This happened twice. And then, the "third day," again "No word from her nor him, / Only another man's note: / 'Dear Pound, I am leaving England.'" The complete poem can be found in the *Selected Poems* (Pound, SPEP, 39–41). In her *Guide to Ezra Pound's Selected Poems* (1983), Christina Froula notes that the poem apparently was written with Henri Gaudier and his "sister" in mind: it was they who promised to show up and didn't. The poem appeared shortly after he had turned thirty, and "Pound feared that Gaudier, six years younger . . . would be bored with him" (Froula, GEP, 60–61). Pound could very well have felt that his 1915 poem applied to the Eliots.

Bishop surely had a note-taking mind, remembering what he heard about the origins and identities of the happenings and characters in Eliot's *The Waste Land*—as Pound continued to reminisce about them while "in his cups": "Mr. Eugenides actually turned up at Lloyds with his pocket full of currants and asked Eliot to spend a weekend with him for no nice reasons. His place in the poem is, I believe, as a projection of Eliot, however. That is, all the men are in some way deprived of their life-giving, generative forces. Phlebas is simply dead. Like the knight in the Gawain version of the Grail. The Fisher King is castrated; the one-eyed merchant a homosexual." Suddenly Bishop pulled back: "I do not, of course, mean to imply that Thomas is that any more than that he is physically nutted [lost his testes]" (quoted in Spindler, 80).

Bishop veers from simply recording Pound's news about Eliot's new poem into a brief but sensitive account of Pound as a person: "[Pound] is inordinately vain, especially where women are concerned, gets tight very quickly, and proceeds to act out every remark, turning over chairs and tables on the way. He is delighted with his nigger, yiddish, and western accents which he employs to wearing excess. Yet in spite of making a continuous ass of himself, there is something rather noble and certainly very sensitive under his buffoonery which appeared chiefly when he recited the Arnaut Daniel passage from the *Purgatorio*." Pound shared Eliot's passion for Dante, but would have been steeped in Arnaut the troubadour. Bishop concludes with certainty that he has "cleared up the meaning of the poem as far as it is possible," having learned from Pound that "it was originally twice as long and included Bleistein and all the old familiar faces." Bishop now felt it to be not "so logically constructed as I had at first supposed and that it is a mistake to seek for more than a suggestion of personal emotion in a number of passages." This last sentence implies that *The Waste Land* is not nearly all personal, but somewhat slightly so "in a number of passages." Bishop concludes by focusing on passages that relate to Eliot's biography: "The Nightingale passage is, I believe, important: Eliot being Tereus and Mrs. E., Philomela. That is to say, that through unbalanced passion, everybody is in a hell of a fix; Tereus being changed to a hoopoe [hawk] and T. S. E. a bank clerk. Thomas's sexual troubles are undoubtedly extreme" (quoted in Spindler, 80–82).

Edmund Wilson answered Bishop in a letter of November 29, 1922, much interested in "Pound's gossip about Eliot" and concluding that "He must be a dreary fellow. But I certainly think you have the wrong dope about the nightingale." At this point, Wilson went systematically through the interpretations that Bishop had sent him and, with great self-assurance, pointed out how they were wrong. As Ronald Bush writes in "T. S. Eliot and Modernism at the Present Time: A Provocation," Wilson explained to Bishop the significance of Eliot's "complicated correspondences" and "recondite references and quotations." Moreover, Bush points out, Wilson had been commissioned by the *Dial*, the publication that had first published *The Waste Land* in the United States and had awarded Eliot a $2000 prize, to write his review. Had he written a review expressing the remarkable sentiments he expressed in his first letter to Bishop about *The Waste Land* ("almost the cry of a man on the verge of insanity"), the *Dial* would have refused to publish it. In effect, Wilson knew his review had to be not just favorable, but emphatically approving (Bush, TSEM, 191–94).

Wilson's review of *The Waste Land* was indeed extravagant in its praise of the poem: its title, "The Poetry of Drouth," indicates something of the theme Wilson found to praise in it. Moreover, Wilson was perhaps the foremost literary critic at the time. Many later reviewers seized upon this theme and followed Wilson's lead in defining the poem and in praising Eliot's skill in supporting the theme with the various allusions, unattributed quotations, and images found in the poem. Indeed, Wilson anticipates the criticism that will be leveled at the poem (after all, his first reaction to it was critical) and points out how the misperceived shortcomings are in reality the poem's virtues: "It is sure to be objected that Mr. Eliot has written a puzzle rather than a poem and that his work can possess no higher interest than a full-rigged ship built in a bottle. It will be said that he depends too much upon books and borrows too much from other men and that there can be no room for original quality in a poem of little more than four hundred lines which contains allusions to, parodies of, or quotations from, the Vedic hymns, Buddha, the Psalms, Ezekiel, Ecclesiastes, Luke, Sappho, Virgil, Ovid, Petronius, the 'Pervigilium Veneris,' St. Augustine, Dante, the Grail Legends, early English poetry, Kyd, Spenser, Shakespeare, John Day, Webster, Middleton, Milton, Goldsmith, Gérard de Nerval, Froude, Baudelaire, Verlaine, Swinburne, Wagner, 'The Golden Bough,' Miss Weston's book, various popular ballads, and the author's own earlier poems" (quoted in Grant, 142).

A cynic might argue that all Wilson had to do to compile this list was to go through the notes and list all the authors and titles. And Wilson anticipates that his overwhelming list might well drive away potential readers of *The Waste Land* by intimidating them. In the final paragraph of his long review he writes: "It is not necessary to know anything about the Grail Legend or any but the most obvious of Mr. Eliot's allusions to feel the force of the intense emotion which the poem is intended to convey. . . . [Eliot's] very images and the sound of the words—even when we do not know precisely why he has chosen them—are charged with a strange poignancy which seems to bring us into the heart of the singer." Seemingly on the edge of mentioning a personal dimension to *The Waste Land*, Wilson drops back: "And sometimes we feel that he is speaking not only for a personal distress, but for the starvation of a whole civilization—for people grinding at barren office-routine in the cells of gigantic cities, drying up their souls in eternal toil whose products never bring them profit, where their pleasures are so vulgar and so feeble that they are almost sadder than their pains. It is our whole world of strained nerves and shattered institutions, in which 'some infinitely gentle, infinitely suffering thing' is somehow done to death—in which the maiden Philomel 'by the barbarous king so rudely forced' can no longer even fill the desert 'with inviolable voice'" (quoted in Grant, 143–44).

This review, written by one of the most widely known and influential reviewers of the time, and presented in one of most important little magazines in America and abroad, established the approach to Eliot's poem that was faithfully followed by many subsequent reviewers and critics. Another important review appeared in the December 6, 1922, issue of the *Nation,* written by Gilbert Seldes. It should be recalled that Seldes was co-owner of the *Dial,* in which the poem first appeared in the United States. Implicated in its publication, he could hardly be expected to write a negative review.

In fact, he spends most of the review surveying Eliot's career and previous works, and gets around to the new poem only in his final paragraphs. And most of these paragraphs are devoted to a descriptive summary: "In essence, 'The Waste Land' says something which is not new: that life has become barren and sterile, that man is withering, impotent, and without assurance that the waters which made the land fruitful will ever rise again. . . . The title, the plan, and much of the symbolism of the poem, the author tells us in his 'Notes,' were suggested by Miss Weston's remarkable book on the grail legend." Following the direction of Eliot's footnotes, Seldes finds no problem in summarizing the poem, and at the end of his review, finds the secret of its unity: "A closer view of the poem does more than illuminate the difficulties; it reveals the hidden form of the work, indicates how each thing falls into place, and to the reader's surprise shows that the emotion which at first seemed to come in spite of the framework and the detail could not otherwise have been communicated." Seldes at the very end sets an example for many other critics to follow by connecting the poem in style and theme to James Joyce's *Ulysses:* "That 'The Waste Land' is, in a sense, the inversion and the complement of 'Ulysses' is at least tenable. . . . More important still, I fancy, is that each has expressed something of supreme relevance to our present life in the everlasting terms of art" (quoted in Grant, 148–50).

Louis Untermeyer, a widely read literary figure of the time, opens his review, which appeared in the *Freeman,* January 17, 1923, with something of an exposé of the way Eliot's poem was launched: "The 'Dial's' award to Mr. T. S. Eliot and the subsequent book-publication of his 'The Waste Land' have occasioned a display of some of the most enthusiastically naive superlatives that have ever issued from publicly sophisticated iconoclasts. A group, in attempting to do for Mr. Eliot what 'Ulysses' did for Mr. Joyce, has, through its emphatic reiterations, driven more than one reader to a study rather than a celebration of the qualities that characterize Mr. Eliot's work and endear him to the younger cerebralists. These qualities, apparent even in his earlier verses, are an elaborate irony, a twitching disillusion, a persistent though muffled hyperaesthesia." When he finally characterizes *The Waste Land,* Untermeyer's terms are blunt and clear: "a pompous parade of erudition, a lengthy extension of the earlier disillusion, a kaleidoscopic movement in bright-coloured pieces fail to atone for the absence of an integrated design" (quoted in Grant, 151).

But in spite of some scattered voices raised in protest, Edmund Wilson's vigorous defense of the poem as a work whose central theme was a "criticism of the contemporary world," i.e., "an important bit of social criticism," not only won the day but held sway throughout most of the twentieth century—and this in spite of the fact that Eliot himself denied the validity of this interpretation in remarks not published until editor Valerie Eliot decided to place them at the beginning of her 1971 edition of the *Waste Land* manuscripts. The quotation included not only Eliot's disclaimer, but also his affirmation as to what his poem was about: "To me it was only the relief of a personal and wholly insignificant grouse against life; it is just a piece of rhythmical grumbling." The citation indicates that Eliot's remarks, as quoted by Professor Theodore Spence and recorded by the poet's brother, were made during his lecture series at Harvard, 1932–33 (*WLF,* 1).

But at this point it seems appropriate to introduce the view of a British critic, I. A. Richards, whose reputation at the time he wrote about Eliot was comparable to that of Ezra Pound. We have discussed his treatment of Eliot and sexuality in Chapter 4, Section 5, but it bears repeating here. In his review of Eliot's *Poems 1909–1925* (the February 26, 1926, *New Statesman,* reprinted in *Principles of Literary Criticism*), he concentrated on *The Waste Land.* After objecting to the poem's "lack of any intellectual thread" and "obscurity," Richards settles on the term "music of ideas" to point to Eliot's redeeming virtue. It is not, however, a term that was picked up and used by later Eliot critics. Before introducing that term, he raises the question of whether "the poem is worth all the trouble it entails." He then begins a list of the sources of the "trouble": "There is Canto XXVI of the *Purgatorio* to be studied—the relevance of the close of that canto to the *whole* [emphasis added] of Mr. Eliot's work must be insisted upon. It illuminates his persistent concern with sex, the problem of our generation as religion was the problem of the last. There is the central position of Tiresias in the poem to be puzzled out—the cryptic form of the note which Mr. Eliot writes on this point is just a little tiresome. It is a way of underlining the fact that the poem is concerned with many aspects of the one fact of sex, a hint that is perhaps neither indispensable nor entirely successful" (quoted in Grant, 236). The question that this comment raises is whether Pound, in his letters to Eliot discussing his excavation of *The Waste Land* from the mass of manuscripts (see Section 1 above), wasn't on some level (below the bawdy vocabulary he used) raising this same question.

In raising the question about Eliot's "persistent concern with sex," and citing especially Canto XXVI (particularly the closing lines) of Dante's *Purgatorio* and the central role of the bisexual Tiresias in *The Waste Land,* Richards focuses on genuine concerns that any reader might have. As we have noted above, Ezra Pound's sexual references in his letters ("Uranian," "mountainy gay") emphasized male-male sex, and even Eliot's letters to Pound in which he quotes lines from his bawdy poem ("The Fall of Admiral Barry") suggest male-male coitus. We have noted in several chapters, beginning with the treatment of the manuscript version of "The Love Song of J. Alfred Prufrock" in Chapter 5, Section 6, Eliot's frequent use of the last two lines from Canto XXVI of the *Purgatorio*. This canto, as we have noted before, is a portrayal of the suffering of the lustful and the hermaphrodites (who followed their lusts "like brute beasts"). The poet Arnaut Daniel appears at the end of the canto and addresses a speech to Dante and Virgil. We find that Eliot used them as an epigraph in the manuscript version of "The Love Song of J. Alfred Prufrock" (Ricks, 39)—but not for the final version of "Prufrock." The title of one of Eliot's volumes of poetry, *Ara Vos Prec*, published in England in 1920, appears in the fourth from the last line of this canto, and is part of Arnaut Daniel's speech; and it is significant that the lead-off poem in *Ara Vos Prec* is "Gerontion"—a poem that introduces the term "unnatural vices" to characterize the title character. And the final line of this canto turns up at the end of *The Waste Land*—one of the several "fragments" that the speaker has "shored against" his "ruins," with the final four lines reprinted in the footnote.

As we have already observed, in his book of essays, *The Use of Poetry and the Use of Criticism* (the Charles Eliot Norton Lectures for 1932–33, 1964 edition), Eliot addresses himself to Richards's comment about Eliot's "persistent concern with sex": "[Richards] observes that Canto XXVI of the *Purgatorio* illuminates my 'persistent concern with sex, the problem of our generation, as religion was the problem of the last.' I readily admit the importance of Canto XXVI, and it was shrewd of Mr. Richards to notice it; but in his contrast of sex and religion he makes a distinction which is too subtle for me to grasp. One might think that sex and religion were 'problems' like Free Trade and Imperial Preference; it seems odd that the human race should have gone on for so many thousands of years before it suddenly realized that religion and sex, one right after the other, presented problems" (*UPUC*, 126–27). Eliot seems here to seize on Richards's mentioning "religion" alongside "sex" to deflect his comment rather than answering it directly. It is too bad that Eliot passed over the opportunity to explain more fully his almost obsessive return in his work to Canto XXVI of the *Purgatorio*.

4. Pound's Financial Scheme for Eliot: "Bel Esprit"

Pound hinted in a letter of March 14, 1922, at "a larger scheme" to get Eliot out of his bank to allow him to devote himself wholly to writing. "Bel Esprit" was the scheme Pound had in mind and wrote about in the *New Age* on March 30 (*LTSE1*, 512–14). Pound wrote urgently to William Carlos Williams on March 18 "that Eliot is at the last gasp. . . . I have been on the job, am dead tired with hammering this machine." He enclosed a carbon outline of the scheme to free Eliot from the "darkness and confusion" of the present age in order to save civilization. The circular sent to subscribers read: "In order that T. S. Eliot may leave his work in Lloyds Bank and devote his whole time to literature, we are raising a fund, to be £300 annually . . . message £10, Fifty dollars . . . payable yearly by 30 subscribers." Pound, Richard Aldington, and May Sinclair were the founding members of this communal plan to support "better literature, not more literature, better art, not more art" (Pound, *L*, 172–75). When Eliot returned from his holiday in Italy he reported to Aldington on June 30 that he had stopped in Verona to see Ezra, who told him further details: Pound would concentrate on France, there were "two or three women in New York" as well as Quinn, and Aldington, Lewis, Schiff would work England, "so that people in each country could keep their own methods." Eliot was appreciative but skeptical, finding the plan "embarrassing and fatiguing," and the method "bordering on the precarious and slightly undignified charity" (*LTSE1*, 536). He preferred the security and independence afforded by the bank.

Eliot reacted to the circular in a letter to Pound on July 28, unhappy that the bank was mentioned and concerned that word would get out, "especially in America, to the effect that I have a family which *should* be providing for my support." He added a postscript: "If this Circular has not gone out, will you please delete Lloyds Bank, to the mention of which I *strongly object*. If it is stated so positively that Lloyds Bank interfered with literature, Lloyds Bank would have a perfect right to infer that literature interfered with Lloyds Bank. *Please see my position*—I cannot jeopardize my position at the Bank before I know what is best. They would certainly object if they saw this. If this business has any more publicity I shall be forced to make a public repudiation of it and refuse to have anything more to do with it" (552–53).

At the beginning of November, Vivien wrote a "PRIVATE" letter to Pound, concerned over the ongoing negotiations with Lady Rothermere and the *Criterion*, wondering if he could "get for T. this money (Bel Esp.) . . . without the condition that he leave the bank *immediately*." Vivien was hoping that Eliot could buy the *Criterion* and she was willing to "provide £500 (it would halve my income) . . . gladly" (588). Eliot showed a similar concern for Vivien in his letter to Pound on November 15. He compared the relationship between Pound and his wife Dorothy (her good health and family financial resources), to that between Eliot and his wife Vivien, whose family resources (encumbered real estate) were a drag, and as for her health—

"she will *never* be strong enough to earn her own living." And Eliot added: "I am responsible toward her in more than the ordinary way. I have made a great many mistakes, which are largely the cause of her present catastrophic state of health, and also it must be remembered that she kept me from returning to America where I should have become a professor and probably never written another line of poetry, so that in that respect she should be endowed. . . . In the bank, I am assured £500 a year and perhaps more, and in case of death a widow's pension increasing according to the size of the salary." Eliot's conclusion was clearly supported by his personal revelations: "I will leave the bank as soon as I have such guarantees—for my life *or for Vivien's life*—as would satisfy a solicitor" (597–98).

By this time the circle of concerned people had widened. In September Virginia Woolf wrote to Eliot saying that Ottoline Morrell had asked her to join "Mr. Aldington's Committee for what they call the Eliot Fellowship Fund" and wanted to verify the details with him. She then wrote Ottoline that Tom told her he needed £500 a year, anything less would "throw him into journalism, and he prefers the Bank." Tom confided to her that the whole matter had become "so very difficult" that it has been "an incessant strain." Virginia thought Tom was responsible for the "muddle . . . if only he would have swallowed his shyness at the beginning, something might have been done" (Woolf, *L2*, 560–61, 564).

Eliot's situation was made even more difficult when he came across a news item about himself that shocked him. He shared it with Aldington, pledging him to secrecy until he had seen his solicitor. It appeared in the *Liverpool Post*, November 16, 1922. The story began with an account of the author of *The Waste Land* and "Mr. Prufrock," who was to be the "first beneficiary under a unique scheme through which a co-operation of English, French, and American enthusiasts, known as 'Bel Esprit,' pledged themselves to give fifty dollars per year for life or as long as the author needs it. . . . Until quite recently Mr. Eliot was earning his livelihood in a London bank. Attempts had previously been made by his admirers to persuade him to give himself up to literature." What followed was false—and perhaps libelous: "Actually, as the amusing tale went at the time, the sum of £800 was collected and presented to Mr. Eliot there and then. The joke was that he accepted the gift calmly, and replied: 'Thank you all very much; I shall make good use of the money, but I like the bank!' That was two years ago, and he held out until last spring, when he suffered a nervous breakdown which necessitated a three-months' leave of absence. Thereupon the society of 'Bel Esprit' was hatched in secret and carried through, the poet's own wishes not being consulted. The poem in *The Criterion* is the initial result" (*LTSE1*, 599).

Eliot was incensed, and he wrote to Pound that he suspected Aldington of planting the story. It appears that these suspicions were unfounded, and Eliot later wrote to Aldington that he knew he was innocent in the matter. He wrote also to the *Liverpool Post* pointing out that the story about him was false: "No such collection or presentation as that mentioned ever took place, and I never made the statement attributed to me. I have not received £800 or any part of such sum, nor have I received any sum from 'Bel Esprit,' nor have I left the bank. . . . Finally the appearance of my poem in the *Criterion* is not the result of any scheme whatever." Eliot concluded his letter with an implied threat: "I trust that you will take immediate steps to put this matter right" (600, 602–3).

Although the *Liverpool Post* printed an apology, confessing that the news story had "no foundation," and paid some reparation, Eliot remained bitter about the matter, writing to Virginia Woolf on December 4 about the whole affair, and remarking: "I do not consider that the reparation offered by the *Liverpool Post* is at all adequate considering the grossness of the accusation" (606). While dealing with these troublesome matters, Eliot found himself the recipient, as he wrote to his brother, of "an anonymous insulting letter offering me sixpence for the collection which the writer had heard was being taken up for me" (609). With all these derailments and the accompanying negative publicity, the Bel Esprit enterprise lost its momentum and quietly expired.

5. Birth of *The Criterion*

October 1922 marked an auspicious event in Eliot's life. Not only was *The Waste Land* published, it appeared in the first issue of the *Criterion*. Eliot took over the job of editing the new magazine without giving up his full-time job at the bank—thus devoting his time on evenings and weekends to requesting and reading manuscripts and putting together issues. Vivien's letter to Schiff tells the story: "I am glad . . . that you like *The Criterion*. It seems to me an achievement, by a man who has only his evenings, tired out by eight hours in the City, and who fills hot water bottles, and makes invalid food for his wretchedly unhealthy wife, in between writing" (*LTSE1*, 584). The birth of the *Criterion* is linked to the death of another little magazine, *Art and Letters*, in which Eliot had published both prose and poems ("Burbank with a Baedeker: Bleistein with a Cigar" and "Sweeney Erect"). *Art and Letters* came into existence in July 1917 and died in the spring of 1920; one of the financial backers was Eliot's friend, Sydney Schiff. Less than a year later, Eliot found himself one of several literary people trying to resuscitate the journal. In a letter of July 14, 1921, Eliot wrote to Ottoline Morrell: "There has been a project for the revival of *Art and Letters,* or rather as it now appears, a quarterly of similar size under a new name. It has undergone various transformations and passed through various hands since it was first broached to me—Schiff has taken part in it, but the person to provide the money is Lady Rothermere" (461).

Lady Rothermere was the wife of the first Viscount Rothermere, owner of *The Daily Mail, The Sunday Dispatch,* and *The Evening News.* According to the editor of *The Letters of T. S. Eliot,* it was through "Thayer, whom she met in New York, that she founded *The Criterion* with TSE." Eliot had come to know her through the independent publisher Richard Cobden-Sanderson— who was, incidentally, Bertrand Russell's godfather. Cobden-Sanderson came from a distinguished family and was interested only in publishing distinguished works of literary importance. (In 1919 he was prepared to publish a collection of Eliot's essays on Renaissance literature, which never got pulled together [331].) Eliot confided to Ottoline his doubts about taking on such a demanding enterprise as the editing of a new literary journal, but he felt that "once started, one feels [it] could be made something of, in time, and would be an interesting attempt just now when there is *nothing* in London. But I cannot tell you how very exhausting and difficult the business has been" (461).

By the beginning of September 1921, Eliot found himself in the middle of making estimates about the cost of publishing a little magazine, but his breakdown and stay at Margate and Lausanne intervened. Vivien informed Thayer in October of Eliot's breakdown and brought him up to date on the proposed journal: "T. and Lady Rothermere have clicked. A Quarterly has been arranged between them, which Tom was to edit in his 'spare' time, and to get what pickings he could from the inadequate sum laid down by her in the name of Literature. Everything is now postponed until January" (478).

Some time between Eliot's return to London in mid-January and early March 1922, he and Richard Cobden-Sanderson met with Lady Rothermere and worked out a series of agreements, revealed in a letter to Ezra Pound, March 12: "She will finance it for three years anyhow, there is enough money to pay contributors at £10 per 5000 words and proportionately (should be 80 pages) and I don't see why it shouldn't be tried and the right people as far as possible (i.e., as far as they can be enlisted) get the money regardless of consequences. Lady R. is a particular admirer of yours and especially anxious for your collaboration, as of course I also consider it an essential condition. Also, my credit with her would suffer seriously if you did not." At this point Eliot made a list of what he would like to receive from Pound: "1. A Paris letter every quarter as per *Dial*, say 1500 words. / 2. Of course cantos etc. except that I suppose you would get more by putting them in the *Dial*, but I shall hope to arrange much higher rates for verse. / 3. Sending over contributions by the best people." Lady Rothermere apparently made it clear that "selection of contributions" would be put entirely in Eliot's hands. And he would have a free hand in making up "special numbers devoted to the work of one man each." Eliot concluded: "Please consider that this venture is impossible without your collaboration, and let me hear from you as soon as possible" (507–8). Almost immediately (March 14) Pound sent his long, harsh reply, denouncing all things "English." Pound was by no means unconcerned, for he was about to launch his Bel Esprit scheme to come to Eliot's rescue at this time. But Pound's list of "minimum conditions" for collaborating were so absurd that they could never be met or, for that matter, ever presented by Eliot to Lady Rothermere (511–13).

Eliot was not deterred from sending out many letters to potential contributors—not only in England but throughout Europe. The German scholar Ernst Robert Curtius recalled that in the summer of 1922 he received a letter "out of the blue" from the unknown T. S. Eliot, proposing that he should contribute to the *Criterion* (Curtius, 119). When Eliot wrote on July 21 thanking Curtius for his promised article, he gave the aims of the review: "to raise the standard of thought and writing in this country by both international and historical comparison. Among English writers I am combining those of the older generation who have any vitality . . . with the more serious of the younger generation, no matter how advanced, for instance Mr. Wyndham Lewis and Mr. Ezra Pound." A week later he wrote more conspiratorially to Pound, saying that he did not want "to concentrate the jailbirds too much at the beginning and I think that if the *Waste Land* bursts out in the first number and you contribute to the second, that Lewis must remain behind the scenes until the third" (550–53). As planned, Pound appeared with "Criticism in General" in the second issue, January 1923. Two chapters of Lewis's *Apes of God* were published in the February and April 1924 *Criterion*. From the start, Eliot had "the new" in mind, in addition to contributors with an international flavor.

To F. S. Flint, whom Aldington had recommended as a contributor, Eliot announced the new review on July 13, and wrote: "I am intending to include a larger proportion of foreign writers," and mentioned his hope to include translations done by "men of letters." As payments were "low—£10 per 5000 words," he could only offer "the usual rate of 15 /—per 1000 words to translaters." He had on hand essays by Ramón Gómez de la Serna, in Spanish, and

Hermann Hesse, in German, both having "the additional interest of being quite unknown in this country." On the same day he wrote to Aldington, asking him to translate the Ulysses section of Valery Larbaud's lecture on Joyce. (Eliot would eventually have to translate it himself "at the last moment," "under great pressure" [578].) He hoped that the *Criterion's* first installment would appear on the first or the fifteenth of October, so that Aldington could arrange publication in America after the middle of October. He confessed that "the stakes" were "serious": "there will be a great many jackals swarming about waiting for my bones. If this falls flat I shall not only have gained nothing but will have lost immensely in prestige and usefulness and shall have to retire to obscurity or Paris like Ezra" (541–43). For Eliot, London was all; Paris, the magnet for so many writers at this time, was linked with "obscurity" and certainly not for Eliot, now on the brink of launching his own review.

Besides Aldington's help, Eliot relied on Vivien, despite the state of her health, which she detailed in a long letter to Pound on June 27. The last doctor had affirmed that she had "colitis" and gave her "some glands to take called Ovarian Opocaps," telling her "this was 'a shot in the dark.'" Eliot added: "Vivien has shown me this letter and I think it is *quite inadequate* as a description of her case, but she is *very* ill and exhausted and I do not think she can do any better now" (532–33). As we have earlier noted, Vivien helped get the *Criterion* off the ground with her secretarial work, and she would also publish her stories there in 1923–24. She also named the review. Pound had coincidentally suggested the same title two days after Vivien's suggestion was accepted, and this, for Eliot, was "a most auspicious confirmation" (538, 544).

Like Vivien, Eliot labored in the face of recurring physical illnesses, as well as mental pressures. His letter of September 21 to Quinn provides us with an account of the *Criterion,* its place with respect to the *Dial* and the *Little Review,* and the fact that he was "not taking a penny from it except a fee for my poem." He also provided a glimpse into the "old symptoms ready to appear" whenever he got tired or worried. Then he found himself "under the continuous strain of trying to suppress a vague but intensely acute horror and apprehension" (573).

Volume 1, No. 1 of the *Criterion* appeared in October 1922. The cover (reproduced in LTSE1, 583) announced an extraordinarily distinguished group of contributors and works: George Saintsbury, "Dullness"; F. M. Dostoëvski, "Plan of a Novel," translated by S. S. Koteliansky and Virginia Woolf; T. Sturge Moore, "The Legend of Tristram and Isolt, I"; T. S. Eliot, "The Waste Land"; May Sinclair, "The Victim"; Hermann Hesse, "German Poetry of Today"; Valery Larbaud, "Ulysses." This table of contents is not the first time, nor the last, that Eliot and Joyce, *The Waste Land* and *Ulysses,* would be linked—a linkage that has survived to this day.

The "*Criterion* is a SUCCESS," wrote Eliot to Pound: "Nearly all the copies are sold (600 printed)." Just as the "*Times Lit Supp*" topped the list of places to advertise in Eliot's letter of September 28, so it came into focus again on November 8, when Eliot asked Aldington, "Who wrote the extremely amiable and, as *I* thought, intelligent notice in the *Times*?" It was Harold Hannyngton Child, English author, who said of *The Waste Land:* "We know of no other modern poet who can more adequately and movingly reveal to us the inextricable tangle of the sordid and the beautiful that make up life" (589, 575, 595). And of the review: "If we are to judge by its first number, *The Criterion* is not only that rare thing amongst English periodicals, a purely literary review, but it is of a quality not inferior to that of any review published either here or abroad" (quoted in Grant, 134).

Eliot's "editorship of those eighteen volumes is as much a part of his literary career as any of his volumes of poetry, drama, or criticism," as John Margolis notes in his study of Eliot's role as editor of the *Criterion* in *T. S. Eliot's Intellectual Development: 1922–1939.* "In his determination of the journal's contents, his own contribution of articles and reviews, and especially his publication of regular 'Commentaries,' Eliot provided an index to his involving concerns." Margolis points out that not until January 1927 did Eliot's name appear as editor on the cover of the *Criterion.* This anonymity was explained by Eliot in a letter to Edmund Wilson (January 11, 1923): "The reason is that I already occupy one 'official' position—in a bank; and it is inconsistent with the obligations of that position to occupy any other and the continued or conspicuous publication of my name in that capacity might be troublesome for me. My conscience is quite clear, because the one work does not interfere with the other" (quoted in Margolis, 33–35).

Lady Rothermere withdrew her support in 1925, the year Eliot left the bank to become a "director" of the publisher Faber & Gwyer. Eliot's new position brought support not only for him but also for the *Criterion.* Faber & Gwyer sponsored it starting in 1926 under its various names—the *New Criterion* (1926), the *Monthly Criterion* (1927), and then once again the *Criterion.* Eliot continued as editor until the outbreak of World War II in 1939.

Eliot would in later years look back on 1922 as the year that was for him a turning point. Indeed, in 1956, he gave a backward glance over his career and observed that 1922 brought to conclusion the opening chapter of his life and prepared for other chapters to come. In a tribute to Ernst Robert Curtius, the German critic and scholar who had appeared in the early pages of the *Criterion* and who later translated *The Waste Land* into German and, by his criticism, assured that it would be widely read in Germany, Eliot wrote for Curtius's Festschrift: "I count [Curtius] . . . among my old friends. In one sense, it is as if I had always known him, for the beginning of our acquaintance coincides, very nearly, with what seems to me my adult life: the period of my life which is marked by *The Waste Land,* and the foundation of *The Criterion,* and the development of relations with men of letters in the several countries of Europe" (BUERC, 25–27). And so Eliot's "adult life" began.

[14]

A Glance Ahead
THE MAKING OF AN AMERICAN POET

On New Year's Eve, 1922, Eliot wrote to his brother about his "problem of living a double or triple life," and his hope that a successful *Criterion* would provide "a partial way out" (*LTSE1*, 617). The *Criterion* did prove success-ful and Eliot's position at Faber and Faber did ease his financial burden, but in some sense Eliot would continue to lead multiple lives. To follow Eliot into what he called the beginning of his "adult life" and beyond would be to explore certain significant events and people across the decades. Those years are beyond the scope of this book; however, we might list some of the markers. Eliot's editorship of the influential *Criterion* would end in 1939, but in his role as editor at Faber and Faber, as Ackroyd has observed, "through his publication and support of certain judiciously chosen poets, he determined the shape of English poetry from the Thirties into the Sixties." His new poets included W. H. Auden, Stephen Spender, and, later, Ted Hughes and Thom Gunn (Ackroyd, 182–83). The year 1927 saw his baptism and confirmation into the Church of England and his embrace of English citizenship.

He lectured throughout his life, most memorably in 1932–33, giving the Charles Eliot Norton Lectures at Harvard and the Page-Barbour Lectures at the University of Virginia, notable for Eliot's reconnection with America and final separation from Vivien. The 1930s also brought important publications, including "Ash-Wednesday," *Selected Essays,* the verse dramas, *The Rock, Mur-der in the Cathedral, The Family Reunion,* and the *Collected Poems 1909–1935,* with the first appearance of "Burnt Norton." The 1940s brought "East Coker,"

"The Dry Salvages," "Little Gidding"—bringing to completion Eliot's other long poem, *Four Quartets,* his last serious poetic work. With Helen Gardner's publication of the manuscript of the *Quartets,* we now know that Eliot consulted with his friend John Hayward, who played a role similar to Pound's role with *The Waste Land.* Hayward, a cultivated man with a passionate interest in languages and literature, suffered from muscular dystrophy and was confined to a wheelchair at the time Eliot moved in with him in 1946. A year later Eliot would learn of Vivien's death. Hayward and Eliot's domestic arrangement came to an abrupt end in January 1957, when Eliot married his secretary, Valerie Fletcher. His second marriage brought him great happiness.

He was to be honored with both the Order of Merit and the Nobel Prize for Literature in 1948, a year when fifty thousand copies of his *Selected Poems* were published, as well as his *Notes Towards the Definition of Culture. The Complete Poems and Plays* in 1952 and *Collected Poems 1909–1962* gathered the work of his life. On September 14, 1964, at the American embassy in London, an ailing Eliot accepted the Presidential Medal of Freedom, America's highest civilian award: "Poet and critic, he has fused intelligence and imagination, tradition and innovation, bringing to the world a new sense of the possibilities in a revolutionary time." Eliot died on January 4, 1965. In 1967 his plaque was placed in the Poet's Corner, Westminster Abbey.

In looking ahead to the many years that Eliot lived after the publication of *The Waste Land* in 1922, we can trace the evolution of his views on several important subjects, two of which will be explored here. The first is his astonishing reversal regarding the great nineteenth-century American poet who preceded him and whose shadow extended deeply into the twentieth century: Walt Whitman. And, related to this change, a radical shift transpired in Eliot's view of his nationality as a poet, as he came to the remarkable realization that he was, indeed, like Whitman, an American poet.

1. T. S. Eliot and Walt Whitman

Two poets, Whitman and Eliot: one the obverse of the other. Their most vital themes, sexuality and mysticism; Whitman arrived at the latter through exalted celebration of the former; Eliot arrived at the latter by suppression and rejection of the former.

Both Whitman and Eliot are great poets, one the joyful singer of nineteenth-century hope, the other the doleful purveyor of twentieth-century despair. Readers who respond to one have often felt the necessity of condemning the other. But there are readers—myself among them—who respond to both these poets and see them not as mutually exclusive, but in the best American sense complementary. Hope and despair are integral and necessary parts of human experience; Whitman and Eliot provide us, through their most compelling lines and passages, ways of comprehending life's highs and lows, exhilarations and depressions. And together their individual talents are part of a great American poetic tradition.

Eliot has a place in my book, *The American Quest for a Supreme Fiction: Whitman's Legacy in the Personal Epic* (1979), where I argue that *The Waste Land* is part of the American tradition of the "personal epic," growing out of *Leaves of Grass.* The following discussion is drawn from the chapter entitled "Personal Mood Transmuted into Epic: T. S. Eliot's *Waste Land.*" Echoes of Whitman sound throughout Eliot's poetry and have been discussed in Sydney Musgrove's important early study, *T. S. Eliot and Walt Whitman* (1952). Both poets in their two long poems share a common purpose: to express an age through expression of self. Of course, if we take Eliot at his word in "Tradition and the Individual Talent," he would have none of any "expression of self" (*SE*, 7). Few today would deny the personal dimension of Eliot's poetry now that scholarship has caught up with what was always there in the manuscripts and with Eliot's own critical comments later in life. We may fully envision Eliot as bent on "expression of self" in his most famous poem, as we might also envision Whitman finding his "objective correlative" in such "personal" poems as "Song of Myself" or "When Lilacs Last in the Dooryard Bloom'd."

Eliot's earliest comments on Whitman might well give pause to anyone seeking a link between the two. In fact, Eliot's references to Whitman are such as to raise questions of deeper connections than those admitted. In his introduction to the 1928 edition of Ezra Pound's *Selected Poems,* Eliot wrote: "I did not read Whitman until much later [than 1908, 1909] in life and had to conquer an aversion to his form as well as to much of his matter, in order to do so" (IEPSP, viii–ix). Eliot's insistence that Whitman could not have influenced Pound is strange, especially in view of Pound's own admission in his 1909 essay, not published until 1955, on Whitman of just such an influence: "Mentally I am a Walt Whitman who has learned to wear a collar" (Pound, *SP*, 145). In "Ezra Pound: His Metric and Poetry" (1917), Eliot wrote: "Whitman is certainly not an influence; there is not a trace of him anywhere; Whitman and Mr. Pound are antipodean to each other" (*TCTC*, 177).

"Not a trace"—the kind of extreme statement to inspire a contrary critic to find a trace—the kind of statement that, by the very nature of its flamboyance, calls itself into question. Indeed, some critics have found several traces of Whitman in Pound, as, for example, Donald Davie in his 1964 work,

Ezra Pound: Poet as Sculptor, referring to the early poetry: "The only poetic voice that [Pound] can command . . . is the voice of Whitman" (Davie, 82). In the 1928 introduction to Pound's *Selected Poems,* Eliot wrote: "I am . . . certain—it is indeed obvious—that Pound owes nothing to Whitman"; and: "Now Pound's originality is genuine in that his versification is a *logical* development of the verse of his English predecessors. Whitman's originality is both genuine and spurious. It is genuine in so far as it is a *logical* development of certain English prose; Whitman was a great prose writer. It is spurious in so far as Whitman wrote in a way that asserted that his great prose was a new form of verse. (And I am ignoring in this connection the large part of clap-trap in Whitman's content.)" (IEPSP, ix, xi). It is somewhat surprising to find Eliot here resurrecting a disreputable theory that Whitman's poetry was not really poetry, but prose instead. And the parting shot at Whitman's content as "clap-trap" betrays an intensity of feeling that the critical point seems hardly to call for. What in Whitman inspired such passionate response? There can be little doubt that it was his themes of democracy and equality that inspired Eliot to characterize Whitman's "content" as "clap-trap": Eliot, as we have seen, identified himself proudly as a "classicist in literature, royalist in politics, and anglo-catholic in religion" (FLA, 7).

By 1944, Eliot's views of Whitman had undergone a change. It was then that Donald Gallup, as a member of the U.S. Army, attended a lecture given by Eliot entitled "Walt Whitman and Modern Poetry." Gallup published the notes he took of the lecture for the first time in *The Southern Review* (1985) in "Mr. Eliot at the Churchill Club." There Eliot spoke of Whitman's "rare" kind of free verse, his "personal rhythm," whose poems "cannot be compressed without mutilation; nor can Whitman's verse be made more rhythmical as poetry. It is perfect, although at first it looks far from it. This singularity is very great and makes Whitman unique in the whole history of literature." In this 1944 lecture, Eliot also compared Whitman and Tennyson, calling Whitman the "greater poet" due to his "depth and universality." Eliot remarked on Whitman's closeness to Wordsworth in his "perception, of strange intensity, of a relationship between individuals by which he wanted society to be governed and which he spent his life communicating to others." This notion of society that Eliot perceived in Whitman was not to be "satisfactorily explained by any sexual peculiarity." Eliot was obliquely referring to Whitman's alleged homosexuality and then parenthetically said, "We do not explain what the eye sees by analyzing the structure of the eye." At this point Eliot stressed that he "shan't attempt to explain this . . . but it is essential to grasp this to understand the poet." Thus ended Gallup's notes of Eliot's formal remarks. (WWMP in Gallup, MECC, 98–99). In Eliot's two attempts at nonexplanation, he seems not to want to associate Whitman's sexuality with his verse, just as he had done earlier in his 1926 review of Emory Holloway's *Whitman: An Interpretation in Narrative.*

Holloway had raised the question of Whitman's ambivalent sexuality following his discovery that a "Children of Adam" poem addressed to a woman had been, in manuscript, originally addressed to a man. In his review, Eliot perhaps touched on the matter that made him so intense in his feeling about Whitman: "Whitman had the ordinary desires of the flesh; for him there was no chasm between the real and the ideal, such as opened before the horrified eyes of Baudelaire. But this, and the 'frankness' about sex for which he is either extolled or mildly reproved, did not spring from any particular honesty or clearness of vision: it sprang from what be called either 'idealization,' or a faculty for make-believe, according as we are disposed. There is, fundamentally, no difference between the Whitman frankness and the Tennyson delicacy, except in its relation to public opinion of the time" (W&T, 426).

This is a strange statement indeed in the context of the revelations of the Holloway book; and the attempt to equate the "Whitman frankness and the Tennyson delicacy" seems far-fetched; clearly Eliot saw himself closer to the Baudelaire "horror." In spite of its general negative thrust, his review of the Whitman biography concluded with a positive assessment, however backhanded: "Beneath all the declamations there is another tone, and behind all the illusions there is another vision. When Whitman speaks of the lilacs or of the mocking-bird, his theories and beliefs drop away like a needless pretext" (426). This last sentence has the passionate ring of one who has been deeply moved by Whitman's major poetry—perhaps even in spite of himself.

To go through Eliot's poetry tracking every echo of Whitman is a task for another book, but one of his poems is highly relevant to my purposes: "Ode on Independence Day, July 4th 1918." As noted earlier, I have discussed the "Ode" in my 1977 book, *T. S. Eliot's Personal Waste Land: Exorcism of the Demons,* but a few comments are in order here. Eliot published the poem in *Ara Vos Prec,* a 1920 limited edition, and never reprinted it. It was only printed again when it was included in Christopher Ricks's 1996 *T. S. Eliot's Inventions of the March Hare.* The second stanza appears intelligible only in a Whitmanian context:

> Misunderstood
> The accents of the now retired
> Profession of the calamus. (IOMH, 383)

Eliot's pervasive technique of literary allusion renders it inevitable that, on encountering the word "calamus," readers recall the major literary use of the word—in Whitman's *Leaves of Grass*. "Calamus" is Whitman's title for a cluster of poems devoted to comradeship, "adhesive" love, and man-man relationships, coming directly after, and in contrast to, "The Children of Adam" cluster of procreational, sexual, or man-woman relationships. There in a short poem are lines expressing intense sexual ecstasy: "O hymen! O hymenee! why do you tantalize me thus? / O why sting for a swift moment only? / Why can you not continue? why do you now cease? / Is it because if you continued beyond the swift moment you would soon certainly kill me?" (Whitman, CPSP, 81). These lines have only ironic meaning for the "tortured" bridegroom in Eliot's "Ode," where we find the lines "When the bridegroom smoothed his hair / There was blood upon the bed. / . . . / Children singing in the orchard / (Io Hymen, Hymenaee) / Succuba eviscerate." "Ode" was probably written in 1918, and Eliot published earlier, in 1917, *Prufrock and Other Observations,* a book containing "The Love Song of J. Alfred Prufrock" and "Portrait of a Lady"—poems portraying (among other things) men who cannot love women.

Another important echo of *Leaves* appears in a passage of *The Waste Land* that Eliot cited as his favorite—what he called the "30 good lines" of the poem, lines of "the water-dripping song" in Part v ("What the Thunder Said"). Among these lines appear the following:

> If there were the sound of water only
> Not the cicada
> And dry grass singing
> But sound of water over a rock
> Where the hermit-thrush sings in the pine trees
> Drip drop drip drop drop drop drop drop
> But there is no water
>
> (lines 353–59)

In view of Eliot's own appreciation of "When Lilacs Last in the Dooryard Bloom'd" (as in the comment above concluding his review of the Holloway biography), the Whitman connection here can be missed only at peril of misreading the meaning. The hermit thrush is an American bird, and Whitman made it his own in his Lincoln elegy. We might even take the "dry grass singing" as an oblique allusion to *Leaves of Grass,* where the grass image evoked is usually green, not dry. There is no "sound of water," there is no green grass growing, there is no hermit thrush singing in the pine trees.

What is missing, then, is not merely a set of sounds, but what the sounds vitally imply: and what they imply can be fully comprehended only in the context of Whitman's "Lilacs."

Whitman's hermit thrush becomes the source of his reconciliation to Lincoln's death, to all death as the "strong deliveress." The poet follows the bird to hear "Death's outlet song of life" as he goes "Down to the shores of the water, the path by the swamp in the dimness, / To the solemn shadowy cedars and ghostly pines so still." Lincoln is never mentioned by name in "Lilacs," but references to him are much in the "calamus" spirit—the poet mourns for his "comrade lustrous," for the dead he "loved so well." If we follow out all the implications of Eliot's evocation of Whitman's "Lilacs" at this critical moment in *The Waste Land* we might assume it has its origins, too, in a death, in a death deeply felt, the death of a beloved friend. But unlike the Whitman poem, Eliot's *Waste Land* has no retreat on the "shores of the water," no hermit thrush to sing its joyful carol of death; rather, only a "cock . . . on the rooftree" to sound mockingly its ambiguous "Co co rico co co rico."

In the history of American poetry, Walt Whitman and T. S. Eliot have often been presented as two possible polarities, two extremes: the personal and the impersonal; the optimistic and the pessimistic. Poets have taken one or the other as a model. But Pound was right when he made his "pact" with Walt Whitman. Nor could Eliot escape. He and Whitman have more in common than has often been thought—in the way they exploit poetically their emotional experience, and in the way they use themselves and their feelings as representative of their time and place. It seems unlikely that Eliot's long poem, in the form in which it was first conceived and written, would have been possible without the precedence of Whitman's own experiments in similar forms. In what he derived from Whitman consciously or unconsciously, and in the way he shaped the poems that came after him, T. S. Eliot must assume a prominent place in the succession of America's poets of the personal epic.

2. An American Poet Discovers His American-ness

"Hawthorne, Poe and Whitman are all pathetic creatures: they are none of them so great as they might have been" (AL, 237). So wrote Eliot in his unfavorable review of *A History of American Literature,* volume 2 of the American Supplement to *The Cambridge History of English Literature,* published in the *Athenaeum* in 1919. By 1953, Eliot's views about American literature had radically changed. That year he returned to the city of his birth, St.

Louis, Missouri, and spoke at the centenary celebration of the University founded by his grandfather in 1853. The University printed five hundred copies of Eliot's talk; the title page reads "American Literature and the American Language, An Address delivered at Washington University on June 9, 1953, with an Appendix 'The Eliot Family and St. Louis' prepared by the Department of English." "American Literature and the American Language" was not widely available until its inclusion in the 1965 volume, *To Criticize the Critic and Other Writings.*

In his address Eliot revealed his views about the language and literature of his country of origin more fully than in any other essay he wrote in his later years. And it disclosed at the end Eliot's answer to the question of whether he thought himself an American or English poet.

Stimulated by his surroundings, Eliot began the address with a brief reminiscence of his early years and concluded with an emphasis on place: "I am very well satisfied with having been born in St. Louis: in fact I think I was fortunate to have been born here, rather than in Boston, or New York, or London." He then turned to the subject of his address, whether there indeed existed an "American Literature" or an "American Language," explaining that the two were "related" and "must be distinguished" and that he did not want to lose his "reputation for affecting pedantic precision." Having disarmed his audience, this distant relative of Noah Webster told of having recently run across a new dictionary that the compilers called a dictionary of "the American Language." Eliot agreed that though there were "differences of spelling and pronunciation" between the languages used by America and England, these appeared to be minor. More important, he said, he discovered that this dictionary contained a number of words "which have not yet found their way into England." The words, he noted, "will either make their way over the Atlantic, or if not they no doubt disappear from the American dictionary." Eliot recalled that as a boy, he was "reproved" by his family for using the vulgar phrase "O.K." Then "O.K." seemed to disappear for a time but some twenty years later "swept like a tidal wave over England" (*ALAL*, 6, 9).

Against those, like Mencken, who seemed "to be issuing a kind of linguistic Declaration of Independence, an act of emancipation of American from English," Eliot told a charming story, based on a true occurrence, one that must have appealed to someone who had been given for his fourteenth birthday Chapman's *Handbook of Birds of Eastern North America* (Soldo, *TTSE*, 6). We might take it as a metaphor for Eliot's own migration. "For the first time, apparently, an American robin, well named *turdus migratorius,* crossed the Atlantic under its own power." He speculated "on the future of this pilgrim": either a mate would follow, thus populating England with "American robins"; or the "lone pioneer" would "breed with the English thrush, who is not *migratorius* but *musicus.*" Should the latter take place, the new species, being a "blend" of the two, "should become known as the troubadour-bird, or organ-grinder." With such an example as the American robin, asked Eliot, "what cannot the American language do?" He cautioned: "Unless you [Americans] yourselves draw a linguistic iron curtain (and I think Hollywood, to say nothing of *Time, Life, The New Yorker* and other periodicals, would object to that) you cannot keep the American Language out of England. However fast the American language moves, there will be always behind it the pattering of feet: the feet of the great British public eager for a new word or phrase." The flow of the English language to America had happened in the past, but the flow at the time he spoke was from west to east. He believed "that there will always be a movement in one direction or the other. So that, against the influences towards the development of separate languages, there will always be other influences tending towards fusion" (*ALAL*, 11–13).

Eliot turned next to his discussion of American literature, for he believed now in the existence of "two literatures in the same language": "Like many other terms, the term 'American literature' has altered and developed its meaning in the course of time. It means something different for us today from what it could have meant a hundred years ago" (13). Embarking on an impressive survey of the primary writers of American literature, Eliot observed that early American writers of the seventeenth and eighteenth centuries, including Jonathan Edwards, Washington Irving, and James Fenimore Cooper, would have been considered English writers in America. It is "only in retrospect that their Americanness is fully visible." And those of the nineteenth century (he lists Longfellow, Whittier, Bryant, Emerson, Thoreau, Robert Frost—"the last of the pure New Englanders"—and Nathaniel Hawthorne—"the greatest among them") would not have been considered American writers but New England writers.

Thus "the landmarks" Eliot chose to identify with American literature were Poe, Whitman, and Mark Twain. By his choice Eliot insists that he is not saying they are "necessarily greater"; nor that the three are "more American" than others; nor that American literature "*derives*" from them; nor that studying them would produce "a formula of Americanism in literature." Eliot is not concerned with "questions of influence." Poe and Whitman have had the greatest reputation abroad, "both in English speaking lands and in countries where they are known in translation." He anticipated objections to the inclusion of Poe since he had so little influence on any good poets in

America or England; whereas Whitman's influence was immense, if exaggerated. And he noted that Twain's influence may prove to be considerable for he had discovered "a new way of writing . . . one of those rare writers who have brought their language up to date, and in so doing, 'purified the dialect of the tribe.'" In this respect, Twain ranked above Hawthorne, not because he was a "finer" stylist or more "profound explorer of the human soul," but because Salem "could not be anywhere but where it is" and the "Mississippi of Mark Twain" is "the universal river of human life." Such powerful praise of *Huckleberry Finn*, similar to that he had given in his 1950 introduction to the book, brought Eliot to the two characteristics that must be found together in any author designated as a "landmark": "strong local flavor combined with unconscious universality" (14–17). Once again we must note Eliot's one extraordinarily puzzling omission: Herman Melville was never mentioned (nor is he referred to in other essays by Eliot). As for Emily Dickinson, Eliot's silence speaks volumes.

Eliot himself acknowledged the puzzle posed by Poe—"What is identifiably local about Poe?" He answered his question by saying that "his was a type of imagination that created its own dream world; that anyone's dream world is conditioned by the world in which he lives; and that the real world behind Poe's fancy was the world of the Baltimore and Richmond and Philadelphia that he knew" (18). Lee Oser, in *T. S. Eliot and American Poetry* (1998), suggests that Eliot's "unexpected" inclusion of Poe in the "landmarks" may have been suggested by Whitman's essay in *Specimen Days* (1882), entitled "Edgar Poe's Significance," which showed Poe as "a product of American culture." Just as Whitman "describes 'a close tally' between Poe and his American environment," listing the cities of "Baltimore, Richmond, Philadelphia and New York," so Eliot repeats Whitman's sequence, and, "like Whitman, connects Poe's singular achievement to his life in American cities" (Oser, 13–14).

Before a country can have its own "national" literature, Eliot suggested that there must have been "several generations of writers" behind the younger writers coming along. Eliot explained his meaning by citing his own experience: "Some of my strongest impulses to original development, in early years, has come from thinking: 'here is a man who has said something, long ago or in another language, which somehow corresponds to what I want to say now; let me see if I can't do what he has done, in my own language—in the language of my own place and time'" (*ALAL*, 19).

It is only rarely that there occurs a literary revolution—when it appears that "tradition has been flouted and that chaos has come. [But] after a time it appears that the new way of writing is not destructive but re-creative." And at this point Eliot came up to the twentieth century: "We might now consider such a revolution as that which has taken place in poetry, both in England and in America, during the last forty years" (20). Indeed, he had reached the point when his own development as a poet was taking place, and he spoke from personal experience. The first decade of the century provided not one poet "at the height of his powers" whose work could point the way to a young poet in search of "a new idiom" (21). Yeats emerged as a great modern poet in 1917, and thus was considered "not as a precursor but as an elder and venerated contemporary." Eliot's changing appreciation for Yeats has been deftly summarized by A. Walton Litz in his introduction and afterword of T. S. Eliot's Dublin lecture, "provisionally" entitled "Tradition and the Practice of Poetry," given in 1936 and first published in 1985. There Litz notes that Eliot's "*rapprochement* with Yeats . . . had to wait upon his own *rapprochement* with the American inheritance and the American scene that took place during and after his visit to the United States in 1932–3." According to Litz, Eliot's writings of this time displayed "a new sense of landscape and regional identity," thus enabling him to see Yeats in a new way (Litz, I&A, 22). In Chapter 1, Section 4, we have discussed Eliot's use of landscape in his poetry, his urban St. Louis imagery, and his New England coastal imagery.

"The starting point of modern poetry," Eliot continued in his 1953 address, "is the group denominated 'imagists' in London about 1910. I was not there. It was an Anglo-American group: literary history has not settled the question, and perhaps never will, whether imagism itself, or the name for it, was invented by the American Ezra Pound or the Englishman T. E. Hulme. The poets in the group seem to have been drawn together by a common attraction towards modern poetry in French, and a common interest in exploring the possibilities of development through study of the poetry of other ages and languages. . . . I think it is just to say that the pioneers of twentieth-century poetry were more conspicuously the Americans than the English, both in number and in quality" (ALAL, 21–22).

It should be no surprise that in this talk Eliot had worked his way up to himself and his associates, especially Ezra Pound, as the leaders of this modern movement. As for the difference between American and English poetry in this movement, he said: "So far as my observation goes, I should say in general, of contemporary verse, that the most dangerous tendency of American versifiers is towards eccentricity and formlessness, whereas that of English versifiers is rather towards conventionality and reversion to the Victorian type." As for the Americans, Eliot set forth an impressive list of his "own generation," including Ezra Pound, W. C. Williams, Wallace Stevens, and Marianne Moore, and "of a somewhat younger generation"—Cummings, Hart Crane, Ransom, Tate. Whereas "Poe and Whitman stand out as solitary international figures" in the nineteenth century, Eliot remarked, "In the last forty years, for the first time, there has been assembled a *body* of American poetry which has made its total impression in England and Europe."

Eliot's conclusion: although there cannot be said to exist two languages, American and English, there have emerged, in the early twentieth century, two literatures. And just as language moved in both directions, each influencing the other, so there have been influences in both directions, to the mutual benefit of literature on both sides of the Atlantic. But English and American poetry do not merge (AL, 23–24).

Eliot's remarks in the 1936 Dublin lecture speak to the point here: "The American writing in English does not write English poetry." Eliot isolates "the different rhythm in the blood," making the rhythms of the American poet "different from those of any English poet you can think of, but you cannot distinguish between what is personal and what he shares with other American poets." Speaking of "Poe and Whitman and the poets of our own time," Eliot noted that "two or three sensitive critics" assured him that "it is clearly present in my own work" (TPP, 17). Eliot, in 1936, was aligning himself with the "blood rhythms" of his fellow American poet, Walt Whitman.

At the end of his St. Louis address, Eliot introduced some remarks about the prominent British poet W. H. Auden (1907–73), whose career was much like Eliot's, but in reverse: as Eliot left America for England, Auden left England for America. Eliot wrote: "I do not know whether Auden is to be considered an English or an American poet: his career has been useful to me in providing me with an answer to the same question when asked about myself, for I can say: 'whichever Auden is, I suppose I must be the other'" (*ALAL*, 23). Eliot would turn to this comparison with Auden again in 1960 in dealing with the question of whether he was, "qua poet, American or English," treating it in a lighthearted way (ILUP, 421). But despite living in America and becoming an American citizen, Auden was and continued to be an English poet, and Eliot, despite living in England and becoming a British citizen, was and continued to be an American poet. Auden, for his part, was to comment that no European would have said, with Eliot: "Tradition cannot be inherited, and if you want it you must obtain it by great labor" (Auden, 366). Pound put it this way in one of his many comments on identity in *National Culture: A Manifesto 1938:* "It can't be said that an alteration on Mr. Eliot's passport has altered the essential Americanness of his work" (Pound, SP, 163). Indeed, in a 1959 interview Eliot was asked whether he considered his poetry as belonging in "the tradition of American literature." He replied: "I'd say that my poetry has obviously more in common with my distinguished contemporaries in America than with anything written in my generation in England. That I'm sure of. . . . In its sources, in its emotional springs, it comes from America" (INT, 110).

This book has been an exploration of Eliot's American "sources," his "emotional springs," and thus I have called my book *T. S. Eliot: The Making of an American Poet*—confident that he would endorse such a title.

[references to works by t.s. eliot]

ACHM   "A Commentary [a review of Henri Massis's *Evocations*]." *Criterion* 13, no. 52 (April 1934): 451–54.

ACIB   "A Commentary [on the death of Irving Babbitt]." *Criterion* 13, no. 50 (October 1933): 115–20.

ACTEH   "A Commentary [on T. E. Hulme, signed Crites]." *Criterion* 2, no. 7 (1924): 231–35.

AL   "American Literature." Review of *A History of American Literature,* vol. 2, ed. William P. Trent et al. *Athenaeum* 4643 (April 25, 1919): 236–37.

ALAL   *American Literature and the American Language: An Address Delivered at Washington University on June 9, 1953.* With appendix, "The Eliot Family and St. Louis" (pp. 25–46). New Series, *Language and Literature,* no. 23. Prepared by the Department of English, Washington University, St. Louis, 1953 (pp. 3–24; reprinted in *TCTC,* 43–60).

ASG   *After Strange Gods: A Primer of Modern Heresy.* The Page-Barbour Lectures, University of Virginia, 1933. New York: Harcourt Brace, 1934; London: Faber and Faber, 1934.

B&B   "Beyle and Balzac." Review of *A History of the French Novel, to the Close of the Nineteenth Century,* by George Saintsbury. *Athenaeum* 4648 (May 30, 1919): 392–93.

BUERC   "Brief über Ernst Robert Curtius." [In English, addressed to Dr. Max Rychner]. In *Freundesgabe für Ernst Robert Curtius zum 14 April 1956* [Festschrift for Ernst Robert Curtius], 25–27. Berne: Francke, 1956.

CPP   *The Complete Poems and Plays, 1909–1950.* New York: Harcourt Brace, 1950.

Dante   *Dante.* London: Faber and Faber, 1929.

DIOT   "Donne in Our Time." In *A Garland for John Donne: 1631–1931,* ed. Theodore Spencer, 1–19. Cambridge, Mass.: Harvard University Press, 1931; reprint, Gloucester, Mass.: Peter Smith, 1958.

E&A   "Eeldrop and Appleplex." In *The Little Review Anthology,* ed. Margaret Anderson, 102–9. New York: Hermitage House, 1953. Reprinted from *Little Review* 4, nos. 1 and 5 (May and September 1917): 7–11, 16–19.

EOT   "The Education of Taste." Review of *English Literature During the Last Half-Century,* by J. W. Cunliffe. *Athenaeum* 4652 (June 27, 1919): 520–21.

EP   "Ezra Pound." With postscript. In *An Examination of Ezra Pound,* ed. Peter Russell, 25–36. New York: New Directions, 1950. Reprinted from *Poetry* 58, no. 6 (September 1946): 326–38.

EPMP   *Ezra Pound: His Metric and Poetry.* In TCTC, 162–82. Reprinted from anonymous booklet (New York: Alfred A. Knopf, 1917 [i.e., 1918]).

FLA   *For Lancelot Andrewes: Essays on Style and Order.* London: Faber & Gwyer, 1928.

HAHJ   "The Hawthorne Aspect [of Henry James]." *Little Review* 5, no. 4 (August 1918): 47–53.

IEPSP   "Introduction." In *Ezra Pound: Selected Poems,* ed. T. S. Eliot, vii–xxv. London: Faber & Gwyer, 1928.

IHF   "Introduction." In *The Adventures of Huckleberry Finn,* by Samuel L. Clemens [Mark Twain], vii–xvi. London: Cresset Press, 1950.

ILBC   "Introduction." In *Leisure, the Basis of Culture,* by Josef Pieper, trans. Alexander Dru, 11–17. London: Faber and Faber, 1952.

ILUP   "The Influence of Landscape upon the Poet." *Daedalus: Journal of the American Academy of Arts and Sciences. Proceedings* 89, no. 2 (Spring 1960): [420]–22.

IMHJ   "In Memory of Henry James." *Egoist* 5, no. 1 (January 1918): [1]–2. Reprinted as "In Memory," *Little Review* 5, no. 4 (August 1918): 44–47.

INT   "Interview." Conducted by Donald Hall. In *Writers at Work: The "Paris Review" Interviews,* introduced by Van Wyck Brooks. Second Series, 91–110. New York: Viking Press, 1963. Reprinted from *Paris Review* 21 (Spring/Summer 1959): [47]–70.

IOMH   *Inventions of the March Hare: Poems 1909–1917 by T. S. Eliot.* Ed. Christopher Ricks. London: Faber and Faber, 1996.

KEPB   *Knowledge and Experience in the Philosophy of F. H. Bradley.* London: Faber and Faber, 1964; New York: Farrar, Straus, 1964.

LTSE1   *The Letters of T. S. Eliot, Volume 1, 1898–1922.* Ed. Valerie Eliot. New York: Harcourt Brace Jovanovich, 1988.

NEO   "The New Elizabethans and the Old." Review of *The New Elizabethans: A First Selection of the Lives of Young Men Who Have Fallen in the Great War,* by E. B. Osborn. *Athenaeum* 4640 (April 4, 1919): 134–36.

NP   "New Philosophers." Review of *Elements of Constructive Philosophy,* by J. S. Mackenzie; *The Self and Nature,* by DeWitt H. Parker; and *Locke's Theory of Knowledge,* by James Gibson. *New Statesman* 11, no. 275 (July 13, 1918): 296–97.

OPP   *On Poetry and Poets.* London: Faber and Faber, 1957; New York: Farrar, Straus and Giroux, 1957; reprint, Noonday Press, 1961.

ORPC   "On a Recent Piece of Criticism." *Purpose: A Quarterly Magazine* 9, no. 2 (April–June 1938): 90–94.

PBOM   "Preface." In *Bubu of Montparnasse,* by Charles-Louis Philippe, trans. Laurence Vail, vii–xiv. Paris: Crosby Continental Editions, 1932.

POO   *Prufrock and Other Observations.* London: Egoist Ltd., 1917.

PPFB   "Publisher's Preface" [anonymous]. In *Fishermen of the Banks,* by James B. Connolly, vii–viii. London: Faber & Gwyer, 1928.

PTAW   "Preface." In *This American World,* by Edgar Ansel Mowrer, ix–xv. London: Faber & Gwyer, 1928.

PWEY   *Poems Written in Early Youth.* Compiled by John Hayward and privately printed with the author's permission in Stockholm, 1950; London: Faber and Faber, 1967; New York: Farrar, Straus and Giroux, 1967.

RCP   "Reflections on Contemporary Poetry [IV]." *Egoist* 6, no. 3 (July 1919): 39–40.

RI   "Revelation I by T. S. Eliot." In *Revelation,* by Gustaf Aulén, Karl Barth, T. S. Eliot, et al., ed. John Baillie and Hugh Martin, 1–39. London: Faber and Faber, 1937.

RK   "Rudyard Kipling." In *A Choice of Kipling's Verse,* ed. T. S. Eliot, 5–36. London: Faber and Faber, 1941. Reprinted in OPP, 265–94.

SE   *Selected Essays: New Edition.* New York: Harcourt Brace, 1950.

SP   *Selected Prose of T. S. Eliot: The Centenary Edition, 1888–1988.* Ed. Frank Kermode. New York: Farrar, Straus and Giroux, 1975.

SPMC   *A Sermon Preached in Magdalene College Chapel.* Cambridge: Cambridge University Press, 1948.

TCTC   *To Criticize the Critic and Other Writings.* London: Faber and Faber, 1965; New York: Farrar, Straus and Giroux, 1965.

TPP   "Tradition and the Practice of Poetry." Talk given in Dublin, January 1936, with introduction and afterword by A. Walton Litz. In *T. S. Eliot: Essays from "The Southern Review,"* ed. James Olney, 7–25. Oxford: Clarendon Press, 1988. Reprinted from *Southern Review* 21, no. 4 (Autumn 1985): 873–88.

UGRK   "The Unfading Genius of Rudyard Kipling." In *Kipling and the Critics,* ed. Elliot L. Gilbert, 118–23. New York: New York University Press, 1958. Reprinted from *Kipling Journal,* London, 26, no. 129 (March 1959): 9–12.

UOM   "Ulysses, Order, and Myth." Review of *Ulysses,* by James Joyce. *Dial* 75, no. 5 (November 1923): [480]–483.

UPUC   *The Use of Poetry and the Use of Criticism: Studies in the Relation of Criticism to Poetry in England.* Charles Eliot Norton Lectures, Harvard University, 1932–33. Cambridge, Mass.: Harvard University Press, 1933.

V&R   "Views and Reviews." *New English Weekly* 7, no. 8 (June 6, 1935): 151–52.

W&T   "Whitman and Tennyson." Review of *Whitman: An Interpretation in Narrative,* by Emory Holloway. *Nation & Athenaeum* 40, no. 11 (December 18, 1926): 426.

WDMM   "What Dante Means to Me." Talk given at the Italian Institute, London, July 4, 1950. In TCTC, 125–35. New York: Farrar, Straus and Giroux, 1965.

WFMY   "What France Means to You." *La France Libre,* London, vol. 8, no. 44 (June 15, 1944): [94]–95. In French.

WJOI   "William James on Immortality." Review of *Human Immortality: Two Supposed Objections to the Doctrine,* by William James. *New Statesman* 9, no. 231 (September 8, 1917): 547.

WLF   *The Waste Land: A Facsimile and Transcript of the Original Drafts.* Ed. Valerie Eliot. New York: Harcourt Brace Jovanovich, 1971.

WRIC   "Why Mr. Russell Is a Christian." Review of *Why I Am Not a Christian,* by Bertrand Russell. *Criterion* 6, no. 2 (August 1927): 177–79.

WWMP   "Walt Whitman and Modern Poetry." Unpublished lecture given in London, 1944, in "Mr. Eliot at the Churchill Club," by Donald Gallup. In *T. S. Eliot: Essays from "The Southern Review,"* ed. James Olney, 97–101. Oxford: Clarendon Press, 1988. Reprinted from *Southern Review* 21, no. 4 (Autumn 1985): 969–73.

Ackroyd
    Ackroyd, Peter. *T. S. Eliot*. London: Hamish Hamilton, 1984.
Adams
    Adams, J. Donald. *Copey of Harvard: A Biography of Charles Townsend Copeland*. Boston: Houghton Mifflin, 1960.
Aiken, KB
    Aiken, Conrad. "King Bolo and Others." In *T. S. Eliot: A Symposium,* ed. Richard March and Tambimuttu, 20–23. Chicago: Henry Regnery, 1949.
Aiken, U
    ———. *Ushant: An Essay.* New York: Duell, Sloan and Pearce, 1952; Boston: Little, Brown and Co., 1952.
Aiken, CJ
    ———. *The Clerk's Journal, Being the Diary of a Queer Man: An Undergraduate Poem, Together with a Brief Memoir of Harvard, Dean Briggs, and T. S. Eliot.* New York: Eakins Press, 1971.
Aiken, SL
    ———. *Selected Letters of Conrad Aiken.* Ed. Joseph Killorin. New Haven: Yale University Press, 1978.
Aldington, ACP
    Aldington, Richard. "A Critic of Poetry." Review of *The Sacred Wood. Poetry* 17 (March 1921): 345–48.
Aldington, LLS
    ———. *Life for Life's Sake: A Book of Reminiscences.* New York: Viking Press, 1941.
Aldrich
    Aldrich, Thomas Bailey. "A Persian Poet." *Atlantic Monthly* 41 (April 1878): 421–26.
Allen
    Allen, Gay Wilson. *Waldo Emerson: A Biography.* New York: Viking Press, 1981.
Anon., EFSL
    "The Eliot Family and St. Louis." Appendix to T. S. Eliot's *American Literature and the American Language,* 25–46. New Series, *Language and Literature,* no. 23. Prepared by the Department of English, Washington University, St. Louis, 1953.
Anon., OHP
    "Obituary of Harold Peters." *Harvard College Class of 1910, 35th Anniversary Report,* 183–84. Cambridge, Mass.: Harvard College, 1945.

Arberry

    Arberry, Arthur J. *Omar Khayyám: A New Version Based upon Recent Discoveries.* New Haven: Yale University Press, 1952.

Arrowsmith, s

    Arrowsmith, William, trans. *The Satyricon, Petronius.* New York: Mentor Books, The New American Library, 1960. First published by University of Michigan Press, 1959.

Arrowsmith, pp

    ———. "The Poem as Palimpsest: A Dialogue on Eliot's 'Sweeney Erect.'" *Southern Review* 17 (1981): 17–68.

Arrowsmith, el

    ———. "Eliot's Learning." *Literary Imagination* 2, no. 2 (2000): 153–70.

Asher, tsei

    Asher, Kenneth. *T. S. Eliot and Ideology.* Cambridge: Cambridge University Press, 1998.

Asher, tsecm

    ———. "T. S. Eliot and Charles Maurras." *ANQ* 11, no. 3 (Summer 1998): 20–29.

Auden

    Auden, W. H. "American Poetry." In *The Dyer's Hand and Other Essays,* 354–68. New York: Vintage Books, 1968.

Babbitt, lac

    Babbitt, Irving. *Literature and the American College: Essays in Defense of the Humanities.* Boston: Houghton Mifflin, 1908.

Babbitt, br

    ———. "Bergson and Rousseau." *The Nation* 95, no. 2472 (November 14, 1912): 452–55.

Beckson

    Beckson, Karl, ed. *Aesthetes and Decadents of the 1890s: An Anthology of British Poetry and Prose.* New York: Vintage Books, 1966.

Bell

    Bell, Clive. *Old Friends, Personal Recollections.* London: Chatto & Windus, 1956.

Benda

    Benda, Julien. *Belphégor.* New York: Payson and Clarke Ltd., 1918.

Benét

    Benét, William Rose, ed. *The Reader's Encyclopedia.* New York: Thomas Y. Crowell, 1948.

Benson

    Benson, A. C. *Edward Fitzgerald.* English Men of Letters Series. New York: The Macmillan Company, 1905.

Bergonzi

    Bergonzi, Bernard. *T. S. Eliot.* New York: Collier Books, 1972.

Bernstein

    David Bernstein. "The Story of Vaslav Nijinsky as a Source for T. S. Eliot's 'The Death of Saint Narcissus.'" *Hebrew University Studies in Literature* 4, no. 1 (Spring 1976): 71–104.

Blanshard, eim

    Blanshard, Brand. "Eliot in Memory." In *T. S. Eliot: Critical Assessments,* vol. 1, ed. Graham Clarke, 217–21. London: Christopher Helm, 1990. Reprinted from *Yale Review* 54, no. 4 (June 1965): 635–40.

Blanshard, EAO
————. "Eliot at Oxford." In *T. S. Eliot: Essays from "The Southern Review,"* ed. James Olney, 27–37. Oxford: Clarendon Press, 1988. Reprinted from *Southern Review* 21, no. 4 (Autumn 1985): 889–98.

Bowra
Bowra, C. M. *The Creative Experiment.* London: Macmillan, 1967.

Boyd
Boyd, S.J., John. "The Dry Salvages: Topography as Symbol." *Renascence* 20, no. 3 (1968): 119–33, 161.

BU
The Bṛhadāraṇyaka Upaniṣad. Trans. Swami Madhavananda. Calcutta: Advaita Ashrama, 1965.

Brinnin
Brinnin, John Malcolm. *Sextet: T. S. Eliot, Truman Capote & Others.* New York: Delacorte Press/Seymour Lawrence, 1981.

Brooks, Cleanth, TWLCM
Brooks, Cleanth. "*The Waste Land:* Critique of the Myth." In *Modern Poetry and the Tradition,* 136–72. New York: Oxford University Press, 1965. First published as "*The Waste Land:* An Analysis," *Southern Review* 3 (Summer 1937): 103–36.

Brooks, Cleanth, TWLPD
————. "*The Waste Land:* A Prophetic Document." *Yale Review* 78, no. 2 (September 1989): 318–32.

Brooks, Van Wyck, AA
Brooks, Van Wyck. *An Autobiography.* New York: E. P. Dutton, 1965.

Brooks, Van Wyck, TWOP
————. "The Wine of the Puritans." In *Van Wyck Brooks, the Early Years: A Selection of His Works, 1908–1925,* ed. Claire Sprague, 1–60. Boston: Northeastern University Press, 1993.

Browning
Browning, Robert. *Poems of Robert Browning.* Ed. Donald Smalley. Boston: Houghton Mifflin, 1956.

Bush, TSESCS
Bush, Ronald. *T. S. Eliot: A Study in Character and Style.* New York: Oxford University Press, 1984.

Bush, NHTSE
————. "Nathaniel Hawthorne and T. S. Eliot's American Connection." In *T. S. Eliot: Essays from "The Southern Review,"* ed. James Olney, 65–74. Oxford: Clarendon Press, 1988. Reprinted from *Southern Review* 21, no. 4 (Autumn 1985): 924–33.

Bush, TSEM
————. "T. S. Eliot and Modernism at the Present Time: A Provocation." In *T. S. Eliot: The Modernist in History,* ed. Ronald Bush, 191–204. Cambridge: Cambridge University Press, 1991.

Butler
Butler, Christopher. "The Search for Salvation." *Times Literary Supplement,* October 28, 1977, 1271–72.

Butscher
Butscher, Edward. *Conrad Aiken: Poet of White Horse Vale.* Athens: University of Georgia Press, 1988.

Carpenter
  Carpenter, Humphrey. *A Serious Character: The Life of Ezra Pound.* Boston: Houghton Mifflin, 1988.
Carrington
  Carrington, Dora. *Carrington: Letters and Extracts from Her Diaries.* With contributions by David Garnett and Noel Carrington. London: Jonathan Cape, 1970.
Catullus
  Catullus, Gaiuis Valerius. Poem #16. In *Latin Poetry,* trans. L. R. Lind. Boston: Houghton Mifflin, 1957.
Chauncey
  Chauncey, George. *Gay New York: Gender, Urban Culture, and the Making of the Gay Male World, 1890–1940.* New York: Basic Books, 1994.
Clark
  Clark, Ronald W. *The Life of Bertrand Russell.* New York: Alfred A. Knopf, 1974.
Cole
  Cole, Merrill, "Empire of the Closet." *Discourse: Theoretical Studies in Media and Culture* 19, no. 3 (Spring 1997): 67–91.
Comley
  Comley, Nancy R. "From Narcissus to Tiresias: T. S. Eliot's Use of Metamorphosis." *Modern Language Review* 74 (1979): 281–86.
Copeland and Rogers
  Copeland, Melvin, and Elliot Rogers. *The Saga of Cape Ann.* Freeport, Maine: Bond Wheelwright Co., 1960.
Corbière
  Corbière, Tristan. "La Rhapsodie foraine. . . ." In *The Centenary Corbière: Poems and Prose of Tristan Corbière,* trans. and with an introduction by Val Warner. Cheadle: Carcenet New Press, 1974.
Cowan
  Cowan, Laura, ed. *T. S. Eliot: Man and Poet,* vol. 1. Orono, Maine: National Poetry Foundation, University of Maine, 1990.
Cox and Hinchcliffe
  Cox, C. B., and Arnold P. Hinchcliffe, eds. *T. S. Eliot: The Waste Land.* Casebook Series. Nashville: Aurora Publishers, 1969.
Crawford
  Crawford, Robert. *The Savage and the City in the Work of T. S. Eliot.* Oxford: Clarendon Press, 1987.
Curtius
  Curtius, Ernst Robert. "T. S. Eliot and Germany." Trans. Richard March. In *T. S. Eliot: A Symposium,* ed. Richard March and Tambimuttu, 119–25. Chicago: Henry Regnery, 1949.
Dacus and Buel
  Dacus, J. A., and James W. Buel. *A Tour of St. Louis; or The Inside Life of a Great City.* St. Louis: Western Publishing, Jones & Griffity, 1878.
D'Ambrosio
  D'Ambrosio, Vinnie-Marie. *Eliot Possessed: T. S. Eliot and Fitzgerald's Rubáiyát.* New York: New York University Press, 1989.

Dante, *Inferno*
> Dante, Alighieri. *The Inferno of Dante Alighieri.* Trans. J. A. Carlyle. The Temple Classics Edition, used by TSE in college. London: J. M. Dent & Sons, 1900.

Dante, *Purgatorio*
> ———. *The Purgatorio of Dante Alighieri.* Trans. Thomas Okey. The Temple Classics Edition, used by TSE in college. London: J. M. Dent & Sons, 1901.

Dante, *Paradiso*
> ———. *The Paradiso of Dante Alighieri.* Trans. P. H. Wicksteed. The Temple Classics Edition, used by TSE in college. London: J. M. Dent & Sons, 1899.

Davie
> Davie, Donald. *Ezra Pound: Poet as Sculptor.* New York: Oxford University Press, 1964.

Day
> Day, F. Holland. *F. Holland Day: Suffering the Ideal.* Ed. with an introduction by James Crump. Santa Fe, N.M.: Twin Palms Publishers, 1995.

DAB
> *Dictionary of American Biography.* New York: Charles Scribner's Sons, 1943–1973.

Douglass
> Douglass, Paul. *Bergson, Eliot, and American Literature.* Lexington: University Press of Kentucky, 1986.

Doyle
> Doyle, Charles. *Richard Aldington: A Biography.* Carbondale: Southern Illinois University Press, 1989.

Drew
> Drew, Elizabeth. *T. S. Eliot: The Design of His Poetry.* New York: Charles Scribner's Sons, 1949.

Edel, *HJ*
> Edel, Leon. *Henry James: The Middle Years, 1882–1895.* Philadelphia: Lippincott, 1962.

Edel, *B*
> ———. *Bloomsbury: A House of Lions.* Philadelphia: Lippincott, 1979.

Egoist
> *Egoist* 5, no.1 (1918): 1–16. Special Issue, *Henry James.*

Eliot, Charlotte, *WGE*
> Eliot, Charlotte Champe. [mother]. *William Greenleaf Eliot: Minister, Educator, Philanthropist.* Boston: Houghton Mifflin, 1904.

Eliot, Charlotte, *S*
> ———. *Savonarola: A Dramatic Poem.* With an introduction by T. S. Eliot. London: Cobden-Sanderson, 1926.

Eliot, H. W., Jr.
> Eliot, Henry Ware, Jr. [brother]. *Harvard Celebrities: A Book of Caricatures & Decorative Drawings by Frederick Garrison Hall '03 and Edward Revere Little '04. Verses by Henry Ware Eliot, Jr., '02.* Cambridge, Mass.: University Press, Frederick G. Hale, 1901.

Eliot, H. W., Sr.
> Eliot, Henry Ware, Sr. [father]. *A Brief Autobiography, 1843–1919.* Manuscript, John M. Olin Library, Washington University, St. Louis.

Eliot, Vivien, UD

Eliot, Vivien. [wife, née Vivienne Haigh-Wood]. Unpublished diaries for the years 1914, 1919, 1934, 1935. MSS Eng. misc. e. 876-8, f. 532, The Bodleian Library, Oxford, England.

Eliot, Vivien, FG

———. [Fanny Marlow, pseud.]. "Fête Galante." *Criterion* 3, no. 12 (July 1925): 557–63.

Eliot, W. G.

Eliot, William Greenleaf. [grandfather]. *Lectures to Young Men.* Boston: Crosby Nichols & Co., 1854; New York: Charles S. Francis & Co., 1854.

Ellis, GP

Ellis, Havelock. "General Preface." In *Studies in the Psychology of Sex,* vol. 1, part 1, xxvii–xxx. New York: Random House, 1901; reprint, 1936.

Ellis, AE

———. "Auto-Eroticism." In *Studies in the Psychology of Sex,* vol. 1, part 1, 161–325. New York: Random House, 1910; reprint, 1936.

Ellis, SI

———. "Sexual Inversion." In *Studies in the Psychology of Sex,* vol. 2, part 2, 1–356. New York: Random House, 1910; reprint, 1936.

Ellmann

Ellmann, Richard. *James Joyce.* New York: Oxford University Press, 1959.

Emerson, L

Emerson, Ralph Waldo. *The Letters of Ralph Waldo Emerson.* Vols. 4 and 6. Ed. R. L. Rush in 6 volumes. New York: Columbia University Press, 1939.

Emerson, SR

———. "Self-Reliance." In *Selected Writings of Ralph Waldo Emerson.* Ed. William H. Gilman. New York: New American Library, 1965.

EB

The Encyclopaedia Britannica. 11th ed. New York: Encyclopaedia Britannica, 1911.

Englebert

Englebert, Omer. *The Lives of the Saints.* New York: David McKay, 1951.

Fitzgerald

Fitzgerald, Edward, trans. *The Rubáiyát of Omar Khayyám.* Garden City, N.Y.: Doubleday Dolphin Books, n.d. (1859/1889). The first edition appeared in 1859 and the fifth, used here, in 1889.

Flandrau, HE

Flandrau, Charles Macomb. *Harvard Episodes.* Boston: Copeland and Day, 1897.

Flandrau, DF

———. *The Diary of a Freshman.* New York: Doubleday, Page & Co., 1902.

France

France, Peter, ed. "Bergson." In *The New Oxford Companion to Literature in French,* 83–84. Oxford: Clarendon Press, 1995.

Froula, GEP

Froula, Christine. *A Guide to Ezra Pound's Selected Poems.* New York: New Directions, 1983.

Froula, EGQ

———. "Eliot's Grail Quest, or, The Lover, the Police, and *The Waste Land.*" *Yale Review* 78, no. 2 (September 1989): 235–53.

Gallup, *TSEB*
> Gallup, Donald. *T. S. Eliot: A Bibliography: A Revised and Extended Edition.* New York: Harcourt, Brace & World, 1969.

Gallup, MECC
> ———. "Mr. Eliot at the Churchill Club." In *T. S. Eliot: Essays from "The Southern Review,"* ed. James Olney, 97–101. Oxford: Clarendon Press, 1988. Reprinted from *Southern Review* 21, no. 4 (Autumn 1985): 969–73.

Gardner, *ATSE*
> Gardner, Helen. *The Art of T. S. Eliot.* London: Faber and Faber, 1949; reprint, 1968.

Gardner, CFQ
> ———. *The Composition of Four Quartets.* New York: Oxford University Press, 1978.

Gautier
> Gautier, Théophile. *The Works of Théophile Gautier.* Vol. 24, *Enamels and Cameos and Other Poems,* trans. Agnes Lee. New York: George D. Sproul, 1903.

Gay
> Gay, Peter. *The Tender Passion,* vol. 2 of *The Bourgeois Experience, Victoria to Freud.* New York: Oxford University Press, 1986.

Gayley
> Gayley, Charles Mills. *The Classic Myths in English Literature and in Art.* Waltham, Mass.: Ginn Blaisdell, 1911.

Gide
> Gide, André. *Marshlands and Prometheus Misbound: Two Satires.* Trans. George D. Painter. New York: New Directions, 1953.

Gordon, EEY
> Gordon, Lyndall. *Eliot's Early Years.* Oxford: Oxford University Press, 1977.

Gordon, ENL
> ———. *Eliot's New Life.* New York: Farrar, Straus and Giroux, 1988.

Gordon, EIL
> ———. *T. S. Eliot: An Imperfect Life.* [Revision of EEY and ENL]. *New* York: W. W. Norton, 1998.

Grant
> Grant, Michael, ed. *T. S. Eliot: The Critical Heritage,* vol. 1. London: Routledge & Kegan Paul, 1982.

Greene
> Greene, Edward J. H. *T. S. Eliot et La France.* Paris: Boivin et Cie Éditeurs, 1951.

Gross
> Gross, Harvey. "The Figure of St. Sebastian." In *T. S. Eliot: Essays from "The Southern Review,"* ed. James Olney, 103–14. Oxford: Clarendon Press, 1988. Reprinted from *Southern Review* 21, no. 4 (Autumn 1985): 974–84.

Habib
> Habib, M. A. R. *The Early T. S. Eliot and Western Philosophy.* Cambridge: Cambridge University Press, 1999.

Hale
> Hale, Nathan G., Jr. *Freud and the Americans: The Beginnings of Psychoanalysis in the United States, 1876–1917.* New York: Oxford University Press, 1971.

Hands
> Hands, Anthony. *Sources for the Poetry of T. S. Eliot.* Oxford: Hadrian Books, 1993.

Hargrove

Hargrove, Nancy D. "'Un Présent Parfait': Eliot and La Vie Parisienne, 1910–1911." In *T. S. Eliot and the Turn of the Century*, ed. Marianne Thormählen, 33–58. Lund, Sweden: Lund University Press, 1994.

Harvey

Harvey, Sir Paul. "Bergson." In *The Oxford Companion to French Literature*, ed. Sir Paul Harvey and J. E. Hesaltine, 60–62. Oxford: Clarendon Press, 1959.

Hastings

Hastings, Michael. *Tom and Viv*. New York: Viking Penguin, 1985.

Headings

Headings, Philip. *T. S. Eliot*. Rev. ed. Boston: Twayne, 1982.

Herodotus

Herodotus. *The Persian Wars*. Trans. George Rawlinson. New York: Modern Library, 1942.

Hoffman et al.

Hoffman, Frederick J., Charles Allen, and Carolyn F. Ulrich. *The Little Magazine: A History and a Bibliography*. Princeton: Princeton University Press, 1947.

Holder

Holder, Alan. *Three Voyagers in Search of Europe: A Study of Henry James, Ezra Pound, and T. S. Eliot*. Philadelphia: University of Pennsylvania Press, 1966.

Holroyd

Holroyd, Michael. *Lytton Strachey: The New Biography*. New York: Farrar, Straus and Giroux, 1994. Expanded version of Volume 1 (1967) and Volume 2 (1968).

Holt, Perry, et al.

Holt, Edwin B., Ralph Barton Perry, et al. *The New Realism: Cooperative Studies in Philosophy*. New York: Macmillan, 1912.

Howarth

Howarth, Herbert. *Notes on Some Figures Behind T. S. Eliot*. London: Chatto & Windus, 1965.

Howink

Howink, Eda. "T. S. Eliot: A Clinician's Perspective." *Yeats Eliot Review* 12, no. 1 (Summer 1993): 27–30.

Hughes

Hughes, Ted. *A Dancer to God: Tributes to T. S. Eliot*. New York: Farrar, Straus and Giroux, 1992.

Hyde and Conard

Hyde, William, and N. L. Conard. *Encyclopedia of the History of St. Louis*, vol. 4. New York and Louisville: Southern History Co., 1899.

Jain

Jain, Manju. *T. S. Eliot and American Philosophy: The Harvard Years*. Cambridge: Cambridge University Press, 1992.

James, Henry, AN

James, Henry. *The Art of the Novel: Critical Prefaces*. London: Charles Scribner's Sons, 1947.

James, Henry, CTHJ

———. *The Complete Tales of Henry James*, vols. 1–12. Ed. Leon Edel. Philadelphia: Lippincott, 1963.

James, William

   James, William. *The Varieties of Religious Experience: A Study in Human Nature.* Originally published 1902. New York: Longmans, Green, 1903; reprint, Garden City, N.Y.: Doubleday Dolphin Books, [1983?] .

Jarrell

   Jarrell, Randall. "Fifty Years of American Poetry." In *The Third Book of Criticism,* 295–334. New York: Farrar, Straus and Giroux, 1969.

Johnson

   Johnson, Loretta. "A Temporary Marriage of Two Minds: T. S. and Vivien Eliot." *Twentieth Century Literature* 34, no. 1 (Spring 1988): 48–61.

Jones

   Jones, A. R. *The Life and Opinions of T. E. Hulme.* Boston: Beacon Press, 1960.

Jonson

   Jonson, Ben. *Selected Works.* Ed. Harry Levin. New York: Random House, 1938.

Julius

   Julius, Anthony. *T. S. Eliot, Anti-Semitism, and Literary Form.* Cambridge: Cambridge University Press, 1995.

Kaye

   Kaye, Richard A. "'A Splendid Readiness for Death': T. S. Eliot, the Homosexual Cult of St. Sebastian, and World War I." *Modernism/Modernity* 6, no. 2 (April 1999): 107–34.

Kearns

   Kearns, Cleo McNelly. *T. S. Eliot and Indic Traditions: A Study in Poetry and Belief.* New York: Cambridge University Press, 1987.

Kenner, *IP*

   Kenner, Hugh. *The Invisible Poet: T. S. Eliot.* New York: Harcourt, Brace & World, 1959.

Kenner, *TSE*

   ———, ed. *T. S. Eliot: A Collection of Critical Essays.* Englewood Cliffs, N.J.: Prentice-Hall, 1962.

Kenner, *UA*

   ———. "The Urban Apocalypse." In *Eliot in His Time: Essays on the Occasion of the Fiftieth Anniversary of The Waste Land,* ed. A. Walton Litz, 23–49. Princeton: Princeton University Press, 1973.

Kermode

   Kermode, Frank. *Continuities.* New York: Viking Press, 1968.

King

   King, Francis. *Yesterday Came Suddenly: An Autobiography.* London: Constable, 1993.

Knight

   Knight, G. Wilson. "Thoughts on *The Waste Land.*" *Denver Quarterly* 7, no. 2 (Summer 1972): 1–13.

Koestenbaum

   Koestenbaum, Wayne. *Double Talk: The Erotics of Male Literary Collaboration.* New York: Routledge, 1989.

Kuklick

   Kuklick, Bruce. *The Rise of American Philosophy: Cambridge, Massachusetts, 1860–1930.* New Haven: Yale University Press, 1977.

Kyd
> Kyd, Thomas. *The Spanish Tragedy.* London: Ernest Benn, 1970.

Laforgue
> Laforgue, Jules. *Poems of Jules Laforgue.* Trans. Peter Dale. London: Anvil Press Poetry, 1986.

Lamos
> Lamos, Colleen. *Deviant Modernism: Sexual and Textual Errancy in T. S. Eliot, James Joyce, and Marcel Proust.* Cambridge: Cambridge University Press, 1998.

Langbaum
> Langbaum, Robert. "Why Was April the Cruellest Month." *New York Times Book Review,* April 17, 1977, 15.

Lanman
> Lanman, Charles Rockwell. *The Beginnings of Hindu Pantheism.* Cambridge: Charles W. Sever, 1890.

Lawrence
> Lawrence, D. H. *Fantasia of the Unconscious.* New York: Thomas Seltzer, 1922.

Lee
> Lee, Hermione. *Virginia Woolf.* New York: Alfred A. Knopf, 1997.

Levy and Scherle
> Levy, William Turner, and Victor Scherle. *Affectionately, T. S. Eliot: The Story of a Friendship: 1947–1965.* New York: Lippincott, 1968.

Lewis, ELE
> Lewis, Wyndham. "Early London Environment." In *T. S. Eliot: A Symposium,* ed. Richard March and Tambimuttu, 24–32. Chicago: Henry Regnery, 1949.

Lewis, BB
> ———. *Blasting and Bombardiering.* London: 1937. 2nd rev. ed., Berkley and Los Angeles: University of California Press, 1967.

Lidderdale and Nicholson
> Lidderdale, Jane, and Mary Nicholson. *Dear Miss Weaver: Harriet Shaw Weaver, 1876–1961.* London: Faber and Faber, 1970.

Little
> Little, Leon Magaw. "Eliot: A Reminiscence." *Harvard Advocate* 100 (Fall 1966): 33.

Litz, EHT
> Litz, A. Walton, ed. *Eliot in His Time: Essays on the Occasion of the Fiftieth Anniversary of The Waste Land.* Princeton: Princeton University Press, 1973.

Litz, I&A
> ———. "Introduction" and "Afterword" to "Tradition and the Practice of Poetry," by T. S. Eliot. In *T. S. Eliot: Essays from "The Southern Review,"* ed. James Olney, 7–25. Oxford: Clarendon Press, 1988. Reprinted from *Southern Review* 21, no. 4 (Autumn 1985): 873–88.

Loucks
> Loucks, James. "The Exile's Return: Fragment of a T. S. Eliot Chronology." *ANQ* 9, no. 2 (Spring 1996): 16–39.

Lyon
> Lyon, Richard Colton, ed. *Santayana on America: Essays, Notes, and Letters on American Life, Literature, and Philosophy.* New York: Harcourt, Brace & World, 1968.

Magill
> Magill, Frank N., ed. "Time and Free Will," 703–6; "An Introduction to Metaphysics," 749–61; "Creative Evolution," 767–73; "The Two Sources of Morality and Religion," 959–63. [Essays on Henri Bergson.] In *Masterpieces of World Philosophy,* vol. 2. New York: Salem Press, 1961.

March, Richard, and Tambimuttu, eds. *T. S. Eliot: A Symposium.* Chicago: Henry Regnery, 1949.

Margolis
> Margolis, John D. *T. S. Eliot's Intellectual Development: 1922–1939.* Chicago: University of Chicago Press, 1972.

Matthews
> Matthews, T. S. *Great Tom: Notes Towards the Definition of T. S. Eliot.* New York: Harper & Row, 1974.

Matthiessen
> Matthiessen, F. O. *The Achievement of T. S. Eliot: An Essay on the Nature of Poetry.* London: Oxford University Press, 1935; reprint, 1947, 1958.

May
> May, Derwent. *Critical Times: The History of "The Times Literary Supplement."* London: Harper Collins, 2001.

Mayer
> Mayer, John T. *T. S. Eliot's Silent Voices.* New York: Oxford University Press, 1989.

Mayne
> Mayne, Xavier. [pseud. Edward Stevenson]. *The Intersexes: A History of Similisexualism as a Problem in Social Life.* Printed privately 1908; New York: Arno Press, 1975.

McCormick
> McCormick, John. *George Santayana: A Biography.* New York: Alfred A. Knopf, 1987.

Meyers
> Meyers, Jeffrey. *The Enemy: A Biography of Wyndham Lewis.* London: Routledge & Kegan Paul, 1980.

Miller, TSEPWL
> Miller, James E., Jr. *T. S. Eliot's Personal Waste Land: Exorcism of the Demons.* University Park: The Pennsylvania State University Press, 1977.

Miller, AQ
> ———. *The American Quest for a Supreme Fiction: Whitman's Legacy in the Personal Epic.* Chicago: University of Chicago Press, 1979.

Miller, FQ
> ———. "*Four Quartets* and an 'Acute Personal Experience.'" In *T. S. Eliot: Man and Poet,* vol. 1, ed. Laura Cowan, 219–38. Orono, Maine: National Poetry Foundation, University of Maine, 1990.

Miller, UM
> ———. "T. S. Eliot's 'Uranian Muse.'" *ANQ* 11, no. 4 (Fall 1998): 4–18.

Monk
> Monk, Ray. *Bertrand Russell: The Spirit of Solitude, 1872–1921.* New York: Free Press, 1996.

Moody, TSEP
> Moody, A. David. *Thomas Stearns Eliot: Poet.* Cambridge: Cambridge University Press, 1979; 2nd ed., 1994.

Moody, CC
———, ed. *The Cambridge Companion to T. S. Eliot*. Cambridge: Cambridge University Press, 1994.

Moody, BFW
———. "Being in Fear of Women." In *Tracing T. S. Eliot's Spirit: Essays on His Poetry and Thought*, 182–95. Cambridge: Cambridge University Press, 1996.

Morison, TCH
Morison, Samuel Eliot. *Three Centuries of Harvard, 1636–1936*. Cambridge, Mass.: Harvard University Press, 1936.

Morison, DSTS
———. "The Dry Salvages and the Thacher Shipwreck." *The American Neptune: A Quarterly of Maritime History* 25, no. 4 (October 1965): 233–47.

Morrell, M
Morrell, Ottoline. *Memoirs of Lady Ottoline Morrell: A Study in Friendship, 1873–1915*. Ed. Robert Gathorne-Hardy. New York: Alfred A. Knopf, 1964.

Morrell, OG
———. *Ottoline at Garsington: Memoirs of Ottoline Morrell, 1915–1918*. Ed. Robert Gathorne-Hardy. New York: Alfred A. Knopf, 1975.

Morse
Morse, Josiah. *Pathological Aspects of Religion*. Worcester, Mass.: Clark University Press, 1906.

Musgrove
Musgrove, Sydney. *T. S. Eliot and Walt Whitman*. Wellington: University of New Zealand Press, 1952.

Neilson
Neilson, William Allan. *Essentials of Poetry: Lowell Lectures, 1911*. Boston: Houghton Mifflin, 1912.

Nerval
Nerval, Gérard de. *Selected Writings of Gérard de Nerval*. Trans. Geoffrey Wagner. Ann Arbor: University of Michigan Press, 1959.

NYT
New York Times. "2 More T. S. Eliot Poems Found Amid Hundreds of His Letters," by Craig R. Whitney. Section 1, November 2, 1991, 13.

Nordau
Nordau, Max. *Degeneration*. New York: D. Appleton, 1895.

Norton
Norton, Charles Eliot. Review of the *Rubáiyát of Omar Khayyám, the Astronomer-Poet of Persia*. *North American Review* 109, no. 225 (October 1869): 565–85.

Olney
Olney, James, ed. *T. S. Eliot: Essays from "The Southern Review."* Oxford: Clarendon Press, 1988.

Oser
Oser, Lee. *T. S. Eliot and American Poetry*. Columbia: University of Missouri Press, 1998.

Ovid
Ovid. *Metamorphoses*. Trans. Rolfe Humphries. Bloomington: Indiana University Press, 1961.

Palmer and Palmer
    Palmer, Alan, and Veronica Palmer. *Who's Who in Bloomsbury.* New York: St. Martin's
    Press, 1987.
Partridge
    Partridge, Frances. *Love in Bloomsbury: Memories.* Boston: Little, Brown, 1981.
Patmore
    Patmore, Brigit. *My Friends When Young: The Memoirs of Brigit Patmore.* Ed. Derek
    Patmore. London: Heineman, 1968.
Pearson
    Pearson, John. *The Sitwells: A Family's Biography.* New York: Harcourt Brace Jova-
    novich, 1979. Published in England as *Façades: Edith, Osbert, and Sacheverell Sitwell.*
    London: Macmillan London, 1978.
Perinot
    Perinot, Claudio. "Jean Verdenal: T. S. Eliot's French Friend." *Annali di ca' Foscari: Riv-
    ista della Facoltá de lingue e letterature straniere dell università di venezia* 35, no. 1–2 (1996):
    265–75.
Perl and Tuck
    Perl, Jeffrey M., and Andrew P. Tuck. "The Hidden Advantage of Tradition: On the
    Significance of T. S. Eliot's Indic Studies." *Philosophy East and West: A Quarterly of
    Asian and Comparative Thought* 35, no. 2 (April 1985): 115–31.
Pervigilium
    Pervigilium Veneris: The Vigil of Venus. Trans. Sir Cecil Clementi. Oxford: Basil Black-
    well, 1911; 2nd ed., 1928.
Peter
    Peter, John. "A New Interpretation of *The Waste Land.*" *Essays in Criticism* 2, no. 3
    (July 1952): 242–66; reprinted with "Postscript," *Essays in Criticism* 19, no. 2 (April
    1969): 140–75.
Petronius
    Petronius. *The Satyricon of Petronius Arbiter.* Trans. W. C. Firebaugh with introduction
    by Charles Whibley. New York: Horace Liveright. 1927.
Philippe
    Philippe, Charles-Louis. *Bubu of Montparnasse.* Trans. Laurence Vail, preface by T. S.
    Eliot. Paris: Crosby Continental Editions, 1932.
Pierpont
    Pierpont, John. *Airs of Palestine and Other Poems.* Boston: J. Munroe, 1840; reprint, 1916.
Poe
    Poe, Edgar Allan. *The Complete Tales and Poems of Edgar Allan Poe.* Ed. Hervey Allen.
    New York: Modern Library, 1938.
PMC
    Poetry Magazine: A Gallery of Voices. Exhibition Catalog. Ed. Kathleen Farley. Chi-
    cago: University of Chicago Library, 1980.
Pound, ww, NC
    Pound, Ezra. "What I Feel about Walt Whitman." [1909]; and "National Culture: A
    Manifesto, 1938." In *Selected Prose: 1909–1965,* ed. William Cookson, 145–46, 161–66.
    New York: New Directions, 1973.
Pound, BN
    ———. "Brief Note." *Little Review: Henry James* 5, no. 4 (August 1918): 6–9.

Pound, L

——. *The Letters of Ezra Pound*. Ed. D. D. Paige. New York: Brace & World, 1950.

Pound, LE

——. *Literary Essays of Ezra Pound*. Ed. and with an introduction by T. S. Eliot. Norfolk, Conn.: New Directions Publishing, 1954.

Pound, SPEP

——. *Selected Poems of Ezra Pound*. New York: New Directions, 1962.

Pound, LPJ

——. *The Letters of Ezra Pound to James Joyce*. Ed. Forrest Read. New York: New Directions, 1967.

Pound, C

——. *The Cantos of Ezra Pound*. New York: New Directions, 1972.

Pound, SP

——. *Selected Prose 1909–1965*. Ed. William Cookson. New York: New Directions, 1973.

Powel

Powel, H. W. H. "Notes on the Life of T. S. Eliot, 1888–1910." Master's thesis, Brown University, 1954.

Rainey

Rainey, Lawrence. *Institutions of Modernism: Literary Elites and Public Culture*. New Haven: Yale University Press, 1998.

RHD

Random House Dictionary. 2nd, unabridged ed. Ed. Stuart Berg Flexner. New York: Random House, 1987.

Read

Read, Sir Herbert. "T. S. E.—A Memoir." In *T. S. Eliot: The Man and His Work,* ed. Allen Tate, 11–37. New York: Delacorte Press, 1966.

Reade

Reade, Brian, ed. *Sexual Heretics: Male Homosexuality in English Literature from 1850 to 1900*. New York: Coward-McCann, 1970.

Richards, PTSE

Richards, I. A. "The Poetry of T. S. Eliot." Appendix B in *Principles of Literary Criticism,* ed. John Constable, 289–95. New York: Harcourt, Brace, 1926; reprint, London: Routledge, 2001.

Richards, TSE

——. "On TSE: Notes for a Talk . . . 1965." In *T. S. Eliot: The Man and His Work,* ed. Allen Tate, 1–10. New York: Delacorte Press, 1966.

Ricks

Ricks, Christopher. *T. S. Eliot and Prejudice*. Berkeley and Los Angeles: University of California Press, 1988.

Rusk

Rusk, L. *The Life of Ralph Waldo Emerson*. New York: Charles Scribner's Sons, 1949.

Ruskin

Ruskin, John. *The Stones of Venice*. 3 vols. Chicago: Bedford, Clarke & Co., 1851–53.

Russell, A

Russell, Bertrand. *Autobiography*. 3 vols. London: George Allen & Unwin, 1967–1975; reprint in one volume, London: Routledge, 1991.

Russell, SL
———. *The Selected Letters of Bertrand Russell,* ed. Nicholas Griffin. Vol. 1, *The Private Years, 1884–1914.* Boston: Houghton Mifflin, 1992.
Saint Augustine
The Confessions of St. Augustine. Trans. E. B. Pusey. New York: Dutton, 1942.
Santayana
Santayana, George. *The Last Puritan: A Memoir in the Form of a Novel.* New York: Charles Scribner's Sons, 1936.
Schmeling and Rebmann
Schmeling, Gareth L., and David R. Rebmann. "T. S. Eliot and Petronius." *Comparative Literature Studies* 12, no. 4 (December 1975): 393–410.
Schuchard
Schuchard, Ronald. *Eliot's Dark Angel: Intersections of Life and Art.* Oxford: Oxford University Press, 1999.
Sedgwick
Sedgwick, Eve Kosofsky. *Epistemology of the Closet.* Berkeley and Los Angeles: University of California Press, 1990.
Sencourt
Sencourt, Robert. *T. S. Eliot: A Memoir.* New York: Dodd, Mead & Co., 1971.
Seymour
Seymour, Miranda. *Ottoline Morrell: Life on the Grand Scale.* New York: Farrar, Straus and Giroux, 1992.
Seymour-Jones
Seymour-Jones, Carole. *Painted Shadow: A Life of Vivienne Eliot.* London: Constable, 2001.
Shakespeare
Complete Plays of Shakespeare. Ed. George Lyman Kittredge. New York: Ginn & Co., 1936.
Shand-Tucci, BB
Shand-Tucci, Douglass. *Boston Bohemia, 1881–1900.* Vol. 2 of *Ralph Adams Cram: Life and Architecture.* Amherst: University of Massachusetts Press, 1995.
Shand-Tucci, AS
———. *The Art of Scandal: The Life and Times of Isabella Stewart Gardner.* New York: Harper Collins, 1997.
Shand-Tucci, CL
———. *The Crimson Letter: Harvard, Homosexuality, and the Shaping of American Culture.* New York: St. Martin's Press, 2003.
Shelley
Shelley, Percy Bysshe. *The Complete Poetical Works of Percy Bysshe Shelley.* Ed. Thomas Hutchinson. Oxford: Oxford University Press, 1923.
Shusterman
Shusterman, Richard. *T. S. Eliot and the Philosophy of Criticism.* New York: Columbia University Press, 1988.
Sigg
Sigg, Eric. "Eliot as a Product of America." In *The Cambridge Companion to T. S. Eliot,* ed. A. David Moody, 14–30. Cambridge: Cambridge University Press, 1994.

Simpson

    Simpson, Louis. *Three on the Tower: The Lives and Works of Ezra Pound, T. S. Eliot, and William Carlos Williams.* New York: William Morrow, 1975.

Smidt

    Smidt, Kristian. *Poetry and Belief in the Work of T. S. Eliot.* Oslo: 1949; Revised edition, London: Routledge & Kegan Paul, 1961.

Smith, Grover, PP

    Smith, Grover. *T. S. Eliot's Poetry and Plays.* Chicago: University of Chicago Press, 1974.

Smith, Grover, TWL

    ———. *The Waste Land.* London: George Allen & Unwin, 1983.

Smith, Timothy

    Smith, Timothy d'Arch, ed. *Love in Earnest: Some Notes on the Lives and Writings of English "Uranian" Poets from 1889 to 1930.* London: Routledge & Kegan Paul, 1970.

Soldo, thesis

    Soldo, John J. "The Tempering of T. S. Eliot 1888–1915." Ph.D. diss., Harvard University, 1972.

Soldo, TTSE

    ———. *The Tempering of T. S. Eliot.* Ann Arbor: University of Michigan Press, 1983.

Southam

    Southam, B. C. *A Guide to the Selected Poems of T. S. Eliot.* 6th ed. London: Faber and Faber, 1994.

Spender, DE

    Spender, Stephen. *The Destructive Element: A Study of Modern Writers and Beliefs.* Boston: Houghton Mifflin, 1936.

Spender, TSE

    ———. *T. S. Eliot.* New York: Penguin Books, 1976.

Spender, WW

    ———. *World within World: The Autobiography of Stephen Spender.* New York: St. Martin's Press, 1994.

Spiller et al.

    Spiller, Robert E., Willard Thorp, Thomas H. Johnson, Henry Seidel Canby, and Richard M. Ludwig, eds. *Literary History of the United States.* 3rd rev. ed. New York: Macmillan, 1963.

Spindler

    Spindler, Elizabeth Carroll. *John Peale Bishop: A Biography.* Morgantown: West Virginia University Library, 1980.

Stead

    Stead, C. K. *Pound, Yeats, Eliot, and the Modernist Movement.* New Brunswick, N.J.: Rutgers University Press, 1986.

Steinberg

    Steinberg, Erwin R. "*Mrs. Dalloway* and T. S. Eliot's Personal Waste Land." *Journal of Modern Literature* 10, no. 1 (March 1983): 3–25.

Stephenson

    Stephenson, Ethel M. *T. S. Eliot and the Lay Reader.* London: Fortune Press, 1944.

Stevens

    Stevens, Walter B. *St. Louis, the Fourth City: 1764–1909.* St. Louis: S. J. Clarke Publishing, 1909.

Stonier
Stonier, G. W. "The Mystery of Ezra Pound." *Purpose: A Quarterly Magazine* 10, no. 1 (January–March 1938): 21–26.
Svarny
Svarny, Erik. *T. S. Eliot and Early Modernism*. Philadelphia: Open University Press, 1988.
Symons
Symons, Arthur. *The Symbolist Movement in Literature*. Rev. ed. New York: E. P Dutton, 1919; original edition, 1899.
Tadié
Tadié, Jean-Yves. *Marcel Proust: A Biography*. Trans. Euan Cameron. New York: Viking, 1966; reprint, 2000.
Tannenbaum
Tannenbaum, Edward R. *The Action Française: Die-Hard Reactionaries in Twentieth-Century France*. New York: John Wiley and Sons, 1962.
Tate
Tate, Allen, ed. *T. S. Eliot: The Man and His Work*. New York: Delacorte Press, 1966.
Thornton
Thornton, R. K. R. *The Decadent Dilemma*. London: Edward Arnold, 1983.
Tinckom-Fernandez
Tinckom-Fernandez, W. G. "T. S. Eliot '10: An Advocate Friendship." *The Harvard Advocate* 125, no. 3 (December 1938): 5–8, 47–48.
Townsend
Townsend, Kim. *Manhood at Harvard: William James and Others*. New York: W. W. Norton, 1996.
Trosman
Trosman, Harry. "T. S. Eliot and *The Waste Land:* Psychopathological Antecedents and Transformations." *Archives of General Psychiatry* 30 (May 1974): 709–17.
Trueblood
Trueblood, Paul G. *Lord Byron*. Rev. ed. Boston: Twayne, 1977; original edition, 1977.
Underhill
Underhill, Evelyn. *Mysticism: A Study in the Nature and Development of Man's Spiritual Consciousness*. 12th ed. London: Methuen, 1930; original edition, 1911.
Unterecker
Unterecker, John. *Voyager: A Life of Hart Crane*. London: Anthony Blond, 1970.
Verlaine
Verlaine, Paul. *Oeuvres Poétiques Complètes*. Paris: Éditions Vialetay, 1955.
Vickery
Vickery, John B. *The Literary Impact of "The Golden Bough."* Princeton: Princeton University Press, 1973.
Villon
The Complete Works of François Villon. Ed. Anthony Bonner. New York: Bantam Books, 1964.
Warner
Warner, Val, trans. *The Centenary Corbière: Poems and Prose of Tristan Corbière*. Cheadle: Carcenet New Press, 1974.

Warren

    Warren, Henry Clarke. *Buddhism in Translations,* vol. 3. Harvard Oriental Series. Cambridge, Mass.: Harvard University Press, 1896; reprint, 1909, 1953.

Watson, George

    Watson, George. "Quest for a Frenchman." *Sewanee Review* 84, no. 3 (Summer 1976): 465–75.

Watson, Steven

    Watson, Steven. *Strange Bedfellows: The First American Avant-Garde.* New York: Abbeville Press, 1991.

Wendell, SOE

    Wendell, Barrett. *Stelligeri, and Other Essays Concerning America.* New York: Charles Scribner's Sons, 1893.

Wendell, LHA

    ———. *A Literary History of America.* New York: Charles Scribner's Sons, 1900.

Weston

    Weston, Jessie. *From Ritual to Romance.* New York: Doubleday Anchor Books, 1957.

Whibley

    Whibley, Charles. "Essay on Petronius." In *The Satyricon of Petronius Arbiter,* vii–xxiii. New York: Horace Liveright, 1927.

Whitman, CPSP

    Whitman, Walt. *Complete Poetry and Selected Prose.* Ed. James E. Miller Jr. Boston: Houghton Mifflin, 1959.

Whitman, SD

    ———. "Nights on the Mississippi" and "Edgar Poe's Significance." In *Specimen Days.* Vol. 1 of *The Collected Writings of Walt Whitman: Prose Works 1892,* ed. Floyd Stovall, 229, 230–33. New York: New York University Press, 1963.

Williams

    Williams, Ellen. *Harriet Monroe and the Poetry Renaissance: The First Ten Years of Poetry, 1912–1922.* Urbana: University of Illinois Press, 1977.

Williamson, TTSE

    Williamson, George. *The Talent of T. S. Eliot.* Seattle: University of Washington Book Store, 1929.

Williamson, RGTSE

    ———. *A Reader's Guide to T. S. Eliot.* New York: Farrar, Straus and Giroux, 1953.

Wilson

    Wilson, Edmund. *Letters on Literature and Politics, 1922–1972.* Ed. Elena Wilson. New York: Farrar, Straus and Giroux, 1977.

Wollheim

    Wollheim, Richard. "Eliot, Bradley, and Immediate Experience." *New Statesman* 52 (March 13, 1964): 401–2.

Woods

    Woods, J. H. *The Yoga-System of Patañjali or The ancient Hindu Doctrine of concentration of Mind. . . .* Harvard Oriental Series. Cambridge, Mass.: Harvard University Press, 1914; reprint, 1927, 1966.

Woolf, D1

    Woolf, Virginia. *The Diary of Virginia Woolf, Volume One: 1915–1919.* Ed. Anne Olivier Bell. New York: Harcourt Brace Jovanovich, 1977.

Woolf, *D2*

———. *The Diary of Virginia Woolf, Volume Two: 1920–1924.* Ed. Anne Olivier Bell. New York: Harcourt Brace Jovanovich, 1978.

Woolf, *D3*

———. *The Diary of Virginia Woolf, Volume Three: 1925–1930.* Ed. Anne Olivier Bell. New York: Harcourt Brace Jovanovich, 1980.

Woolf, *L2*

The Letters of Virginia Woolf, Volume Two: 1912–1922. Ed. Nigel Nicolson and Joanne Trautmann. New York: Harcourt Brace Jovanovich, 1976.

Woolf, *L3*

The Letters of Virginia Woolf, Volume Three: 1923–1928. Ed. Nigel Nicolson and Joanne Trautmann. New York: Harcourt Brace Jovanovich, 1977.

Ziff

Ziff, Larzer. *The American 1890s: Life and Times of a Lost Generation.* New York: Viking Press, 1966.

Index

Freud, Sigmund, 55–56
Freudian Wish, 166
"From Narcissus to Tiresias: T. S. Eliot's Use
of Metamorphosis," 251
Frost, Robert, 1, 223, 421
Froula, Christine, 390, 398
Frye, Roger, 275
Fugitive Slave Law, 12
"Function of Criticism, The," 269
Furst, Henry, 136–37, 226

Gallup, Donald, 343, 416
Gardner, Amory, 136
Gardner, Augustus Peabody, 56
Gardner, Helen, 214, 378, 414
Gardner, Isabella Stewart, 4, 6–7; Boston
Bohemians and, 56–61, 135–39, 274; Eliot's
acquaintance with, 173, 226, 307
Gardner, Joseph Peabody, 57
Gardner, William Amory, 57
Gardner Museum, 136. *See also* Fenway Court
Garland for John Donne: 1631–1931, A, 107
Gaudier, Henri, 398
Gay, Peter, 13, 54–55, 124
Gay American History, 53
*Gay New York: Gender, Urban Culture, and the
Making of the Gay Male World, 1890–1940,*
xix, 105–6
George Santayana, 186
"German Poetry of Today," 409
"Gerontion," 35, 172; creation and publication
of, 350–60; homosexual motif in, 106–7,
403; influence of *Rubáiyát* on, 265; Pound-
Eliot correspondence concerning, 391–92;
reviews of, 344
Gibson, James, 166
Gide, André, 118, 121, 126–27
Ginsberg, Allen, 264
Giraudoux, Jean, 118
Gloucester, Eliot's early experiences in, 41–45
Golden Ass, The, 97
Golden Bough, The, 346
Goldman, Emma, 56
Goldthorpe, Rhiannon, 140
Gómez de la Serna, Ramón, 408
Goodhue, Bertram, 59
"Good-Morrow, The," 108–9
Gordon, Lyndall, xvii–xviii; on Eliot's early
work, 69, 77, 214, 242; on Pound's
correspondence with Eliot, 388; on
Virginia Woolf and Eliot, 378; on *The
Waste Land,* 371

Gourmont, Rémy de, 300
Granite Review, 6, 154
Gray, John, 246
*Great Tom: Notes Towards the Definition of
T. S. Eliot,* xvii, 70, 213–14
Green, Martin, 59
Greene, William C., 204
Gross, Harvey, 242, 244–45
Guide to Ezra Pound's Selected Poems, 398
Guide to the Selected Poems of T. S. Eliot, 68
Gunn, Thom, 413

Habib, M. A. R., 142–43
Haigh-Wood, Charles, 221–23
Haigh-Wood, Maurice, xviii–xix, 230–31, 240
Haigh-Wood, Rose, 222
Haigh-Wood, Vivien. *See* Eliot, Vivien
(Haigh-Wood)
haiku, Imagism movement and, 270
Hale, Emily, 211–15, 219
Hall, Donald, 36, 310
Hallam, Arthur Henry, 134, 365–66
"Hamlet and His Problems," 328, 348
Handbook of Birds of Eastern North America,
420
Hargrove, Nancy D., 140–41, 245–46
Harper, Charles G., 385
Harriet Monroe and the Poetry Renaissance, 200
Harvard Advocate, 36, 57, 62–65, 69, 199;
TSE's poetry in, 70–78, 102–3; TSE's
reviews in, 110
Harvard Celebrities, 51, 58
Harvard Episodes, 59–60
Harvard University: bohemian life at, 56–61;
Brooks's recollections of, 112–14; courses
TSE enrolled in, 79–80; Dante cult at,
95–97; free elective course system at,
80–81; friends of Eliot at, 62–64;
philosophy department at, 7, 161–89;
psychology courses at, 175–81; TSE
considered for position at, 187–89; TSE's
lectures at, 32–34; TSE's student life at,
2–4, 6–7, 24–27, 34–35, 49–56, 79–114
Hastings, Michael, xviii–xix, 218, 230–31, 236,
377–79, 387; challenges to work of, 378,
383
Hatch (Mr.), 39
Hawthorne, 295
Hawthorne, Nathaniel, 9–10, 22, 295, 419,
421; Wendell's comments on, 88
"Hawthorne Aspect [of Henry James]," 22,
52, 295–96